D0344675

EMBRACING DEFEAT

Japan in the Wake of World War II

John W. Dower

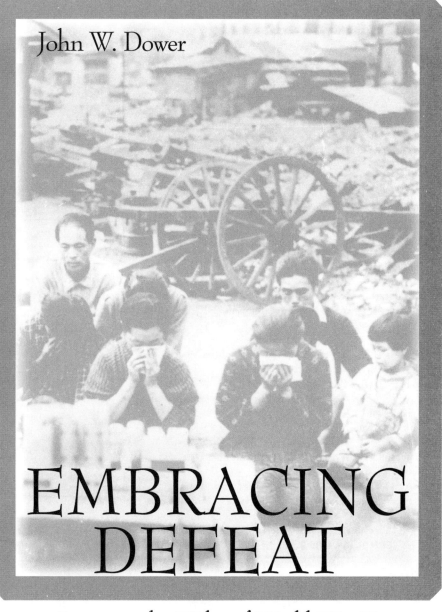

EMBRACING DEFEAT

Japan in the Wake of World War II

W. W. Norton & Company / The New Press

Copyright © 1999 by John W. Dower

All rights reserved
Printed in the United States of America
First Edition

For information about permission to reproduce selections from this book, write
to Permissions, W. W. Norton & Company, Inc., 500 Fifth Avenue, New York,
NY 10110.

The text of this book is composed in Bernhard Modern
with the display set in CairHeart
Composition by ComCom, Inc.
Manufacturing by the Maple-Vail Book Manufacturing Group
Book design by Lane Kimball Trubey
Cartography by Jacques Chazaud

Library of Congress Cataloging-in-Publication Data

Dower, John W.
    Embracing defeat : Japan in the wake of World War II / by John Dower.
        p.   cm.
    Includes bibliographical references and index.
    ISBN 0-393-04686-9
    1. Japan—History—1945–   I. Title.
DS889.D69   1999
952.04—dc21   98-22133
                                                                     CIP

W. W. Norton & Company, Inc., 500 Fifth Avenue, New York, N.Y. 10110
                    http://www.wwnorton.com

W. W. Norton & Company Ltd., 10 Coptic Street, London WC1A 1PU

1 2 3 4 5 6 7 8 9 0

for
Howard B. Schonberger
(1940–1991)

*who never lost sight of the ideals
of peace and democracy*

CONTENTS

ACKNOWLEDGMENTS

This book has taken a long time to prepare, and would have taken forever without great contributions from two people. My wife, Yasuko, helped to survey a broad range of materials; and our conversations, woven into the fabric of everyday life, became an important way of mulling over themes and probing nuances. We covered a great deal of ground together—not only figuratively, exploring the past, but also literally, in various places in Japan and the United States. This is a heavy debt, as well as a rewarding way to do history.

At a certain point these labors came together in an exceedingly long manuscript, and I called on an old friend to help me get untangled. Tom Engelhardt responded with patience and an exceedingly sharp pen. His critical scrutiny extended beyond language to structure, and beyond structure to themes and concepts. The manuscript reads differently (and faster) because of his friendship and skill.

I am indebted to others as well. Sodei Rinjirō, General MacArthur's Japanese biographer and a master of knowledge about occupied Japan, has directed me to many Japanese materials. My reliance on some of his writings, especially his analysis of letters written by ordinary Japanese to MacArthur, is obvious here. Ever since a long sojourn in Kamakura early on in this project, I have turned to Aketagawa Tohru to track down

Japanese sources. I also shared materials with Herbert Bix and had numerous helpful conversations with him about the role of Emperor Hirohito.

Takao Toshikazu directed me to one of the most remarkable texts I have introduced here, the diary-memoir of Watanabe Kiyoshi. Alex Gibney shared transcripts of some of the excellent interviews he conducted concerning the American drafting of a new Japanese constitution. Murakami Hisayo called attention to interesting materials in the Gordon Prange collection of Japanese publications submitted for vetting by the occupation's censors and now housed in the McKeldin Library at the University of Maryland; it was she who showed me what I regard as a little gem, the 1946 cartoon history of the occupation by Katō Etsurō. James Heisig made me aware of Tanabe Hajime, the formidable nationalistic philosopher of "repentance." James Zobel at the MacArthur Memorial identified a number of important archival documents. Years ago, when I began exploring Japan's transition from war to peace, I had the good fortune of being associated for a year with the "postwar financial history project" of the Japanese Ministry of Finance, headed by Hata Ikuhiko; and I still ride on some of the materials collected then.

One summer Yasuko and I secluded ourselves at Farm Island Lake in Minnesota and did economic policy in a cabin generously made available to us by Jerry and Aiko Fisher. I also received advice, materials, or assistance from Takemae Eiji, Matsuo Takayoshi, Sumiya Mikio, Igarashi Takeshi, Yui Daizaburō, Koseki Shōichi, Katō (Yasuhara) Yoko, Miura Yōichi, Eiji Yutani, Yuki Tanaka, Kozy Amemiya, Laura Hein, Marlene Mayo, David Swain, Frank Schulman, Andy Coopersmith, Peter Grilli, Edward Friedman, Glen Fukushima, and Steve Rabson. At the Massachusetts Institute of Technology, student projects by Abigail Vargus, Jennifer Mosier, and Ann Torres helped illuminate aspects of the Japanese scene immediately after the war; Leslie Torrance typed several chapters; Dianne Brooks and Mabel Chin were of unfailing help in navigating the practical world; and in various ways the university administration generously supported my research. At one point early on, our daughter Kana turned some handwritten chapters into computerized ones. Ed Barber and Andre Schiffrin have been my patient mentors at W. W. Norton and The New Press, respectively, and Georges Borchardt has been my literary agent. Barbara Gerr copyedited the manuscript. Sarah Holt and Alan Tolliver at Boston's WGBH television station shared photographs collected for a documentary on General MacArthur. Funding that has supported the project has come from the Japan Foundation as well as MIT. On several occasions, Tokyo University generously extended institutional access to its facilities.

Japanese publications pertaining to Japan's defeat in World War II and the American-led occupation that followed defy counting. They include excellent archives-based academic studies and an extraordinary range of edited popular volumes containing articles published at the time, letters written to newspapers during the occupation, day-by-day chronologies, photos, capsule summaries of films, song lyrics, special topics (like the war crimes trials and the black market), lists and summaries of postwar best-sellers, what have you. As the endnotes indicate, I have drawn heavily on such published Japanese materials, and on certain subjects I have taken it as my task to present some of the findings of Japanese scholars to English-language readers. These scholars deserve special mention here. On war crimes, exceptional research and analysis have been done by Awaya Kentarō, Yoshimi Yoshiaki, Yoshida Yutaka, and Ōnuma Yoshiaki. Koseki Shōichi has published the most incisive scholarship on the Japanese side of constitutional revision. The expert on popular magazines of the early postsurrender period, especially the "pulps," is Fukushima Jūrō; he is a major source for my treatment of this lively subject. On SCAP censorship, I have drawn many examples from the writings of Furukawa Atsushi, Etō Jun, and Matsuura Sōzō, among others. Where Japanese films of the immediate postsurrender period are concerned, the invaluable benchmark study is in English, by Kyoko Hirano. Considerations of space having precluded the inclusion of a separate bibliography, the lengthy endnotes contain (with a few clearly noted exceptions) full citations for each source the first time it is cited in any particular chapter. Credits for the illustrations are given at the end of the book.

A note on Japanese names: Throughout the text, I have followed the Japanese convention in which the family name or surname precedes the given or personal name (thus, for example, Prime Minister Yoshida's full name is Yoshida Shigeru). Of necessity, however, this rule is reversed in two situations: where Japanese living outside the country have chosen to follow the opposite (Western) order, and in identifying the authors of publications in English. If uncertainty arises, readers can usually resolve this by referring to the index, where individuals are listed alphabetically by their family names.

EMBRACING DEFEAT

Japan in the Wake of World War II

INTRODUCTION

Japan's emergence as a modern nation was stunning to behold: swifter, more audacious, more successful, and ultimately more crazed, murderous, and self-destructive than anyone had imagined possible. In retrospect, it seemed almost an illusion—a ninety-three-year dream become nightmare that began and ended with American warships. In 1853, a modest fleet of four vessels, two of them coal-burning "black ships," had arrived to force the country open. In 1945, a huge, glistening armada came back to close it.

When all this began with the arrival of Commodore Matthew Perry, Japan was a small country with few obvious resources. For over two centuries, intercourse with foreigners had been largely prohibited by its feudal shoguns Although the economy had become commercialized in those long years of seclusion, no industrial revolution had taken place, nor had there been any striking advances in science. If Americans and Europeans found these island people capable and clever as well as exotic, no one thought to say of them, as Napoleon had of neighboring China with its vast territories, its awesome population, and its millennia of high civilization, that here was a sleeping giant.

In 1868, dissident samurai drove out the shogun and established a government in the name of the emperor, hitherto a remote, powerless figure.

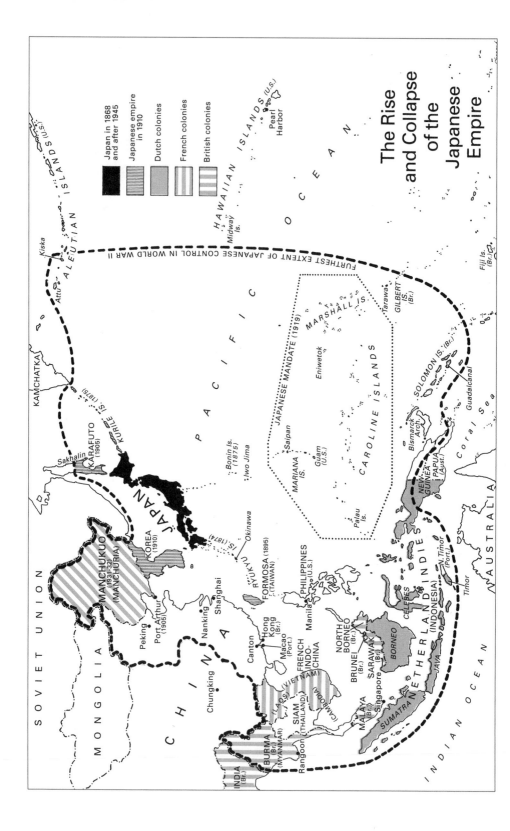

The Rise
and Collapse
of the
Japanese
Empire

Japan in 1868
and after 1945

Japanese empire
in 1910

Dutch colonies

French colonies

British colonies

PACIFIC OCEAN

HAWAIIAN ISLANDS (U.S.)
Pearl Harbor

ALEUTIAN ISLANDS (U.S.)
Kiska
Attu

FURTHEST EXTENT OF JAPANESE CONTROL IN WORLD WAR II

Midway Is.

KAMCHATKA

Sakhalin
KARAFUTO (1905)
KURILE IS. (1875)

JAPAN

KOREA (1910)

Port Arthur (1905)
Peking

SOVIET UNION

MONGOLIA

MANCHUKUO
(1931-32)
(MANCHURIA)

Chungking

C H I N A

Nanking
Shanghai

Canton
Hong Kong (Br.)
Macao (Port.)

Bonin Is. (1875)
Iwo Jima

Okinawa
RYUKYU IS. (1874)

FORMOSA (1895)
(TAIWAN)

PHILIPPINES
(U.S.)
Manila

JAPANESE MANDATE (1919)

MARIANA IS.
Saipan

Guam (U.S.)

Palau Is.

MARSHALL IS.

Eniwetok

CAROLINE ISLANDS

Tarawa
GILBERT IS. (Br.)

SOLOMON IS. (Br.)
Guadalcanal

Bismarck Arch.

NEW GUINEA
PAPUA (Aust.)

Coral Sea

AUSTRALIA

FRENCH INDO-CHINA
(LAOS, VIETNAM)

(CAMBODIA)

SIAM (THAILAND)

BURMA (Br.)
(MYANMAR)
Rangoon

INDIA (Br.)

MALAYA (Br.)
Singapore

NORTH BORNEO (Br.)
BRUNEI (Br.)
SARAWAK (Br.)

BORNEO

CELEBES

NETHERLAND INDIES
(INDONESIA)

SUMATRA

JAVA

Timor
N. Timor (Port.)

INDIAN OCEAN

Fiji Is. (Br.)

Their new nation-state proved a quick study, learning the modern arts of war as well as peace and showing itself particularly adept at understanding how to survive in an imperialist world. As a line in a popular Japanese song of the 1880s put it, "There is a Law of Nations, it is true, / but when the moment comes, remember, / the Strong eat up the Weak."[1] While most of the rest of the world fell under the control of the Western powers, Japan emulated them and joined their banquet. In 1895, the imperial army and navy brought China to its knees; this decisive victory on the Asian mainland, capped by an enormous indemnity, precipitated a scramble for international concessionary areas torn from the very body of the sleeping giant. "Slicing the Chinese melon" was the pleasant way westerners came to speak of this.

The war brought imperial Japan its first colony, the island of Formosa. Triumph over czarist Russia ten years later, after costly battles on land and a sensational victory at sea, gave the nation an internationally recognized foothold in Manchuria and paved the way for taking Korea as a second colony. Loans raised in New York and London helped to finance this war, and the Western powers turned a deaf ear to the appeals of Korean patriots. In World War I, Japan joined the hostilities on the Allied side, moving against German holdings in China, and was rewarded by being seated as one of the "Big Five" nations at the Versailles peace conference, where the victors met to punish Germany and rearrange the world. No other nonwhite, non-Christian people at that time could have imagined playing the great game of global power and influence at this level; nor could anyone anticipate the disastrous breakdown of security that lay ahead. World War I, after all, had been the war to end all wars.

In the 1920s and 1930s, as the world plunged into depression and instability, the country's leaders responded (and contributed) to this disorder with an increasingly frantic quest for control over the markets and resources of Asia. *Dai Nippon Teikoku*—the "Great Empire of Japan"— spread like a monstrous stain. (On Japanese maps, the empire was always colored red.) Nineteen thirty-one saw the takeover of Manchuria; 1937, the launching of all-out aggression against China; 1941, the attack on Pearl Harbor as part of a strategy of seizing control of the southern reaches of Asia and the Pacific. At the peak of its expansion in early 1942, Japan bestrode Asia like a colossus, one foot planted in the mid-Pacific, the other deep in the interior of China, its ambitious grasp reaching north to the Aleutian Islands and south to the Western colonial enclaves of Southeast Asia. Japan's "Greater East Asia Co-Prosperity Sphere" briefly embraced the Netherlands East Indies, French Indochina, the British colonial possessions of Burma, Malaya, and Hong Kong, and America's Philippine colony. There was talk of reaching further to take India, Australia, possibly even Hawaii. *Banzai* cries to the glory of the emperor's holy war and the invincibility of his loyal soldiers and sailors pierced the heavens in myriad places at home and overseas. Poets, priests, and propagandists alike extolled the superiority of the "Yamato race" and the sublime destiny of the Imperial Way.

The Co-Prosperity Sphere was but a chimera; the euphoria of the first half-year of the Pacific War but a dream within a dream, soon dismissed by Japanese themselves as the "victory disease." They had run amok, badly miscalculating both the resilience of Chinese resistance and the resources, psychological as well as material, that the United States could bring to a protracted conflict. They had, at the same time, become prisoners of their own war rhetoric—of holy war, death before dishonor, blood debts to their war dead, the inviolability of the emperor-centered "national polity," the imminence of a decisive battle that would turn the tide against the "Chinese bandits" and stay the "demonic Anglo-Americans." Long after it had become obvious that Japan was doomed, its leaders all the way up to the emperor remained unable to contemplate surrender. They were psychologically blocked, capable only of stumbling forward.

Perry, said the Americans (with their charming habit of neglecting such historical inconveniences as imperialism, colonialism, and the breakdown of the global economy) had let the genie out of the bottle—and that genie had become a blood-soaked monster. From the rape of Nanking in the opening months of the war against China to the rape of Manila in the final stages of the Pacific War, the emperor's soldiers and sailors left a trail of unspeakable cruelty and rapacity. As it turned out, they also devoured themselves. Japanese died in hopeless suicide charges, starved to death in the field, killed their own wounded rather than let them fall into enemy hands, and murdered their civilian compatriots in places such as Saipan and Okinawa. They watched helplessly as fire bombs destroyed their cities—all the while listening to their leaders natter on about how it might be necessary for the "hundred million" all to die "like shattered jewels." The most obvious legacy of the Greater East Asia Co-Prosperity Sphere was death and destruction. In China alone, perhaps 15 million people died. The Japanese lost nearly 3 million—and their entire empire as well.

After this terrible fury, Japan entered a strange seclusion.

It withdrew from the world again—not willingly, but under orders from the victors; and not alone, as in the centuries before Perry, but locked in an almost sensual embrace with its American conquerors. And soon enough, it became apparent that the Americans could not or would not let go. Beginning with Pearl Harbor and ending with the emperor's capitulation after the atomic bombings of Hiroshima and Nagasaki, the war between Japan and the Allied powers lasted three years and eight months; the occupation of the defeated nation began in August 1945 and ended in April 1952, six years and eight months later, almost twice as long as the war itself. In those years, Japan had no sovereignty and accordingly no diplomatic relations. No Japanese were allowed to travel abroad until the occupation was almost over; no major political, administrative, or economic decisions were possible without the conquerors' approval; no public criticism of the American regime was permissible, although in the end dissident voices were irrepressible.

Initially, the Americans imposed a root-and-branch agenda of "demilitarization and democratization" that was in every sense a remarkable display of arrogant idealism—both self-righteous and genuinely visionary. Then, well before their departure, they reversed course and began rearming their erstwhile enemy as a subordinate Cold War partner in cooperation with the less liberal elements of the society. Yet despite the ultimate emergence of a conservative postwar state, the ideals of peace and democracy took root in Japan—not as a borrowed ideology or imposed vision, but as a lived experience and a seized opportunity. They found expression through a great and often discordant diversity of voices.

There was no historical precedent for this sort of relationship, nor anything truly comparable elsewhere in the wake of the war. Responsibility for occupied Germany, Japan's former Axis partner, divided as it was among the United States, England, France, and the Soviet Union, lacked the focused intensity that came with America's unilateral control over Japan. Germany also escaped the messianic fervor of General Douglas MacArthur, the postsurrender potentate in Tokyo. For the victors, occupying defeated Germany had none of the *exoticism* of what took place in Japan: the total control over a pagan, "Oriental" society by white men who were (unequivocally, in General MacArthur's view) engaged in a Christian mission. The occupation of Japan was the last immodest exercise in the colonial conceit known as "the white man's burden."[2]

It would be difficult to find another cross-cultural moment more intense, unpredictable, ambiguous, confusing, and *electric* than this one. The Americans arrived anticipating, many of them, a traumatic confrontation with fanatical emperor worshippers. They were accosted instead by women who called "yoo hoo" to the first troops landing on the beaches in full battle gear, and men who bowed and asked what it was the conquerors wished. They found themselves seduced (far more than they realized) by polite manners as well as by elegant presents and entertainments. Most of all, they encountered a populace sick of war, contemptuous of the militarists who had led them to disaster, and all but overwhelmed by the difficulties of their present circumstances in a ruined land. More than anything else, it turned out, the losers wished both to forget the past and to transcend it.

Understandably, these early postwar years have been described positively as Japan's "American interlude" or, more negatively, as an epoch of unusually crude and forced "Americanization." In either case, what has usually been emphasized is the imposition of America's will on an alien land. Winning, more than losing, has defined the moment. It is the victors who capture attention, just as they took command of the war itself. The occupiers and their agenda hold pride of place in most accounts, whereas the vanquished country itself is located in the postwar context of a world falling into antagonistic Cold War camps and discussed in terms of a vision of that moment which was distinctly American. The once-formidable Japanese enemy becomes miniaturized, the conquered people but shadow figures on the margins of a new global drama.

Such story lines are hardly surprising. The Allied triumph was stupendous, and where Japan was concerned it was in the fruits of this victory that the story seemed so clearly to lie. At the end of August 1945—in the still-inaugural years of what had been proclaimed as the "American century"—history in the form of a unique occupation with a compellingly visionary agenda approached a ruined, shriven land in a world careering in alarming new directions. What else of remotely comparable import remained to be said about that thoroughly defeated and demoralized nation? For journalists, and later for historians as well, what the Americans would do to the Japanese was the story of most compelling interest. Until recently, it has been difficult to imagine the occupation as an "embrace," or to consider what effect the losers might have had on the victors and their agendas, or how that "American interlude" might have reinforced rather than altered tendencies within the defeated country. It has been difficult, certainly for outsiders, to grasp the defeat and occupation as a lived *Japanese* experience.

Half a century later, however, we can begin to see things differently. Shattered lands, shattered peoples, shattered empires, and shattered dreams have been one of the central stories of our times. Certainly, there is much to be learned from the world as viewed through the eyes of the defeated—not only about misery, disorientation, cynicism, and resentment, but also about hope, resilience, visions, and dreams. In the chapters that follow, I have tried to convey "from within" some sense of the Japanese experience of defeat by focusing on social and cultural developments as well as on that most elusive of phenomena, "popular consciousness"—departing, in the process, from the approach taken in most historical accounts, including my own earlier writings.[3] To put it a little differently, I have tried to capture a sense of what it meant to start over in a ruined world by recovering the voices of people at all levels of society. World War II did not really end for the Japanese until 1952, and the years of war, defeat, and occupation left an indelible mark on those who lived through them. No matter how affluent the country later became, these remained the touchstone years for thinking about national identity and personal values.

Much as we may desire to simplify peoples and problems, there was no single or singular "Japanese" response to the defeat apart from a widespread abhorrence of war. On the contrary, what is fascinating is how kaleidoscopic such responses were. This was a far cry from what many of the "old Asia hands" in Washington and London had predicted, fixated as they were on the idea that Orientals were, at their essence, an "obedient herd." The victors arrived with briefing papers outlining salient features of "the Japanese personality," some of which were perceptive but many of which were cartoons. (Japanese intelligence agencies, in turn, were waiting with their own lists of "American characteristics.")[4] No one on either side, however, predicted how diverse and spirited would be the responses to defeat—and to liberation from war and wartime regimentation. Because the defeat was so shattering, the surrender so unconditional, the disgrace of the militarists so complete, the misery the "holy war" had brought home so personal, starting over involved not merely reconstructing buildings but also rethinking what it meant to speak of a good life and good society.

In the immediate wake of defeat, a great many individuals at the highest levels displayed no concern at all for the good of society. They concentrated instead on enriching themselves by the wholesale plunder of military stockpiles and public resources. The mystique of racial and social solidarity that had saturated wartime propaganda and behavior seemed to disappear overnight. Police operatives tore their hair at the spectacle of such rampant personal aggrandizement (when not themselves looting and hoarding), and ordinary men and women expressed disgust at the venality of yesterday's respected leaders and compatriots. Before the victors ever set foot in Japan, defeat had profoundly altered how people thought and behaved.

It was in this atmosphere of flux and uncertainty that the Americans proceeded to dismantle the oppressive controls of the imperial state. It remained for the vanquished themselves to fill this new space, however, and they did so in often unexpected ways. Support for socialist and communist agendas exceeded anything the Americans had anticipated, as did the explosive energy of the nascent labor movement. Mid-level bureaucrats emerged as initiators of serious reform. Prostitutes and black-market operatives created distinctive, iconoclastic cultures of defeat. Publishers responded to a huge hunger for words with publications that ran the gamut from sleazy pulp magazines to incisive critical journals and books as well as wide-ranging translations of Western writings. Portmanteau concepts such as "love" and "culture" were discussed obsessively, and the adjective "new" was coupled with promiscuous abandon to almost every noun in sight. Private attachments supplanted the old state-enforced dictates of public morality. Connoisseurs of decadence emerged as popular critics of the unsavory wartime cult of "wholesomeness." New heroes and heroines were discovered and idolized, new celebrities rocketed to pop-culture fame. Messianic religions flourished, and pretenders to the throne emerged. Millions of ordinary people spoke out in community meetings and in letters to the press as well as in a small avalanche of communications to the occupation authorities. Tens of millions found themselves longing for material affluence of the sort their American overlords so conspicuously enjoyed.

This was untidy. It was also energetic and emancipating, and for the first few years even the Communists found it easy to speak of the occupation forces as an "army of liberation." Just as the dynamism of the Japanese in defeat has been underestimated, however, so too the nature of the "Americanism" of the occupiers has generally been oversimplified. The reforms that the victors introduced were unique to both moment and place. They reflected an agenda inspired by heavy doses of liberal New Deal attitudes, labor reformism, and Bill of Rights idealism of a sort that was in the process of being repudiated (or ignored) in the United States. This agenda was never introduced to other American-occupied areas in Asia such as the southern half of Korea and the southern reaches of Japan itself—Okinawa and the Ryukyu Islands—where harsh strategic considerations held sway. Even in its most idealistic early phases, moreover, the occupation's "Americanism" was schizophrenic. Visions of "democratization" that would have seemed extreme if proposed within the United States went hand in hand with severe authoritarian rule.

We normally see August 1945 as a great divide between militarist Japan and a new democratic nation. This *was* a watershed moment, but it is also true that Japan remained under the control of fundamentally military regimes from the early 1930s straight through to 1952. However high minded they may have been, General MacArthur and his command ruled their new domain as neocolonial overlords, beyond challenge or criticism, as inviolate as the emperor and his officials had ever been. They epitomized hierarchy—not merely vis-à-vis the defeated enemy, but within their own rigidly layered ranks as well as by their white-men's rule. One of the most pernicious aspects of the occupation was that the Asian peoples who had suffered most from imperial Japan's depredations—the Chinese, Koreans, Indonesians, and Filipinos—had no serious role, no influential presence at all in the defeated land. They became invisible. Asian contributions to defeating the emperor's soldiers and sailors were displaced by an all-consuming focus on the American victory in the "Pacific War." By this same process of vaporization, the crimes that had been committed against Asian peoples through colonization as well as war were all the more easily put out of mind.

Because the victors had no linguistic or cultural entrée to the losers' society, they had little choice but to govern "indirectly," through existing organs of government. This was unavoidable. As actually put into practice, however, this indirect rule led to several incongruous developments. For all practical purposes, General MacArthur's supergovernment relied on the Japanese bureaucracy to carry out its directives, creating in effect a two-tiered mandarinate. When the Americans departed, the native mandarins carried on, stronger than they had been even during the war. For ideological purposes, MacArthur also chose to rely on Emperor Hirohito, in whose name all of Asia had been savaged. He went so far as to secretly discourage queries about Hirohito's abdication that came from the emperor's own entourage while publicly praising him as the leader of the new democracy.

This American royalism would have been inconceivable without the determination of the general and his closest aides to exonerate the emperor of all war responsibility, even of moral responsibility for allowing the atrocious war to be waged in his name. The emperor's active contribution to his country's aggression had not been negligible, although serious investigation of this was thwarted by the occupiers. His moral responsibility, in any case, was transparent; and in choosing not merely to ignore this but to deny it, the Americans came close to turning the entire issue of "war responsibility" into a joke. If the man in whose name imperial Japan had conducted foreign and military policy for twenty years was not held accountable for the initiation or conduct of the war, why should anyone expect ordinary people to dwell on such matters, or to think seriously about their own personal responsibility?

The ramifications of such decisions and practices were enormous. The victor's own modus operandi contributed to the institutionalization, as it were, of oxymorons: "bureaucratic democracy" and "imperial democracy." At the same time, the obsequious treatment of the emperor, coupled with the peculiar way in which a handful of top military and civilian leaders were found guilty of war crimes in a showcase trial convened by the victors in Tokyo, reinforced a strong popular inclination to ignore what the men of Yamato had done to others in their frantic quest for empire and security. After the occupation, foreigners seized on such developments as evidence of distinctive Japanese inclinations—areas where, it was suggested, the victor's idealistic vision had failed to take hold. In fact, such phenomena were, if peculiar at all, then binationally so. Much that lies at the heart of contemporary Japanese society—the nature of its democracy, the intensity of popular feelings about pacifism and remilitarization, the manner in which the war is remembered (and forgotten)—derives from the complexity of the interplay between the victors and the vanquished.

To many Japanese, looking back, the few years that followed defeat constitute a period of unusually chaotic vitality when the adoption of political models other than a state-led capitalism seemed possible, and one could at least dream of an international role other than creeping remilitarization under America's nuclear umbrella. Hardship often has its retrospective attractions, and nostalgia sometimes sweetens the recollections of that time. Personal memories have, in recent years, been buttressed by an outpouring of publications in Japan that shows little sign of abating. Books, articles, and special issues of magazines continue to address the experience of defeat and occupation from every conceivable perspective—ranging from policy documents and exhaustively researched scholarly studies to diaries and reminiscences, letters and journalistic pieces, photographs and day-by-day chronologies. Many celebrities who made their names in the wake of defeat are only now passing away; and each such departure is usually accompanied by a piercing and poignant evocation of those years, so long ago and yet still so palpably connected to the present. It has been a daunting task to try to grasp and share this, in no little part because there is always so much more that could be told, and of course so much more to be learned.

Something about Japan invites people to view it hermetically, and the sealed space of the years following defeat can all too easily come to seem but an exaggerated version of "typical" Japanese uniqueness. It is not just outsiders who tend to isolate and insulate the Japanese experience; no one makes more of a fetish of the supposed singularity of the national character and the national experience than the country's own cultural essentialists and neonationalists. Even during that passing moment in the 1980s when Japan seemed to have emerged as the master of global capitalism, it was the peculiarly "Japanese" dimension of its practices that drew greatest attention at home as well as abroad. Although all peoples and cultures set themselves apart (and are set apart by others) by stressing differences, this tends to be carried to an extreme where Japan is concerned.

The years following defeat certainly did comprise an exaggerated moment. As William James once wrote about the religious experience, however, it is such moments of extremity that often best reveal the essence of things. I myself find the concrete details and textures of this extraordinary experience of a whole country starting over absorbing, but they do not strike me as alien, exotic, or even mainly instructive as an episode in the history of Japan or U.S.–Japanese relations. On the contrary, what is most compelling from my own perspective is that defeat and occupation forced Japanese in every walk of life to struggle, in exceptionally naked ways, with the most fundamental of life's issues—and that they responded in recognizably human, fallible, and often contradictory ways that can tell us a great deal about ourselves and our world in general.

The ease with which the great majority of Japanese were able to throw off a decade and a half of the most intense militaristic indoctrination, for instance, offers lessons in the limits of socialization and the fragility of ideology that we have seen elsewhere in this century in the collapse of totalitarian regimes. (That Japan's monarchy was propped up while so many other imperial houses were toppled offers, in itself, a suggestive comparative story in politics and ideology.) Or again, American veterans of the Vietnam War will surely experience a shock of recognition on learning how the emperor's soldiers and sailors struggled to come to terms with the contempt with which they were commonly greeted upon returning from their lost war. Similarly, the preoccupation with their own misery that led most Japanese to ignore the suffering they had inflicted on others helps illuminate the ways in which victim consciousness colors the identities that all groups and peoples construct for themselves. Historical amnesia concerning war crimes has naturally taken particular forms in Japan, but the patterns of remembering and forgetting are most meaningful when seen in the broader context of public memory and myth-making generally, issues that have deservedly come to attract great attention in recent years. "Responsibility," addressed in many contexts in the cauldron of defeat and reconstruction, is hardly an insular concern.

When the Japanese ransacked their national history for precedents pertinent to their "new" circumstances—for the roots of a native democracy, examples of principled resistance to militarism, or indigenous formulations of repentance and atonement—the examples they came up with were naturally specific to their past. What they were doing, however, was what all people do in moments of traumatic change; they were finding—inventing, if need be—something familiar to hold on to. Everyday language was itself a bridge that enabled many men and women to cross from war to peace without experiencing complete psychological disorientation—for many totemic words, catchphrases, even texts that had been popular during the war proved perfectly adaptable to radically altered interpretations and objectives in the postwar years. Again, giving familiar language new meaning is one of the ways people everywhere rationalize and legitimize substantive change.

One can, of course, recross such "bridges" and head back in directions presumably left behind. Neonationalistic voices are strong in contemporary Japan, and some of the loudest of these have zeroed in on precisely the years discussed here, depicting the period of defeat and occupation as an overwhelmingly humiliating epoch when genuinely free choice was repressed and alien models were imposed. My own assessment of the vitality of the period and dynamism of the Japanese role in shaping postwar consciousness is (however qualified) more positive. What matters is what the Japanese themselves made of their experience of defeat, then and thereafter; and, for a half century now, most of them have consistently made it the touchstone for affirming a commitment to "peace and democracy." This is the great mantra of postwar Japan. These are the talismanic words that individuals filled with their own often disparate meanings and continue to debate today; and neither the concepts, nor the debates, nor the weight of historical memory in these struggles are peculiar to Japan.

Part I

VICTOR
and
VANQUISHED

chapter one

SHATTERED LIVES

It was August 15, 1945, shortly before noon. What followed would never be forgotten.

Aihara Yū was twenty-eight years old then, a farmer's wife in rural Shizuoka prefecture. Through the decades to come, the day would replay itself in her memory like an old filmstrip, a staccato newsreel in black and white.

She was working outdoors when a messenger arrived breathless from the village. It had been announced that the emperor would be making a personal broadcast at noon, he exclaimed before rushing off. Everyone was to come and listen.

The news that America, the land of the enemy, had disappeared into the sea would hardly have been more startling. The emperor was to speak! In the two decades since he had ascended the Chrysanthemum Throne, Emperor Hirohito had never once spoken directly to all his subjects. Until now the sovereign's words had been handed down in the form of imperial rescripts—as printed texts, pronouncements humbly read by others.

Half a century later, Aihara could still recall every detail. She rushed to the village, repeating over and over to herself a line from the Imperial Rescript on Education, which everyone knew by heart from daily recitation during their school years. "Should any emergency arise," it went, "offer yourselves courageously to the State." She knew the country's situation was desperate and could only imagine that the emperor was going to exhort every Japanese to make even greater efforts to support the war—to be prepared, indeed, to fight to the bitter end.

The villagers had gathered around the single local radio over which the single state-run station was received. Reception was poor. Static crackled around the emperor's words, and the words themselves were difficult to grasp. The emperor's voice was high pitched and his enunciation stilted. He did not speak in colloquial Japanese, but in a highly formal language studded with ornamental classical phrases. Aihara was just exchanging puzzled glances with others in the crowd when a man who had recently arrived from bombed-out Tokyo spoke up—almost, she recalled, as if to himself. "This means," he whispered, "that Japan has lost."

Aihara felt all strength drain from her body. Before she knew what happened she found herself lying face down on the ground. Others who collapsed around her—as she later pictured the scene—lay on their backs. The emperor's voice was gone, but the radio droned on. An announcer was speaking. One of his sentences burned itself into her mind, where it would remain for the rest of her life: "The Japanese military will be disarmed and allowed to return to Japan."

With this, Aihara Yū experienced a flood of hope. Her husband, who had been drafted into the army and sent to Manchuria, might soon return! All that day and through the night, she prayed, "Please, my husband, don't commit suicide." Japanese fighting men had been indoctrinated to chose death over surrender, a path Aihara feared her husband might take as a proper and moral response to this extraordinary moment.

For three years, Aihara continued to pray for her husband's return. Only then did she learn that he had been killed in a battle with Soviet forces five days before she was summoned from the fields to hear her sovereign's voice. The war had, after all, permanently shattered her life.[1]

Euphemistic Surrender

The millions of Japanese who gathered around neighborhood radios to hear that broadcast were not "citizens" but the emperor's *subjects,* and it was in his name that they had supported their country's long war against China and the Allied Powers. In Japanese parlance, it had been a "holy war"; in announcing Japan's capitulation, the forty-four-year-old sovereign faced the challenge of replacing such rhetoric with new language.

This was a formidable challenge. Fourteen years earlier, in the sixth

Emperor Hirohito's subjects hear his voice for the first time, in the
unforgettable radio broadcast of August 15, 1945, in which he announced
Japan's capitulation and exhorted the populace to "endure the unendurable."

year of his reign, Emperor Hirohito had acquiesced in the imperial army's
takeover of the three Chinese provinces known collectively as Manchuria.
Eight years previously, Japan had initiated open war against China in the
emperor's name. From that time on, Hirohito had appeared in public
only in the bemedalled military garb of commander in chief. In December 1941, he issued the rescript that initiated hostilities against the United
States and various European powers. Now, three years and eight months
later, his task was not merely to call a halt to a lost war, but to do so without disavowing Japan's war aims or acknowledging the nation's atrocities—
and in a manner that divorced him from any personal responsibility for
these many years of aggression.

It was Hirohito himself who first broached the idea of breaking precedent and using the airwaves to speak directly to his subjects. The text of
his announcement, not finalized until close to midnight the previous
night, had been composed and delivered under great pressure. Much intrigue was involved in recording and then hiding it from military officers
opposed to a surrender. Despite its chaotic genesis, the rescript emerged
as a polished ideological gem.[2]

Although many shared Aihara Yū's difficulty in comprehending the emperor's words, his message (which was simultaneously transmitted to Japanese overseas by shortwave radio) was quickly understood by everyone. Sophisticated listeners such as the Tokyo man in her village explained the broadcast to their puzzled compatriots. Radio announcers immediately summarized the rescript and its import in everyday language. Newspapers rushed out special editions reproducing the emperor's text accompanied by editorial commentary.

Like insects in amber, lines and phrases from the broadcast soon became locked in popular consciousness. The emperor never spoke explicitly of either "surrender" or "defeat." He simply observed that the war "did not turn in Japan's favor, and trends of the world were not advantageous to us." He enjoined his subjects to "endure the unendurable and bear the unbearable"—words that would be quoted times beyond counting in the months to come.

With this rescript, the emperor endeavored to accomplish the impossible: to turn the announcement of humiliating defeat into yet another affirmation of Japan's war conduct and of his own transcendent morality. He began by reiterating what he had told his subjects in 1941 when Japan declared war on the United States—that the war had been begun to ensure the survival of Japan and the stability of Asia, not out of any aggressive intent to interfere with the sovereign integrity of other countries. In this spirit, Hirohito now expressed deep regret to those countries that had cooperated with Japan "for the liberation of East Asia." With reference to the recent atomic bombings of Hiroshima and Nagasaki, the emperor went on to present Japan's decision to capitulate as nothing less than a magnanimous act that might save humanity itself from annihilation by an atrocious adversary. "The enemy has for the first time used cruel bombs to kill and maim extremely large numbers of the innocent," he declared, "and the heavy casualties are beyond measure. To continue the war further could lead in the end not only to the extermination of our race, but also to the destruction of all human civilization." By accepting Allied demands to end the war, the emperor declared it was his purpose to "open the way for a great peace for thousands of generations to come."

He then proceeded to offer himself as the embodiment of the nation's suffering, its ultimate victim, transforming the sacrifices of his people into his own agony with a classical turn of phrase. When he contemplated those of his subjects who had died in the war, the bereaved kin they left behind, and the extraordinary difficulties all Japanese now faced, he exclaimed, "my vital organs are torn asunder." For many of his listeners, this was the most moving part of the broadcast. Some confessed to being overcome by

American sailors at Pearl Harbor celebrate the news of Japan's capitulation.

a sense of shame and guilt that, in failing to live up to their sovereign's expectations, they had caused him grief.

To evoke such emotions in August 1945 was an impressive accomplishment. Close to 3 million Japanese were dead, many more wounded or seriously ill, and the country in ruins as a consequence of the war waged in the emperor's name, yet it was his agony on which his loyal subjects were expected to dwell. That this was the first time the emperor had spoken directly to the public made the appeal all the more effective. Perhaps he was indeed not just a symbol of their suffering, but the most conspicuous victim of the lost war. Certainly his subjects could imagine that previous imperial exhortations to fight and sacrifice had not reflected his true intentions, but had been extracted by evil advisers. Only now, as sentimental royalists would soon put it, were people actually hearing the sovereign's *true* voice. It was "as if the sun had at long last emerged from behind dark clouds."[3]

Although the emperor reaffirmed his faith in "the sincerity of my good and loyal subjects" and assured them that he would "always be with" them, he also admonished them not to fall out among themselves in the chaos and misery of defeat. It was essential to remain united as a great family, firmly believing in "the invincibility of the divine country" and devoting every effort to the reconstruction of a nation that would preserve its traditional identity while keeping pace with "the progress and fortune of the world."

Behind these brave but nervous words lay a gnawing fear of future revolutionary upheaval in defeated Japan—a dire prospect the emperor had been warned about for months. This was, then, not merely the official closing statement of a lost war, but the opening pronunciamento of an urgent campaign to maintain imperial control as well as social and political stability in a shattered nation.[4]

Responses to the emperor's broadcast varied greatly. Some residents of Tokyo did make their way to the imperial palace, still standing amid a ruined cityscape. (U.S. policy makers had excluded this as a bombing target, although part of it had been inadvertently destroyed anyway). Photographs of them kneeling on the gravel in front of the palace, bowing in sorrow for having failed to live up to the emperor's hopes and expectations, later were offered as a defining image for the moment of capitulation.

This was, in fact, a misleading image. The number of people who gathered before the imperial residence was relatively small, and the tears that ordinary people everywhere did shed reflected a multitude of sentiments apart from emperor-centered grief: anguish, regret, bereavement, anger at having been deceived, sudden emptiness and loss of purpose—or simple joy at the unexpected surcease of misery and death. Kido Kōichi, the lord keeper of the privy seal and Emperor Hirohito's closest confidant, captured the palpable sense of relief in a diary entry in which he noted that some people were actually cheering in front of the palace. It was clear, he observed with some ambivalence, that they felt a great burden had been lifted.[5]

As Aihara Yū's prayers indicated, it did not seem unreasonable to anticipate that great numbers of Japanese might chose death over the dishonor of defeat. Through the long years of war, fighting men had been forbidden to surrender. There was no greater shame than this, they were told. As the war drew closer home, civilians had also been indoctrinated to fight to the bitter end and die "like shattered jewels," as the saying went. In the wake of the emperor's words, however, the number who actually chose the jeweled path was fewer than had been imagined. Several hundred individuals, most of them military officers, committed suicide—just

Word of the victory reaches enlisted men in the U.S. Navy's Special
Construction Battalion in the Pacific theater.

as many Nazi officers did on the capitulation of Germany, where there
never had existed a comparable cult of patriotic suicide.[6]

Indeed, at the official level, the most notable immediate response to the
momentous broadcast of August 15 was pragmatic and self-serving. Military officers and civilian bureaucrats throughout the country threw themselves frenetically into the tasks of destroying their files and disbursing
vast hoards of military supplies in illicit ways. Although the emperor's
broadcast put an end to the American air raids, it was said, with a fine
touch of hyperbole, that the skies over Tokyo remained black with smoke
for days to come. Bonfires of documents replaced napalm's hellfires as the
wartime elites followed the lead of their sovereign and devoted themselves
to obscuring their wartime deeds.

Unconditional Surrender

The victors did not witness these bonfires, for the first major contingents of Allied occupation forces did not arrive in Japan until two weeks

Malnourished American
and British POWs
liberated on Formosa in
late September 1945.

after the emperor's broadcast. With them came a new, imperious figure
of authority in the person of General Douglas MacArthur, who had
been designated the Supreme Commander for the Allied Powers in
Japan. On September 2, in an imposing ceremony on the deck of the
U.S. battleship *Missouri* in Tokyo Bay, MacArthur, representatives of
nine other Allied powers, and Japanese officials signed the instruments
of surrender.

The ceremony was laden with symbolism. Missouri was the home
state of President Harry S. Truman, whose major decisions regarding
Japan had been to use the atomic bombs on two Japanese cities and to
hold firm to the policy of "unconditional surrender" of his deceased predecessor Franklin D. Roosevelt. One of the flags displayed on the *Missouri* was the same Old Glory that had been flying over the White
House on December 7, 1941, when Pearl Harbor was attacked. Another,

rushed by plane from Annapolis, was the standard with thirty-one stars used by Commodore Matthew Perry on his flagship *Powhatten* when his gunboat diplomacy forced Japan to end more than two centuries of feudal seclusion. The appearance of Perry's small, mixed fleet of sailing vessels and coal-fueled, smoke-belching "black ships" in 1853 had propelled Japan onto its ultimately disastrous course of global competition with the Western powers. Now, a shade under a century later, the Americans had returned with a gigantic navy, army, and air force that reflected technology and technocracy of an order Perry could not have envisioned in his wildest dreams—flaunting the commodore's old flag as a reprimand.

Two Japanese officials signed the surrender documents: General Umezu Yoshijirō, representing the imperial armed forces, and the diplomat Shigemitsu Mamoru, representing the imperial government. Shigemitsu had lost a leg in 1932 in a bomb attack by a Korean protesting Japan's colonization of his country, and his awkward gait on the rolling deck of the American battleship conveyed an uncanny impression of a crippled and vulnerable Japan. Those present to sign the surrender documents, however, stood in the shadow of those who were missing: for the emperor did not participate in these proceedings, nor did any representative of the imperial family or the Imperial Household Ministry. This concession on the part of Allied authorities caught observers in the camps of both victor and vanquished by surprise. Until the end of the war, even unabashedly proimperial American officials such as the former ambassador to Japan Joseph Grew had assumed that the emperor would and should sign the formal articles of surrender. And even after the Japanese learned that the emperor would be personally spared this ordeal, they still assumed that an intimate representative from the court, perhaps blood kin to the sovereign, would be required to sign the surrender documents on his behalf. The emperor's complete exclusion from the great morality play of September 2 was a heartening signal to the Japanese side, for it intimated that the victors might be willing to disassociate the emperor from ultimate war responsibility.[7]

In his address on the *Missouri*, MacArthur spoke eloquently about the hope of all humanity that "a better world shall emerge out of the blood and carnage of the past—a world founded upon faith and understanding—a world dedicated to the dignity of man and the fulfillment of his most cherished wish—for freedom, tolerance and justice." In words directed explicitly to his fellow Americans, he reported that "the holy mission has been completed," and warned that the utter destructiveness of modern

The enormity of the defeat did not really sink in until the formal surrender
ceremony on the USS *Missouri* on September 2, 1945, where the Japanese
delegation was surrounded and almost literally overwhelmed by the armaments
and personnel of the victorious Allied forces.

war meant that "Armageddon will be at our door" if the world did not
learn to live in peace. Where defeated Japan was concerned, the supreme
commander declared that the terms of surrender committed the victors
to liberate the Japanese people from a "condition of slavery" and to ensure that the energies of the race were turned into constructive channels—what he referred to as expanding "vertically rather than
horizontally." These were stern but solemn and hopeful words, and their
high-minded tone offered a modicum of further comfort to Japanese lead-

ers who were still nervously attempting to gauge what the victors might have in store for them.[8]

Still, to most patriots the surrender ceremony "spelled doom," as one American general present on the *Missouri* put it. "Although the inscrutable faces of their representatives gave no indication of their feelings," he recalled, "their demeanor was so extremely somber as to indicate that they fully realized that their once-proud empire had been humbled into dust and that their national hopes and aspirations were at an end."[9] The future remained terribly uncertain, and the enormity of the nation's humiliation had only begun to sink in. The country's utter subjugation was reinforced by the dramatic setting of the surrender ceremony itself. The imperial navy had long since been demolished. Apart from a few thousand rickety planes held in reserve for suicide attacks, Japan's air force—not only its aircraft, but its skilled pilots as well—had virtually ceased to exist. Its merchant marine lay at the bottom of the ocean. Almost all of the country's major cities had been fire bombed, and millions of the emperor's loyal subjects were homeless. The defeated imperial army was scattered throughout Asia and the islands of the Pacific Ocean, its millions of surviving soldiers starving, wounded, sick, and demoralized. But Tokyo Bay was clogged with hundreds of powerful, well-scrubbed American fighting ships. At a thunderous theatrical moment, the sky was all but obscured by a fly-by of some four hundred glistening B-29 bombers accompanied by fifteen hundred Navy fighter planes. The imperial soil was being desecrated by the landings of wave upon wave of well-fed, superbly equipped, supremely confident GIs—an army of occupation whose numbers, in a short time, would surpass a quarter of a million. A country that had celebrated its mythic "2,600-year anniversary" in 1940, and prided itself on never having been invaded, was about to be inundated by white men.

In Japanese eyes, the inescapable impression of September 2, 1945, was that the West—which meant, essentially, the United States—was extraordinarily rich and powerful, and Japan unbelievably weak and vulnerable. This was a simple observation, but it carried enormous political implications. The scene in Tokyo Bay, coming in the wake of the nuclear destruction of Hiroshima and Nagasaki, offered a stunning lesson in the kind of material strength and affluence that might be attained under American-style democracy. Although it took a while for this equation of democracy with wealth and power to sink in, it took very little time for the scale of Japan's defeat to become apparent. Nine days after the surrender ceremony, MacArthur observed at a press conference that Japan had fallen to the status of "a fourth-rate nation"—a blunt statement of reality guaranteed to tear asunder the vital organs of every Japanese leader from the emperor on down. From the moment Commodore Perry had forced Japan open, its leaders had been obsessed with becoming an *ittō koku*, a country of the first rank. Indeed, fear that such status was being denied Japan was commonly evoked with great emotion as the ultimate reason for going to war against the West. Japan would be relegated to "second-rate" or "third-rate" status, claimed Prime Minister Tōjō Hideki among others, if it failed to strike out and establish a secure imperium in Asia. Like a reopened wound, the term *yontō koku*—"fourth-rate country"—immediately became a postsurrender catchphrase.[10] Shortly after this, MacArthur framed the nation's plight in even more alarming terms, evocative of the wrathful God of the Old Testament. Speaking about the demobilization of Japan's armed forces, he declared that "they are thoroughly beaten and cowed and tremble before the terrible retribution the surrender terms impose upon their country in punishment for its great sins."[11]

In the weeks that followed, the victors continued to be taken aback by the extent of the country's devastation. In mid-October, in a memorandum to President Truman summarizing conversations with MacArthur and his aides, the special presidential envoy Edwin Locke, Jr. reported that "the American officers now in Tokyo are amazed by the fact that resistance continued as long as it did." Indeed, so great was the economic disarray, he added, that in the opinion of some Americans the atomic bombs, "while seized upon by the Japanese as an excuse for getting out of the war, actually speeded surrender by only a few days." Locke went on to note that "the entire economic structure of Japan's greatest cities has been wrecked. Five millions of Tokyo's seven million population have left the ruined city."[12] Later investigative missions from Washington, led by analysts for the prestigious U.S. Strategic Bombing Survey, similarly concluded that presurrender estimates of Japan's capacity for continuing the war had been greatly exaggerated.[13] This was ex post facto conjecture, but it reflected a common observation that Japan at war's end was vastly weaker than anyone outside the country had imagined—or anyone inside it had acknowledged.

Virtually all that would take place in the several years that followed unfolded against this background of crushing defeat. Despair took root and flourished in such a milieu; so did cynicism and opportunism—as well as marvelous expressions of resilience, creativity, and idealism of a sort possible only among people who have seen an old world destroyed and are being forced to imagine a new one. In such circumstances, it was hardly surprising that few Japanese had the energy, imagination, or desire to dwell on how many other lives they had shattered in the course of carrying out their emperor's holy war.

Quantifying Defeat

The ravages of war can never be accurately quantified. Even when large bureaucracies are put to the task of calculating total casualties and estimating the extent of physical destruction, the results are typically a potpourri of implausibly precise numbers masking areas of uncertainty. In defeated Japan, it took years to arrive at generally accepted estimates of the price Japan paid for its lost war.[14]

The number of deaths usually cited for the armed forces—1.74 million up to the time of surrender—is probably fairly accurate. On the other hand, estimates vary considerably where civilian deaths in air raids are concerned. When war-related military and civilian deaths outside Japan *after* August 15, 1945 are taken into consideration, the picture becomes even murkier. Japan's postsurrender governments tended to be evasive on such painful matters. All told, probably at least 2.7 million servicemen and civilians died as a result of the war, roughly 3 to 4 percent of the country's 1941 population of around 74 million. Millions more were injured, sick, or seriously malnourished. Approximately 4.5 million servicemen demobilized in 1945 were identified as being wounded or ill, and eventually some three hundred thousand were given disability pensions.[15]

In the most sweeping of material calculations, it was estimated that the Allied assault on shipping and the bombing campaign against the home islands destroyed one-quarter of the country's wealth. This included fourfifths of all ships, one-third of all industrial machine tools, and almost a quarter of all rolling stock and motor vehicles. General MacArthur's "SCAP" bureaucracy (SCAP, an acronym for Supreme Command[er] for the Allied Powers, was commonly used to refer to MacArthur's command) placed the overall costs of the war even higher, calculating early in 1946 that Japan had "lost one-third of its total wealth and from one-third to one-half of its total potential income." Rural living standards were estimated to have fallen to 65 percent of prewar levels and nonrural living standards to about 35 percent.[16]

Sixty-six major cities, including Hiroshima and Nagasaki, had been heavily bombed, destroying 40 percent of these urban areas overall and rendering around 30 percent of their populations homeless. In Tokyo, the largest metropolis, 65 percent of all residences were destroyed. In Osaka

Over sixty cities were heavily damaged in air raids before Japan capitulated.
This U.S. military photo looks down on a B-29 Superfortress on a bombing
mission over Osaka in June 1945.

and Nagoya, the country's second and third largest cities, the figures
were 57 and 89 percent. The first American contingents to arrive in
Japan—especially those that made the several-hour journey from Yokohama to Tokyo—were invariably impressed, if not shocked, by the mile
after mile of urban devastation they encountered. Russell Brines, the first
foreign journalist to enter Tokyo, recorded that "everything had been flat-
tened . . . Only thumbs stood up from the flatlands—the chimneys of
bathhouses, heavy house safes and an occasional stout building with heavy
iron shutters."[17] The first photographs and newsreel footage from the
conquered land captured these endless vistas of urban rubble for American audiences thousands of miles away who had never really grasped what
it meant to incinerate great cities.

Even amid such extensive vistas of destruction, however, the conquerors
found strange evidence of the selectiveness of their bombing policies. Vast

The first victors to enter defeated Japan were stunned by the extent of urban destruction they confronted. This aerial view takes in downtown Tokyo by the Sumida River.

areas of poor people's residences, small shops, and factories in the capital were gutted, for instance, but a good number of the homes of the wealthy in fashionable neighborhoods survived to house the occupation's officer corps. Tokyo's financial district, largely undamaged, would soon become "little America," home to MacArthur's General Headquarters (GHQ). Undamaged also was the building that housed much of the imperial military bureaucracy at war's end. With a nice sense of irony, the victors subsequently appropriated this for their war crimes trials of top leaders. Railways still functioned more or less effectively throughout the country (Tokyo residents, for example, had been able to ride directly to distant Hiroshima to see if their kin had survived the atomic blast). Outside of devastated poor people's neighborhoods, most utilities including electricity and water were also still in working order. Wittingly or not, U.S. bombing policy, at least in the capital city, had tended to reaffirm existing hierarchies of fortune.[18]

Close to 9 million people were homeless when the emperor told them

A Japanese soldier walks through the leveled landscape of Hiroshima,
September 1945.

they had fought and sacrificed in vain. "In every major city," as one
American described the scene, "families were crowded into dugouts and
flimsy shacks or, in some cases, were trying to sleep in hallways, on sub-
way platforms, or on sidewalks. Employees slept in their offices; teachers,
in their schoolrooms"—if, of course, they were fortunate enough to still
have offices or schoolrooms to sleep in. The streets of every major city
quickly became peopled with demoralized ex-soldiers, war widows, orphans, the homeless and unemployed—most of them preoccupied with
simply staving off hunger.[19] Yet even these individuals were relatively fortunate. At least they were in their own country.

Coming Home . . . Perhaps

In the wake of defeat, approximately 6.5 million Japanese were stranded
in Asia, Siberia, and the Pacific Ocean area. Roughly 3.5 million of them
were soldiers and sailors. The remainder were civilians, including many

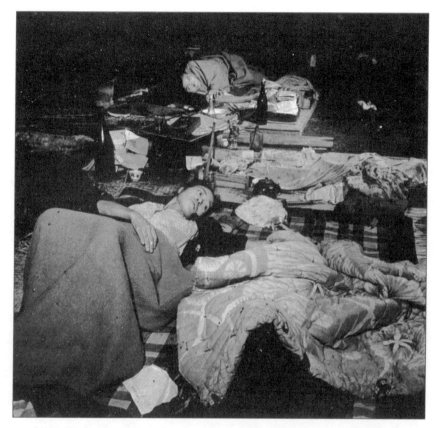

Atomic-bomb survivors in a makeshift hospital in Hiroshima, September
1945. The bedding is covered with flies, and the woman is gazing at her
injured infant, all but invisible under the quilt.

women and children—a huge and generally forgotten cadre of middle-and
lower-class individuals who had been sent out to help develop the imperium. Some 2.6 million Japanese were in China at war's end, 1.1 million dispersed through Manchuria. In addition, almost six hundred
thousand troops laid down their arms in the Kurile Islands and the
Darien–Port Arthur enclave in southern Manchuria. Over five hundred
thousand Japanese were in Formosa (Taiwan) and nine hundred thousand
in Korea, the countries Japan had colonized in 1895 and 1910, respectively.
The number in Southeast Asia and the Philippines was close to nine hundred thousand at war's end, mostly military personnel. Hundreds of thousands of other remnants of the emperor's shredded army were stranded on
scattered islands in the Pacific.[20]

For years after the defeat, many city dwellers continued to eke out a
precarious existence in shantytowns such as this.

All of these individuals naturally looked forward to returning home
quickly, and their kin anxiously awaited them. For many, however, repatriation would take years not months, and hundreds of thousands were destined to die without seeing their homeland again. For these millions of
individuals, surrender merely marked the beginning of a new stage in lives
of escalating uncertainty and brutalization. They became victims of the
chaos that reigned in war-torn "liberated" Asia, of epidemic diseases, and
of maltreatment by the victorious Allies. In September 1946, more than
a year after the emperor's broadcast, over 2 million Japanese still remained unrepatriated and the government acknowledged that the whereabouts of 540,000 others were unknown.[21]

The fate of these Japanese is a neglected chapter among the countless
epic tragedies of World War II. In Manchuria alone, it is estimated that
179,000 Japanese civilians and 66,000 military personnel perished in the
confusion and the harsh winter that followed capitulation.[22] Uprooted
civilians in Manchuria and elsewhere in northern China usually were able
to bring with them only what they could carry, which commonly meant
little more than their smallest children and paltry, soon-to-be-exhausted
quantities of food. A lifetime's possessions were abandoned. Many of these
refugees were also driven to leave their youngest children with poor Chi-

nese peasant families, in the desperate hope that those so abandoned would have a better chance of survival.[23]

Entering into the formal channels of repatriation did not guarantee a swift and safe return. Diseases ravaged many groups of returnees, and as a consequence repatriation became delayed by the need to conduct medical examinations, immunizations, and occasional quarantines. The spring and summer of 1946 were especially harsh in this regard. Repatriation from central China was impeded by a smallpox epidemic in April, a typhus epidemic in May, and an outbreak of cholera in June. Cholera epidemics also broke out in both southern Korea and northern Indochina in May, and in Manchuria in August.[24]

For servicemen in all theaters, repatriation was often delayed by local Allied authorities who chose to use their prisoners for specific postwar purposes. Until the closing months of 1946, the United States retained almost seventy thousand surrendered Japanese as laborers to help phase out wartime facilities in the Philippines, Okinawa, the Pacific Ocean area, and Hawaii. The British, in charge of the repatriation of approximately three-quarters of a million Japanese from south and southeast Asia, made no bones about their intention to hold on to a large number for projects in areas where the European powers, having ousted the Japanese aggressors, were intent on reasserting their own colonial authority. In mid-1946, they announced that they would retain 113,500 POWs for local work until some time in 1947. Of this number, 13,500 were later turned over to the Dutch, engaged in reimposing their rule over the former Netherlands East Indies. The last of the Japanese detained by the British in Malaya and Burma were not repatriated until October 1947.[25]

The total number of Japanese who surrendered to Chinese forces and were forced to work or fight for either side in the Chinese civil war is unknown. More than a year after surrender, it was reported that some sixty-eight thousand Japanese taken prisoner in Manchuria were still being employed by Chinese forces, mostly on the communist side. The Kuomintang (Nationalist) government, for its part, delayed the repatriation of over fifty thousand Japanese with useful technical skills for much of 1946. As late as April 1949, on the eve of the communist victory, more than sixty thousand Japanese were still believed held in communist-controlled areas.[26]

By far the most extensive, protracted, and abusive treatment of surrendered forces came at the hands of the Soviets, who entered the war on August 8, one week before the emperor's broadcast, and accepted the Japanese surrender in Manchuria and northern Korea. American and

Japanese authorities estimated that between 1.6 and 1.7 million Japanese fell into Soviet hands, and it soon became clear that many were being used to help offset the great manpower losses the Soviet Union had experienced in the war as well as through the Stalinist purges. The first contingent of prisoners released by the Soviets did not reach Japan until December 1946. By the end of 1947, a total of 625,000 men had been formally repatriated. During this same period, an estimated 294,000 who had surrendered in northern Korea "unofficially" made their way to disembarkation ports in the American-controlled southern part of the peninsula. Between May and December of the following year, after a delay of four months, roughly three hundred thousand more were allowed to return home. Then, once again, the flow of repatriates was stopped, ostensibly because of adverse weather conditions.

Popular animus against the Soviet Union dated back to the turn of the century, well before the Bolshevik revolution, when czarist Russia and imperial Japan emerged as rival expansionist powers in northeast Asia. The excruciatingly prolonged nature of the repatriation process, together with Soviet unwillingness to provide accurate information about the number and identity of their prisoners, greatly exacerbated this animosity. By 1948, it had also become obvious that the Soviets were delaying repatriation in order to subject prisoners to intensive indoctrination, so that they might contribute to communist agitation on their return.[27]

In the spring of 1949, after repeated prodding by occupation authorities, the U.S.S.R. announced that only ninety-five thousand prisoners remained, all of whom would be returned by the end of the year. According to American and Japanese calculations, the actual number should have been around four hundred thousand. Suddenly, more than three hundred thousand Japanese were unaccounted for. Over four decades later, the Soviet Union finally released the names of some forty-six thousand Japanese known to be buried in Siberia. The overall numbers never jibed.[28]

The chaos of these numbers—hundreds of thousands of soldiers, sailors, and civilians simply disappearing overseas—suggests how essentially meaningless the formal dating of "war's end" was for many Japanese. Year after year, wives, children, and parents waited for kin to return—often learning, like Aihara Yū, that they had been bereaved all the while; or, even worse, never learning anything at all. In 1950, *Sazae-san*, the country's most popular family-oriented comic strip, could still play on the theme of a boy pathetically awaiting his father's return from "Soren," the Soviet Union.[29]

In April of that year, General MacArthur received a remarkable appeal

At a meeting sponsored by the Buddhist Nichiren sect in Tokyo's Hibiya Park
in February 1950, women and children pray for the return of POWs still held
by the Soviet Union four-and-a-half years after the war ended.

from some 120,000 individuals living in Shiga Prefecture, all of them relatives of still-missing soldiers. It was accompanied by an unusual gift, la-
boriously made over an eight-month period: an embroidered portrait of
MacArthur, to which all 120,000 petitioners had each contributed a
stitch. The inspiration for this striking present lay in one of the more
intimate symbolic acts of the war years—the practice of sending soldiers
cloth stomach warmers sewn with a thousand stitches, each by a different person. Both making and wearing the *sennin-bari haramaki*
("thousand-stitch belly bands") were affirmations of the closeness between
men fighting abroad and their communities, especially their womenfolk,
back home. A short letter accompanying the gift thanked the supreme
commander for his "immeasurable compassion" in ensuring the repatriation of millions of Japanese, and pleaded for his continued endeavors on
behalf of those who still remained abroad.[30] Four and a half years after
the surrender, great numbers of people still wrestled with grief and uncertainty, and cherished the hope that their shattered lives might be
made whole again.

Displaced Persons

From a logistical standpoint, the repatriation process was an impressive accomplishment. Between October 1, 1945 and December 31, 1946, over 5.1 million Japanese returned to their homeland on around two hundred Liberty Ships and LSTs loaned by the American military, as well as on the battered remnants of their own once-proud fleet. Another million finally touched native soil again sometime in 1947.[31] While this was taking place, a "reverse repatriation" was underway to return aliens who had spent the war in Japan to their native lands. The first priority of the victors naturally was to secure the release of Allied prisoners of war in Japan. Scattered in more than a hundred prison camps, these POWs were malnourished, some suffered from tuberculosis, and in notorious facilities such as the Ofuna camp some had suffered severe abuse as well. The Americans also learned of outright atrocities against prisoners in the home islands, including vivisections conducted at Kyushu Imperial University. A total of 31,617 American POWs were freed and processed through Manila by October 31, 1945, of whom 187 remained hospitalized.[32]

By far the largest number of aliens in Japan were other Asians, the great majority Koreans who had been conscripted to perform heavy labor. Some 1.35 million Koreans were resident at the time of surrender, and most desired to leave. By the first week of 1946, 630,000 Koreans had already been repatriated. The total reached over 930,000 by the end of that year. At the same time, some Koreans who encountered confusion and hardship in their native country, now divided into American and Soviet occupation zones, attempted to reenter Japan. Others, including many who had served in the Japanese military, chose to be repatriated from overseas to Japan, not Korea. Repatriation of Asians also involved the return of over 31,000 Chinese POWs and collaborators to China, and roughly the same number of former Formosan colonial subjects to Formosa.[33]

In the desperate final stages of the war, Japan's top leaders including the emperor had chosen to sacrifice Okinawa in a futile but devastatingly brutal battle that, it was hoped, would dissuade the Allies from attempting to invade the home islands. More than ten thousand Americans died in that battle, which lasted from April to June 1945. Imperial forces numbering over 110,000 men were virtually wiped out, and approximately one-third of the civilian population—possibly as many as 150,000 men, women, and children—were killed. Repatriation simply marked a new stage of suffering for Okinawans, for prior to the battle some 160,000 is-

Children orphaned during the repatriation of Japanese civilians from
Manchuria arriving at Tokyo's Shinagawa station in December 1946, sixteen
months after the surrender. The youngster at the right carries, in a white sash
suspended from her neck, a box containing the cremated bones and ashes of
her family.

land residents had been evacuated to the main islands of Japan. Although
they desired to return to their native place quickly, this was impossible.
Okinawa had been so devastated that there was not enough food and shelter for the much reduced population of survivors already living there. As
a consequence, Okinawans became yet another group of displaced persons,
forced to languish and suffer unrepatriated in "repatriation camps" in
Japan.[34]

Accounts from such repatriation camps convey a stark impression of chaos and demoralization. A contemporary description of the Kamoi Repatriation Center in Uraga captures this. Opened in November 1945 to handle civilian repatriates from the Pacific, the camp was intended to accommodate thirteen hundred people but quickly became responsible for three times that number, about half of whom were children. The camp administration was incapable of staving off malnutrition. Its typical menu consisted of a meager daily ration of mixed rice and wheat, accompanied by bean-paste soup for breakfast, cooked cabbage for lunch, and cooked cabbage and white radish for dinner. Many of the repatriates had no place to go to. Stealing became commonplace, and gambling absorbed the energies of many of the men. Kuramitsu Toshio, the camp director, wrote in January 1946 that four doctors, eighteen nurses, and four medical aides served the center, with critically ill people being sent to one of six neighboring hospitals as expeditiously as possible. Despite this, fifteen to twenty people died in the camp of malnutrition or other causes every day. Burial groups appointed to carry bodies to the crematorium were unable to keep up with the deaths, and bodies were frequently left lying as they had fallen until rigor mortis set in.[35]

In December 1946, Kuramitsu recorded a conversation he had with Watanabe Chizuko, a seven-year-old girl who was among the first group of orphans to return from Manchuria. Of thirty-six children aged four to twelve, twenty-three including Chizuko were immediately hospitalized. Most of them suffered from scabies and malnutrition, and four had severe cases of tuberculosis. A photograph of Watanabe Chizuko had appeared in many newspapers that covered the arrival of the orphans. She was singled out because she had arrived with the by-then familiar white box that contained ashes of the dead hanging by a sash around her neck. Kuramitsu found the little girl sitting up on an adult-size bed, the box of ashes on a nearby shelf next to a small doll. He recorded a bit of his conversation with her:

"Where did your father die?"

"Mukden."

"Your mother?"

"Karafuto."

"Your little sister Sadako?"

"Sasebo."

The place names marked successive stages in Chizuko's long journey from Manchuria. It was the Japanese custom to give the deceased a posthumous Buddhist name. Because nothing was written on the box on the shelf but a single such name, Kuramatsu could not tell whether it con-

In the prolonged confusion of defeat, the fate or whereabouts of many ex-servicemen as well as civilians remained unknown to family and friends. Ten months after the surrender, a Red Cross worker reads signs posted by individuals trying to locate missing persons.

tained Chizuko's father's, mother's, or sister's ashes, or perhaps a mixture of all of them.[36]

While the spectacle of a child bearing the ashes of her immediate family was newsworthy a year after Japan surrendered, it was commonplace to see demobilized soldiers returning from abroad with the ashes of deceased comrades, which they had undertaken to return to surviving kin. Civilian returnees, too, routinely carried the small white boxes among their meager belongings. Sometimes, however, even the remains of the dead had no clear final destination. On August 1, 1946, it was reported that the repatriation vessel *Hikawa Maru* had put in at Uraga with seven thousand boxes of unclaimed ashes.[37]

Many adults who returned after years abroad found that their families had been shattered. Urban neighborhoods had been obliterated. Parents, wives, and children had been killed in the air raids or had dispersed to the countryside. Throughout the country, makeshift notice boards carried handwritten notes asking for information about missing family members or providing information about the writer's own whereabouts. This was not just a phenomenon of the months immediately following surrender. Beginning in January 1946, a radio program called *Returnee News* provided ongoing information concerning the names of incoming repatriates as well as their vessels and ports of entry. When this proved inadequate, a program called *Missing Persons* was introduced in June 1946. Almost immediately, the station was inundated with four to five hundred written inquiries a day in addition to dozens of phone calls. By August, broadcast time had been increased to twice daily, five days a week. For a while the program included a special segment—"Who Am I?"—devoted to inquiries from disoriented returned veterans. *Missing Persons* had considerable success in accomplishing its mission. Initially, some 40 to 50 percent of the inquiries it broadcast were answered, and until 1950 the program continued to clear up the whereabouts or announce the deaths of significant numbers of individuals. *Missing Persons* continued on the air until March 31, 1962.[38]

Despised Veterans

When repatriated prisoners began returning from the Soviet Union reciting communist propaganda, it was charged that their indoctrination had been designed to create "class hatreds between officers and enlisted men."[39] It had, but many demobilized veterans returned from other places than the U.S.S.R. cynical and contemptuous of the officers who had led them in battle. This was especially true among soldiers who had been ordered to fight to the bitter end in the fanatic and futile final campaigns of the war. The group cohesion and discipline of the military hierarchy had not been built, as its propagandists intoned, on some idealized notion of "loyalty" or "harmony," but on a structure of authoritarian coercion that transferred oppression downward. Superior officers commonly commanded fear rather than respect even in the best of times, and defeat unleashed deep, hitherto repressed resentments. In extreme cases, such hatred led to the murder of former officers.

After the surrender, these feelings were vented openly for the first time. In May 1946, a veteran wrote a typically anguished letter to the *Asahi,* one of the country's leading newspapers, recalling the "hell of starvation" he and his fellow soldiers had endured on a Pacific island and the abuse they suffered at the hands of their officers. He noted that enlisted men had died of starvation at a far greater rate than officers and asked how he could give comfort to the souls of his dead comrades who, in effect, had been killed by the tyranny of their own leaders. He quoted an old samurai saying about bringing a souvenir to hell, which originally had meant killing an enemy at the time of one's own death. Most of his comrades, he said, died wishing to take not an enemy but one of their officers with them as their souvenir.[40]

Several months later, a report in the *Asahi* about an abusive officer "lynched" by his men after surrender triggered eighteen reader responses, all but two of which supported the murder and offered their own accounts of brutality and corruption among the officer corps. A soldier who had served in Korea described the womanizing and drinking of officers there. A marine bitterly recalled how they beat one of his comrades. Another veteran confessed that he frequently had felt like attacking his officers, but restrained himself because he feared adverse consequences for his family back home. Even the two letters critical of the lynching incident took a defensive stance. Not all officers, each said, were bad.[41]

Such confessions, unthinkable before the surrender, exposed the fatuity of wartime propaganda about "one hundred million hearts beating as one." Even hardened veterans, however, were often ill prepared for the shock of returning home. The communities that had sent them off with parties and parades and kept them supplied with comfort packages and "thousand-stitch" belly warmers often did not welcome them back. They were, after all, losers. Their unkempt appearance seemed a mockery of the heroic ideals and imagery that had saturated wartime propaganda.

In addition, in the wake of defeat discipline collapsed, and men stationed in the home islands deserted their units in droves. More than a few staggered home with as much loot from military stores as they could carry—like "stragglers" from a routed force, as several police observers put it. Even survivors from the suicide squadrons, who had been prepared to take off on their sublime one-way missions when the war ended, leaped into the wild scramble for goods. One such pilot greeted the surrender by filling his plane with military commodities, flying it to an airfield near his home, carting his spoils to his house, and then returning to set the plane on fire. The emperor's loyal soldiers and sailors seemed to have metamorphosed overnight into symbols of the worst sort of egoism and atomization. Officers as well as enlisted men engaged in looting, sometimes on a grand scale, and police reports expressed fear that public disgust would extend upward to "grave distrust, frustration, and antipathy toward military and civilian leaders," even "hatred of the military" in general.[42]

Sometimes, just the unexpected fact that a repatriated soldier was still
alive could cause consternation. A number of ex-soldiers returned to discover that they had been declared dead long before, their funerals conducted and grave markers erected. In the sardonic phrase of the times,
such men became known as the "living war dead."[43] To grieving kin, the
appearance of someone believed to be dead could be simultaneously joyous and traumatic, even heartbreaking. Stories circulated about men who
made their way home after years of hardship only to find that their wives
had remarried, frequently to a brother or close friend.

For a great many ex-soldiers and sailors, the greatest shock of returning home lay in finding themselves treated, after all their travails, as pari-
ahs in their native land. By 1946, when the tide of repatriates became a
flood, those at home were already being exposed to a steady flow of information concerning the shocking range of atrocities committed by the
imperial forces in China, Southeast Asia, and the Philippines, as well as
against Allied prisoners generally. As a result, many ex-servicemen found
themselves regarded not just as men who had failed disastrously to accomplish their mission, but also as individuals who had, it was assumed,
participated in unspeakable acts. References to the reproachful glances that
acquaintances and strangers alike directed at them became a familiar refrain in veterans' letters to the press. Some frankly and sincerely expressed regret for their crimes. Others protested their innocence and the
injustice of being treated as war criminals. They pleaded that the public
had to make distinctions between soldiers or military men *(gunjin)* and the
"military cliques" *(gunbatsu)* who were ultimately responsible for the war
and its conduct.

An anonymous letter published in the *Asahi* on June 9, 1946 captured
the bleakness of such "homecomings":

> I returned to Japan from the southern regions on May 20. My house
> was burned, my wife and children missing. What little money I had
> quickly was consumed by the high prices, and I was a pitiful figure.
> Not a single person gave me a kind word. Rather, they cast hostile
> glances my way. Tormented and without work, I became possessed
> by a devil.

His "devil" was the impulse to turn to crime. The writer went on to describe how he accosted a young man on a dark street, intending to rob
him, only to discover that he was assaulting an off-duty policeman. His
story, as it turned out, had an uplifting ending. The policeman did not arrest him, but gave him a hundred yen and some of his own clothing, while

urging him to have faith in his ability to surmount his difficulties. Though the writer was still without wife or child or home or job or money, his letter was offered as a public vow that he would go straight thereafter.[44]

Stigmatized Victims

Many of the most pathetic Japanese war victims now became the country's new outcasts. Despite a mild Buddhist tradition of care for the weak and infirm, despite Confucian homilies about reciprocal obligations between social superiors and inferiors, and despite imperial platitudes about all Japanese being "one family" under the emperor, Japan was a harsh, inhospitable place for anyone who did not fall into a "proper" social category. There existed no strong tradition of responsibility toward strangers, or of unrequited philanthropy, or of tolerance or even genuine sympathy (as opposed to occasional sentimentality) toward those who suffered misfortune.

This is no doubt true to some degree of all cultures and societies, but it was an especially conspicuous phenomenon in Japan at war's end, when whole new categories of "improper" people felt the sting of stigmatization. These included the survivors of Hiroshima and Nagasaki, with their taint of—really, their *pollution* by—radiation; war orphans and street children, forced to live by their wits outside "proper" society; war widows, especially if poor, in a society inherently unkind to women without men; and homeless ex-servicemen or any of the other abandoned people who clogged public places such as Tokyo's Ueno Station.

Veterans suffering from battle shock were commonly shunned. Although a number of emperors and shoguns were known to have been deranged, mental illness remained a taboo and those in need of help were usually consigned to the shadows and back rooms. Physical handicaps or deformities provoked a similar public aversion. Many maimed veterans, having nowhere to turn, defied these taboos and flaunted their disabilities—more accurately, their pain and hardship—by donning distinctive white clothing and begging in public. In Tokyo, such outcast figures haunted public places until the late 1950s. Others simply gave up the struggle for survival after returning home to find, as one wrote to a newspaper, that "the existence of us injured and ill veterans is forgotten." Writing from a sanitarium, he described the suicides of despairing fellow convalescents and concluded with the announcement that "I myself am five minutes away from hanging."[45]

Disabled veterans were doubly stigmatized, having lost the war as well

Street children near Tokyo's Ueno station, 1946.

as their physical or mental wholeness. Similarly, once sentimental effusions had been dispensed with, the war's youngest victims were treated abysmally. War orphans and homeless children almost by definition became "improper" children. Forced to scramble for daily survival on the streets, they became treated as incorrigible delinquents. Long after the war ended, the government not only had no effective policy for caring for these children, but scant grasp of the dimensions of the problem. In July 1946, the Ministry of Health and Welfare estimated that there were approximately 4,000 war orphans throughout the country. A February 1948 report put the number of orphaned and homeless children combined at 123,510. Of this number, 28,248 had lost their parents in air raids; 11,351 were orphaned or lost contact with their parents during the traumatic repatriation process; 2,640 were identified as "abandoned"; and an astonishing 81,266 were believed to have lost their parents, or simply become separated from them, in the turmoil that accompanied the end of the war.[46]

Many of these children lived in railroad stations, under trestles and railway overpasses, in abandoned ruins. They survived by their wits—shining shoes, selling newspapers, stealing, recycling cigarette butts, illegally selling food coupons, begging. Some orphan boys who picked pockets earned the nickname *charinko* or *"charin* kids."* (Apparently *charin* was coined as an onomatopoeia for the sound of coins clinking together.) Some teenage girls unsurprisingly turned to prostitution. A minority of these street children learned to survive well indeed by their wits. A Tokyo police roundup in April 1947 netted 285 homeless children, of whom only 76 were without jobs of any sort. In a year when the average *monthly* salary of a college-educated, white-collar public employee was around 1,240 yen, nineteen averaged an astonishing daily income of 100 yen, and 67 others were earning between 30 and 50 yen daily.[47]

One of the most fashionable slogans of the early postsurrender period envisioned Japan becoming a "nation of culture." In October 1946, Hayashi Fumiko, a well-known fiction writer from an impoverished background herself, argued in a popular magazine that no country so indifferent to the plight of orphans and the homeless could claim to be cultured.[48] Over two years later, Osaragi Jirō, a distinguished author respected for his humanism, wrestled frankly with the same issue. A British acquaintance, he wrote, had asked why the Japanese did nothing about their street children. His immediate response was that they lacked the financial resources, but on reflection he realized this was disingenuous. In fact, he concluded, as a people they simply lacked love toward strangers. He himself was no exception. In all honesty, he had to admit that he had no desire to take in these filthy urchins and try to straighten out their characters. Could it be, Osaragi mused, that Japanese were shallower than other peoples when it came to love?[49]

Homeless children were commonly rounded up and loaded on trucks like cattle—by no means a strained metaphor. Police or city officials directly engaged in these roundups often counted the children aloud not in the way that human beings are counted in Japanese (*hitori, futari,* and so on), but rather in a vocabulary used for counting animals (*ippiki, nihiki,* and so on). Detention centers were usually militaristically authoritarian, with physical abuse not uncommon. Some boys were even kept naked to prevent them from attempting to escape. In certain locales, it took years before such children were mainstreamed from orphanages into the regular educational system, and even then they were scorned for being parentless "institution creatures."[50]

War widows, ennobled in public rhetoric, also often endured neglect and discrimination. All but the well-to-do were forced to support themselves and their children in an environment in which military salaries had ceased to arrive, wartime factory jobs had been abolished, and millions of men back from overseas as well as others laid off from defunct wartime industries were competing for scarce jobs. Those who could muster the strength and will to make their anguish public spoke in a common voice in the media. A rural woman whose missing husband had abandoned the family business to "fight for the emperor" wondered why the world had turned cold to her three children and herself. The delivery of food rations had ceased, she wrote, and despite the fact that she lived in the countryside, she could not afford to purchase vegetables. By working at home until midnight, she was able to bring in 2 yen a day, at a time when less than 4 kilograms of potatoes cost 35 yen. A widow asked that same month why war widows should starve while former officers and military men were embezzling military goods. Was there no way, she inquired, that she could get just one month's military salary, or some of the war goods herself, or even a single blanket?

Another woman, whose husband was still missing, complained that soldiers demobilized at home received severance pay, a rice ration, and clothing. She and her children, in contrast, could only anticipate death. Then, plaintively, she asked what the use of talking about such things as woman suffrage was when she and others like her were starving.[51] This was a question that arose in many quarters, as people confronting shattered lives in a shattered land were asked to contemplate seemingly abstract political ideals.

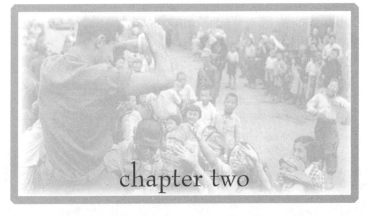

chapter two

GIFTS FROM HEAVEN

"You think you can make Japan a democratic country? I don't think so."
—Prime Minister Yoshida Shigeru

"We can try."
—Colonel Charles Kades, Government Section, GHQ[1]

In August 1946, the talented cartoonist Katō Etsurō wrote the preface to a little collection of his illustrations documenting the first year under American occupation. Katō confessed that he had lacked the courage to oppose the war, which was an understatement. He had, in fact, thrown his considerable skills wholeheartedly into the war effort. It was he who had produced one of the more grisly war posters of 1942, depicting Roosevelt and Churchill (or Uncle Sam and John Bull, for these personal and national renderings tended to shade into one another) as figures with bestial hindquarters, being speared by a gleaming Japanese bayonet. The legend on the poster read, "The Death of These Wretches Is the Birthday of World Peace."

Using a convoluted metaphor to explain a convoluted sketch, Katō commented that until capitulation he had drawn not with his hand but with a foot wrapped in military gaiters. From the moment of unconditional surrender, his pen had returned to his hand—that is, to its proper, right-side-up place—but it hadn't been easy to get going again. He offered this

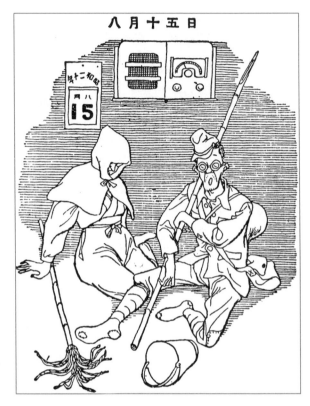

On the first anniversary of the surrender, the cartoonist Katō Etsurō conveyed the widespread feeling of how stupid the war had been in this graphic of an exhausted man and woman contemplating the emperor's surrender broadcast on August 15, 1945. The couple muses on the folly of pitting fire-fighting buckets and bamboo spears against atomic weapons.

modest selection of drawings as a record of what the past year had meant to him. The title he choose was *Okurareta Kakumei*, a phrase best rendered in English as "The Revolution We Have Been Given."[2] Katō's beastly enemy wretches had been transformed, almost overnight, into liberators— the agents of a revolution from above.

Katō's evocative title captured a dominant sentiment of the early years of the occupation, and he conveyed its essence within a few pages. His opening illustration depicted an exhausted couple sprawled on the ground on August 15, 1945. The woman wore the ubiquitous *monpe* pantaloons of the war years as well as the protective hood donned when fighting fires from the air raids. The man, in baggy ex-soldier's garb, clutched a bamboo spear. A fire-fighting bucket lay on its side. Behind them was a radio, representing the emperor's surrender broadcast. The caption spoke of the stupidity of pitting bamboo spears against atomic bombs. Before feeling joy at moving from war to liberation, it said, people were simply in a daze.

On the next page, Katō's husband and wife were taking down the blackout papers that had covered their windows and filling in a trench they had dug in their backyard for protection from air raids. They really had assumed, each confided to the other, that this was going to be their grave.

Immediately after this simple depiction of relief and joy at quite literally letting the light back into one's life, Katō introduced his central theme. A crowd of Japanese stretched their arms heavenwards, where the sky was filled with parachutes carrying canisters labeled "Democratic Revolution." The graphic bore the heading "A Gift from Heaven," and had this caption:

> The downpour of bombs and incendiaries abruptly ceased. Then, from the very same sky, the gift of peace began to descend. So-called democratic revolution! Bloodless revolution!
>
> Well, we Japanese, who lost in war, who were exhausted by war, how did we receive this gift? How *are* we receiving it . . . ?

The pages that followed, at once ironic and yet hopeful, presented a lively panorama of the first year of defeat. Katō ridiculed the initial ramshackle postwar cabinet, headed by Prince Higashikuni Naruhiko, as a shop advertising merchandise but with nothing to sell. He mocked the facile converts to the "bloodless revolution"—the militarist donning the morning coat of "democracy," the politician writing "liberalism" over his wartime slogans, the right-wing boss trimming his handlebar mustache to look like a modern labor leader, the student replacing Hitler's portrait with Marx's, *Mein Kampf* with *Das Kapital*.

The government and civilian elites came off poorly indeed in Katō's new nation. Financial and economic policies did little more than enable big capitalists to weather the disruptions of defeat. Rampant inflation plunged the society into anxiety and imperiled democracy. The "epoch-making" election law that paved the way for the first general election under universal suffrage in April 1946 was a Pandora's box (Urashima Tarō's box, in the Japanese idiom) that produced a reactionary cabinet under the conservative former diplomat Yoshida Shigeru. In Katō's eyes, no serious alternative to these bankrupt policies and policy makers could be expected from the fractious political left. In one illustration the Socialist Party issues divorce papers to the Communist Party, while a geisha (representing old-guard conservatives) smirks in the background.

Katō also turned his pen with vigor and bemusement to the vagaries and difficulties of ordinary life. Street children smoked cigarettes. Workers bickered over the chicken-and-egg causes of economic stagnation. ("No food, no coal. No coal, no fertilizer. No fertilizer, no food. No food, no coal . . . Whoa, getting dizzy!") Armed robbers broke into houses and

天降る贈物

In Katō's exuberant rendering, the reformist agenda introduced by the occupation force was a "gift from heaven" welcomed by the populace. The canisters being parachuted in by the victors to a joyous reception read "democratic revolution."

couldn't find anything left to steal. ("Well, you could take the empty bureau," says a tied-up housewife.) Black marketeers advised prostitutes to organize themselves, while the black market itself emerged as a droll facsimile of the larger political economy. Former military helmets turned upside down were being sold as democracy cooking pots. ("Come on, come on . . . Handy thing—you can use it immediately as a metal helmet again in times of crisis.") A thin, intellectual-looking vendor sold "empty-theory bread" (nonfilling, but good for whetting the appetite). An empty-handed huckster solicited advance orders for whatever he might be able to come up with in the future, down payment required.

Into such tumult came the victor's revolution from above. Like the hand of God reaching down from heaven, the United States, in another illustration, made a present to Japan of "the key to freedom" that unlocked restrictions on speech and expression. As if wielding giant scissors from the sky, America cut the chains that had bound ordinary Japanese and granted them civil liberties. With the arms of a great deity, MacArthur's headquarters levered the crushing burden of the old *zaibatsu*—the gigantic financial and industrial oligopolies that dominated the presurrender economy—off the backs of the exploited people. While Japan's leaders slept, the Americans—again, godlike hands extended from on high—provided food for the near-starving people.

"Revolution from Above"

Katō, a master of perspective as well as line, had a distinctive but by no means peculiarly Japanese style. His renderings of the conquerors certainly would have seemed familiar enough in the United States. American cartoonists who turned their attention to occupied Japan routinely depicted the victors as omnipotent and godlike. Indeed, they frequently resorted to a virtually identical "hand of God" iconography by depicting little Japan in the palm of the Allies, or receiving MacArthur's orders from on high. More broadly, during the occupation and after, the victors as well as the vanquished commonly referred to the American agenda for the defeated country as an attempt to impose a "democratic revolution from above." General MacArthur himself rarely lost an opportunity to call attention to the political, economic, and "spiritual" revolution being carried out under his aegis.[3]

This revolution from above received an early endorsement from none other than Tokuda Kyūichi, a fiery Communist Party leader who had been imprisoned for eighteen years. Upon exiting the prison gates early in October 1945, when occupation authorities "cut the chains" of political repression, Tokuda immediately read an "Appeal to the People" that began with this declaration: "We express our deepest gratitude that the occupation of Japan by the Allied forces, dedicated to liberating the world from fascism and militarism, has opened the way for the democratic revolution in Japan." Later, when the Cold War intensified, this would become a point of embarrassment to the Communists, who lamely rationalized Tokuda's words by pointing out that the reference to "Allies" included the Soviet Union.[4]

This was backtracking revisionism. Until 1947, leftists as well as liberals commonly regarded the overwhelmingly American occupation force as an army of liberation, and the notion of achieving a "democratic revolution" under the eagle's wing was so widespread as to become an almost instant cliché. Various catchphrases conveyed the idea that a political and social revolution was being induced under the tutelage—indeed, under the commands—of the conquerors. In addition to Katō's "received revolution" and the "gift" or "present" of democracy that he frequently mentioned, Japan-

鎖 は 切 断 さ れ た

Here, in one of Katō's numerous renderings of the liberation brought about by early occupation policies, giant American shears cut the chains that had held down "the people," while old-guard power brokers and militarists flee in the background. The specific reference was to SCAP's "civil liberties" directive of October 4, 1945.

ese also spoke of a "Potsdam revolution," alluding to the terms of surrender set forth by the United States and other Allies in the Potsdam Declaration of July 26, 1945. "Reform from on high" was a comparable phrase.[5]

Such phrases did not, however, invariably convey approbation, for in many circles the democratic revolution was regarded with reservation or even outright alarm. To conservatives, this revolution from above reeked of "red" manipulation, and Tokuda's embrace of the "liberation army" did little to dispel such paranoia. More subtle and cynical observers savored the mordant observation of Kawakami Tetsutarō, a detached man of letters, who in October 1945 described the U.S. policy as one of "rationed-out freedom." His clever expression captured the inherent contradiction of democracy by fiat as well as the irony of promoting freedom in the context of unconditional surrender. Its twist came from evoking the food rationing the Japanese endured under their wartime leaders and continued to experience under the Americans.[6]

Even Katō Etsurō's applause had a cautionary aspect to it, and the abiding interest of his little book lies in the way his enthusiasm for the ideals of a democratic revolution was mixed with apprehension that this "gift" had not been earned. The commentary that went with those giant American scissors, for example, read: "Chains were cut—but we must not forget that we did not shed a drop of blood, or raise a sweat, to cut these chains." His final drawing depicted a figure lying lazily in a house full of gifts. "We Japanese seem to have gotten accustomed to the sweetness of the revolution we have received," the caption warned, "and to have become extremely sparing in our efforts to turn this valuable gift into our flesh and blood."

As time passed, more than a few commentators called attention to the passivity and superficiality implicit in the very notion of a democratic revolution from above. Just as ordinary people had been manipulated by militarists and ultranationalists during the war, the argument went, now they were following a new set of leaders. The playwright and critic Yamazaki Masakazu, who returned from Manchuria as a ninth grader in 1948, later recalled being impressed with how "everything was being given." Democracy came "too easily" in such a milieu and so failed to establish deep roots. Democratization from above, others observed, tended to reinforce the unfortunate "logic of irresponsibility" whereby everyone was socialized to bow to orders from superiors.[7]

This sense of the precariousness of the new democratic revolution was conveyed late in 1949 by one of its most articulate supporters, the Christian president of Tokyo University, Nanbara Shigeru. Speaking in Washington, D.C. as one of the first Japanese allowed to leave his occupied country, Nanbara characterized World War II as a war of "spirit against spirit" as well as "people against people," which had exposed terrible failings in his compatriots. He embraced the ideals of the European Renaissance, identifying them as the establishment of individual character and a free search for truth. His country, he declared, now had to experience its "own renaissance." Looking back at the Meiji era that followed the opening to the West in the mid-nineteenth century, Nanbara observed that this earlier epoch of reform had created only the "external appearance" of a modern nation. It had emphasized only the establishment of state power and the expansion of national wealth. Humanistic values had been, at best, subordinated to these goals. Although it was "not too late to correct this mistake," it was certainly too early to applaud the establishment of a new, democratic Japan. "Unlike America, political democracy in Japan has not acquired true life," Nanbara commented. The possibility that reac-

The most effective "gifts from heaven" purveyed by occupation troops were often the simplest: sweets, cigarettes, and chewing gum, accompanied by offhanded friendliness. "Give me chocolate" became a catch phrase for the approach children adopted toward the conquerors within days after the first GIs arrived. Here schoolchildren crowd around a soldier passing out candy from his jeep in September 1945.

tionary forces would reestablish themselves was by no means out of the question.[8]

The critic Kamei Katsuichirō, writing in one of the country's most popular monthlies immediately after the occupation ended, deftly captured the view that the heralded revolution was more than a charade but less than a real struggle for democracy. Instead of revolutionizing consciousness, Kamei wrote, the occupation had tended to reinforce a "colonial mentality." Certainly, looking back on what was actually accomplished, democracy fell far short of the initial hopes and ideals captured in Katō Etsurō's little book. In some ways, the occupation reminded Kamei of a noose of silk floss with a thin wire hidden in it; in other ways, it reminded him of a Hollywood movie set.[9]

The occupiers themselves naturally looked on their "revolution from above" more positively. Yet in many ways, even from their elevated and righteous vantage point, this was a moment when idealism and cynicism meshed, when democratic aspirations became entangled with colonial mentalities in unexpected, not to say unprecedented ways. The reformers were also proconsuls. They were, as has been said of other Americans in other situations, sentimental imperialists. As administrators whose careers were altered and accelerated by the victorious war, they possessed what John Kenneth Galbraith, in a related context, characterized as "an arrogant certainty of high purpose."[10]

Demilitarization and Democratization

Formally, the period from August 1945 to April 1952 when Japan was subject to foreign control was known as the Allied occupation of Japan. This was a misnomer. Although two international advisory boards representing the victorious powers were created to deal with the occupation, their influence was negligible.[11] From start to finish, the United States alone determined basic policy and exercised decisive command over all aspects of the occupation.

Accordingly, it was policy makers in Washington who drafted the three basic documents that established the initial objectives of the occupation: the Potsdam Declaration in which the United States, Great Britain, and China announced the terms of surrender; the "United States Initial Post-Surrender Policy Relating to Japan" that was sent to MacArthur in late August and made public on September 22; and a comprehensive military directive elaborating postsurrender policy that the Joint Chiefs of Staff also sent to the supreme commander in draft form in late August. Although the first two quickly became public documents, the third—which many occupation authorities regarded as their basic guide—remained secret until November 1948.[12]

Douglas MacArthur's singular command over the occupation—indeed, his very title of Supreme Commander—epitomized the American monopoly on policy and power. No other Allied nation could challenge his authority. The huge occupation force under his control, engaged in both military and civil affairs, was American with but token exceptions (such as the stationing of British and Australian forces in nuclear-bombed Hiroshima). The high-level advisory missions that would visit MacArthur and his general headquarters in Tokyo over the years that followed all came from Washington and were made up almost exclusively of Americans. There was nothing covert about this domination. Indeed, the initial policy document sent to MacArthur in late August and made public the following month explicitly stated that in the event of differences among the Allies, "the policies of the United States will govern."

The top-level war-crimes trials that accompanied the occupation, formally known as the International Military Tribunal for the Far East, also were misleadingly named. An international panel of judges did preside and the president of the tribunal was Australian, but the Tokyo trial was a predominantly American show. Americans dominated the "International Prosecution Section" that set the agenda for the tribunal, and they brooked scant internal dissent from other national contingents.

The objectives of the occupation set forth in the three fundamental policy documents were broad and ambitious—in an ever-*accelerating* manner. That is, the postsurrender policy made public in September called for more extensive democratization than the Potsdam Declaration had really intimated. In turn, the lengthy, secret Joint Chiefs of Staff directive that elaborated how this public policy was to be implemented—not actually finalized until November—made clear to MacArthur and his headquarters that they were expected, in effect, to micromanage a democratization agenda.

Behind this development lay a byzantine history of interbureaucratic debate and struggle in Washington, in which, as the war approached its eleventh hour, conservative State Department Japan specialists who scoffed at the notion of "democratizing" that country found themselves overruled by more liberal and progressive reformers. Katō Etsurō's canisters of "democratic revolution" parachuting into Japan came not from the "old Japan hands" but from individuals, a number of whom were associated with the War Department,[13] who were framing the issues of war and peace in Asia in broader and more radical ideological terms.

The Potsdam Declaration was by no means a tame document. It assured the Japanese that they would not be enslaved or destroyed as a nation, although they would lose their empire. On surrendering, the country would be placed under military occupation; "stern justice" would be meted out to war criminals; the authority and influence of those who had "deceived and misled the people of Japan into embarking on world conquest" would be eliminated "for all time"; "just reparations in kind" would be exacted; military forces would be "completely disarmed"; the economy would be demilitarized but eventually permitted to return to world trade; and the government would be required to "remove all obstacles to the revival and strengthening of democratic tendencies among the Japanese people," and to establish freedom of speech, religion, and thought, as well as respect for fundamental human rights. The occupation would be terminated when "there had been established in accordance with the freely expressed will of the Japanese people a peacefully inclined and responsible government." Although sometimes interpreted as signaling that they would be allowed to retain the imperial institution, this last phrase was, in fact, left deliberately ambiguous. The emperor's subjects, after all, had never had been entirely free to express their views and did not at that time possess the right to choose their form of government.

To these stern but general terms, the other policy documents added several objectives that transformed the occupation from a moderate exercise in demilitarization and political reform into an unprecedented experiment in induced democratization. These documents made clear that disarmament and demilitarization were not merely to be "complete" but also "permanent." They also specified that the purging of individuals who had advocated militarism or militant nationalism would be broader than might have been imagined from the Potsdam Declaration, extending even into "the economic field."

Beyond this, the guiding directives incorporated a potent emerging notion among policy bureaucrats, namely, that the occupation authorities should become actively engaged in attempting to change the psychology of the Japanese people. Underlying this immodest objective was a growing sense of urgency that the country should not only be "democratized" to prevent the reemergence of militarism, but simultaneously immunized against a rising tide of communist influence. Such a policy of reeducation, it was stipulated, would require not only the active promotion of American objectives throughout the media, but also "minimum control and censorship" of the press, radio, film, and private communications.[14]

The policy blueprints finalized after Potsdam also extended ideals of democratization to the economic field. On the one hand, it was emphasized that occupation authorities bore no responsibility "for the economic rehabilitation of Japan or the strengthening of the Japanese economy." Apart from preventing economic crises that could lead to chaos (averting starvation, for example), U.S. policy called for letting the Japanese stew in their own juices. At the same time, the post-Potsdam formulations explicitly mandated the promotion of policies "which permit a wide distribution of income and of the ownership of the means of production and trade." To this end, planners in Washington called for "dissolution of the large industrial and banking combinations which have exercised control of a great part of Japan's trade and industry." This amounted to ordering a direct attack on both the older zaibatsu that had dominated the nation's economic growth since the early twentieth century and the "new zaibatsu"

The shipment of emergency foodstuffs to Japan by the victors beginning in
1946 helped alleviate severe shortages and prompted many public expressions
of gratitude. This celebration in a Tokyo suburb coincided with traditional
Obon observances, when festive dances accompany the annual return of the
souls of the dead.

that emerged in the course of the country's mobilization for war. In tandem with such an antitrust campaign, the supreme commander was directed to promote labor unions and carry out a sweeping land-reform program.

This was a strikingly ambitious reformist agenda. Outlaw Japan was to be rendered a peaceful, democratic, law-abiding nation by eradicating the very *roots* of militarism that had led it so recently to war. In the famous opening lines of the "Initial Postsurrender Policy," the ultimate objectives of the occupation were framed as follows:

(a) To insure that Japan will not again become a menace to the
     United States or to the peace and security of the world.

(b) To bring about the eventual establishment of a peaceful and
    responsible government which will respect the rights of
    other states and will support the objectives of the United
    States as reflected in the ideals and principles of the Char-
    ter of the United Nations. The United States desires that
    this government should conform as closely as may be to
    principles of democratic self-government but it is not the re-
    sponsibility of the Allied Powers to impose upon Japan any
    form of government not supported by the freely expressed
    will of the people.

The key to legitimizing radical top-down reform lay in the reference
to "the freely expressed will of the people." Under imperial Japan's existing political, economic, and social institutions, the reformers argued, the
people had had little if any control over their lives. To enable them to truly
express their will freely required dismantling this authoritarian structure
root and branch, even while disclaiming any intention to "impose" an alien
system of government on the defeated foe. The very logic of the argument
dictated the imposition of reforms that would create a society in which the
"will of the people" prevailed, thereby eliminating the "will to war" that
had made Japan the scourge of Asia.

Shortly after the occupation began, Assistant Secretary of State Dean
Acheson formulated this vision in blunt terms. The goal of the occupation, he stated, was to ensure that "the present economic and social system in Japan which makes for a will to war will be changed so that the
will to war will not continue."[15] This bumpy, redundantly will-full prose
succinctly conveyed the Americans' crusading sense of purpose, as did the
plain metaphors with which the reformers routinely described their mission. It became commonplace to speak of *rooting out* the sources of aggression. Colonel Charles Kades, an idealistic and influential lawyer in
GHQ's Government Section, expressed this nicely when pointing out the
difference between the mild postsurrender reforms proposed by Japanese
leaders and the radical policies GHQ forced them to adopt: "They wanted
to take a tree that was diseased and prune the branches—cut off the
branches. We felt it was necessary to, in order to get rid of the disease,
take the root and branches off. Otherwise we find new branches and the
same disease in the tree."[16] In the shorthand of the times, SCAP's mission was nothing less than to carry out the "demilitarization and democratization" of Japan.

Such an audacious undertaking by victors in war had no legal or his-

As part of its massive "demilitarization" program, the occupation forces
physically destroyed vast quantities of Japanese armaments. In this scene
deceptively reminiscent of the inferno of war, U.S. tanks spewing napalm jelly
and flames torch over fifty war planes at the famous Sasebo base in northern
Kyushu.

torical precedent. With a minimum of rumination about the legality or
propriety of such an undertaking, the Americans set about doing what no
other occupation force had done before: remaking the political, social, cultural, and economic fabric of a defeated nation, and in the process changing the very way of thinking of its populace. It is not surprising that the
Japanese did not know what to expect. The conquerors were embarking
on uncharted terrain, and in early autumn 1945, as the war in Asia hur-
tled toward its denouement, they were still defining their grand mission
as they went along. Initially, they themselves had only an imprecise picture of what concrete reforms this mission would require.

To a certain degree, comparable occupation policies were followed in
Germany. Indeed, the "Europe-first" policy the United States pursued
from the beginning of its involvement in World War II made Germany's
prior surrender inevitable and meant that policies adopted for that defeated
nation would be used as guidelines in drafting postsurrender policy for
Japan. Nonetheless, differences were notable. Most obviously, of course,
all of Japan was placed under American control, whereas occupied Germany had been divided into U.S., British, French, and Soviet zones.

Beyond this, the enemy in Asia was also subjected to "MacArthur-
esque" control—a unique experience on which personality indisputably

One of the most notorious episodes in the destruction of "war-related" material occurred in November 1945, when the Americans cut apart the cyclotron at Tokyo's Riken laboratory with blowtorches and dropped the pieces in Tokyo Bay. Expressions of outrage from scientists around the world eventually prompted a statement of regret from military officials in Washington.

left its imprint. MacArthur and the cadre of reformers who initially gathered under his command conveyed a messianic fervor that had no real counterpart in Germany, and American Eurocentrism in the immediate postwar period left MacArthur's GHQ with an unusually free hand. While policy makers in Washington concentrated their attentions on Soviet policies in eastern Europe and the reconstruction of western Europe, the imperious MacArthur until 1948 reigned as a minor potentate in his Far Eastern domain. In 1951, explaining the authority he had wielded in Japan to a U.S. Senate committee, MacArthur pointed out that "I had not only the normal executive authorities such as our own President has in this country, but I had legislative authority. I could by fiat issue directives."[17]

Race and culture also set Japan apart. Unlike Germany, this vanquished enemy represented an exotic, alien society to its conquerors: nonwhite, non-Western, non-Christian. Yellow, Asian, pagan Japan, supine and vulnerable, provoked an ethnocentric missionary zeal inconceivable vis-à-vis Germany. Where Nazism was perceived as a cancer in a fundamentally mature "Western" society, Japanese militarism and ultranationalism were construed as reflecting the essence of a feudalistic, Oriental culture that was cancerous in and of itself. To American reformers, much of the almost sensual excitement involved in promoting their democratic revolution from above derived from the feeling that this involved *denaturing* an Oriental adversary and turning it into at least an approximation of an acceptable, healthy, westernized nation.

The anomaly of attempting to make Japan "law abiding" in the Western mode by pursuing occupation policies unprecedented in international law was rationalized by the argument that World War II had been a catastrophe of unprecedented destructiveness, and any stable new world order required breaking with the mold of the past. The plain crusading ardor of the victors was thus mixed with high levels of fear, hope, and idealism, and with a clear consciousness of creating new norms of international behavior.[18] This attitude was most evident to the general public in the war-crimes trials of top leaders, in which policies adopted toward Japan and Germany rested on similar—and novel—legal premises. Following the rules established for the Nuremberg trials, accused "Class A" war criminals were held accountable for committing "crimes against peace" and "crimes against humanity" that had no precedent in international law. B. V. A. Röling, the Dutch judge at the Tokyo trials, later acknowledged the many "unfair features" and "grave errors" of these proceedings, but still expressed faith that the trials contributed "to a legal development that mankind urgently needed." "International law," in his words, "was *en route* to banning war and rendering it a criminal offense."[19] In Japan, a similar idealism, arrogance, and wishfulness—a similar missionary sense of being called on to *create* new norms that might eradicate forever the "will to war"—initially governed the "demilitarization and democratization" policy as a whole.

Imposing Reform

In this intensely ideological and emotional milieu, the defeated Japanese were made the subjects of an unprecedented experiment—audacious in its ethnocentrism but also in its ambition and, until devoured by the Cold War, its idealism. This was an undertaking plagued from the start by contradictions, among them the very notion of "revolution from above." Enduring political and social revolutions generally emanate from below. Certainly, they must ultimately come from within the indigenous society. Never had a genuinely democratic revolution been associated with military dictatorship, to say nothing of a neocolonial military dictatorship—which, when all was said and done, is what MacArthur's command was.

Virtually all of the Americans involved in this crusade were aware of these contradictions, but this did not daunt them. It took months, however, before the reformers actually worked out the full, concrete implications of their ambitious agenda and conveyed this to the other side. Japanese officials had carefully scrutinized the Potsdam Declaration and initially gamely insisted that the manner in which they had accepted its terms signified a contractual and conditional surrender. On this critical issue, they were crisply informed that their capitulation was and always had been unconditional. As the Japanese national press dutifully and dourly reported, they were "not equal" to the occupation authorities.[20] What ultimately impressed Japanese at all levels with the truly ambitious nature of the Americans' intentions, however, were two SCAP directives issued with fanfare more than a month after the surrender ceremony in Tokyo Bay.

On October 4, the supreme commander ordered the dissolution of restraints on political expression. The Peace Preservation Law of 1925, under which thousands of (usually left-wing) critics of the government had been arrested, was abrogated. Governmental restrictions on assembly and speech were lifted. The Special Higher Police, or "thought police," of the Home Ministry were abolished. The heads of the Home Ministry and the national police force were purged. Political prisoners were ordered released from jail, paving the way for the return to public life of Tokuda Kyūichi and hundreds of his stalwart communist colleagues who had held firm to their principles during upwards of eighteen years of incarceration. Prior to this directive, the Cabinet headed by Prince Higashikuni had made it clear how unthinkable it was for communist prisoners to be released. On the day following the issuance of what came to be called MacArthur's "civil-liberties directive," Higashikuni and his whole cabinet resigned.[21]

One week later, the new premier, Shidehara Kijūrō, met MacArthur for the first time and received a succinct order that made the previous directive seem mild. In addition to the "liberalization of the constitution," the government was commanded to extend the franchise to women, promote labor unionization, open schools to more liberal education, democratize the economy by revising "monopolistic industrial controls," and in general eliminate all despotic vestiges in society. Suddenly, abstract statements about promoting democracy had become exceedingly specific.

Supporters as well as critics of this October 11 directive interpreted it as a signal expression of America's commitment to a genuinely radical agenda of "democratization," and the months that followed proved them correct. Beginning in early November, GHQ initiated a frontal attack on the giant zaibatsu conglomerates, starting with the forced dissolution of the "holding companies" through which zaibatsu families controlled their vast empires. Eventually both "antimonopoly" and "deconcentration" legislation was passed, and hundreds of large enterprises were earmarked as targets for breakup. At roughly the same time, an agrarian land reform was initiated that within a few years would virtually dispossess the rural landlord class, destroying a system in which exploitative tenancy had been widespread and creating in its place a huge constituency of small owner-farmers. Arrests of accused "Class A" war criminals, modestly initiated in September, accelerated during the final months of the year.

The government-sponsored cult of state Shinto, a bulwark of emperor-centered ultranationalism, was abolished on December 15. Under GHQ pressure, a Trade Union Law guaranteeing workers the right to organize, strike, and bargain collectively was approved by Japan's parliament, the Diet, on December 22. In the same month, President Truman's special envoy on reparations, Edwin Pauley, called for extensive reparations in kind to be taken from the country's already prostrate industrial plant. For the old guard, the new year of 1946 began with more inauspicious tidings, including the first of a series of purge directives that would eventually prohibit some two hundred thousand individuals—mostly but by no means exclusively former military officers—from holding public office.

And this was but the beginning of the revolution from above, which over the next two years would extend to the reform of civil and criminal law, elimination of the "feudalistic" family system that had legally rendered women inferior, extension of the right to vote to women, decentralization of the police, enactment of a progressive law governing working conditions, revision of both the structure and the curriculum of the education system, renovation of the electoral system, and promotion of greater local autonomy vis-à-vis the central government. In the single most brazen and enduring act of the democratic revolution, a reluctant government was forced to introduce an entirely new constitution that retained the imperial system but simultaneously established the principle of popular sovereignty and guaranteed a broad range of human rights. It was under this charter that the emperor's erstwhile subjects became citizens.

The new national charter—initiated by GHQ in February 1946 and promulgated nine months later, after extensive public and parliamentary discussion—was the crown jewel of the reformist agenda. It not only codified the basic ideals of "democratization," but wedded them to "demili-

Women voting, for the first time, in the general election of 1946. Several still
wear the *monpe* pantaloons that were commonplace during the war years. The
granting of woman suffrage was sometimes referred to as "the vote received
from MacArthur."

tarization" by explicitly prohibiting Japan from resorting to war as a
means of resolving international disputes. The imperial army and navy had
already been demobilized, the military establishment already abolished.
Under the "renunciation of war" provisions in the new constitution's preamble, as well as in its Article 9, the country formally committed itself
to a pacifist course. This was a stunning innovation, enacted at General
MacArthur's initiative but at the same time entirely consistent with the
objectives set forth in the basic policy directives.

The radicalism of these policies shocked the elites who held power
when the war ended. Had men of influence from the emperor on down
been left to their own devices, they would never have dreamed of initiat-
ing anything remotely approximating such drastic reforms; and had the
government actually been conceded a "conditional" surrender in the closing stages of the war, it might have been in a position to cut American
reformers off at the knees. To conservatives, the overriding tasks of the
postdefeat period were to thwart social upheaval, preserve unchanged the
emperor-centered "national polity," and put the country back on its feet

economically. They rejected all arguments about the "root" causes of militarism, repression, and aggression, choosing instead to depict the recent war as an aberration brought about by irresponsible and conspiratorial elements within the imperial military. This being the case, their argument continued, sweeping structural and institutional reforms were unnecessary. On the contrary, all that needed to be done was to return the state and society to the *status quo ante* of the late 1920s, before the militarists took over. On their own, these civilian elites might have conducted a mild postwar purge of military leaders and perhaps instituted some small political reforms aimed at preventing military excesses in the future.[22]

Cabinet members wept openly when confronted with the most draconian reforms they were ordered to implement, distraught at their inability to prevent what they saw as the destruction of sacrosanct "traditional" ways. The few conservative leaders who were cantankerous enough to speak bluntly to the conquerors—for instance, Yoshida Shigeru, who served as prime minister in 1946–1947 and again from 1948 to 1954— belittled the very possibility of making Japan democratic. In Yoshida's typically elitist argument, the Japanese people were not capable of genuine self-government, and anyone who argued otherwise was either blinded by ethnocentrism or hypnotized by left-wing propaganda. Yoshida and his colleagues were, of course, terrified by the spectacle of the Katō Etsurōs of their country enthusiastically embracing the unexpected "gifts from heaven" that the Americans were bestowing.

This was an extraordinary, and extraordinarily fluid, moment—never seen before in history and, as it turned out, never to be repeated. Like Katō, many Japanese would indeed welcome the revolution from above. It kindled their hopes and sparked their imaginations. The American regimen cracked open the authoritarian structures of the old society in a manner that permitted unprecedented individual freedoms and unanticipated forms of popular expression to flourish.

Katō feared that the exhaustion of defeat, the resilience of the old guard, and the lack of grass-roots struggle inherent in the very notion of a revolution "from above" might prevent the Japanese from ever making the democratic revolution their own. In this regard, his fears resonated with Yoshida's hopes. No one really had any idea what the future would bring.

Part II

TRANSCENDING DESPAIR

chapter three

KYODATSU:
EXHAUSTION AND DESPAIR

Even though the United States and Japan had been locked in the bitterest of wars, the Americans who arrived in Tokyo Bay might well have come from a different planet. An enormous abyss separated the experience and outlook of victor and vanquished. The Americans, brimming with pride and self-righteous confidence, bursting with plans for a golden future, confronted a populace that, in the apt phrase of the perceptive observer and scholar Tsurumi Kazuko, had undergone intense "socialization for death."

For Americans, World War II began in December 1941 and ended three years and eight months later. Japan's war, in contrast, began with the conquest of Manchuria in 1931 and expanded to all-out war against China in 1937. The Japanese had been geared for war for fifteen years; and as their situation became increasingly desperate, what had begun as the indoctrination of young men for death in battle became expanded into a frenetic and fanatical campaign to socialize the entire population for a final suicidal fight. The "hundred million" would die defending the sacred homeland, just as selfless young *kamikaze* pilots were doing. "Good men and women," observed the communist critic Ara Masato, "remained committed to collective suicide right up to the moment at which unconditional surrender was announced." Or, if not committed, at least resigned. Like

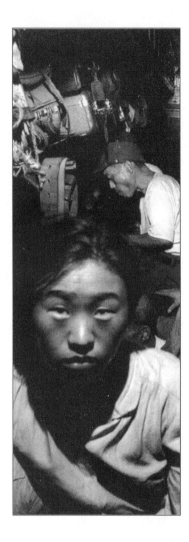

The *"kyodatsu* condition" of exhaustion and
despair that overwhelmed many Japanese after
the defeat emerges strongly in this photo of a
woman on a train crowded with repatriated
servicemen and civilians returning to their
homes in September 1945.

their fighting men abroad, those on the home front were rarely able to
imagine a future other than struggle and probable death.[1]

In this all-consuming milieu, the immediate meaning of "liberation" for
most Japanese was not political but psychological. Surrender—and, by association, the Allied victory, the American army of occupation itself—
liberated them *from death*. Month after month, they had prepared for the
worst; then, abruptly, the tension was broken. In an almost literal sense,
they were given back their lives. Shock bordering on stupefaction was a
normal response to the emperor's announcement, usually followed quickly
by an overwhelming sense of relief. But that sense of relief all too often
proved ephemeral. Exhaustion and despair followed quickly in its train—

a state of psychic collapse so deep and widespread that it soon became popularly associated with *kyodatsu,* a previously technical term. The populace, it was said, had succumbed to the *"kyodatsu* condition."

Near the end of 1946, the Japanese-language page proofs of an interesting pocket-size dictionary were submitted to censors in the occupation bureaucracy for prepublication approval. Entitled *Explanation of Postwar New Terms,* it included a substantial entry on the *kyodatsu* concept. Originally, it explained, this had been a clinical term used to describe physical or emotional prostration in individual patients. Only after the surrender did it gain wide usage as a way of characterizing the "distracted" and "dejected" condition of the people as a whole. It was widely believed, according to the little lexicon, that this despondency posed the greatest of all possible dangers to the country—that it had become "the great enemy that could destroy Japan."[2]

In fact, it is possible to find references to collective manifestations of a *"kyodatsu* condition" in the confidential observations of presurrender officials, who were acutely sensitive to the physical exhaustion and declining morale of the populace long before the war ended. When the emperor made a rare visit to inspect damage from the March 1945 air raids in Tokyo and was not treated with proper deference by local residents, for instance, his alarmed military aide attempted to explain this in terms of a rising scourge of demoralization, or *kyodatsu.*[3] Whether in war or in defeat, such collective exhaustion did indeed appear to be "the great enemy" to a vast array of observers. Just as it could erode reverence for the throne, so it might impede postwar reconstruction—not to mention undermining the whole idealistic enterprise of promoting democracy in a shattered land.

Hunger and the Bamboo-Shoot Existence

Ultimately, of course, the persistence of widespread exhaustion and despair was rooted in material conditions. In the climate of the times, the American decision to adopt a hands-off policy toward economic reconstruction seemed perfectly natural. Misery was accepted as proper punishment for a defeated adversary that had brought so much misery to others. It was in any case inconceivable to think of assisting in Japanese reconstruction when America's own allies were struggling to recover from the devastation of the recent war. What this meant in practice, however, was that the Americans found themselves promoting their "revolution from above" in a society plagued by stagnating productivity and runaway

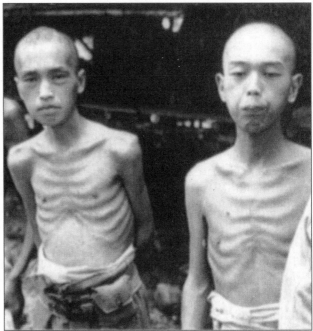

By war's end, Japanese troops in the field were perishing in huge numbers from malnutrition and disease. This is one of several photographs taken by American military photographers depicting starvation among the imperial forces as they surrendered on Saipan.

inflation. Until 1949, while Japan's political, bureaucratic, and corporate leaders stumbled and dragged their heels—biding their time until reparations, "economic democratization," and the reform agenda as a whole had run their course—most Japanese were preoccupied with merely obtaining the bare essentials of daily subsistence. Simply putting food on the table became an obsessive undertaking. Hunger and scarcity defined each passing day.

Hunger was not simply a product of defeat. Rather, it derived from the desperate prolongation of the emperor's lost war, besides being compounded by a disastrous harvest and exacerbated by the confusion, corruption, and ineptitude of the postsurrender elites. A majority of Japanese already were malnourished at the time of surrender. Food shortages had begun to appear in some parts of the country even before Pearl Harbor, and by 1944 theft of produce still in the fields led police to speak of a new class of "vegetable thieves" and the new crime of "field vandalizing." That year, officials in Osaka prefecture estimated that 46 percent of all economic crimes in their jurisdiction involved food. Entrepreneurial individuals formed illegal "procurement troops" that specialized in obtaining rural produce for sale in the cities. In a typical case that August, well before the systematic destruction of urban centers by air raids, 30 percent of the work force at the Mitsubishi glass factory in Tsurumi was found to be suffering from beriberi. By 1945, food shortages were disrupting the war effort and rending the social fabric. Factory absenteeism rose nation-wide, in large part because workers took time off to bargain and barter for food in the countryside. By July, absentee rates in major cities stood at 40 percent or more, with the food problem being cited as a major con-tributing factor.[4]

The Allied policy of "economic strangulation" had sent most of the navy and merchant marine to the bottom of the ocean by mid-1945, choking off supplies to the home front as well as to the war front. In the Southeast Asian and Pacific theaters, starvation became a major cause of death among fighting men. The home islands themselves were heavily dependent on Korea, Formosa, and China for basic foodstuffs. Before Pearl Harbor, imports from these areas accounted for 31 percent of Japan's rice consumption, 92 percent of its sugar, 58 percent of its soy beans, and 45 percent of its salt. Defeat abruptly severed access to these resources.[5]

As the war neared its end, it was a rare family anywhere that regularly ate white rice as a staple. The most common household diet consisted of barley and potatoes, but even these had fallen into short supply. It was in such circumstances that authorities in Osaka recommended an emergency diet that suggested how precarious daily subsistence had become. Based on a research report by local army officials, the emperor's loyal subjects were encouraged to supplement their starch intake by introducing such items as acorns, grain husks, peanut shells, and sawdust to their house-hold larder. (Sawdust, it was explained, could be broken down with a fer-menting agent, transformed into a powder, and mixed in a ratio of one to four with flour to make dumplings, pancakes, or bread). For minerals, peo-ple were encouraged to introduce used tea leaves and the seeds, blossoms, and leaves of roses to their diet. Protein deficiencies could be remedied by eating silkworm cocoons, worms, grasshoppers, mice, rats, moles, snails, snakes, or a powder made by drying the blood of cows, horses, and pigs. Well sterilized, the researchers reported, mice and rats tasted like small birds, but it was important to avoid eating their bones since it had been demonstrated that this caused people to lose weight. The press reproduced these dietary recommendations shortly before the emperor's surrender broadcast under such headlines as "Eat This Way—Endless Supplies of Materials by Ingenuity."[6]

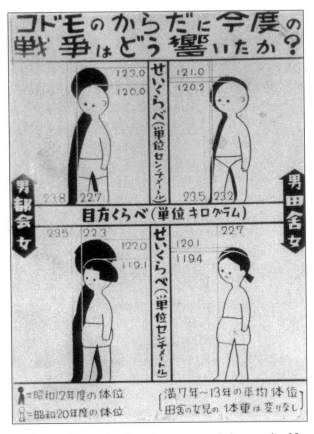

This 1946 poster illustrating how the war stunted the growth of Japanese children shows the average height and weight of youngsters between the ages of seven and thirteen in 1945 (the foreground figures) and 1937 (the black background figures). Urban boys and girls (on the left) were bigger than their rural counterparts (on the right) in 1937 and suffered far more conspicuous malnutrition over the course of the war.

The average calorie intake per person had by this time declined to far less than deemed necessary even for an individual engaged in light work. Elementary-school children were on the average physically smaller in 1946 than they had been in 1937. Births had dropped precipitously. Infant mortality rose.[7] Even Kawakami Hajime, the elderly, humanistic pioneer scholar of Marxism, spent much of his time before and after the surrender dreaming of food. Between July and September 1945, the old Communist wrote himself a series of poems expressing his craving for *manjū*, a bun filled with bean paste once widely available.[8] A young schoolgirl's first thought on hearing the emperor's broadcast was that she would not have to look eyeball to eyeball at frogs anymore—a reference to the practice of sending children out to catch frogs to eat. As it turned out, her intimation of relief was premature.[9]

Defeat did not merely sever Japan from the food supplies of Asia. It also occurred in midsummer, when the previous year's rice harvest was running out. With the empire now cut off and millions of exhausted civilians and demobilized soldiers about to return, it was imperative that there be a bumper crop. Instead, due to adverse weather, manpower shortages, insufficient tools, and a fall-off in fertilizer production, 1945 saw the most disastrous harvest since 1910, a shortfall of almost 40 percent from the normal yield. The deities appeared truly to have abandoned the Land of the Gods.[10]

Bureaucrats and farmers also abandoned their countryfolk, for a large part of the crop immediately moved onto the black market. Rumors spread that millions would die of starvation over the coming fall and winter. In early October, the minister of agriculture was shocked to learn that Tokyo had on hand only a "three-day" supply of rice (mixed with soybeans and *mamekasu,* the residuum of processed soybeans)—an estimate based on rations barely sufficient to keep a nonactive adult alive. His colleague the minister of finance informed the United Press that as many as 10 million Japanese might starve to death if food imports were not immediately forthcoming. This huge (and exaggerated) figure became accepted as gospel.

On October 28, the press reported an exemplary death that seemed a harbinger of things to come: Kameo Hideshirō, a professor of German language at the elite Tokyo Higher School, had died of malnutrition. On November 1, a newly formed citizens group called "The People's Association for a Policy Against Starvation" announced that as many as six individuals a day were dying of malnutrition and related causes among the homeless in Tokyo's Ueno Station. *Eiyō-shitchō*—malnutrition, or dystrophy—became a watchword of the times. In mid-November, it was reported that 733 individuals had died of starvation in Kobe, Kyoto, Osaka, Nagoya, and Yokohama—the country's five largest cities after Tokyo. In the capital, the situation was so chaotic that there were no cumulative statistics. A rough estimate put the number of deaths from malnutrition in Tokyo in the three months after surrender at more than one thousand.[11]

Food shipments from the United States helped avert the anticipated disaster—and, in the process, enhanced the image of the United States as a generous benefactor. A yearbook of the time described such shipments from America as coming "like a merciful rain during a drought"; in the words of a local history, they "kindled a light of hope in the hearts of depressed residents." Consisting primarily of staples such as wheat, flour, corn, legumes, sugar, small quantities of rice, powdered milk, and tinned goods such as corned beef, such assistance came under the auspices of several aid programs and continued until the end of the occupation.[12] Still, hunger remained a constant companion. Although rice was nominally the mainstay of the diet, for a great many families this treasured staple was encountered mostly in the form of a thin, watered-down gruel. A survey of families of elementary-school students found that in mid-1946 gruel took the place of boiled rice at least once a day. For a quarter of the families, gruel constituted the major part of all meals. Soups with leafy vegetables were another mainstay of the daily diet, as were homemade bread and dumplings along with steamed sweet potatoes. Typical diets of desperation also included acorns, orange peels, roots of the arrowroot plant, rice-bran dumplings, and a kind of steamed bread made from a wheat bran that in normal times was fed to horses and cattle.[13]

Kōdansha, the great conservative publishing house that dominated the mass-circulation market, was in general quite bewildered about how to make the transition from militaristic propaganda into an era of new topics. Its earliest postwar magazines, however, unhesitatingly zeroed in on the food crisis. The first postsurrender issue of its housewife-oriented magazine *Fujin Kurabu* (Housewives Club) devoted many pages to family vegetable gardens and how to make nutritious meals in a time of scarcity. The August–September issue of *Shōjo Kurabu* (Girls Club) included such articles as "How to Eat Acorns" and "Let's Catch Grasshoppers." The grasshoppers, like the acorns, were not part of a nature-appreciation study for young readers, but a potential source of protein.[14]

Despite efforts by occupation authorities as well as the government, the collection and distribution of even the most basic foodstuffs remained chaotic for years. In February 1946, to combat the diversion of rice and other staples to the black market, the government introduced a system of "compulsory deliveries" enforced by the police. Since they were often backed up by American military police, in popular parlance these became known from the MP's vehicles as "jeep deliveries." Although the new system doubled government payments to farmers, the black market remained a vastly more attractive market for the producer. In June, for example, black-market rice sold for thirty times more than rice allotted through the official rationing system. Two years later the black-market price was still roughly 7.5 times the official price.[15]

Many farmers engaged in a gratifying barter trade with once-

In the immediate aftermath of defeat, the food crisis was so acute that even bombed-out areas in downtown Tokyo were turned into vegetable gardens. This photograph was taken near Shinbashi station, in the heart of the city, in October 1945.

condescending city folk who flocked to rural areas in search of food. Kimonos as well as watches, jewelry, and other treasured possessions were traded for food, giving rise to one of the most famous phrases of the time: *takenoko seikatsu,* the "bamboo-shoot existence." The edible bamboo shoot can be peeled off in layers, and the *takenoko seikatsu* phenomenon referred to city people stripping off their clothing, as well as other possessions, for food. Similarly, people spoke of an "onion existence," with the clear implication of weeping as one peeled off layer upon layer of precious belongings.

Official data from the unsettled years of 1945 and 1946 are by and large unreliable or simply nonexistent. The spotty records of government food deliveries, however, convey a graphic impression of the unpredictability of a system on which all families were theoretically supposed to depend for survival. Tokyo residents failed to receive a full month's ration in six out of twelve months of 1946. Despite a normal harvest, deliveries in 1947 were worse. In both years, deliveries were commonly a week or two late nationwide, and the allotment of rice dropped off drastically between late spring and early fall, with various kinds of flour being increased in compensation.[16]

Hardly a day seems to have passed when food was not a major topic of discussion. Citizens' groups quickly emerged to protest the government's miserable delivery system. In this manner, hunger and scarcity served as a stimulus to grass-roots political activism. One of the most popular radio programs of the postwar period—an unprecedented audience interview show called *Gairoku* ("Sidewalk Interview")—made its debut in May 1946 by asking passersby on Tokyo's Ginza thoroughfare what became the most familiar question of the new era: "How do you manage to eat?" Many local schools reported closing for a few weeks or shifting to morning-only classes because they were unable to provide lunches. As late as July 1947, a teacher in Kobe wrote to the press about a middle-school student who asked to be demoted to elementary school so that he might partake of the free lunches there. Absentee rates among civil servants taking time off to search for food ran to 15 percent or more, and even the Tokyo metropolitan police took to providing monthly "food holidays" for their employees.[17]

Food-fixated activities and stories mesmerized the public. In September 1946, "bread-eating races" became a fad at elementary-school athletic contests. Competitors in this popular event had to run up to a roll suspended on a string and then eat it without using their hands. In such a race, needless to say, there were no losers. Around the same time, it became common for people in Yokohama to bring their own rice balls to weddings in lieu of a banquet provided by the new couple. Leftovers from restaurants, even the garbage of places where the more privileged dined, became depended-on sources of sustenance. The press carried cruel and pathetic reports about elderly, respectable people who had been arrested for the petty theft of a few potatoes or the like. A hotel proprietor plagued by rats had to give up scattering poisoned food because people were picking it up and eating it.[18]

By the government's own standard, an adult needed to consume approximately 2,200 calories a day in order to be able to carry out a light level of activity. In December 1945, rations supplied only a little better than half of this required amount. During mid-1946 and mid-1947, when the delivery system broke down most abysmally, the figure sometimes dropped to little more than one-quarter or one-third of what was required.[19] In these circumstances, virtually everyone broke the law and found themselves turning to the black market. As late as 1948, it was still a grim joke that, as one magazine editorialized, "in today's Japan, the only people who are not living illegally are those in jail."[20] For the average family, becoming dependent on the black market was a daunting prospect. Not only were prices there many times greater than official ones, but all this was occurring in the midst of runaway inflation. At this point, families already living precariously commonly felt themselves swept into the maelstrom.

Enduring the Unendurable

On November 7, 1945, the Osaka edition of the *Asahi* printed the following letter under the heading "I Am About to Commit Suicide":

I am a mere common laborer. I write this now standing at the dividing point between life and death. My mind has become empty. There is only resentment toward our incompetent government. With five children, I worked hard and even managed to meet the responsibility of saving a little in these hard times, but the government's incompetence regarding food supplies kept getting worse and finally I became unable to work even half the month. I felt sorry for the children, though, and thinking that even our children may be useful for the country in the future, I fed them by buying food on the black market. That couldn't go on forever, however, and we reached our limit. In the end, I even borrowed money at high interest to get food, but I can no longer do this and so we have not eaten for four whole days. My wife collapsed yesterday, and two of the children are losing spirit. The government just talks and does nothing. I understand that high officials are filling their stomachs, but there is nothing we can do. On the other hand, evil merchants involved in the black market—there are two or three of them in this neighborhood alone—make what amounts to 50,000 or 60,000 yen a year.

    At last, I have resolved to commit suicide. I am going to die, reproaching the incompetent, merciless government. Indirectly, I've asked neighbors and the head of the neighborhood association to look after my wife and children. Please give us enough food so that we can work, even thin rice gruel. Uneducated people like us cannot understand difficult theories, but I feel there must be enough rice and wheat. Look, if you have the money, five or ten bushels of rice and wheat can be obtained instantly. It's not that there isn't any. High officials—get rid of your indifference and willingness to let others suffer for years, and show some human heart! Now, for the first time, I realize that Japan does indeed qualify as a fourth-rate country. Without really good policies, it can sink to a fifth- or sixth-rate country. When this letter reaches you, I may already be dead. I have written this gathering up all the spirit I have left.

The letter was signed "A Laborer." In a short postscript, the editors urged the writer to abandon thoughts of suicide and seek immediate help for himself and his family by going to the local police station.

Responses from readers were published within a week. Going to the police station, one writer commented, would simply result in the writer of the letter being treated like a criminal. Another agreed that indifferent officials were nothing new. Wartime and postwar, they were the same. Prices were indeed extraordinarily high, but if the writer of the November 7 letter was still alive, he urged him to be brave and live. A third reader wrote that he cried all day after reading the suicide letter. Citing the emperor's surrender address, he urged the writer to "endure the endurable." He asked that the man—or his family, if it were too late—send him his name and address, for he wished to share some potatoes with them.[21]

If, indeed, the letter writer did resolve to endure the unendurable, he almost surely faced at least four more years of hardship and uncertainty. For millions of blue-collar and white-collar families, life—mere daily survival—did not begin to regain a semblance of "normality" until 1949 or later. Statistics quantify the miserable economic conditions of these years, but it is to personal accounts that one must turn to appreciate not only the emotional and psychological nature of the so-called *kyodatsu* condition, but also how long it took for many individuals to escape their exhaustion and despondency.

Fifteen months after "a laborer" wrote his suicide note to the public, a housewife in Saitama prefecture, north of Tokyo, used a letter to the national press to vent her bitterness at the unchanging wretchedness of her life. She painted a vivid picture: rushing out at a moment's notice, baby on her back, to get rice and other rationed goods; picking up scraps of wood wherever she happened to be walking to supplement the inadequate supply of fuel at home; rising first and retiring last, unable to afford a movie or even a cup of coffee; giving the rare piece of beef or other de-

A typical scene of a destitute man and woman peddling makeshift items on the street. The man's cap, jacket, and gaiters identify him as a demobilized soldier, wearing all the clothing he possesses.

licious food to the rest of the family; going without makeup, still dressed in her baggy, worn-out *monpe* pantaloons; losing youth, losing intelligence, losing everything to the daily grind for survival. This, she made clear, was not just a self-portrait, but the sorry lot of most housewives of her acquaintance.[22]

Early in November 1947, the entire country was shocked by an incident that cast the government's incompetence addressing the food crisis in an almost pathological light. Belatedly, the press reported the death by starvation twenty days earlier of a thirty-three-year-old judge named Yamaguchi Yoshitada. He had presided over a small subsection of the Tokyo municipal court devoted to petty economic crimes, where the great bulk of cases involved transactions on the black market. Serious profiteers had almost never appeared before him. Virtually all the individuals on whom he had been required to pass judgment were desperate men and women struggling to make ends meet.

Yamaguchi's wife, herself the daughter of a judge, later recalled one case her husband told her about, involving a seventy-two-year-old woman whose son had not returned from the war and whose daughter-in-law had been killed in an air raid. When arrested, she had been attempting to feed her two grandchildren by selling such personal possessions as her kimonos and buying food on the black market. Because she was a repeat offender, the judge had no alternative but to sentence her to jail.

Judge Yamaguchi's little courtroom amounted, in effect, to one small stage in a national theater of the absurd. While industrialists, politicians, and former military officers made killings on the black market, while government officials lavishly wined and dined their American overlords, some 1.22 *million* ordinary men and women were arrested for illegal black-market transactions in 1946, a number that rose to 1.36 million and then 1.5 million in the next two years. From the young judge's personal perspective, he had no alternative but to find those brought before him guilty. Yet his own family also relied on the black market for basic commodities. A half-year before his death, a popular magazine featured a short article that concluded that if all black-market regulations were strictly enforced, everyone in the country would have had to go to prison.[23]

The young judge's response to this moral dilemma was not to challenge the law, but rather to live by it personally—to perform his duties with a clear conscience, as he told his wife, and at the same time share the suffering of the people. Sometime in 1946, he asked his wife to feed him nothing beyond his rationed allotment, although it was understood that she might buy black-market food for their children and herself. Thereafter, most of the family's legally obtained food, particularly the rice, went to the children. Yamaguchi's widow later recalled days when she and her husband consumed nothing more than salted water. Judge Yamaguchi died on October 11, 1947.[24]

Widely analyzed at the time, the death provoked shock and praise, as well as a scattering of criticism. When it became fashionable to compare Judge Yamaguchi to Socrates, for example, one citizen demurred. Would it not have been wiser, he asked, to die fighting for good laws instead of insisting on observing lethal ones? In a frank discussion shortly afterwards, Mibuchi Tadahiko, the chief justice of the Supreme Court, observed that the laws Judge Yamaguchi had been required to enforce, though inefficient, did have the ultimately beneficial objective of curbing black-market activity and making basic commodities more readily available. At the same time, he conceded, staying alive was more important than not violating the food laws.[25]

On December 24, 1947, two years and four months after the surrender, a midnight raid by Japanese police on the underground passages in Tokyo's Ueno station led to the roundup, depicted here, of 744 men, 200 women, and 80 children who were living there.

The judge's exemplary death, in any case, changed little. Shortages of staple foods persisted. The black market continued to flourish. Unemployment remained severe. Inflation continued to mount at a dizzying rate. In 1948, women still scavenged for firewood and waited hours to buy sweet potatoes. Housewives still spoke bitterly of the indignity and exhaustion of standing in long lines with "dusty, dry, messy hair," as one wrote that February, "and torn *monpe,* and dirty, half-rotten blouses . . . like animal-people made of mud." The homeless still starved to death. As late as February 1949, the press was reporting that "only" nine homeless people had died in Ueno railroad station that winter, in contrast to the hundred or more deaths in each of the previous three winters.[26]

Okano Akiko, a middle-class Osaka housewife writing for a women's magazine early in 1950, offered an intimate picture of what "enduring the unendurable" had been like for her family. Her husband, a teacher at a military-affiliated school, became unemployed after the surrender but soon found a low-level job as a clerk at a salary of 300 yen a month. At that time, about a quart and a half of rice cost 80 yen, so to make ends meet they began selling off their belongings.

In the confusion of early 1946—when a "new yen" was introduced in a futile attempt to curb inflation—the company employing Okano's husband went out of business, leaving him with a mere 900 yen in severance pay. Lacking anything more than casual light footwear, neither she nor their two sons, aged five and three, were able to venture far from home. Okano, pregnant and unable to consider outside employment, could find no work that could be done in her own residence. The price of rationed rice tripled early in 1946, but, out of principle as well as poverty, the family tried to use the black market as little as possible.

Eventually, her husband found a new job as a schoolteacher at a salary of 360 yen per month. They had little choice but to continue to sell their possessions, purchasing black-market goods about eight times monthly, at a cost of roughly 400 yen per month. Okano supplemented their diet of rice and grains by picking wild parsley, rocambole, and fernbrake. Meat or fish were largely beyond their means, and the two children began to show signs of malnutrition. Food became an obsession. The young woman's account was extremely graphic on this. The youngest boy in particular, his stomach distended, began to look like a frog. There were times the children screamed in hunger; times when all four family members shared 20 grams of roasted beans and tea for breakfast; times her husband had no lunch at all. The family consumed everything that seemed edible: the leaves and stems of pumpkins, potato vines, plants from the roadside. They tried to raise chickens, but the chickens were hardly able to stand and took a year and a half to begin to produce eggs. For a twenty-day period they were unable even to afford potatoes and lived solely on pumpkins. Her husband lost his job again when the school ran into financial difficulties, this time receiving only 50 yen as severance pay. He, too, began to suffer noticeably from malnutrition, his entire body beginning to swell up. The children ceased screaming and lay motionless. Only feeble cries from the newborn baby broke the silence.

The next two years offered but slight relief. In 1947, Okano found a job doing spinning at home, sometimes rising at 3:00 A.M. to work. Such household piecework—sewing, making cigarettes (often from discarded cigarette butts), and the like—was a major source of income for many families. In 1948, the food situation improved somewhat, although potatoes remained the mainstay of the family diet. Both wife and husband fell seriously ill that year and went deeply in debt. In 1949, another child was born, and meat and fish finally became plentiful again, although it was still a struggle to make ends meet, as rent and food prices continued to climb. As 1950 began, her husband found a teaching position at a college. For the first time since the war ended, they could live on his income; and so, Okano wrote, she was finally able to think about the quality of family life, not mere survival.[27]

Most middle- and lower-class Japanese had comparable stories, some of which, at least in the telling, had a kind of Rabelaisian energy to them. Control of bowels and bladders, for example, often required tactical planning. People who spent hours riding crowded trains to and from the countryside to barter for goods frequently had to refrain from eating or drinking en route because there was no way to get to the toilets. Extended families that had crowded into a single residence without plumbing or regular sanitation services had to devise strategies for relieving themselves elsewhere. Crowding also meant furtive competition for scarce resources. Thus, a young husband and his pregnant wife vividly recalled smuggling a chocolate bar into the bath, that being the only place they could share it without envious relatives looking on.[28] A popular novel serialized in the *Yomiuri* newspaper provided a catchphrase—"Saturday wife"—that captured the frustration of married couples who had to escape to an inn or some such place on Saturday nights just to have a little privacy.[29]

Compounding all this, a plague seemed to have quite literally descended on the country. Communicable diseases, widespread during the war, now flourished in the filth, chaos, and poverty that accompanied defeat. Deaths from dysentery nearly doubled to over 20,000 in 1945. Between 1945 and 1948, over 650,000 people were reported to have contracted cholera, dysentery, typhoid fever, paratyphoid fever, smallpox, epidemic typhus (spotted fever), scarlet fever, diphtheria, epidemic meningitis, polio, and encephalitis. Of this number, official records reported the deaths of 99,654 individuals.[30]

Tuberculosis carried off far more victims than all the other diseases combined. The annual tuberculosis death count had increased steadily from the mid-1930s. The disease claimed 130,763 lives in 1935, 160,398 in 1942. Impressionistic evidence suggests even greater numbers over the next four years. In 1947, when official statistics resumed, 146,241 persons were reported to have died of TB, and it was not until 1951 that total annual deaths dropped below 100,000.[31] For every person who died of tuberculosis, several others contracted the disease. Following surrender, the total number of TB cases annually was probably well over a million.[32] Like radiation sickness, like physical disability, like being a war orphan or a poor war widow or a "third-country person," having tuberculosis was a social stigma. In this instance, the communicable nature of the disease made fear of contact reasonable, but the social consequences were comparable. Both patients and their families commonly were shunned by their communities.[33]

Sociologies of Despair

On the morning after the emperor's surrender broadcast, farmers in Kanagawa prefecture did something unprecedented: they slept late.[34] What is one to make of this? Had years of physical and emotional exhaustion caught up with them? Was this collective behavior an all too human response to the shock of defeat? Is it best seen as a homely harbinger of the enervating *"kyodatsu* condition"? Surely, the farmers' fatigue was all of these.

Acknowledging defeat *was* traumatic, and this trauma found immediate expression in a rhetoric of despair. People spoke of the "shame and dishonor" of unconditional surrender. For many, sudden confrontation with the hitherto unspeakable words *maketa sensō*—"lost war"—was almost stupefying. Since the early 1930s, the Japanese had been told they were fighting for the purest and most noble of objectives—that they were a "great country" and a "great empire," a "leading race" destined to overthrow Western imperialism and bring about a "Greater East Asia Co-Prosperity Sphere," a people possessed of a unique and indomitable "Yamato spirit."

Now, what could one say to the war dead? How was one supposed to survive, spiritually as well as materially, in the midst of such a stupendous abandonment of purpose? Any people mobilized to fight a holy war and then, after prolonged sacrifice, told that they had been totally defeated, that it was now incumbent on them to go along with whatever the victor commanded, might have responded similarly. However elusive the term *kyodatsu* might have been, little was peculiarly Japanese about the state of depression and disorientation it described insofar as the immediate psychic numbing of defeat was concerned.

To attribute the *"kyodatsu* condition" simply to the shock of defeat would be misleading, however, for exhaustion of a deep and complex sort had set in long before August 15, 1945 as a result of the government's policy of wasting its people in pursuit of impossible war objectives. In the final year of the war, the secret records of the police as well as diaries from the privileged elites were shot through with expressions of apprehension concerning the war weariness and declining morale of the populace.[35]

Similarly, the fact that exhaustion and despondency lasted for years did not so much reflect the lasting trauma of defeat as the manner in which wartime fatigue was compounded by incompetence and outright corruption on the part of the postsurrender leadership. In the long view of history, Japan rebounded quickly from defeat. For ordinary people, however, the postwar recovery seemed agonizingly slow.

Public discouragement was exacerbated by a recognition that privileged groups continued to prosper in defeat as they had in war. Sixteen months after the surrender, a laborer described with anger and resentment activities centering around two expensive restaurants in his neighborhood. A Western-style establishment with "incredible food and drink" never lacked bureaucrats, bankers, company executives, and policemen as regular customers. A nearby Japanese-style restaurant was packed nightly with men who arrived in cars and, once the drinking was under way, entertained themselves by singing the patriotic songs of the recent war. This was a far cry, the worker observed, from the "democracy" people were supposed to be creating.[36]

The media were indefatigable in reporting on all events symptomatic of social breakdown. Police roundups of homeless people received regular coverage, and early in 1947 it was duly noted that the younger brother of the former general and prime minister Tōjō Hideki, then on trial for war crimes, had been discovered among vagrants living in Osaka's Namba district. Near the end of that year, it was reported that the crown prince's pet dog was missing; fears were expressed that, like many other unfortunate albeit nonimperial canines, it had become minced meat on someone's table. The *sandoicchi-man*, or sandwich-board man, became a symbol of postwar disorientation, especially after the media discovered in 1948 that one of the forlorn figures shuffling along the street wearing advertising boards was the son of the former admiral Takahashi Sankichi, another of yesterday's men of influence. It was also in 1948 that lingering exhaustion in the general population translated into widespread popular criticism of one of the occupation's most minor innovations, the introduction of American-style daylight savings time. Called *sanmā taimu* ("summer time") in the marvelous new pidgen terminology of the moment, setting the clock forward an hour was opposed on the grounds that it simply extended the difficulty of "daily" life. People preferred that darkness come earlier, although they did not succeed in getting daylight savings time repealed until September 1951.[37]

One development that drew attention as being emblematic of the desperate struggle to transcend the *kyodatsu* condition was the *shūdan miai* or

One of the more striking innovations spawned by the postsurrender confusion was the "group marriage meeting." Here young men and women seeking spouses pose for a solemn photo at the Hachimangū shrine in Kamakura in 1948. Each wears a number that corresponded to the forms they had filled out concerning their background and interests.

"group marriage meeting," in which young men and women gathered for the explicit purpose of finding marriage partners. The traditional *miai* was an arranged meeting between two marriage prospects and their parents, a meeting in which the prospective bride and groom—especially the young woman—often had relatively little say in the final decision. In the confusion of the time, such matchmaking arrangements proved difficult due to the disruption of families and communities as well as a shortage of the individuals who customarily had served as intermediaries or marriage brokers. It was young women of marriageable age who found themselves in the most desperate circumstances, for the demography of death in the recent war had removed a huge aggregation of prospective husbands. In 1940, there had been more men than women between the ages of twenty and twenty-nine; seven years later, women in this age group outnumbered men by over one million. A large cohort of women, most of them born between 1916 and 1926, confronted the prospect not merely of coping with postwar hardships without a marriage partner, but of never marrying at all.

This was the background to the unprecedented spectacle of the "group *miai.*" The first such gathering, sponsored by a commercial marriage-service magazine named *Kibō* (Hope), took place on November 6, 1947. Held outdoors by the Maruko bridge on the bank of the Tamagawa river in Tokyo, it attracted some 386 men and women. A second group *miai* at the same site the following spring drew upwards of four thousand participants and received congratulatory messages from both the current and former prime ministers, Ashida Hitoshi and Yoshida Shigeru. Later that year, a major women's magazine ran an article by the critic Kon Hidemi about a smaller group *miai* held at the imposing Hachiman Shrine in Kamakura. He described the atmosphere as a combination of desperation and remarkably businesslike procedures, taking particular note of how carefully the women checked the men's resumes and how aggressively they sought out those who seemed most attractive. Kon was impressed by the courage and vitality that the young women displayed in struggling to create a normal life under abnormal circumstances, and touched by the painful sense of urgency that seemed to grip all the participants.[38]

Noting harsher indices of the *kyodatsu* condition, the media called attention to a rise in alcoholism, drug addiction, and violent as well as nonviolent crimes. Alcoholism, never a rarity in male society, became a gaudy symbol of social disintegration in part because the cheap liquor available was frequently made with dubious and dangerous ingredients. *Kasutori shōchū,* an exceedingly popular lower-class drink made from sake dregs (*kasu,* hence the name), was said to render most drinkers unconscious after three cups. An entire subculture known as "*kasutori* culture" developed around this inebriated world. The ravages of cheap alcohol were sometimes swift and stark, particularly when drinkers turned to another favorite concoction, the *bakudan* or "bomb" in which methyl alcohol was mixed with a variety of other liquids. In November 1946, the government reported that there had been 384 known deaths from methyl alcohol poisoning since the surrender, and impressionistic evidence suggests that a large number of individuals were permanently blinded by this crude intoxicant. So familiar were the effects of the "bomb" that they became the subject of sick jokes. The illustrated magazine *Asahi Gurafu*, for example, ran a cartoon of a blind, disabled veteran in dark glasses standing by a roadside food-and-drink stand saying, "Even if it's methyl, that's okay."[39]

The black market, a major source of both methyl alcohol and the foul *kasutori shōchū*, also became a major source of illicit drugs, including heroin and philopon *(hiropon)*, which had been used as a stimulant to induce wakefulness among pilots during the war. Although drug abuse did not become widespread among the general populace, it was prevalent among the writers, artists, and performers who constituted the more flamboyant members of the *kasutori*-culture demimonde.[40]

To the extent that these stimulants became associated with a bohemian culture of writers and artists, their abuse acquired a certain cachet of fashionable decadence. More alarming by far as a sign of social breakdown was the seeming ubiquity of avarice and crime. In the midst of unprecedented hardship, all the homilies about Japan's unique racial and cultural harmony, its "beautiful customs" and "familial" sense of social solidarity, proved to be hollow. Corruption on a grand scale was taken for granted. Gouging on the black market came to be expected. Suddenly it seemed possible that anyone at all might become a victim of predatory crime. Although military men had murdered, raped, and robbed abroad with appalling casualness, the crime rate at home had declined during the war years. Thereafter, to judge at least by media accounts—which is what people did judge by—lawlessness spread with alarming speed. Certain incidents were singled out for their symbolism. It was reported, for example, that surviving members of the virtually deified Tokkōtai—the "special forces" who flew suicide missions in the final stages of the war, and were better known in the West as *kamikaze* pilots—were turning to strong-arm robbery. The phrase *Tokkōtai kuzure*, literally "degenerate Tokkōtai," suggestive of a thoroughly destructive fusion of drinking, womanizing, and criminal activity, came into vogue. Here was a world turned upside down.[41]

The press also published piquant pleas from robbery victims. A pregnant woman begged an unknown thief to return stolen baby clothes, for she had no way to replace them. A child similarly asked a thief to return clothes stolen from his family. Certain gangs, it was reported, specialized in robbing exhausted repatriated civilians and ex-servicemen as they left disembarkation centers.[42] Armed robbers accosting men or women on the streets or in their homes became a ubiquitous subject of black humor among cartoonists and comedians. A radio comedy show of 1947 suggested that the number of men carrying knives, cleavers, and pistols and committing burglary, armed robbery, and murder had become so numerous that—like other workers—they probably should form a union.[43]

Demoralized, unemployed men did not prowl this new criminal landscape alone. Students were apprehended in robberies. And in July 1946, the police announced that they had broken up an all-female gang of fifty or more members who were formally divided into a "prostitution unit" and a "blackmail unit." The latter specialized in robbing and intimidating other prostitutes. Their name had a nice, old-fashioned nationalistic ring to it: they called themselves the "Blood Cherry Gang."[44]

Sensational murders intensified the growing sense of social disintegration. On the morning of March 16, 1946, the sixty-five-year-old Kabuki actor Jinzaemon was brutally slain with a hatchet in his home, along with his young wife, infant son, and two maids, one of whom was only twelve years old. The murderer turned out to be a twenty-two-year-old writer living on the verge of starvation in a detached house on the actor's property. Investigators later estimated that his daily diet averaged 920 calories. Apparently when he complained bitterly about Jinzaemon's comfortable lifestyle, a row ensued and the actor ordered him off the property, whereupon the writer carried out the murders in a frenzy of resentment.[45]

This sensational crime sent a tremor of apprehension through the country, intensified a month later when a twenty-four-year-old man killed his father because, as he explained, his father had refused to share his black-market food with him. Four months later, police arrested a decorated ex-soldier (who in all likelihood had committed atrocities in China) for kidnapping and murdering two young women. They soon discovered that they had a serial murderer of at least ten women on their hands. Even in his pathological crimes a connection to hunger was found. He had enticed all his victims with offers of food.[46]

Police records convey a less sensational impression of postsurrender lawlessness. The number of arrests was not exceptional by American standards. On the other hand, crime rates were noticeably higher than they had been between 1937 and 1945, when aggression abroad was accompanied by intensified authoritarian controls at home. Compared with rates of the mid-1930s, the murder rate had probably not changed, and arrests for so-called intellectual offenses such as fraud and embezzlement were actually lower. Unsurprisingly, armed robbery, theft, and the handling of stolen goods had indeed increased significantly over prewar levels. Thus, in 1934, 2,126 persons were arrested for robbery and 724,986 for theft, whereas the comparable average yearly figures for the period from 1946 through 1949 were 9,485 and 1,177,184. The number of young offenders also appears to have increased dramatically. In April 1949, it was reported that individuals between the ages of eight and twenty-five were committing half of all serious crimes in Japan (murder, assault, armed robbery, blackmail, arson, and so on), at the alarming rate of one offense every two minutes.[47]

Child's Play

Children's games can provide a barometer of their times. With consumerism of any sort still in the distant future, youngsters were thrown back on their imaginations, and their play became a lively measure of the obsessions of adult society. Not long before, boys in particular had played war with a chilling innocence of what they were being encouraged to become. They donned headbands and imagined themselves piloting the planes that would, in fact, never return. They played at being heroic sailors long after the imperial navy began to be decimated. Armed with wooden spears and bayonets, they threw themselves screaming at mock-ups of Roosevelt and Churchill and pretended they were saving the country from the foreign devils.[48] In defeat, there was no such clear indoctrination behind children's games. Essentially, they played at doing what they saw grownups do. It was a sobering sight.

There were not many commercial toys in this world, although the first popular one after the war was revealing. In December 1945, a toy maker in Kyoto produced a jeep not quite 10 centimeters long that sold for 10 yen. The stock of one hundred thousand quickly disappeared from store shelves, heralding the modest revival of the toy industry. The quintessentially American nature of the product was appropriate, for the child's world was defined, in generally positive and uncritical ways, by an acceptance of the fact of being occupied. Jeeps were associated with the chocolate and chewing gum handed out by cheerful GIs, and thus with the few delicious amenities imaginable in these war-torn lives. "Hello," "good-bye," "jeep," and "give me chocolate" were the first English words most youngsters learned. They also learned to fold newspapers into soft GI-style hats rather than the traditional samurai helmets of the past. To older, nationalistic Japanese, a good part of child's play seemed to involve finding pleasure in being colonized.

The games *were* happy—that was the point of playing, after all—but in ways that almost invariably tended to sadden grownups, for they highlighted so clearly and innocently the pathos that war and defeat had brought into their lives. Early in 1946, for example, it was reported that the three most popular activities among small boys and girls were *yamiichi-*

Panpan asobi—pretending to be a GI and prostitute—became a popular activity among young boys and girls. Other inventive children's games included imitating black-market activities, labor demonstrations, and overcrowded trains.

gokko, panpan asobi, and *demo asobi*—that is, holding a mock black market, playing prostitute and customer, and recreating left-wing political demonstrations.

Black-market games—hawkers and their wares—might be seen in retrospect as a kind of school for small entrepreneurs, but to grownups at the time they were simply another grim reminder of the necessity of engaging in illegal activity to make ends meet. *Panpan asobi,* prostitution play, was even harder for parents to behold, for *panpan* was a postwar eu-

phemism for freelance prostitutes who catered almost exclusively to the
GI trade. A photograph from early 1946 shows laughing youngsters in
shabby clothes reenacting this—a boy wearing a soft GI hat, his arm
hooked into that of a little girl wearing patched pants. In the *"demo"*
game, children ran around waving red paper flags. As youngsters grew
older, play shaded into practice. The press took care to note when
roundups of prostitutes included girls as young as fourteen, while school-
boys as well as orphans and runaways quickly learned how to earn pocket
money as pimps by leading GIs to women. "You like to meet my sister?"
became, for some, the next level of English after "give me chocolate."

As time passed, the playtime repertoire expanded. In mid-1947, a
teacher in Osaka reported that his pupils seemed absorbed in playing
"train" games, using the teacher's platform at the front of the classroom
as the center of their activities. In "repatriate train," children put on their
school knapsacks, jammed together on the dais, shook and trembled, and
got off at "Osaka." "Special train"—obviously a takeoff on the railway cars
reserved for occupation personnel—allowed only "pretty people" to get on.
A "conductor" judged who was favored and who wasn't. A button missing? Rejected. Dirty face? Rejected. Those who passed these arbitrary hur-
dles sat in leisure on the train. Those rejected stood by enviously. In
"ordinary train," everyone piled on, pushing and shoving, complaining
about being stepped on, crying out for help. Every so often, the conduc-
tors balancing on the edges of the platform announced that the train had
broken down and everyone had to get off. It was, the teacher lamented, a
sorry spectacle to behold: from playing war to playing at utter confusion.

Well into 1949, children continued to turn social disorders into games.
In *runpen-gokko* they pretended to be homeless vagrants. The game took
its name from the German word *lumpen,* which had come to Japan earlier as "lumpenproletariat" and then acquired the everyday meaning of
being an unemployed vagrant. The atmosphere of lawlessness was reen-
acted in "catch a thief" *(dorobo-gokko)* and "pretending handcuffs" *(tejō-
gokko).* "Catch a thief," it was said, had replaced hide-and-seek in
popularity. Desire to strike it rich was captured in a lottery game. Predictably, child's play also included *kaidashi-gokko,* pretending to leave
home to search for food.[49]

Inflation and Economic Sabotage

The postwar scourge of material shortages coupled with spiraling inflation
lasted for over four years, longer than the Pacific War itself had lasted. Al-

though economic chaos was an inevitable legacy of the foolhardy lost war, the protracted nature of the postwar crisis was in large part the result of policy shortcomings on both the Japanese and American sides, compounded by outright corruption and economic sabotage. Government attempts to curb inflation by issuing a "new yen," imposing wage and price controls, and promoting "priority production" by funneling reconstruction loans to strategic industries proved to be woefully inadequate. While the victors dithered and delayed in finalizing and implementing their announced policies of claiming industrial reparations and promoting economic "deconcentration," capitalists and business managers hesitated to reinvest in productive facilities that might have no future. And while the judicial system brought more than a million individuals to the dock annually for petty economic crimes, most of the opportunistic capitalists, former military officers, corrupt politicians, and powerful gang leaders who crassly manipulated the system and benefited most from the black market went scot free.

Although inflationary trends first became apparent in late 1942, they did not get out of hand until the final months of the war, when huge sums were expended in preparation for an anticipated "decisive battle" on the home islands. In theory, the military budget for fiscal 1945 (April 1945 through March 1946) had seven months remaining when the war ended. In fact, approximately 70 percent of this sum already had been spent at the time of the emperor's broadcast. The remaining 30 percent (26.6 billion yen out of a total military budget of 85 billion yen) was hastily disbursed before the arrival of occupation forces, mainly to military contractors.[50]

The diversion of military funds and supplies into private hands actually began the day before the emperor's broadcast and unfolded in several distinct phases. On August 14, in one of its last acts before resigning, the cabinet headed by Admiral Suzuki Kantarō agreed to turn all materiel over to unit commanders for disposal at the local level. This decision, issued in army circles as "Secret Instruction No. 363" the following day, stipulated that war supplies should be distributed to local governments, public organizations, private factories, and private citizens as appropriate. "As a principle," the order stated, these goods should be given free of charge to local governments and sold in other cases—but "where goods are sold it is not necessary that payment be made at once."

On August 20, in its "General Order No. 1" handed to a Japanese surrender delegation in Manila, the Americans made it clear that all military supplies were to be maintained intact. This order was ignored by the new cabinet headed by Prince Higashikuni until two days before General MacArthur was scheduled to arrive. Even then, although the secret disposal orders were canceled, no attempt was made to identify or regather the dispersed materials. Needless to say, there were no easily accessible records concerning their whereabouts. During this same period, the Bank of Japan turned its energies to extending massive loans to erstwhile war contractors for the ostensible purpose of facilitating conversion to "peaceful" production. The impression one gains from later investigations into these activities is that during the turbulent two weeks following the emperor's broadcast, a great many men of influence spent most of their waking hours looting military storehouses, arranging hasty payments from the military budget or from the Bank of Japan to contractors and cronies, and destroying documents. In the greatest moment of crisis in Japanese history, it was a rare officer, official, or executive who devoted himself with sincerity and foresight to serving the well-being of the general populace. No wise men or heroes, no commendable statesmen, emerged from among the old elites.

It was later estimated that approximately 70 percent of all army and navy stocks in Japan were disbursed in this first frenzy of looting—and this for a force of some 5 million men at home, over 3 million overseas. That, however, was not the end of it. Some months after the surrender, occupation authorities naively turned over to the government a major portion of the military stocks that had been properly maintained intact, with instructions that these be used for public welfare and economic reconstruction. A substantial portion of these goods consisted of construction materials and machinery, and the Home Ministry proceeded to entrust their disposal to a committee consisting of five representatives from zaibatsu enterprises. The total value of goods involved was estimated to be roughly 100 billion yen—and these materials, too, quickly disappeared almost without a trace. In pathetic testimony before a parliamentary committee investigating these scandals in August 1947, Ishibashi Tanzan, who had served as minister of finance in 1946, ruefully observed that "nobody knows where a hundred billion yen worth of stuff has gone to."

Where the stuff had gone to, of course, was either myriad places of concealment or directly into the black market. At the same time, defeat prompted a run on previously blocked savings deposits. During the war, these controlled funds sitting in banks and other financial institutions had been known as "stand-by purchasing power." They constituted a huge resource (264 billion yen, by one estimate) that quickly vanished after the surrender, largely into the black market—in this instance due less to corruption than to the desperation of ordinary individuals who exhausted their savings simply to make ends meet.

These developments were compounded by certain immense governmental expenditures associated with defeat. One of these—the cost of repatriating millions of servicemen and civilians—was predictable. A second fiscal drain, however, caught the government by surprise. Only after the Americans arrived did the Japanese learn that they would be required to pay a major portion of the costs of housing and supporting the gigantic army of occupation. As it turned out, these latter expenditures amounted to a staggering one-third of the regular budget at the beginning of the occupation. Nor was this a one-time burden. Although outlays directly supporting the American presence declined as a percentage of the annual budget, they remained one of the government's single largest expenditures in the years that followed. As a budget line, they were euphemistically disguised as "war termination costs" or simply "other expenses" in compliance with orders from occupation authorities.[51]

It would be difficult to exaggerate the material as well as psychological ramifications of requiring the Japanese to contribute in a major way to the maintenance of the occupation army. While some 3.7 million families still lacked housing of their own as of 1948, the government was required to direct a substantial portion of its annual budget to providing housing and facilities for the conquerors—and, indeed, ensuring that these met American living standards. While war widows begged to little avail for relief, the government had no choice but to pay the expenses of, say, an American officer who desired to "modernize" the private residence requisitioned for him by upgrading the electricity and plumbing, painting the interior, introducing modern appliances (phones, stoves, and toilets), and perhaps converting the garden pond into a swimming pool.[52] While the unbearable press of passengers on the national railways was dramatized by the suffocation, in December 1945, of an infant strapped to its mother's back, the government was required to run special cars or even "exclusive occupation army trains," often nowhere near full, for the free use of occupation personnel. Few Americans gave any thought to such "costs of occupation," but they were readily apparent to many Japanese.

In the legal market where official price controls applied, wholesale prices doubled by the end of 1945 and continued to multiply rapidly thereafter, increasing by 539 percent in the first year of occupation, 336 percent in the second year, 256 percent in the third year, and 127 percent in the fourth. A *shō* (1.4 kilograms) of rice that cost 2.7 yen at official rates in June 1946 cost 62.3 yen by March 1950. The celebrated radio comedian Miki Torirō captured the runaway nature of this hyperinflation with a slapstick song about riding on a train and finding the price of oranges higher at every stop.[53]

Naturally, in the black market (sometimes pleasantly called the *jiyū ichiba* or "free market") the same inflationary curve was observed but at much higher levels. If there were no oranges left to buy at official prices, one could only sing a very rueful song indeed. Until the end of 1951, the government maintained close scrutiny of black-market prices for some fifty "basic consumer goods"—led by the so-called five staple foods (rice, barley, flour, sweet potatoes, and potatoes)—and its findings provide a rough approximation of the gouging that took place. In the first half year after the surrender, black-market prices amounted to around 34 times the "official" price for comparable commodities. Thereafter, the "free market" became somewhat more restrained. For the remainder of 1946, prices for the fifty basic consumer goods averaged fourteen times greater than official prices. In 1947 the multiple was nine, in 1948 it dropped to less than five, and by 1949 prices in the illegal market were roughly double official prices.[54]

Consumer goods, however, constituted only a portion of the products that found their way onto the black market, which also dealt in an immense variety of producer's goods: coal, coke, gasoline, lumber, cement, plate glass, *tatami* straw matting, pig iron, rolled steel, galvanized steel, copper sheeting, aluminum, tin, electric wire, electric motors, fertilizers, industrial chemicals (sulfuric acid, caustic soda, soda ash), mechanic oil, rubber tires, farm equipment, alcohol, paints, dyestuffs, textiles, paper, and so on.[55] Obviously, the farmers who diverted their rice and potatoes to the black market had nothing to do with these items. Where had they come from? The answer was obvious: from the militarists, industrialists, bureaucrats, and politicians who had looted military stockpiles and hidden them away. To a degree impossible to measure, shortages persisted, inflation ran unchecked, industrial reconstruction languished, and the black market flourished because this was exceedingly profitable for a large number of well-placed people.

This massive diversion of military stockpiles did not begin to receive serious criticism until 1946, when it was subjected to informal and unofficial investigation by Sekō Kōichi, a Home Ministry official who subsequently was elected to the lower house of the Diet. Even then, it was not until the latter part of 1947 that the scope of this betrayal of public trust became widely known. As the scandal unfolded, investigators routinely complained about encountering "tremendous opposition" at every level from the cabinet and central bureaucracy through the ranks of Diet members, notorious political fixers, and the "nouveaux riches," down to petty officials and policemen at the local level. Indeed, a good portion of the profits from black-market sales of the plunder was being used to finance political campaigns, especially but by no means exclusively among politicians affiliated with the conservative parties.

Even when the House of Representatives belatedly and reluctantly created a "Special Committee for Investigation of Concealed and Hoarded Goods" in July 1947, the would-be investigators were initially given only limited powers and allotted *no* public funds. Despite these impediments, the committee, headed by Katō Kanjū, a well-known Socialist, was at least able to evaluate the broad ramifications of the pillage. In a famous report published at the end of the year, the Katō committee concluded that "the goods thus diverted from their proper channels and the individuals thus enriched have remained throughout the Occupation as a cancer threatening the economy of this country." With the "hoarded goods scandal," structural corruption was established as one foundation stone of the postwar political economy.

The materials looted by men of position and privilege were obviously of enormous value. They were, after all, being stockpiled to supply a gigantic home army for a protracted "decisive battle." They were also, in many cases, materials capable of being concealed indefinitely. Large quantities of diamonds and other personal jewelry that patriotic women had donated to support the war effort were among the items stolen; so were drugs and rare precious metals such as titanium brought back from overseas. The sporadic hoards of goods that investigators did manage to track down provided an ongoing menu of tantalizing tidbits for the general public. In April 1946, for instance, a cache of silver ingots was found sunk near the shoreline in Tokyo Bay. Almost a year later, a raid on a single chemical company uncovered "10 tons of naphthalene, 26 tons of caustic soda, 45 tons of lubrication oil, 150 tons of edible oil, 16 tons of industrial salt, 50 tons of steel tube, 50 tons of steel bars, 30 tons of iron sheet, 45 electric motors and other miscellaneous iron, textile and rubber goods." Although the absence of reliable records makes an accurate calculation of the scale and worth of the diverted goods impossible, a patchwork estimate of a very rough sort suggests that their value in 1947 may have exceeded 300 billion yen. The significance of this sum becomes apparent when it is set against the regular national budget for that year, in which total government expenditures were placed at 205 billion yen. By another calculation, the dispersed stocks would have weighed something on the order of 300 million tons—a crude estimate indeed, but a fair indication of the physical scale of the goods involved and the large number of persons needed simply to transport and conceal them. Despite the enormity of the scandal, no major perpetrators were ever indicted.[56]

Obviously, far more than a massive looting of the public treasury underlay the economic chaos and social hardships of these years. Sudden conversion from an industrial structure geared to war to a nonmilitarized economy would, under the best of circumstances, have proved a staggering task. Permanent loss of the overseas empire—not so much the ephemeral "Greater East Asia Co-Prosperity Sphere" of 1941–1945, but the imperialist structure embracing Korea, Formosa, and northern China including Manchuria—stripped the economy of access to raw materials and markets that had been absolutely critical to its previous economic growth. This loss of empire was compounded by the termination of normal trade and diplomatic relations. Until the final years of the occupation, Japanese were not even permitted to travel abroad.

In critical industrial sectors such as coal production, moreover, the country paid dearly for long years of class and racial oppression. By the time of the surrender, much of the most onerous heavy labor—especially in the coal mines—was performed by conscripted Korean laborers or Chinese prisoners. When liberation came, they deserted their hellholes en masse. One result was that the basic energy sources necessary to fuel industrial reconstruction recovered at a dismal rate. By the end of 1945, preoccupation with human malnutrition had its industrial counterpart in the new concept of a "coal famine." In many critical industrial sectors, productivity declined precipitously after the defeat before beginning to show improvement. In most sectors, it was not until at least 1950 that output returned to the levels of the mid-1930s.[57]

All this contributed to the *kyodatsu* condition. To be called on to endure the unendurable was something the Japanese people had grown used to over long years of war. Then, at least, the exhortation carried a clear sense of purpose: their nation, their culture, their "national polity," people were led to believe, were imperiled by external forces. To be told to endure the unendurable in the postwar quagmire was a different matter, and the Diet report on the hoarded-goods scandal went a good way toward explaining why, for so many, physical and emotional exhaustion persisted for so long. "Private individuals have profited fabulously and have nourished the black market," the investigators concluded, whereas attempts to expose the scandal and retrieve looted materials had been "frustrated by a combination of fraud and legal barriers" at every level. Of the men of influence who profited from the scandal, it was observed that "they wear a mask of democracy but in reality they swagger on the black markets," revelling in the prolongation of economic confusion.

In these circumstances, it was not surprising that a pervasive victim consciousness took root, leading many Japanese to perceive themselves as the greatest sufferers from the recent war. The misery on hand was far more immediate and palpable than accounts of the devastation that the imperial forces had wreaked on strangers in distant lands. To many political idealists, the hardships of everyday life also seemed to pose a formidable obstacle to bringing about popular support for progressive reforms. A well-known newspaper photo in March 1946, on the eve of the first postwar general election, was taken to be representative of this dilemma. It showed people crowding to purchase sardines from open street stands, completely ignoring a political candidate on a soapbox.[58]

Antidotes to such pessimism, however, were to be found almost everywhere one looked. Early in 1946, the poet Horiguchi Daigaku conveyed his own feelings about transcending exhaustion and despair with these lines:

> The country has become small
> and powerless,
> food scarce,
> shame plentiful,
> life fragile.
> Stop grieving!
> Raise your eyes
> to the treetops,
> to the sky.[59]

Few people read this, for it appeared in an obscure new poetry magazine; but, each in his or her own way, millions of individuals did stop grieving and fixed their gaze on clear targets. Defeat stimulated skepticism and outright anger at established authority. Poverty radicalized many workers. Blatant corruption often prompted healthy criticism. Sardonic humor flourished alongside despair, and for every personalized story of emotional exhaustion and shattered lives, it usually was possible to find an uplifting counterexample of resilience, hope, and accomplishment. A veritable torrent of diverse publications accompanied the lifting of the old police-state restrictions on free expression. The film industry prospered. Radio became lively again. Intellectuals ran on as if there were no tomorrow. New formulations of "culture" were debated alongside new models of "love," both carnal and pure. "Decadence" itself emerged as a provocative challenge to old orthodoxies.

chapter four

CULTURES OF DEFEAT

It is a testimony to human resilience that the great majority of Japanese transcended exhaustion and despair to refashion their lives in diverse and often imaginative ways. Some took years to do so. Some threw off the psychological prostration of *kyodatsu* within days. Others never succumbed to it at all. They experienced a sense of liberation and opportunity from the moment they heard the scratchy recording of the emperor's voice. People splurged on a fancy meal or a special celebratory dish such as *sekihan* (boiled white rice with red beans). They hastened to remove the blackout paper from their windows, letting light back into their lives. Millions of them began to consider what it might mean to create a private life free from the dictates of the state.[1]

Recalling all this years later, a critic spoke of a new "space" suddenly existing in society.[2] People behaved differently, thought differently, encountered circumstances that differed from any they had previously experienced—or would ever experience again. It was a rare moment of flux, freedom, and openness when new patterns of authority and new norms of behavior were still in the process of forming. People were acutely conscious of the need to reinvent their own lives.

If cynical opportunism was everywhere visible, so was opportunity— the chance to do things, say things, think about things in ways that had

been impossible under the militarists. The occupation was a military dictatorship, of course, but in its early stages it destroyed enough of the authoritarian controls of the previous elites to allow for a generally
unpredictable efflorescence of popular sentiment and initiative. At the
popular level, these developments involved the refashioning of the very
meaning of "Japan" in ways that encouraged greater personal autonomy.
Prior to August 15, the state had defined in the most doctrinaire terms
imaginable what the "cardinal principles of the national polity" were;
what the correct "way of the subject" was; how it was essential to observe
one's "proper place" in the established hierarchies of class and gender;
which "decadent" and "corrupting" foreign thoughts or cultural expressions were forbidden; what could be said or not said in virtually every situation.

When ideologues rhapsodized about "one hundred million hearts beating as one," Japan's enemies commonly took this at face value. During the
war, the Americans and others simply used this racial self-praise to reinforce the racist stereotype of a robotic, ferociously brainwashed people.
What defeat showed, to the astonishment of many, was how quickly all the
years of ultranationalistic indoctrination could be sloughed off. Love of
country remained, but mindless fanaticism and numbing regimentation
were happily abandoned. By deed as much as word, people everywhere
demonstrated relief at the collapse of the authoritarian state and receptivity to, or at least tolerance of, an immense variety of pleasures and activities.

The most flamboyant early expression of the casting off of despair and
the creation of new space was to be found on the margins of "respectable
society." There, distinctive subcultures of defeat emerged, shocking yet
mesmerizing symbols of the collapse of the old order and the emergence
of a new spirit of iconoclasm and self-reliance. Not all marginalized groups
came to possess such an aura, of course. Many "third-country people"—
Koreans, Formosans, Chinese (and Okinawans, too, in the view of most
Japanese)—played defiant roles on the margins, but with few exceptions
they were largely rendered all but invisible by the society at large.[3]

The marginal groups that electrified popular consciousness came from
three overlapping subcultures: the world of the *panpan* prostitute, whose
embrace of the conqueror was disturbingly literal; the black market, with
its formidable energy and seductively maverick code of behavior; and the
well-lubricated "*kasutori* culture" demimonde, which celebrated self-
indulgence and introduced such enduring attractions as pulp literature and
commercialized sex. All three marginal worlds came to exemplify not

merely the confusion and despair of the *kyodatsu* condition, but also the vital, visceral, even carnal transcending of it.

Servicing the Conquerors

Two incidents gave prostitution a face in occupied Japan. On September 29, 1946, the *Mainichi* newspaper published a letter from a twenty-one-year-old prostitute. The young woman described how she had been repatriated from Manchuria and, without relatives or resources, ended up living in the cavernous reaches of Tokyo's Ueno station:

> I slept there and looked for work, but could not find anything, and there were three consecutive days when I went without eating. Then on the night of the third day a man I did not know gave me two rice balls. I devoured them. The following night he again brought me two rice balls. He then asked me to come to the park because he wanted to talk with me. I followed him. That is when I sank into the despised profession of being a "woman of the dark."[4]

Even though the press was full of letters expressing the anguish of ordinary people, this one caused a sensation, albeit in an unusual and delayed manner. The letter inspired "In the Flow of the Stars," a maudlin popular song released with little notice in December 1947. Almost a year later, the song belatedly became a great hit, and its refrain of *konna onna ni dare ga shita*—essentially, "Who made me such a woman?"—was taken up as a serious social question. The proper answer was usually understood not to be the sleazy procurers and pimps who took advantage of such destitute young women, but an incompetent government and bureaucracy.

Between the publication of the *Mainichi* letter and the release of the song, a national radio broadcast of an interview with a nineteen-year-old streetwalker shocked the public and captured quite a different view of the nether world of prostitution. Caught on a hidden microphone in April 1947, she was identified on the program as "Rakuchō no Otoki"—that is, Otoki of the Yūrakuchō district in Tokyo, where many streetwalkers operated—and was described as a leader among the prostitutes in that area. Otoki's interviewer painted a vivid word picture of her. She was tall and sharp looking, he said, wearing navy slacks and a lavender sweater, her hair tied stylishly with a yellow band. Her face was quite beautiful, the skin almost transparently white, eyebrows strong, lips thickly rouged. However, when she talked, he observed, she had a habit of twisting her mouth in an unsavory way reminiscent of a gangster. A photograph of Otoki from this time captures the curl of her lip.

Otoki's words made an even stronger impression than her appearance:

> Of course it's bad to be a hooker. But without relatives or jobs due to the war disaster, how are we supposed to live? . . . There aren't many of us who do this because we like it . . . but even so, when we try to go straight and find a job, people point their fingers at us and say we were hookers. . . . I've turned many of these girls straight and sent them back into society, but then . . . they all [her voice becomes tearful] get picked on and chased out and end up back here under the tracks. . . . You can't trust society. They despise us.

Nine months later, as in a perfect parable of fall and redemption, the interviewer received a letter from Otoki saying that she had been shocked to hear her own voice on the radio. It sounded "like a devil," and as a consequence she had left the streets and found a job. Society was still harsh to her, she continued, and her resolve often came close to breaking, but she was determined to hold on.[5]

These sentimentalized images of "women of the dark" left a great deal unsaid, and necessarily so; for a great part of the prostitute's trade involved catering to the huge army of occupation. The sexual implications of having to accommodate hundreds of thousands of Allied servicemen had been terrifying, especially to those who were aware of the rapacity their own forces had exhibited elsewhere as well as of the huge numbers of non-Japanese women who had been forced to serve the imperial troops as *ianfu* or "comfort women." In the wake of the emperor's surrender broadcast, rumors spread like wildfire that "the enemy, once landed, will violate women one after the other." The Home Ministry's intelligence analysts immediately recognized the link between these rumors and the behavior of their own forces abroad. As one internal police report put it, "many of those who speak of pillage and rape, unsettling people's minds, are returnees from the war front."[6] Urban families were urged to send their womenfolk to the countryside. Women were advised to continue to wear the baggy *monpe* pantaloons of the war years rather than more enticing feminine attire. Young girls were cautioned not to appear friendly. Still, it was taken for granted that the foreigners would demand sexual gratification. The question was simply: who would provide it?

The government lost no time in answering this question. On August 18, the Home Ministry sent a secret wireless message to regional police officials throughout the country instructing them to prepare special and ex-

This classic photograph of a *panpan* or "woman of the night" was taken by Yoshida Jun in Tokyo's Yūrakuchō district. In a later collection, the photo was captioned with a famous song title from the time: "Who Made Me Such a Woman?"

clusive "comfort facilities" for the occupation army. Such preparations were to be made with maximum discretion. Responsibility for staffing such facilities should be assumed by local chiefs of police, who were to mobilize local entrepreneurs and individuals already engaged in providing sexual services. On the same day, high police officials in Tokyo met with "entrepreneurs" operating in the Tokyo-Yokohama area and promised them 50 million yen in financial backing, with the understanding that they should raise a similar amount themselves.[7]

On the following day, Vice Premier Prince Konoe Fumimaro asked the national police commissioner to personally take charge of this urgent matter. "Please defend the young women of Japan," the prince, a former prime minister, is said to have implored him. Within a matter of days, however, a new approach would be taken. General Kawabe Torashirō, one of the officers who had met with General MacArthur and his staff in Manila to arrange the surrender, returned to Tokyo and urged that the government not become directly involved in managing these facilities.

Thereafter, the government's role consisted primarily of formally endorsing the project and providing it with loans and police support. The businessmen encouraged to undertake the task solicited private investment with a circular announcing official support from the Home Ministry, Foreign Ministry, Ministry of Finance, national commissioner of police, and Tokyo municipal government. On September 6, the official Kangyō Bank advanced upwards of 30 million yen as the presumed first installment on a government loan for these activities. Ikeda Hayato, a rising young star in the Ministry of Finance who was instrumental in arranging government backing, was later quoted as saying that "a hundred million yen is cheap for protecting chastity." The entrepreneurs publicly expressed their gratitude for this lucrative opportunity to serve the nation by gathering in front of the imperial palace and shouting "Long live the emperor!"[8]

Enlisting a small number of women to serve as a buffer protecting the chastity of the "good" women of Japan was well-established policy in dealing with Western barbarians. Special pleasure quarters had been set up for foreigners immediately after Commodore Perry forced the country to abolish its policy of seclusion, and in modern mythology one young woman who gave her body for the nation had already been glorified as a patriotic martyr. Her name was Okichi, and she had been assigned as a consort for Townsend Harris, the first American consul, who assumed his duties in 1856. The procurers of 1945 appropriated her sad, sensual image in defining their own task. The women they were assembling, they declared, would be *Shōwa no Tōjin Okichi*, "the Okichis of the present era."

To the government's surprise, professional prostitutes proved reluctant to become latter-day Okichis. By one account, they were fearful that the Americans, commonly portrayed as demonic figures in wartime propaganda, possessed oversized sexual organs that could injure them. The organizers of the special comfort facilities thus undertook to recruit ordinary women by posting a large signboard addressed "To New Japanese Women" in the Ginza district of downtown Tokyo. "As part of urgent national facilities to deal with the postwar," this read, somewhat vaguely, "we are seeking the active cooperation of new Japanese women to participate in the great task of comforting the occupation force." The solicitation also mentioned openings for "female office clerks, aged between eighteen and twenty-five. Housing, clothing, and food supplied."[9]

Most of the women attracted by this advertisement arrived for their interviews shabbily dressed. Some, it is said, were even barefoot. The great majority had no experience in the "water trade" of the red-light districts, and most left when informed what their actual duties would be. Among those who remained, some claimed to be attracted not so much by the assurance of food and shelter as by the appeal to give their bodies "for the country." This was, after all, essentially the same message of patriotic self-sacrifice that had been drilled into them all their lives. By August 27, 1,360 women in Tokyo had enlisted in what soon would become known in English as the R.A.A., short for Recreation and Amusement Association (*Tokushu Ian Shisetsu Kyōkai* in Japanese).

The next day, just as the first small contingents of occupation forces were arriving, an inaugural ceremony for the R.A.A. was held in the plaza in front of the imperial palace. On this occasion, the following "oath," couched in ornate Japanese, was read:

> Although our family has endured for 3,000 years, unchanging as the mountains and valleys, the rivers and grasses, since the great rending of August 15, 1945, which marked the end of an era, we have been wracked with infinite, piercing grief and endless sorrow, and are about to sink to the bottom of perilous, boundless desperation. . . .
>
> The time has come, an order has been given, and by virtue of our realm of business we have been assigned the difficult task of comforting the occupation army as part of the urgent national facilities for postwar management. This order is heavy and immense. And success will be extremely difficult. . . .
>
> And so we unite and go forward to where our beliefs lead us, and through the sacrifice of several thousands of "Okichis of our era" build a breakwater to hold back the raging waves and defend and nurture the purity of our race, becoming as well an invisible underground pillar at the root of the postwar social order. . . .
>
> A word as we conclude this proclamation. We absolutely are not flattering the occupation force. We are not compromising our integrity or selling our souls. We are paying an inescapable courtesy, and serving to fulfill one part of our obligations and to contribute to the security of our society. We dare say it loudly: we are but offer-

GIs attempt to strike up a conversation with young women in Yokohama on
August 31, 1945, three days after the first occupation forces arrived in Japan.

ing ourselves for the defense of the national polity. We reaffirm this.
This is our proclamation.[10]

A statement was also issued by the seven professional associations engaged in the water trade who were to run the Tokyo R.A.A. collectively.
After paying solemn homage to "the great spirit of maintaining the national
polity by protecting the pure blood of the hundred million," these patriotic
procurers moved with almost breathtaking agility into the facile new rhetoric
of these rapidly changing times. Through the R.A.A., they declared, "we
hope to promote mutual understanding between [the Allied occupation
forces] and our people, and to contribute to the smooth development of people's diplomacy and abet the construction of a peaceful world."[11]

Several hundred GIs on that day quickly found their way to an R.A.A.

facility in Tokyo's Ōmori district, where a small number of mostly inexperienced recruits had been gathered. Neither beds, futons, nor room par-
titions were yet available, and fornication took place without privacy
everywhere, even in the corridors. Later Japanese accounts of the scene
tend to be irate, speaking of shameless "animalistic intercourse" that
showed the "true colors" of so-called American civilization. The local police chief is said to have wept.[12]

One naive recruit to the R.A.A. later recalled the terror of her first day,
when she was called on to service twenty-three American soldiers. By one
estimate, R.A.A. women engaged between fifteen and sixty GIs a day. A
nineteen-year-old who previously had been a typist committed suicide almost immediately. Some women broke down or deserted. By mid-
September, however, this grotesque exercise in "people's diplomacy" had
become more or less routine. In his diary entry for September 13, the

Japanese waitresses pose with members of the U.S. Strategic Bombing Survey
who were rushed to Japan to evaluate the effects of the wartime air raids.

writer Takami Jun recorded a conversation with a taxi driver who reported seeing a woman in a flashy kimono—like something from an operetta, he said—greeting an American soldier outside one of the comfort facilities. She leaped up, threw her arms around his neck, and said *Harō*—"Hello." It was, for both Japanese men, a depressing scene.[13]

Since the greater part of Tokyo had been incinerated in the air raids, initially there were not many areas where comfort facilities could be provided. In the latter part of September, Dr. Yoshino Mitsuru, the head of the municipal government's hygiene department (and eldest son of Yoshino Akiko, a celebrated feminist and poet), was summoned by GHQ and asked to help apportion the prostitutes into separate districts to be reserved for use by U.S. officers, white enlisted men, and black enlisted men. Initially, women designated for use by black soldiers were said to have been horrified—until they discovered that many black GIs treated them more kindly than the whites did. In their meticulous preoccupation with race and racial hierarchy, some Japanese concluded that such relative kindness derived from the fact that black soldiers had been socialized to regard them as "whites."[14]

Such "recreation and amusement" centers expanded rapidly in Tokyo—there were soon thirty-three by one count—and spread almost as quickly to some twenty other cities. Not surprisingly, they proved popular among U.S. servicemen. They were, among other things, inexpensive. The price for a short visit with an R.A.A. prostitute was 15 yen, or one dollar—about the same as half a pack of cigarettes on the Japanese market. Two or three times that amount purchased an entire night of personal diplomacy.[15] Although these services did not prevent rape and assault, the incidence of rape remained relatively low given the huge size of the occupation force—much as the government had hoped.[16]

Despite its popularity and initial support from the victors, the R.A.A. did not survive the early months of the occupation. In January 1946, occupation authorities ordered the abolition of all "public" prostitution, declaring it undemocratic and in violation of women's human rights. Privately, they acknowledged that their major motivation was an alarming rise in venereal disease among the troops. By the time the prohibition went into effect a few months later, almost 90 percent of the R.A.A. women tested positive for infection. Around the same time, syphilis was detected in 70 percent of the members of a single unit of the U.S. Eighth Army, and gonorrhea in 50 percent. It was largely to combat such diseases that the first U.S. patents for penicillin were sold to Japanese companies in April of that year.[17]

Alarmed by the threat of widespread venereal disease, U.S. military
authorities quickly established "prophylactic stations" outside places of
prostitution that catered to the GI trade—here, conveniently lettered in
English, the popular "Oasis of Ginza."

The women who had been recruited by the R.A.A. were sent off without severance pay, but with uplifting speeches to the effect that they had
"served the country" and been a "dike of chastity," albeit not their own.[18]
Ending formal public prostitution did not, of course, mean the end of
prostitution itself. The trade simply was carried out more privately—and
venereal disease naturally remained difficult to control. Nonetheless, the
transition did have its precious moments. Outside the new comfort facilities that had been created exclusively for the foreigners, in one licensed
quarter of the traditional geisha-centered "floating world," the last day of
public prostitution was memorably recorded in a photograph of kimono-
clad young women standing before an American flag affixed to the wall of
their brothel and throwing up their arms in the familiar *banzai* cheer of
celebration.[19]

In responding to SCAP's orders, Japanese bureaucrats revealed a rare
and unusually fine appreciation of human rights. In December 1946, the
Home Ministry declared that women had the *right* to become prostitutes,
and this became the ostensible rationale behind designating "red-line"
districts in which it was understood by all parties that they would continue to ply their trade. (The "red-line" designation came from markings
on the city maps used by the police; in areas outlined in blue, such activity was not allowed). In the years that followed, an estimated fifty-five
thousand to seventy thousand women, many of "third country" origin,
worked these areas as full-time or part-time prostitutes.[20]

"Butterflies," "Onlys," and Subversive Women

This was the milieu epitomized by the panpan—tough, vulnerable figures
remembered for their bright lipstick, nail polish, sharp clothes, and sometimes enviable material possessions. They became inseparable from the
urban nightscapes and memory landscapes of postwar Japan. Photographs
of them remain among the most melancholy and evocative of this period:
the leaning figure in the dark, wearing a kerchief, handbag on her arm,
often lighting or smoking a cigarette. They were known by many euphemisms—women of the night, women of the street, women of the
dark—but *panpan* was the most familiar. Although male prostitutes also
emerged to cater to the GI trade, little public mention was made of them
and they failed to capture the popular imagination.[21]

The origin of the word *panpan* is obscure, although it was said to have
been picked up by Americans in the South Seas during the war as a term
for available women. A book published in 1948 observed that Japanese
sailors repatriated from the southern areas also sometimes spoke of panpan. Among GIs, the term provoked ridicule, pity, compassion, exoticism,
and plain eroticism. When prostitutes used the label themselves, it conveyed a similarly mixed impression—a sense of *jikiyake* and *awareshimi*,
"desperation" and "misery," as popular accounts put it, coupled with a
proud defiance of conventional norms, a sensual *joie de vivre*.

Although "Rakuchō no Otoki" spoke bitterly of being treated with
contempt by "society," she and her companions also came to seem at-
tractively bold and subversive in the popular mind. An opinion column
in the humor magazine *Van* hinted at this. "What is the oldest (most feudalistic) feature of contemporary Japanese society?" *Van* asked a selection
of famous people, "and what is the newest (most democratic)?" In the
opinion of Tatsuno Takashi, a well-known social critic and scholar of

French literature, "politics" was the oldest and most unchanged feature of the present-day scene, for it still had no meaningful connection to people's lives. The newest and most democratic? "The panpan girls," Tatsuno responded, "because they have transcended racial and international prejudice."[22]

The comment was clever and barbed, even if only half true. In certain areas, the panpan trade was strictly organized not merely into territories (called *shima*, literally, "islands"), but also in regard to clientele. Some panpan serviced only Japanese customers; others, much more numerous, serviced Americans. The distinction was rigidly observed in certain *shima*, and panpan who transgressed either turf or race could be subjected to abuse or even torture by other prostitutes. Still, Tatsuno's glib reply, mocking the political charades that often masked themselves as "democracy," had a ring of truth to it. He was calling attention not merely to the most intimate manifestation of "international relations" in his occupied country, but also to its racial dimensions. Thousands of panpan consorted openly and comfortably with both white and black GIs. Even while being looked down upon, they came to exemplify a certain tolerance toward other races and an undeniable independence in their defiant behavior as a whole.

Despite the tawdry nature of their lives, the panpan became associated with the liberation of repressed sensuality—a world of erotic indulgence that had found earlier expression not merely in the pleasure quarters of the late feudal period, but in the bawdy relationships and amorous dalliances celebrated in popular tales and courtly romances of ancient times. Their self-indulgent carnality was as sharp a repudiation as could be imagined of the stultifying austerity and discipline the militarists had demanded. Although some men may have been shocked by their sexual frankness, more than a few found themselves attracted to it as well. To numerous entrepreneurs, the panpan heralded an oncoming commercialization of sex that would flourish long after they themselves disappeared.[23]

The very reasons that young women gave for becoming panpan in the first place reflected the ambiguous persona of these women of the night. One survey of street women found that many were war orphans, or—virtually as devastating in terms of economic and social security—had no fathers. A considerable number were eldest daughters who professed to feeling an especially strong sense of responsibility for the well-being of their parents and siblings. The same survey also noted, however, that a majority of those interviewed had lost their virginity "willingly" outside of marriage, and that many had turned to prostitution for reasons other than economic desperation. Although some used their incomes frugally to support themselves or their families, others threw their money away on ephemeral pleasures—displays of extravagant indulgence that defied the general poverty of the times. Surveys of panpan rounded up by the police in 1946 and 1947 found a substantial number who frankly said they chose their way of life simply "out of curiosity."[24]

Police transcripts recording the "life histories" of arrested prostitutes sometimes conveyed their candid acknowledgment of sexual pleasure in considerable detail. An eighteen-year-old in Kyoto told of how, while attending a dressmaking school in Nara the previous year, she had lost her virginity to a young GI in a park on a summer night. Several months later, after their romantic liaison broke up, she decided almost casually to become a prostitute and moved to Kyoto to do so. Most of her customers were GIs. If a customer was especially good looking, she blandly told the police, she often did not charge him. Despite illness and hospitalization, she claimed to have no serious second thoughts about pursuing this way of life.[25]

Prostitution usually paid far better than other jobs available to most women, and the argot of the profession tended to romanticize the panpan in subtly traditional ways. A prostitute who flitted indiscriminately from customer to customer was known, in borrowed English, as a *bata-furai* or "butterfly." She was seen, in her way, as a modern-day counterpart of "the woman who loved love," the promiscuous heroine of a famous work by the great seventeenth-century writer Ihara Saikaku. Panpan who specialized in the GI trade were also called *yōpan*—the ideograph for *yō* connoting foreign or Western. They were the new Okichis, counterparts of a group of women known as *rashamen* who became the mistresses or wives of foreigners in the mid-nineteenth-century treaty ports of newly opened Japan (and who have survived in photographs as evocative and melancholy as those of the panpan). Panpan who were loyal to a single American patron were identified, again in borrowed English, as *onrii* ("only"), short for *onrii wan* ("only one"). Here the reworking of old values was subtle indeed. Like the samurai and his lord or high-ranking geisha and their privileged patrons, a panpan, too, could exemplify loyalty. The virtue remained; only the object it was directed toward had changed.

Like accomplished courtesans of the past, the panpan also possessed special talents—most notably, in their case, the ability to communicate in a polyglot form of English, a hybrid mix of hooker's Japanese and the GI's

The wound to masculine pride of having to kowtow to an army of occupation
was compounded by the ubiquitous fraternization of the victors with Japanese
women. Endō Takeo's undated cartoon of a disabled veteran encountering a
burly GI was accompanied by a long caption observing that things had
changed greatly since the two men had confronted each other at Guadalcanal
several years earlier.

native tongue that was humorously identified as "panglish." Getting along
in this second language, broken or not, was a skill highly valued in postsurrender Japan—hundreds of thousands of men were also struggling to
survive by dealing with the conqueror in the conqueror's tongue (*their* pid-
gin English was sometimes laughed off as "SCAPanese"). And here lay the
rub. The panpan arm in arm with her GI companion, or riding gaily in
his jeep, constituted a piercing wound to national pride in general and
masculine pride in particular. Yet at the same time, these women were
striking symbols of the whole convoluted phenomenon of "Americanization" in which everyone was in some way engaged. The panpan openly,
brazenly *prostituted* themselves to the conqueror—while others, especially
the "good" Japanese who consorted with the Americans as privileged
elites, only did it figuratively. This was unsettling.

In the heat of war, the Japanese enemy was commonly regarded as subhuman by the victors. In this photo from December 1944, American sailors in the Pacific theater gather to observe a newly captured prisoner being "deloused."

In their embarrassing way, the panpan were the exemplary pioneer materialists and consumers of the postwar era. In those years of acute hunger and scarcity, the material comfort of the Americans was simply staggering to behold. What made America "great" was that it was so rich; and, for many, what made "democracy" appealing was that it apparently was the way to become prosperous. Among ordinary people, no group tapped the material treasures of the conquerors as blatantly as the panpan. They were the recipients of goods from the U.S. military exchange posts (the famous PXs) that in those impoverished days truly seemed like treasure houses from a magic land: crammed not only with basic foodstuffs, but with liquor and cigarettes, sweets and delicacies, voluptuously decadent feminine things such as lipstick and nylon stockings.

The appeal of *this* "America" can hardly be exaggerated. Otoki's brightly rouged lips and colorful clothing were not merely a prostitute's regalia, but part of a mystique of American glamour and fashion that

The eroticization of defeated Japan in the eyes of the conquerors took place almost immediately, creating a complex interplay of assumed masculine and feminine roles that has colored U.S.–Japan relations ever since.

made a spectacular impact after the drab parsimony of the war years. The sensual panpan was as close as anyone in Japan might hope to get, in the flesh, to Hollywood. Even Shiseidō, the premiere purveyor of cosmetics, with a *haut bourgeois* prewar tradition, was caught up in this. The company's first new postwar product was a "nail stick" resembling lipstick that was used to color fingernails. It was especially popular among women who consorted with GIs.[26] To women who had been denied make-up, permanents, and colorful clothing ("extravagance is an enemy" was a wartime slogan), the application of a bit of cosmetics could be a touching and understandable way to try to transcend despair and exhaustion, even if just for a moment. A journalist recalled how nylons, never seen before, arrived along with the Americans just as women were shedding their ugly *monpe* pantaloons. Their hearts were tempted, she observed acidly, and some were known to have exchanged their chastity for a pair of stockings.[27]

The bearing of gifts, a routine practice among enlisted men in the occupation force and their paramours, was carried out on a far more lavish
level when occupation officers engaged in such personal diplomacy. The
sheer quantitative dimensions of this intercourse—in terms of material exchange as well as sexual relations—are impressive to contemplate. Regular force rotations continued to bring in hundreds of thousands of new
troops to staff the quarter-million-man occupation army, and those who
chose the path of chastity during their tour of duty were by all accounts
exceptional. By one estimate, almost half of the many tens of millions of
dollars that occupation personnel spent on "recreation" passed through the
hands of the Okichis of that era.[28]

At that time, the panpan was perhaps the most obvious symbol of a new
phenomenon in intercultural relations: the "horizontal" westernization of
Japan. Previously, such influences had penetrated the country vertically,
almost invariably introduced by the elites. Even seeming exceptions like
the spread of flapper culture in the 1920s, with its "modern boys" and
"Clara Bow girls," tended to involve only the comfortable bourgeoisie,
while ordinary people remained relatively unaffected. The lower-class
panpan represented an unprecedented phenomenon—a popular westernization "from the side." Figuratively as well as literally, these tough, ani-
mated young women were closer to the Americans than anyone else. No
one surpassed them as the harbingers of a hedonistic, materialistic,
American-style consumer culture.[29]

The ubiquitous sexuality linking conqueror and conquered had far-
reaching ramifications insofar as American perceptions of the defeated nation and its people were concerned. To some members of the occupation
force, native women came to be regarded as little more than available sexual objects. This characteristic colonial attitude led to a notorious incident
in which all the women on a commuter train were detained by American
MPs and forced to submit to medical examinations for venereal disease.
Every Japanese woman, in a word, was potentially a whore.[30] More strikingly, the defeated country itself was feminized in the minds of the Americans who poured in. The enemy was transformed with startling
suddenness from a bestial people fit to be annihilated into receptive ex-
otics to be handled and enjoyed. That enjoyment was palpable—the panpan personified this. Japan—only yesterday a menacing, masculine
threat—had been transformed, almost in the blink of an eye, into a com-
pliant, feminine body on which the white victors could impose their will.
At the same time, fraternization between the occupation forces and Japanese women—both within and outside the structures of prostitution—also

became, for some, a starting point for interracial affection, mutual respect, even love. There was metaphor here too. For all parties, this was—however one engaged in it—a phenomenal cultural event.

Black-Market Entrepreneurship

Nothing was truly sacred any longer, and everything seemed interconnected. Among the numerous cynical sayings of those days was *onna wa panpan, otoko ga katsu giya*—women become panpan, men become carriers for the black market. The word for "black market" was *yami-ichi*, for "woman of the dark" it was *yami no onna*—written with the same ideograph for *yami* (darkness) in each case. *Manga*, a humor magazine with a wartime pedigree of brilliant propagandistic articles and illustrations, captured the connection between the two worlds with a cartoon of a large, unshaven thug in an old army uniform accosting a trembling citizen. "Who made me such a man?" its caption asked, mocking the maudlin song about the poor fallen woman of Ueno.[31]

There were striking differences between these two dark worlds, however. The realm of the panpan was highly Americanized, whereas the black market, even when GIs roamed through it, was first and last for the Japanese. Its distinctive argot derived from the gangster underworld in contrast to the "panglish" of the panpan. Renting a spot for a stall in the black market in Osaka, for example, required *shoba dai*, "place money." *Shoba* was the gangster inversion of *basho*, the conventional word for "place."[32] Where the world of the panpan was fundamentally sexual and only occasionally violent, that of the black market was almost perpetually carnivorous. Men carried weapons. Order was enforced. No one gave anything away because the customer was good looking—or pathetic, or desperate, or starving to death. There was little room for sentimentality. These outlaw activities often were camouflaged by gentle euphemisms—not only the "free market" but also the lovely "open-sky" or "blue-sky" market—but when all was said and done, the black market remained a place of hardened hearts and harsh dealings.

Whereas the economic significance of the panpan was greater than commonly realized, no one could fail to be aware of the enormous economic role of the black market. For many Japanese, this was virtually *the* economy. It emerged almost simultaneously with capitulation. Indeed, a week before the emperor's broadcast, the *Asahi* published a letter warning, in a grim pun, that the approaching enemy would try to exploit *yami*—that is, take advantage of both dark emotions and the illicit mar-

ket.[33] On August 18, the postwar black market received a grand send-off
with the publication of a large advertisement in Tokyo's major newspapers.
Presented as an "Urgent message to factories and entrepreneurs engaged
in conversion," the ad, promising sales at "proper prices," invited people
to bring samples of their products to the organization that had placed the
ad: the Kantō-area Ozu gang.

Small-factory owners whose livelihood as military subcontractors had
come to a sudden end poured into the gang's office in the Shinjuku district, and its boss quickly emerged as one of the most energetic entrepreneurs of the new Japan. As the folklore of the market had it, he
encouraged manufacturers to convert their swords into household cutlery,
their battle helmets into pots and pans. Within two days, he had engineered the opening of the Shinjuku black market, a congeries of outdoor
stalls and stands selling sundry goods and already sporting a happy motto:
"Brightness from Shinjuku." By September, that slogan was spelled out
in a large sign made up of 117 hundred-watt bulbs, visible as far away as
neighboring stations on the rail line. In the night darkness of a shattered
city only weeks removed from air raids, the literal "brightness from Shinjuku" provided a memorable vision of optimism for a despairing people.
Initially, the media greeted these developments with enthusiasm.[34]

"Blue-sky markets" materialized in most large cities by early September, often springing up without plan. In some instances, ex-servicemen
and discharged factory workers went to the countryside, returned with
knapsacks full of goods, and started selling right out of their packs. Such
spontaneous entrepreneurs soon gained a name—*tachiuri*, literally, "stand
and sell" people. One marketeer told of "opening his store" by plopping
a bucket of edible live frogs down on the street. Some he sold some for
money, the rest he traded for potato powder, dumplings, dry bread, and
the like—and with that, his new profession was launched. A returned soldier reportedly got into business on the spur of the moment by selling the
pants he was wearing. Surely the blackest of black-market stories concerned the emerging market in Osaka, where a brisk trade quickly developed in blankets and clothing taken from the dead. Many such items
came directly from sanitariums and were still stained with blood coughed
up by tuberculosis victims. The Osaka entrepreneurs who dealt in such
goods referred to them among themselves as *oshaka*—a ghoulishly pious
reference, for *shaka* refers to the Buddha or buddhas.[35]

By October 1945, an estimated seventeen thousand open-air markets
had blossomed nationwide, mostly in the larger cities. Only months later,
there were many as seventy-six thousand stalls, each averaging over forty

customers a day, in Tokyo's numerous markets alone. With this came organizational rationalization, a sometimes brutal process commonly led by *yakuza gumi*—gangster gangs headed by godfather-type individuals. In Tokyo, the division of black-market territories among various gangs was fairly clear cut. The market in the Shinbashi district was controlled by the Matsuda gang, Asakusa by the Shibayama gang, the Ginza area by the Ueda gang, Ikebukuro by the Sekiguchi gang, and Shinjuku by the Ozu and Wada gangs.[36]

Gang control of the Osaka "free market" followed similar lines. Morimoto Mitsuji, who organized the Umeda market there, was a particularly flamboyant figure. He took pleasure in identifying with the tradition of the noble gangster who uses his influence to protect the weak against the rapacious. Repatriated from the Philippines in late 1945, he arrived home a month after the death of his father, who had been a man of influence in local political circles. At the request of the speaker of the municipal assembly, he moved in with his followers to clean up the Umeda market which, as he described it, was a hodgepodge of amateurs who were being shaken down by a small number of toughs. "It was a time," in Morimoto's words, "when the strong ate the weak in cold blood. I did what I could to prevent it, but it was a miserable time to be Japanese." Morimoto's workday attire included a leather jacket, a knife by his breast, and a pistol on his hip. When the police proved ineffective, he "took care" of things himself. Before long, there was a substantial price on his head. Before long, there was also a colossal Osaka black market extending far beyond Morimoto's turf. In July 1946, city officials estimated that approximately one hundred thousand individuals were supporting themselves by such activity, of whom around 80 percent were either repatriated soldiers or former factory workers who lost their jobs when the war ended. Sixty percent of the market's regular operatives were men; 30 percent, women; and the remaining 10 percent, children.[37]

Some of the buying and selling in these markets was legitimate, essentially a replacement for the countless small urban retailers whose businesses had been destroyed in the air raids. On the other hand, a great deal of the activity was illegal. The black market under the Matsuda gang in Tokyo, which had some two thousand members at its peak, exemplified the complexity and volatility of these arrangements. The gang's influence was established when the *oyabun* or "patron" (in the feudalistic vocabulary of this demimonde) Matsuda Giichi began organizing petty vendors unloading their knapsacks and setting up stands around Shinbashi station. The Tokyo municipal government and local police threw their support be-

Organized gangs such as the Matsuda *gumi* played an open and major role in
organizing the black markets that dominated the economy until around 1949.

hind Matsuda, who proceeded to assume responsibility for approving vendors (for a fee) and organizing such practical and essential services as lighting, toilets, and trash collection. He relied on his own gang members
rather than the police to enforce order.[38]

By early 1946, the Shinbashi market had a well-rationalized structure,
nominally under the oversight of the police, that operated through an association known as the Tokyo Stall Vendors Professional Union. Vending
licenses had to be obtained through local police stations, and generally
were reserved for individuals who fell into one of the following fairly in-
clusive categories: war wounded, family of someone killed in the war,
handicapped persons, former vendors or street-stall operators, or retail
merchants who had lost their shops in the war. An unusually large number of vendors in the Shinbashi market—some 80 percent—were registered in this way, but elsewhere in Tokyo around 80 percent of participants
were reported to be unregistered.

The market was supplied, both legally and illegally, by tapping into food
supplies in the countryside, sea products from coastal fishing communi-

ties, and former military stockpiles. Many American goods also made their way onto the market, often arriving by way of panpan who received them from their patrons. Vendors also struck private deals with occupation personnel. The Ueno outdoor market even featured an "America Lane" specializing in such goods. A hierarchy of brokers soon emerged— from top-level dealers handling lots valued in the millions of yen down through two or three levels of wholesalers to individuals known as *oroshiya* who delivered the goods directly to vendors. At each step on this ladder, a profit of between 20 and 30 percent was normal. A tough operator working a particular marketplace might pocket as much as 8,000 yen a *day* in these early months; even the most modest vendors—sometimes called "peanuts," apparently in mocking reference to the lowly status of peanut sellers—could earn as much as 50 yen a day. In Shinbashi, the Matsuda-gumi normally relied on approximately one hundred fifty underlings to maintain or enforce order, collect fees, and the like. They enjoyed the old-fashioned prestige of being called *oniisan* or "big brother" by those they policed, and earned a regular monthly income of 600 to 1,000 yen. In addition to the black market per se, the Matsuda organization was also involved in construction and supplied and supervised daily laborers requested by the occupation forces.

Fierce rivalries accompanied these activities. In June 1946, for example, two months after grandly proclaiming the creation of the "Shinbashi New Life Market," Matsuda Giichi, the gang's boss, was assassinated by a former gang member. Territorial conflicts were seriously exacerbated, moreover, by racial tensions. Like the world of prostitution, the black market had a large representation of "third-country people" who had chosen not to be repatriated to their native lands. Well-organized Korean and Formosan gangs vied with Japanese gangs, and in July these simmering tensions erupted in spectacular violence. A fight involving hundreds of Formosan vendors and over a thousand Matsuda-gumi toughs spilled over into the neighboring Shibuya district, culminating in a gunfight outside the Shibuya police station that left seven Formosans dead and thirty-four injured. One policeman was killed and another critically injured.

Repercussions from the "Shibuya incident" extended in many directions. The hostility that already existed between the police and the Formosan and Korean communities was rubbed rawer. Prejudice against "third-country people" increased, and much of the public's anger against both black-market abuses and the rising crime rate came to fall on non-Japanese Asians. In addition, the inability of law-enforcement officers to control the black market effectively was exposed, prompting ridicule of the police and demoralization in their ranks. Although U.S. authorities attempted to encourage greater control over the black market following the incident, their efforts were largely unavailing.[39]

The police emerge poorly in accounts of the illegal markets—venal if not thoroughly corrupt, harried and hapless if not completely incompetent. This was nicely captured in a banal vignette: the case of the stolen overcoat. The coat's owner almost immediately noticed it was missing from his office in Osaka's city hall and with unerring instinct rushed to the local black market, where he found it two hours later—on sale for 3,500 yen. He summoned two police detectives, who advised him to negotiate the matter with the market bosses, who in turn spoke to the vendor selling the stolen coat, who graciously sold it back to its owner for 500 yen. The owner's base salary as a city employee at that time was 700 yen a month.[40]

The top-to-bottom corruption of the system did little to foster faith in politics or confidence in the heralded programs of "democratization" that were being promoted elsewhere. In addition, the undisguised junglelike nature of the "free market" had an effect much like shock therapy on a people who had been indoctrinated to believe that as a race and culture they possessed a unique "familial" consciousness that bound them together in mutual support. As the writer Sakaguchi Ango observed at the time, this predatory world was an extraordinary thing to behold. Men who only months earlier had been willing to die for their country—to fall with the purity and beauty of the cherry blossom, as the mesmerizing cliché of the war years put it—were now mercilessly gouging their compatriots.

Some of the market's petty operators later acknowledged this of themselves—with awe, much like former soldiers of any time or place who look back, as if at total strangers, on the horrors and atrocities they themselves once witnessed or committed. Thus, Furusawa Kōtarō, who later became a journalist, recalled that when the war ended he and his fellow students had parted pledging with high idealism to work hard to rebuild the country. What he actually did, for a half-year or more, was prey on the weak. Exhausted mothers with crying children came to him to barter a precious kimono, and he would beat them down by calling it a moth-eaten rag. He even did this to one of his own relatives, knowing that her home had been bombed and her mother lay sick in bed. "Yamato race" solidarity did not matter, nor did kinship, nor politics. "The emperor's renunciation of divinity, and the liberal, democratizing policies issued by the occupation

"Blue-sky" black markets flourished in every major city. In this 1946 scene near Tokyo's Ueno station, vendors are selling metal household utensils. Such consumer products had virtually disappeared during the war, when basic resources such as metal were diverted to the production of military goods.

forces," Furusawa recalled, "all seemed irrelevant to the dark faces gathered in the black market."

In this milieu, men and women drank to excess, just as many panpan squandered their earnings in hedonistic indulgence. A timid participant in the Osaka market framed this piquantly: "I bargained for things saying whatever was necessary, and sold them the same way. To numb our consciences and gain courage, many of us merchants did business while drinking *kasutori* liquor. For me, faint hearted, every day was difficult and full of wounds." A less faint-hearted marketeer recalled the exhilaration of raking in, in a single day, what would take the average salaried worker a full month to earn. No one had any thought at all of saving for the future. After all, there *was* no clear future beyond, it appeared, endless runaway inflation. And so, after putting aside that part of the day's earnings necessary for the next day's business, he and his companions would squander the rest on prostitutes and liquor. "I drank," as he put it, drawing on time-worn imagery, "trying to forget a life that hung suspended like a floating weed."

Sometimes life in the market assumed an almost exquisite merging of delicacy and degeneration. For the right price, all sorts of things were for sale. In one corner of one market, vendors who regularly made a killing would gather around a third-country person who sold an ungodly drink made of alcohol used in aircraft lubricants mixed with artificial sweetener. With this, he served—and this would have been a rare delicacy at any time in Japan—jellyfish in sea-urchin sauce. Although the chronicler of this story could not afford such elegant depravity, he did manage to drink virtually nonstop for a half year after becoming a black-market vendor—and to live to tell the tale.[41]

A great many other unedifying stories—none of them destined to appear in exemplary accounts of Japan's postwar recovery—also reveal this sheer spirit of individual survival. The other side of greed and decadence was a brazen vitality. Toughs flaunted their defiance of "good" society by attiring themselves in what became known as their "three sacred regalia," an irreverent takeoff on the sanctified regalia of the emperor. In place of the imperial mirror, sword, and jewel, they were identified by their predilection for aloha shirts, nylon belts, and rubber-soled shoes.[42] Men on black-market runs to the countryside took over whole train cars, where they sang until drunkenness overcame them. Men intent on cornering the fish market put out to sea in boats of their own, surrounding fishing vessels and paying them two to three times the fixed market price to transfer their catches right there on the ocean. Farmers, mythically the most humble and subservient of the emperor's loyal subjects, turned aside even the most desperate of city folk if they could not meet black-market rates. Such rural hard trading was so commonplace that city dwellers even embraced the rumor that farmers held a celebration whenever their pile of hundred-yen bills became a foot (one *shaku*) high.[43]

The life force here was unmistakable. Entrepreneurs dealt in everything from a stew made out of leftovers from GI bases and hotels catering to occupation personnel (known as *zanpan* or *gotteri* stew) to job lots of pilfered machinery and construction materials to loan sharking. They did not spend their time stroking the Americans or engaging in polite, hypocritical conversation. In their peculiar way, they were more honest than the prominent politicians, capitalists, and former military officers who snuggled up to the conquerors and put on righteous faces while secretly profiting from the black market.

Despite its pervasive tensions and outright eruptions of violence, the black market was also one of the few arenas where interactions between the Japanese and other Asians took place on a regular and more or less equitable basis. In the view of more romantic Japanese historians, poor Japanese, Koreans, and Formosans came together here in unprecedented

When the victors arrived in Japan, they encountered a country with few privately owned vehicles. Of those, moreover, a great many were powered by charcoal rather than gasoline. This taxi driver, caught by the camera in October 1945, is stoking up his charcoal-driven car.

ways. Considerations such as class background, education, or former employment had little bearing on personal relationships; and although race and nationality mattered, interracial relationships were taken for granted far more than was the case among the broader public. From this perspective, the marginal black marketeers posed a challenge to society that went beyond the illegality of many of their activities.[44]

From a plainer perspective, the men and women who worked the market exemplified, without varnish, a pragmatic materialism and even an exemplary work ethic. In a letter to the *Asahi*, a young boy asked what was wrong with this. His brother was a black marketeer who got up at 2:00 or 3:00 A.M. every day, rode crowded trains, scratched for small profits, and somehow managed to support his mother and four siblings—and he admired him for it. He was more impressive by far, the boy opined, than those laborers running around in demonstrations and sabotaging work. When he himself graduated from middle school, he intended to follow his brother's path.

A week or so later, a sixth-grade girl responded that working the black market was not more admirable than engaging in labor protests. What would happen, she asked, if the whole working class turned into black marketeers. "I think," she concluded, "that the government is at fault for creating such a society as this. The goal of constructing a new Japan should be aimed at creating a country where people can live without a black market."[45]

One way or another, the black market/free market/blue-sky market challenged everyone to define where they stood.

"Kasutori Culture"

The *kasutori shōchū* that made the faint hearted bold and the strong hearted wild also apparently made prolific those with countercultural proclivities. It was, in any case, the drink of choice among those artists and writers who made a cult out of degeneracy and nihilism. It was a vile liquor—best downed, it was said, while holding one's nose—and it gave its name to a chaotic subculture that proved a natural complement to the worlds of the panpan and black marketeers: the *"kasutori* culture" *(kasutori bunka)*.

Kasutori culture flourished into the 1950s and left a gaudy legacy of escapism, titillation, and outright sleeze—a commercial world dominated by sexually oriented entertainments and a veritable cascade of pulp literature. Like the panpan and the black marketeers, however, the denizens of kasutori culture also exhibited an ardor and vitality that conveyed a strong impression of liberation from authority and dogma. This aura of iconoclasm was reinforced by the emergence of a kind of barroom intelligentsia—wittily nicknamed, in the usual hybrid manner, the *kasutori-gencha* or "kasutori-gentsia"—whose writings purported to impose a semblance of meaning and even quasi-philosophical structure on a wildly degenerate life-style. Thanks to the pulp publications and to more serious writers alike, life on the margins became intertwined with theories of decadence as the only true honesty and authenticity, of the carnal body as the only body worth venerating. In some of these formulations, sex, degeneracy, and "love" even became equated with "revolution."

Pulp magazines, the flashiest product of kasutori culture, eventually became generically known as *kasutori zasshi* or "kasutori magazines," a term that in itself captured the mordant humor of the counterculture. The label rested on an elaborate pun equating the fleeting nature of consciousness when drinking *kasutori shōchū* with the ephemeral existence of most of these early periodicals. The third cup of kasutori liquor, the saying went, usually rendered the drinker unconscious; and similarly, very few of these escapist magazines ever got beyond three issues. (Although written with different ideographs, "three cups" and "three issues" are both pronounced *sango*, thus giving rise to the pun *sangome de tsubureru*, "gone by the third.") Beyond this joke lay a larger double meaning. While the "kasutori magazines" celebrated a fugitive world of hedonistic and even grotesque indulgence, they also evoked more sobering images of impermanence, a world of no tomorrow, the banishment of authority, the absence of orthodox or transcendent values.[46]

Publishers of the pulps denied having any serious purpose whatsoever. The classic formulation of their ethos was presented in the maiden issue of a magazine named *Ryōki* (Bizarre), whose editors emphatically declared that they had "no audacious ambition to enlighten or educate readers," but on the contrary simply desired to provide a moment of pleasure to those who had become "totally exhausted physically and mentally in attempting to construct a nation of peace." More often than not, the covers of the kasutori magazines featured illustrations of sensual women, or occasionally paired lovers, with a high percentage of Caucasians among them. The first seminude photographs of women appeared in the monthly *Aka to Kuro* (Red and Black) in late 1946, and drawings or paintings of nude or partially nude women became commonplace as cover designs by the summer of the following year.

The sexual fantasies in these publications, read mostly by young men, provided a kind of counterpart to the sexual encounters through which a large part of the occupation army was simultaneously viewing Japan. While hundreds of thousands of young GIs were coming to regard the accommodating panpan as representative of the conquered country, a large audience of Japanese males was being encouraged to think of the West in terms of its women—and these women, in turn, as voluptuous sexual objects. From this time on, the idealized Western female figure, long limbed and amply proportioned, became an object of male lust—and an ideal for young Japanese women to emulate.

The titles of the pulps were usually as colorful as their cover designs. *Ryōki*, for example, inspired such clones as *Ōru Ryōki* (All Bizarre), *Sei Ryōki* (Sex Bizarre), and even *Ryōki Zeminaru* (Bizarre Seminar). Borrowed and bastardized English titles included *Ōru Romansu* (All Romance), *Madamu* (Madam), *Kyabaree* (Cabaret), *Guro* (Grotesque), *G-men* (G-Men), *Chi to Daiyamondo* (Blood and Diamonds), *Buinasu* (Venus), *Suriru* (Thrill), *Hū Danitto* (Who Dunnit), *Neo-riberaru* (Neoliberal), *Pinappu* (Pinup), *Saron* (Salon), and *Nanbā Wan* (Number One). The last of these was produced as a sideline by some hard-up students at Tokyo University. From the French came *Shikku* (Chic), and from the German *Riibe* (Liebe). There was also *Seppun* (Kiss), the perfect title for a period when even

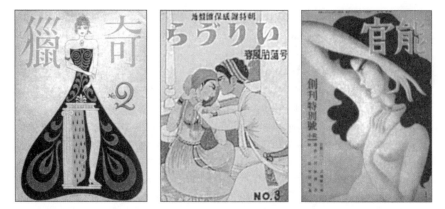

"The Pulps": magazines associated with the counterculture revived a popular craze known in borrowed English as *ero-guro-nansensu* ("erotic, grotesque, nonsensical") that had flourished in the 1920s and the early 1930s.

some American reformers were promoting kissing as an expression of liberation from the feudal constrictions of the past. Editors of the pulps accepted this particular gift from heaven with open arms by publishing pieces on, for example, "a theory on the rehabilitation of kissing"—and then proceeded to challenge the constrictions of the *present* by focusing on topics that tested the limits of the occupation's censorship apparatus. They got away with a good deal. A study based on some sixteen hundred issues of kasutori magazines found that the "symbolic images" that tended to dominate the genre included kissing, strip shows, underpants, panpan and "leisurely women," chastity, incest, masturbation, and lonely widows. This was not edifying, but it was undeniably a far cry from the mystique of living and dying for the emperor that had governed life until just recently.[47]

The visual accompaniment to the "rehabilitation of kissing" initially came to occupied Japan by way of Hollywood. Films such as *Prelude to Spring,* starring Deanna Durbin, and *Madame Curie,* with Greer Garson, proved immensely popular—partly because, contrary to presurrender practice, their kissing scenes remained uncut. Emboldened by this and encouraged by the Americans, local film studios ventured to add osculation to their own repertoire. The first platonic kiss was landed in the Daiei Studio's oddly titled *He and She Go,* which opened in mid–April of 1946. A friendly peck followed in the same studio's *An Evening's Kiss,* released on May 23. Film history truly was made the next day when Shōchiku's *Springtime at Twenty* opened, featuring a close-up scene of hero kissing heroine. Unknown to spellbound viewers, the passion of this moment had been sanitized by a piece of gauze soaked in hydrogen oxide that the lovers placed inconspicuously between their lips. What the actor Ōsaka Shirō mainly recalled of the great event was the taste of disinfectant, whereas the actress Ikuno Michiko staunchly proclaimed that she had simply closed her eyes and done her job. *Kinema Jumpō*, a leading film journal, primly observed that the kiss was contextually unnecessary. Still, there was no turning back.[48]

The diversification of the commercialization of sex proceeded relatively smoothly thereafter. January 15, 1947 marked a dubious milestone of sorts in this regard, for on that date two signal events occurred. The first Western-style beauty contest to be held culminated in the crowning of "Miss Ginza." (She was 158 centimeters tall, weighed 50 kilograms, and had bust and hip measurements of 95 and 88 centimeters respectively.)[49] In a separate, more imaginative adaptation of Western ways, the inaugural performance of the first "picture-frame nude show" *(gakubuchi nūdo shyō)* took place the same day in Tokyo's Shinjuku district. This featured motionless women posed inside huge mock picture frames as if they were famous Western works of art. The curtain opened; the models held their poses for several tens of seconds; then the curtain closed again while another European masterpiece arranged itself.

The nudes-in-frames show was the brainchild of a wayward scholar of German culture and translator of Goethe's *Faustus* named Hata Toyokichi, and its premiere presentation was elegantly entitled "The Birth of Venus." Lines of male devotees of Western art, the story has it, extended from the

More Pulps: Even the woman scientist (who is actually a well-known actress)
serves as cover girl to a "special issue on sex problems."

The "nudes-in-frames show," ostensibly replicating great works of Western art, helped inaugurate the postwar culture of commercialized sex. It was the brainchild of a university professor.

performance hall down five flights of stairs and out into the street. The star of the show was a statuesque half-Russian young woman named Naka-mura Shōko, who draped gauze over her bosom and loins. Kai Miwa, the second Venus to achieve fame, did so by being genuinely half nude. She was admired not only for being tall but also for having unusually "white" skin. The latter quality was a virtue in the old, traditional canons of per-sonal attractiveness, although now with an obvious overlay of bringing one closer to the Caucasians. Being tall and amply bosomed were new crite-ria of feminine beauty.

Hata Toyokichi later claimed that he had charitable motives for his frozen format. Tall "Venuses" were rare, he explained, and he did not think it flattering or appropriate to ask short-legged women to dance. This was somewhat misleading, for stocky chorus girls already had kicked and hopped their way across theatrical stages in the interwar period, and disrobing sometimes accompanied the more licentious dances performed for male patrons in the private rooms of elite inns and geisha houses. In any case, other entrepreneurs were less chivalrous than Hata, and the strip show soon made its debut with a rather tame revue called "Tokyo Follies," which climaxed with dancers striking a pose, reaching behind their backs, and unhooking the tops of their costumes. A Tokyo University student is given credit for introducing this theatrical finale. By 1948, a less academic interpretation of the strip show had emerged in Asakusa, one of Tokyo's liveliest and earthiest "low city" amusement areas. From Asakusa, stripping spread throughout the country.

The strip show, like its "nudes-in-frames" predecessor, created new celebrities who succeeded in captivating not merely popular audiences but also some of Japan's most accomplished creative artists. "Mary" Masubara,

By 1947, American-style strip shows, such as this in Tokyo's Asakusa amusement district, had introduced new perspectives on "democratization."

one of Asakusa's star strippers, for example, became a favorite of the distinguished writer Nagai Kafū. Her charisma apparently derived not merely from her on-stage routine, but also from her wonderfully incongruous background—for she had graduated from an excellent girls' high school and previously been employed as a secretary in the House of Peers, the upper house of the pre-1947 parliament. Another Asakusa star, Shimizu Toshiko, was heralded as Japan's "Gypsy Rose," after America's most famous ecdysiast, Gypsy Rose Lee. Gypsy Rose Shimizu was almost literally worshipped for her "Caucasian" features, physical allure, and attractive personality. To the prolific wood-block artist Munakata Shikō, she had "flesh like a goddess." The Western-style oil painter Onozawa Sanichi found the entire kasutori-culture milieu of cabarets, revues, and strip shows stimulating in the most inspirational sense. As with Toulouse Latrec, this demimonde would become the major subject of his art.[50]

Despite its obvious borrowings from the West, however, the kasutori counterculture remained fundamentally indigenous. Like the black market, this was a world the conqueror could never really enter—an environment as colorful as the gaudy covers of its pulp magazines and as gritty as the black-and-white photographs that record its bars, dance halls, and hole-in-the wall eateries, its narrow, crooked streets and cluttered backstage dressing rooms. The conqueror's ideas had only negligible impact on this world, which seemed so awash in the glitter of American popular culture. Apart perhaps from Hollywood and popular music, "America" often tended to signify little more than an amorphous alien army of occupation, vaguely present, that in and of itself was the ultimate symbol of Japan's degradation. Similarly, although the barroom intelligentsia often delighted in dropping names and terms from the European intellectual tradition, more often than not these were just set adrift like exotic flotsam and jetsam on a sea of self-indulgence. The term *apure*, for example—a contraction of the post–World War I French term *après-guerre*—was first applied to a small group of young existentialist and nihilist writers who argued that the wreckage of the recent war included all absolute values. Before long, however, *"apure"* became indiscriminately attached to any young person who defied traditional norms. The counterculture came from within.

Decadence and Authenticity

Self-indulgence and eroticism found expression at many levels. Such distinguished writers as Tanizaki Junichirō and Kawabata Yasunari, curbed by censorship during the war, reemerged as connoisseurs of sensuality. Other literary figures in the lofty strata of the *bunkajin,* or "men of culture," also became associated with the primacy of individual passions. The classical poet Kawada Jun gained lasting fame when, at age sixty-eight, he stole the much younger wife of one of his disciples, sang of his passion in a poem which declared that "to an old man approaching the grave, love holds no fear," and then had the good karma to live for almost two more decades in close companionship with his purloined lover.[51]

While these literary engagements with love and sexuality resonated with the lubricious eroticism of kasutori culture, three younger writers—Sakaguchi Ango, Tamura Taijirō, and Dazai Osamu—dramatically linked degeneracy and carnal behavior to authenticity and individuality. In his short essay "On Decadence," published in April 1946, Sakaguchi offered a impassioned critique of the "illusory" nature of the wartime experience, contrasting it to the intensely human and truthful decadence of postwar society. Sakaguchi's public persona was as turbulent and anarchistic as his preachments. He rode through the postsurrender years on adrenaline and

Sakaguchi Ango's 1946 essay "On Decadence" is often cited as the most succinct expression of the repudiation of traditional values that many writers and intellectuals espoused in the wake of defeat. This photo by Hayashi Tadahiko conveys some of the flavor of Sakaguchi's talent for disruption.

a variety of less natural stimulants, and left his image to posterity in several memorable photographs in which he sits at a low table, almost literally buried in trash (old newspapers, books, magazines, crumpled manuscript pages, empty cigarette packages, torn-open envelopes, and a rumpled towel or blanket). He wears an inside-out undershirt that appears sweaty; his mouth is pursed; he gazes mournfully up at the camera out of horn-rimmed glasses, which reflect the light. He is writing—almost certainly about decadence.[52]

For decadence was Sakaguchi's métier; and, in the view of some critics, his essay on this subject captured the essence of its time as brilliantly as any piece of writing in Japan's long history. "On Decadence," according to a later commentary, "freed people from the possession of war, returned to them their rightful selves, and gave them the confidence to live."[53] Part of Sakaguchi's appeal lay in the fact that he wrote with candor of the psychological *attractiveness* of the recent war—of the mesmerizing grandeur of massive destruction and the "strange beauty" of people submissive to fate—and then, in the same intense prose, repudiated it. It was in "On Decadence" that Sakaguchi observed how former kamikaze pilots who had intended to die like scattered cherry blossoms were now working the black market, while wives who heroically saw their husbands off to battle and then knelt in prayer before their memorial tablets had already begun casting around for other men. "The look of the nation since defeat is one of pure and simple decadence," he declared—and in this lay the beginning of truth, of the return to a genuine humanity:

> Compared to the banality of decadence, its banal matter-of-factness, one feels that the beauty of those people obedient to destiny, the beauty of the love in the midst of that appalling destruction, was a mere illusion, empty as a bubble. . . .
>
> Could we not say that the kamikaze hero was a mere illusion, and that human history begins from the point where he takes to black-marketeering? That the widow as devoted apostle is mere illusion, and that human history begins from the moment when the image of a new face enters her breast? And perhaps the emperor too is no more than illusion, and the emperor's true history begins from the point where he becomes an ordinary human. . . .
>
> Japan was defeated, and the samurai ethic has perished, but humanity has been born from the womb of decadence's truth. . . .
>
> Humans don't change. We have only returned to being human. Humans become decadent—loyal retainers and saintly women be-

come decadent. It is impossible to halt the process, and impossible to save humanity by halting it. Humans live and humans fall. There is no easy shortcut to the saving of humanity outside this.[54]

Much of the shock of this critique lay in its seeming so simple and sane. Although "healthy" and "wholesome" were treasured words of the wartime ideologues and censors, the world so described had in actuality been morbidly sick. In contrast, to be decadent and immoral was truthful, realistic—and supremely human. Only by starting with a humble attitude toward decadence could people begin to imagine a new, more genuine morality. "We must discover ourselves, and save ourselves, by falling to the best of our ability," Sakaguchi concluded. In so doing, each individual would have to create his or her own "samurai ethic," his or her own "emperor system." In his distinctive way, Sakaguchi was affirming something that moral philosophers and other intellectuals were also wrestling with: that no society not based on a genuine *shutaisei*—a true "subjectivity" or "autonomy" at the individual level—could hope to resist the indoctrinating power of the state.[55]

Sakaguchi's perceptions were almost literally fleshed out in the writings of Tamura Taijirō, who had spent seven years fighting in China and was under no illusions about the horrendous realities of his nation's "holy war." Beginning in the latter part of 1946, Tamura published a series of novels and essays extolling the truth and honesty of *nikutai*, or "flesh," as opposed to the delusions of abstract "thought" or "ideas" *(shisō)*. The most sensational of these writings was the novel *Nikutai no Mon* (Gate of Flesh). The title became a popular catch phrase, and the book was made into a long-running play that premiered in Tokyo in 1947 as well as a movie that made its debut the following year.

In celebrating *nikutai*, or the carnal body, Tamura was engaging in a potent act of linguistic demolition, for his choice of language amounted to sacrilege bordering on outright lese majesty. Ever since the late nineteenth century, all Japanese had been indoctrinated to believe that the supreme object of veneration was the *kokutai*, or emperor-centered "national entity"—a misty concept written with two ideographs meaning literally "country" and "body." From the mid-1920s on, criticism of the *kokutai* was a major criminal offense. Glorifying *nikutai*, as Tamura did with spellbinding effectiveness, amounted to a complete repudiation of *kokutai*, a shocking inversion of the body *(tai)* to be worshipped. Now the only body deserving of veneration was the "flesh" *(niku)*—the sensual body—of the individual. The abstract "nation body" or nation state was meaningless, and all patriotic blather about it was duplicitous. What mattered—all that was indisputably real, honest, fundamental—was the solitary physical individual. For a people who had been deformed by a long tradition of so-called spiritual ideas, Tamura explained at one point, the "gate of flesh" was the "gate to modernity."[56]

An entire genre of "flesh novels" *(nikutai shōsetsu)* emerged in mimicry of Tamura's carnal vision, but even his extraordinary popularity did not surpass that of his charismatic and doomed colleague Dazai Osamu. In the manner of his death as much as of his life and work, Dazai came to epitomize the captivating degeneracy of kasutori culture. He, too, lives on in a small number of photographs. One captures him typically perched on not one but two bar stools, sleeves pushed up untidily, necktie loosened, cigarette in hand, a magazine half falling from his trouser pocket. He is fairly good looking, and it is easy to imagine him engaging in witty conversation before he topples off his perch.[57]

Dazai was well born, well regarded, and well on his way to self-annihilation through self-indulgence long before surrender—an example of exhaustion and despair years before the *"kyodatsu* condition" became identified as a collective malaise. He became addicted to drugs before the Pacific War even began and appears to have long courted and cultivated the mystique of the self-destructive artist. Dazai's personal demons, however, came to seem emblematic of the confusion and demoralization of the postwar years. Gifted and tormented, he lived like a degenerate and often wrote like an angel. His 1947 novel *Shayō* (The Setting Sun) lamented the demise of true noblesse oblige and professed to find a philosophy for the current epoch in the motto "love and revolution." When, the year after the novel appeared, an alcohol-saturated Dazai committed suicide with his mistress by drowning in a reservoir, he ensured himself immortality as the tragic symbol of a world without moorings.[58]

The Setting Sun was a flawed and uneven novel. It frequently fell into maudlin romanticism and suffered from the familiar "kasutori-gentsia" habit of scattering vacuous European terms and references about like confetti. Nonetheless, its almost immediate status as a classic came from more than just the morbid conjunction of the decadence and suicide it depicted with the decadence and suicide of the author. No other work captured the despondency and dreams of the times so poignantly. Whatever he may have lacked, Dazai was not lacking in a self-pity that resonated strongly with the deep strain of victim consciousness then pervading society. At the same time, he found beauty in decay and intimated, however feebly, that it might be possible to transcend despair through love. Al-

Dazai Osamu, who died in a double
suicide with his mistress in 1948,
shortly after completing the novel
The Setting Sun, lived on as a
memorable symbol of the
dislocation, degeneracy, and unstable
romanticism of the early postwar
years.

though conceived in peculiarly Dazai-esque terms, this vision of "love and revolution" struck another popular chord.

In *The Setting Sun*, this credo is articulated not by the artistic, suicidal younger brother who so resembled Dazai but by his sister Kazuko. Like her brother, Kazuko refuses to go on living in mindless compliance with what society demands. Unlike him, however, she resolves to live rather than die, accepting the fact that this means she must commit herself to "struggle with the world." Kazuko expresses this in a famous passage:

> I had never longed for revolution and had not even known love. Until now, the grownups around us taught that revolution and love were the most foolish and despicable things, and before and during the war we believed that to be the case. But after the defeat we became distrustful of the grownups around us and came to feel that the true way of living existed in the opposite of whatever they said. We came to believe that revolution and love in fact are the best and most delicious things in this life, and it is precisely because they are such

good things that grownups perversely lied that they were sour grapes. I want to believe firmly. *Humans were born for love and revolution.*[59]

Although he had flirted with left-wing activities, Dazai showed no interest either in doctrinaire Marxism or the more liberal agenda of "democratic revolution." In *Ningen Shikkaku* (No Longer Human), the novel that followed *The Setting Sun,* he ridiculed orthodox leftism mercilessly. Economics was hardly sufficient as a causal explanation for human behavior, Dazai's semi-autobiographical protagonist declared. He simply found the aura of illegitimacy that surrounded the leftists more comfortable than "the world of legitimate gentlemen."[60]

His attitude toward the occupation was just as caustic. Where the Americans themselves appeared in Dazai's work, it was usually only as an unwelcome, marginal presence. Occasionally, as in a story called "Winter Fireworks," he revealed a deeper nationalistic resentment. Although occupation censors excised the strongest line in the text, the pertinent passage (with the censored portion in brackets), spoken by a woman, went as follows:

> "We say defeated, defeated, but I don't think that's so. We've been ruined. Destroyed. [From one corner to the other, the country of Japan is being occupied, and every single one of us is a captive.] Rural people who don't find this shameful are fools. . . ."

Three months after being censored, Dazai enjoyed a small measure of revenge by smuggling the following implicitly anti-American ditty into a short play titled *Dry Leaves in Spring:*

> Not you
> Not you
> It was not you
> we were waiting for.

In a later story, he got another dig in with the observation that "from now on in Japan there's equality of the sexes even for horses and dogs."[61]

Since Dazai had turned his back on both the Marxist and the American versions of radical change, it was entirely in character that the "revolutionary" vision he did offer in *The Setting Sun* was highly idiosyncratic. In the final analysis, his heroine Kazuko declares in her rambling way, revolution is nothing more than a defiant love that repudiates the "old morality," a passion beyond understanding, or even the sorrow that comes from such passion. Revolution and love are the same thing. In Kazuko's case, to be a revolutionary meant to bear and raise the illegitimate child of her disreputable elderly lover. That, she declares in the letter that concludes the novel, "will be the completion of my moral revolution."[62]

This was not a revolutionary credo for everyone, nor did Dazai pretend that it was. He was not in the business of politics, after all, but of expressing emotions—and, as it emerged, of being obsessed with victimization. This was anything but a subtle leitmotif in the novel. Kazuko's suicidal brother was a "little victim" of life. Her seedy, alcoholic lover had "the face of a victim. A noble victim," and she herself spent much of her time murmuring about the "extreme desolation of being alive." Indeed, the novel ends on a ghastly note—a letter from Kazuko to her sodden lover in which revolution becomes equated with victimization, and victimization with beauty.

> A bastard and its mother.
>
> Nevertheless, we intend to struggle against the old morality to the end, and live like the sun.
>
> Please, you too continue to fight your battle.
>
> The revolution still hasn't taken place to the slightest degree.
>
> Many, many more precious, noble victims seem to be necessary.
>
> In the present world, the most beautiful thing is a victim.[63]

The passage is not only mawkish, but also redolent of the sort of wartime rhetoric that extolled the beauty of falling victim to causes greater than oneself. Like so much else, Dazai's celebrated novel revealed tortured, twisted links between the "old" and "new" Japan.

Many commentators were appalled by the literary developments exemplified by popular writers such as Dazai, Sakaguchi, and Tamura. The critic Kawakami Tetsutarō savaged *The Setting Sun* as a novel by an effete author about effete characters that appealed to effete readers.[64] Sakaguchi's affirmation of the compelling passions of war led him to be denounced for espousing violence. Tamura, whose *Gate of Flesh* included graphic scenes of the slaughter of a bull and the torture of a prostitute, was similarly condemned for displaying an attraction to violence that was not fundamentally different from the brutality of the war years. In a free-flowing and highly abstract discussion published in 1949, the political scientist Maruyama Masao managed to equate "carnal literature" not only with both the abnormality of war writings and the sensual preoccupations of the more traditional "autobiographical novel," but also with the bankruptcy of contemporary "carnal politics." Although carnal literature might appear to be "soaring away in unhampered freedom" with its exaggeration of the sordid, Maruyama observed, "actually it's grubbing around on its hands and knees in quite a commonplace world." For him this situation had dire implications. "If we don't control carnal literature and carnal politics in one way or another," he concluded, "then it's senseless to talk about Japan as a democratic and cultured nation."[65] The influential literary scholar Nakamura Mitsuo had these trends in mind when, at the end of occupation in 1952, he declared that nothing of originality or value had been written in Japan since the surrender.[66]

Nakamura's cranky judgment can be disputed. Whatever their literary stature, however, the writers of escapist stories and carnal literature, the apostles of "decadence" and philosophers of the flesh, the sodden romanticizers of love and revolution, the *après-guerre* existentialists and nihilists all roiled popular consciousness and called doctrinaire modes of thinking into question in ways their intellectual critics rarely succeeded in doing. They were spirited, iconoclastic, and influential to a degree the academic elites were loath to acknowledge. They might not have constituted the basis for a genuinely revolutionary transformation of Japan, but their challenge to old verities proved unforgettable.

"Married Life"

The carnal body remained, for most people, a literary construct. Sensuality, on the other hand, did not. A mainstream reconsideration of sexuality in conjugal relations led not to ridicule of "wholesomeness," as in kasutori culture, but rather to reconsideration of what a *healthy* sensuality between marriage partners might involve. Ancient Japanese poetry and prose had embraced an ideal of reciprocal love in which men and women shared sexual pleasure. In medieval times, however, the feudal elites had drawn an increasingly strict distinction between love and marriage, and certainly between sensual pleasure and marriage. "Good" women were taught that they were inherently inferior to men; that their entire lives were to be subordinated to the patriarchy of three generations of males (father, husband, and, in old age, son); that although men might find it natural to indulge in erotic lovemaking, such desires and behavior were utterly improper for a well-bred woman. The ideologues of the modern state carefully reformulated these feudal prescriptions as a code of behavior for "modern" married couples. In their hierarchical subjugation of private worlds, women bore by far the heavier burden. A woman's destiny was to become *ryōsai kenbo*, a "good wife and wise mother." Her overriding duty was to serve the male-dominated family—and the duty of the family, in turn, was to serve the imperial state.

Not surprisingly, to esteem genuine reciprocity in the conjugal relationship, including not only "love" but also mutual sexual gratification, became one way of defying authority and elevating the primacy of individual feelings and private worlds. In the wake of the defeat, such sentiments emerged in many guises, including a variety of popular publications emphasizing not only the appropriateness of enjoyable sex in marriage, but also appropriate techniques for achieving this. In time, the kasutori magazines would turn promoting a sexually satisfying "married life" into a distinct commercial genre. The impetus to this trend, however, was the remarkable popularity of a serious text on conjugal relations that rose onto the "top-ten" bestseller list in 1946 and remained there for over a year.

Titled *Kanzen naru Kekkon* (The Complete Marriage), this surprising publishing phenomenon was a translation of a clinical manual originally published in German in 1926 by the Dutch obstetrician T. H. Van de Velde. A portion of Van de Velde's long opus had actually been translated into Japanese in 1930 under the title *Kanzen naru Fūfu* (The Complete Couple). Its first translator was a Communist; its original publisher churned out erotic books; and it was quickly banned as "unwholesome" by prewar authorities. Despite the book's suppression, its reputation as a work of "sexual liberation" remained alive among the left-wing intelligentsia. The German edition as well as an English translation also remained popular among medical students and young doctors in the 1930s and early 1940s.

Van de Velde's work was retranslated in its entirety by a group of medical students at Tokyo Imperial University after an inquiry in the *Asahi* asking if anyone would be interested in such a book elicited one hundred or more responses in a single day. According to one of the translators, the students drew lots to determine who would get to do the most explicit chapters on sexual techniques. Their translation was quickly followed by a cheaper, less academic, abridged version that soon hit the number-three spot on the bestseller list.

Many readers undoubtedly were attracted to *The Complete Marriage* because of its "erotic" reputation, an allure heightened by its earlier suppression. This had been Van de Velde's first book, written when he was in his early fifties after twenty years of medical practice. Its intended audience had primarily been medical practitioners and educated husbands, and one of its basic premises—impressively enlightened for its time—was that "sex is fundamental to marriage." The book's major contribution to Japanese sexual consciousness lay in the way it called attention to a "sexual sensibility curve," especially in women, and stressed such concepts and practices as foreplay, afterplay, and orgasm. Van de Velde's notion that "man is the teacher" in sexual intercourse may appear now old fashioned, but in these years his sensitivity to women's sexual feelings and needs in the conjugal relationship seemed startling.[67]

The popular appeal of such a frank discussion of conjugal sex was exploited in 1949 by a new monthly magazine, *Fūfu Seikatsu* (Married Life). Its first issue followed the prescribed pattern for a legendary publication. The first printing of seventy thousand copies sold out in a day. A second printing of twenty thousand was snapped up immediately. With a wayward touch usually reserved for postage stamps, that printing was rushed out in such haste that many covers had only the magazine's name on a blank white background, thereby becoming collector's items. *Fūfu Seikatsu* soon reached a monthly printing of over three hundred thousand copies. So sensational was its success that it is sometimes said to have marked the end of the "kasutori magazine" genre and the beginning of a new epoch in mass publishing. Although a substantial portion of its articles were devoted to explicit discussions of sexual techniques, it differed from its pulp predecessors in a fundamental way. By linking sex to marriage, *Fūfu Seikatsu* made sex a legitimate rather than a furtive activity—and turned sexual reciprocity and mutual pleasure into symbols of gender equality.[68]

Although the publishers of *Fūfu Seikatsu* drew on such American periodicals as the journal *Sexology* as models, they were not charting entirely new territory. *Hanashi* (Story), a prewar magazine backed by the well-known writer Kikuchi Kan, had attempted to introduce serious articles on sexual practices as early as 1933. In essentially resurrecting this unsuccessful prewar venture, *Fūfu Seikatsu* also took up and transformed some familiar rhetoric from the recent past. Thus, the new magazine emphasized that the family was the fundamental unit of society, which sounded very much like what ideologues of the patriarchal "family system" and "family state" had long said. By going on to identify compatible, reciprocal sexual relations between husband and wife as essential to the family, however, the magazine undermined the old ideology. As would happen again and again in postdefeat Japan, words and phrases seemed to remain little changed, but what they signified altered dramatically.

Letters to *Fūfu Seikatsu* suggested that, unlike the pulps, this new periodical was attracting female as well as male readers. Although the magazine received many critical letters in its early days—especially, one editor recalled, from "intellectuals"—positive letters of support poured in from wives as well as husbands. Among other things, such letters revealed that, like people everywhere, many Japanese were troubled by fears of sexual inadequacy. The two most common anxieties expressed by male readers involved small penises and premature ejaculations, while the most common inquiry from women was whether it was possible to have an operation to make their vaginas smaller.

Despite its serious objectives, *Fūfu Seikatsu* proved susceptible to the kasutori-magazine disease. The line between seriousness and sensationalism soon blurred, and erotica increasingly took the place of genuine concern with the physical and emotional complexities of sexual reciprocity and marital happiness. At the same time, the magazine's success inspired the birth of copycat periodicals that rarely added anything of a substantial nature to the genre, but certainly reinforced in popular consciousness the desirability of physical intimacy in marriage. Newsstands were flooded with magazines whose titles and contents picked up the romantic new outlook on married couples *(fūfu)* and, indeed, on daily life *(seikatsu)* itself. Typical titles included *Fūfu Nikki* (Couples' Diary), *Modan Fūfu Jitsuwa* (Modern Couples' True Stories), *Fūfu Sekai* (Couples' World), *Shin Fūfu* (New Couples), *Fūfu no Shinshitsu* (Couples' Bedroom), *Fūfu no Seiten* (Couples' Sex Manual), *Kanzen nara Fūfu Seikatsu no Tomo* (Complete Couples' Life Companion), *Aijō Seikatsu* (Love Life), and *Romansu Seikatsu* (Romance Life).[69]

The blurred boundary between escapism and engagement with serious issues was typical of kasutori culture as a whole, and some critics, particularly on the political left, offered a Machiavellian interpretation of such developments. In their view, sex was part of a broader "three-S" policy encouraged by occupation authorities and conservative politicians to divert popular energies and resentments away from genuinely radical politics and protest movements—the other two "S's" being sports and "screen," that is, both domestic and imported movies of an escapist nature.[70] As this austere conspiracy thesis had it, the commercialization of sex was given tacit if not overt encouragement because, like sporting events and films, it was seen as an effective safety valve for a society beset by hunger and scarcity, confusion and despair. What seemed a revolutionary counterculture to some was deemed a counterrevolutionary conspiracy by others.

As theories go, this was unusually harsh, priggish, elitist, and paranoid.

Hayashi Tadahiko's *"kasutori* culture" photograph of a young woman in a
white bathing suit, lying on a balustrade high above the shabby streets of
Tokyo, captured the ambience of the cultures of defeat.

A more enduring comment on kasutori culture could be found in a posed photograph taken by Hayashi Tadahiko in 1947, depicting a model in a white two-piece bathing suit lying on a filthy balustrade high above the grimy train tracks and smutty city streets. The hardship of those days is readily apparent, but so also is the *esprit* of hardship and a humorous, even defiant élan. The photo is witty and sad, naturalistic and contrived, erotic and strangely innocent. Decades later, it remains an icon of the cultures of defeat as memorable for what it excludes as for what it depicts. We see no Americans here, no politicians preaching democracy, no figures in military uniform, no hints of nostalgia for the past, no vestiges of the state—just the bittersweet ambiance of life on the margins in a defeated land.[71]

chapter five

BRIDGES OF LANGUAGE

Words matter; and, as if a dam had broken, defeated Japan was engulfed in words. The kasutori magazines and the literature of degeneracy were but currents in a great river of communication. People came alive through words. They crossed from past to future on bridges of language.

Familiar words and slogans cushioned the shock of defeat, providing a comforting sense of continuity even when the very import of these words and phrases was turned topsy turvy. Defeat jokes flourished as satire became a weapon for dispelling despair. Bright, dipsy song lyrics lightened people's days and encouraged hope in the future. Radio reached into every household with a startling range of new programming, closely guided by the American reformers. A cacophony of political rhetoric filled the air. Serious publishing flourished, promoting liberal and left-wing ideas as well as a broad range of translated works that left the old ideologues sputtering and gnashing their teeth.

This conversion of language from war uses to peace uses was part of a more general tumult involving all sorts of transformations from war to peace, sometimes of the most literal nature. Former sword makers began producing kitchen cutlery. Steel helmets were converted into cooking pots. A former manufacturer of machine guns redesigned its plant to turn out sewing machines. Publishers, faced with acute paper shortages, figured out how to make cheap recycled paper with a process formerly used to make "balloon" bombs. By the end of 1946, Kobe's famous Motomachi shopping district had been substantially rebuilt using metal and bulletproof glass that came from former aircraft factories.

In the process, the former enemy became an entirely new kind of target. Optics technicians who until recently had been engaged in producing lenses for military use emerged with a "Baby Pearl" camera aimed at GI buyers. Former designers of fighter planes for Nakajima Aircraft (now renamed Fuji Industry) came up with the "Rabbit," a motor scooter based on a U.S. military model and made from tail parts for the Ginga bomber. American habits and customs derided only yesterday as alien and uncouth now put a gleam in the eyes of small businessmen. Within a year after the surrender, some four hundred companies were making chewing gum.

It took only months for a new business sector to emerge catering to the holiday needs of the conqueror. By November 1945, small entrepreneurs had obtained enough paper through the allotment system to meet the GI demand for exotic "Greetings from Tokyo" Christmas cards. Some 5.5 million cards were printed, mostly reproducing winter scenes from traditional wood-block prints. For the GIs as well as their families and acquaintances back home, no sharper contrast could possibly be imagined to the images that had prevailed only a few months previously. The Japanese landscape was now dotted with temples and shrines rather than pillars of smoke and pockets of flame, while graceful geisha under parasols in the snow took the place of the monkey-men hiding in tropical jungles.

The GI desire for cigarettes was met almost immediately by the government itself, which held a monopoly on tobacco sales. Three new brands were produced specifically for the occupation forces with the romanized names of Rose, Salon, and Gion (after the famous Gion geisha quarter in Kyoto). Indigenous liquor manufacturers, who only a few years earlier had been toasting Japan's spectacular initial victories against the "devilish Anglo-Americans," quickly came to market with a smooth intoxicant (so the story goes) bearing the friendly and reassuring label "Special Six-Year-Old Brandy, Brewed Especially for the Occupation Forces."[1]

Housewives welcomed, if not the victor personally, then at least his lingo and diet into their kitchens. In mid 1946, as rice rations disappeared, it was announced that "the era of flour has arrived." An Osaka electric company responded to the challenge with an immensely popular device known as the *Hōmu Beikā*, Japanese-English for "Home Baker." This consisted of a crude wooden box lined with metal sheets connected to an electric cord. One poured in batter or corn meal (a new taste sen-

sation, courtesy of food imports from America), and that was it—although
the Home Baker also emitted an unintended blue sparkle that was regarded
as aesthetically pleasing. The earliest advertisements proclaimed this to be
"The First Step in Kitchen Culture—A Bread Maker That Does Not
Need Charcoal, Gas or an Electric Burner."[2]

Bread making was integral to plain survival, of course. At the same
time, it also was a small manifestation of the horizontal westernization that
reached into every corner of society. Another example was the "dressmaking boom." Western-style dressmaking quickly emerged not only as an
attractive practical skill, but as a symbol of liberation from the drab
poverty and anti-westernism of the war years. Dressmaking schools, fashion magazines, and a variety of style books all blossomed amid the ruin.
When the designer Sugino Yoshiko decided to reopen her "Doreme"
dressmaking school early in 1946, she prepared only thirty application
forms. On the day set for registration, she was astonished to find "a thousand and several hundred" women patiently queued up in the cold outside the school gate. Chain schools like Sugino's quickly spread through
the country. The colorful, broad-shouldered "bold look" associated with
American women became the rage for those able to indulge in a touch of
fashion and the dream of those still too poor to do so.[3]

Mocking Defeat

Witty language accompanied many of the quick adjustments to peace. Military uniforms *(heitai fuku)*, worn by men even years after the surrender,
were rechristened "defeat suits" *(haisen fuku)*. Similarly, military footwear
became "defeat shoes." By October 1945, brass Japanese-style pipes for
smoking tobacco were already available on the black market. Sometimes
said to be Japan's first postwar manufacture, the pipes, about 10 centimeters long with a very small bowl, were made from the casings of machine gun cartridges and antiaircraft-gun shells. Their popular name?
"Defeat pipes," of course.[4]

Such cynicism helped to diminish the pain and disgrace of defeat; and,
indeed, mocking defeat became something of an impromptu cottage industry. Nothing was sacred. Sentimental children's songs were given parody lyrics ("Big Sunset, Little Sunset," the most saccharine of them,
became "Big Black-Marketeer, Little Black-Marketeer"). A famous
fourteenth-century satirical text entitled "What's Fashionable in the Capital Now" was rewritten stem to stern as a description of precarious contemporary life in Tokyo—from armed robbers and chameleon officials

down to "pencils that break when sharpened" and "screws that bend when turned."[5] Well-known clichés were recycled with wicked intent. "Thanks to our fighting men" *(Heitaisan no okage desu)*, one of the most pious expressions of the war years, became overnight a bitter, nasty comment on how Japan had come to find itself in its current predicament. In an unusually grim application of new meanings to old sayings, the pictorial weekly *Asahi Gurafu* (Asahi Graphic) ran a photo of the mushroom cloud over Hiroshima in its 1946 New Year issue, accompanied by the old-saw caption "Truth that emerged out of lies." The scorn for discredited ideologues and military leaders apparent in these new applications of old sayings was typical.[6]

The celebration of each new year became a particularly opportune occasion for mocking defeat, for since ancient times it was customary to play sound-association card games on the first day of the year. Known as *iroha karuta*, or "syllabary cards," the game might be compared to our pastime of making alphabet associations ("A is for apple, B is for boy"), but with the open-ended possibility of more elaborate connections (such as "A is for 'All that glitters is not gold' "). Phonetically, Japanese can be broken down into almost fifty basic sounds, which meant that every New Year irreverent wordsmiths could make roughly fifty satiric observations about the current situation.

These jokes, puns, and turns of phrase tend to defy effective translation, but they lightened hard times for many—particularly because the *"iroha"* associations made after defeat posed such a sardonic contrast to the solemn way the game had been deployed during the war years. A few examples may convey some sense of this. For the sound *su*, a wartime set of syllabary cards used the slogan "Advancing Japan, radiant globe" *(Susumu Nippon, kagayaku chikyū)*, with an accompanying illustration of a fluttering rising-sun flag against the sky. By contrast, an early postsurrender rendering for *su* offered the phrase "Morale deteriorates, fights blossom" *(Sutaru dōgi ni saku kenka)*, with a drawing of two shabby repatriated men slugging it out. Similarly, a wartime association for the sound *o* was the patriotic legend "Mother goes to the Women's National Defense Association" *(Okāsan wa Kokubō Fujinkai e)*, accompanied by a drawing of a young boy waving good-bye to his mother, who is carrying a small Japanese flag. In a postwar rendering, *o* was tied to the phrase "For parent and child alike—malnutrition" *(Oya mo ko mo eiyō-shitchō)*, illustrated with a drawing of a thin mother and child, hand in hand. No one reading the postwar *karuta*, with their mocking illustrations, could fail to smile ruefully.

Such language-play defeat jokes greeted new year after new year as the occupation continued. A cartoon *karuta* sequence in 1946, for example, offered for the syllable *ka* the impudent saying "The Divine Wind didn't blow" *(Kamikaze mo fuki sokone)*. A year later, in the midst of the runaway inflation, another publication offered this inspired though for *ka:* "Steal when poor, spend madly when prosperous" *(Kasshite wa dorobo, uruoeba ranpi)*. The new year of 1948 was greeted with this seemingly refined association for the syllable *re:* "A cultured person who comprehends manners" *(Reisetsu o shiru bunkajin)*. The barb here lay in the accompanying illustration, depicting a GI bowing in front of a Shinto shrine.[7]

The victors dropping gifts from heaven never really had the slightest idea that this level of popular joking about defeat existed, but the mordant wit itself was not necessarily antithetical to their aims. Certainly, the iconoclasm here was by no means hostile to some of the messages of "democracy." It simply found its own idiosyncratic voice.

Brightness, Apples, and English

There had been no tolerance of satire in Emperor Hirohito's war-mobilized nation, and precious little place for frivolity. This may help explain why the first great popular expression of relief and hope after the defeat involved an utterly frivolous paean to an apple: forbidden fruit.

Within weeks of surrender, a spirit of optimism could be seen emerging in publishing, radio, popular music, and film. The media continued to speak of *kyodatsu*, but simultaneously began to focus on what was "bright" *(akarui)* in the present and in an imagined future. Indeed, an emphasis on "brightness" and "newness" became the ubiquitous rhetorical antidote to all that was dark and despairing. While the purveyors and consumers of kasutori culture spoke of finding authenticity through degeneracy, others repudiated the recent past by emphasizing the bright, pure, liberating prospects of "the new Japan."

In many recollections of these years, the moment when hope dawned can be dated exactly to October 11, 1945, the day on which an otherwise unmemorable film opened with a buoyant tune, *Ringo no Uta*—"The Apple Song"—that captured everyone's fancy. The song began inanely:

> Red apple on my lips,
> silently watching the blue sky.
> The apple doesn't say a thing,
> but the apple's feeling is clear.

"The apple's lovable, lovable's the apple," went the refrain, followed by three more stanzas whose lyrics became, remarkably enough, ever more inane. The song ended:

> Shall we sing the apple song?
> If two people sing, it's merry.
> If everyone sings, it's more and more delightful.
> Let's pass on the apple's feeling—
> Apple's lovable, lovable's the apple.

"The Apple Song" launched the singing career of a young actress named Namiki Michiko, whose wartime experience resembled the shattered lives of many of her admirers. Her mother had been killed in the devastating March 10, 1945 fire bombing of Tokyo, and she herself had to be rescued from the Sumida River after the raid. Her father and elder brother had not returned from the war. She was a new face in the Shōchiku movie troupe, and by her own account never forgot the taste of an apple she ate on location—at a time when apples cost 5 yen each and a young actress's monthly salary was between 100 and 300 yen.

Namiki's sudden success made her a symbol of escape from hard times. At concerts, she threw apples to her audience while singing and they, it was suggested, tried to catch them as if reaching for happiness. That spirits were lifted by a peppy jingle about something edible was hardly surprising at a time when food was an overriding concern. Beyond intimations of deliciousness, however, the song lightened people's hearts with its frivolity, while its unforgettable red-apple, blue-sky imagery gave palpable color to a drab psychic landscape. Virtually every commentator on the song refers to a sensation of "brightness," even "marvelous brightness," in attempting to convey its appeal. Whether or not the "Apple Song" craze deserves such fulsome praise as a catalyst of postwar optimism is beside the point. It was a perfect example of the emergence of brightness (alongside exhaustion) as a code word for the times. For tens of millions of Japanese, the past was dark, the present grim, but the future brighter.[8]

Sometimes such expressions of optimism were deliberately crafted. Postwar publishers generally took care to offer upbeat and entertaining fare to their readers. Films and serious prose often moved, stylistically, from darkness to light. Even practical undertakings such as teaching English were carefully wedded to an explicit philosophy of accentuating the positive. "Come Come English" *(Kamu Kamu Eigo),* an enormously popular daily radio program that premiered on February 1, 1946, became famous not only for its conversation lessons, but also for *its* cheery theme song.

Here the lyrics were in English, set to the melody of a bouncy old Japanese children's song:

> Come, come everybody—
> How do you do, and how are you?
> Won't you have some candy?
> One and two and three, four, five.
> Let's all sing a happy song—
> singing tra la la.

Hirakawa Tadaichi, the moderator of the program, later explained the unusual decision to adopt a theme song for an educational program as being motivated by a keen feeling that this would help foster confidence in the new Japan. "In the dark Japanese society of immediately after the war," he recalled, "we couldn't sing military songs, and wanted an English song to sing proudly that would make people's feelings brighter."

Hirakawa's lessons were designed to convey a sense of good humor while fostering an appreciation of democratic practices in everyday life. Here, too, the pedagogy rested on an almost Manichean vision of darkness and light. "I thought in those days," as he put it, "that there could be no reconstruction of Japan until brightness was regained—unless people's hearts became bright and they began to look forward with positive feelings. I seriously feared Japan would collapse if the situation continued where people forgot to even laugh and didn't know what to do. . . . So when I was asked to do an English program . . . I took it as a solemn opportunity the gods gave me to make Japan bright." By all accounts, "Come Come English" lived up to Hirakawa's expectations. The program remained on the air for seven years, and was regularly listened to in an estimated 5.7 million households. Half a million textbooks were published in conjunction with the program, and half a million fan letters were received between 1946 and 1952. Hirakawa himself became a greatly respected celebrity.[9]

Such visions of a bright and democratic society stood as a sharp contrast to the ponderous pronouncements of the wartime ideologues. Yet a certain elasticity in wartime rhetoric and values made it possible to pursue such bright new hopes without feeling thoroughly disoriented. Language—vague, emotional, evocative discourse of the most formulaic sort—proved to be a bridge on which people could move from the militarist past toward a more peaceful future, while still retaining a sense of familiarity, consistency, even integrity of a sort.

"Brightness" itself was a good example of this, for the word and the

images and connotations associated with it—light, radiance, the rising
and shining sun, clarity of purpose, purity of motive—had been ubiquitous during the war years. In July 1941, on the fourth anniversary of the
outbreak of war with China, for example, the government exhorted its
people to carry on under numerous slogans including "The Hundred Million Fighting, Bright and Strong." One of the pithier slogans of 1943
called on the Japanese to "Extinguish America and Britain and Make a
Bright World Map." Slogan after slogan sought to instill bright attitudes
and confidence on both the battlefield and the home front—and also to
project Japan as the radiant hope of all Asia. ("Light of Asia" was one of
the propaganda names the Japanese used in Southeast Asia.) When the
boss of the Ozu gang opened the "Light from Shinjuku" market, he was
moving from wartime to peacetime sloganeering without even breaking
stride.[10]

Kōdansha, Japan's largest publisher and an enthusiastic supporter of the
war effort, responded similarly to defeat by accentuating the positive. As
an editor recalled, it was decided that people really wanted and needed to
read not serious, soul-searching tomes about the war, but rather "enjoyable novels, fun novels, bright novels." Kōdansha's staff, however, was really doing little more than reaffirming the company's long-held policy of
avoiding serious social and political criticism. In 1931, following Japan's
seizure of Manchuria, it was none other than this same publishing house
that had adopted the slogan "Bright and Just, with All Our Might."[11]

Wartime rhetoric proved malleable when it came to postwar objectives
because it was largely constructive and idealistic to begin with. The Japanese did not march off to war shouting "Long Live Militarism and Aggression!" They declared that they were fighting for peace and security,
coexistence and co-prosperity, a bright future for their nation and all of
Asia. All lies, declared the victorious Allies, the kasutori-gentsia, the political left in general. A more ordinary response, however, was to say:
wartime rhetoric reflected decent, even noble ideals, but we were disastrously deceived and misled by our leaders in our pursuit of them. From
this perspective, it became possible to imagine that the ideals for which
so many had been willing to die might also aid in the creation of a new,
prosperous, and peaceful nation. At the very least, it could be argued that
serving the country did not mean simply serving it in war.[12]

Early in 1947, a first-grade teacher offered an example of how the
same words or texts could be interpreted differently before and after surrender. He described for the press how "Momotarō, the Peach Boy," a
classic of children's literature and a favorite tool of wartime propagandists,

was now used in his classroom. During the war, Momotarō had been seen as a nationalistic parable of a divine, quintessentially Japanese hero who saved the country from conquest by demons (the Anglo-American enemy) and returned with their treasure as booty. Postwar children, as this teacher told it, were now more interested in the treasure than the demons; and as there were no illustrations in their postsurrender textbooks, they were left to speculate on the nature of the treasure. Money and food, they concluded. When asked what should be done with these, his pupils engaged in considerable discussion—itself a contrast to wartime classrooms—before finally deciding, by a 38–2 vote, that they should be divided equitably and dispensed to the poor.[13]

The carry-over of catch phrases, images, even whole texts from the war years was in itself neither progressive nor reactionary. Invariably, however, this continuum of familiar language conveyed a sense of stability, and so functioned as psychological balm at a time of acute stress and unusually drastic change. Sometimes rhetoric of the recent past fit neatly, almost like fine joinery, with the new agendas of defeat. The two most familiar slo-

The single most popular catch phrase in postsurrender Japan was surely *Heiwa Kokka Kensetsu:* "Construct a Nation of Peace." Schoolchildren practiced this as a matter of course in their calligraphy lessons—as seen in this sample by the then twelve-year-old crown prince, Akihito, who succeeded his father Hirohito as emperor in 1989.

gans of the early postwar period—"Construct a Nation of Peace" *(Heiwa Kokka Kensetsu)* and "Construct a Nation of Culture" *(Bunka Kokka Kensetsu)*—resurrected two key themes of wartime propaganda, construction and culture, and turned them into rallying cries for the creation of a nation resting on democratic, antimilitaristic principles. Schoolchildren throughout the country wrote and rewrote these slogans as part of their calligraphy lessons. Even the young crown prince Akihito participated in this exercise.[14]

Because such antiwar sentiments reflected the sincere feelings of millions of war-weary Japanese, it was easy to overlook how firmly the rhetoric of "construction" and "culture" was grounded in wartime discourse. After all, the great rallying cry in World War II had been "Construct a Greater East Asia Co-Prosperity Sphere." Japan's war against China and the Western Allied powers had been accompanied by slogans such as "Muster the Yamato Heart for Construction" and "Everyone Serving for Construction." Similarly, the phrase makers of the 1930s and early 1940s rang "culture" like a bell—commonly coupling it with images of brightness and radiance. "Rising-Sun Land, Superior Culture" was a typical slogan from the China War. After Pearl Harbor, the propagandists were even more explicit in emphasizing that culture, dynamic and regenerative, emanated from Japan. "Imperial Culture Is the Light of Asia" was a rallying cry from 1942. As another slogan of that year expressed it, Japan was in the process of creating "A New Culture Tied to a Radiant Past."[15]

Catchphrases were like valises, waiting to be emptied of their old contents and filled with something new.

The Familiarity of the New

The most hackneyed beseechments of wartime sloganeering—"cooperate" *(kyōryoku suru)*, for example, and "give your all" *(gambaru)*—also became staples of postwar exhortations to work for reconstruction, peace, democracy, or the new Japan. It was the rhetoric of "newness" itself, however, that most revealed how old and familiar many of the "new" slogans and exhortations really were. The cult of the new was omnipresent. In the publishing world alone, well over one hundred magazines that appeared during the first three years after the war used the ideograph for "new" in their name, either in compound words (read *shin*) or in its adjectival form (read *atarashii*). A number of magazines even used the English for new *(nyū)* in their titles. The areas of interest in which these magazines specialized reveal how avidly the blessing of newness was dispensed. Among other things, readers could embrace a new age, new culture, new democracy, new education, new geography, new history, new hope, new labor, new life, new movies, new salaried man, new school, new poetry, new sports, new way, new women, new world, newborn democratic Buddhism, new literature, new haiku, new marriage, new self-government, new era, new freedom, new free people, new society, new science, new farmer, new farm village, new youth, new police, new family, new beauty care, and even a new happy star.[16]

As the wartime slogan "A New Culture Tied to a Radiant Past" indicates, however, newness (like culture and brightness) was a concept that lay at the very heart of the ideology of imperial Japan. This fixation on transformation was often obscured by those strains of Western and Japanese propaganda that stressed the "old," "traditional," or "unchanging" aspects of presurrender culture and policy. In actuality, renovation was one of the central ideals of the war years, just as rapid change had been the watchword of millions of Japanese ever since the mid-nineteenth century.

From the Japanese perspective, the war years were an attempt to throw off the status quo—to transcend the global depression and to catch up with the more advanced industrial economies of the West. People's lives were transformed dramatically after 1931, as the country mobilized for "total war," and the wartime goals of "construction" were explicitly renovationist. Internationally, this vision—like the Nazi "New Order"—was encapsulated in the formulation of an "East Asia New Order," or simply "New East Asia." Domestically, the renovationist sentiment found expression in the ideal (as announced by the second Konoe Cabinet in 1940) of a "New Economic Structure" coupled with a "New Political Structure." Typically, the emperor's subjects were expected to be bright and cheerful as they threw themselves into supporting this new policy. As a 1941 slogan put it: "Always Smiling Faces—the New Structure."[17] All this made it easier to embrace the inevitability and even the desirability of postwar transformations.

"Change," in a word, was itself a continuity. The Japanese had not been socialized to preserve the status quo. On the contrary, ever since the Meiji Restoration in the 1860s they had been involved in a whirlwind of change. The war years represented an acceleration of this process in innumerable ways. The sense of crisis intensified; so also did the depth of dissatisfaction with the status quo. When the war ended in disaster and utter defeat, it was obvious that the "New Order" and the "New Structure" had been miserably conceived. It seemed no less self-evident that the quest for a new domestic structure and a new place in the global political economy had to go on.

The point is not complicated, only generally neglected: renovation and iconoclasm were strains as deeply imbedded in consciousness as were reverence for the past or acquiescence to the powers that be. For almost a century, the Japanese had been socialized to anticipate and accommodate themselves to drastic change. When World War II ended, they were well prepared—not merely by the horrors and manifest failures of the war, but also by the socialization of the past and even the psychic thrust of wartime indoctrination—to carry on the quest for a "new" Japan. In other words, it was entirely "traditional" to find pundits gathering soon after the surrender to engage in a "roundtable discussion on 'changing the world.' "[18] What changed, and drastically so, was how men and women now chose to define what that new world should be like.

Turning familiar rhetoric and preoccupations in new directions smoothed the passage from war to peace in numerous other ways. The postsurrender fixation on "enduring the unendurable" was rooted in a sense of vulnerability and victimization that predated the China and Pacific wars and traced back, in its modern guise, to the gunboat diplomacy and unequal treaties with which the Western powers had forced Japan out of its feudal isolation. The wartime demonization of "devilish Anglo-Americans" proved easily transferable to new incarnations of evil—to "militarists," "ultranationalists," and "feudal elements" during the early radical days of reformism, and to demonic "communists" or, in the eyes of the left, demonic "U.S. imperialists" thereafter. A wartime emphasis on purity elided easily into postwar fixations on purification, or cleansing, or rectification. It was in this context that there emerged substantial popular support not only for top-level war crimes trials and a purge of militarists and untranationalists, but also for the general reformist policy of cleansing politics and society of "feudalistic" and "militaristic" vestiges. Even conspiracy theories provided a kind of comforting, or at least familiar, continuity between the epochs of war and peace. Before surrender, the Japanese were indoctrinated to attribute their troubles to the machination of Western imperialists on the one hand and canny Communists on the other. It required only a slight turn of mind to conclude that the real conspirators had been Japan's own *gunbatsu*, its military cliques.

More obvious legacies from the past—especially the premilitarist past—reinforced such subtle rechanneling of popular sentiment in helping people look to the future with a sense of continuity and hope. Conservative and liberal antimilitarists could, for instance, point to a number of "democratic" precedents in the prewar period: the "Charter Oath" of 1868, in which the new government pledged to overthrow the "evil practices" of the feudal past; the Western-inspired ideals of "civilization and enlightenment" and "liberty and people's rights" that had flourished in the 1870s and 1880s; the practice of parliamentary government under a constitutional monarchy initiated as early as 1890; and the emergence of greater political pluralism in the 1910s and 1920s (a promising development known as "Taishō democracy," in reference to the reign years of Emperor Hirohito's father). For more radical men and women, defeat and the temporary disarray of the old guard made possible the revitalization of left-wing traditions as well. When two hundred fifty thousand people assembled in front of the imperial palace on May 1, 1946, they were able to announce that they were celebrating May Day for the seventeenth time in Japan—merely resuming a tradition that had been repressed in 1936.

In these manifold ways, language and history contributed immeasurably to the resources people drew on in engaging the prospects of a "new" Japan.

Rushing into Print

Although actual hunger preoccupied most people in the months, if not years, following capitulation, more figurative hungers beset them as well. Notable among these was a craving for words that went beyond sloganeering. Under the militarists and ultranationalists, free expression had been severely suppressed. What passed the censors gave meager sustenance at best. Despite formidable obstacles, publishing was one of the first commercial sectors to recover in defeated Japan.

This was an impressive development. The efflorescence of the publishing industry represented a triumph of intellectual and entrepreneurial spirit, for both censorship and material obstacles continued to plague publishers. Under the occupation, a considerable range of subjects was placed off limits, including criticism of the Allies and their policies, as well as praise of values that the victors deemed in any way militaristic or ultranationalistic. Many printing plants had been destroyed, and start-up capital was in short supply. Insolvency was a commonplace among would-be publishers. Until 1951, paper remained in critically short supply and was subject to complicated and onerous rationing regulations. Despite all this, the recovery was rapid and vigorous.[19]

Dry statistics convey some sense of the hunger for words in print. At war's end, there were approximately three hundred publishing companies in Japan. Eight months later, the number had increased to almost two thousand. In 1948, it peaked at around forty-six hundred, a majority of which did not survive the recession that began the next year. Nonetheless, in 1951, as the occupation drew to a close, about nineteen hundred publishers were still in operation—a sixfold increase over August 1945.[20]

Where magazines were concerned, the publishing situation was so turbulent that exact figures are impossible to come by. Many periodicals ceased publication temporarily in the confusion of defeat, but returned to newsstands weeks or months later. Others, suppressed by the militarists, made a postwar comeback. Still others navigated the passage from war to peace with a hasty, expeditious name change. The former "Wartime Woman" *(Senji Josei)* became "Ladies Graphic" *(Fujin Gahō)*, for example, while "Wartime Youth" *(Senji Seinen)* was rechristened "Constructive Youth" *(Kensetsu Seinen)*, "Wartime Economy" *(Senji Keizai)* was neatly deregulated into "Investment Economy" *(Tōshi Keizai)*, and "Wartime Medicine" *(Senji Igaku)* entered postwar practice as "Integrated Medicine" *(Sōgō Igaku)*. In the same spirit, "National Administration" *(Keikoku)* became "New Era" *(Shin Jidai)*, "Weapons Technology" *(Heiki Gijitsu)* underwent rapid conversion to "Peace Industry" *(Heiwa Sangyō)*, and "Mechanics Friend" *(Kikaikō no Tomo)* experienced a mysterious conversion and emerged as "New Opinion" *(Shinron)*. The Youth Culture Association East Asia Culture Sphere Company, a propagandistic wartime publisher whose very name cried out for a good copy editor, resurfaced as the Cultural Association for Construction of a New Japan and replaced its imperialistic flagship journal, "East Asia Culture Sphere" *(Tōa Bunkaken)*, with a new magazine titled simply "Culture" *(Bunka)*. It exhorted readers to join "kindred souls" throughout the world and "drive out the enemies of culture" that existed around them as well as in their own hearts and minds.[21]

Some name changes resembled a woman taking back her maiden name on the dissolution of a failed marriage. In 1943, Kodansha's mass circulation magazine "King" *(Kingu)* became *Fuji* (one of the most evocative of nationalistic symbols), when the company decided to give its all to winning the "thought war." After surrender, the name "King" was resumed. The confusion resulting from such stops, starts, and rechristenings was compounded by the sudden appearance and equally sudden disappearance of genuinely new periodicals. At the same time, many small publications aimed at local audiences tended to be neglected in comprehensive publishing statistics, although some were of high quality.[22]

It is estimated that between surrender and the end of 1945 slightly fewer than 200 different magazines appeared on national newsstands, of which 60 or 70 may have been brand new. During the first half of 1946, at least 400 additional magazines appeared, of which around 85 percent were new. Thereafter, the number of periodicals increased exponentially. In 1946 alone, some 114 magazines were identified as catering exclusively to women readers. From surrender to late 1949, the censorship section of the occupation command surveyed some thirteen thousand different periodicals. Over the same period, circulation figures for daily newspapers rose from 14.2 million to 26.6 million. In this area, SCAP's zealous censors surveyed an estimated 16,500 different newspapers between 1945 and 1949.[23]

Book publishing similarly showed no evidence of succumbing to the *kyodatsu* condition. Close to one thousand new books had appeared by the end of 1945, including many by authors who had been suppressed under the militarists or on topics that had been declared taboo. The total number of books and pamphlets submitted to SCAP's censorship detachment prior to the latter part of 1949 was in the neighborhood of 45,000. By SCAP's own count, between November 1945 and April 1948 new translations of some 1,367 foreign-language works had been produced, amounting to over three translations every two days. Contrary to what one might have expected under an occupation regime controlled by the United States, books by American authors constituted but a small portion (7.6 percent) of the total. The list was genuinely cosmopolitan, with French authors accounting for 350 works, Germans 294, Russians 251, British 194, Americans 104, Chinese 43, and Italians 37; the remaining 94 titles came from various other countries.[24]

Although a good portion of postwar publishing was escapist and ephemeral, much was serious and idealistic. The "statements of purpose" with which new and revived magazines and journals introduced their first postwar issues are suggestive in this regard, because in many cases they were formulated before the occupation authorities had fully articulated their own reformist agenda. "Democracy" was in the air, of course, as anyone remotely familiar with the Potsdam Declaration or General MacArthur's early pronouncements was aware. Still, as a random sample of such early statements reveals, publishers across the political spectrum lost little time in advancing their own visions of what this still-vague idea of democracy should entail.

The editors of *Kyōryoku Shimbun* (Cooperative Press) were fairly typical in the way they set about redefining national purposes in their maiden postsurrender issue. A labor-oriented publication dating back to the Taishō era and originally named *Shōkō Shimbun* (Worker Encouragement Press), it had devoted its wartime issues to encouraging labor support for national policy. The first renamed edition, dated September 1—a day before the surrender ceremonies on the *Missouri*—was identified as a "Guide to Recovery Issue." Turning an old image to new purposes, the cover reproduced a drawing that had been used four years earlier when Japan initiated war against the United States, depicting people kneeling in front of the imperial palace. Of course, it sported a new caption: "We have cried all we can—now let's smile and stand up." The feature article was an exchange between the publisher and Tsurumi Yūsuke, a famous parliamentarian, awkwardly but provocatively headlined "The World Has Changed! Questions and Answers—Think about Japan Being Reborn as a Great Nation of Culture and Do Collective Repentance About the Past."

Typically of the more conservative responses to defeat, *Kyōryoku Shimbun* told its readers that no experience, not even staggering defeat, was without value. Japan, the United States, the world as a whole could learn from the Great East Asia War. Indeed, for the sake of future peace and prosperity, the entire world had to engage in "self-reflection" (a cherished term of the times) and repentance. Where the Japanese were concerned, one could only "tremble in awe" before the emperor's magnanimity in concluding the war. At the same time, it was necessary to recognize that the "hundred million" as a whole, not just militarists such as General Tōjō, bore responsibility "as war criminals and for the defeat."

That said, *Kyōryoku Shimbun*'s editors urged readers to concentrate on the future. "First of all," they observed, "we need to work three to five times more than the Americans," study harder, and be more inventive. Before the war, the country was said to be twenty years behind the United States in science and industry. Now, the technological gap probably amounted to the equivalent of thirty to fifty years, and was compounded by a comparably formidable gap in "government, economics, and culture."

Despite the daunting challenge of catching up with the United States, there was hope for a bright future if the hundred million could succeed in wedding pragmatic flexibility to their own unparalleled history and culture. Here, the editors of the former propagandistic publication found it possible to retain some of their old patriotic rhetoric. "Our divine Japan, with a national polity that is unsurpassed in the world and a proud history of three thousand years, possesses brains as well as absolute loyalty and morality. Although possessing such exemplary environment and quality, we do need to absorb the good points of the United States and the rest of the world. At the same time, however, we also must rid ourselves of the 'imitate-and-follow-ism' of the past, and make the most of ourselves and what is Japanese. Thus, we firmly believe that war-defeated Japan can win over war-victorious America culturally, and come to have many things to teach Britain."[25]

Such attempts to salvage a modicum of honor and self-esteem in the midst of humiliating defeat were commonplace. Just as common, however, were heartfelt acknowledgments of failure and of the necessity of starting over. The editorial send-off for the September 1945 issue of *Geien* (Garden of Art), a magazine for young women, was characteristically candid and earnest. "The war which we had believed to be just was lost, our writings about victory turned into wastepaper, and we young editors plunged into depths of despair," it read. "The same must be true of you readers. Since you believed in the war and dedicated yourselves to the home front, forgetting the seasons and youth and dreams, your shock must have been all the greater." This said, the editorial immediately went on to declare that the pressing demands of "tomorrow's Japan" did not permit wallowing in confusion and perplexity. Youth in particular now faced the task, indeed the duty, of building a "new Japanese culture" and establishing "a nation of culture and peace." Other women's publications were more exuberant. *Shin Tsubaki* (New Camellia), a local magazine that began publishing in Osaka in March, opened with a strong endorsement of the Potsdam ideals of creating a democratic and peace-oriented nation. From the moment Japan threw down its arms, the statement exclaimed, women were liberated "from everything." The magazine went on to call for the elimination of unscientific elements from scholarship and irrationality from all aspects of social behavior.[26]

Shin Jidai (New Era), the peppy postdefeat spawn of a magazine prosaically titled *Keikoku* (National Administration), also was expansive in defining the challenges ahead. Irresponsible leaders of the Shōwa era had betrayed the glorious legacies of the earlier Meiji and Taishō periods, the editors declared. Moral deterioration and loss of pride as a race were major causes of defeat, and serious self-reflection was in order. The war could be seen as a mirror in which both the beauty and ugliness of the people were reflected, and the most obvious manifestations of ugliness were feudalistic legacies, irrationality, and antiscientific attitudes—a position that would soon be *de rigueur* in American pronouncements about the Japanese malaise. When all was said and done, *Shin Jidai*'s born-again editors continued, the people had failed to completely understand and assimilate "modern civilization." It behooved them to do so now, and to win their freedom by their own abilities—their own self-governing creativity—

instead of merely relying on the occupation force. "Even on this difficult road of thorns there is a ray of light," the editors concluded, "and in this sense the new era is an era of liberation."[27]

Other periodicals even more emphatically repudiated the past. *Shinsei* (New Life), a typical new magazine, proclaimed that "make-believe and slippery excuses no longer work. The old Japan has been completely defeated. Completely. We must engrave this in our hearts and embark from here toward a newborn Japan." "Newborn Japan" *(Shinsei Nihon)* was in fact the name of a new periodical that made its appearance in November, featuring as its cover an illustration of a tall American GI helping an elderly Japanese woman with a heavy load on her back. Here the editorial send-off called for shedding old clothes, gazing unflinchingly at "the real figure of defeated Japan," and considering all social phenomena in a genuinely critical spirit—while at the same time reaffirming that love of country remained absolutely unchanged.[28]

By year's end, left-wing publications were contributing loudly to the chorus heralding change. *Jinmin* (The People), one of the most relentless magazines when it came to castigating wartime collaborators among the intelligentsia, made its debut in December with a stinging denunciation of militarists, landlords, zaibatsu, and the emperor-centered bureaucratic system. "People are suffering in this ruined land," its editors declared, "but for the first time in history they are also liberated from oppression. Great sacrifices were made, but if for the first time Japanese history is being transferred to the people's hands, then all was worth it." The Allied blow to the ruling classes was described as "a valuable gift from the world to the peace-loving, democratic Japanese people." Like most commentators, the editors of *Jinmin* found it politically and psychologically imperative to identify indigenous seeds of democracy in Japan, calling attention to "the passionate desire for democracy" seen in the "liberty and people's rights movement" of the early Meiji period and in the proletarian movements of the early twentieth century.[29]

Most of the senior editors and writers who gave voice to such views were products of an eclectic prewar intellectual tradition that had accommodated serious engagement with Marxist as well as liberal discourse. For them, defeat amounted to the resumption of an interrupted critical tradition that, in a few instances, had continued for longer than most of Japan's antagonists realized. This was the case with the monthly *Kaizō* (Reconstruction), which along with the equally famous *Chūō Kōron* (Central Review) had provoked suppression by the imperial government as late as mid-1944. When *Kaizō* resumed publication in January 1946, its lead article was an essay on "Constructing a Peaceful Japan" by Morito Tatsuo, a well-known Marxist. The magazine commented editorially that although it was natural for people to view their own country's actions as just, from an objective perspective it was apparent that Japan's past attitudes and actions had been "a dark mass of ambition," especially where China was concerned.[30]

Kaizō's resurrection was complemented by the appearance of a distinguished new progressive periodical, the monthly journal *Sekai* (World), published by Iwanami. Iwanami was to serious intellectual publishing what Kodansha was to books and magazines aimed at mass consumption. Indeed, "Iwanami culture" and "Kodansha culture" were already familiar catchphrases for the separate worlds of elite and popular publishing. Many of the greatest writers of the West, including Marxist as well as prerevolutionary Russian authors, already were present on Iwanami's backlist of translations, some of them suppressed during the war and most of them destined for renewed promotion in the wake of defeat. Impressive numbers of Japan's most incisive critics and progressive intellectuals were already in Iwanami's stable or soon flocked to it.

Even amid the deluge of old, reconstituted, and new periodicals, *Sekai*'s

The hunger for words in print is vividly captured in this July 1947 scene of customers sleeping outside the Iwanami bookstore in Tokyo's Kanda district, waiting to buy a new edition of the collected works of the philosopher Nishida Kitarō. The queue began three days before the announced date of publication and grew to some two hundred persons over the next two days.

birth was notable, and its opening statement of purpose was fairly representative of liberal and left-wing opinion in general. Surrender, the new journal observed, was unprecedented and humiliating, and darkness, chaos, and suffering clearly lay ahead. At the same time, defeat had exposed the "unreasonableness, fraud, bluff, and injustice" of the war years, and opened the possibility of the Japanese people's making a new start based on realistically facing up to the truth. Bereft of armaments and empire, denied economic freedom and restrained from overseas activity, they had no alternative but to try to create a world "of broad and bright morality and culture." Evoking a biblical metaphor, *Sekai*'s editors described this as "breaking through a narrow gate." What lay ahead, they said, was a road of extreme difficulties, but at the same time a road of glory. If the war experience had exposed "the powerlessness of culture, emptiness of morality, and laziness, cowardice, and irresponsibility of the cultured, intellectual class in our country," the redemptive task that lay ahead was to develop a culture and morality that the whole world could applaud.

By the time *Sekai* appeared on the scene, U.S. occupation ideals had been clearly articulated. The editors summarized these as democracy, respect for individuality, freedom of speech and religion, and world peace—and then took care to emphasize that these ideals were to be pursued not because the victors had ordered this to be done, but "because they are based on the demands of human nature and universal justice." The list of tasks to be accomplished was endless, but central to all endeavors was the creation of a society based on social justice and responsive to the will of the people. Only that kind of society would prevent tyranny and dictatorship from arising ever again in Japan.[31]

Such sentiments—painful, earnest, self-critical, intensely idealistic—found expression in hundreds of postsurrender periodicals.

Bestsellers and Posthumous Heroes

The first sensational postwar bestseller was a short English-language conversation book conceived on the day of the emperor's surrender broadcast. The brainchild of an editor named Ogawa Kikumatsu, this phenomenal little success story quickly earned a place in publishing lore and held the record as the country's all-time best-selling publication until 1981.

As the story goes, Ogawa was on a business trip when he heard the broadcast. His eyes still moist with emotion, he boarded a train back to the capital and immediately began to consider how to get rich from the changed situation. By the time the train pulled into Tokyo, he had hit upon his great idea; and, like so many enlightenment experiences, it was the essence of simplicity. As soon as the country was occupied, people would be clamoring for an easy guide to everyday English conversation. He would provide it.

Ogawa, who evidently had no particular competence in English, sold his idea to a publisher. He and his more skilled collaborators then took two conversation books from the war years as models. One was a Japanese-Chinese manual that had proven useful in quite a different occupation situation (no one seems to have noted the black humor in this); the second was a Japanese-Thai manual. Accounts vary as to whether it took one day or three to complete the full draft of the little book. In any case, *Nichi-Bei Kaiwa Techō* (Japanese-English Conversation Manual) made its debut exactly one month after those tears came to Ogawa's eyes. It was thirty-two pages long, and its initial printing of three hundred thousand copies disappeared almost immediately.

By the end of 1945, 3.5 million copies had been sold. All over Japan, people prepared to meet their conquerors by turning to page 1 of this handy guide, which began:

> Thank you!
> Thank you, awfully!
> How do you do?

The English phrases were accompanied not only by equivalent Japanese in both ideographic and romanized form, but also by phonetic *(katakana)* renderings of the English. These, too, revealed a touch of inspiration, for they were not precise, formal renderings, but had a comfortably colloquial feel to them—as if Ogawa and his associates had managed to spend an evening (or three) in a bar with a woozy native speaker before rushing the draft to the printer. Thus, on encountering their first GI, Japanese could be ready to say phonetically:

> *San kyu!*
> *San kyu ofuri!*
> *Hau dei* (or, alternatively, *Hau dei dou*)

The last, apparently, came from "Howdy" and "Howdy-do."[32]

Fortunately for the world of letters, this astonishing little publication did not set the pattern for subsequent bestseller lists. Although academic critics have tended to look down on the literary output of these years, the world of book publishing proved unusually open to broad questioning of an impressively fundamental sort. Scholarship flourished in numerous areas that had been proscribed by the militarists, including academic Marxism, which experienced a strong revival. Eminent literary figures who had chafed under or been censored by the militarists—such as Nagai Kafū, Tanizaki Junichirō, Kawabata Yasunari, and Osaragi Jirō—became celebrities again.

The "top ten" bestsellers from 1946 to 1949 collectively conveyed an impression of cosmopolitan breadth and serious purpose never again to be matched, as ordinary citizens proved responsive to writings that addressed abiding issues of human nature and social responsibility. As one commentator has put it, these writings tended to be preoccupied with "life" in the broadest sense.[33] Even in retrospect, the early bestseller lists remain full of surprises. Postwar readers, for instance, immediately turned in large numbers to the greatest of their modern writers, Natsume Sōseki, who died in 1916. Sōseki's collected works, issued in several new editions, remained on the top ten lists through 1948. Much of his attractiveness during these uncertain years lay in the unflinching candor with which his fiction explored intimate personal relationships. Affairs of the heart constituted the essence of Sōseki's many novels, including the revered *Kokoro* (Heart and Soul).

The Sōseki boom seems to have reflected not so much nostalgia for a period in modern history before war and defeat, but a desire for a renewed engagement with the torments and solaces of the individual. In a famous lecture in 1914, Sōseki had already spoken strongly about the need to maintain a spirit of "individualism" vis-à-vis the state. As a novelist, he was a masterful delineator of how difficult it was to maintain one's balance and integrity in a nation that was inexorably undergoing frenetic change. In the final works of his brief but extraordinarily productive career, love between man and woman—painful, conflicted, irresistible—was his most obsessive concern.

In Sōseki's world, love always was placed on a higher plane than the demands of society, even when this meant social ostracism, personal torment, or self-destruction. The protagonist of *Sorekara* (And Then), for example, becomes a heroic (and tragic) figure by giving himself entirely to "a love that obeyed the will of heaven but violated the laws of man."[34] Of the isolated married couple whose life is described in *Mon* (The Gate), readers were told that "when the cold was hard to bear, they found warmth in each other's embrace, relying only on one another."[35] In this regard, the old master's writings were consistent with the concern for private worlds that now preoccupied so many Japanese. They were also a powerful reminder that the intellectual and psychological crises which men and women were then confronting were not at all unprecedented. On the contrary, this was but the latest stage in an ongoing dilemma—how to define and assert one's identity and individuality in an age of traumatic and irresistible "modernization" and "westernization." Sōseki addressed such issues with unsurpassed sensitivity.

He was by no means the only author to remain on these bestseller lists for more than a year. Remarkably, seven other writers did likewise. In addition to Van de Velde's text on marital relations, the top ten publications of 1946 included three other foreign works in translation: Jean Paul Sartre's *Nausée*, André Gide's *Intervues Imaginaires* ("Imaginary Interviews," translated as *Kakū Kaikenki*), and Erich Maria Remarque's *Arc de Triomphe*. Interestingly, no American author rose into the top ten until the translation of Margaret Mitchell's *Gone with the Wind* appeared in 1949. Sartre and Gide were the only two authors who did not reappear in the top ten lists of 1947, although interest in existentialism remained keen among intellectuals. Remarque's novel, like Sōseki's collected works, remained a bestseller for three years in succession.

In addition to Sōseki, Japanese books at the top of the 1946 bestseller list included *Sempū Nijūnen* (The Twenty-Year Whirlwind), a journalistic account of Japan's road to war and destruction; Nagai Kafū's *Udekurabe* (Rivalry), a novel about competition in the geisha quarters that was written during the war but withheld from publication; the autobiography of Kawakami Hajime, a pioneer Marxist scholar and early member of the Japan Communist Party who passed away a few months after the war ended; Miki Kiyoshi's *Tetsugaku Nōto* (Philosophical Notes), consisting of previously published essays by a well-known philosopher who had died in prison; and the prison letters of the executed spy Ozaki Hotsumi. Four of the Japanese authors on the bestseller list were dead; and of them, only Sōseki had seen his writings reach a large audience in his lifetime.

Miserable defeat brought with it a cultural crisis of a very specific nature: the old, nationalistic heroes had been toppled, but who would take their place? Textbooks had to be rewritten. Postage stamps had to be redesigned. Publishers had to come up with exemplary new native sons. In the last case, the best-selling writings of Kawakami, Miki, and Ozaki helped meet this need. The three men shared much in common. They were associated with Marxism and communism, although their intellectual horizons were not bound by either. Each had been imprisoned for political reasons. They were all principled individuals who embodied qualities of independent thought and personal autonomy that appeared rare and admirable in a country where most people had caved in completely, in many cases enthusiastically, to the authoritarian state.

It also helped that they wrote well. Kawakami and Ozaki were particularly effective stylists, and Miki, in his posthumous *Tetsugaku Nōto* (Philosophical Notes), conveyed his ideas on tradition, genius, leadership, morality, "ideology and pathology," and "constructing a world view" in an accessible language rare among his philosopher colleagues. In addition, the three men surely appealed to Japanese readers because they were victims— even though they were in a sense victims of many of the same people who now found them attractive.

Kawakami, the oldest of the three, had made a mark on popular consciousness in 1916, when he published an impassioned denunciation of exploitation titled *Bimbō Monogatari* (A Tale of Poverty), a subject of keen renewed interest three decades later. Imprisoned from 1933 to 1937 because of his communist activities, he disappeared from public view during the eight years of the China and Pacific wars. He did not speak out against his country's aggression, but neither did he lend himself actively to the imperial cause, as so many of his erstwhile leftist comrades had. Essentially, he became invisible; and when he spoke up again through his writings after the surrender, it almost seemed as if a legendary figure had suddenly risen from the dead. A small "Kawakami boom" ensued, involving the publication of articles, poems, letters, prison recollections, and miscellaneous pieces.

The boom was highlighted by the appearance of the lengthy autobiography Kawakami had written secretly between 1943 and 1945, which began to be serialized in a progressive journal in February 1946. Eventually published in four volumes, this was extravagantly praised as being unprecedented in Japanese letters and comparable to such odysseys as Rousseau's *Confessions* and Goethe's *Sorrows of Young Werther;* but the old revolutionary never witnessed his full apotheosis as what one critic called "a seeker after truth who chose the difficult path." He died on January 31 at the age of sixty-seven, just before the first installment of the autobiography appeared.[36]

The death of forty-eight-year-old Miki Kiyoshi was more shocking, for he succumbed to illness in prison on September 26, 1945—six weeks after the war ended, but before U.S. occupation authorities had effected the release of political prisoners. An eclectic philosopher and social critic, he had been imprisoned in 1944 for allowing a Communist friend to hide in his home. From 1922 to 1925, Miki had studied in Germany, where he became an acquaintance of Karl Mannheim and was influenced by both

Marxist thought and the methodology of Martin Heidegger. In 1930, he was briefly arrested as a Communist sympathizer. His intellectual quest led him to attempt to reconcile existentialism and religion, and he became increasingly involved with Japanese systems of thought—particularly the ideas of his eminent contemporary the philosopher Nishida Kitarō (who sought to meld Western philosophical ideas with the insights of Zen Buddhism) and the teachings of the iconoclastic thirteenth-century religious leader Shinran. In the late 1930s, however, Miki emerged as a sophisticated apologist for Japan's "pan-Asian" mission, and in 1942 he accepted a position as a publicist for the imperial army in the Philippines. His fatal decision to harbor his fugitive Communist acquaintance was a personal rather than ideological act. Like Kawakami, Miki's appeal to postsurrender readers lay as much in the intellectual quest he had undertaken as in the answers he may have arrived at and was greatly enhanced by his personal generosity.[37]

Of the trio of best-selling posthumous heroes, surely the most fascinating was Ozaki Hotsumi. Ozaki had been a well-known journalist with a particular expertise in Asian affairs, but the writings that brought him adulation in the wake of defeat were private and intimate—a selection of prison letters he wrote to his wife and daughter between the time of his arrest in October 1941 as a Comintern spy and his execution in November 1944, at the age of forty-three. Ozaki had been the major Japanese contact for the master spy Richard Sorge, whose reports had provided the Soviet Union with invaluable information about Japanese strategic thinking prior to Pearl Harbor. He was the only Japanese to be formally tried and hanged for treason during the war—an extraordinary traitor in the eyes of his compatriots prior to August 15, 1945, and an even more remarkable hero and martyr figure thereafter.

Cynics may well take the Ozaki case as an example of the frivolity of popular sentiment, but no one could deny the exceptional appeal of the letters themselves. The aura they evoked was captured in the emotional title chosen for the collection: *Aijō wa Furu Hoshi no Gotoku* (Love Is Like a Shower of Stars), which was suggested by a letter in which Ozaki wrote that "I have lived feeling deep human love everywhere. Reflecting upon my life, sincere love is like brightly shining stars." The appeal of the executed spy obviously lay outside communist doctrine per se.

Although he had served the Comintern through his connection with Sorge, Ozaki had never joined the Japan Communist Party. This did not prevent the postwar party from trying to identify him as an "iron communist," but they faced fierce competition in trying to claim him as their

own. That Ozaki had a revolutionary and utopian vision of a new socialist world order that would arise from the war was indisputable. The
prison letters made this clear, but these same writings also made it easy
and natural for other admirers to regard him as a great "humanist"—a
label not at all pleasing to the Communists.

Ozaki's letters revealed with rare intimacy the intellectual and moral deliberations of a cosmopolitan man. While under arrest, he voraciously
read a wide range of literary, political, economic, and historical works including the writings of Goethe and Machiavelli's *Prince*. In attempting—
unsuccessfully, as it turned out—to write a "recantation" for the judicial
authorities, he immersed himself in Japanese classics. As his execution approached, he became increasingly interested in Zen Buddhism. Beyond any
doubt, however, the greatest appeal of the published letters was the love
directed to his wife and daughter—to the real, nuclear family, that is, as
opposed to the "family state."

Prior to his imprisonment, Ozaki had been an unfaithful husband who
had not shared his thoughts with his wife, Eiko, or told her about his activities. She knew nothing about his espionage work until he was arrested.
In the prison letters themselves, he acknowledged that he had not desired
children because of the demands of his clandestine life.[38] The couple had
only one daughter, Yōko, who was twelve at the time of her father's arrest. Imprisonment, of course, put an end to Ozaki's philandering, but it
also led him to initiate an intimate intellectual as well as emotional relationship with Eiko as well as Yōko. The prison letters, hundreds of them
over the course of three years, were addressed to both wife and daughter.
In them, Ozaki conveyed his ideas and feelings unreservedly and expressed his affection openly. This was not characteristic "Japanese" male
behavior, but it was a level of open emotional and intellectual sharing that
many men and women were ready to admire.

Indeed, the popular embrace of these letters was yet another indication
of how much the war and defeat had prepared the ground for elevating
the preciousness of intimate personal relations. Until the surrender, the
state and its ideologues had dictated that the primary love a human should
feel was patriotism or love of country, ultimately expressed through devotion to the emperor. To the very moment of surrender, official myths
about parents and wives gladly sending sons and husbands off to war with
patriotic fervor, and men happily giving their lives for the emperor, had
prevailed. Only later did accounts slowly emerge of soldiers and sailors
sobbing in their billets in the dark after receiving letters from home, and
of dying men calling out their mother's names, not the emperor's, with

their last breath. In this context, Ozaki's prison letters, even while describing his grand visions of global revolution and world peace, simultaneously could be read as confirming the importance of private worlds. The frank, affectionate, intellectual nature of the prison letters became a kind of model of attractive "technique" in relations between husband and wife, father and daughter—a complement, as it were, to Van de Velde's very different but also liberating emphasis on sharing and reciprocity.

Ozaki's publishers, like Van de Velde's, were not so exalted as to lose sight of the popular market for love and romance that emerged in the wake of defeat. Komorida Kazunori, the publisher of *Aijō wa Furu Hoshi no Gotoku,* had himself suffered at the hands of the wartime censors. He also, as it happened, had spent three years as the editor of a woman's magazine and was keenly aware of the heightened evocativeness of the word *aijō*—love—among women. The title, which was thoroughly in tune with any number of popular songs of the day, apparently was proposed by Komorida specifically with the idea of attracting female readers. Communist ideologues, on the other hand, emphasized Ozaki's revolutionary love of freedom, peace, and the proletariat (although he wrote, and apparently thought, very little indeed about the working classes as such). When the Communists published the commemorative proceedings of a memorial meeting held three years after Ozaki's execution, they titled it "The Great Love" *(Idai naru Aijō).*[39]

Yet a third, more subtle kind of love came to be associated with Ozaki—beyond the revolutionary love that the Communists chose to emphasize and the more personal, humanistic love revealed in his family relations and intellectual inquiries. For an erstwhile traitor, this involved a spectacular metamorphosis—for increasingly Ozaki came to be seen as a true patriot, a man who loved his country in a deeper, more genuine way than all the self-righteous ultranationalists and superpatriots. After all, those who had claimed to love Japan actually brought it to disaster, whereas Ozaki had been one of the few individuals intelligent enough, independent enough, and courageous enough to oppose them to the end. His love of country transcended doctrinaire emperor worship and acquiescence in the policies of exploitative, narrow-minded elites. Those who emphasized Ozaki's love of country after the surrender discovered that an unlikely figure had preceded them on this interpretive path. Takada Tadashi, the judge who sentenced him to death in 1944, privately stated after the secret trial that he regarded Ozaki as not merely a man of virtue and ideals, but as a model patriot—hardly the observation one would have expected from a hanging judge.[40]

In these various ways, Ozaki's exceptional qualities appeared to offer one model—a *Japanese* model—for exceptional times. He served a popular need for icons of Japanese suffering on the one hand and symbols of hope on the other. From the liberal or leftist perspective, Ozaki, like 2 million fighting men and hundreds of thousands of civilians, had been sacrificed by a murderous, militarist state. Less important than the precise identity of the victimizer, however, was the sense of being victimized. In the years to come, Ozaki's wife and daughter would both be active and effective in keeping his reputation alive; and, as a widow and a fatherless daughter, each in her own right enhanced the popular preoccupation with victimization.

Simultaneously, like any true martyr, Ozaki became a symbol of hope to his admirers. His vision of world revolution and ultimate peaceful "universalism" was almost breathtakingly utopian. In the despair of defeat, he could easily be held up as an eloquent visionary of that "bright" new world so many Japanese were groping toward in the three years that *Love Is Like a Shower of Stars* remained on the bestseller lists.[41] Ozaki's widow conveyed this sentiment succinctly in the foreword she wrote for the first, abbreviated edition of the letters in 1946. The title of her essay, like the title of the book itself, evoked the dreams and hopes of the time: "I Believe That Dawn Is Approaching."[42]

Heroines and Victims

Heroines also graced the early bestseller lists. One of the first Hollywood films to be shown after the defeat was *Madame Curie,* starring Greer Garson and based on the biography by the renowned scientist's daughter Eve. In 1947, carried by the great popularity of the movie, the translation of the biography itself rose to the top ten list. Madame Curie's brilliant accomplishments in a hitherto "masculine" intellectual domain were in and of themselves inspirational to women, and the story of her achievements had an incalculable impact in dramatizing the case for gender equality. But the story was also a romance of the most exhalted sort imaginable—involving not merely the marital love of Marie Curie and her scientist-husband Pierre, but their equitable sharing of grand ideas.

A genuine Japanese heroine also appeared on the bestseller lists in 1947 in the person of Miyamoto Yuriko, a prolific writer and indefatigable radical organizer whose younger husband, Miyamoto Kenji, was one of the small number of prewar Communists who refused to recant and consequently languished in prison from 1933 until October 1945. As a woman separated from her spouse by the authoritarian state, Miyamoto Yuriko became an incarnation of sacrifice and suffering. As a loyal wife who not only awaited her husband's release but actively shared his radical politics, she personified both romance and liberation.

Beyond her celebrated marriage, Miyamoto Yuriko's huge talent and prodigious energies made her a charismatic figure in her own right. She had burst to fame as a writer in 1916 when, as a seventeen-year-old college student, she published a novel titled *Mazushiki Hitobito no Mure* (A Flock of Poor People). Beginning in 1927, she spent three years abroad, mostly in the Soviet Union. Between 1932 and 1942 she was arrested for left-wing activities on five separate occasions and spent a total of more than two years in prison. She was released in 1942 only after suffering heat prostration and falling into a coma. Subsequent ill health led to her early death in 1951, at the age of fifty-two.

After the war, despite her physical weakness and an endless round of organizing activities for the Communist Party, Miyamoto managed to turn out a succession of widely read articles, stories, and novels that captured the frenetic energy with which individuals on the left responded to the defeat and disarray of the old regime. *Banshū Heiya* (The Banshū Plain), a thinly disguised account of her activities in the wake of surrender, remains one of the most celebrated descriptions of the immediate postwar scene. Both thematically and stylistically, this novella moves from darkness to brightness, despair to hope, disarray to purposefulness. *Fūchisō* (the name of a flower), the best-selling sequel, described the heady and hectic days when Miyamoto Yuriko and Kenji, reunited, threw themselves with great optimism into communist activities aimed at creating a truly new Japan. Several years later, a selection from the thousands of letters Miyamoto had written to her imprisoned husband was published to critical acclaim under the title *Jūninen no Tegami* (Twelve Years of Letters)—a feminist and humanist counterpart to the prison letters of Ozaki Hotsumi.[43]

As time passed and the occupation's censors permitted greater freedom in publishing materials about the war, visions of hope and dreams of peace found provocative new forms of expression. In 1948, as the trial of accused top-level war criminals finally drew to a close, three books emerged as bestsellers that, almost like a kaleidoscope, offered varying perspectives on the issue of victimization. One of these was Dazai Osamu's *The Setting Sun;* another was the translation of Dostoyevsky's *Crime and Punishment.* The third was Nagai Takashi's *Kono Ko o Nokoshite* (Leaving These Children), one of the first books permitted by occupation authorities about the atomic bombings. Nagai, a young scientist dying of radiation sickness in Nagasaki, mesmerized the country with his reflections on nuclear destruction and future redemption. His rumination on what would happen to his young son and daughter when he died was joined as a bestseller the next year by another of his contemplations, *Nagasaki no Kane* (The Bells of Nagasaki), which was published only after a protracted give-and-take with SCAP censors.

Like many Japanese in Nagasaki, Nagai was a Christian. He also, by ironic happenstance, was a medical doctor specializing in radiology and had been exposed to radiation poisoning before the Nagasaki bomb was dropped. His wife was killed by the bomb, and he himself died in 1951 at the age of forty-three. He thus wrote about the nuclear age from a unique perspective—as scientist, Christian, and victim—and the passion with which he spent his final years confronting the meaning of the atomic

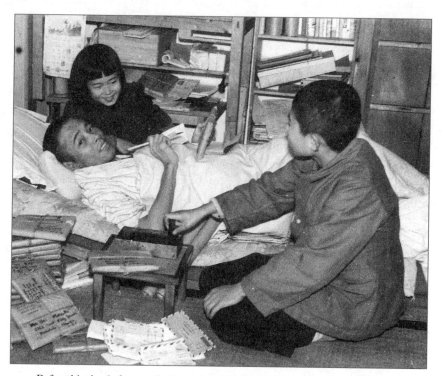

Before his death from radiation sickness in 1951, the Catholic scientist Nagai Takashi had become idolized as "the saint of Nagasaki" for his prolific writings on the meaning of the nuclear age. Nagai's wife had been killed in the Nagasaki blast, and he was often photographed with his young son and daughter by him as he lay on his sickbed.

bombs led him to be called, in his own lifetime, the "saint of Nagasaki." The pope paid tribute to Nagai. Helen Keller visited him at his sickbed, as did Emperor Hirohito. In 1950, *The Bells of Nagasaki* was made into a movie, and the theme song of the film proved immensely popular.

Nagai's message bordered on the mystical. Essentially, he regarded the bombings of Hiroshima and Nagasaki as the act of a Christian God meant to bring the world to its senses. That the second atomic bomb fell on a city with a long tradition of Christianity only reinforced his sense of divine intervention. In a typically apocalyptic passage, he asked: "Was not Nagasaki the chosen victim, the lamb without blemish, slain as a whole-burnt offering on an altar of sacrifice, atoning for the sins of all nations during World War II?"

Radical Japanese found such religious fatalism unpalatable, not to say fatuous, but even they could not deny Nagai's contribution to the swelling of pacifist sentiment in Japan. At the same time, his emotional prose, his melodramatic martyr's descent into death, and the belated emergence of such writings on the nuclear-bomb experience gave substance to a growing sense of victimization at the very moment the victors' war-crimes trials were bringing judgment against the Japanese for crimes against peace and humanity. In this milieu, war itself became the greatest "victimizer," while the Japanese—personified by the saintly father/doctor/scientist dying in a nuclear-bombed city—emerged as the most exemplary victims of modern war. Here was a new symbol for the familiar sentiment of grievous Japanese suffering and noble Japanese sacrifices. That the popular theme song for the film version of *The Bells of Nagasaki* was written by Koseki Yūji, the country's most famous composer of sentimental war songs, seemed entirely natural in these circumstances.[44]

In 1950, Japanese readers got their first unvarnished view of the Pacific War from the perspective of the American fighting man when the translation of Normans Mailer's novel *The Naked and the Dead* appeared and quickly became a bestseller. As an enduring impression, however, Mailer's gritty novel paled before a selection of letters and other writings by university students killed in the war. Edited by progressive intellectuals and evocatively titled *Kike—Wadatsumi no Koe* (Listen—Voices from the Deep), this extraordinary exercise in transforming war words into peace words was inspired by the belief that these intimate communications from the very maw of the war itself would be read as an eloquent cry for peace. The letters rocketed to the top ranks of bestsellers and almost immediately became the basis for a movie of the same name.

Kike—Wadatsumi no Koe was like a two-way hinge on a door in time, opening onto the past, then swinging toward the future. "Wadatsumi no Koe" associations were formed by relatives of the war dead, and the book remained in print over the decades that followed. The entries, some seventy-five in all, had been selected with great care by a team of liberal and leftist scholars. They were literate, reflective, cultured—and extraordinarily moving, for one read them knowing that these young men would be cut down before fulfilling their obvious promise. Although they wrote under military censorship and accepted, sometimes even embraced, the mission of dying for their country, there was an underlying hunger for life, not death, in what they wrote. The overwhelming tone of the collection was a sense of wasted lives and tragic loss. *Listen* was compiled as an antiwar statement, and its impact was greatly enhanced by the fact that it appeared at the same time as the outbreak of the Korean War, the U.S. decision to rearm Japan, and the rise of an anti-American "peace movement" in Japan.

Superficially, the use of wartime writings as peace statements resembled the more rudimentary carry-overs from war to peace of simple catchwords such as *reconstruction, brightness, culture,* and *new*. In practice, the publication of this collection proved far more complicated. Whatever the editors' intentions may have been, *Listen* perpetuated an image of sacrifice that came perilously close to the imagery the militarists had promoted. These were pure young men. Their deaths were noble. They could not be faulted, certainly not criticized, for having offered no resistance to militarism. It was their deaths, rather than the deaths of those they might have killed, that commanded attention and were truly tragic. Indeed, there were no non-Japanese victims in this hermetic vision of the war. It was, moreover—and here the class bias of the academic compilers revealed itself—their literacy, their status as elite university students, that made these young men's deaths so worth noting. They were selected as figures to mourn because they wrote so well, but also because it was easy to imagine them as the future leaders of Japan.

As in the writings of Nagai Takashi, war was understood and repudiated primarily in terms of its destructive effects on Japanese. The compilers of *Listen* were aware of the ideological ambiguity of their undertaking from the beginning, for their collection had a revealing pedigree. This was not the first, or even the second publication of letters from elite student conscripts. A similar collection, entitled *Haruka naru Sanka ni* (In Distant Mountains and Rivers), published in 1947, had sold some seventy thousand copies before its editors stopped reprinting it in response to criticism that they were perpetuating wartime thinking. This collection, which had drawn exclusively on letters from students at the very apex of the university hierarchy, Tokyo Imperial University, was in turn based on letters that had been published in *Teikoku Daigaku Shimbun,* the university newspaper, as a regular feature over the course of 1944.[45]

Despite the fact that the editors of the 1950 book took care to include students from other universities among their writers, and despite their fervent antiwar and antimilitarist intentions, they could not really shake off the past. Even the title of the collection carried ambiguous, muted echoes. *Wadatsumi no koe*—"voices from the deep"—was an evocative phrase from one of the militarists' favorite source books, the great eighth-century poetic anthology *Man'yōshū.* These bridges of language, so crucial to maintaining a sense of identity and purpose, were awesome indeed, for they carried an ambiguous traffic. People used them to escape the past and move on to new destinations. At the same time, there was always the possibility—even the temptation—of crossing back.

Part III

REVOLUTIONS

chapter six

NEOCOLONIAL REVOLUTION

From the Japanese perspective, the prospect of experiencing a "revolution from above" was hardly unprecedented. Ever since the mid-nineteenth century, ruling elites had exhorted the populace to industrialize, modernize, westernize, throw off the past, become new men, become new women, become new subjects of a new-born nation state. Starting in 1868, the government had carried out extensive reforms under the explicitly Europe-oriented slogan "civilization and enlightenment." Beginning in the 1880s, the state promoted modern nation building under the more conservative top-down aegis of a reconstituted emperor system. Even the military and civilian autocrats of the 1930s and 1940s carried out their imperialistic and militaristic policies under renovationist and revolutionary slogans.

The fact that authoritarian, top-down exhortations to dramatically alter the status quo were not new does help explain—but only in part—why the American reformers succeeded as well as they did. General MacArthur, quintessential American that he was, easily became a stock figure in the political pageantry of Japan: the new sovereign, the blue-eyed shogun, the paternalistic military dictator, the grandiloquent but excruciatingly sincere Kabuki hero. MacArthur played this role with consummate care. Like the emperor and the feudal shoguns, he ensconced himself in his headquarters, never associated with the hoi polloi, granted audiences only to high

General MacArthur's charisma was as great as his authority among the
defeated Japanese.

officials and reverential distinguished visitors, issued edicts with imperious panache, and brooked no criticism.

Victors as Viceroys

The supreme commander never actually saw the Japan over which he
presided. From the moment he arrived in Tokyo, his travels were restricted to morning and afternoon commutes between his residence in the
old U.S. embassy facilities and his nearby office at SCAP headquarters in
the former Daiichi Insurance building. He never socialized with Japanese;
and, according to one intimate observer, "only sixteen Japanese ever spoke
with him more than twice, and none of these was under the rank, say, of
Premier, Chief Justice, president of the largest university." The general's

evenings were largely devoted to watching Hollywood movies, particularly Westerns. Sometimes he also viewed newsreel-type footage of Japan shot by U.S. military cameramen, enabling him to at least keep in celluloid touch with the country he governed.

For five years, the general's movements were as predictable as a metronome. Prior to the outbreak of the Korean War in June 1950, he left Tokyo only twice for brief visits to Manila and Seoul. Like Emperor Hirohito prior to 1946, MacArthur spoke in intimate, paternalistic terms about the sentiments and accomplishments of the tens of millions of Japanese under his aegis but never had the slightest meaningful contact with them, never observed first hand how they actually lived. The general thrived on veneration, believed that "the Oriental mind" was predisposed "to adulate a winner," and assumed that democracy would take root only if people believed him when he said it should. And, indeed, the response of huge numbers of Japanese was that the supreme commander was great, and so was democracy.[1]

MacArthur was the indisputable overlord of occupied Japan, and his underlings functioned as petty viceroys. At the hub of GHQ activities in the unbombed section of downtown Tokyo, a cadre of American military and civilian bureaucrats (roughly fifteen hundred in early 1946, peaking at thirty-two hundred in January 1948) operated what Theodore Cohen, an energetic participant, aptly characterized as a "new super-government." This super-government interpreted and promoted basic political, economic, social, and cultural policy, while cultivating the art of "noncommands with the force of commands." Even mid-level staff offered advice or suggestions to Japanese functionaries that, though technically not orders, effectively operated as such. Faubion Bowers, who served as an assistant military secretary to MacArthur, described this heady authority as involving, in practice, a policy of "demand, insist, enforce, ban, burn" (and a basic pattern of behavior that often, in his rich phrase, "became buffonic").[2] In the postoccupation period, when the Japanese bureaucracy itself proved adept at such "administrative guidance," Americans would denounce this practice as yet another peculiarity of the Japanese state. Such authoritarian legacies of the neocolonial revolution would rarely be acknowledged.

This extraordinary concentration of power at the center was complemented not only by the stationing of both civilian and military personnel throughout the country, but also by a hands-on manipulation of the educational system and everyday culture. The conquerors were keenly aware that meaningful democratization involved more than simply instigating legal and institutional reforms. It was also essential, as one of the initial planners of occupation policy put it, "to get at the individual Japanese and remold his ways of thinking and feeling" to enhance a deeper appreciation of freedom and democracy.[3]

To this end, occupation authorities created a web of programs designed to reach every man, woman, and child in the country. They dispatched teams of Americans, mainly men but some women as well, to local communities to provide grass-roots tutelage in American-style civics. Until the end of the occupation, they required that every textbook be translated into English for their scrutiny and approval.[4] They exerted immense influence over the mass media—negatively through censorship and positively through active input into the articles the press published, the programs public radio broadcast, and the foreign and domestic films movie houses put on screen.

The conundrum of inducing democracy autocratically was apparent at every level and easily abused by functionaries who found themselves suddenly possessed of authority they could never have dreamed of wielding in their own country. Case after case demonstrated how seductive such power could be. To ensure a single voice of "democracy" in the crucial medium of radio broadcasting, to give but one small example, occupation authorities chose to perpetuate the total monopolization of the airwaves by the national broadcasting station (named "NHK" at this time, in emulation of CBS and NBC). The fixation on top-down social engineering was so great that GHQ deliberately thwarted the development of rival commercial stations until 1951. Only through such tight control, the reformers believed, could the archetypal "Joe Nip" (their counterpart to "John Doe") be molded into a good facsimile of an American-style democrat.[5]

The ramifications of the viceroy role extended beyond policy making per se, for the huge army of occupation—including military officers and their dependents, civilian employees of SCAP and their dependents, and eventually close to a million ordinary GIs *in toto*—constituted a privileged caste, class, and race. They made up a "little America" in Japan, literally so in downtown Tokyo; and they practiced clear-cut segregation. Year after year—while the Cold War intensified, the nuclear arms race accelerated, the European powers struggled to reestablish themselves in Southeast Asia, the Communists emerged victorious in China, and war erupted in Korea—American domination remained a constant in defeated Japan. Under the new constitution that came into effect in 1947, the Japanese in theory became citizens and no longer just the "subjects" of their emperor. In practice, however, they remained the subjects of the occupation.

Beyond doubt, many of the conquerors conveyed an impressive ideal-ism and generosity of spirit. GIs became famous for their offhand friend-liness and spontaneous distribution of chocolates and chewing gum. Individual Americans demonstrated serious interest in aspects of Japan-ese culture and a sense of bearing responsibility toward strangers that was unfamiliar and attractive (or sometimes just bizarre) to their Japanese neighbors. They took people unknown to them to hospitals and did favors without expecting repayment. They practiced simple charity in uncalcu-lating, matter-of-fact ways.[6]

The conquerors also bestowed significant practical gifts upon their new subjects: penicillin, streptomycin, blood banks, and genuinely public li-braries, for example, as well as tutoring in such technological practices as statistical quality control, which would be of immense value in the coun-try's eventual economic reconstruction. Close personal relationships based on mutual respect were forged between individual Americans and their Japanese counterparts in a variety of settings; but when all was said and done, such relationships were impressive, in part, precisely because they defied the inevitable inequalities of binational relations under a military oc-cupation. And even such intimate personal relationships usually rested on the assumed superiority of American culture. With very few exceptions, all relationships were defined and conducted in the conqueror's tongue.

Daily reminders of American superiority were unavoidable. The most redundant phrase in the defeated land, posted in public places and reiter-ated in a myriad public and private settings, was *Shinchūgun no meirei ni yoru*—By order of the Occupation Forces. Petty as well as grand activi-ties were governed by directives from GHQ and encumbered by all the tedious paperwork and micromanagement this entailed. Numerous stores, theaters, hotels, buildings, trains, land areas, and recreational facilities like golf courses were designated "off limits" to Japanese. Ordinary SCAP of-ficers and civilian officials who would have lived plain middle-class lives at home resided in upper-class houses requisitioned from their owners, hardly the most persuasive demonstration of respect for the rights and property of others. There, they might employ three, four, five, or even six servants, all paid for by the Japanese government (cook, "boy," maid, gar-dener, nursemaid, and laundress was considered an ideal roster). Bowers, an irrepressible aficionado of Kabuki, managed to obtain two personal cooks, one for Western-style and the other for Japanese-style cuisine. "I and nearly all the Occupation people I knew," he later mused, "were ex-tremely conceited and extremely arrogant and used our power every inch of the way."[7]

This U.S. Navy photo from August 1947 was part of a series illustrating the lives enjoyed by occupation personnel. "There is no talk about the high cost of living among some 125 Navy families in Yokosuka, Japan," the Navy's caption read. "For $27.00 a month they occupy from five to seven rooms furnished complete with electric ranges, telephones, refrigerators and house boys." Japanese would find this breakfast scene odd, in that the maid on the right is wearing far too elaborate a kimono for the occasion.

The few square miles of downtown Tokyo that had been spared by the air raids became known to all as "Little America." Christmas decorations appeared on those streets annually starting in December 1945, almost simultaneously with SCAP's directive ordering the disestablishment of state Shinto and the absolute separation of church and state. American flags hung from the numerous large buildings the foreigners had taken over, whereas any display of the Japanese rising-sun flag ("the meatball" in GI slang) was severely restricted and singing of the national anthem prohibited; a man who improperly displayed the national flag in Yokohama in June 1948 was sentenced to six months' imprisonment at hard labor.[8]

Thousands upon thousands of Americans worked and played in Little America. They renamed streets and buildings (there was a MacArthur Boulevard and an Ernie Pyle Theater, for example), and clogged the area with jeeps, military buses, and new automobiles brought over from the United States. In a daily vignette that perfectly symbolized the U.S.–Japan relationship, an American MP and a Japanese policeman directed traffic together at the busy Hibiya intersection—with the Japanese always giving his signals a moment after the MP's. "We could walk from one end to the other" of Little America, the wife of an American colonel recalled, "without being out of sight of an American face or an American vehicle." This gave the occupiers a sense of familiarity and security—and provided a stark contrast to the surrounding "mile upon mile of wasteland, heaped with ashes, charred wood and rusty metal," where their subjects were attempting to reconstruct their lives.[9] For some, the separation between these two worlds was unbridgable, and properly so. "To me," a woman attached to the occupation as a civilian employee recalled with unbridled contempt, "the world beyond our brightly lighted Allied billets, offices and railroad coaches was largely peopled by warped and ugly creatures from some Oriental Nibelungenlied; often I think I must have stared at them as hard as they ever gaped at any member of the conquering masters."[10]

While Japanese turned to the black market to survive, Americans shopped at PXs and commissaries filled to the brim with luxury items as well as hardy staples. "There was always a crowd of Japanese outside the PX," the colonel's wife observed, "watching the customers come in and out, flattening their noses against the show windows, gazing in silent awe at the display of merchandise: the souvenirs, candy bars, cameras, milk shakes, shoes, wool sweaters, silk kimonos and guaranteed curios of the Orient." Ragged onlookers watched in silence as the Americans staggered out with "meat in fifteen-pound hunks, rice in fifty-pound sacks, vegetables and fruit in mess-size tins." Occasionally the officer's wife deliberately knocked a few loaves of freshly baked bread to the ground while loading her jeep, so that a small, hollow-eyed boy, who always seemed to be present, could make off with them. Even the mustard came in one-gallon jars, obviously more than a healthy American family needed; and so, "rather than have it go bad, the servants ate it with a spoon." Faubion Bowers was visited every morning by a master sergeant who asked, "What do you want?"—to which, in his exuberant retelling, he would reply, "Eighteen chickens and three hamhocks!" He entertained a lot, Bowers explained, but also gave many of these provisions "to the starving Kabuki actors."[11]

As in any colonial enclave, individuals in the conquering force possessed inordinate authority. MacArthur's devoted aide Courtney Whitney, a lawyer who had been his personal attorney before the war, became chief of GHQ's Government Section while still a colonel and exercised decisive influence in supervising the purges, policies regarding the emperor and the imperial institution, revision of the constitution, and all matters pertaining to the cabinet, Diet, electoral system, courts, and civil service. Comparable if not greater power accrued to Major General William Marquat, who had been a professional boxer, journalist, and low-ranking army officer specializing in antiaircraft tactics before emerging as one of MacArthur's trusted aides. Appointed chief of the Economic and Scientific Section, Marquat assumed responsibility for nothing less than supervising all developments in finance, economics, labor, and science, including the dissolution of zaibatsu holding companies and the promotion of economic deconcentration. Every major government financial and economic institution reported to his section, including the Ministry of Finance, the Ministry of Commerce and Industry, the Bank of Japan, the Economic Stabilization Board, the new Ministry of Labor, the Board of Trade, and eventually the new Ministry of International Trade and Industry as well.[12]

Farther down the chain of command, young Americans in their twen-

The hierarchies of race and privilege were apparent in virtually every interaction between victor and vanquished. These GIs, in jinrikisha pulled by yesterday's battlefield foe, posed for a U.S. Army photographer in front of the imperial palace.

ties or thirties, short on practical experience and unversed in the native language, were empowered to tell more elderly Japanese how to conduct their business and rearrange their minds. Individuals who did not speak a second language judged the intelligence of those they dealt with by their competence in English and joked about their pidgin-English mistakes. Americans accused of crimes against Japanese were tried by their own government, not in local courts, and their crimes went unreported in the press. Indeed, any criticism of the alien overlords whatsoever was forbidden. The mass media were not permitted to take issue with SCAP policy or speak negatively of any of the victorious Allied powers, nor were they allowed to mention that they were operating under such restraints.

Although as a rule the victors conducted themselves with far greater discipline than the Japanese military had exercised in occupied areas of Asia, assault and rape inevitably occurred. None of this was reported in the press, and more than a few incidents went unreported to the police as well. Victims had little faith in the possibility of fair redress. After the occupation, mass-circulation magazines ran articles about rapes by American servicemen, and Japanese men resentfully recalled incidents of being randomly, almost whimsically, assaulted in public.[13] The sexual opportunities enjoyed by men affiliated with the occupation forces, including foreign journalists—with their gifts of tinned goods, chocolates, nylon stockings, cigarettes, and liquor—humiliated and infuriated Japanese males. GIs regarded themselves as experts on "Babysan's world" and, in a racial idiom they found amusing, joked that this gave them a unique "slant" on Japan. Some spoke with contempt of the "gook girls." Mixed-blood children became one of the sad, unspoken stories of the occupation—seldom acknowledged by their foreign fathers and invariably ostracized by the Japanese.[14]

In numerous such ways, the contradictions of the democratic revolution from above were clear for all to see: while the victors preached democracy, they ruled by fiat; while they espoused equality, they themselves constituted an inviolate privileged caste. Their reformist agenda rested on the assumption that, virtually without exception, Western culture and its values were superior to those of "the Orient." At the same time, almost every interaction between victor and vanquished was infused with intimations of white supremacism. For all its uniqueness of time, place, and circumstance—all its peculiarly "American" iconoclasm—the occupation was in this sense but a new manifestation of the old racial paternalism that historically accompanied the global expansion of the Western powers. Like their colonialist predecessors, the victors were imbued with a sense of manifest destiny. They spoke of being engaged in the mission of civilizing their subjects. They bore the burden (in their own eyes) of their race, creed, and culture. They swaggered, and were enviously free of self-doubt.

It was inevitable that relations between the victors and the vanquished be unequal, but this inequality was compounded by authoritarian practices that were part and parcel of the American modus operandi independent of the situation in Japan. To begin with, the administrative structure that the Japanese encountered was itself organized in the most rigid hierarchical manner imaginable. MacArthur's command, after all, was a military bureaucracy, the very organizational antithesis of democratic checks and balances. The caste distinction between officers and enlisted men was hard and fast, and each individual's "proper place" in the chain of command minutely prescribed. Women were excluded from authority in this governing apparatus. Blacks were segregated and relegated to low-ranking positions.

This working *model* of authoritarian governance was compounded by the manner in which the occupation regime implemented its directives. Contrary to the practice of direct military government adopted in defeated Germany, this occupation was conducted "indirectly"—that is, through existing organs of government. This entailed buttressing the influence of two of the most undemocratic institutions of the presurrender regime: the bureaucracy and the throne. As with the basic reform agenda itself, the decision to rely on already existing machineries of government was formalized at the eleventh hour. Until the literal eve of arrival, MacArthur and his staff were operating under secret orders, code-named "Blacklist," that called for the establishment of direct military government. These plans were altered in the "Initial Post-Surrender Policy" document, which stipulated that "the Supreme Commander will exercise his authority through Japanese governmental machinery and agencies, including the Emperor, to the extent that this satisfactorily furthers United States objectives."[15]

The rationale behind this fundamental policy change was eminently practical: the occupation force lacked the linguistic and technocratic capacity to effectively govern the country directly. In principle, the supreme commander retained the authority to change the existing machinery of government, depose Emperor Hirohito, even eliminate the imperial institution altogether if given approval to do so by his superiors in Washington. In practice, these options never were given serious consideration. Although the military establishment was eliminated and the repressive

Home Ministry dismantled, the civilian bureaucracy was left essentially untouched and the emperor was retained. The American proconsuls depended so heavily on an indigenous technocratic elite to implement their directives that, under SCAP's aegis, the bureaucracy actually attained greater authority and influence than it had possessed even at the height of the mobilization for war.[16]

In the end, MacArthur's imperious personal role as the supreme symbol of the new democratic nation would be transferred back to the emperor who had reigned through all the years of repression, war, and atrocity; and GHQ's modus operandi as a "super-government" would be carried on, long after the conquerors departed, by the bureaucratic mandarins it had left in place. Still, Japan would be a different country after the victors who arrived as reformist viceroys finally left. It would take a Jonathan Swift to do full justice to such political and ideological convolutions. And this was only the half of it.

Reevaluating the Monkey-Men

The very notion of democratizing Japan represented a stunning revision of the propaganda Americans had imbibed during the war, when the media had routinely depicted all Japanese as children, savages, sadists, madmen, or robots. In the most pervasive metaphor of dehumanization, they were portrayed in word and picture as apes, "jaundiced baboons," or, most often, plain "monkey-men." There had been scant place in popular consciousness for "good Japanese," as there usually had been for "good Germans." The wartime incarceration of over one hundred thousand American citizens and residents of Japanese ancestry, with scarcely a murmur of protest, was stark testimony to this animus. In *On to Tokyo*, an instructional film produced by the War Department after Germany had been defeated and the Nazi concentration camps exposed, General George Marshall, the chairman of the joint chiefs of staff, took care to emphasize that the "barbarism" of the Japanese "has even exceeded that of the Germans." In the War Department's *Know Your Enemy—Japan*, which was released only weeks before surrender, the Japanese were relentlessly depicted as a people devoid of individuality, as alike as "photographic prints off the same negative."[17]

This was hardly promising material for a democratic revolution. Once policy shifted from killing the monkey-men to turning them into democrats, it became necessary to reeducate not merely the Japanese but the American public as well. Demeaning and dehumanizing wartime stereotypes had to be corrected. When it still was assumed that direct military government would be imposed in defeated Japan, for example, Americans being trained at the Civil Affairs Staging Area in California were given instructional materials couched in the following terms:

> Under the heat of wartime emotions the Japanese were commonly seen as treacherous, brutal, sadistic, and fanatical "monkey-men."
> It is true that individuals and even groups have at various times demonstrated these traits—as witness the rape of Nanking, Bataan, Pearl Harbor, etc. Without attempting to defend or excuse the Japanese for these horrors it should be emphasized that it is a mistake to think that all Japanese are predominantly the monkey-man type. It would be just as wrong to picture all Americans as constantly being engaged in mob-lynching, gangsterism and race rioting.

A "realistic, balanced knowledge of the Japanese character," the civil affairs guide went on to explain, would equate Japanese treachery with an extreme manifestation of the Western notion that "all's fair in love and war." In this regard, they simply went too far and did not understand or appreciate the Western sense of fair play. Where wartime acts of brutality and sadism were concerned, these were to be understood as the outbursts of men who had been subjected to a lifetime of repression. In the words of the military handbook, "The docile, meek little Japanese when put in uniform, ruthlessly trained and turned loose, has an opportunity for the first time in his life to express himself, and he may go completely berserk, indulging in outrageous orgies of terror and brutality." When all was said and done, however, the despised "monkey-men" were not in fact all that different from other people:

> There are other traits of character—reliability, ingenuity, industriousness, thrift, bravery, aggressiveness, honesty. With some exceptions, depending on individual personality, sex, age, social standing, income, profession and so forth, the average Japanese displays these characteristics in about the same manner and measure as other people in other lands.[18]

Other materials directed to American audiences, especially troops assigned to occupation duty, similarly endeavored to convey the notion that the "little Japanese" were almost humans like themselves. In November 1945, when the War Department sent a short instructional film titled *Our Job in Japan* over to SCAP for viewing by occupation forces, officials demanded that the film be revised because it still hewed too closely to the wartime portrayal of the Japanese as dangerous and untrustworthy. In the altered version received early in 1946, grisly images of the "disgusting, revolting, obscene" war they had waged were offset, in the film's final minutes, by footage depicting friendly Americans mingling with attractive, earnest Japanese women and children.[19]

Our Job in Japan began with the observation that the Japanese were a people "trained to play follow-the-leader." The problem the victors faced could be stated in a word: it was the Japanese *brain,* which could "make trouble" or "make sense." Viewers were presented with a close-up of a Japanese man's head in profile—and then watched as a literal representation of a spongelike brain filled his cranium and expanded until the head itself was obliterated and the brain, now gigantic, held the center of the screen, floating against a background of countless other tiny brains crowded together like so many beans in a box. "Our problem's in the brain inside of the Japanese head," the narrator intoned. "There are seventy million of these in Japan, physically no different than any other brains in the world, actually all made of exactly the same stuff as ours. These brains, like our brains, can do good things [here appeared a still photo of a bearded elderly man, seemingly in a Christian church] or bad things [the screen now showed a famous wartime atrocity photo of a Japanese beheading a kneeling, blond soldier], all depending on the kind of ideas that are put inside."

Throughout the film, that giant brain repeatedly materialized and receded, while the GI audience was informed of the terrible things it had been taught by the "warlords" and the "military gang." Turning ancient Shinto beliefs into a weapon of modern indoctrination, the militarists had saturated that brain with "ancient nightmares" and "ancient hatreds," with "bloody fairy tales and pagan superstitions," with the "mumbojumbo" of a "murky past." When the narrator made passing reference to "an old, backward, superstitious country," the screen showed scenes of people burning incense outside a Buddhist temple.

In wartime propaganda films, it was standard practice to convey the utterly alien nature of the enemy by introducing jarring montages of the "most exotic" Japanese behavior—such as footage depicting seasonal festivals and traditional dances, in which distinctive garments were worn and the accompanying music was inevitably atonal and offensive to Western ears. *Our Job in Japan* exploited this familiar formula, while the toughtalking narrator proceeded to hammer home another basic theme: all

Japanese were indoctrinated to believe—and here the point was deemed so central that it was printed across the screen as well—that "The Sun Goddess Created the Japanese to Rule all Other Peoples of the Earth." Although Japan's leaders in fact had never contemplated "world conquest," this had been a staple of wartime American propaganda and was not about to be repudiated now. On the contrary, it was averred that this was the most basic idea "that was sold to the Japanese brain"; and this, in turn, clarified the victor's task. "That same brain today remains the problem, our problem," the narrator intoned. "It will cost us time, it will cost us patience. But we are determined that this fact will sink in: THIS IS JAPAN'S LAST WAR." For emphasis, these last words were again emblazoned across the screen.

Turning to the demilitarization policies already under way in the defeated nation, the film suddenly became lyrical, surely reflecting the more positive outlook that SCAP had demanded. Smiling GIs were shown talking with kimono-clad women no longer gyrating in strange dances or singing in nasal voices, sharing a book with an earnest boy, receiving a bouquet of flowers from a doll-like girl. The Americans would be vigilant and tough with tricksters, the narrator declared, "but the honest ones, the sincere ones, the ones who really want to make sense are being given every opportunity they need. At the same time, these people, these honest ones, are looking to us to help them prove that our idea is better than the Japanese idea." Their job, the GIs were told, was simply to be themselves:

> By being ourselves we can prove that what we like to call the American way, or democracy, or just plain old Golden Rule common sense, is a pretty good way to live. We can prove that most Americans don't believe in pushing people around, even when we happen to be on top. We can prove that most Americans do believe in a fair break for everybody, regardless of race or creed or color [two black GIs flitted across the screen at this point, hitherto and hereafter invisible].

Our Job in Japan was a near-perfect expression of an American sense of righteous mission and manifest destiny, not to speak of secular saintliness. It was America's task, the film concluded, to enable the Japanese to read, speak, and hear the truth; and "when they've read enough truth, when they've heard enough truth, when they've had enough first-hand experience with the truth, they'll be able to lead their own lives" in a constructive and peaceful manner. With the Liberty Bell tolling on screen, the narrator summed it all up:

> We're here to make it clear to the Japanese brain that we've had
> enough of this bloody barbaric business to last us from here on in.
> We're here to make it clear to the Japanese that the time has now
> come to make sense—modern, civilized sense. That is our job in
> Japan.

Much of the film's footage, apart from its concluding images of a ruined and occupied land, had been cannibalized from earlier wartime films.
Conspicuously missing when compared with propaganda such as *Know
Your Enemy—Japan* were any critical references to the emperor, reflecting SCAP's belief that the imperial brain, too, was capable of being democratized. The most striking aspect of the film, apart from its eerie
floating brains, however, was its fundamentally optimistic message. Neither blood, culture, nor history drove the Japanese to war, but rather socialization and indoctrination of recent vintage. When all was said and
done, reeducation did not in fact seem to be such an insuperable task. The
title of an article in the weekly *Saturday Evening Post* four months after
surrender captured the new outlook succinctly: "The G.I. Is Civilizing the
Jap."[20]

The Experts and the Obedient Herd

In characterizing the Japanese as people "trained to play follow-the-
leader," the War Department film was tapping into a conservative view
that carried great implications for the development of democracy. Among
the American and British elites who claimed special knowledge of Japan,
this observation was virtually gospel; and to many of these specialists, the
logical inference was that any notion of inducing a democratic revolution
from above was absurd. With few exceptions, the "old Japan hands" were
second to none in belittling the capacity of ordinary Japanese to govern
themselves.

In Washington, by far the best known expert on Japan during the war
was Joseph Grew, the undersecretary of state who had served as ambassador to Tokyo from 1931 to 1941. In May 1945, Grew told President Truman that while the imperial institution was undeniably a relic of feudalism,
"from the long range point of view the best we can hope for in Japan is
the development of a constitutional monarchy, experience having shown
that democracy in Japan would never work." Eugene Dooman, a language

specialist and Grew's key advisor on things Japanese, similarly emphasized that the country was "a communalism, that is a graduated society, in which the top of the social structure formulated purposes and objectives and the people down below conformed." The emperor capped this social hierarchy and performed the crucial role of providing social cohesion as "a living manifestation of the racial continuity of the Japanese people." Joseph Ballantine, another influential Japanese-speaking specialist in the State Department, thought the notion of bringing forth new political leadership was ludicrous, for ordinary Japanese were simply "inert and tradition bound."[21]

British Asia specialists tended to be similarly disdainful. Prior to the surrender, for instance, the prestigious Royal Institute of International Affairs issued an influential report that referred to the Japanese people as an "obedient herd"—a standard phrase of the time—and expressed grave "misgivings regarding Japanese ability to operate democratic institutions." In the opening stages of the occupation, the British representative in Tokyo used the formation of a new cabinet under Shidehara Kijūrō—a former ambassador to London famous for his impeccable English—as an occasion for wiring the Foreign Office that the Japanese were "as little fitted for self-government in a modern world as any African tribe, though much more dangerous."[22]

Such views, which gained wide currency in the writings of journalists and academics who also enjoyed reputations for being Asia experts, reflected something more complex than just ethnocentric contempt for the "obedient herd" or "monstrous beehive" (another pet phrase) of Orientals. Many Western experts, diplomats in particular, had spent a good part of their careers ingratiating themselves in upper-class circles in Japan. When they spoke disdainfully of the capacity of ordinary Japanese to govern themselves, they were reflecting not only their own elitism but also the reverential monarchism and fearful contempt for "the masses" they had heard their Japanese counterparts express time and again.[23]

Had these erstwhile Asia experts had their way, the very notion of inducing a democratic revolution would have died of ridicule at an early stage. As happened instead, the ridicule was deflected by the views of experts of a different ilk—behavioral scientists who chose to emphasize the "malleability" of the Japanese "national character," along with planners and policy makers of liberal and left-wing persuasions who sincerely believed that democratic values were universal in their nature and appeal. Although these latter viewpoints pulled in opposite directions, toward the "particularistic" on the one hand and "universal" on the other, both offered reasons to be optimistic that democratic institutions could indeed be established in Japan.

The wartime mobilization of behavioral scientists attracted an impressive contingent of American and British anthropologists, sociologists, psychologists, and psychiatrists into the general areas of intelligence analysis and psychological warfare. By the final year of the war, their work had led them to the conclusion that the Japanese national character was pendulumlike, capable of swinging from one extreme to another—and consequently capable of shifting from fanatical militarism to some form of qualified democracy. Numerous variations on this theme were offered in confidential intelligence reports, all essentially in one way or another imposing the findings of individual clinical psychology on the Japanese as a collectivity.

A representative sample of where such thinking led can be seen in a routine paper prepared for the U.S. Office of War Information (OWI) in December 1944, which observed that "the Japanese civilization pattern seems to be most closely akin to the clinical picture of an obsessional neurosis." Such neurosis, it was argued, was manifest in their concern with "ritual and avoidness [sic]," as well as in their masochism, violent reaction to frustration, and "general rigidity of behavior." Insofar as future policy was concerned, the most interesting "practical upshot" of this diagnosis lay in the question the OWI investigator posed: "Which are the individuals and social groups who set the pattern of thoughts and attitudes likely to be imitated by the rest of Japan?"[24]

Practical responses to this familiar query took several forms. As suggested most famously by the cultural anthropologist Ruth Benedict, a member of the OWI intelligence team, the Japanese were said to behave in accordance with situational or particularistic ethics, as opposed to so-called universal values as in the Western tradition. The same person might be polite and generous under some circumstances, harsh and callous under others. What mattered was the social context and the individual's prescribed role in each and every situation. In exceptional circumstances, where roles and constraints had not been defined, the individual had no core values, no clear subjectified self, to fall back on.

More particularly, the analysis went, the Japanese responded submissively to authority. This was the social scientists' more circumspect way of referring to an "obedient herd," and it would soon provide a good basis for rationalizing policies that promoted democracy under the emperor's aegis. Such OWI analysts as Clyde Kluckhohn and Alexander Leighton, who went on to distinguished academic careers, argued that the emperor, the supreme authority in Japan, was fundamentally an empty vessel. Just as he had been followed as the embodiment of ultranationalism, so he would be followed if turned into a symbol of some sort of imperial democracy. All this seemed to have been borne out by the American experience with POWs. Many of these prisoners had been captured against their will, unconscious or severely injured and so unable either to fight to the bitter end or to take their own lives. As prisoners, however, they quickly proved docile and obedient to their captors, even to the point of assisting in drafting surrender appeals to their erstwhile comrades. This experience gave analysts further grounds for believing that, by an adroit combination of authority, example, and symbolic manipulation, the victors could provide a "democratic" model, however modest, that postwar Japanese might seek to imitate and emulate.

The cautious optimism of this revised vision was itself soon challenged. With the benefit of hindsight, it is possible to look back on the last half year of the Pacific War not only as murderous folly on the part of the imperial government, but also as a futile prolongation of conflict that permitted the emergence of a more radical occupation policy in Washington. Had Japan surrendered in early 1945, as the emperor was strongly urged to do by some intimate advisors, the country would not merely have been spared the air raids, atomic bombs, and deaths of well over a million of its people; it also might have escaped the occupation's revolution from above. As of early 1945, there was no plan to induce a democratic revolution in the defeated nation. The old Japan hands who still controlled postsurrender planning anticipated a mild reform agenda at best.

The more progressive, less racially and culturally condescending argument that ultimately shaped much of postsurrender policy emerged from several overlapping groups: New Deal liberals, leftists, and Asia specialists more associated with China than Japan. The New Dealers—whose influence over domestic policy was waning as the war entered its final stage—placed their faith in the universal applicability of democratic ideals, aspirations, and policies. Such "universalism" held that people everywhere were fundamentally the same and that the ideal government was one in which all individuals were equal before the law. At the same time, the bedrock principles of democratization espoused by the New Dealers contained a strong component of economic democracy, which in practical terms meant the active encouragement of organized labor, opposition to excessive concentrations of economic power, and policies aimed at ensuring a more equitable distribution of wealth. In addition, of course, the New

Dealers had few compunctions about supporting interventionist governmental policies to achieve their goals.[25]

Where the liberal New Deal approach minimized the significance of cultural constraints in Japan, a more radical line of analysis—found in left-wing publications such as *Amerasia* as well as the Institute of Pacific Relations periodicals *Far Eastern Survey* and *Pacific Affairs*—called attention to the existence of a genuine potential for democratization from below. Leftists denounced support of the emperor and the old-guard civilian "moderates" as appeasement. At the same time, they applauded the revolutionary potential of the lower-class groups that the old Japan hands deemed incapable of democracy—or, worse yet, highly susceptible to Communist demagoguery.

To T. A. Bisson, the prolific editor of *Pacific Affairs*, authentic "liberals" were to be found among men and women "who led political parties, trade unions, or peasant organizations that were suppressed prior to 1941" and had "spoken publicly and unequivocally against the war, and have perhaps languished in jail for their temerity." Only such Japanese, Bisson argued, could establish a new order that was truly "based on the will of the people and dedicated to democracy and peace."[26] In his book *Dilemma in Japan*, published in September 1945 and sometimes referred to as "the Bible" for radical reformers in the early stages of the occupation, the young left-wing researcher Andrew Roth similarly argued that a true potential for democracy was to be found among industrial workers, peasants, students recruited for onerous war work, small shopkeepers, political prisoners, brutalized and disillusioned ex-soldiers, and former prisoners of war in China who had been subjected to "anti-fascist" reeducation by such Japanese Communists as Okano Susumu (the pseudonym of Nosaka Sanzō) in Yenan and Kaji Wataru in Chungking.[27]

As the Pacific War entered its final stages, such views gained greater prominence in the government and in the media. At the same time, the Japan experts increasingly came to be regarded as special pleaders for the conservative causes of their Japanese contacts and acquaintances, as men befuddled and bamboozled by too many elegant, silken prewar encounters with the privileged. In the State Department, such criticism of the "Japan crowd" arose primarily among those who had been more involved with China. Such individuals, the "China crowd," were harsher in their critique of the civilian Japanese elites and more sanguine about the possibilities of cracking open the structures and institutions of ruling-class control to release democratic forces from below. They rejected, among other orthodoxies, the Japan crowd's depiction of the zaibatsu leaders as "moderate" businessmen and argued that the existing economic system itself was one of the "roots of war" that had to be dug out and eliminated.

The best-known public spokesman for the views of the China crowd was Owen Lattimore, a distinguished, if caustic, scholar of China and central Asia. Although British, Lattimore was a conspicuous figure on the American scene—teaching at Johns Hopkins University, editing *Pacific Affairs* before the war, working for OWI after Pearl Harbor, and serving as a regular consultant to the State Department. In 1945, he reached out for a popular audience with a short, polemical book, *Solution in Asia,* in which he skewered the Japan crowd. The only "solution" for postwar Asia, as he saw it, was the thoroughgoing democratization of Japan, combined with a maximal leveling of economic capabilities throughout Asia. Otherwise, Japan would sooner or later resume its exploitative, imperialist policies. Reparations would be one step toward such leveling, serious economic deconcentration of the economy another.[28]

The "Japan crowd" and "China crowd" were of course emblematic terms in a complex struggle over the evaluation of Japan's prospects for democracy. Much of this debate took place behind the scenes in Washington, and the issue did not come to a head until the final weeks of the war, when critics of Grew and his backers emerged triumphant in the State Department and also found support in the War Department, where a sympathetic assistant secretary of war, John J. McCloy, was directing the revision and finalization of basic policies for Japan. This shift in influence reflected broader policy struggles within the bureaucracy and was, in part, related to the change of guard that occurred in the wake of President Roosevelt's death.[29]

In symbolic terms, the eclipse of the conservative Japan specialists can be precisely dated. On August 11, 1945, Dean Acheson replaced Grew as undersecretary of state, and Acheson's comments soon thereafter about eradicating the forces in Japan that made for a "will to war" reflected his identification with the more radical reformers. In a striking insult to the Japan crowd, the first State Department appointee as political adviser to MacArthur was George Atcheson, Jr., a China specialist, rather than one of the department's senior Japan experts such as Dooman or Ballantine. In the years that followed, the advisory missions that regularly shuttled between Washington and Tokyo invariably comprised well-briefed technical experts. One would be hard pressed to find a single Japan specialist among them.

At GHQ headquarters in Tokyo, Japan specialists were likewise conspicuous by their absence. In his unique way, the supreme commander himself exemplified this. He was, in many ways, the most ethnocentric of men, given to extraordinary generalizations about the "Oriental" personality. "The general," President Truman was informed by an envoy to Tokyo in mid-October of 1945, "stated that Oriental peoples suffer from an inferiority complex which leads them to 'childish brutality' when they conquer in war and to slavish dependence when they lose." Yet at the same time, MacArthur was also capable of speaking expansively about the irrelevance of "racial characteristics"; and, even in the midst of the war, he had often taken time to expound on how "the lands touching the Pacific with their billions of inhabitants will determine the course of history . . . for the next ten thousand years."

The supreme commander had no serious first-hand experience with Japan, apart from war. There is no evidence that he read widely about the country, apart from intelligence reports. He did talk on occasion with knowledgeable, non-elitist scholars such as the Canadian historian and diplomat E. H. Norman, but most of his "conversations" tended to end up as monologues. Bowers observed that MacArthur rarely if ever asked his staff questions about the country, and he certainly did not seek information from the Japanese themselves. His only guides, he often intimated, were Washington, Lincoln, and Jesus Christ (pictures of the first two adorned the walls of his office in Tokyo); and, essentially, he seemed to operate on the assumption that the four of them together could—with help from the emperor—"democratize" Japan. However one may categorize this mixture of prejudice, presumption, and grand bromides, it was not to be confused with expertise on Japan or Asia. It did, however, enable MacArthur to throw himself wholeheartedly behind the early agenda of "demilitarization and democratization" with an almost messianic zeal.[30]

From top to bottom, the general's "super-government" in Tokyo reflected an aversion to area specialists as such. Colonel Charles Kades, an exemplary New Dealer who would play a pivotal role in such critical Government Section initiatives as the drafting of a new constitution, later spoke frankly of his own background in this regard. "I had no knowledge whatsoever about Japan's history or culture or myths," he recalled. "I was blank on Japan, except of course I knew about the atrocities that had occurred during the war and I was aware of their expansion into China and Southeast Asia. But I had no knowledge other than what one would glean from a daily newspaper about Japan."[31]

There were exceptions, but by and large Kades's case was typical. Indeed, at the level of daily operations GHQ appears deliberately to have excluded most individuals who possessed even slight credentials in Japanese matters. The several thousand Americans trained in Japanese language and culture during the war in anticipation of being assigned to military-government duties often found themselves sent elsewhere than Japan. MacArthur and his staff did not want them. Of those who actually made it there, some were shunted off to Okinawa—an American version of exile to the gulag, where U.S. policy eschewed reform and focused instead on turning the war-savaged archipelago into an impregnable military base. Alternatively, these bright, eager, new speakers of Japanese might be assigned to the Eighth Army in Yokohama and deposited at the lowest level of occupation activity: grass-roots prefectural work. Whatever their ultimate assignment, they were excluded from serious policy-making positions. As the consummate GHQ insider Theodore Cohen put it, "they were firmly kept out of Tokyo." Rather than utilize these neophyte Japan specialists, SCAP conducted an intensive "in-house" recruitment campaign to tap the numerous "lawyers, bankers, economists, industrial technicians," and other professionals who willy-nilly happened to find themselves in Japan at war's end.[32]

Alfred Oppler, a jurist born and educated in Germany who was recruited to assume the heady responsibility of overseeing revision of all civil and penal codes, was a perfect product of this cult of exclusion. When interviewed by an Army colonel, Oppler "volunteered the confession that, although I had some familiarity with European affairs, I did not have any knowledge of things Japanese."

He could not have advanced his case more felicitously. "Oh, that is quite all right," the colonel responded. "If you knew too much about Japan, you might be prejudiced. We do not like old Japan hands."[33]

chapter seven

EMBRACING REVOLUTION

When Kobayashi Masaki was finally repatriated after being detained for a year by the U.S. military to perform labor services in Okinawa, he was astonished at the political scene that greeted him. "Japan had become extremely democratic," he recalled. "Everyone was moving in that direction. Everyone was racing off in the direction of a democratic kind of humanist freedom and union activity." Kobayashi, who went on to become a distinguished director of antiwar and humanistic films, had grave misgivings about this sudden enthusiastic embrace of democracy. "The conformism seemed just the same as before the war, only then everyone had jumped on the militarist band wagon," he observed. "I don't mean that the change of consciousness was necessarily wrong, it's just in the *way* it happened."[1]

From a different perspective, Yoshida Shigeru also expressed grave reservations about the "democratic revolution." The gruff, English-speaking Yoshida served as foreign minister and a chief liaison to SCAP shortly after the surrender, headed a hapless coalition cabinet of his own in 1946–1947, and returned to the premiership with greater staying power and effectiveness in late 1948. He is given credit for one of the more enduring conservative witticisms of the occupation period. Whenever he thought of GHQ, the joke went, what ran through his mind was "Go Home Quickly."[2]

Contrary to Yoshida's hopes, the Americans stayed and stayed; and contrary to his expectations, he and his conservative allies found it impossible to completely undo the reformist agenda. The neocolonial revolution did force the ruling structure to introduce and institutionalize progressive reforms that would not otherwise have been undertaken; and despite the doubts of conservatives and progressives alike, the popular forces released by these policies often proved to be vigorous, diverse, resilient, even radical. Although Yoshida held on to the premiership until the end of 1954 and was credited with leading postwar Japan's conservative resurgence, he later reflected ruefully on his accomplishments. "There was this idea at the back of my mind," he observed of his government's inescapable acquiescence to the reformist agenda, "that whatever needed to be revised after we regained our independence could be revised then. But once a thing has been decided on, it is not so easy to have it altered."[3]

Embracing the Commander

In Japanese parlance, the conformism that Kobayashi worried about and non-Japanese observers ridiculed as the psychology of the "obedient herd" usually was framed in more benign terms. Particularly in rural areas, where most people still lived or had their roots, this was simply *junpū bizoku*, "good morals and manners." A strong sense of hierarchy and proper place was integral to such consciousness, but this was hardly the whole of it. "Good morals and manners" also encompassed a cultural world of values, activities, and symbols that were familiar and comforting. The rising-sun flag and national anthem, both banned by GHQ, were associated with this world of "beautiful customs." So were village festivals and portable shrines, folk dances, traditional weddings and funerals, lachrymose popular songs, tea ceremonies, the martial arts, filial piety, diligence and industriousness, respect for elders, a catalog of feminine virtues, a romanticized sense of tension between "duty" and "emotion" *(giri* and *ninjō)*, considerations of appearance and "face," esteem for harmony *(wa)*, and so on. Sentimental as well as slavish attitudes toward the emperor were part of this popular consciousness. So also, in many instances, was a healthy skepticism toward overly Westernized or overly facile intellectuals.[4]

When informed that such attitudes and practices might impede certain projected reforms, one GHQ section chief imperiously retorted, "Make them change their folkways."[5] This was easier said than done, of course; but the larger question was how extensively the "folkways" really needed to be changed to lay the groundwork for a meaningful grass-roots acceptance of the victors' revolution from above. Although such "old consciousness," as the scholar Hidaka Rokurō called it, may not have seemed particularly ripe for democratization, neither was it inherently hopelessly reactionary. As it turned out, spontaneous popular responses to the victors and their policies were more vigorous than almost anyone had predicted, and ideologically more ambiguous.

This was dramatically reflected in the response to General MacArthur personally and to GHQ more generally. Japanese at all levels of society embraced the new supreme commander with an ardor hitherto reserved for the emperor, and commonly treated GHQ with the deference they had until recently accorded their own military leaders. Obviously, such behavior seemed to lend credence to the fear that the new vogue of "democracy" was little more than the old obsequiousness in new garb. The reasons people gave for embracing the victors varied greatly, however, and often were intensely personal.

One of the most unexpected responses to SCAP's policies took the form of letters and postcards addressed directly to General MacArthur or simply to GHQ. Hundreds of these arrived daily throughout the occupation, and although some involved organized petitions or letter-writing campaigns, the great majority reflected spontaneous individual initiatives. Virtually all such communications were read and analyzed by occupation personnel. Many were translated, or at least summarized in English, and eventually between three and four thousand of them ended up in General MacArthur's personal files. Much of the supreme commander's optimism about peace and democracy being sincerely embraced by ordinary Japanese may well have come from reading these remarkable (and carefully screened) communications.

There was a brief prologue to this correspondence. On August 31, 1945, media coverage of MacArthur's arrival was complemented by almost equal attention to the comments of Prime Minister Higashikuni, who urged his compatriots to express their hopes and concerns by writing him directly. Although this was part of the government's campaign to defuse anger and stifle protest, it was nonetheless an unprecedented solicitation of popular opinion. Within a few days, forty to fifty letters and postcards began arriving at the prime minister's residence daily. On October 1, the *Mainichi* reported that responses had reached a peak of 1,371 in one day.

The collapse of the Higashikuni Cabinet on October 5 ended this flow of missives to the prime minister, but not the flow itself. On the contrary, it soon became a torrent directed to the supreme commander and his staff.

When General MacArthur's name was raised as a possible Republican
candidate for president in 1948, many Japanese, including the proprietor of
this optimistically named "instant construction company," took the occasion
to express their admiration of the supreme commander and his policies.

SCAP's own records do not reveal a tabulation of communications received
during the first year of occupation, when the correspondence was greatest. For the period from September 1946 through May 1951, however, the
official record cites 441,161 letters and cards read and processed by the Allied Translator and Interpreter Service (ATIS). These letters and cards
came from all walks of life—some written in English, the great majority
in Japanese. Most writers identified themselves and wrote with great emotion. Professor Sodei Rinjirō, who has edited and analyzed a fascinating
sample of this correspondence, observes that this was an unparalleled exchange between a vanquished people and their conquerors—involving, in
the end, unsolicited communications from roughly three-quarters of 1 percent of the adult population.[6]

As vetted for the supreme commander, these communications certainly fed his vanity, for he was addressed with veneration and profusely thanked for his boundless generosity. Writers praised the general's "exalted and godlike benevolence" and called him a "living savior." An elderly man in Aomori wrote of worshipping MacArthur's portrait mornings and evenings just as he had done previously with the emperor's portrait. A local cultural association in the Kobe area commissioned a Japanese-style painting of Christ delivering the Sermon on the Mount and presented this to MacArthur with a letter equating his leadership with this sublime moment.[7] The general was praised for his Buddhalike compassion, likened to the "friend from afar" mentioned in the Confucian *Analects*, venerated for having liberated the Japanese from the nightmare of war, thanked for having given hope and happiness to people who initially were terrified by the unknown prospects of alien occupation.[8] Ordinary men and women confessed their past militarist sins to him as if he were a priest. They unburdened themselves of their deepest fears and hopes as to a psychiatrist. They equated him with the great transmogrified concept of these years: love. Their letters over and over again spoke of peace and democracy, as if the words themselves were talismans. The supreme commander may have been likened to the emperor in his august power, but clearly he was deemed more approachable, more directly accessible. Here lay the paradox, and challenge, of an authoritarianism that offered the promise of democracy.

MacArthur was also showered with gifts—and, more often than not, accepted them. Although it was traditional practice to give gifts to superiors and benefactors, the number of offerings to the alien overlord exceeded anything the former military leaders had elicited. Some gestures were modest and charming. A fisherman wrote MacArthur in the midsummer heat of 1948 to say that he had been thinking deeply about how to express his heartfelt gratitude that the general, "with your outstanding ideas and capabilities," was making it possible for the Japanese to achieve "what we could not have attained even in many years of bloody struggle." All he could do, the writer had concluded, was share what he knew best—the river fish *(ayu)* he caught for a living, which were now at their "fattest and most delicious." He looked forward to hearing when it might be convenient for MacArthur to join him catching and eating these local fish. By contrast, the most formal and elaborate of the gifts to MacArthur was surely a brocade kimono and sash. The embroiderer had secluded himself in Kyoto's Shimo Kamo Shrine in November 1946 and spent three years on his task, praying each day and ultimately working some 70 million stitches into his masterpiece. In this instance, the gift was accompanied by a Shinto prayer and offered to the general "as a symbol of the pure hearts of our 70 million people"—each stitch obviously meant to represent one living Japanese.[9]

Between the dancing fish and the ornate brocade, an amazing cascade of gifts and invitations fell on the supreme commander. He received dolls, lamps, ceramics, lacquer work, bamboo products, feudal manuscripts, books, miniaturized *bonsai* trees, *bonkei* tray landscapes, animal skins, armor, and swords, as well as paintings and sculptures that sometimes included renderings of himself. MacArthur was sixty-five years old when the occupation began and his age not only enhanced his aura of wisdom but also prompted writers to express sincere concern for his continued good health. This led to innumerable gifts of canes and walking sticks (as well as at least one girdlelike stomach supporter). Fruits and flowers arrived in season, along with edibles such as mushrooms, tea, red beans, lotus roots, mountain potatoes, salted salmon, dried chestnuts, soybeans, honey, rice, and rice cakes.

Officials and prominent citizens from Kanagawa Prefecture stand with a bronze bust of MacArthur presented to him in the name of the people of the prefecture on the occasion of his seventy-first birthday in January 1951. The general received gifts beyond counting.

A Japanese baker begged permission to come and bake a birthday cake for the supreme commander (his request was accepted). A group of aborigine Ainu in Hokkaido killed a deer and sent MacArthur the skin and antlers "as a token of our grateful appreciation for what he has done to secure land for our people and give to Japan a democratic society, based on law and order." A dozen live hens arrived and became part of the "embassy farm." A canary with an auspicious black cross on its head was sent as a gift. So were two hanging scrolls dating from 1935, on which, in minuscule ideographs, the entire Bible was allegedly written. One elated citizen celebrated the coming into effect of the new constitution by sending the general a fan on both sides of which he had written, again in tiny characters, the entire national charter. A ten-year-old youngster kept a daily journal about the development of a pumpkin he grew from seeds received from the United States and made a copy of this for the general. His father contributed an oil painting of the full-grown pumpkin, and his mother wrote the letter accompanying this collective family expression of thanks. In most cases, these gifts were offered as simple expressions of gratitude to the supreme commander, not as the more calculated ritual gestures of reciprocity and dependency that characterized gift giving in the purely Japanese context (or in the shrewd politics that lay behind gifts from the imperial household or prominent public and corporate figures to MacArthur and other SCAP officials).[10]

Most of the letters, cards, and petitions sent to the supreme commander and his headquarters addressed the specific concerns as well as hopes of the writers. Well over half dealt with the repatriation of family and acquaintances from overseas. Many focused on specific economic problems and policies. A small but striking percentage of the mail directed to GHQ involved fingering individuals whom the writers believed should be arrested, purged, or even brought to trial as war criminals. Local residents denounced officials who had been oppressive during the war. High-school and university students called attention to militaristic teachers. Former military men volunteered the names of individuals who had abused Allied POWs. Specific organizations, including religious sects, were identified as having promoted ultranationalism. Denouncing others extended to the contemporary scene as well. Complaints were submitted about the behavior of the local police; names were named in connection with hoarding, black-market activity, corruption, and gangsterism; people were reported for having hidden their heirloom swords instead of turning them in as ordered by SCAP; individuals were denounced for harboring "anti-American" or "anti-democratic" sentiments. Judging only by such relentless missives as these, one might be forgiven for concluding that yesterday's nation of patriots had turned into a nation of informers. Another startling category of letters urged that the country be annexed or turned into a permanent colony by the United States. Otherwise, some such writers declared, the democratic reforms would soon be undone.[11]

It was not always a pretty picture, and one ATIS translator, a Japanese-American whose family originally came from Okinawa, told Professor Sodei that reading such letters had actually made him despise the Japanese. They seemed to be weather vanes, many felt, turning as the wind blew. Yet they also turned in many individual directions; and the very fact that hundreds of thousands of people felt motivated to express their views openly to the new authorities was not an inconsequential development. Although these communications usually expressed support for occupation policies, ordinary men and women did not hesitate to offer criticism and advice. Protect the emperor, many letters entreated, a few written in blood or at least sealed with a bloody thumbprint. Get rid of the throne, advised a much smaller contingent. (The emperor was the biggest egotist in Japan, wrote one writer; he was a "vampire," declared another.) The war-crimes trials revealed blatant double standards on the part of the United States, an outspoken primary-school teacher complained. The trials went nowhere near far enough, declared an exceedingly embittered man, who believed that no fewer than a hundred thousand militarists deserved to be executed. A policeman opined that the purge should be restricted to former top officials of the Special Higher Police (the thought police). On the contrary, urged another letter writer, the purge of public officials should be extended down to the level of town and city mayors. Former landowners denounced the confiscatory nature of SCAP's land reform. Some individuals urged that the reform agenda be pushed more vigorously at the local level. Letter writers who accepted the occupation's ideals deemed it necessary and appropriate to call attention to GI abuses. One poor woman was emboldened to complain to the supreme commander that the incessant flights of U.S. aircraft over her neighborhood were driving her crazy, carrying as they did all the terrifying sounds and images associated with the air raids. Some writers were deranged—such as the artist who presented MacArthur with a painting depicting the common identity of Jesus Christ, Santa Claus, and *tengu* or mountain goblins. Others were unmistakably sycophants or cranks. When all was said and done, the torrent of letters constituted, at the very least, yet one more example of the alacrity with which people filled the unaccustomed "space" of defeat with new forms of personal expression.

The letters also suggested the latent—and sometimes not so latent—sexual dimension of the occupation. Like the United States generally, MacArthur was perceived to be a dominant albeit magnanimous masculine figure by men as well as women. (Even the supposedly enlightened *Asahi* newspaper referred to him, in a rather Catholic manner, as "our father"). His headquarters shared in this masculinity. It is not difficult to discern an abiding psychology of dependency in the communications addressed to the supreme commander and GHQ, and many writers obviously made no clear distinction between embracing MacArthur, embracing paternalistic authority, and embracing democracy. Most blatant in this regard was a distinctive strain of letters written to the general by women that bemused analysts dubbed the "I-want-to-have-your-baby" genre. Here, the embrace of the conqueror, at least as wish if not actuality, became literal.[12]

Intellectuals and the Community of Remorse

In contrast to the often inchoate nature of such private expressions of ordinary individuals, intellectuals responded to defeat with notable theoretical vigor. With few exceptions (but many internecine differences), the intelligentsia assumed the mantle of being "progressive men of letters" *(shinpoteki bunkajin)* and rallied behind the causes of democracy and liberation. Maruyama Masao, one of the most influential of these intellectuals, once called attention to the peculiarity of the identity he and his colleagues assumed. Not only was "progressive men of letters" a new catchphrase, but it also was unique to Japan. There were no counterpart terms for the "conservative men of letters" or "centrist men of letters."[13] To be taken seriously as an intellectual in these years, it was *de rigueur* to be an apostle of democratic revolution.

This was a virtuoso turnabout for the intelligentsia, precious few of whom had opposed the war. Although the occupation's purge of militarists and ultranationalists eventually included a few hundred academics and writers, most prewar liberals and leftists had recanted their beliefs by the mid-1930s; in one way or another, they had supported the war.[14] Several hundred communists, a fraction of the original party, resisted apostasy and maintained a critical stance toward the imperial state—in prison or, in a few cases, abroad in the Soviet Union or communist-controlled areas of China. Only a handful of academics emerged from the war with their reputations enhanced for not having been swept along by the tides of ultranationalism—economists such as Arisawa Hiromi and Ōuchi Hyōe, for example, who were purged from the imperial universities for leftist ideas

The rituals of accommodation the Japanese government promoted vis-à-vis
the conquerors sometimes seemed to have been choreographed by Gilbert and
Sullivan. Here geisha welcome a U.S. military plane landing at Yokota Air
Base in 1947 in the course of a round-the-world flight.

in the late 1930s. There was no counterpart to the principled resistance
that a small but heroic number of intellectuals, leftists, church people, and
military officers had mounted against National Socialism in Germany in
the same period. There was very little indeed in which intellectuals could
take pride where their behavior prior to August 15, 1945 was concerned.

To many ordinary Japanese of the "good morals and manners" persuasion, the sudden postsurrender appearance of intellectuals, politicians,
and a host of other public figures spouting paeans to democracy and demilitarization smacked of hypocrisy and opportunism. The "progressive
intellectuals" naturally put a different spin on their new radicalism. In part
they emphasized, not unreasonably, how this represented the resumption
of a serious engagement with liberalism and Marxism that had been repressed in the late 1920s and early 1930s. Beyond this, however, the commitment of many intellectuals to progressive and radical politics reflected
what Maruyama later characterized as the formation of a "community of
remorse."

To many academics and men of letters like Maruyama, defeat and occupation involved (as he described it) a joyous feeling of hope for the future mixed with deep regret for the past, a sense of political and

intellectual liberation combined with self-reproach for having failed to resist the blandishments and awesome power of the state. Among the intelligentsia, politics and ideology thus became thoroughly entangled with
remorse and self-criticism. Individually as well as collectively, many
dwelled openly on their guilt and responsibility for having failed to take
a principled stand against repression and aggression. They resolved, as
Maruyama put it, to make a new start and turn the "rationed-out freedom" of the occupation into a spontaneous embrace of demilitarization and
democratization.[15]

For both intellectual and psychological reasons, Marxism offered special attractions for the repentant community of intellectuals—even for
those who, like Maruyama, drew eclectically from the European intellectual tradition and maintained their distance from the Communist Party.
To most of the progressive men of letters, Marxism offered a theoretical
(and "scientific") framework that seemed to go far in helping to explain
the recent disaster in terms of feudal remnants, capitalist contradictions,
false consciousness, and ruling-class intrigues. This dovetailed well with
the Americans' structural analysis of Japan's "will to war" while giving

Geisha in Yokohama greet a U.S. vessel arriving with servicemen's dependents
in early 1952.

that analysis a more precise and formulaic cast. Marxism also buttressed revolutionary optimism. The war, as the Marxists saw it, had exposed the grossly incomplete nature of the Meiji "revolution," whereas defeat and liberation by the Allied powers clearly accelerated the inevitable transition to a democratic—and ultimately socialist—society.

That the most principled resistance to the war had come from dedicated Communists gave these individuals considerable status. When Tokuda Kyūichi and several hundred other Communists were released from prison, they became celebrities and instant heroes in a society whose old heroes had all suddenly been toppled. Similarly, Nosaka Sanzō's arrival in January 1946 after a long journey from China attracted a great crowd. He, too, received a hero's welcome; even conservatives, it was said, joined in. Within a few months, Nosaka was elected to the Diet in the first general election held under occupation auspices. Defeat gave such Communist leaders charisma, imbuing them with an aura of integrity and political acuity. By the same token, defeat helped establish Marxism and the Communist Party itself as sources of clear, secular, universal principles that transcended the disastrous, particularistic values of the imperial state.

The embrace of one form or another of Marxism by individuals engaged in a wide range of activities was a dramatic feature of the early post-surrender scene, and it caught most American planners by surprise. They had failed to anticipate the radical fervor with which an entire stratum of privileged intellectuals would attempt to propel the American revolution beyond the boundaries of bourgeois democracy. Some of these intellectual campaigns for a more radical emancipation became mired in polemics, but many transcended formulaic Marxism to raise fundamental questions concerning the "modern self," the "modern ego," or the "establishment of a modern person" that were believed to be the basis of any genuine democratic revolution. Without such a clear sense of selfhood or "autonomous subjectivity," it was argued with great passion, individuals could not be expected to stand against the state in defense of democratic values. Since Japanese culture seemed to offer few models for establishing such an autonomous modern self, the intellectuals found themselves looking to Europe, Russia and the Soviet Union, and to a lesser degree the United States, for exemplary individuals and ideas.[16]

Multiple traumas of identity were embedded in this quest for a "modern self": acknowledging personal failure; repudiating one's own history and culture; looking for models in a Western world that itself had engaged in repression, imperialism, and war. Nonetheless, the appeal of foreign models to a remorseful intelligentsia was immense. To one degree or another, many nonintellectuals also felt this attraction, and likewise shared the heady sense of being now firmly embarked on the path of "inevitable" historical progress. Just as often, however, the intellectuals themselves called attention to the opening of a great divide between their cosmopolitan radicalism and the sentiments of those who still held on to the comfort and security of familiar ways. Intellectual writings concerning the defeat, observed Shimizu Ikutarō, a highly visible "progressive man of letters," tended to be "based more or less on the social sciences, and to convey a tone of optimism to the effect that 'everything's going to work out well now.'" Ordinary readers, in Shimizu's view, generally felt detached from such approaches and far more ambivalent about issues of guilt and responsibility.[17]

However remote their ivory towers may have seemed to be, the impact of the intellectuals was far reaching. Many of the most influential postsurrender economists, for example—including men of towering repute such as Arisawa and Ōuchi—worked within a Marxist or neo-Marxist framework. So did leading specialists on labor and industrial relations such as Ōkōchi Kazuo, a future president of Tokyo University. The most intense postsurrender academic debates concerning history, economics, and political economy were grounded in positions established by two factions that had dominated prewar contention among Marxist academics. Entire academic departments, such as Tokyo University's esteemed economics faculty, gave the elite students of the nation an eclectic education in Marxism as well as in classical and neoclassical economics.[18]

In the natural sciences, researchers and theoreticians such as the eminent physicist Sakata Shōichi became active in new organizations such as the Union for Democratic Scientists, which committed its members to using science to achieve democratic and pacifist goals. "To practice and propagate true science which is useful to the people," the union declared, "cannot be done unless we cooperate with various popular struggles. The people are eagerly awaiting such cooperation." Almost immediately, scientists began reaching out to a broader public by publishing books with such titles as "Our Science" and "Democratic Science."[19]

Literary circles were also buffeted by the winds of "revolutionary" consciousness. Most famously, the closing days of 1945 witnessed a gathering of around one hundred writers in Kanda, the famous booksellers' quarter of Tokyo, to announce the formation of the Shin Nihon Bungakukai, or "New Japanese Literature Association." Many well-known figures were among the group's founders, and they wasted little time establishing their radical credentials. The association's announced purpose was to "unify all democratic literary people and fight for the advancement of democratic literature." It was made emphatically clear that writers who had collaborated actively with "the imperialist war" were not welcome. Organizers invited some 322 politically vetted individuals to join them, of whom 173 did.

The "democratic literature" envisioned by these writers was to be international in nature but particularly responsive to the people of China and Korea, Japan's recent victims. *Shin Nihon Bungaku* (New Japanese Literature), the group's monthly journal, devoted its inaugural issue to "The Record of August 15." The writer Odagiri Hideo caused an uproar in a later issue by declaring twenty-five prominent writers guilty of "war responsibility." Other new literary magazines also engaged in such fraternal bloodletting. Through 1946, for example, *Bungaku Jihyō* (Comment on Current Literature) ran a regular feature titled "Literary Prosecution," devoted to exposing the war responsibility of well-known literary figures. Famous writers such as Nakano Shigeharu wrote frankly about the difficulties of achieving revolutionary change under a foreign occupation that operated through the existing mechanisms of the Japanese state, but still remained sanguine that the basic structures for achieving democracy were being established and a new "people's culture" was in the process of formation.[20]

This was the ideological atmosphere in which the rebirth of serious publishing took place, and the cosmopolitanism of the "community of remorse" was reflected in the breadth of foreign writings that publishers rushed to make available. Early issues of the new journal *Sekai*, to take but one example, advertised both new and reissued translations of works by Tolstoy, Gorky, Chekov, Dostoevsky, Goethe, Balzac, Gide, Malraux, Anatole France, Stendhal, Plato, Kant, Spinoza, Rousseau, Locke, Adam Smith, Hegel, Marx, Engels, Lenin, Spengler, and a host of others. In this way, "Marxism" was reintroduced to public debate in the context of the intellectual tradition to which it was indebted and in which it was embedded.

The range and vigor of this response to defeat and democratic opportunities went far beyond anything the American or English "old Asia hands" had believed possible. Indeed, these experts had rarely been able to come up with anything more than a short list of geriatric "old liberals" who might be expected to respond positively to reform (and who usually, like Yoshida Shigeru, did not). They had no inkling of who constituted the intelligentsia, what their personal or scholarly backgrounds were, or how they might respond to defeat and liberation. In this regard, the nonexperts who introduced a more radical line to postsurrender policy came much closer to the mark with their more abstract and ideological assumptions about the "universal" appeal of democratic reform.

Even the New Deal liberals and leftists, however, failed to predict that hundreds of intellectuals would be deeply influenced by the sentiments of the "community of remorse," or that they would find European thought, including Marxism, so crucial to redefining their responsibilities. Nor did anyone really anticipate how swiftly intellectual discourse would percolate to a national audience through the mass media. Such "progressive" intellectual ferment exceeded American expectations and was alien to mainstream American intellectual activity, and occupation authorities responded accordingly. While the more radical reformers within GHQ cultivated and encouraged left-wing intellectuals, the vigilant anticommunists placed their names on blacklists and bided their time until Cold War emotions made it acceptable to move to discredit them.

Grass-Roots Engagements

Psychologically, the more doctrinaire forms of leftism played to the notion that the Japanese people as a whole did indeed have to be guided by their superiors to achieve a democratic revolution. The very notion of a left-wing or communist vanguard rested on the premise that the masses were backward and in need of such leadership. In this regard, left-wing elitism was not all that different from the conqueror's, or from that of the conservatives who sought to retain power under the aegis and aura of the emperor. MacArthur's GHQ, the old-guard Japanese who reluctantly went along with his reformist agenda, the "progressive men of letters," and the Japan Communist Party were, each in their own way, practitioners of imperial democracy.

Where allegiance to the Communist Party itself was concerned, there was a further psychological consideration virtually inborn in the community of remorse. Because so many intellectuals felt personal guilt over their prewar apostasy and their failure to resist the imperial state, they often adopted a never-again attitude of fidelity to the postwar party that demanded strict adherence to its Central Committee pronouncements. Like MacArthur and GHQ, the Communist Party insisted on unquestioning obedience to its prescription of the correct path to the democratic revolution. Such discipline stifled internal criticism and turned many in the community of remorse into followers of a new source of dogma and authority.[21]

Whereas left-wing discourse about dialectical negation and contradiction may have alienated nonintellectuals or simply put them to sleep, the intellectuals' more humanistic sense of liberation and individual self-worth did strike responsive chords in popular consciousness and culture. Letters to the editor in national newspapers reflected an impressive nationwide engagement with the meaning of "democratization." An early letter to the *Asahi*, often quoted in later writings, suggested how out of touch the foreign Japan experts were when they dismissed as an "obedient herd" those they had not met at upper-crust gatherings in Tokyo. It read as follows:

> It seems that four countries—the United States, Great Britain, China, and the Soviet Union—but especially the United States and Britain, emphatically desire that Japan become a democratic country. If you interpret democracy as an idealistic liberation of humanity, then nobody would oppose this. The problem, however, is what form Japanese democracy should have—a Japan that has three thousand years of tradition and was a late-developing country in capitalism.
>
> Just looking at the political systems in the United States and Britain, it cannot be denied that there are different democracies. This applies to the Soviet Union and China as well. Thus, I am concerned that the United States, which sits at the center of the occupation, may out of kindness aim at a democratization in which everything follows the American way.
>
> It must be recognized that even Japan's feudal leaders did not resort to feudal things just to maintain their own power. They also gave consideration to the development of Japan and made adjustments to the Japanese situation. It is possible that American kindness, which regards only American-style democracy as democracy, may lead Japan into an unfortunate situation. We have suffered for a long time from fetters on speech and it would be distressing if American-style fetters were added the minute the old ones are removed. This may be worrying too much, but I wish to call the attention of knowledgeable people everywhere to this point.[22]

Other Japanese who accepted the occupation agenda were severe in criticizing the superficiality of their compatriots' embrace of "democracy." D. T. Suzuki, the well-known interpreter of Zen Buddhism, wrote the *Asahi* to warn readers to be wary of prominent Buddhist leaders who had supported the militarists and now suddenly presented themselves as apostles of democracy.[23] A housewife's letter expressed concern that woman suffrage was being imposed too quickly, before women could fully grasp its meaning.[24] A female writer was ridiculed by another for lavishing praise on a wartime military leader, then shifting almost immediately to praise of American military men.[25] Radio satirists tried to lampoon the political sign repainters in an early skit on the postwar paper shortage. The situation was so bad, one comic exclaimed, that people were making "Democracy" posters on the backs of old wartime placards extolling "Eight Corners of the World under One Roof."[26]

There was certainly a great deal to ridicule or lament in the haste with which so many people seemed to have become, almost overnight, admirers of the Americans and apostles of "peace" and "democracy." Cynics played the conversion game crassly, and were easy targets for satire about repainting signs and changing coats. More troubling were responses to the victors that in one way or another seemed exceptionally naive, accommodating, or superficial. Even in nuclear-bombed Nagasaki, residents welcomed the first Americans with gifts (a doll in a glass case, given to the head of a scientific team investigating radiation effects), and shortly afterward joined local U.S. military personnel in sponsoring a "Miss Atomic Bomb" beauty contest. A comic strip embraced democracy (*demokurashi* in the direct Japanese rendering) by introducing characters named "Little Demo" and "Little Cra" (*Demo-chan* and *Kura-chan;* conservative wordplay, in contrast, spoke of "demo-kurushii," *kurushii* meaning "painful" or "tormenting"). Petitioners from one community wrote General MacArthur to thank him for bringing democracy to Japan—and to request that he *order* a certain highly qualified but reluctant local individual to run for office.[27]

Although it was easy to take such episodes as evidence that the democratic revolution had no roots, it was just as easy to call attention to the emergence of an engaging and persistent "democracy folklore." The media were indefatigable in recounting incidents and activities that gave personality and individuality to grass-roots thinking about what embracing democracy might mean. Sometimes these stories were offered as outright comedy. When fuel shortages forced a bathhouse operator to heat just half his tubs and open his establishment to men and women on alternate days, for instance, he found his plans disrupted by an old woman who marched in on the men's day, started undressing, and resisted expulsion on the grounds that the country now had gender equality. "What are you talking about," she scolded in rich, colloquial Japanese. "Unlike the old days, now women and men have equal rights!"[28]

Other accounts of individuals asserting themselves were eminently serious. Shortly after surrender, students at a high school in Mito city attracted nationwide attention by boycotting classes and forcing their militaristic principal to resign. In Tokyo, female students at an upper-level secondary school caused a sensation by denouncing their male principal as corrupt and demanding classroom reforms. Their actions—doubly defiant in involving not only students but women—were followed by spontaneous protests at a number of higher schools and universities calling for the resignations of militaristic administrators and teachers and the granting of greater student rights. In November 1945, university students in Tokyo, Kyoto, Nagoya, and Kyushu began establishing autonomous student federations that laid the basis for the postwar student movement.[29]

Prewar leaders of the women's movement met on August 25, 1945 to plan strategy. One month later, they petitioned the government to grant woman suffrage—well before General MacArthur made this part of his basic civil liberties directive. By the first week of November, the first nationwide women's organization had been established. The postwar consumers' movement sometimes is dated from October 9, when fifteen women in Osaka formed a "Housewives Association" and held a demonstration to demand rice. That same month, nurses at the Tokyo Police Hospital formed the first women's union and succeeded in negotiating a wage increase. When the first Diet election in which women were empowered to vote took place in April 1946, seventy-nine women entered as candidates, and thirty-nine were elected.[30] The first spontaneous uprisings of male workers occurred in October among Korean and Chinese coal miners, a militancy soon emulated by Japanese miners.[31] Upheavals also took place in the nation's news rooms beginning in October, with high-level newspaper executives and editorial staff being pressured by employees to resign as a gesture of acceptance of their war responsibility. Major shakeups took place in some forty-four newspapers nationwide, including the *Yomiuri, Asahi,* and *Mainichi.*[32]

Many initiatives took place locally without garnering headlines. When a neighborhood festival was resumed in Yokohama in the summer of 1946, for example, after a hiatus of five years due to the war, women for the first time ever were allowed to participate in carrying the *mikoshi,* or portable shrine. They thereby joined men at the center of the festivities and stepped within a Shinto circle that traditionally had excluded them for being physically and morally impure. In such ways, cherished practices associated with the "good morals and manners" of the past began to be transformed subtly from below.[33] At the same time, intense grass-roots discussion about the democratic revolution was carried out in inconspicuous publi-

Many Japanese embraced SCAP's revolution from above with ardor. Here a
woman running for political office in January 1949 addresses a sidewalk crowd
that includes many children baby-sitting their siblings.

cations such as the local press, school papers, and company or union
newsletters. A great deal of political communication also took place in
local meetings and through new American-style forums such as the *paneru
disukasshion* (panel discussion) and the public-opinion poll. As the *Mainichi*
put it, surveys of public opinion were yet one more way of "whipping up
the democratization of newly born Japan." Within a matter of months,
people were being asked what they thought about a spectrum of topics
ranging from the emperor system to neighborhood associations. (Never,
however, were they asked what they thought about the occupation itself.)[34]

Radio also elicited entirely new levels of participation. In March 1946,
it was estimated that household radios were being kept on for an average
of five hours a day, making the airwaves at least as important as the
printed word as a vehicle of communication and politicization. At its
peak, *Truth Box* (Shinsō Bako), a controversial program on the war years,
received between a thousand and twelve hundred written queries weekly
from listeners. The popular *Broadcast Discussion* (Hōsō Tōronkai), featur-

ing a variety of experts on particular topics, traveled through the country responding to questions from local audiences regularly numbering in the thousands.[35]

Political candidates commonly were given air time on NHK. Prior to the general election of April 1946, some two thousand candidates took advantage of this opportunity, and a poll in 1949 revealed that an overwhelming number of voters "chose candidates by radio."[36] The most sensational of all broadcast innovations was the introduction of a wildly popular "Amateur Hour" for vocalists. This program offered a remote promise of fame and fortune, but its initial spirit involved a simple, unprecedented, and remarkably good-natured egalitarianism. Before the surrender, it was unthinkable for ordinary people to be heard on the national airwaves. Now, contestants ranging from four-year-olds to the elderly flocked to present themselves to the nation.[37]

Such grass-roots activities were not necessarily "revolutionary" or even "political" in the sense that the progressive intelligentsia used such concepts, but they subverted old hierarchies and reflected a popular receptivity to a more open society that was often spontaneously creative. They were also but the tip of the iceberg where embracing democracy was concerned.

Institutionalizing Reform

The men and women who wrote letters to SCAP and took part in local panel discussions did not engage peace and democracy in a vacuum. They lived in a world of tumultuous institutional renovation that touched their lives directly. Old laws were abrogated and new laws, civil as well as criminal, introduced. Basic structures of authoritarian control were undermined in fundamental ways. Land reform all but eliminated exploitative landlordism and rural tenancy. Electoral reform strengthened the bicameral legislature as a major political actor. Constitutional reform established the principle of popular sovereignty for the first time, guaranteed a more extensive range of human rights than even the U.S. Constitution, and set antimilitarist ideals at the very center of the national charter. Labor reforms gave workers basic rights hitherto unknown. Educational reform liberalized curricula, promoted coeducational egalitarianism, and broadened access to the elite track of the universities. Reform of the civil code eliminated the legal underpinnings of the patriarchal family system and strengthened the position of women in critical areas such as divorce and inheritance.

These innovations did not merely create an arena in which democracy might flourish but also involved the Japanese themselves in creating such an arena. Virtually all basic reforms were implemented, if not instigated, by a huge cadre of Japanese bureaucrats, technocrats, and outside advisers; frequently their input was creative and constructive. Testimony to the voluntary contributions of reformist Japanese came from every side. Alfred Oppler, who oversaw revision of the civil code, for instance, gave them credit for completely abolishing the patriarchal "house system" under which male domination within the family unit had been legally constituted. His staff never ordered or even urged its complete abolition, Oppler recalled, and "watched with eager interest how the Japanese would adjust it to the principles of the Constitution. They did a more thorough job than we had expected."

Like other occupation officials, Oppler found that the shock of defeat had stimulated "the revaluation of all values," even to the point of prompting a thoroughgoing iconoclastic feeling of "damn what you have adored and adore what you have damned." In the opening stage of the occupation, the reformist ardor of the Americans thus was complemented by a striking "open-mindedness to innovations" on the other side. In these circumstances, Oppler and his colleagues claimed that they "made the greatest effort not to order our Japanese counterparts around, but to work with them on an equal level. Free discussion, persuasion, and compromise rather than fiat brought about agreements."[38]

Such claims naturally cannot be taken at face value. The relationship was inherently unequal, and even in ostensibly free exchanges there usually remained a tacit understanding that the suggestions of GHQ officers and officials were not to be ignored. Even Theodore Cohen, the master of "noncommands with the force of commands," however, acknowledged the impressive degree to which Japanese initiatives supported and occasionally exceeded the mission of his own Labor Division. The basic Trade Union Law of December 1945, under which workers for the first time gained the right to organize, bargain collectively, and strike was almost entirely the work of an unusually large advisory commission headed by Suehiro Izutarō, an eminent legal scholar. The commission consisted of a working committee of three Welfare Ministry bureaucrats and two scholars, a steering committee of thirty members (including the Communist firebrand Tokuda Kyūichi), and an overall membership of some 130 individuals representing universities, corporations, political parties, the bureaucracy, social workers, and labor. Similarly, the September 1947 establishment of a Labor Ministry was "from the first, a Japanese project." Even a bar hostess at the Daiichi Hotel left her mark on labor practices by successfully recommending that labor recruitment agencies, known as "labor encouragement offices" during the war, be renamed "employment security offices." Her exact relationship to GHQ's policy makers is unclear, and perhaps best left so.[39]

One of the most progressive pieces of postwar labor legislation, the Labor Standards Law of 1947, which governed working conditions, came about largely at the unlikely initiative of a former member of the thought police named Teramoto Kōsaku. In the summer of 1946 Teramoto appeared at Cohen's office, unannounced and unknown, with a massive draft of a labor-protection bill. He was, it turned out, head of the Labor Standards Section in the Welfare Ministry and had been working on the project with his staff for several months. Such a bill was not part of GHQ's mission, nor was it high on the government's own agenda. In Cohen's lively telling of the story, the Labor Standards Law was a splendid example of middle-level initiatives in support of democratization.

Essentially, Teramoto took advantage of the confusion of the postwar scene to persuade a wide range of industrialists, bureaucrats, and politicians that GHQ was demanding vigorous regulation of working conditions. Under this misleading cover, he and his small staff, almost entirely on their own, drafted a comprehensive code of protective legislation based not only on prewar provisions suspended by the militarists, but also on a close study of International Labor Organization conventions. GHQ knew nothing of the project until Teramoto appeared at Cohen's door—but once the Labor Division gave this unexpected initiative its blessing, Teramoto was able to tell the interest groups on his side that they had little choice but to go along with these desires of the Americans. There were some touchy moments when it appeared the game might be exposed, but in the end the little team of secretive reformers had its way. The bill even included a provision for menstrual leave—which the American female chief of Cohen's Wages and Working Conditions Branch deemed unprecedented, unnecessary, and frivolous. The provision stayed. Article One of the new law eloquently conveyed the sense of individual worth on which so many now agreed that any meaningful democratic revolution had to rest. It declared that "working conditions must meet the needs of a worker living a life worthy of a human being"—not exactly words one might have anticipated from a former member of the thought police.[40]

The intricate dance involving fiat and "persuasion" on the one hand and genuine cooperation and volunteerism on the other was nowhere more apparent than in the field of education. Until the end of the occupation,

SCAP's Civil Information and Education Section rode herd to see that democratization was promoted here. As a result, the Ministry of Education, which had been a vigilant watchdog of emperor-system ultranationalism, was transformed into one of the country's most systematic and zealous proponents of "peace and democracy." No one repainted their signs more frenetically than the educators, and no doubt this was accompanied by audible curses within the sanctity of the ministry's walls. Here again, however, the occupation's demands cracked open an oppressive system in a manner that permitted new voices to express and explore their genuine sense of liberation. The effect on educators and educated alike was incalculable.

Until new texts could be introduced, students were required to go through their schoolbooks with the guidance of their teachers and systematically excise with brush and ink all passages deemed to be militaristic, nationalistic, or in some manner undemocratic. This practice of "blackening over" *(suminuru)* actually was initiated by the government before the Americans even set foot in Japan. For pupils and teachers alike, this was a visceral undertaking—simultaneously a ritual exorcism of teachings that had only yesterday been deemed sacrosanct and a practical exercise in encouraging criticism of received wisdom. Yuri Hajime, who lost his father, brother, and uncle in the war and was thirteen when hostilities ended, was typical in never forgetting this experience. After his home in Yokohama was destroyed by bombing, he was evacuated to the countryside and entered a poor middle school where it was necessary to make his own hand copy of the language textbook used by his class. Following the arrival of the occupation forces, classes were suspended for a period of months in the three subjects deemed most pervasively nationalistic—ethics, Japanese history, and geography (in which Japan's overseas empire had been extolled)—while the Ministry of Education and a host of publishers hastened to produce new textbooks appropriate to the times. In the meantime, he was required to deface his painstakingly copied language text. The experience was traumatic. The mutilated text struck him as "abnormal and even grotesque," but the episode left him with a lasting awareness that received knowledge could be challenged and education itself could be a relative thing. Decades later, Kurita Wataru recalled the same formative experience. "We held the splotched pages up to the sunlight and if the words could still be read, we applied a fresh coat of ink. That day, for the first time, I felt beseiged by a jumble of contending values, a feeling that has persisted ever since."[41]

The tenor of the intense campaign to democratize education was conveyed in *Shin Kyōiku Shishin* (New Educational Guidance), issued by the Ministry of Education in May 1946. A number of scholars had been enlisted to prepare the original draft, which was then simplified by the ministry before being distributed to educators nationwide. The goal of the new system, it was stated, was to contribute to constructing "a democratic, peaceful nation of culture." To this end, it was imperative to develop "an autonomous and cooperative attitude among educators themselves." In this spirit, teachers and administrators were called on to engage in deep reflection on the shortcomings of society that had led to the war and to the country's present sorry state.

Modernization since the Meiji period, the guide continued, had consisted primarily of borrowing material aspects of Western civilization while ignoring the basic spirit behind them. The Japanese had "learned how to use trains, ships, and electricity, but did not sufficiently develop the scientific spirit that produced them." At the same time, war and defeat had come about because the people did not have proper respect for "human nature, personality, and individuality." Failure to develop a rational, critical spirit had allowed militarism and ultranationalism to arise and, "in this sense, responsibility for the war must be borne by the entire populace, and the people must deeply apologize to the world for their crime." Such an apology could only be made by carrying out the terms of the Potsdam Declaration and the orders of Allied occupation authorities, thereby constructing a new country. In this task, educators had a pivotal role to play. The guide then offered a detailed discussion of the "Fundamental Problems in Constructing a New Japan." Six successive chapters dealt with (1) self-reflection concerning Japan's present state; (2) eliminating militarism and ultranationalism; (3) promoting respect for human nature, personality, and individuality; (4) raising scientific standards and philosophical and religious refinement; (5) carrying out thoroughgoing democracy; and (6) constructing a peaceful nation of culture. A further seven chapters addressed in ever more specific terms the task of educators in promoting respect for individuality, civic education, women's education, scientific knowledge, physical education, art and culture, and vocational education.

However much Ministry of Education officials may have acted under duress in articulating and promoting such an agenda, the "self-reflection" (that cherished term of the times) apparent throughout their guide certainly had a provocative and home-grown feel to it. At one point, the agenda suggested that Japan was a nation but not really a society in that people were loyal to the state and knew how to behave as good family members but lacked a broader sense of public morality due to their weak sense of individuality. This corresponded to what the "progressive men of letters" were saying in their passionate intellectual debates about establishing an autonomous subjectivity, only here the issue was being brought into the country's classrooms in far plainer language.[42]

The sweeping reformist flavor of this early handbook was replicated in scores of other publications sponsored or approved by the ministry, including new classroom textbooks. A typical elementary-school text, *Shōnen Shōjo no tame no Minshu Tokuhon* (Democracy Reader for Boys and Girls), pointed out that in the contemporary world, democratic ideals extended beyond politics per se to economics and daily life. Freedom was to be cherished, young readers were told, but also was to be distinguished from selfishness. It had to be exercised with responsibility. Equality also was central to democracy, but should not be confused with sameness. Equality meant equal opportunity.

The "Democracy Reader for Boys and Girls" addressed the nation's occupied status forthrightly. "Is democracy being promoted in Japan now because we have to do so by order of the Allied powers?" The textbook's yes-but-no answer was expressed in terms that elementary-school youngsters might grasp easily: "In accordance with the Potsdam Declaration, the Allied nations have been exerting themselves so that Japan will realize democracy quickly and be able to rejoin the world. Even without the Allied nations saying so, however, if we look at the history of humankind, to become a democratic nation and democratic people is true to the way people should be." The text went on to introduce pacifism as the means by which Japan, as well as other countries, could best promote civilization and become a cultured nation of "learning, art, and morality."[43] This was not greatly different from what the sophisticated intellectual journal *Sekai* had said in its inaugural issue—hardly surprising, since many of the authors of these new school texts were liberal and left-wing academics who identified closely with the community of remorse.

Millions of young students were exposed to such ideas on a daily basis and imbibed them in a classroom atmosphere that usually was noticeably free and open compared to the militant regimen they had previously experienced. The impact of defeat on teachers in general was exceptionally traumatic. Until the moment of surrender, they had been the drill sergeants of emperor-system orthodoxies. Now, overnight, they were told not merely to think differently but to teach the *new* orthodoxies with the same passion they had brought to the old ones. Naturally, individual responses varied greatly. Some teachers introduced the new course material and the idea of a more democratic give-and-take between teachers and pupils with sarcasm and a twisted self-mockery. "What shall we study today?" one person recalled his middle-school teacher asking. "Since we have democracy, I must ask your opinion."[44] The great majority of teachers adapted quickly to the new situation, however. Many of them felt a particularly keen and painful sense of responsibility on confronting the lost war, for so many of those who had died, and died in vain, had been their pupils.

Filled with grief over the deaths of their young charges, often overwhelmed with guilt for having encouraged them on a pathway to destruction, many teachers embraced the ideals of peace and democracy with fervor. Their new-found radicalism was reinforced by the miserable living conditions they faced. Teachers unionized in great numbers and, as if to atone for past subservience to the state, commonly adopted a confrontational stance vis-à-vis the power structure. Nikkyōso, the most powerful of their unions, was closely affiliated with the Communist Party. By 1948, distraught SCAP officials were traveling the country to denounce "Red" influences in the schools.[45]

The idealistic ambiance of early postwar educational innovations was captured in an acclaimed collection of student writings published in 1951 under the title *Yamabiko Gakkō* (Echo School). Edited by Muchaku Seikyō, a man in his early twenties who had taken a teaching post at a small middle school in the mountains of Yamagata prefecture, this bestseller contained essays, poems, and reports by some forty-three pupils written over the course of three years. Muchaku and his students became celebrity symbols of an ideal relationship of discussion and exchange between teachers and students, and his pupils' writings became the most famous examples of a nationwide pedagogical movement to promote "compositions about everyday life."

Media people flocked to Muchaku's little school after the book became famous, and with virtually one voice they called attention to the open, democratic environment that existed there. Only about 10 percent of the students went beyond middle school, but everyone praised the curiosity and initiative their young teacher nourished in them. These poor, rural youngsters and their mentor became inspirations for the whole country. One pupil later recalled how impressed he had been when the newly arrived teacher first spoke about how "the sprout of democracy growing in Japan now is borrowed from America and not yet our local product." Muchaku's emphasis on writing compositions about daily life was part of his belief that the purpose of education was "to nurture energy for social change."

Local parents, the former student recalled, burdened with daily hardships and in turmoil because of tensions induced by the new land reform legislation, did not always appreciate what the young teacher was doing, but his impact on the students and the community as a whole had been an enduring one.[46]

Democratizing Everyday Language

The Americanization of the education system was revealed in the emergence of a new lexicon of borrowed terms. *Karikyuramu, gaidansu, hommu rummu, hommu purojekuto, cossu obu sutadei, kurabu akutibiti*—that is, "curriculum," "guidance," "home room," "home project," "course of study," and "club activity"—all these bastardized, imported terms and concepts became part of everyday pedagogical vocabulary.[47] These terms, however, were but a small part of the new classroom environment, just as the regular school system itself was only one part of the sweeping education in democracy then taking place. Beginning in 1947, adult education programs were introduced that were explicitly designed to help grownups "learn the consciousness, habits, and lifestyles of a democratic people."[48] Beyond this, the very nature of the language as a whole was permanently altered by the introduction of hundreds of terms and phrases that helped define the ethos of the new world of defeat and democratization.

This revolution in everyday language had two great historical precedents. Ancient and medieval society had been profoundly transformed by wholesale borrowings of texts and concepts from China, not to mention the adoption of its ideographic writing system. The opening of feudal Japan to the outside world in the mid-nineteenth century ushered in another epoch of voracious intellectual borrowing, this time from Europe and to a lesser degree the United States. Here, then, was the beginning of a third cycle of assimilating foreign ideas and practices. With their typical energy, publishers immediately proceeded to try to catalog the new conceptual influx by publishing annual books of popular *shingo,* or "new terms."

Usually these were magpie collections—glittery, eclectic, ranging over every possible field, containing weighty items alongside frivolous baubles. The Americanization of popular culture was evident in Japanicized-English entries for such imports as the pinup, the jitterbug, boogie-woogie, and the whodunit *(hūdanitto).* A 1948 compilation included such essential borrowed English as *alibi, "casting vote," ecstasy, scandal, up-to-date, Achilles' heel,* and *Amen*—along with four suggestive slang words:

baloney, corny, hot, and *phony.* "Dark horses" galloped without translation onto the linguistic terrain. "Hubba-hubba" became popular, albeit with the distinctive meaning of "hurry, hurry" rather than its original association with men ogling women.

Odd made-in-Japan English neologisms sometimes leaped from the page. *Mane-moon,* or "money-moon," was one such creation, defined as "a honeymoon for those who married for money." The borrowed English term "bestseller" was accompanied by *sekkusu serā* or "sex seller," referring to an erotic book. Caustic new idioms jostled against foreign imports, among them the wonderful *go-seru* or "five lets" by which to appease government officials: let them eat, drink, grab money, sleep with women, and put on airs. This catchy term, so irreverent and open, flew in the face of the traditional homily about "revering officials" *(kanson)* and conveyed a pungent taste of the iconoclasm of these years.

In this street scene from early 1950, figures representing the cartoon characters Blondie and Dagwood advertise a film version of the immensely popular *Blondie* comic strip. Serialized in a national newspaper from 1946 until the end of the occupation, *Blondie* featured a "typical" middle-class American family and had an incalculable influence in shaping popular envy of the consumerism and material comforts of American-style "democracy."

Many of the popular handbooks in which such new terms were item-ized were pocket size to permit handy access. Taken as a whole they gave a lively sense of how the very nature of popular discourse was being re-vised on the run and yet in fundamental ways. Readers of these little guides could look up a range of borrowed terms, translated terms, native terms, and resurrected terms (concepts repressed by the militarists) that in one way or another captured the spirit of the new era of change. "Open shop" and "closed shop" were defined in such lexicons along with "picket" and "scab." So were "class consciousness" and "social revolution," "fem-inism" and "feminist," "public opinion" and "popular sovereignty," the "four freedoms" and "transgression of human rights."[49]

The other side of this burst of fashionable new terminology was the abrupt disappearance of such once-ubiquitous terms and slogans as "eight corners of the world under one roof" or the evocative compound *hōkoku*, made up of two ideographs literally meaning "repay the country." Until the defeat, *hōkoku* had been among the most overworked of terms, attached to almost every imaginable activity. *Sangyō hōkoku* evoked images of "pa-triotic industrial service," for example; *genron hōkoku* meant "public ex-pression in the service of the nation." Now, *hōkoku* and a host of companion terms were buried without ceremony. In a grotesque observa-tion that somehow escaped GHQ's censors, the editors of a 1948 volume of contemporary words and phrases noted that these familiar expressions had been obliterated by the atomic bombs "along with the residents of Hi-roshima and Nagasaki." By far the most popular new term, these lexi-cographers went on to say, was "democratization." Indeed, "the situation is such that one can't even receive rations without wearing a democrati-zation suit."[50]

"Democratization" obviously produced its own sarcastic chroniclers, but that in itself said something about the institutionalization of SCAP's revolution from above.

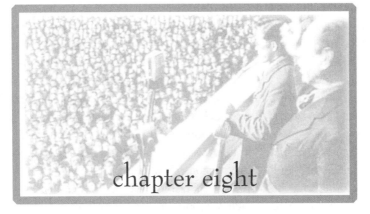

chapter eight

MAKING REVOLUTION

The potpourri of fashionable postsurrender words and phrases included many references to radical activities. Two of the earliest terms to appear were *united democratic front* and *democratic people's front*, referring to an envisioned coalition of Communists and Socialists that ultimately failed to coalesce. That such rhetoric and agitation caught the victors by surprise was understandable. Few people outside Japan were capable of imagining any behavior from the defeated enemy other than obsequiousness to their leaders. Judging from their own domestic experience, moreover, most Americans simply regarded genuinely radical politics as beyond the pale.

"Food May Day" was another left-wing initiative that seemed threatening to the carefully controlled revolution from above. This was the name adopted for a nationwide demonstration against the government's disastrous rationing system on May 19, 1946. "May Day" itself (established by the International Socialist Congress of 1889 as an expression of worker solidarity) had been observed annually by Japanese workers from 1920 until banned by the government in 1936. Celebrations were resumed on the traditional May 1 date after the war ended, and "Food May Day" was an imaginative embellishment on this traditional expression of solidarity and protest. That same month, university students declared their own "Student May Day." All of this confounded the conquerors.

Seisan kanri—"production control"—confounded them too, and in this instance for month after month beginning in 1946. This referred to a largely spontaneous shop-floor movement in which white-collar as well as blue-collar workers seized control of enterprises and kept production going without the managerial class.

In retrospect, it seems obvious that the victors contributed unwittingly to the circumstances in which such radical activities flourished by deciding to promote political freedom and social reform without taking an active role in rehabilitating the economy. In practice, production stagnated and inflation raged under this hands-off policy. Working-class people became understandably receptive to a range of left-wing appeals, and a large cadre of professionals in academic circles and the mass media hastened to endorse these radical agendas. If one of the offspring of shattering defeat was the *kyodatsu* condition of exhaustion, and another a heartfelt hope for "peace" and "democracy," a third was the notion of making revolution as Marxists had long spoken of it—from below with the guidance of an enlightened vanguard. This could be done, it was argued, without violence and bloodshed. The challenge was to turn the conqueror's democratic revolution peaceably into a socialist one.

Lovable Communists and Radicalized Workers

In the chaos of the war's end, early reforms such as the release of political prisoners, legalization of the Communist Party, and introduction of strong prolabor legislation such as the Trade Union Law of December 1945 had virtually guaranteed the emergence of movements more radical than the victors anticipated or desired. Free to organize, Socialists and Communists moved rapidly onto the political stage. Free to unionize, bargain collectively, and strike, workers did so with astonishing speed and vigor. Both radical and moderate Socialists attracted substantial support among voters and in the labor movement; the newly reconstituted Communist Party commanded immense media attention and made even stronger initial inroads into the ranks of organized labor.

The Communist Party's appeal was broadened after the charismatic Nosaka Sanzō returned from his long sojourn with the communist forces in China in mid-January 1946 and immediately spoke in soothing terms of promoting a peaceful revolution in compliance with the occupation

agenda and the desires of the people. While still on the train between
Hakata, his port of arrival, and Tokyo, Nosaka made an instantly famous
statement about creating a "lovable Communist Party," a label that struck
some observers as an astounding oxymoron but proved extremely seductive to others. Nosaka's arrival at party headquarters in Tokyo was treated
like a celebrity event. (One newspaper wrote bemusedly about young girls
in both kimonos and Western dress gathered like fans awaiting a star at
the stage door, and quoted one gushing afterwards, "It was wonderful!
Everyone waved red flags! It was swell!") In his first public address,
Nosaka spoke of his shock on encountering the vast scale of the country's
physical devastation. He warned that the privileged classes, reactionary bureaucrats, and "militarists and war criminals" still posed grave obstacles
to democratization and assured his attentive audience that the creation of
a democratic people's front "absolutely does not mean that we are trying
to realize socialism by overthrowing capitalism today." In a fine example
of turning wartime rhetoric to new purposes, Nosaka lambasted "so-called
patriots" for destroying the nation and declared that "we Communists are
the true patriots and the true service brigade for democracy." His influence was readily apparent in the party platform adopted the next month,
which declared that "the Japan Communist Party takes as its immediate
and fundamental goal the achievement through peaceful and democratic
methods of our country's bourgeois democratic revolution, which already
is in progress."

Nosaka also personally softened the party's previously uncompromis-
ing position on the emperor by arguing that, although it was necessary to
oppose the imperial institution as a "national system," the broader issue
of the emperor as religious leader could be left to a popular vote once a
genuine people's democracy had been established. (This was a position he
had originally advanced in April 1945, while with the Chinese communists
in Yenan.) That February, some forty thousand individuals were present
to hear Nosaka describe the envisioned democratic front itself (and not just
the party) as "a patriotic front with new meaning."[1]

Even though Nosaka and four other party members were elected to the
Diet in the general elections of April 1946, the Communist Party's greatest influence lay not in parliamentary politics but in organizing labor and
mobilizing mass protest. Fierce struggles took place among the Communists and the radical and moderate Socialists before the party succeeded
in asserting its control over roughly two-thirds of organized labor. This
was a signal accomplishment, given the rapid growth of the union movement. By the end of 1945, unions claimed some 380,000 members. A

month later, over one million workers had been added to this number. The number of organized workers rose to around 5.6 million by the end of 1946 and peaked at some 6.7 million in mid-1948, comprising by that date more than half of the nonagricultural work force.[2]

Because the corrosive effects of inflation affected white-collar and blue-collar workers alike, these years saw a narrowing of wage disparities between the two sectors. One consequence of this was a responsiveness to unionization among white-collar employees. Since pay scales in the public sector tended to lag considerably behind those in the private sector, public employees proved particularly receptive to the more aggressive agendas of the Communists. Freshly unionized workers did not hesitate to use their new rights to bargain collectively and strike, and throughout the occupation the incidence of labor disputes remained fairly high. Between the beginning of 1946 and end of 1950, some 6,432 disputes involving over 19 million workers were recorded, including 3,048 strikes supported by close to 5 million workers. The majority of disputes focused on wages and were settled fairly quickly.[3]

The baseline for such rapid unionization had actually been established during the war years when workers were organized at company, industry, and national levels as part of the mobilization for "total" war. Once the wartime *raison d'être* for patriotic service had been destroyed, these existing unions and national federations proved easily mobilized by the political left. At the same time, and more surprisingly, radicalization at the shop-floor level also took place outside the formal structures of organized labor in the form of the "production control" movement. Lacking official support from either the Communists or the Socialist factions, production control appeared to represent the emergence of a truly radical anticapitalist ethos at the grass-roots level. Employees in individual enterprises, acting largely on their own initiative, simply took over the offices, factories, or mines where they were working and ran them without consulting the owners or the managerial elite.

Initially, production control amounted to a radical tactic rather than an end in itself. Instead of striking and shutting down enterprises, workers seized control of production until management met their demands. The first sensational instances of this—involving the *Yomiuri* newspaper, the Keisei electric railway, and the Mitsui Bibai coal mine—all took place in the closing months of 1945 and were settled with employees gaining many of their demands and then relinquishing the managerial functions they had usurped. It quickly became obvious, however, that this tactic held explosive implications. Seizure of enterprises often reflected a belief

on the part of employees that owners and managers were deliberately sabotaging economic recovery in the hope that this would prompt the Americans to jettison their democratization plans. By keeping production going,
workers identified themselves as individuals eager to help solve the economic crisis. Beyond this, their takeovers revealed a growing confidence
that they were capable of making basic decisions previously regarded as
the exclusive prerogative of management. For some radicals, production
control seemed to signal the emergence of nascent "soviets" in defeated
Japan.

Certainly the movement dramatically challenged the clear-cut distinction between labor and management characteristic of capitalist relations,
and in the chaos and scarcity of the immediate postsurrender period it
mesmerized onlookers to a degree beyond what the mere number of plants
taken over might seem to have called for. Workers' commitment to maintain production often gained them public support. In many instances, they
actually succeeded in increasing output, thereby confirming both their
own managerial capabilities and the ineptitude or calculated sabotage of
the managers and owners they had elbowed aside. Success seemed to be
breeding success. Thirteen incidents of production control were reported
in January 1946, twenty in February, thirty-nine in March, fifty-three in
April, fifty-six in May. Tens of thousands of workers were involved each
month, concentrated most heavily in the Tokyo area and in the machine-
tool industry. Thereafter the numbers tapered off, but not enough to offer
comfort to the government and the business community. Between June
1946 and the following February, an average of thirty cases of production
control occurred each month.[4]

The government and, in time, GHQ accused labor and the left of seriously disrupting economic recovery. This was disingenuous. Labor's demands were almost always reasonable, aimed at attaining living wages in
a period of economic chaos. Although unions made good use of the newly
acquired right to strike, most strikes were of short duration; indeed, one
popular tactic was a twenty-four-hour "demonstration strike." SCAP statistics indicate that through July 1948, with the exception of only one
month, the number of "man-days" lost in strikes never exceeded 1 percent of total man-days available.[5] Slight additional time was lost through
slowdowns or other tactics, but this was negligible when set against capitalist hoarding of strategic materials, diversion of goods to the black market, and deliberate heel dragging—to say nothing of the government's
colossal ineptitude in addressing the fiscal and economic crisis. The real
issue, in any case, was whether the "revolution from below" actually

threatened to go beyond the parameters of conventional bourgeois labor practices and electoral politics.

"A Sea of Red Flags"

The impression of such a rising tide of revolution grew stronger in the spring of 1946. Yoshida Shigeru, who formed a cabinet for the first time on May 22 after tortuous backstage maneuvering, later spoke emotionally of assuming power amid "a sea of red flags."[6] His recollection was quite literal. The rising-sun flag he venerated had been banned by the conquerors and in its place, for a short while, red banners fluttered in the streets.

The flags Yoshida remembered so vividly, largely associated with worker solidarity rather than the Communist Party per se, began filling the streets prior to the general election scheduled for April 10. Women were to go to the polls for the first time, and voters confronted some 2,770 candidates representing no less than 363 political parties. Hundreds of old-

When May Day commemorations were resumed in 1946 after having been suppressed for a decade, these workers tried out their English in calling for a "people's front" of socialist and communist forces (and, also slightly misspelled in the background, for protection for working mothers). The tradition of women participating in popular and labor demonstrations traced back to the prewar period, before the militarists took over.

The impetus behind the dramatic "Food May Day" demonstrations of mid-
May 1946 came from neighborhood rallies such as this, in which local
housewives protested the government's miserable food delivery system. The
straw-mat banner, reading "Feed us enough so that we can work," has a
distinctly indigenous feel—calling to mind the rice riots that wracked Japan in
the wake of World War I and that also were ignited by grass-roots protests led
by housewives.

guard politicians having been purged, 95 percent of these candidates had
never before held public office, although slightly over half were affiliated
with one of the five major parties. Conservative candidates had a clear advantage, having inherited the electoral bailiwicks of their now-purged predecessors, whereas leftist candidates were still struggling to create new
bases of support.[7]

Three days before the election, a rally sponsored by sixty-nine "labor-
farmer" groups and forty-five "cultural" groups attracted some seventy
thousand people to Hibiya park in downtown Tokyo. The rally was presented as a "people's assembly" to overthrow the reactionary Shidehara
cabinet. More than fifty trucks provided by a transportation union carried
people to the park from every ward in Tokyo. Members of the national
railway union arranged for trains to bring farmers in from nearby prefec-
tures free of charge. Korean laborers, who had their own organizations,
sent thousands of participants. Even the trees were full of people, reported
the *Asahi,* with red flags waving everywhere and banners standing "like a
forest."

The *Asahi*'s effusive coverage made the demonstration sound rather like a battle scene from one of Japan's medieval war chronicles, although the inscriptions on banners and placards were distinctly contemporary: "Overthrow the Shidehara cabinet—supporter of the rich and enemy of the people!" "Create a people's government and end starvation!" "A democratic constitution by the hands of the people!" Communist and Socialist speakers were joined by liberals such as Ishibashi Tanzan, soon to emerge as Yoshida's beleaguered finance minister. The crowd heckled him, yelling that he should step down until he cut his ties with the conservatives. Various resolutions were passed by acclamation, including one to overthrow the government through a "democratic revolution."

Incited by this rally, some fifty thousand people proceeded to the prime minister's residence to present their demands. A disorderly confrontation ensued in which (according to police claims) several policemen suffered minor injuries. They, in turn, fired their pistols after the crowd broke through the gate and began to converge on the residence. Although no serious injuries resulted, U.S. military police with armored vehicles and machine guns mounted on jeeps intervened to restore order. A delegation of thirteen individuals, led by Tokuda Kyūichi, was finally permitted to enter the residence and submit its demands, but Shidehara himself did not meet with them until the following afternoon. At one point in that meeting, Tokuda told the prime minister that he was so fat he could not possibly be living within the 500-yen limit on monthly income imposed on the nation by the government. The protesters' rhetoric became so abusive that the frightened, elderly premier eventually fled the room.[8]

The general election returned a disparate and disorganized contingent to the Diet and left Shidehara in a lame-duck situation that lasted some six weeks, until Yoshida finally cobbled together a coalition cabinet. While the politicians bickered, food deliveries fell further and further behind schedule and the popular dissatisfaction found creative expression in the separate commemorations of "May Day." On May 1, rallies occurred in major cities nationwide. Police put the total number of participants at 1.25 million, but more sympathetic sources placed it at twice that number. The turnout in Tokyo was stunning, with as many as half a million men, women, and children flooding into the plaza before the imperial palace.

The previous day, a worker in Yokohama had made a brief notation in his diary: "Yesterday, the emperor's birthday, was not a holiday, but for tomorrow's May Day we have the day off. . . . How the world has changed!" Press coverage conveyed a similar sense of transformation. "Historical May Day in Harmony with the World," proclaimed the first

tier of headlines in the *Asahi;* "Unity of Working Millions," exclaimed the
second tier; "Reassuring Progress toward Democratic Japan," read the
third. Mark Gayn, a sympathetic left-wing American journalist who witnessed the occasion, described it in his diary as a day of incessant singing
and unusual ebullience and joy. "Despite the gray skies," he wrote, "this
was a joyous meeting, filled with enthusiasm and more confidence than I
have yet seen in Japan." Elsewhere he spoke of "a day filled with a curious kind of joy—perhaps the kind of luminous joy a war prisoner feels on
regaining freedom." The red flags, Gayn observed, were associated with
labor rather than with revolt. When, through his interpreter, he asked a
worker why he was demonstrating, he was told, "Because I believe that in
a democracy power should belong to the people." Placards such as "Let
us eat enough to be able to work!" called attention, as usual, to the food
crisis. Others called for "Immediate formation of a democratic people's
front!" The new sense of gender equality found expression in slogans like
"Equal wages for men and women in equal work!"[9]

To the *Asahi*'s enthusiastic commentators, these events represented "a
powerful step toward construction of a democratic Japan, rising like a
phoenix out of the devastation of war." The executive committee that organized the May Day observance presented itself—naively, as it turned
out—as acting within the spirit of the Potsdam Declaration and subsequent Allied policies toward Japan. In a message prepared explicitly for
SCAP and the Allied Powers, the organizers began with these words:

> We express our sincerest appreciation for the measures taken by the
> Allied Powers to liberate the people, grant freedom, and extend the
> rights to labor and agricultural groups.
>
>   Inspired by this, we hope to uproot feudalistic and despotic op-
> pression; establish a popular government, based on the true will of
> the people never to break the peace of the world again; realize po-
> litical, economic and social conditions which will not jeopardize the
> livelihood of the people; and be recognized internationally as a peace-
> ful and democratic nation.

The message then went on to itemize many ways in which "bureaucrats,
capitalists, landowners, and other controlling interests" had been inter-
fering with the realization of these objectives, thereby revealing themselves
to be "in truth enemies of the democratic revolution."[10]

On May 12, residents of Shimouma in the Setagaya ward of Tokyo held
a small "give us rice" demonstration that became the inspiration for the
second "May Day" celebration of the month: Food May Day. Nosaka ap-

peared unexpectedly on the scene and, perhaps carried away with the new spirit of "lovable" revolution, made the astonishing announcement that there was no other recourse but to appeal directly to the emperor. This was seconded by other speakers, and various resolutions were approved and packaged as a "Voice of the People" to be presented to Emperor Hirohito. Participants in the small Shimouma demonstration then split into two groups, one carrying their demands to the neighborhood government office and the other to the imperial palace.

At the palace a small nonviolent confrontation with security guards occurred, following which 113 men, housewives, and children carrying a smattering of red flags were permitted to enter the palace grounds and deliver their demands to a representative of the Imperial Household Ministry. Times had changed indeed! In the course of this unprecedented intrusion, they actually succeeded in inspecting the imperial kitchen, where they naturally found foods not seen on ordinary people's tables. Their act inspired local "food demonstrations" in front of rationing stations in other parts of Tokyo, and became the spark that culminated in Food May Day one week later.

When appointed local officials in Setagaya composed a letter humbly begging imperial pardon for this insolence, local residents forced them to resign and demanded that they be replaced by elected officials. This was an impressive expression of grass-roots democratic consciousness, for under the prewar regime, even before the militarist ascendancy, authoritarian control had been implemented through a dense web of appointed officials reaching into every neighborhood. Now local residents, including a strong contingent of housewives, were not only defying this authority but demanding that it be changed.

On Food May Day itself, some 250,000 people gathered in front of the imperial palace—christened "People's Plaza" for the occasion. Although women always participated in such demonstrations, on this occasion the presence of housewives and children, as well as contingents of female students with their teachers, was especially striking. A frail mother with an infant strapped to her back told the crowd how her neighborhood had received no rice rations for two weeks. She was unable to nurse her child, she said, while "sipping rice gruel and eating dumplings made of wild grass." As she spoke, the child's wailing could be heard over the loudspeaker. A fifth-grade boy made a similarly intimate appeal. He was eager to catch up on schoolwork disrupted by the war, he told the crowd, but it was impossible to do so because the food crisis had led to shortened school days. Tokuda made well-received jokes about the emperor. ("We are starving. What about him? . . . Maybe the emperor can only say, 'Ah so, ah so.' ")[11]

These events of mid May proved to be an ideological crazy quilt, however, in great part because the protest became framed as an appeal to the emperor. Resolutions approved on May 19 were soon packaged as a formal memorial to the throne in which the emperor, identified in traditional language as "the holder of sovereign power" and "the highest authority," was respectfully asked to take appropriate measures in response to the people's will. Such measures, the petitioners stated, would entail repudiation of the corrupt politicians, officials, capitalists, and landlords who had brought Japan to the brink of starvation and ruin. In their place, the emperor was asked to support a united front involving workers and farmers, Socialists and Communists.[12]

The conceptual muddle of revolution from below was vividly captured in this petition—which the emperor unsurprisingly refused to receive. Just as personal letters to General MacArthur revealed an often contradictory mixture of obsequiousness and paeans to peace and democracy, so too did the avowed leftists contaminate the campaign for the creation of a democratic people's government with this curiously traditional appeal to the supreme authority of the emperor. Tokuda may have enjoyed his little jokes about Hirohito, but the big joke was the monarchism his own party chose to practice at this moment of intense confrontation.

Appealing to the emperor as "the highest authority" was all the more remarkable when one considers the context in which this appeal took place. The draft of a new constitution proclaiming popular sovereignty had just been released; the first general election with female as well as male universal suffrage had just been held; workers were defying traditional authority in the corporate sector; women were emerging as a political force; students were clamoring for greater self-governance; people for the first time felt free enough to make public jokes about the emperor—and radical leaders chose this moment to appeal respectfully to him to redress the food crisis, repudiate his loyal servants, and assume a leading role in the revolutionary cause. The international history of popular democratic movements has few moments more farcical than this.

Emperor Hirohito's eventual response was predictable. On May 24, in his first broadcast since the epochal moment of capitulation, he essentially reiterated his appeal for national solidarity. As he had throughout the war, the emperor expressed deep personal concern for the people's suffering. In these trying circumstances, he concluded, "I hope that everyone will carry out the beautiful tradition of our country, namely the family state, in coping with the situation, forgetting individual selfish desires and striving ahead on the path of reconstructing the country." This was utterly formulaic, familiar from two decades of oppression and war. The broadcast was repeated three times that day.[13]

Ideological contradictions in the popular movement were expectable at this early date. What was unexpected, and of far greater consequence than the demonstrators' misplaced monarchism or the emperor's predictable canards, was the harsh response of SCAP. The question of acceptable "use of force" by the Japanese people in bringing about a more democratic government had been directly addressed in the initial (and publicly accessible) American postsurrender policy document. This stipulated that where such actions were directed toward eliminating feudal and authoritarian tendencies, the supreme commander should intervene against them only in cases where the security of his forces or other basic objectives of the occupation were threatened.[14]

The demonstrations of May 1946 did not go anywhere near this far. There was some disorderly conduct. Both the prime minister's residence and his dignity suffered a bit of damage. The imperial kitchen was contaminated by the entry of hoi polloi. Although several million individuals ultimately were involved in rallies and protests nationwide, there was no mayhem, no serious violence, no death or serious injury, virtually no destruction of property, and not even a discernible whisper of incitement to revolt. There was not the slightest threat whatsoever to the security or authority of the occupation forces. Nonetheless, on May 20 MacArthur saw fit to warn the Japanese people "that the growing tendency towards mass violence and physical processes of intimidation, under organized leadership, present a grave menace to the future development of Japan."

The supreme commander's warning went on to condemn "excesses by disorderly minorities"—a phrase that was rendered as *bōmin demo* in Japanese and carried with it chilling memories of the language in "peace preservation" legislation that SCAP had ordered abrogated only a half year previously. The dictionary definition of *bōmin* is "mob, rioters, insurgents," while *demo* is borrowed English for "demonstration." With this ominous phrase, the popular turbulence of April and May—full of contradictions but also representing a historic expression of popular defiance of corrupt and inept government—became tarred as a mere step toward mob rule.

"The statement had a startling effect," Mark Gayn noted in his diary. "I could actually recall no American move that matched this pronouncement in its repercussions. There was consternation in union headquarters and in the offices of the left-wing parties. In conservative quarters, there was undisguised jubilation." On the following day, MacArthur summoned Yoshida, who was still struggling to patch together a new government, and promised additional U.S. food shipments to avert starvation. The next day the hitherto despondent Yoshida announced that he had succeeded in forming a cabinet.[15]

This was but one of several signals that the victors had now drawn a clear line between permissible and impermissible ways of bringing about their democratic revolution, and had drawn this line on the conservative side. While MacArthur and the emperor were issuing their tandem statements, the U.S. representative to the four-power Allied Council that met in Tokyo similarly seized the occasion of the May protests to launch an anticommunist campaign simultaneously directed against the Soviet Union and the popular movement, which he intimated were in intimate collusion. Even the message which organizers of the May 1 commemorations had delivered to Allied authorities, he declared with no justification, bore earmarks of having been translated from a "foreign" language. What he meant was that the Russians wrote it—a cavalier, contemptuous, and soon-to-be conventional dismissal of any serious radical expression.[16]

This impression of a conservative crackdown was reinforced by a celebrated episode known as the "placard incident," which captured many of the ambiguities of Food May Day—spontaneity from below, a curious mocking of the emperor while appealing to him, and the emperor worship of the Americans themselves. The placard involved was a crudely lettered sign brought to the demonstration by Matsushima Shōtarō, a Communist employee of a precision tool company. Couched partly in colloquial language and partly in the language reserved for the august sovereign himself, it read:

> *Imperial Edict*
> The national polity has been maintained.
> I am eating my fill.
> You people, starve and die.
> —Imperial sign and seal.

The other side of the placard contained a less often quoted statement: "Why are we starving no matter how much we work? Answer, Emperor Hirohito!"[17]

The mock imperial edict was cleverly irreverent, and whether Matsushima or the Communist Party group at his company actually thought it up, it was an indication, presumably, of healthy iconoclasm after decades of emperor-centered thought control. The government did not view matters this way, and on the day of the emperor's "family nation" homilies issued a warrant for Matsushima's arrest for the crime of lese majesty, that is, violating the dignity of the sovereign. At that moment, revision of the penal code was taking place under GHQ auspices and the issue of whether lese majesty would be allowed to remain was a bone of contention. The placard incident became a test of how far the conservative government could go in isolating the emperor from criticism and ridicule.[18]

To many Japanese who had embraced the idea of civil liberties, it was nothing short of shocking—and again shockingly reminiscent of the world of the peace-preservation laws—that the occupation authorities permitted the case to be dragged into the courts. While the Americans eventually did require the government to drop lese majesty provisions from the penal code, they nonetheless allowed Matsushima to be brought to trial. He was indicted on June 22. In October, apparently in response to GHQ pressure, the charge was changed to "libel" of the emperor. On November 2, the Tokyo District Court found Matsushima guilty and sentenced him to eight months imprisonment, but on the following day he was released under a general imperial amnesty that had been announced in conjunction with the proclamation of the new constitution.

Matsushima appealed the guilty sentence. In June 1947 an appeals court judged that he had indeed been guilty of lese majesty (rather than libel), but was qualified for pardon under the imperial amnesty. When the hapless placard carrier attempted to bring his case to the Supreme Court, he was turned down (in May 1948) on the grounds that the amnesty had voided his right of appeal. From the imperial perspective, this was all a splendid way of demonstrating how the emperor's magnanimity extended even to his most ungrateful subjects. To many ordinary people, the placard incident seemed more like a signpost indicating the limits of the new imperial democracy.[19]

Unmaking the Revolution from Below

While MacArthur's indictment of "disorderly minorities" chilled the popular movement, it certainly did not freeze it. One week after Food May Day, a thousand students representing some twenty universities, colleges, and technical high schools in the Tokyo area sponsored a third round of "May Day" demonstrations under the name "Student May Day." They called not only for self-government by faculties, students, and staff, but also for students to take an active role in ferreting out "war-criminal professors." With a certain imperiousness, these privileged young students also affirmed their solidarity with "the masses" in the democratic revolution.[20]

The date selected for Student May Day revealed an abiding feature of the democratization process—namely, that it worked best when linked in some way to domestic precedents. The May 1 rallies had been presented as the seventeenth celebration of May Day in Japan. The "give-us-rice" demonstrations that culminated in Food May Day were linked in people's minds to the great rice riots at the end of World War I, when housewives initiated a nationwide series of protests against food shortages that helped usher in the era of "Taishō democracy." Similarly, the date chosen for Student May Day was the thirteenth anniversary of the well-known "Takigawa incident," in which a professor had been expelled from Kyoto Imperial University for his liberal ideas. Out of these student demonstrations emerged a rhetoric of antimilitarism and a skepticism toward established authority that led to the formation the following year of the radical student federation Zengakuren (National Federation of Self-governing Student Associations).

Although U.S. food shipments averted the calamitous shortages of basic stables anticipated in mid-May, a corrosive inflation continued unchecked, relentlessly wiping out each and every wage increase won by workers. Early in 1947, the union of national railway employees typically calculated that the average salary of its members barely covered a quarter of family expenses.[21] In these circumstances, labor activists enjoyed impressive organizational successes even after MacArthur's reprimand. Both the anticommunist, Socialist-led labor federation Sōdōmei (All Japan General Federation of Trade Unions) and its rival, the Communist-penetrated Sanbetsu (National Congress of Industrial Unions), were established in August 1946. Two months later, the latter took the lead in mobilizing a nationwide "October offensive" in which, for the first and only time, "man-days" lost to labor disputes exceeded 1 percent of the total labor output theoretically available. This offensive, inspired partly by government threats to fire large numbers of national railway workers and other public employees, was followed by the most dramatic moment in Japanese working-class history: plans for a general strike that was to commence on February 1, 1947.

Initially supported by neutral and anticommunist as well as procommunist unions representing some 3 million workers, the proposed general strike marked a watershed for the radical vision of "peaceful revolution"—and, indeed, a turning point for left-wing anti-Americanism. Government offices and key industries were to be closed down, along with all telecommunications except those necessary for the effective operation of the occupation regime. The strike planners gave assurances that food deliveries would not be impeded and that the national railways would continue to service the occupation forces. As the first day of February approached, tension mounted throughout the country. Posters supporting the strike appeared even in remote rural areas. "Youth corps" were organized to protect strikers. Trains on the national railway, where communist sympathies ran strong, carried signs calling for the overthrow of the Yoshida government.

When negotiations between labor leaders and the government broke down completely on January 30, the momentum toward a general strike seemed irresistible. Late the following day, General MacArthur intervened to announce that he would not permit "the use of so deadly a social weapon." With this, the "two-one [February 1] strike" entered the realm of political legend. Conservatives who had merely been jubilant on May 20, when MacArthur condemned "disorderly minorities," were now ecstatic. Labor leaders wept openly, and the more radical among them now looked upon the United States with bitterness as a duplicitous opponent of any genuine "people's" democracy.

This new left-wing image of the victor as more hypocrite than liberator was memorably conveyed by Ii Yashirō, the chief coordinator of the strike's organizing committee, whose account of SCAP's intervention became an indelible part of postwar labor history. As Ii told the story, he was summoned by General Marquat, the head of GHQ's Economic and Scientific Section, on January 31 and ordered to sign a statement canceling the strike. He responded by asking: "What kind of democracy is this?" Japan's unions were democratic, he declared, and decided policy by majority vote. That being the case, he had no authority to cancel the proposed strike. He vainly tried to assure Marquat that the strikers had no intention of impeding occupation activities or food deliveries. At that point, Marquat evidently banged the table in fury and some seven or eight military police spilled into the room brandishing their pistols. Ii, in his own turn, erupted. He asked the Americans why they were threatening violence, and exclaimed: "Japanese workers are not American slaves! Japanese workers are not fools!" Once Marquat had calmed down, he ordered the MPs to leave and brought in another labor leader, who persuaded Ii that many unions had experienced a change of heart. Ii agreed at this point to draft a statement calling off the general strike, which was translated on the spot and approved by Marquat. Ii's reluctant conclusion that there was no alternative was confirmed when, at the NHK broadcasting building, the ubiquitous and usually ebulliently radical Tokuda materialized and murmured, "Stop the strike."

In this, his darkest moment, Ii still managed to convey an impression of integrity and hope. In broadcasting his statement calling off the strike, he embellished on the text approved by Marquat. One must often, he told his labor constituency, take one step back for every two steps forward. He offered a *banzai* cheer for "workers and farmers." And, voice hoarse and heavy with emotion, he wept. Photographs of a trenchcoat-clad Ii holding his glasses in one hand and wiping tears from his eyes fixed his anguish in popular memory. Many of his listeners sobbed also. This too became part of the mythic story—"tears of limitless anger," as later leftwing accounts put it, "that workers instinctively felt toward the Japanese government and Americans." Some years later, Ii called this the pivotal moment at which it became clear that the American occupation authorities were "deceiving the Japanese people with democracy only at the tip of their tongues." Although the general election of April 1947 resulted in the formation of a short-lived Socialist-led coalition cabinet and union membership continued to rise, suppression of the general strike marked the beginning of the end of the possibility that labor might be an equal partner in the sharing of "democratic" power.[22]

GHQ and the Japanese conservatives were not alone in mistrusting the Communists, for labor and leftist leaders were fiercely factionalized among Communists, fellow travelers, social democrats of varying color, and virulent anticommunists. The party's contribution to the early struggle for a "peaceful democratic revolution" was, to say the least, double edged. Without question, the Communists were more effective than any other single group in encouraging and organizing popular energies against an antireformist government and a paralyzed corporate sector. At the same time, the radical left often tended to be cavalier regarding "bourgeois" issues of political democracy, and to denigrate the importance of the political and civil rights promoted by SCAP.

"Kempō yori meshi da"—"food before a constitution"—read a typical communist banner during the popular upheavals of May. Given that hunger and runaway inflation threatened to squeeze the life out of ordinary people, this emphasis may have been understandable. It did not, however, reflect an impressive commitment to institutionalizing political democracy. Consistent with its prewar position, the party tended to focus more on the elimination of "feudal vestiges" or the "reactionary government" than on the creation and extension of rights and protections. In-

ternally as well as publicly, it was hardly a champion of divergent views. That such a group anointed itself the vanguard of the movement for a genuine people's democracy ultimately undermined the emergence of a truly effective, broad-based democratic coalition. On the other hand, no other progressive group, liberal or socialist, possessed an élan or sense of purpose remotely comparable to the "lovable JCP" of these years.[23]

As the economy continued to founder, a predictable vicious circle ensued. The Communists and the radical wing of organized labor became more militant, alienating GHQ and making the Americans ever more receptive to abandoning reformism and embracing the civilian old guard; the occupation regime's increasing conservatism, in turn, goaded militants into stronger statements and more alienating actions. Early on, GHQ began compiling internal lists of undesirable "Reds" in public life, and these lists quickly became catholic in their embrace. In the summer of 1948, MacArthur reversed occupation labor policy by withdrawing the right to strike from public employees, who commonly were in the vanguard where

After initially heralding the victorious Allied forces as an "army of liberation," the legalized Communist Party began to emerge as a major critic of the "reverse course" in occupation policy. The party's considerable appeal is suggested in this photo of the turnout for a speech by its charismatic leader, Tokuda Kyūichi, in February 1949.

miserable pay, layoffs, and radical unionism were concerned. Simultaneously, occupation authorities worked diligently behind the scenes to promote the emergence of a virulently anticommunist "democratization" *(mindō)* movement within organized labor.

By 1949, "Red purge" had become one of the fashionable new terms of the occupation, appropriately expressed in Japanized English *(reddo pāji)*. Initially referred to within GHQ simply as a "troublemaker purge," the Red purge involved close collaboration among occupation officials, conservative politicians, government bureaucrats, and corporate managers. A major objective was to break radical unions at the company and industry level, and to this end some eleven thousand activist union members in the public sector were fired between the end of 1949 and the outbreak of the Korean War on June 25, 1950. After the war began, the purge was extended to the private sector (including the mass media), resulting in the dismissal of an additional ten to eleven thousand leftist employees by the end of 1950. Side by side with the "Red purge" came the "depurge"—a reference to the return to public activity of individuals previously purged "for all time" for having actively abetted militarism and ultranationalism.[24]

Following severe open criticism from the Kremlin-controlled Cominform in January 1950, Nosaka personally was forced to eat humble pie for the "lovable JCP" policy he had promoted, and the party was thrown into turmoil. On May 18, the central committee issued (with Politburo approval) a militant fifty-two page "thesis" that hostile chroniclers aptly characterized as constituting "the last rites for the "lovable Communist Party." For the Communists and radicals, the aftermath of these developments was swift and disastrous. On May 30, a celebration of America's Memorial Day in the plaza before the imperial palace was disrupted by Communist demonstrators (an apogee, of sorts, for the cartoonlike symbolism that so often marked the occupation). In the first violent confrontation between Japanese and Americans to mar the occupation, four Americans were stoned and roughed up; and when eight demonstrators were arrested for this, the Communist party newspaper recklessly carried their photographs and hailed them as "patriots." On June 6, MacArthur ordered the government to "remove and exclude from public service" all twenty-four members of the party's central committee; the next day he extended this purge to seventeen top editors of the party newspaper. Although party and paper were not suppressed, most top leaders including Tokuda and Nosaka went underground for the duration of the occupation. Tokuda made his way to China, where he died six years later.[25]

Despite its ultimate marginalization, the left contributed in major and enduring ways to defining the contours of democratization. As in much of Western Europe, Marxism in various versions became established as an integral part of political thought and activism, and radical or heterodox concepts became a familiar part of everyday life. Given their dynamic successes in mobilizing mass demonstrations, labor and the left established themselves as forces that, however weakened, still had to be accommodated. Economically, one result was the emergence of a style of capitalism that differed in significant ways from the American model. Influential economic policy makers (often taught by distinguished Marxist or neo-Marxist educators in elite universities) embraced the necessity and desirability of active state intervention in the economy. The goals of establishing job security and eliminating gross economic disparities became widely accepted. And, even as they undercut the emergence of a radical and autonomous labor movement, business executives and management collaborated with labor leaders to promote corporatist structures of "enterprise unionism" that were genuinely responsive to many of labor's demands.

Although the "reverse course" helped establish a domestic conservative hegemony of politicians, bureaucrats, and businessmen that remained dominant to the end of the century, Communists and Socialists continued to be elected to the Diet and to command serious attention in debates over public policy. They became the country's most articulate critics of acquiescence in U.S. Cold War policy—and (no small irony) the staunchest defenders, for decades to come, of the initial occupation ideals of demilitarization and democratization.

Part IV

DEMOCRACIES

chapter nine

IMPERIAL DEMOCRACY: DRIVING THE WEDGE

Until Japan surrendered, the emperor was the heart and soul of ideological indoctrination. Every soldier went to battle carrying the pocket-size *Senjinkun* or Field Service Code, whose opening sentence was this: "The battlefield is where the Imperial Army, acting under the Imperial command, displays its true character, conquering whenever it attacks, winning whenever it engages in combat, in order to spread the Imperial Way far and wide so that the enemy may look up in awe to the august virtues of His Majesty." In *Shinmin no Michi* (The Way of the Subject), a major tract issued four months before the attack on Pearl Harbor, the government's ideologues dwelled on the direct descent of the emperor from the sun goddess Amaterasu and characterized the national polity as a "theocracy" in which "the way of the subject is to be loyal to the Emperor in disregard of self, thereby supporting the Imperial Throne coextensive with the Heavens and with the Earth." Filial piety and loyalty were the supreme virtues of the imperial state, and *Shinmin no Michi* was at pains to denounce the "individualism, liberalism, utilitarianism, and materialism" that imperiled those virtues. Emperor Hirohito was sacrosanct. His war was holy. The virtues he embodied were unique and immutable.[1]

Hirohito was also, as it turned out, resilient and malleable, blessed by the heavens—and by General MacArthur more particularly—to survive and prosper while, all around him, his loyal subjects were denounced, purged, charged with war crimes, even executed. The emperor's role in Japan's aggression was never seriously investigated. He was dissuaded by the Americans from acknowledging even moral responsibility for the repression and violence that had been carried out in his name and with his endorsement. When members of the imperial entourage raised the possibility of his abdication, SCAP opposed this emphatically. Indeed, the occupation authorities chose not merely to detach the emperor from his holy war, but to resituate him as the center of their new democracy.

The political and ideological ramifications of this magical transmutation were enormous. Justice was rendered arbitrary. Serious engagement with the issue of war responsibility was deflected: if the nation's supreme secular and spiritual authority bore no responsibility for recent events, why should his ordinary subjects be expected to engage in self-reflection? Postwar political consciousness became muddled. Although the new constitution drafted by GHQ redefined the emperor as "the symbol of the State and of the unity of the people, deriving his position from the will of the people with whom resides sovereign power," the retention of the throne and remythologizing of Hirohito personally—two separate issues, although usually conflated—severely compromised that popular sovereignty. Hereditary privilege was reaffirmed by the "symbol" sovereign, who simultaneously remained his country's preeminent emblem of patriarchal authority. Although empresses had reigned in earlier times, the victors allowed the monarchy to retain its modern tradition of permitting only males to succeed to the throne. In addition, the emperor remained the incarnation of a putative racial purity as well as cultural homogeneity.

From this perspective, the "unity of the people" amounted to a new way of phrasing the old "family nation" ideology. Harmony and hierarchy were valued over contention and individuality, and the new symbol-emperor still embodied the nineteenth- and early twentieth-century invention of a "Yamato" identity that excluded Koreans, Formosans, Chinese, Caucasians—aliens of whatever ethnic origin—from becoming "Japanese." Despite the formal separation of church and state, the emperor also remained high priest of the indigenous Shinto religion, conducting esoteric rites in the palace and reporting to his divine ancestors at the great Ise shrine. All of this left him as the supreme icon of genetic separateness and blood nationalism, the embodiment of an imagined timeless essence that set the Japanese apart from—and superior to—other peoples and cultures.

The practice of reckoning contemporary time in accordance with the reign year of the sovereign was also left unrevised (this particular "tradition" dated back only to the mid-nineteenth century); and so the "Shōwa" era, which began with Hirohito's ascension to the throne in 1926, carried on unbroken, a calendrical declaration of fundamental continuity with the past.[2] The Shōwa era lasted until 1989, when the former "manifest deity" of the prewar ideologues finally passed away at the age of eighty-nine. In the Japanese manner of recording time, the emperor died in the sixty-fourth year of Shōwa, the period of occupation ("Shōwa 20" to "Shōwa 27") but a momentary interlude in his reign. For conservatives, this was a marvelous way of shrinking the importance of the era of defeat, and to the end of his life the emperor himself continued to emphasize that there had been no change in Japanese values.[3]

The charisma of the imperial institution was undeniably awesome. Even the Communists stumbled, foundered, and made fools of themselves when it came to the emperor. Yet the throne—and certainly Hirohito himself—were exceedingly vulnerable at the time of Japan's defeat. In their own lifetimes, the Japanese elites had witnessed the collapse of many great and seemingly powerful monarchies throughout the world, usually in the wake of war. Within the country, iconoclasts were emboldened to mock the emperor openly. In the victorious Allied nations, voices calling for Hirohito's indictment as a war criminal were loud and insistent. Even foreign defenders of the imperial institution such as the former ambassador Joseph Grew believed that, at the very least, there was no way the emperor could avoid responsibility for having signed the declaration of war. Months after the surrender, Grew still assumed that "Hirohito will have to go."[4] Many of the emperor's intimate advisers feared that this might indeed be the case, and well into 1946 much of the government's energy was devoted to ensuring the survival of not only the "national polity" but the incumbent sovereign himself.

In his memoirs, Yoshida Shigeru praised MacArthur as the "great benefactor" of his country, referring not to the gift of democracy (which Yoshida regarded with grave reservations) but to the supreme commander's preservation of the throne and protection of its august occupant in a time of unprecedented peril.[5] Yoshida was correct: SCAP's influence in these matters was decisive. It was also, in retrospect, predictable, for the reasoning behind the supreme commander's policies regarding the emperor was firmly established before surrender.

Psychological Warfare and the Son of Heaven

Psychological-warfare specialists in MacArthur's wartime command were naturally preoccupied with immediate military objectives rather than post-surrender planning. Nonetheless, the proposals they advanced for hastening the surrender of Japanese forces in the field and undermining morale in the home islands rested on an analysis of enemy patterns of behavior that remained unaltered after the surrender. Some of the key personnel who developed these wartime studies would accompany MacArthur to Tokyo and continue to advise him on affairs affecting the throne.

No one was more influential in this regard than Brigadier General Bonner F. Fellers, MacArthur's military secretary and the chief of his psychological-warfare operations. Fellers cut his teeth as an analyst of the Japanese psyche while attending the Command and General Staff School at Fort Leavenworth as an army captain in 1934–1935. While there, he prepared a research study entitled "The Psychology of the Japanese Soldier" that was prescient and remained dear to his heart. In this study, Fellers anticipated war between Japan and the United States over four years before it broke out and even predicted the adoption of suicidal *kamikaze* tactics once the war situation deteriorated. The intensity of Japanese loyalty and military discipline fascinated him, particularly because of its sharp contrast to high American desertion rates in World War I. "In methods of thought," he concluded, "the Japanese and the Americans are today as different as if each had always lived on different worlds, separated by hundreds of *light years.*" The Japanese, he noted in passing, looked on Western democracy as being of a "temporary character." In the summer of 1944, when MacArthur's command began seriously promoting Japanese surrenders in the field, Fellers produced "Answer to Japan," a report that amounted to a revised version of his "Psychology" study and was used as an orientation guide for Allied intelligence personnel. In addition, Fellers continued to circulate his old essay to military acquaintances. "Today I'd not change a line in this study," he told one of them in 1944.[6]

Although he was on the receiving end of enormous quantities of raw and processed intelligence materials including captured documents, letters and diaries from battlefield corpses, translations from the press and radio, and interrogations of prisoners, not to mention reports from various intelligence agencies, Fellers relied to a great degree on readily available English-language publications. Indeed, "the very best book in existence on Japanese psychology," he claimed, was a turn-of-the-century classic: Lafcadio Hearn's *Japan—An Attempt at Interpretation.*[7] The psychological profile that Fellers and his staff prepared from these various internal and public sources had, at least, the virtue of consistency. As with most official documents, once an observation had been put on paper by MacArthur's men, it tended to be recycled in subsequent reports. By sheer repetition, tentative early observations soon assumed the aura of gospel.

By mid-1944, Fellers had formulated a view of the role of the emperor in language that would remain essentially unchanged thereafter. MacArthur's policies regarding the throne clearly had their genesis not in any serious investigation after defeat of the actual situation in Japan, but rather in these wartime analyses that he received from the amateur psychologists and anthropologists in his own command. The earliest scripts for his later pronouncements and initiatives are to be found in the recommendations Fellers and his staff prepared.

As a basic rule, MacArthur's propaganda specialists observed a wartime policy of not provoking the enemy by attacking the emperor.[8] This was consistent with general U.S. war policy, which opposed military attacks against imperial sites or even the verbal denigration of Emperor Hirohito. Although the stated rationale for such restraint was that the Japanese regarded their sovereign with religious awe and would be even more inclined to fight to the death if he were attacked, other considerations were at work. As an internal report by the Office of Strategic Services (O.S.S.) noted in July 1944, "the desirability of eliminating the present Emperor is questionable; it is probable that he inclines personally toward the more moderate faction and might prove a useful influence later."[9]

Like the O.S.S. and other intelligence agencies, by the latter stages of the war MacArthur's command believed that the emperor held the key not only to surrender but also to postwar change. The task, as Fellers and his men put it, was to "drive a wedge" between the military leadership and the emperor (with his subjects) by persuading the Japanese that "gangster militarists" had not only duped them but betrayed their sacred leader. The Western propagandists, in a word, were ready to take a hand in reimagining an emperor divorced from the policies imperial Japan had pursued in his name, under his authority, and with his active cooperation for almost two decades.

At one point, Fellers flatly acknowledged that "as Emperor and acknowledged head of state, Hirohito cannot sidestep war guilt. He is a part of, and must be considered an instigator of, the Pacific War."[10] In the conclusion to his "Answer to Japan," however, he struck a different note. The emperor, he indicated, would be indispensable not only for effecting a surrender of the enemy's fighting forces but also as the spiritual core of a peacefully inclined postwar government that, it was assumed, would be made up of the now elderly conservative elites, including titled scions of the high nobility, who had controlled the country before the militarists gained ascendancy. This conclusion is worth quoting at length, for over one year and several million deaths later these observations would be resurrected by Fellers to help MacArthur justify not only retention of the throne, but of Hirohito as well:

An absolute and unconditional defeat of Japan is the essential ingredient for a lasting peace in the Orient. Only through complete military disaster and the resultant chaos can the Japanese people be disillusioned from their fanatical indoctrination that they are the superior people, destined to be the overlords of Asia. Only stinging defeat and colossal losses will prove to the people that the military machine is vincible and that their fanatical leadership has taken them the way of disaster.

The Japanese are tough physically and spiritually. But sometime during this extreme agony for the Japanese home people, it is to be hoped that in one quick moment calm-minded conservatives may see the light and save themselves before it is too late.

Enormous military reverses will make it clear to all that the gangster militarists have duped their people.

But this is not all. To the masses will come the realization that the gangster militarists have betrayed their sacred Emperor. They have led the Son of Heaven, Divine Ruler of the Empire, to the very precipice of destruction. Those who deceive the Emperor cannot exist in Japan. When this moment of realization arrives, the conservative, tolerant element of Japan which has long been driven underground possibly may come into its own. They may have sufficient leadership to take over the government, make the necessary concessions to save what remains of the archipelago, their people, and their Emperor. With Imperial Sanction of a peace, it will be acceptable to all. In this way it is possible that our war against Japan may end before it is necessary completely to lay waste to the land.

There must be no weakness in the peace terms. However, to dethrone, or hang, the Emperor would cause a tremendous and violent reaction from all Japanese. Hanging of the Emperor to them would be comparable to the crucifixion of Christ to us. All would fight to die like ants. The position of the gangster militarists would be strengthened immeasurably. The war would be unduly prolonged; our losses heavier than otherwise would be necessary.

There are those among us who advocate slaughter of all Japanese, a virtual extermination of the race. The Asiatic War has brought so much suffering and taken so many lives that no fate seems too awful for the Japanese. However, once Japan's armed forces are destroyed, the military clique wiped out and the people thoroughly acquainted with the horror of war, it will be safe to stop the slaughter. The more civilians who are killed needlessly, the more bitter and lasting will be the feeling of those who survive. It would dislocate the mental equilibrium of our youth who performed the slaughter. It would belie our Christianity.

America must lead, not follow events. At the proper time we should permit the driving of a wedge between the Emperor and the people on the one hand, and the Tokyo gangster militarists on the other. Years of blood baths may possibly be avoided if we understand clearly our enemy and handle him intelligently. After Japan is *totally defeated*, American justice must be the way and light.

An independent Japanese army responsible only to the Emperor is a permanent menace to peace. But the mystic hold the Emperor has on his people and the spiritual strength of the Shinto faith properly directed need not be dangerous. The Emperor can be made a force for good and peace provided Japan is totally defeated and the military clique destroyed.

The Government must have a system of checks and balances. The Emperor must be surrounded by liberal civilian leaders. The military must be limited to an internal police force, responsible to civil authority. . . .

Once the Tokyo gangster militarists are dead, once the armed forces are destroyed and a liberal government formed under the Emperor, the Japanese people—sadder, fewer, and wiser—can begin the reorientation of their lives.[11]

This respectful appraisal of the emperor's benign potential and virtually totalitarian "spiritual" control over the Japanese psyche would become the bedrock of postwar policy. In the spring of 1945, MacArthur's command convened a meeting of psychological-warfare personnel from the combined U.S. and British forces in Manila. By then, Fellers and his staff had compressed "Japanese behavior patterns" that could be exploited by the Allies into a fifteen-point mantra: "inferiority complex, credulousness, regimented thought, tendency to misrepresent, self-dramatization, strong sense of responsibility, super-aggressiveness, brutality, inflexibility, tradition of self-destruction, superstition, face-saving tendency, intense emotionality, attachment to home and family, and Emperor worship."[12] The Manila conference did not linger on the emperor per se, but among the propaganda slogans proposed was "Give the Emperor back to the people." A "wedge" policy was agreed upon, as was the idea of using the emperor "to further our aims" at a "proper time." At one point, the naval intelligence officer for the British fleet in the Pacific suggested, apparently in all seriousness, that *kamikaze* suicide attacks might be deterred by painting the emperor's picture on the sides of Allied ships.[13] Merely imagining the sight of such an Allied armada (and how it might have played in newsreels back home) boggles the mind, but it does convey a sense of how the problem of the emperor obsessed these men.

The most impassioned commentary on the emperor came from Colonel Sidney Mashbir, head of the large Allied Translator and Interpreter Section (ATIS) and one of Fellers' trusted associates. In an oral presentation (including parenthetical asides) unimpeded by coherence, Mashbir was recorded as declaring that "It would be the height of folly to kill the Emperor who is merely the product of 2,500 years of biological ungodliness (inbreeding). You cannot remove their Emperor worship from these people by killing the Emperor (who is only a part of the family ancestor worship system) any more than you remove the godhead of Jesus and have any Christianity left." Responding to a question, Mashbir emphasized the need to "really depend upon their blind obedience to the Emperor."[14]

The bluntness with which participants at the Manila meeting were told that "closely-knit, Western logic is not in accordance with Japanese psychology" and that the Japanese were utterly incapable of comprehending American-style democracy is striking in retrospect. One of the secret papers Fellers distributed on this occasion expressed this in the following unequivocal terms:

> The people of Japan, who believe themselves to be gods, are unaware of and absolutely cannot understand either democracy or American political idealism as expressed in:
>   (1) Our Declaration of Independence.
>   (2) Our Constitution.
>   (3) The Atlantic Charter.

(4) Racial and religious tolerance.
(5) No punishment without fair trial.
(6) Opposition to slavery.
(7) Dignity of the individual.
(8) Supreme faith in the people.[15]

In the month preceding Japan's capitulation, the Psychological Warfare Branch of MacArthur's command had the opportunity to apply the wedge tactic directly to the home islands by way of shortwave radio. Colonel Mashbir played a major role in drafting and delivering a series of Japanese-language broadcasts, and his approach was blunt to the point of crudeness. The "militarists" or "military clique" were ridiculed and berated for having broken their "sacred pledge" to the emperor "and plunged the country into this catastrophe"—or, again, for "allowing these disasters to befall the Emperor's country." Mashbir asked rhetorically: "Have the officers of Japan recently served the Emperor with that utter loyalty expected of warriors?" It was the Allied mission to "drive out the demon of the military clique which is in possession of the Japanese people" in order to reacquaint the emperor with the wishes of his subjects." (Mashbir's broadcasts sometimes sounded as if he were soliciting a job in the emperor's inner circle.)[16]

Fellers' thinking about Japan was far more polished and complicated than his aide's. In a personal letter written after the surrender, he confided that he had "loved Japan since 1922." This was certainly a rare sentiment for an American officer to maintain through the Pacific War, and Fellers' responses to the horrors of that conflict were illuminating. When an army captain informed him in January 1945 that U.S. troops in the field were routinely killing Japanese who were attempting to surrender, Fellers deplored this on rather technical grounds. Since the Americans were dropping leaflets urging Japanese to surrender, he felt it "a matter of national honor that we make good our word, most of all with the enemy. Moreover, we want the prisoners because they all talk freely and, as you know, intelligence saves lives." Where the U.S. saturation bombing of Japanese cities was concerned, however, his condemnation was unqualified. In an internal memorandum dated June 17, 1945, Fellers described this as "one of the most ruthless and barbaric killings of non-combatants in all history."[17] As the war in Asia drew to its terrible denouement, he also forthrightly characterized it as a race war. "The war in Europe was both political and social," he wrote one week before surrender, whereas "the war in the Pacific was racial." In planning for peace, it was imperative to recognize that "the white man as overlord of the Orient is finished." "The American position in the Orient cannot be founded upon the theory of white supremacy," he insisted. "The Oriental must be placed on the basis of absolute equality with our people. . . . There must be no taboo because of race."[18]

Fellers had personal ties to well-placed Japanese, the most intimate tie being his cousin Gwen's marriage to the diplomat Terasaki Hidenari. In the aftermath of defeat, Terasaki was attached to the imperial court and worked as a liaison to Fellers as well as other GHQ officers, greatly facilitating a concordance of views between court circles and the highest level of the occupation command. MacArthur had no such personal ties, but his long pre–Pearl Harbor sojourn as field marshal in the Philippines had likewise persuaded him that Asia would be of central importance in the future global balance of power, and it was thus essential for Westerners to move toward rectifying the inequalities of the past. At the same time, since this vision existed side by side with his belief that Asia was culturally and politically backward, and that "the Oriental mind" had been socialized to kowtow to authority, MacArthur took for granted that the nations of the Far East still had to be led into this new era by such authority figures as himself. Where defeated Japan was concerned, this outlook made it natural to think of exercising a potent *double* authority by utilizing the emperor.

MacArthur had embraced the wedge policy long before he was actually appointed to head the Allied occupation. Roger Egeberg, his personal physician and sometimes confidante, recalled that in Manila in May 1945, the general poked a finger into his chest and "said he wanted peace to bring democracy to Japan. Further, he thought the Emperor was a captive of Tōjō and the warlords, that they were really responsible for the war and that Hirohito would be instrumental in permanently changing the structure of the Japanese government." On August 6, the day Hiroshima was bombed (but before word of the bombing reached him), MacArthur described the emperor as "a figurehead but not quite a stooge" at an off-the-record press conference. While in Manila, preparing for his newly assigned mission to Japan, he told Colonel Mashbir, "I have no desire whatever to debase [the emperor] in the eyes of his own people, as through him it will be possible to maintain a completely orderly government," adding that he desired the emperor to visit him once he was settled in Japan—an invitation Mashbir conveyed to the Japanese the day after the surrender ceremony on the *Missouri*.[19]

Purifying the Sovereign

The emperor's surrender broadcast was, in effect, a stage cue that set in motion a grandly choreographed strategy by court and government to "preserve the national polity." Seven hours afterward, Prime Minister Suzuki Kantarō informed the nation by radio that "His Majesty gave the sacred decision to end the war in order to save the people and contribute to the welfare and peace of mankind. The illustrious power of His Majesty's gracious benevolence is itself the protection of the national polity." The old, retired admiral went on to declare that the nation "sincerely apologized" to the emperor, it being understood that these were apologies for failing to attain victory. "Under any circumstances, whether we live or die, our role as subjects is to assist the imperial destiny which is as eternal as heaven and earth."[20]

The grand themes of the new imperial drama were spelled out in such early statements. While the emperor was portrayed as a magnanimous peacemaker, his subjects as a whole were to assume responsibility, not for the rise of militarism and aggression, but for failing to win the holy war. The Japanese race was now divided into the emperor on the one hand and everyone else on the other; and where responsibility for defeat was concerned, the lowliest subject was suddenly equal to the most beribboned and bemedaled officer or official. On the matter of blame, the old guard hastened to espouse the purest sort of democracy imaginable.

Public figures reiterated these themes ceaselessly during the two weeks before MacArthur's arrival, and the mass media followed their lead. On August 28, the notion of collective (but not imperial) guilt was given its consummate expression at a press conference in which Prince Higashikuni Naruhiko, who had succeeded Suzuki as premier, declared that "the repentance of the hundred million" was the essential first step toward national reconstruction. Addressing the opening session of the eighty-eighth Imperial Diet on September 4, Higashikuni lavished praise on the emperor for having paved the way "for the establishment of an eternal peace in order to save the people from hardships." "We deeply regret," the prime minister exclaimed, "to have caused Him so much anxiety."[21] An alien from another planet listening to these speeches might easily have concluded that Emperor Hirohito had ascended the throne in August 1945, just in time to end a terrible war, and that no one's feelings other than his mattered.

Foreign Minister Shigemitsu Mamoru, who signed the surrender documents on behalf of the emperor and the government, gave irreproachably devoted service to his sovereign in the traumatic days that followed the victors' arrival at the very end of August. To the Americans, he praised the emperor's innate pacifism and—just as Fellers had done in his wartime reports—warned of the revolutionary upheaval that would greet any attempts to eliminate the throne. At the same time, he offered thoughtful counsel to the emperor, advising him on ways to ride the inevitable tide of reform. In a long imperial audience on September 1, Shigemitsu read a memorandum from "Your Loyal Servant Mamoru" which amounted to a Japanese version of the wedge strategy.

The demands in the Potsdam Declaration were flexible, he assured the emperor, and contained nothing that would hinder Japan's reconstruction. The mistakes of the recent past had occurred because the identity between the emperor's heart and the people's heart had been lost after the Meiji period, when the military succeeded in inserting itself between the sovereign and his subjects. The true "spirit of Japan," essentially democratic, included respect for fundamental human rights as well as freedom of thought, religion, and expression. The democracy demanded by the Potsdam Declaration would be realized when the emperor's thoughts and his subjects' wishes were again unified. The "empire" should commit itself to democratic reforms with a zeal double that of the early Meiji period. Shigemitsu concluded this emotional presentation by submitting two poems to the emperor. In one he spoke of himself as a shield for the throne. In the other he anticipated a day when the nation would be so prosperous that people would look back and scorn his (Shigemitsu's) name—as the person, presumably, to whom had fallen the humiliating task of signing the document of surrender.[22]

There was, of course, an implausible aura to all this, as if the antidemocratic rhetoric of "The Way of the Subject" that the emperor's loyal servants had been spouting only yesterday had been no more than a slip of the tongue. Had Shigemitsu been so foolhardy as to openly declare that the national polity was compatible with Western-style democracy one month earlier, in all likelihood he would have been jailed (or committed to a mental institution); and in all likelihood the emperor would have observed his disappearance in silence, just as he had the repression of other critics of the policies and orthodoxies proclaimed in his name. In the new circumstances of defeat, however, the emperor expressed agreement with his foreign minister's observations and filed them away in his mind for future use.

On September 3, Shigemitsu acted out his renewed vow to shield the throne by conveying the thesis of imperial innocence and militarist conspiracy directly to General MacArthur in a private meeting. The foreign minister's immediate purpose on this occasion was to persuade the supreme commander to abandon plans to administer the country through direct military government. Throughout history, he told the general, "our emperors always have been thoroughly pacifistic," and Emperor Hirohito was no exception. He had opposed the recent war, been ever diligent in seeking peace, and played a decisive role in ending hostilities. Shigemitsu emphasized that the emperor understood the terms of the Potsdam Declaration and was fully prepared to support them. Moreover, he enjoyed the "total admiration" of his subjects. It followed that the easiest way for SCAP to enforce the Potsdam stipulations would be to work indirectly "through the Japanese government instructed by the emperor."[23]

As Shigemitsu told the tale, MacArthur accepted his argument immediately and ordered direct military government to be abandoned while the foreign minister was still sitting in the general's office. (Unknown to him, the supreme commander already had received instructions from Washington sanctioning indirect governance.) This was the beginning of a concerted campaign by former high-ranking officials and officers to "brief" occupation authorities about the emperor's noninvolvement in war policy up to the moment when, as the soon-famous story had it, he intervened to break a deadlock among the six military officers and civilian ministers who constituted his supreme war council and cast the deciding vote for capitulation. In their turn, MacArthur's staff actively encouraged the emperor's entourage to keep burnishing this image of an essentially pacifistic sovereign.[24]

Shigemitsu was subsequently indicted as a "Class A" war criminal, found guilty of contributing to the diplomatic policies that fostered Japanese aggression, and sentenced to imprisonment—his sovereign's shield to the end.

The Letter, the Photograph, and the Memorandum

The Shōwa emperor was not an eloquent man; he had never been socialized to be capable of even normal conversation. He was intelligent, but gave no hint of engaging in self-reflection. His education as heir apparent had been rigorous and inflexible, particularly so, perhaps, because his father, the Taishō emperor, was mentally incompetent. He rarely if ever conveyed self-doubt, but neither did he display overweening arrogance. He was scrupulously, almost compulsively, attentive to detail. There is no evidence that, prior to the defeat, "democracy" was of any genuinely serious interest to him apart from being a threat that might get out of control. There is ample evidence, on the other hand, that he moved pragmatically with the prevailing winds. On occasion, both prewar and postwar, he took initiative on matters of policy.

The emperor's lack of self-reflection concerning the war emerged in a rare short letter he wrote on September 9 to his eldest son, the crown prince Akihito, then twelve years old. It might have been expected that such a communication at such a time would have been philosophical as well as practical. There was precedent for such reflection in traditional Japanese writings, but this was not the emperor's *métier*. His letter to his son was cryptic and dry. It concerned, just as most official sermonizing then did, not the war itself but rather "the reasons for defeat." In this most private of communications, at this extraordinary moment, the emperor stressed the ineptitude of his military advisers and made no mention at all of the democratic ideals Shigemitsu had preached about so fervently.

Japan lost the war, Hirohito explained, because "our people" took the Americans and British too lightly. The military had overemphasized spirit and neglected science. Whereas the Meiji emperor had been blessed with great generals and admirals, officers of the post–World War I period failed to grasp the big picture. They knew how to advance but not how to retreat. Had the war continued, the emperor concluded, he could not have protected the "three holy regalia" (the imperial mirror, sword, and jewel), and most of his subjects would have perished. Thus, holding back his tears, he accepted defeat "to preserve the seeds of our people."[25]

It may seem odd that the emperor chose to evoke the imperial regalia so emotionally in the same breath with criticism of the military's irrationality, but he had also dwelled on these objects when agonizing over surrender and would do so again the following spring when dictating his version of the war to court aides. The hallowed mirror, sword, and jewel appear to have obsessed Hirohito not merely as symbols of legitimacy and majesty, but as sacred objects that dated back, as the national foundation myths maintained, to the divine origins of the imperial line. The regalia exemplified the "spirit of Japan" in the most rarefied sense, and it must be assumed that mention of them, along with the awkwardly phrased reference to the "seeds of our people," was the emperor's way of conveying his sense of being the inheritor of a sacred kingship. Never, not even in his heralded "declaration of humanity" four months later, would Emperor Hirohito repudiate his mythic descent from the sun goddess Amaterasu.[26]

In another rare, private document of the times, the crown prince's diary, we have an even more cryptic (and amusing) indication of how defeat was explained in court circles. On the day of his father's broadcast, Akihito dutifully recorded that Japan had lost the war for two fundamental reasons: material backwardness, particularly in science, and individual selfishness. One on one, Japanese were superior to Americans, the earnest young heir apparent noted, but the Americans were superior when it came to working as a group. The key to the future thus lay in developing scientific prowess and learning to work harmoniously as a nation as the Americans did. So much for cultural canards about egoistic Westerners and group-oriented Japanese![27]

The emperor's letter and the crown prince's diary were private writings that remained unknown to the public for many years. The great campaign to drive the wedge, demonize the military, make the emperor a pacifist, and construct an imperial democracy, on the other hand, was eminently public. Both the Japanese and the Americans used the mass media to advance their ultimately convergent positions. On September 21, for example, MacArthur told the United Press that "untold savings in American life, money, and time" had resulted from retaining the emperor.[28] Three days later, under a front-page headline reading "Hirohito in Interview Puts Blame on Tojo in Sneak Raid; Says He Now Opposes War," the *New York Times* published an unprecedented "interview" with the emperor, based primarily on a written response to questions submitted in advance. The most significant of these responses, which had actually been drafted in Shigemitsu's Foreign Ministry, had the emperor asserting "that he had had no intention of having his war rescript employed as former Premier Hideki Tojo had used it when Japan launched her sneak attack on Pearl Harbor. He said that he had expected Tojo to declare war in the usual, formal manner, if necessary." In a complementary article, Kido Kōichi, the emperor's most intimate advisor, was paraphrased as stating that "Hirohito knew nothing in advance about the Pearl Harbor attack, learning about it later from the palace radio."[29]

This was camouflage, but it was precisely what the wedge theorists in MacArthur's headquarters wanted to hear. A confidential report to the emperor's astute vice chamberlain Kinoshita Michio some weeks later indicated how misleading the answer really was. The military attaché who wrote this concluded, "it is obvious that, as the ruler, he [the emperor] bears responsibility for the nation's war unless he is a robot." As evidence of the sovereign's responsibility, the attaché noted, insofar as the opening of hostilities were concerned, Emperor Hirohito understood and gave orders for preparations for war, deployment of the fleet, the mission of the fleet, the decision to pull out the fleet if last-minute diplomatic negotiations with the United States succeeded, and the time for beginning hostilities.

What the emperor had not expected was merely what no one, including Tōjō himself, had anticipated: that the attack on Pearl Harbor would be launched before the U.S. government received a note from the Japanese embassy in Washington formally breaking off relations. The message had not been delivered on time because of an absurdly human faux pas: an embassy staff member took too long typing it. Apart from this unforeseen development, which without question made the surprise attack seem especially "treacherous," Hirohito was well briefed on the Pearl Harbor strategy, right down to the reason for choosing Sunday ("a day of rest") for the surprise attack. Contrary to the impression conveyed in the widely cited *Times* "interview," he signed the declaration of war with full knowledge of the military's intentions.[30]

As it transpired, however, parts of the bureaucracy were not yet in on the strategy for saving the emperor, notably, the Home Ministry, which—six weeks after the capitulation and a month after the Americans' arrival—still controlled the police and practiced censorship. When the emperor's comments in the *Times* were reported in the Japanese press on September 29, Home Ministry officials attempted to confiscate the offending editions. They opposed domestic publication of the statement about Pearl Harbor not on the grounds that it was untrue, but because it was beneath the dignity of the sovereign to single out his officials for public criticism. "Inappropriate" *(mazui)* was the term used by the official in charge.

This was the setting in which the entire country was confronted with The Photograph—the most famous visual image of the entire occupation period, which appeared in the same newspapers. This overshadowed accounts of the emperor's "interview," appalled the Home Ministry's censors (a banner day indeed for the watchdogs), and was another reason that they attempted to recall those press runs. The photo depicted MacArthur and the emperor standing together in the general's quarters, and there was no mistaking who possessed greater authority. The supreme commander, wearing an open-necked khaki shirt and no medals, held himself almost casually, hands behind his hips, arms slightly akimbo. He towered over the emperor, who stood stiffly to his left in full morning dress. Even the age difference between the two leaders reinforced the general's seniority. MacArthur was sixty-five years old at the time. The emperor, forty-four, was young enough to have been his son.

The idea for this meeting, which took place on September 27, usually is attributed to Yoshida Shigeru. Colonel Mashbir, on the other hand, claimed he conveyed the invitation to Okazaki Kazuo of the Foreign Ministry the day following the surrender ceremony.[31] Be that as it may, the idea for the photograph was MacArthur's, and his decision to make it public revealed the deft touch of a man who had spent much of his career practicing public relations. The photo established MacArthur's authority for all to see, while simultaneously demonstrating his receptivity to the emperor. As an unplanned bonus, SCAP also was able to override the Home Ministry's attempt to censor the newspapers carrying it, thereby turning the occasion into an affirmation of freedom of the press.

In all, three photographs were taken on this occasion. Two were unusable because the subjects were not ready for the camera (in one, MacArthur's eyes were closed and the emperor's mouth open; in the other, the emperor was again gaping). On such slender margins, the moment of a shutter's blink, often rest our renderings of compelling events. Rigid royalists like the Home Ministry's censors immediately saw the published photo as an appalling sort of lese majesty. In virtually every way, the iconography of height, posture, age, and locale placed the emperor in an inferior position. This reading of the situation was correct, but also unimaginative. The photograph is often said to mark the moment when it really came home to most Japanese that they had been vanquished and the Americans were in charge. At the same time—and this is what the censors and the more overwrought superpatriots missed—it also made it plain that SCAP was hospitable to the emperor, and would stand by him.[32]

The meeting was arranged with little fanfare and took place not in MacArthur's office but at his personal residence in the former American embassy building. The emperor arrived promptly at ten o'clock in his custom-made Rolls Royce, formally dressed in cutaway and top hat and unexpectedly accompanied by several carloads of imperial guards and court attendants. On the American side only a few individuals witnessed his arrival, among them Fellers and the exhuberant Kabuki lover Faubion Bowers. As Bowers later described the event, there was a touch of Gilbert and Sullivan, if not Kabuki, in the opening sallies of this first encounter between the two imperial presences. Fellers and Bowers saluted the emperor, whereupon His Highness bowed and shook their hands. Bowers then took Hirohito's top hat, which seemed to alarm the sovereign, who understandably must have arrived with dire forebodings that all sorts of things might be taken away from him.

This famous photo taken at the first meeting of General MacArthur and
Emperor Hirohito on September 27, 1945, created a sensation when published
in the Japanese press. In a single stroke, it established both MacArthur's
authority and the fact that he would stand by the emperor.

MacArthur burst upon the scene at that point, "saying, in that stentorian voice of burnished gold that thrilled everyone who heard it, 'You are very, very welcome, sir!' " It was the first time Fellers had ever heard the general say "sir" to anyone. The supreme commander reached out to clasp the emperor's hand, and the emperor simultaneously bowed so deeply that the handshake ended up taking place above his head. MacArthur then whisked the emperor inside, accompanied only by the imperial household interpreter Okumura Katsuzō, leaving Fellers and Bowers in unsuccessful pursuit of a topic of conversation with the stranded court retainers. Bowers brought up Kabuki, and later said he might as well have brought up rodeos. When Fellers mentioned having been an attaché to King Farouk in Egypt and spoke of duck hunting along the Nile, one of the chamberlains asked if he would like to hunt ducks on the palace grounds—an idle bit of conversation that later led to a steady stream of invitations to GHQ officers to take part in "imperial duck hunts."[33]

The general and the emperor spent around forty minutes together, and in theory both parties agreed to keep the details of what they discussed confidential. The two men would meet again on ten occasions, in all of which the same policy of official secrecy prevailed. Apparently no notes were ever taken on MacArthur's side, and minutes by the Japanese interpreters were—with two exceptions—never made public.[34] By this practice, SCAP in effect extended the life of the "chrysanthemum curtain" that surrounded the throne, even enhancing its aura of transcendence and inviolability. In the months that followed, occupation authorities would, in fact, draw the curtain tighter by refusing to permit serious investigation of the emperor's war responsibility or even to let him be interrogated concerning the events for which his loyal servants were about to be brought to trial.

This secrecy enabled both sides to leak selective versions of what actually transpired in the momentous meeting of September 27. MacArthur proceeded to use the occasion to embellish his portrait of the emperor as the "first gentleman of Japan." He told his aides that Hirohito had offered to take responsibility for the war upon himself, and later offered this same heroic narrative to the public in his memoirs.[35] The Japanese side, on its part, actually went public on a parallel track within a few days. A Home Ministry spokesman, adroitly scrambling to regain lost ground, stated that MacArthur had made a "tremendous impression" on the emperor, who in turn had declared himself "well satisfied" with the occupation's progress thus far. The spokesman went on to emphasize that General MacArthur "expressed the opinion that the smooth occupation was really due to the Emperor's leadership." This was duly reported in the Western press and never repudiated by GHQ.[36]

Like many of MacArthur's oft-told tales, his statement that the emperor volunteered to take responsibility for the war upon himself appears to have been, at best, a creatively ornamented version of what actually was said. For, as it happened, detailed minutes written immediately afterwards by Okumura, the emperor's interpreter, eventually did see the light of day three decades later. They tend to confirm the Home Ministry's version of events. In this confidential reconstruction, the emperor is never quoted as offering to assume responsibility for the war, whereas the supreme commander emerges almost as a fawning courtier awed by his proximity to "Your Majesty" and extraordinarily solicitous in his comments.

On the basis of Okumura's transcript, it is difficult to say who was having an audience with whom, although MacArthur clearly dominated the conversation. After some introductory courtesies, the general launched into a lengthy monologue about the horrors of modern war, so vividly revealed by the atomic bombs. Then, almost as if echoing lines from the emperor's rescript, he praised Hirohito for his "great prompt decision" to end hostilities and spare his people immeasurable suffering. In obvious reference to the chorus of world opinion calling for the emperor's indictment as a war criminal, the general went on to lament the "hatreds and feelings of revenge" that arise among people who never actually have been to war, referring specifically to the "regrettable" cacophony of public opinion in the American, British, and Chinese media.

At this point, according to Okumura's account, the emperor intervened to state that he had wanted to avoid the war and regretted its occurrence. MacArthur seized on this to emphasize that he appreciated how much the emperor had hoped for peace, and how difficult it had been for him to lead the public in one direction while it was moving so strongly in another. Only history could judge both men, he solemnly observed, long after they were dead—surely a reassuring comment considering the fear in court circles about Hirohito being judged imminently, while still alive. The emperor then intervened again. It went without saying, he stated, that he and his subjects deeply understood the fact of defeat and that he intended to do his best to carry out the stipulations of the Potsdam Declaration while helping to reconstruct a new Japan on the basis of peace.

And so it went, the supreme commander paying respect to the commander in chief and being given assurance of cooperation in return. MacArthur praised the emperor's "august virtue" (*miitsu*, in Okumura's rendering) as manifest in the discipline with which his order to lay down arms had been carried out. This, he said, should be encouraging to the emperor as he confronted the tasks ahead of him. "Needless to say," Okumura quoted MacArthur as saying, "there is no one else who knows as much about Japan and its people as you." The general encouraged the emperor to pass on any advice he might have in the future through his grand chamberlain or officials of his choice, and assured him that any such communications would remain confidential. After touching on other topics, the emperor departed expressing his hopes that he would have many more opportunities to meet with MacArthur. The supreme commander, in turn, spoke of the great honor of having met with the emperor.

Prior to this meeting, intimate court sources tell us, Hirohito had been tense and uncertain. Bowers noticed that he was trembling when he arrived (the *New York Times* interviewer of a day earlier had made a similar observation). He left the meeting buoyed in spirit, visibly more relaxed and confident—obviously with good reason. The emperor immediately told Kido Kōichi about the compliments MacArthur had paid him, and Kido was immensely relieved. As he later noted, if this meeting had not occurred, it would have been exceedingly difficult to defend the emperor against charges of war crimes. On the following day, the empress sent Mrs. MacArthur a bouquet of spider chrysanthemums mixed with lilies grown on the palace grounds. The next week, the MacArthurs received an elegant lacquered writing box embossed in gold from the emperor and empress.[37]

Had the imperial household been privy to communications at the top level of GHQ, they would have been ecstatic, for there was little fundamental difference between their hopes and SCAP's intentions. On October 1, MacArthur received through Fellers a short legal brief that made absolutely clear that SCAP had no interest in seriously investigating Hirohito's actual role in the war undertaken in his name. The brief took as "facts" that the emperor had not exercised free will in signing the declaration of war; that he had "lack of knowledge of the true state of affairs"; and that he had risked his life in attempting to effect the surrender. It offered, in awkward legalese, the one-sentence "Conclusion" that "If fraud, menace or duress sufficient to negative intent can be affirmatively established by the Emperor, he could not stand convicted in a democratic court of law." And it ended with the following "Recommendation":

a. That in the interest of peaceful occupation and rehabilitation of Japan, prevention of revolution and communism, all facts surrounding the execution of the declaration of war and subsequent position of the Emperor which tend to show fraud, menace or duress be marshalled.

b. That if such facts are sufficient to establish an affirmative defense beyond a reasonable doubt, positive action be taken to prevent indictment and prosecution of the Emperor as a war criminal.[38]

On the next day, General Fellers prepared a long memorandum for MacArthur's exclusive perusal that spelled out in richer detail why it was imperative that such mitigating "facts" be marshaled. Fellers's memo was written before SCAP's "civil liberties" directive, before free discussion existed in Japan, before political prisoners had been released from prison, before the most basic questions of "war responsibility" had been clearly formulated, before trends in popular sentiment had been seriously evaluated, before it was even legal for Japanese to speak such phrases as "popular sovereignty." It read, in full, as follows:

The attitude of the Japanese toward their Emperor is not generally understood. Unlike Christians, the Japanese have no God with whom to commune. Their emperor is the living symbol of the race in whom lies the virtues of their ancestors. He is the incarnation of national spirit, incapable of wrong or misdeeds. Loyalty to him is absolute. Although no one fears him, all hold their Emperor in reverential awe. They would not touch him, look into his face, address him, step on his shadow. Their abject homage to him amounts to a self abnegation sustained by a religious patriotism the depth of which is incomprehensible to Westerners.

It would be a sacrilege to entertain the idea that the Emperor is on a level with the people or any governmental official. To try him as a war criminal would not only be blasphemous but a denial of spiritual freedom.

The Imperial War Rescript, 8 December 1941, was the inescapable responsibility of the Emperor who, as the head of a then sovereign state, possessed the legal right to issue it. From the highest and most reliable sources, it can be established that the war did not stem from the Emperor himself. He has personally said that he had no intention to have the War Rescript used as Tojo used it.

It is a fundamental American concept that the people of any nation have the inherent right to choose their own government. Were the Japanese given this opportunity, they would select the Emperor as the symbolic head of the state. The masses are especially devoted to Hirohito. They feel that his addressing the people personally made him unprecedentally close to them. His rescript demanding peace filled them with joy. They know he is no puppet now. They feel his retention is not a barrier to as liberal a government as they are qualified to enjoy.

In effecting our bloodless invasion, we requisitioned the services of the Emperor. By his order seven million soldiers laid down their arms and are being rapidly demobilized. Through his act hundreds of thousands of American casualties were avoided and the war terminated far ahead of schedule. Therefore having made good use of the Emperor, to try him for war crimes, to the Japanese, would amount to a breach of faith. Moreover, the Japanese feel that unconditional surrender as outlined in the Potsdam Declaration meant preservation of the State structure, which includes the Emperor.

If the Emperor were tried for war crimes the governmental structure would collapse and a general uprising would be inevitable. The people will uncomplainingly stand any other humiliation. Although they are disarmed, there would be chaos and bloodshed. It would necessitate a large expeditionary force with many thousands of public officials. The period of occupation would be prolonged and we would have alienated the Japanese.

American long range interests require friendly relations with the Orient based on mutual respect, faith and understanding. In the long run it is of paramount, national importance that Japan harbor no lasting resentment.[39]

SCAP's commitment to saving and using the emperor was firm. The pressing, immediate task was to create the most usable emperor possible.

This seemed a daunting challenge at the time, given the loud chorus of hostile public opinion in the Allied camp. SCAP was under no illusions about the depth of animosity toward the emperor in the United States itself. While many planners in Washington were inclined to regard the emperor as a figure of "hollow" charisma, who could be used as easily for peace as he had been for war, mainstream opinion showed little tolerance for such notions. A Gallup poll conducted six weeks before the war ended indicated that 70 percent of Americans favored executing or harshly punishing the emperor. The Senate joined this clamor on September 18, and on October 16 MacArthur was instructed by the Joint Chiefs of Staff to "proceed immediately to assemble all available evidence of Hirohito's participation in and responsibility for Japanese violations of international law." Official policy concerning whether to reform the imperial institution or possibly even abolish it completely remained unresolved through the end of 1945. At the same time, the creation of the multination Far Eastern Commission, whose inauguration as an advisory committee to the occupation was delayed until early 1946, introduced the possibility of an imminent coordinated campaign against the throne from representatives of such recent enemies as China, Australia, the Philippines, and the Soviet Union. Authorities in Tokyo, following these developments closely, felt an understandable sense of urgency to change the emperor's image quickly before outside pressure forced their hand.[40]

In this atmosphere, Fellers and others did not hesitate to offer private words of encouragement and advice to the royalists. Near the end of October, Fellers went so far as to remind a well-connected Japanese general that the problem of the emperor's responsibility for the attack on Pearl Harbor was still the "most important and critical" issue on the American side, urging him to come up with a good "general defense" of the emperor that would help MacArthur override public opinion in the United States and elsewhere. It was clear, this contact reported to the chief cabinet secretary, that "both MacArthur and Fellers have very warm feelings toward His Majesty," and were "thinking of how to solve this problem without causing trouble for the emperor." Had such clandestine advice to manipulate the historical record become known at the time, it would have been deemed scandalous.[41]

In the months that followed, the royalists and their American supporters engaged in an clumsy dance on the matters of how best to protect and use the emperor, sometimes listening to different music, often out of step. Yet in the end their collaboration proved remarkably effective in dressing the emperor in new clothes, ensuring his personal security, and redefining the throne as the centerpiece of the new democracy. In the process, a striking relationship of open social fraternization between court circles and the upper echelons of the occupation staff was cultivated. The imperial household took the initiative in this, quickly revealing a genius for grasping the Americans' love of aristocratic pomp and pageantry. Invitations were regularly extended to high occupation officials to participate in the court's genteel pastimes. Geisha parties became bonding places for the middling elites, but the upper-class activities to which high-ranking members of the occupation force were invited were refined to a fault: firefly catching, cherry-blossom viewing on the palace grounds, bamboo-sprout hunts, traditional sword-fighting exhibitions at the palace, even an occasional wild-boar hunt. Nothing was more prized, however, than being invited to an imperial duck hunt. The first such invitation was extended to some twenty high GHQ officers on November 4, and in the years that followed there were sometimes as many as two or even three such hunts a week. General MacArthur himself never deigned to participate in these or any other such affairs, but his wife and young son Arthur joined in happily. So did the president of the Tokyo war-crimes tribunal and the American head of the prosecution staff, who were in the process of hanging or incarcerating some of the emperor's most devoted servants.[42]

The imperial duck hunts bore no resemblance to the Western practice of detaching wild fowl from their heartbeats with shotguns. Guests assembled at an imperial preserve where mallards, teals, and other game birds had been attracted to narrow ditches or channels baited with rice. There they were greeted by a court chamberlain, who conveyed a cordial welcome from the emperor and briefed them on how the ducks were to be caught. Each hunter was given a net that looked like a gigantic trout-fishing net and then waited behind a blind until a gamekeeper gave the signal to move in on a channel full of feeding ducks. The guests netted the startled fowl as they attempted to take flight, then regrouped and moved on to another ditch.

As one American major general described the sport, "four or five of us rushed in on each side of the ditch with our nets held high at which time the ducks took off straight up. We swooped and swished with our nets as the ducks passed and usually came up with a bird. My best batting average was 60 percent, which is good in any league." Ducks that escaped the hunters were sometimes picked off by falcons, an elegant royal touch indeed. After the swooping and swishing was finished, guests adjourned to a nearby building where they sat Japanese style at low tables and sipped *sake*. Imperial chefs assisted them in grilling duck filets on small charcoal hibachis.[43]

For many Allied officers and high civilian officials, the imperial duck hunt was the most memorable moment of their fleeting interlude as nobility in a foreign land. On these or other occasions, they might even hope to receive a small gift embossed with the sixteen-petal imperial chrysanthemum crest. While the media in the United States were chuckling and enthusing over the "Americanization" of Japan, the Japanese were quietly and skillfully Japanizing the Americans.

It was all part of the challenge of conquering the conqueror.

chapter ten

IMPERIAL DEMOCRACY:
DESCENDING PARTWAY
FROM HEAVEN

When ordinary Japanese were asked directly whether they wished to retain the emperor and the imperial institution, an overwhelming majority
answered affirmatively. Initially, most were thunderstruck simply at being
asked, for the question itself (not to speak of a negative response) would
have been treasonous prior to October 1945. Subsequent polls continued
to indicate strong support for retaining the throne, but this was misleading if interpreted—*pace* Fellers—as revealing widespread enthusiasm or
deep awe and veneration comparable to that of the war years. In a curious way, the emperor's surrender broadcast punctured emperor worship.
When the holy war ended, so also did the worship of its high priest and
erstwhile "manifest deity." In place of this, to judge from police reports
and other impressionistic evidence of the times, a great many people came
to regard the throne as if they were just spectators to its fate.

Becoming Bystanders

Put in Japanese terms, the emperor worship that so mesmerized Fellers
and other Western analysts appeared to have been in large part *tatemae*, a
facade. Once defeat came home and the military state collapsed, the *honne*
or true sentiment of ordinary Japanese revealed itself to be closer to mild

attachment, resignation, even indifference where the imperial system and the vaunted national polity were concerned. This detachment emerged in secret reports prepared in the Home Ministry during and immediately after the war. Police files prior to the surrender revealed mounting concern that incidents of lese majesty were increasing as the situation deteriorated. Even children, it was suggested, were becoming the bearers of incipient sedition. In one incident, the police apprehended a youngster who had cut a photograph of the emperor out of the newspaper and hung it from his neck in imitation of the boxes containing ashes of the war dead. Another nervous entry in the police dossiers, recorded shortly after the air raids over Tokyo began, noted that little children were blithely singing a jingle anticipating the imperial palace burning down.[1]

These presentiments were unnerving not simply in and of themselves, but also because the conservative elites were aware that history was not on their side. The Japanese had discarded their feudal shogunate and the samurai-led social structure on which it rested in the mid-nineteenth century, cast them off like worn-out garments after almost eight centuries of exalted existence. They had experienced less than a century of modern imperial rule, beginning with Hirohito's grandfather, the Meiji emperor, in 1868. No other regime in their history, no other leader, had ever presided over such devastation and disaster as Hirohito. No one else had opened the door to a conquering army from abroad. These were not reassuring matters to contemplate.

The cosmopolitan royalists were also aware of the high mortality rate of monarchies generally in the twentieth century. The Chinese imperial system, which was said to reflect the "mandate of heaven" and traced its origins back two millennia, had fallen in 1911. World War I witnessed the collapse of once-powerful and presumably revered imperial systems in Germany, Austria-Hungary, Russia, and Turkey. While the Japanese pondered the fate of their imperial institution, the monarchy in defeated Italy hung in the balance. In June 1946, the House of Savoy, which claimed to be the oldest ruling house in Europe (and to rule "by the grace of God and the will of the people"), was repudiated in a popular referendum. Looking abroad as well as within, to the past as well as at the present situation, royalists saw sufficient reason to fear that defeat might precipitate, if not active antagonism to the throne, at least popular indifference to whatever happened to the remote figure in the imperial palace.

The thought police continued to operate for many weeks after the victors set up shop, and their internal reports for August, September, and early October gave ample indication that although fears of large-scale antagonism toward the throne had been off the mark, indifference was another matter entirely. This is not to say that the old fears were dispelled quickly and entirely. Early in September, a secret report of the Kempeitai (the military police) anticipated "ideological confusion" arising in many forms, including "popular-sovereignty ideology" and a "mercenary ideology" stimulated by Western liberalism. Police in Shiga Prefecture reported that "just before the conclusion of the war, and afterwards, the general public's distrust and antipathy toward the military and those who govern intensified, and words and deeds against the emperor especially have tended to increase, so we are trying to control this." A September report dealing with popular responses to Prime Minister Higashikuni's statement that Hirohito was not responsible for the surprise attack on Pearl Harbor concluded that informed opinion was skeptical of this. People found it difficult to reconcile this picture of the emperor's nonresponsibility with either the imperial order under which the country went to war or the then-current hoopla about the emperor's crucial role in the decision to end hostilities.[2]

The voluminous police reports also itemized rumors about the emperor. He had died of anxiety after delivering the surrender broadcast. He had taken to bed with a facial tic. He had committed suicide. There were reports of his abdication, some replete with detail. As the person responsible for the war, he had stepped down in favor of the young crown prince, Akihito, who had already gone to the United States to study. In his absence, Hirohito's brother Prince Chichibu was serving as regent. A gallows was being erected in front of the imperial palace, obviously intended for the emperor. More striking yet, in the vast majority of surveys of popular sentiment the emperor was invisible, a non-presence. There was no indication that ordinary people were giving him much thought. If they did, it was with the casualness of bystanders. A gallows in front of the imperial palace? What next?[3]

Although the police reports expressed concern about widespread "grave distrust, frustration, and antipathy toward military and civilian leaders," the emperor was in fact only rarely included in such denunciations. Even Socialists and Communists displayed restraint, not to mention respect, when it came to the sovereign.[4] To royalists obsessed with preserving the "national polity," the situation was thus simultaneously hopeful and ominous. Popular "hatred of the military" (another police-dossier phrase) made it easy and natural to do precisely what Fellers and his aides advocated: drive a wedge between the emperor and the "gangster militarists." At the same time, the swift descent of parts of the populace into greed, antisocial behavior, and fatalism suggested that the Japanese really might be thoroughly "situational" in their allegiances. Even honest homeless people had moved into shrines and temples and were said to be hanging diapers in the holiest sanctuaries.[5] Although they may not have been about to repudiate the throne, anyone inclined to paranoia might see precious little sacred ground left.

Some field-level American analysts offered similar appraisals of the situation. In mid-December 1945, an intelligence unit in metropolitan Tokyo came to this conclusion: "With regard to the Emperor system, it is the opinion of observers especially as far as the middle classes are concerned that the Allies are unduly apprehensive of the effect on the Japanese if the Emperor were removed. It is claimed that at the most there might be demonstrations, particularly in the rural districts, but they would soon pass. People are more concerned with food and housing problems than with the fate of the Emperor." On December 29, two days before the emperor's "declaration of humanity," the same unit reported that "informed sources claim that many people have reached a state where it is almost immaterial to them whether the Emperor is retained or not." Four days after the New Year's Day rescript, they observed that "generally the people are grasping the idea that the Emperor is simply a human being. Reports are being received that the better educated younger generation are not regarding him with the same degree of dignity as formerly, and that he has even become the 'point' of many jokes in the past three months." Shortly after this, the U.S. Strategic Bombing Survey conducted a survey asking Japanese what their feelings had been when they heard Japan had given up in the war. In a striking demonstration of the extent to which ordinary people had become bystanders where the emperor was concerned, only 4 percent checked off "worry about Emperor, shame for Emperor, sorrow for him."[6]

Jokes about the emperor and flippancy in speaking of him were another small sign that awe toward the sovereign was not so great as the royalists or Fellers and MacArthur insisted. After the famous photograph of the general and the emperor appeared, Hirohito even emerged as the butt of the most salacious riddle of the occupation period. This rested on a hitherto unmentionable pun: the fact that the imperial "We"—pronounced *chin*—was a homonym to a slang word for penis (or "prick"). Why was General MacArthur the belly button *(heso)* of Japan? Because, the rude joke went, he was above the prick/emperor.[7]

Other developments at the popular level also indicated that the emperor might be less than irreplaceable. In February, for instance, SCAP's local intelligence people reported a rumor current in the Shimonoseki area to the effect that the emperor's ancestors came from India, and that he therefore "was not Japanese." As a result of this "revelation," which was said to be verifiable by records in a temple in Shimane Prefecture, "some Shimonoseki residents have expressed their preference for a Japanese president rather than an Emperor of Indian ancestry."[8]

This was entertaining or unsettling depending on where one stood, as was true also of one of the more widely publicized developments of the period: the emergence of a dozen or more individuals, each of whom claimed to be the legitimate heir to the throne or a genuine descendent or incarnation of the sun goddess Amaterasu. Contemplating this parade of imperial pretenders and daughters of heaven became one of the small amusements by which people lightened the hardships of these times, and they had a motley assortment of would-be royals and goddesses to contemplate. "Emperor Sakamoto" surfaced in Okayama, "Emperor Nagahama" in Kagoshima, "Emperor Sado" in Niigata, and "Emperor Yokokura" in Kōchi. Aichi Prefecture produced not one but two pretenders, "Emperor Tomura" and "Emperor Miura."

The most intriguing claimant to the chrysanthemum throne first brought his case to GHQ in September 1945 and saw it emerge as a topic of public interest in January. He was a fifty-six-year-old variety-store proprietor from Nagano named Kumazawa Hiromichi, who attracted particular interest because his claim rested on a genuine genealogical dispute tracing back to the early fourteenth century, when the imperial line had split into fiercely contentious "northern" and "southern" courts. Hirohito belonged to the northern line, but there were serious grounds for arguing that the southern line—from which Kumazawa claimed descent—was the more legitimate and should have carried on the imperial tradition.

The fact that three of Kumazawa Hiromichi's relatives each soon claimed that he was the true family head gave this challenge added zest, and the very durability of the story in the media seemed to reveal one more way in which Hirohito's authority was eroding. Kumazawa Hiromichi toured the country, gathering a small number of supporters and a considerable amount of curiosity. His celebrity status, coupled with his spirited public statements, certainly suggested that some Japanese, at least, were less enamored of the current occupant of the throne than were the victors ensconced in the Daiichi Building. "I consider Hirohito a war criminal," the pretender was quoted as saying—to which he immediately added (whether as shrewd politician or true believer is unclear): "MacArthur is heaven's messenger to Japan." Among other things, Kumazawa's claim cast serious doubt on the vaunted ideology of *bansei ikkei* ("ten thousand generations in a single line") by which the modern imperial institution claimed unbroken descent from time immemorial.[9]

This myth of an unbroken imperial line tracing back to the sun goddess—around which many of the emperor's unique sacerdotal activities revolved—was soon challenged at the grass-roots in other ways. The directive disestablishing Shinto as the state religion opened the door to a resurgence of popular religions. Some that had been repressed under the prewar Peace Preservation Law, often on the specific grounds of lese majesty, reemerged as vigorous centers of spiritual attraction. Sōka Kyōiku Gakkai was reestablished as Sōka Gakkai, Omotekyō as Aizenen, Tenri Hondō as Honmichi. In one form or another, various Shinto-affiliated organizations that had been marginalized also resumed independent activity, among them Risshō Kōseikai (which split off from the prewar Reiyūkai) and Seichō no Ie.

Dynamic as many of these revived religions were, they paled in terms of immediate media appeal before two postwar religions founded by women who claimed special connection to the sun goddess and promised their devotees this-worldly benefits. The Jiu religion was established by Nagaoka Yoshiko, who called herself Jikōson, claimed to be the reincarnation of Amaterasu, and predicted that a series of natural calamities would occur to correct a world in disarray. Jikōson tapped a traditional strain of "world renewing" millenialism and numbered among her devotees Futabayama, a near legendary former sumo grand champion, and Go Seigen, a celebrated master of the board game *go*. Her new religion became a journalist's delight in 1947 when the police raided its facilities on the grounds that illegal foodstuffs were stored there and were tossed around by Futabayama.

The second of these new religions, called Amaterasu Kōtai Jingūkyō (Religion of the Great Shrine of Amaterasu), was founded three days before the war ended by Kitamura Sayo, a housewife in a farming family in Yamaguchi prefecture. Claiming that something had entered her body in 1944 and placed her in receipt of direct messages from the sun goddess, Kitamura preached through songs and promoted an ecstatic "selfless dance." She spoke harshly of all authorities including the emperor, and attracted upward of three hundred thousand followers within a few years.[10]

In Japanese parlance, this efflorescence of postsurrender religions eventually became known as "the rush hour of the gods." The royalists continued to insist that the throne was the unshakable center of the national

belief system, but countless numbers of people were finding spiritual solace elsewhere.

Becoming Human

The campaign to dress Emperor Hirohito in new clothes and turn him
into a symbol of peace and democracy was conducted on several fronts.
Immense care was taken to exempt him from indictment in the impending showcase war-crimes trials in Tokyo. Although his formal exoneration
from war responsibility did not actually come until June 1946, well before
that date the emperor cast aside his commander-in-chief's uniform,
donned a Western suit, and embarked on a series of tours that eventually
would take him to almost every prefecture in the country. Suggestions that
the emperor abdicate, some of them emanating from court circles, were
quickly suppressed. The emperor's constitutional status was drastically revised, depriving him of formal power; and in a single deft declaration, he
managed to satisfy many of his foreign critics that he no longer claimed
divinity.[11]

The last of these acts was accomplished in the form of a "Rescript to
Promote the National Destiny" printed in newspapers nationwide on New
Year's Day. This was the emperor's first formal address to his subjects
since August 15, but its greatest impact was among foreigners. Popularly
known as his "declaration of humanity" *(ningen sengen)*, it was immediately hailed by the Americans and the British as the emperor's "renunciation of divinity," a clear sign that he had sincerely repudiated the pretense
to divine descent that had constituted the core of prewar emperor worship and ultranationalism.[12]

The idea for the declaration came not from among the emperor's top-
level advisors or SCAP's high planners, as might have been expected, but
from an expatriate British aesthete and a middle-level American officer.
As a communication in the Japanese language, moreover, it fell considerably short of being the sweeping "renunciation of divinity" Westerners
wishfully imagined it to be. Through the use of esoteric language, Emperor Hirohito adroitly managed to descend only partway from heaven.
Largely thanks to his personal intervention in the drafting process, the rescript seized the initiative for the throne by identifying it with a "democracy" rooted neither in the reformist policies of the victors nor in popular
initiatives from below, but in governmental pronouncements dating back
to the beginning of the reign of Hirohito's grandfather, the Meiji emperor.
The New Year's Day declaration offered an excellent preview of what a

many-colored raiment the emperor's new clothes would prove to be. How he would be seen depended largely on the eye of the beholder.

To Westerners, Christians in particular, the notion of "emperor worship" was blasphemous. To speak of the emperor as the Son of Heaven, as he was commonly termed in English, seemed perilously close to equating him with Christ, the Son of God. Americans devoted a great deal of attention to this issue. The prolific missionary writer Willis Lamott discussed the need for the emperor to renounce his divinity as early as 1944, in his popular book *Nippon: The Crime and Punishment of Japan*. Analysts in the U.S. Office of War Information came to a similar conclusion before the war ended. Experts consulted in a Columbia University poll likewise concluded that "emperor worship" somehow had to be eliminated. In November 1945, Otis Cary, a young Japanese-speaking officer with a missionary background in the country, met the emperor's brother Prince Takamatsu on a social visit and boldly offered his personal suggestion that the emperor publicly deny he was a god. In mid-December, another young specialist from a missionary family prepared a memorandum in the State Department devoted to this same theme. Edwin O. Reischauer, later a distinguished Japan scholar and ambassador to Japan, recommended that the supreme commander "should exert every effort to influence the emperor voluntarily to demonstrate by word and deed to his people that he is an ordinary human being not different from other Japanese or from foreigners, that he himself does not believe in the divine origin of the imperial line or the mystical superiority of Japan over other lands, and that there is no such thing as the 'imperial will' as distinct from government policy."[13]

Issues of church and state, sacredness and authority, were in the air in other ways as well. SCAP's directive prohibiting the propagation of Shinto as a state religion referred explicitly to "the perversion of Shinto theory and beliefs into militaristic and ultra-nationalistic propaganda designed to delude the Japanese people and lead them into wars of aggression." Such pernicious ideology included the belief that "because of ancestry, descent, or special origin" the emperor was superior to the heads of other states, just as the people of Japan were superior to the people of other lands.[14] Although the Shinto directive struck at the heart of ultranationalistic emperor ideology, it provoked no criticism—and indeed, no great interest—among the populace. Court circles naturally were more keenly attentive to its implications. On December 22, the emperor and a small number of intimate associates listened to a presentation by a Japanese scholar who informed them that using this-worldly words to try to talk about the "other world," as the directive did, was like "cutting smoke with scissors." This helped to persuade the emperor that issuing a statement defusing the question of imperial divinity would be useful for foreign consumption.[15]

A small group of individuals had already been at work for weeks on such a statement, a project that had its beginnings in a casual conversation between Lieutenant Colonel Harold Henderson, an American special adviser to the Civil Information and Education (CI&E) section, and Dr. Reginald E. Blyth, a British citizen. Both men were Japan specialists with a scholarly interest in literature and culture. Henderson, born in 1889, had lived in Japan in the 1930s, studying its language and art. He had taught Japanese at Columbia University, published a well-regarded introduction to *haiku* poetry *(The Bamboo Broom)*, administered a Japanese language program for the government in the war years, and participated in the preparation of propaganda leaflets urging Japanese soldiers to surrender in the New Guinea and Philippine campaigns.

Nine years younger, Blyth had spent two years in prison as a conscientious objector during World War I. He first became involved with things Japanese in 1926, when he took a teaching position at the Japanese colonial university in Seoul, Korea. Fluent in Japanese, he had divorced his British wife and married a Japanese woman, published a highly original comparative literary study *(Zen in English Literature and Oriental Classics)*, and spent the war years in detainment in Japan. In his 1941 book, Blyth had referred to Henderson's *haiku* anthology as "a little masterpiece." The two men obviously had a great deal in common. In October, Blyth appeared at CI&E to explore the possibility of working as an interpreter or translator. Soon, however, he found a more interesting niche as a teacher at Tokyo's prestigious Gakushūin, or Peers' School, and also as a liaison between court circles and GHQ.[16]

Japanese officials relied heavily on informal contacts with GHQ personnel to ascertain which way the occupation winds were blowing. This was as true for the imperial household as it was for other agencies and ministries, and CI&E, which dealt with the democratization of ideology and ideas, was a major focus of the court's intelligence gathering and lobbying. Sometimes the line between exchanging views and obtaining American support through lavish entertainment and valuable presents became blurred. Much of this interaction was aboveboard, however, and no individual proved more valuable to court circles in this capacity than Blyth.[17]

It was Blyth's practice to visit CI&E once or twice a week, always driven in a government car. Henderson was one of Blyth's regular contacts, and apparently unwittingly initiated a fateful conversation late in November, when he shared his thoughts concerning the 1890 Imperial Rescript on Education, which had been turned into a prop of emperor-centered militarism in the 1930s. Before peace and democracy could grow, he observed, it was necessary to eliminate false notions of national superiority and imperial divinity. Perhaps, he mused, this could be accomplished by a new imperial rescript.

The following week, Blyth returned to CI&E with the unexpected announcement that he had conveyed this proposal to his contacts and had received word that the emperor was anxious to comply. These contacts, however, desired further advice on exactly what it might be appropriate to say. Brigadier General Ken R. Dyke, the head of CI&E, was absent at the time, and at Blyth's insistence Henderson agreed to draft a sample statement himself. This he did during his lunch break in his room at the Daiichi Hotel—lying on a bed with a pad and pencil imagining that he was the emperor of Japan renouncing his divinity. There were no witnesses to this creative moment, but the wonderful American presumption and casualness of it all rings true.

Henderson and Blyth both regarded this hasty lunch-break text as an entirely unofficial suggestion. To Henderson's astonishment, however, Blyth returned a day or two later with both a "silly" request and a bombshell. First, at the request of the head of the Imperial Household Ministry, Henderson and Blyth burned Henderson's draft. Then Blyth produced a draft of his own, which followed Henderson's quite closely on key points, and asked Henderson to show this draft to his superiors. Henderson took it to General Dyke, who immediately brought it to MacArthur. Both generals expressed surprise and pleasure that court officials were contemplating such a statement, and Blyth hastened back to convey their favorable response to his contacts. For all practical purposes, Henderson and Blyth had become the emperor's ghost writers—but a great deal more was to come.[18]

Blyth's draft was translated into plain vernacular Japanese by his Peers' School contacts, and this became the basis for secret Japanese deliberations on an imperial "declaration of humanity." Until the end of the year, when the entire cabinet was convened to comment on the proposed rescript, no more than a dozen people, ranging from the head of the Peers' School to the emperor himself, were involved. Their sense of secrecy, prompted by fear of violent ultranationalistic protests, was acute. At one point, in a moment even sillier than the burning of the Henderson memo, then–foreign minister Yoshida Shigeru clandestinely received a copy of the working draft of the declaration in the men's room reserved for members of the cabinet. No one seems to have questioned the appropriateness of such a locale for an exchange involving the emperor's divinity.[19]

The imperial rescript released on January 1 was a distinctly Japanized rendering of the Blyth draft. It retained the essence of what Henderson and Blyth had proposed, but in a submerged, sublimated, adroitly altered form. The subtly of the final statement becomes apparent when it is set against initial versions based on the Blyth draft. Blyth's text began with hopes for "a new world with new ideals, with Humanity above nationality as the Great Goal." In its second paragraph, it renounced the emperor's divinity in a passage apparently taken almost verbatim from Henderson's draft. "The ties between us and the nation," it stated, "do not depend only upon myths and legends" and "do not depend at all upon the mistaken idea that the Japanese are of divine descent, superior to other peoples, and destined to rule them. They are the bond of trust, of affection, forged by centuries of devotion and love."

In its third paragraph, Blyth's draft emphasized that loyalty within family and nation "always has been the great characteristic of our nation in all our religious and political belief." It then went on, "Just as our loyalty to the nation has been greater than that to the family, so let our loyalty to humanity surpass our loyalty to the nation." A fourth paragraph acknowledged present-day hardships and looked forward to Japan's reconstruction as a free nation that would make a "unique contribution to the happiness and welfare of mankind." In conclusion, Blyth's text stated unequivocally that "His Majesty disavows entirely any deification or mythologizing of his own Person."[20]

It is easy to see why this text by the two foreigners was received positively in court circles. The affirmation of "centuries of devotion and love" existing between sovereign and subjects differed scarcely at all from imperial myths popularized in the 1930s. Until the latter part of the nineteenth century, ordinary Japanese had little or no awareness of the throne, and the imperial house was comparably indifferent to, if not utterly contemptuous of, ordinary people. Blyth's praise of loyalty as the supreme and eternal Japanese virtue was similarly fallacious historically, although it is easy to see why he chose to emphasize loyalty as a means of calling for a "loyalty to humanity" that would transcend mere nationalism.

While court circles could hardly have hoped for a more encouraging signal of SCAP's good will at a time when the emperor's status was officially still undecided, this did not prevent them from revising the Blyth draft in substantial ways. The final version retained Blyth's references to traditional loyalty to family and nation and went on to speak of the necessity of extending this spirit to a "love of mankind." In this way, much of the sentiment of the English text was retained, but with a subtle reservation. Loyalty to the nation was no longer explicitly subordinated to an obligation to humanity.

In addition, the draft was revised to warn against falling prey to what had only recently been called "dangerous thought" but now went under the rubric of "confusion of thought" *(shisō konran)*. The emperor came down strongly on this. "The protracted war having ended in defeat, our people are liable to become restive or to fall into despondency. The extremist tendencies appear to be gradually spreading, and the sense of morality is markedly losing its hold on the people. In effect, there are signs of confusion of thought, and the existing situation causes me deep concern." This was not in the Blyth draft, but it was uppermost in the minds of the royalists.

In the most dramatic revision, the New Year's Day rescript opened by quoting in its entirety the five-article "Charter Oath" proclaimed by the youthful Meiji emperor at the beginning of his reign in 1868. This, Meiji's grandson now declared, would be the basis for discarding "old abuses" and creating a new Japan devoted to the pursuit of peace and the attainment of an enriched culture. (There was no mention of democracy in the rescript.) For many conservatives, this was the very heart and soul of the New Year's Day proclamation. The Charter Oath would become a touchstone, a talisman, a comforting historical and psychological anchor by which they could claim that the "new Japan" was firmly grounded in the past.[21]

It was at the emperor's personal instigation that the entire focus of the statement was shifted from "renouncing divinity" to emphasizing the Meiji-era oath.[22] By this simple revision he accomplished many things. He obscured the autocratic, theocratic, and imperialistic nature of the Meiji state. He gave the emerging postwar system a peculiarly Japanese (and mid-nineteenth-century) patina. He ignored (apart from a vague mention of "old abuses") the repression and virulent emperor-centered indoctrination, rooted in his grandfather's time, that had characterized his own reign. He aligned himself publicly with the "moderates" and "old liberals" of the school represented by Shidehara, Shigemitsu, and Yoshida (just as he had once publicly aligned himself with the militarists). Most important, he undercut the ostensible purpose of the rescript, the renunciation of divinity. In the process, the emperor made himself a champion of the Charter Oath—which, for the preceding two decades of his reign, he had rarely mentioned and certainly never had exalted as a touchstone of the national polity.

In the emperor's later words, this affirmation of the ideals of the Charter Oath was the "primary object" of his declaration, and the issue of divinity only a "secondary matter." His emphasis was not only endorsed but made stronger by MacArthur. As Hirohito told the story, it was his intention simply to begin the rescript by alluding to the oath, which was familiar to all educated Japanese. When MacArthur was shown a draft to this effect, however, Hirohito was informed that the general had not only praised the Meiji emperor (fourteen years old when the oath was promulgated) for "having done such a splendid thing," but also urged that the five-article oath be reproduced in its entirety.[23]

Cutting Smoke with Scissors

With the Charter Oath now at the beginning of the rescript, the "declaration of humanity" was buried in the text. With the emperor's intimate involvement, the text was also reworked to eliminate language in the early vernacular translation of the Blyth draft that referred unequivocally to the "deification" (*shinkakuka*) of the emperor as well as language that clearly repudiated the belief that both the emperor and the Japanese people were "descendants of the deities" (*kami no shison* in the initial draft, *kami no sue* in interim drafts). The formerly key paragraph was, in the final statement, tucked three-quarters of the way through and read as follows in the official English version:

> I stand by my people. I am ever ready to share in their joys and sorrows. The ties between me and my people have always been formed by mutual trust and affection. They do not depend upon mere legends or myths. Nor are they predicated on the false conception that the Emperor is divine, and that the Japanese are superior to other races and destined to rule the world.

The emperor minimized the importance of this "renunciation of divinity" because, he said, it essentially amounted to little more than a semantic game necessary to mollify the Westerners. He was never a "god" in the Western sense of omnipotence and omniscience, he argued when the issue arose late in 1945, nor was he ever a *kami* or "deity" as Japanese understood this admittedly ambiguous concept. Yet he had certainly never before taken issue with being treated as divine. Tailors never touched his august body, for example, nor did ungloved physicians or anyone else except, presumably, his consort. He had literally been a man devoid of ordinary human contact. Virtually every daily act had signaled his transcendence.

Typically, the emperor now chose to discuss this with his advisers only in the most oblique of ways. He turned to second-hand anecdotes, especially the case of an early seventeenth-century emperor, Go-Mizunoo. It was a simple, bordering on simplistic, tale he had heard from the scholar who offered him advice on the Shinto directive. Go-Mizunoo contracted chicken pox, but as a reigning "manifest deity" *(akitsumikami)* he was not permitted to be treated with moxibustion, a popular remedy that involved cauterizing the skin with tiny points of burning substance; and so he abdicated. (One of many comparable anecdotes in the imperial canon involved an emperor who abdicated so that he could indulge his taste for *soba,* or buckwheat noodles, instead of subsisting primarily on the "sacred" white rice ruling monarchs were required to eat.) Hirohito apparently repeated the Go-Mizunoo story to both Prime Minister Shidehara and Education Minister Maeda Tamon in justifying his endorsement of the Henderson-Blyth initiative. It was appropriate, he opined, to put such absurdities to rest.[24]

What all this meant was, of course, more complicated than poxes and noodles. In practical terms, however, the issue was not terribly arcane. The emperor was willing to deny that he had ever been a "god" in the Western sense or even in the more ambiguous Japanese sense, but he was unwilling to deny that he was a descendent of the sun goddess as the ancient eighth-century mytho-histories had set forth, as the Meiji emperor's own constitution had proclaimed, as the entire cycle of rituals he performed as a Shinto high priest had indicated, and as twentieth-century ideologues had reiterated ad nauseam.[25]

This issue came to a head two days before the New Year's Day declaration had to be submitted to the press. In addition to recommending inclusion of the full text of the Charter Oath, MacArthur made a single, precise editorial change in the English-language draft shown him, which contained reference to "the mistaken idea that the Japanese are of divine descent." The reference here, the supreme commander said, should be not to "the Japanese" but to "the emperor." Now, at virtually zero hour, those around the emperor had to consider the vocabulary by which this should be expressed. More cutting smoke with scissors, as it turned out, was required.

To this point, revisions of the Blyth draft had retained rather straightforward language denying that the emperor and Japanese were "descendants of the gods" *(kami no shison; kami no sue)*. To Kinoshita Michio, the emperor's vice chamberlain, however, this was intolerable. On December 29, he persuaded the emperor that, although it might be acceptable to deny that the people were descendants of the *kami*, it was absolutely unacceptable to say that imperial descent from these deities was a "false conception." To get around this, he proposed that they resort to more esoteric language and deny that the emperor was a "manifest deity" or *"kami* in human form" *(akitsumikami)*. The emperor agreed wholeheartedly to this revision.

The more literal "descendant of the gods" language that had survived earlier drafts was now deleted. The final version simply denied that the Japanese were "superior" to other peoples, or that the emperor was an *akitsumikami*, or manifest deity. *Akitsumikami* was not an entirely obscure term, but neither was it an everyday word. It was certainly more esoteric than the plain word "divine" that was used in the official English translation. Wartime ideologues had used this archaic compound (the three ideographs literally mean "visible exalted deity," and the phonetic reading is totally idiosyncratic) to deify the emperor, but even well-educated people had difficulty identifying the term when confronted with it in writing, or explaining it if asked to do so.

Kinoshita's lively diary, for example, contains an indignant entry in which Foreign Minister Yoshida is dismissed as an imbecile for failing to know what *akitsumikami* meant. The vice chamberlain also observed with dismay that when the near-final version of the rescript was submitted to the cabinet on December 30, a phonetic reading *(furigana)* was written alongside the ideographs for *akitsumikami* so that the ministers would be able to grasp the reference. In Japanese, in short, the "renunciation of divinity" was far more obscure than was apparent in the official translation—or than had been the case in earlier drafts. Neither on this occasion, nor later, did the emperor unequivocally repudiate his alleged descent from the gods. He could not do so, for his entire universe rested on this mythological genealogy.[26]

The emperor did not broadcast the New Year's Day rescript. It appeared in the press accompanied by a commentary by Prime Minister Shidehara. While the text was intelligible to educated readers, the final version had typically been worked over by a scholar of classical language and was couched in the stiff and formal prose reserved for imperial pronouncements. The prime minister's gloss, on the other hand, was in the vernacular and, following the usual practice, was regarded as the official interpretation of the emperor's words. It, too, was an example of cutting smoke with scissors, for the prime minister dwelled exclusively on the prior existence of democracy in Meiji Japan. "Upholding the imperial message," he concluded, "we can construct a new nation of thoroughgoing democracy, pacifism, and rationalism, and thus hope to ease the Emperor's mind." His emphasis was a familiar one: until now, the people had failed to live up to the sovereign's expectations. The prime minister did not make even passing reference to the emperor's divinity or renunciation thereof.[27]

American responses to the January 1 declaration were extremely positive. The *New York Times* editorialized that with this rescript Emperor Hirohito "made himself one of the great reformers in Japanese history" (and, in the process, dealt the "jungle religion" of Shinto "a blow from which it can scarcely recover"). General MacArthur was equally extravagant. He informed the world that by this declaration the emperor "undertakes a leading part in the democratization of his people. He squarely takes his stand for the future along liberal lines." In a single stroke, the supreme commander had identified Hirohito as a *leader* of democratization, and indicated that he would continue to be so "for the future."[28]

Privately, some loyal subjects who had sincerely believed what they were told during the war were shocked by the emperor's new clothes and felt betrayed. There was not, however, a single instance of the right-wing violence that the drafters had feared. Education Minister Maeda was astonished to personally hear only one complaint, from an elderly man who came to see him.[29] By and large, most people seemed to take the "declaration of humanity" in stride as a matter of less than momentous interest. The media were now free to comment on the sovereign's personality in a manner hitherto impermissible, and in this way Hirohito did indeed become accessible to the public in more intimate and "human" ways.

Many readers probably found more meaning in the emperor's "New Year poem" than they did in his New Year's Day rescript. In heralding the advent of each new year, the court customarily assigned a thematic topic on which members of the imperial household as well as ordinary people would compose thirty-one-syllable *waka*, with commoners invited to submit their verses for evaluation by experts assembled by the court. Early in the new year, the best poems would be published alongside *waka* by the emperor and other eminent figures—a high honor indeed for an amateur poet. In October of that year of bitter defeat, it was announced that the theme for the coming year's poem would be "snow on the pine," a classic image of beautiful endurance. The emperor's own poem, widely disseminated in the media on January 22, was as follows:

Courageous pine—
enduring the snow
that is piling up,
color unchanging.
Let people be like this.[30]

This was an exquisite expression of defiance, and few who read it could have missed its meaning. When all was said and done, the sovereign had not changed his color. Neither should his subjects.[31]

chapter eleven

IMPERIAL DEMOCRACY:
EVADING RESPONSIBILITY

While the emperor was descending partway from heaven, the machinery for Allied war crimes trials of top leaders was slowly being assembled. Accusations and arrests came in unpredictable waves. The first arrests were announced on September 11, followed by an ominous lull until a second such announcement on November 19. In the first week of December, scores of high-ranking officers and officials were added to the list of prospective "Class A" defendants, including Prince Konoe, the former prime minister, and Kido Kōichi, who had been the emperor's closest adviser as lord keeper of the privy seal. Joseph Keenan, President Truman's appointee as chief prosecutor, arrived in Tokyo with forty aides on December 6, and MacArthur established the International Prosecution Section (IPS) for the impending trials two days later—by the Japanese calendar, on the fourth anniversary of the attack on Pearl Harbor. The International Military Tribunal for the Far East was formally inaugurated by the supreme commander on January 19, 1946, but the designation of who among those arrested would be brought to trial immediately was not announced until March 11. The trials themselves began on May 3. Until then, SCAP and the IPS might still—in theory—have accused Emperor Hirohito of war crimes.

Confronting Abdication

In court circles, the very idea of the emperor's being guilty of crimes was naturally inconceivable, but the notion that he should somehow assume responsibility for the war and defeat was taken quite seriously. Before SCAP revealed itself to be so adamantly opposed to any policy other than *using* Hirohito, the emperor himself gave thought to this. On August 29, the day before the victors set foot on the sacred soil, he spoke to Kido about abdication as a way of possibly absolving his faithful ministers, generals, and admirals of responsibility for the war. Kido told him this was not desirable. In mid-September, the cabinet headed by Prince Higashikuni, Hirohito's uncle by marriage, secretly discussed abdication with the emperor's knowledge. Whereas some ministers emphasized that the emperor had no constitutional responsibility for the war, others stressed that he bore moral responsibility to the nation, to the dead, and to his bereaved subjects for the defeat.[1]

In the first week of October, Prime Minister Higashikuni met privately with his nephew and recommended that he step down. Higashikuni offered to give up his own status as a member of the imperial family. His suggestion reportedly was turned down on the grounds that "the time is not yet right." A few weeks later, Hirohito matter-of-factly informed his vice chamberlain that, if he had to renounce the throne, he wished to find a good researcher to assist him in his studies of marine biology (an area of academic inquiry chosen years earlier to help establish his *bona fides* as a "modern" man).[2]

On January 4, as public discussion of war crimes grew and a wide-ranging "categorical" purge of individuals deemed to have held positions that abetted militarism and ultranationalism began, the emperor asked Fujita Hisanori, Kido's successor as privy seal, to investigate whether GHQ now wished him to abdicate. Fujita demurred at making such an inquiry. Ever keen on the study of imperial precedent, in late January the emperor had a scholar lecture to him on the abdication of Emperor Uda, who had reigned from 887 to 897 and then stepped down from the throne at the age of thirty-one. He also had his officials brief him on the practice of abdication in the British monarchy, which he had often looked to as a model of regal propriety in the modern world.[3]

The abdication issue quickly spilled over into the media. Late in October 1945, Prince Konoe had caused a commotion by publicly raising the prospect of abdication and then amending his statements under pressure from the cabinet. Konoe was unusually outspoken in his belief that the emperor bore grave personal responsibility both for failing to prevent the war with the United States and for failing to end it sooner. On February 27, the issue was again catapulted into the public realm when the *Yomiuri Hōchi* newspaper reported that Prince Higashikuni, the former prime minister, had informed an Associated Press correspondent that abdication was being seriously discussed at the highest levels, and would have the support of the entire imperial family if Hirohito himself chose this path. A few days later, Higashikuni told the Japanese media directly that he had personally urged his nephew to consider three "timely opportunities" to abdicate. Although the first of these had already passed without action, being "when the surrender was signed," the other two appropriate moments still lay ahead. As Higashikuni saw it, Hirohito should consider stepping down either when the constitution had been revised or when a peace treaty ending the occupation had been signed. Speculation in the press ran to the emperor's brother Prince Takamatsu as the most probable regent until the crown prince came of age.[4]

The publication of the sensational *Yomiuri Hōchi* story coincided with a tense meeting of the Privy Council in the Imperial Household Ministry quarters, at which the emperor's thirty-one-year-old youngest brother, Prince Mikasa, indirectly urged the emperor to take responsibility for defeat. The government and the imperial family as a whole, Mikasa argued, had to transcend "old thinking" and "take bold action now." Welfare Minister (and later prime minister) Ashida Hitoshi, who was present, recorded in his diary that "everyone seemed to ponder" Mikasa's words and that "His Majesty's face was never so pale with anxiety."[5]

Anxious as he may have been, it was at about this time that the emperor evidently resolved not to step down. He told Vice Chamberlain Kinoshita Michio that he was not confident anyone was qualified to take his place. Of his three brothers, Prince Takamatsu had been too openly "prowar," Prince Chichibu was too frail physically, and Prince Mikasa was too young and inexperienced. (Mikasa, at thirty-one, was eleven years older than Hirohito had been when he became regent in 1921). He regretted his uncle's careless words to the press, the emperor told Kinoshita.[6]

Well-known public figures across the political and ideological spectrum were beginning to speak up in favor of abdication. Nanbara Shigeru, a liberal Christian educator recently appointed president of Tokyo Imperial University, spoke warmly of the imperial institution in general but argued that Hirohito should abdicate on moral grounds. Sasaki Sōichi, a conservative constitutional scholar who had assisted Konoe in drafting a proposed revision of the Meiji Constitution, also advanced moral reasons for abdication. Tanabe Hajime, an austere conservative philosopher deeply engaged in elaborating a Buddhist-oriented concept of "repentance" for Japan, hoped the emperor would retire and become a symbol of poverty and emptiness. He also recommended that the resources of the imperial household be turned over for the relief of impoverished people.[7]

The most sensational public call for Hirohito's abdication came in an essay by Miyoshi Tatsuji, a well-known poet. Titled "The Emperor Should Abdicate Quickly," this essay appeared in the June 1946 issue of the popular magazine *Shinchō*. Miyoshi made it clear that he was not concerned with war responsibility in the sense that supporters of the Tokyo war-crimes trials used the term—that is, direct, policy-making responsibility for aggression and atrocity—but neither did he accept the benign image of a peace-loving but helpless monarch that the royalists were promoting. What was at issue, he emphasized, was "not simply responsibility for defeat in war." Rather, in unusually strong language, Miyoshi accused the emperor of being "extremely negligent in the performance of his duties" and "responsible for betraying the loyal soldiers who laid down their lives in battle for him."

The emperor had presented himself as commander in chief, Miyoshi declared, but had failed to curb the violence of the military. He spoke paternalistically of his subjects as his "children," but then urged them to obey to the death an army and navy he knew to be out of control. As head of state, he should now set a moral example by taking responsibility for the disaster. He had been incompetent in his wartime leadership, in appraising and responding to situations, in choosing personnel, in his perception of the people's sentiments, and in his judgments about when and how to end the war. Having announced he was not a "manifest deity," he should now act as an ordinary mortal and follow the dictates of reason by abdicating.[8]

Had the occupation authorities chosen to encourage Hirohito's abdication, it seems clear that there would have been no insurmountable obstacles to such an act. The emperor's entourage acknowledged this. However sadly, the public would surely have accepted an imperial announcement of abdication as easily as they had accepted defeat itself. Conservatives would have rationalized the abdication as a reaffirmation of the moral integrity of the imperial institution. Imperial democracy could still have been promoted under a new sovereign, but Hirohito's disastrous Shōwa era—so mockingly ironic in its nomenclature, since the two ideographs for

"Shōwa" meant "radiance and peace"—would have been closed and the issue of "responsibility" would have been cast in a sharper light.

MacArthur and his aides appraised the situation very differently, of course, and made their position clear to the Japanese side. On November 26, when the former admiral and prime minister Yonai Mitsumasa, who remained a close imperial confidant, solicited MacArthur's views on abdication, the supreme commander replied that this would not be necessary.[9] A month later, one of the court's Japanese contacts with GHQ reported that General Dyke, the head of CI&E, had suggested that the emperor might remove himself from the limelight by leaving Tokyo and reestablishing his court in Kyoto, which had been the traditional seat of the imperial household prior to the mid-nineteenth century. One day later, three Japanese intermediaries who had relations with CI&E brought Vice Chamberlain Kinoshita a remarkable, long memorandum that summarized General Dyke's views on "The Problem of the Imperial House." It began with the flat assertion that maintenance of the emperor was absolutely essential to constructing a democratic Japan.[10]

Early in March 1946, the vice chamberlain was informed that General Fellers was worried about "funny people" around the emperor who seemed to be giving him bad advice—a reference, presumably, not only to such imperial heretics as Prince Higashikuni and Prince Mikasa, but also to the court advisers who had arranged the lectures on Emperor Uda's abdication and British-style royal departures.[11] Fellers, who often emerged as the *deus ex machina* in MacArthur's imperial intrigues, could be unusually blunt in telling his Japanese opposites that they could maintain the throne and should keep Hirohito on it. Thus, at one point, the general informed former admiral Yonai that the emperor was the "best ally" for the occupation authorities and "the emperor system should continue so long as the occupation does." Fellers rationalized this policy as essential to thwart Soviet-led "communization of the entire world," and told Yonai that "un-American thought" was on the rise even at high levels in the United States, where influential voices still called for arresting Hirohito as a war criminal.

According to the Japanese record of the conversation, Fellers then urged Yonai to ensure Emperor Hirohito's survival by fixing testimony by defendants in the impending war-crimes trials. "It would be most convenient," Fellers is recorded as having said, "if the Japanese side could prove to us that the emperor is completely blameless. I think the forthcoming trials offer the best opportunity to do that. Tōjō, in particular, should be

made to bear all responsibility at his trial. In other words, I want you to
have Tōjō say as follows: 'At the Imperial Conference prior to the start of
the war, I had already decided to push for war even if His Majesty the
emperor was against going to war with the United States.' " The "Class
A" defendants led by Tōjō were to be asked, quite literally, to die to protect their sovereign in the halls of justice rather than on the battlefield.
Yonai readily agreed to pass on this message.[12]

On March 20, Fellers invited Terasaki Hidenari, Terasaki's wife (and
Fellers's cousin) Gwen, and their young daughter to dinner. Afterwards the
court aide bluntly asked what MacArthur thought about the emperor abdicating. Taking care to point out that he could not presume to speak for
his commander, Fellers then emphasized that MacArthur was the emperor's "true friend." The general, he told Terasaki, had recently informed Washington that, were the emperor to be indicted, Japan would
be plunged into chaos and a significantly larger occupation force would be
required. He had taken this position even though the emperor bore "technical" responsibility for the war. Insofar as abdication was concerned, it
might also cause chaos by posing various problems of succession. For this
reason, Fellers believed MacArthur did not desire Hirohito's abdication.
Terasaki asked if the supreme commander could publicly express his opposition to abdication to put a stop to the "disrespectful so-called abdication discussion" in the press, thus enabling the Japanese people to feel
that "dark clouds" had been dispelled and they were again "beholding the
sun." This, Fellers responded, would be extremely difficult.[13]

What Fellers was disclosing to emperor's aide was the gist of a secret
cable from MacArthur to General Dwight D. Eisenhower, the army chief
of staff. In this response to Washington's call for an investigation of the
emperor's war responsibility, MacArthur pulled out all the stops in defending him. "Investigation has been conducted," the supreme commander had informed Eisenhower on January 25, and no evidence had been
found that connected Hirohito to political decisions during the past
decade. MacArthur characterized the emperor as "a symbol which united
all Japanese," and warned that if he were indicted the nation would experience "a tremendous convulsion," "disintegrate," initiate a "vendetta for
revenge . . . whose cycle may well not be complete for centuries if ever."
Government agencies would break down; "civilized practices will largely
cease"; guerrilla warfare could be expected; all hopes of introducing modern democracy would disappear; and once the occupation forces left,
"some form of intense regimentation probably along communistic line[s]
would arise from the mutilated masses."

This was not pleasant to contemplate, and to maintain order in the midst of such chaos, MacArthur declared, he would need at least a million troops, in addition to an imported civil service of several hundred thousand, for an indefinite number of years. If this passionate cable amounted to a reprise of the memorandum Fellers had submitted to his commander on October 2, the doomsday rhetoric was inimitably MacArthur's. Although it was not until over four months later that the International Prosecution Section (IPS) of the International Military Tribunal for the Far East publicly exonerated the emperor from war crimes, MacArthur's cable essentially marked the end of the issue as a topic of serious internal consideration.[14]

Before the war crimes trials actually convened, SCAP, the IPS, and Japanese officials worked behind the scenes not only to prevent Emperor Hirohito from being indicted, but also to slant the testimony of the defendants to ensure that no one implicated him. Former admiral and prime minister Yonai, following Fellers's advice, apparently did caution Tōjō to take care not to incriminate the emperor in any way. The collaborative campaign to shape the nature of the trials went considerably beyond this, however. High officials in court circles and the government collaborated with GHQ in compiling lists of prospective war criminals, while the hundred or so prominent individuals eventually arrested as "Class A" suspects and incarcerated in Sugamo Prison for the duration of the trial (of whom only twenty-eight were indicted) solemnly vowed on their own to protect their sovereign against any possible taint of war responsibility.[15] The sustained intensity of this campaign to protect the emperor was revealed when, in testifying before the tribunal on December 31, 1947, Tōjō momentarily strayed from the agreed-on line concerning imperial innocence and referred to the emperor's ultimate authority. The American-led *prosecution* immediately arranged that he be secretly coached to recant this testimony.[16]

The counterpoint to this active tampering involved the simplest of tactics: nonaction. Despite the charge to do so, neither SCAP nor the IPS ever conducted a serious investigation of the emperor's involvement in promoting aggression. No close, impartial textual analysis of the documentary evidence was undertaken that focused on the emperor's political, military, and ideological role from the beginning of his reign. No one seriously questioned the claim of the emperor's apologists that his acts were constrained by his strict sense of being a "constitutional monarch"—when, in fact, under Meiji-era stipulations concerning the military's "right of supreme command," much of Japan's aggression was formulated outside the cabinet in conferences involving only the military and its commander in chief.[17] Serious interrogation of former high officials concerning the emperor was taboo, although GHQ's door always was open to the sovereign's defenders. When Prince Konoe, the least beguiled participant in inner court circles, spoke critically of the emperor's responsibility, the Americans recoiled in horror. "One of the American generals who has interviewed Konoe several times," a British official reported, "described him to me as a rat who was quite prepared to sell anyone to save himself and even went so far as to call his master, the Emperor, 'the major war criminal'." With the full support of MacArthur's headquarters, the prosecution functioned, in effect, as a defense team for the emperor.[18]

These endeavors to insulate Hirohito from any taint of war responsibility, which went beyond the emperor's own expectations, resulted in a lost opportunity to use him to help clarify the historical record. As the formal commencement of the Class A trials drew closer, the emperor apparently assumed that he would eventually be called on to give his own version of the wartime decision-making process. Whatever his motivation, between March 18 and April 8 he spent a total of eight hours dictating a "monologue" about the major policy decisions of his reign to his aides. By no means did these recollections amount to an acknowledgment of personal responsibility. On the contrary, he used the occasion to lay the onus for disastrous policies on his subordinates. At the same time, however, this unprecedented recitation offered a window into his exceptionally detailed knowledge of personalities, procedures, and concrete decisions at the highest levels.

At the time, every top Japanese leader apart from the emperor was being subjected to interrogation by the IPS. It seemed natural to assume that the victors also would wish to tap the emperor's unparalleled inside knowledge, and the "monologue" essentially amounted to an imperial dress rehearsal for such anticipated questioning. As it transpired, chief prosecutor Joseph Keenan had already informed his international staff that the emperor was off limits and, if they couldn't agree with this, they should "by all means go home immediately." Both Fellers and General Charles Willoughby, MacArthur's chief of counterintelligence, appear simply to have buried materials related to the emperor's presentation that were provided to them by court sources.[19]

This successful campaign to absolve the emperor of war responsibility knew no bounds. Hirohito was not merely presented as being innocent of any formal acts that might make him culpable to indictment as a war criminal. He was turned into an almost saintly figure who did not even bear moral responsibility for the war. For cynical practitioners of Realpolitik, this was an easy and natural undertaking. Brigadier General Elliott Thorpe, an intelligence specialist who was assigned responsibility for both ensuring the emperor's physical security and compiling initial lists of probable war criminals, looked back on his activities with bemusement. He was all in favor of keeping Emperor Hirohito on the throne, he recalled, "because otherwise we would have had nothing but chaos. The religion was gone, the government was gone, and he was the only symbol of control. Now, I know he had his hand in the cookie jar, and he wasn't any innocent little child. But he was of great use to us, and that was the basis on which I recommended to the Old Man [MacArthur] that we keep him." For more thoughtful insiders, such pragmatism was more agonizing. In a long report to President Truman early in 1946, for example, George Atcheson, the State Department's representative in Tokyo, frankly stated his belief "that the Emperor is a war criminal" and "that the Emperor system must disappear if Japan is ever to be really democratic." Nonetheless, in the present circumstances Atcheson too believed that chaos could be averted and democracy best served if the imperial system were maintained and Hirohito exempted from charges of war responsibility. Abdication, he ventured, was a potentially attractive future course, but best postponed until constitutional revision could be effected.[20]

Atcheson was killed in a plane crash shortly afterward, and so did not live to witness how the abdication issue unfolded. Although the government formally announced in September 1946 that the emperor had no present intention of stepping down, the possibility of his doing so resurfaced on two occasions. In 1948, as the Tokyo trial approached judgment, the issue of the emperor's moral responsibility was rekindled. Long before sentences were announced, it was obvious that Hirohito's loyal servants would be condemned to death or imprisonment. How should the emperor respond? In a discussion published in a mass-circulation magazine, Mibuchi Tadahiko, the chief justice of Japan's Supreme Court, joined the constitutional scholar Sasaki Sōichi and the liberal critic Hasegawa Nyozekan in a frank exchange in which Mibuchi and Sasaki agreed that it would have been appropriate for the emperor to have taken the blame for the war upon himself as soon as hostilities ended. A poll conducted in Osaka found over a quarter of respondents in favor of Hirohito abdicating right away or at an opportune moment. Other sources speculated that if a vote were actually taken, popular support for abdication would probably run around 50 percent—and much higher if the emperor personally stated it to be his wish to step down. It was known that these matters were being discussed at high levels, and rumored that Hirohito himself was torn by conflicting feelings.[21]

As usual, the Americans weighed in to squelch any such prospects. Although Fellers had retired and left Japan over a year previously, in July 1948 he hastened to write a personal letter to Terasaki expressing his alarm at the "frequent mention of the Sire's abdication in the American press." Such an act, he declared, "would be a victory for all Communists and especially the Russians who hold it is naive to claim that Japan can be democratized so long as the Emperor remains on the throne." It "would be a blow to the MacArthur occupation as the General's success has made the very best use of the emperor's prestige and personal leadership." By stepping down, moreover, Hirohito would unravel the whole mystique of imperial innocence that had been so carefully nurtured to that point:

> His abdication, especially if it coincided with the announcement of war crimes punishments, would, in the eyes of the world, identify the Sire as one of the Military clique. This of course is absolutely untrue. It would reverse public opinion in this country [the United States] which is beginning to turn to the impression that the Emperor was *not* responsible for the war. Abdication would fix the Sire's place in history as one who sympathized with the war criminals and, as a gesture of his sympathy for them, gave up his throne. . . .
>
> Today Japan is absorbing the terrific impact of Western civilization. She needs, in fact Japan must have, the stabilizing influence which only the Sire can give. He is part and parcel of the new Japan which is surely emerging. He must help Japan's reentry into the family of nations.

No Japanese royalist could have surpassed such homage to "the Sire," but Fellers was not alone among Americans in his passionate feelings about this issue. In the closing days of October, former prime minister Ashida Hitoshi informed William Sebald, Atcheson's replacement as the State Department representative in Tokyo, that the emperor did indeed seem to be thinking about abdicating. Sebald immediately brought this to MacArthur's attention, and in a "Personal and Top Secret" letter to his superior in Washington conveyed the startling information that MacArthur feared that, under the strain of the impending military tribunal judgments, Hirohito might consider not merely abdicating but even committing suicide. The two men agreed, in any case, that abdication "would play directly into the hands of communism and chaos in Japan," and MacArthur declared that as soon as he saw the emperor "he would tell him that any thought of abdication is not only ridiculous and preposterous, but that it would result in a major disservice to the Japanese people." Sebald on his part hastened to convey the same message to Terasaki, stating that he believed this to be "the position of Washington" as well as of the supreme commander.

The notion that the emperor might commit suicide when the Tokyo tribunal handed down its judgments was a strange reading of Emperor Hirohito's personality (Sebald concurred that this was a possibility, "especially as the Emperor is both Oriental and Japanese"). Be that as it may, in an ultrasecret personal message on November 12, the emperor set MacArthur's mind at ease. With renewed resolution, he told the supreme commander, he intended to work together with his people for the reconstruction of Japan and the promotion of world peace.[22]

When the occupation ended three and a half long years later, the emperor faced the moment for which his old confidant Kido had told him to prepare when bidding farewell as he left for prison in December 1945. The honor of the imperial house, Kido had then emphasized, demanded that he take responsibility for losing the war, but the proper moment to do that would only be when the occupation ended and a peace treaty was signed restoring sovereignty to Japan. In October 1951, still imprisoned under the sentence meted out to him by the Tokyo tribunal, Kido recorded in his diary that he had sent a message to the emperor reiterating these sentiments. Abdication, he counseled, would be an act of "compliance with the truth." It would console the bereaved, including the families of condemned war criminals, and "make a very important contribution to national unity centered on the imperial house." Should the emperor fail to seize this opportunity, he observed, "the end result will be that the imperial family alone will have failed to take responsibility and an unclear mood will remain which, I fear, might leave an eternal scar."[23]

Kido's conception of the emperor's responsibility, like that of most Japanese, was inner directed. The emperor should assume responsibility "for defeat." He should clear the historical record by apologizing to his subjects who had suffered, died, or been bereaved in a war waged in his name. In this manner, he would cleanse the throne of the bloody stain of the most terrible interlude in Japanese history.

But the moment came and went, and this time there was no MacArthur serving as Hirohito's alter ego. In November, word filtered back to Kido that the emperor was giving serious thought to abdicating and once again was being encouraged in this direction by some of his most intimate advisers. Nothing came of this. The rescript with which the emperor greeted

the long-awaited restoration of sovereignty announced his intention to remain on the throne and contained no mention whatsoever of personal responsibility, although earlier drafts had included the expression, "I deeply
apologize to the nation for my responsibility for the defeat." Why was the
apology finally deleted? Because, the story is told, the emperor was persuaded by the rhetorical query of one of his advisers: "Why now is it necessary for His Majesty to apologize in such strong terms?"[24]

Imperial Tours and the Manifest Human

While these intrigues were unfolding, the conservative elites collaborated
with GHQ on a massive public relations campaign designed to transform
the emperor into, to coin a phrase, a "manifest human." The sovereign,
it was agreed, should literally descend to the level of his subjects by tour-
ing the country and mingling with the poor, hungry, and wretched. These
tours, known in plain Japanese as *junkō*, inevitably carried the special aura
of being *gyōkō* or "august imperial visits." They also marked the beginning of what became known as the "mass-communications emperor system"—the transformation of the monarch into a celebrity.

    These costly imperial processions continued through the occupation pe-
riod and eventually brought Hirohito into every prefecture except Okinawa. The sovereign whom millions had known almost exclusively as a
manifest deity and bemedaled commander astride his famous white horse
now suddenly appeared standing alongside them, awkwardly trying to
make conversation with kinds of people he had never spoken to before,
shuffling awkwardly in his new clothes (a soft felt hat and a Western coat
and tie). By the time the tours ended in August 1954, they had consumed
a total of 165 days and covered some 33,000 kilometers. Much of the planning behind them was shrewd. Hardly by chance, the emperor descended
on Hiroshima on the sixth anniversary of the attack on Pearl Harbor, presumably offsetting one act with the other in a little game of binary symbolism. Later he also appeared at the Nagasaki bedside of Nagai Takashi,
the best-selling author who lay dying of radiation sickness.

    The tours represented an extraordinary undertaking for the painfully
formal Hirohito and, in ways both planned and unplanned, they contributed greatly to the creation of his new persona. The vaunted "identity of sovereign and subject" never seemed more viable than in those
hardscrabble years when the emperor left pomp behind, dressed like an
accountant or a small-town school principal, and tried to talk to his subjects. That, of course, was the purpose of the tours: to drive the wedge,

meld emperor and people, and secularize popular veneration of the throne. At the same time, Emperor Hirohito carried out these engagements with such stolid, uncomplaining discomfort that, in unanticipated ways, he actually became an intimate symbol of the suffering and victimization of his people. As often as not, they felt sorry for him.

Although the precise genesis of the tours is obscure, high court officials such as Iriye Sukemasa later indicated that Hirohito personally thought of going out among his subjects shortly after the surrender. On December 8 of that year, some ordinary subjects volunteered to help clean the grounds of the imperial palace and much was subsequently made of the fact that the emperor exchanged a few words with them. On January 1, in its coverage of the emperor's rescript, the *Asahi* described the sovereign as a "gentle gentleman" and broached the need for more effective public relations. Two days later, the same newspaper published an article on the British royal house and its effective interaction with the public.[25]

Hirohito had been deeply impressed by the British royal style ever since his visit to Great Britain as crown prince in 1921, and around the end of 1945 his advisers provided him with an illustrated English-language book about the British royal family. This included photographs of the king mingling with the public and even descending into coal mines to observe miners at work. The book was introduced to the Imperial Household Ministry by Yamanashi Katsunoshin, the head of the Peers' School who was also Reginald Blyth's point of entree to court circles.[26] Whether the book came from that avid British Zen royalist is unclear, but he soon emerged as a major catalyst in the campaign to have the emperor demonstrate, and not merely proclaim, his humanity.

The English expatriate wrote a memorandum, translated and shown to the emperor on January 13, stating that the time was ripe for him to offer positive suggestions to MacArthur about his future course of action. "The Emperor must reign, not rule," Blyth emphasized. "He must show himself really interested in the people not only by words but by coordinated action and speeches, appealing to their pride, their love of country." More specifically, the emperor should travel around the country, visiting coal mines (the power of picture books!) and farming districts, listening to the people, talking to them, asking questions.

> He should uncork some feeling, pull out the vox humana stop, and appeal to the Japanese to share their stocks [of food]. . . . He should tell the Japanese that they are still a great people potentially, and have

In the two decades between his ascension to the throne in 1926 and the end of
the war, Emperor Hirohito played an increasingly prominent public role as the
commander in chief—and unassailable ideological center—of his country's
runaway militarism. His most memorable public appearances involved
reviewing the imperial forces from his handsome horse, White Snow.

their unique contribution to make to world culture, particularly in
the fields of literature and religion, and mode of life.[27]

The Japanese had a saying that "you can gaze upon the lords, but looking at the shogun will make you blind; and the emperor cannot be seen
at all." To starchier court officials, it was inelegant to contemplate the sovereign literally descending to mingle with ordinary people, not to mention
the terrifying thought that he might be assassinated by Communists. But
the emperor responded positively to Blyth's proposal and General
MacArthur threw his enthusiastic support behind the tours.[28]

Again, the Meiji period provided a precedent. Between 1872 and 1885,
the Meiji emperor had made six royal tours to different parts of the country to help mobilize popular support behind the emerging emperor-
centered modern state. There was one especially striking similarity
between the public excursions of the two sovereigns. Each set of tours was

undertaken at a time of domestic confusion and instability, when radical ideologies were being trumpeted and support for the imperial system seemed precarious. Whatever precedent Hirohito may have seen in his grandfather's processionals, such excursions were unprecedented in his own reign, not to speak of the fact that they ran against the grain of his introverted personality and the rigidly aloof style he had cultivated until then.[29]

The emperor's very unpreparedness for mingling with ordinary people proved to be an immense public-relations advantage. His attempts at conversation were so stumbling and ill at ease that they provoked a wave of popular sympathy for so sheltered and vulnerable a soul. This almost disconcerting awkwardness also reinforced an impression of him as someone uniquely pure and innocent. That the emperor was willing and even eager to undertake these tours despite his obvious discomfort strengthened the argument that this was a sovereign truly devoted to his subjects. His social ineptitude made him seem all too human, and simultaneously unworldly—an essentially "spiritual" essence after all.[30]

The imperial discomfort also tapped a strain of guilt in the populace. Up to the war's end, Japanese had been indoctrinated to apologize to the

The emperor's tours, which began in 1946 and eventually took him to every prefecture but Okinawa, placed him in unprecedented contact with his subjects. His modest civilian attire and habit of tipping his hat to the crowd (an unthinkable gesture before the defeat) became essential parts of his new persona as an erstwhile "manifest deity" who had declared his "humanity."

emperor for each and every failure to advance the nation's cause. In their peculiar way, the imperial tours revitalized and refocused this mass psychology of self-criticism and apology. Obviously, the emperor was undertaking these excursions for the people's sake. Just as obviously, this was not a natural or an easy thing for him to do. A feeling emerged that one should, as in the past, apologize for embarrassing and inconveniencing His Majesty. Here was imperial veneration transmogrified, although whether it had anything at all to do with "democracy" was another matter entirely. By coming down from "above the clouds," as the hoary trope had it, to walk on the same burned earth his subjects trod, the emperor also came to personalize the plight of a once-proud nation brought low. Somehow he managed, almost in spite of himself, to touch a sad and subdued chord

Bewildered by the rapid twists and turns of imperial politics, an elderly woman searches for the newly humanized emperor while standing next to him.

Photographs of the emperor's tours rarely showed, as here, the role played by
U.S. military personnel in his entourage.

of nationalism, or at least national regret, even as he remained the one
clear figure of Japanese authority amid an overwhelmingly Caucasian
army of occupation.

Jaundiced Western journalists did not share much of this sentiment.
They were more taken by the contrast between the transcendent former
Son of Heaven and this remarkably ordinary physical specimen. As Russell Brines of the Associated Press described it, the emperor's subjects
suddenly learned "that he was short, slight, and round-shouldered, that his
coordination was so poor he seemed constantly on the verge of toppling
over. He was weak-chinned. His conversation consisted of inanities in a
high pitched voice. His face was covered with moles—a Japanese omen of
good luck. Apart from a stubby mustache his beard was straggly and he
often needed a shave. Thick, horn-rimmed glasses shielded his weak eyes.
His clothes were unkempt and his shoes scuffed. He was sorely in need
of an alert valet." The emperor responded to cheering crowds, Brines

noted, by constantly hoisting his fedora and bobbing his head "as though afraid to face silence again."[31]

The emperor's awkwardness was apparent from the first moments of his very first tour. On February 19, 1946 he visited a factory and black market in Yokohama. The black market, he said, was "interesting." The next day he appeared at a camp for repatriated people, where he asked an official two questions. The first was, "What sort of feelings do these military and civilian repatriates have when they return to Japan?" The second concerned what was being done so that former Formosan and Korean colonial subjects could return home "with true gratification." These "conversations," recorded by NHK public radio, were broadcast on February 22 and included the emperor's characteristic response, then and afterwards, to any answer he was givenn: *Ah, sō?* (Oh, is that so?). As the NHK commentators put it, he was as stiff in actions and words as if he had just come out of a box.[32]

The emperor attracted large crowds. People gawked and on rare occasions wept. They sent emotional letters and poems to newspapers. They grew rapturous about "the sun appearing from behind dark clouds." They saved the emperor's bath water in bottles and picked up pebbles where he had walked. Even ostensible Communists found themselves waving illegal rising-sun flags.[33] Although it was said that, as time passed, his discomfort with ordinary people eased and his comments became more articulate, this was not always readily apparent. His response to Hiroshima, almost two years after the tours began, was, "There seems to have been considerable damage here."[34]

The throngs that engulfed the emperor were not exclusively Japanese. Foreign journalists and American servicemen were prominent among them. This pattern was established on the initial visit to Yokohama, when GIs surrounded the emperor's car, climbed on the hood, and jostled to shake his hand. "Proximity to the throne" proved as infectious for the Americans as it was for the Japanese. If the underlying sentiments differed, as surely they did, there was still a common denominator of awe in the presence of royalty, intoxication in the presence of celebrity.

Even more striking was the formal, almost feudal role the Americans came to play in the ritual choreography of the tours. Wherever the emperor went, he was protected by GIs including military policemen, who usually preceded him like an honor guard. This protection had been requested by the government, ever fearful of attacks by left-wing or right-wing radicals that never materialized. In complying, SCAP provided far more than simple physical security, however. It demonstrated, in the most concrete manner, American support for the throne and for the emperor personally—all this beginning when abdication was a live issue and the emperor in theory still indictable for war crimes. A composition by a third grader captured this particular dimension of the imperial visits. People packed both sides of the street, the youngster wrote, and the first thing that appeared was a jeep, followed by American MPs with rifles on their shoulders . . . and then the emperor. On occasions when the crowds became confused, the emperor's American guardians cleared the way by driving their jeeps into the melee or shooting blank cartridges into the air.[35]

Amid all the wonder and excitement, the imperial visits also provoked a healthy quota of irreverence. "Emperor Ah-sō" became a ubiquitous tag line, while the tours themselves became known as one of the "three world-renewing kō's" (yonaoshi sankō)—a joke that rested on the appearance of the phonetic syllable kō in three lively media events of the time: the ecstatic new religion of "Jikōson," the hoarded-goods scandal that had been first exposed by a Diet member named Sekō Kōichi, and the tours (junkō) themselves. A slapstick addition to the emperor's retinue materialized in Nagoya in October 1946, when an uninvited auto appeared at the tail end of the imperial motorcade. Its passenger was none other than the would-be "Emperor Kumazawa," the local pretender who claimed to represent the true imperial line.[36] The element of carnival was always lurking just beneath the surface.

Through his tours, the emperor became known as "the Broom"—and was depicted in a few left-wing cartoons with bristles for a head—because every place he was scheduled to visit got cleaned up. While the emperor persuaded himself that he was seeing how his subjects lived, he was, of course, only taken to clean, well-lighted places. Roads were repaired and buildings rebuilt where he was to pass. Streams were cleared out. He lodged in immaculate dwellings. Paths were covered with matting, and platforms erected near the rice fields he was to observe. In the words of a GHQ report, "pillars, columns, and arches, usually covered with flowers and branches" were erected along the course of the royal procession. Enormous sums were spent to ensure that the emperor did not really encounter reality, to the point of sometimes devastating the budgets of local governments.[37]

As the tours became routinized, local politicians began to solicit imperial visits to enhance their personal prestige. At the other end of the procession, as many as one hundred court officials sometimes accompanied the new symbol of democracy, and corrupt members of the imperial entourage used the local visits to requisition black-market rice or other "gifts" for their personal use. (Even bluebloods felt the food shortage.)[38] Partly due to such excess and turpitude, the tours were suspended at the beginning of 1948, by which time the emperor had beyond question become a different figure than the manifest deity of the war years—although still possessed of certain extraordinary qualities. This was conveyed in an article headlined "Emperor Hirohito—He Holds Japan Together" in the English-language *Nippon Times,* which applauded the fact that "the Emperor's present attempt at humanizing himself fortunately has not been marred by any mishaps." Enumerating the many talents of the human emperor, the paper pointed out that "it isn't everybody who can take a fan between his toes and fan himself. Not only can Emperor Hirohito perform this stunt but he is able to do so while swimming. He can also swim in the rain holding an open umbrella in one hand."[39]

The imperial tours were resumed in the spring of 1949. Even then, all was not unalloyed imperial charisma, as Kojima Ken, a court physician, discovered when he accompanied the emperor to the southern island of Shikoku. In the city of Uwajima the imperial entourage lodged at an inn that had been virtually rebuilt in anticipation of this sublime visit, but the emperor had a slight cold and so chose not to bathe. In such cases, it was customary for people accompanying the sovereign to use the bath that had been prepared for him, so Kojima and a fellow doctor took to the tub. While they soaking, the water suddenly drained out, leaving the two men shivering in an empty *ofuro*. The explanation for this bizarre happening, it turned out, lay in the fact that the inn had tried to recoup some of its reconstruction expenses by selling bath space to dignitaries such as the mayor and the head of the local assembly—all of whom were anticipating soaking in the same hot water the emperor had used. When the emperor failed to perform his ablutions, the local dignitaries hovering in eager anticipation outside were so infuriated that they pulled the plug. Kojima caught cold and ran a fever for several days.[40]

Less amusing was the emperor's visit to Kyoto in November 1951, when the occupation was nearing an end and fierce debates raged over rearmament and alignment with the United States in the Cold War. Radical students at Kyoto University prepared an open letter filled with hostile questions to be presented to the emperor and sang a "Peace Song" instead of the national anthem in his presence. This was the first open act of protest against the imperial tours. The university refused to present the students' petition to the emperor, and indefinitely suspended eight students for lack of proper decorum.[41] To anyone who recalled the suppression of "dangerous thought" a scant decade or two earlier, the new imperial democracy did indeed seem rooted in the past.

One Man's Shattered God

In 1983, *Shattered God (Kudakareta Kami),* a unique and incisive critique of the emperor's abrupt transformation from god to mortal, from supreme symbol of a holy war to ambiguous symbol of "democracy," was published. Its author, Watanabe Kiyoshi, had been an ex-serviceman with little formal education when he wrote this journal-diary covering the period from September 1945 to April 1946. Watanabe turned twenty years old that November, but it would be erroneous to say that he celebrated his birthday. He was a man consumed by rage at having been betrayed by his sovereign.[42]

Watanabe had enlisted in the navy at the age of fifteen and served in the decisive losing battles in the Marianas in 1942, when the tide of war turned against Japan. Almost miraculously, he survived the sinking of the great battleship *Musashi* in which most of his comrades perished. He was among the earliest group of servicemen demobilized, arriving back at his home village in Kanagawa Prefecture about two weeks after the emperor's broadcast. Unlike others, he returned empty handed, with no looted military supplies—for which his mother berated him, comparing him unfavorably with the more practical demobilized sons of her neighbors.

As a young fighting man, Watanabe had revered the emperor as ardently and unreservedly as any "emperor worshipper" who ever appeared in the behavioral profiles prepared by MacArthur's psychological-warfare experts. He believed every word the emperor said about the "holy war" and expected to die fighting. When defeat came, it was rumored on his battleship and then later in his village that the emperor would be executed. Watanabe assumed he would commit suicide. To him this seemed the natural way to take responsibility for the defeat and avoid being demeaned by the enemy. When this did not happen, he wondered if the emperor were staying on so as not to make the confusion of defeat worse. Perhaps he intended to abdicate once most of his soldiers and sailors had been demobilized. It was inconceivable that he would not in some way demonstrate responsibility for and to those who had died following his orders.

Watanabe's journal began on September 2, the day of the surrender ceremony in Tokyo Bay. Seeing even Japanese vessels flying the enemy's flag tore him apart. There could be no greater humiliation, he wrote. For days after returning home he hardly moved. He even ate his meals apart from his family. When Allied troops poured into Tokyo, he felt as if muddy military boots were trampling on his heart. Tōjō's botched suicide attempt disgusted him, and the emperor's first visit to MacArthur shocked him beyond belief. Seeing the famous photograph of the two leaders standing side by side like friends made him want to vomit. It also impressed on him the finality of the fact that "together with the emperor, we truly lost." His sense of despair went beyond the norm, for he simply could not comprehend why the emperor showed no sense of shame. "The emperor threw away his divinity and authority by himself and bowed his head like a dog," Watanabe wrote. And so, for him, "the emperor died on this day."

In the months that followed, he was a man obsessed—tormented by a sense of betrayal, frightened by his own anger. He found it no longer possible to trust anything or anyone, including himself. If the emperor truly did not want the war, then why had he signed the declaration of war? Why did he seem to be trying to pass responsibility for Pearl Harbor on to Tōjō? Why could he not simply say this was done by his order? The press, too, appalled him. Newspapers that only yesterday had been trumpeting every slogan of the "holy war" were now talking about a conspiracy by the militarists, bureaucrats, and zaibatsu. Someone, Watanabe noted with approval, said that the only truth in the press was to be found in the obituaries.

The sudden vogue of media praise for American-style democracy and "yesterday's enemy becoming today's friend" struck him as fatuous. If friendship was so important, why had they gone to war in the first place? Why had he risked his life? What—here, in early October—was one supposed to make of the "repentance of the hundred million" that the government was promoting? For every Japanese to express repentance for defeat was meaningless. On the other hand, it might make sense for those directly responsible for starting the war, including the emperor, to express repentance to the people.

A female acquaintance told him that he was simply wrong. The emperor had been a robot, not responsible for what was done in his name. The photograph with MacArthur was just a "performance." However, for Watanabe, who like many poorly educated teenage soldiers and sailors had never doubted that the emperor was a kind of divinity, a supreme value in whom one could place absolute trust, it was all too real. By mid-October he was so consumed with rage that he began to fantasize about burning down the imperial palace, hanging the emperor upside down from a pine tree by the palace moat, and beating him with an oaken stick (as was done to sailors in the imperial navy). He even imagined dragging the emperor to the bottom of the ocean to make him view the thousands of corpses lying there as a result of the war his orders had begun. He saw himself seizing the emperor by the hair and banging his head against the rocks on the ocean floor. He believed he was going crazy.

In the latter part of October, he mused about putting the imperial system to a popular referendum. Most Japanese, he conceded, would support the emperor. Watanabe absolutely opposed arresting him, for this would only involve a vengeful trial by the victors. In his village, people already were beginning to speak of MacArthur as the new emperor, or a new king who stood over the emperor. Their fickleness sickened him. His fellow Japanese simply snuggled up to whomever was most powerful at the moment. "Times change," people kept saying, but Watanabe wanted no part of such shallow pragmatism.

On November 7, Watanabe recorded his disgust at the saccharine "Apple Song" that had caught everyone's fancy. Several days later, he noted that the emperor had been outfitted with a new uniform that made him look like a railroad employee. This indicated, he thought, that the imperial house felt confident the emperor would neither be arrested, nor abdicate. But what were *his* thoughts? he wondered. In mid-month he listened to a village dignitary lecturing about how the "holy war" had actually been a war of aggression and recalled how the same man had given speeches supporting the war.

When GHQ began arresting prominent figures for war crimes, Watanabe recorded his opposition. The Japanese should conduct such trials on their own. In late November, upon hearing that the emperor had visited Yasukuni Shrine, dedicated to those who died in war for the imperial cause, he wondered how the souls of the dead greeted the sovereign—and then concluded that there could be no such souls, for if there had been, they would already have slain the emperor with their curses. A few days later, he heard that a new photograph of the emperor was to be distributed to the schools. This led him to remember the day the *Musashi* sank, when he had watched an officer clutching the emperor's heavy, enclosed sacred photo in his arms as he leapt into the ocean. The weight of it must have carried the man to his death.

When Watanabe saw a Communist poster calling for the overthrow the emperor system, he found himself laughing at the vagaries of language. During the war it had been common to speak of loyalty to the emperor as *sekishin*, literally "red heart." Now, he found himself agreeing with the poster. He realized that he had come to possess a "red" heart of an en-

tirely different nature. Early in December, he resolved to judge everything
for himself, never again accepting without question what others said.

On December 15, the day the directive disestablishing State Shinto was
issued, Watanabe was severely beaten up by five "gangsters" who belittled
him as an "ex-soldier." Lying in bed with his bruises, he imagined himself back on the *Musashi*, aiming its 46-centimeter shells at random all over
Japan. He wrote this curse:

> What is the emperor?
> What is Japan?
> What is love of country?
> What is democracy?
> What is "country of culture"?
> All this, all of this eats shit.
> I spit on it!

On December 21, an acquaintance from Yokosuka visited Watanabe and
asked him about his own responsibility for having believed so blindly in
the emperor. The man left him two books by the Marxist humanist
Kawakami Hajime—a history of modern economic thought and a copy of
his old classic *Bimbō Monogatari* (A Tale of Poverty). He also gave Watanabe three packs of Lucky Strike cigarettes. Watanabe threw the American
cigarettes in the river, but the books provided him an entree into a new
world.

On the last day of 1945, Watanabe recorded that SCAP had issued a
progress report on Japanese democratization, claiming that the Shinto directive had destroyed the last evil element supporting the emperor system
and that feudalistic elements were being eliminated one by one. This was
a lie, Watanabe observed, so long as the emperor remained. The SCAP
pronouncement reminded him of comparable pronunciamentos by the
wartime military high command. On January 1, the day of the emperor's
"declaration of humanity," he finished reading Kawakami's history of economic thought. He found the chapter on Marx especially illuminating.

When he read the emperor's New Year's Day rescript, which he had
assumed would be an abdication announcement, Watanabe's rage again became physical. He felt dizzy; "cold blood" rushed up from his feet; he felt
like "vomiting" his anger. He was particularly incensed by the emperor's
denial that he ever had been a "manifest deity." It was as if Hirohito were
playing games with the people, as if it were merely a "contest of foxes and
badgers" (trickster figures in Japanese folklore).

The rescript's warning against "radical tendencies" and declining morality also outraged him. Who, if not the emperor, was responsible for causing such conditions? How could he even speak about the people's declining morality when he himself had not yet taken responsibility for the war? Feudal lords, Watanabe observed, took responsibility when their castles fell. Captains bore responsibility for the loss of their ships. Then it struck him: neither the August 15 nor the January 1 rescripts contained a single line saying, "I was to blame. I apologize." When the press published MacArthur's praise of the emperor for playing a leading role in the democratization of Japan, Watanabe dismissed this as a contradiction, like sugar that is not sweet. True democratization *(minshuka)* could only be created by the people *(min)*. That was why democracy was rendered <u>min-shushugi</u> (the four ideographs literally mean people-sovereign-ism). For a recently devoted emperor worshiper with only eight years of formal education, Watanabe had traveled a long way, driven by his rage.

In the wake of the "declaration of humanity," Watanabe began to ponder more deeply his own responsibility for having believed in the emperor. He expressed disappointment in the Communist Party's abandonment of opposition to the emperor and the emperor system. At the same time, he was disgusted to hear a neighbor tell his father that Japan should become the forty-ninth state of the United States. The same man, he recalled, had run around urging people to fight the "devilish Anglo-Americans." Formal announcement of the war-crimes trials in late January troubled him, for although it seemed appropriate for Chinese and Southeast Asians to judge the Japanese, the situation was not so clear cut where the Americans were concerned. He agreed Pearl Harbor had been wrong, but wondered how people who had dropped atomic bombs could speak so easily of Japan as the "enemy of peace and morality."

Late in January, Watanabe finished reading Kawakami's *Tale of Poverty*. He admired it greatly, but took issue with a passing point. Kawakami had written critically about a store selling expensive cosmetics to the poor daughters of tenant farmers, using this as an example of the exploitation of the poor. To Watanabe, himself a rural boy, it was entirely appropriate for poor country girls to wish to become pretty like any other young women. On February 1, he recorded his shock on hearing of Kawakami's death. The old scholar was a true teacher and had opened his eyes to the way he had blindly followed along. "Ignorance," Watanabe wrote, "is the most terrifying thing."

Early in February, Watanabe was shocked by GHQ's revelation of the immense assets of the imperial family. He had never connected the emperor with money and goods—another indication, he felt, of his own ignorance. Watanabe continued to wrestle with the question of his own war responsibility. He came to accept the fact that the war had been one of aggression. Although he had not realized this at the time, his ignorance did not, he felt sure, erase his responsibility. It had taken millions of deaths, blood sacrifices, and then defeat to bring him to this realization. He now thought not only about the comrades who had died around him, but also about the countless shells he had fired to kill Americans. When, in mid February, a relative encouraged him to return to school, he expressed cynicism about this. "Scholarship, art, culture"—all seemed meaningless, since they had not succeeded in preventing such a war.

On February 22, Watanabe read or heard an account of the emperor's conversation with a soldier repatriated from Saipan. "Was the war severe?" asked the emperor. "Yes, it was severe," the man replied. "You really worked hard. It was a lot of trouble," the emperor added in response. "Keep on working hard. Advance along a fine path as a human being." Once again, Watanabe was plunged into despair. Perhaps, he thought, the emperor simply lacked the normal sense of responsibility other people possessed. Could he not at least have said, "I am sorry to have caused you so much difficulty"?

It puzzled Watanabe that people accepted the emperor's hat-waving tours so easily, and he placed some of the blame for this on the failure of the media to face the emperor's war responsibility squarely. The fashion was to blame militarists and big capitalists for the war, and present the emperor as their victim—a "poor robot" or a "true pacifist." Since the media had kowtowed to the military themselves, he speculated, perhaps this was part of their tactic for absolving themselves of responsibility. He continued to wonder about the "psychological influence" the emperor's behavior was having on the people as a whole. If the entire nation followed the emperor, Watanabe feared, they would end up with only one guiding rule: "Even the emperor gets away without taking responsibility, so there is no need for us to take responsibility, no matter what we did."

On March 8, Watanabe, recording his thoughts on the newly announced draft constitution, marveled at the emperor's ability to change forms from "god" to "human" to "symbol" so rapidly. He bitterly exclaimed that a sardine's head might be a better symbol. A few days later he had a conversation with some veterans from the China theater, much older than he, and was shocked to hear about the atrocities one of them committed there, apparently without a bit of remorse. Was that man's irresponsibility a reflection of the emperor's? Might he himself have casually engaged in such acts had he been sent to China?

In mid-March, Watanabe got into a brawl with a GI walking with a Japanese woman who was wearing bright lipstick and a red dress. Refusing to step aside, Watanabe bumped the woman's arm, whereupon the GI kicked him and they traded punches. A crowd gathered and four Japanese policemen eventually broke up the fight. Watanabe was brought to the police station for a lecture. He had never been so close to the enemy before. The American smelled like an animal and he concluded that the term "hairy barbarian" was well chosen. The next day, still boiling with anger, he thought of Filipina women who had refused to go with Japanese men. Some even shot Japanese soldiers. He found them impressive. The vogue for English-language terms—*thank you, hello, good-bye, okay, I love you*—disgusted him.

In early April, Watanabe's former elementary school teacher told him that, although it was sad Japan had been defeated, in a way it was better to have lost the war. Otherwise, the Japanese would not have dreamed of democracy. This same teacher had once exhorted his young charges to join that war and Watanabe naturally wondered if he thought about this. A few days later he recorded an incident: a soldier, long given up for dead, had returned home to find his wife seven months pregnant by his younger brother. Tears and violence followed, and the man ran away to stay with relatives.

On April 20, Watanabe left his village to take a job in Tokyo. He had heard that anyone could write a letter to the emperor now, and he did so before leaving. He used the familiar "you" *(anata)*, unthinkable before the surrender, in addressing him. He had fought hard for the emperor in accordance with his orders, Watanabe wrote, but since the defeat he had lost all trust and hope in him. As a result, he wished to sever their relationship. He then offered an accounting of all the salary that he had been paid by the imperial navy and every article he could remember having received in his years of service—a long list indeed, itemizing food as well as clothing and other goods. The total, as he calculated it, came to 4,281 yen and 5 sen. With his letter, he enclosed a check for 4,282 yen.

"Thus," the letter concluded, "I owe you nothing."

chapter twelve

CONSTITUTIONAL DEMOCRACY: GHQ WRITES A NEW NATIONAL CHARTER

Early in 1946, virtually on the spur of the moment, General MacArthur initiated what he later called "probably the single most important accomplishment of the occupation"—nothing less than the replacing of the "Meiji Constitution" of 1890 with a new national charter.[1] The Americans had long looked askance at the Meiji charter, deeming it incompatible with the healthy development of responsible democratic government. This critique was developed in a number of confidential internal studies and policy papers. It was also expressed unusually vividly in a *Guide to Japan* that was prepared for U.S. forces around the time of the surrender. Readers of the guide, after being informed that the early Meiji government was dominated by powerful former samurai associated with the former feudal domains of Satsuma and Chōshū, were told that these oligarchs had looked west for a constitutional model and emerged with an unholy hybrid. "The new Japanese Constitution, with Prussian tyranny as its father, and British representative government as its mother, and attended at its birth by Sat-Cho [Satsuma and Chōshū] midwives," the guide declared, "was a hermaphroditic creature."[2]

Regendering this hermaphroditic creature in 1946 involved casting aside the authoritarian German legal model on which it was based (and in which most Japanese legal specialists continued to be trained), and replacing it with a charter rooted in basic ideals from the Anglo-American legal tradition. On March 6, 1946, a draft outline of a new constitution was presented to the public as the government's own handiwork and subsequently submitted to the Diet for deliberation and adoption. In actuality, it had originally been written in English by members of GHQ's Government Section in a secret week-long session in the Daiichi Building in Tokyo. The Americans who participated in this extraordinary undertaking called it *their* "constitutional convention." They had scooped the old Meiji Constitution hollow; only its "structure, headings" were left, as an internal GHQ memo put it. The old shell was then refilled with Anglo-American and European democratic ideals—and more. Under the new charter, Japan also renounced belligerency as a sovereign right of the state.

No modern nation ever has rested on a more alien constitution—or a more unique wedding of monarchism, democratic idealism, and pacifism; and few, if any, alien documents have ever been as thoroughly internalized and vigorously defended as this national charter would come to be. Although it bore the unmistakable imprint of the conqueror and shocked Japan's conservative elites—indeed, although it was hermaphroditic in its own manner—it tapped into popular aspirations for peace and democracy in quite remarkable ways.[3]

Regendering a Hermaphroditic Creature

The rationale for constitutional revision lay in several ambiguous sections of the Potsdam Declaration. Section 6 declared, "There must be eliminated for all time the authority and influence of those who have deceived and misled the people of Japan into embarking on world conquest." Primarily, this provided justification for war-crimes trials and an extensive purge of individuals associated with militaristic and ultranationalistic activities and organizations. It could, however, also be interpreted as requiring the establishment of constitutional protections against future abuses of authority. Section 10 required that "the Japanese government shall remove all obstacles to the revival and strengthening of democratic tendencies among the Japanese people. Freedom of speech, of religion, and of thought, as well as respect for fundamental human rights, shall be established." Also pertinent was Section 12, which promised that "the occupying forces of the Allies shall be withdrawn from Japan as soon as these objectives have been accomplished and there has been established in accordance with the freely expressed will of the Japanese people a peacefully inclined and responsible government."[4]

On the basis of these statements, reinforced by later directives from Washington that reiterated the general objective of "modifying the feudal and authoritarian tendencies of the government," MacArthur and his staff in Tokyo concluded that their mission could not be accomplished without fundamental changes in the nation's constitutional structure.[5] Policy makers in Washington submitted their indictment of that structure to MacArthur in a top-secret cable early in January 1946, calling for changes in the "governmental system" to create genuinely representative suffrage, popular control over the executive branch, a strengthened elective legislature, guarantees of fundamental civil rights, and greater local autonomy. In one significant way, Washington's critique was more radical than prevailing sentiment within SCAP: the cable went on to recommend that the Japanese "should be encouraged to abolish the Emperor Institution or to reform it along more democratic lines."[6]

Although the Americans in Tokyo were clear on the need for constitutional revision, initially it was MacArthur's policy that any amendments to the old constitution should come from the government. Even here, the usual incongruities were apparent. The Americans were ordering the Japanese to adopt democracy by their "freely expressed will" through constitutional revision. They were acting, moreover, as if the postsurrender conservative cabinets actually represented the will of the people— which no one, including SCAP, the populace, and or the rapidly revolving governments themselves believed for a moment.

Still, SCAP initially did as much as could be expected under the circumstances. By October 1945, it had conveyed privately and publicly to the other side that constitutional revision was expected. In the months that followed, no obtrusive attempts were made to interfere while occupation officials awaited the Japanese response. As it turned out, the public grasped the American intent quite quickly. Both private groups and political parties took the initiative to draft and publicize constitutional proposals, several of which were impressively liberal. The media followed these activities with interest; and GHQ, in turn, followed the media closely. The government, in contrast, moved like a tortoise and remained tone deaf to the Potsdam language even when the Americans reiterated it to them. Of all revisions proposed by Japanese, the government's were among the last to appear and the most transparently cosmetic in content. The public greeted the proposals drafted by the cabinet's revision committee with derision, and GHQ seized the moment to convene its own audacious, secret "convention." Where constitutional revision was concerned, the conservative old guard dug its own grave.

At the official level, the Americans actually set two separate constitutional inquiries in train, one of which became a tragedy of sorts, the other a farce. The tragedy began on October 4, when MacArthur personally encouraged Prince Konoe, then serving as minister without portfolio in the Higashikuni cabinet, to look into the problem of constitutional revision. Several days later, George Atcheson discussed this project with Konoe in greater detail. Although the Higashikuni cabinet resigned on the day after Konoe met MacArthur, Konoe continued to regard himself as the anointed patron of constitutional matters. With the warm approval of Atcheson and the supreme commander, he discussed the issue of revision with the emperor, moved his activities under the aegis of the imperial household, and assembled a small group of constitutional experts to assist him. Konoe took his new responsibilities seriously. With the panache of the comfortable nobleman, he even rented at his own expense the entire third floor of an inn in Hakone, where his team could work without disturbance. To all public appearances, constitutional revision now had become an imperial enterprise. The media presented it as the emperor's own initiative.

Despite the vagueness of his official position, Konoe was a man of exceptional influence and personal charisma. He had served as prime minister on two separate occasions in the critical period between 1936 and 1941, which enhanced his prestige immensely but ultimately was to prove his undoing. It was during Konoe's premiership, in 1937, that Japan launched its "war of annihilation" against China. He also was prime minister in 1938 when Japan declared a "New Order" in East Asia, and it was his government that brought Japan into the Axis Pact with Nazi Germany and fascist Italy in 1940. The wonder was not that he was identified as a war-crimes suspect before the year was out, but rather that both MacArthur and Atcheson, the top American military and civilian representatives in Japan, initially deemed him an appropriate person through whom to promote constitutional democratization.

MacArthur's headquarters publicly dissociated itself from Konoe's project on November 1. It had practical reasons for doing so, but these did not lessen the sting of betrayal. Konoe had become a liability, for it was increasingly clear that he would be indicted as a war criminal; secret memoranda as well as mounting media criticism made this apparent. In addition, the Shidehara cabinet grew more restive and resentful as the weeks passed, criticizing the fact that an undertaking as important as constitutional revision was being pursued outside its purview.

It was the prince's own flair for publicity and self-promotion that brought things to a head—and revealed, in the process, the intricacy of

imperial politics. In late October, in the provocative interview in which
he suggested that emperor might abdicate, Konoe also referred to his
conversation with MacArthur and revealed that the supreme commander
had "stated the necessity for a liberal constitution in a very stern tone and
suggested I take the leadership in this movement." SCAP had welcomed
the impression that the initiative for constitutional revision had come
from the emperor. Konoe's frank disclosure upset this pretense.

Despite this misstep, Konoe carried on with his inquiries. On November 22, he presented the emperor with an "outline" itemizing twenty-
two specific constitutional problems or concerns. His primary focus was
on clarifying the emperor's authority while offering ways to prevent
abuses of power in the name of the throne, but his recommendations also
revealed that he had listened carefully to many of the specific concerns
conveyed to his aides and informants by the Americans. His very first
point stipulated, "The Emperor shall be the superintendent of sovereignty
and shall be the exerciser of it, but it shall be made especially clear that
its exercise shall be dependent on the support of the people." Since "the
misfortune of today" derived primarily from abuses by the armed services, in Konoe's view, care also had to be taken to clarify the military's
subordination to the cabinet and Diet, and thus to "the will of the people."

Concerning human rights, Konoe showed himself receptive to the criticism that under the existing constitution these rights were always hedged
by the phrase "unless otherwise stipulated by law." It should, he recommended, "be made clear that the freedoms of the people take precedence
over the law." Konoe went further on this score, proposing the abolition
of prerogatives by which people's rights could be suspended in time of
emergency. Ministers of state, hitherto responsible only to the emperor,
would be made responsible to the Diet as well, and fixed procedures
would be established for the selection of the prime minister. The prince
also proposed abolishing the elite, extraparliamentary Privy Council.

For all practical purposes, this was the end of the Konoe initiative. No
official text of his outline was ever released, although the *Mainichi* newspaper printed an accurate version a month later. The Konoe project seems
to have made no lasting impression upon SCAP officials. Still, notwithstanding his provocative comments about abdication, the prince had performed a subtle service for the throne. His well-publicized activities
helped refurbish the emperor's image as a monarch devoted to peaceful
rather than military concerns.

That SCAP actively acquiesced in Konoe's initiative for a while reinforced the impression that the Americans would be amenable to modest constitutional revisions aimed at creating some sort of balance between imperial prerogatives and electoral politics. This impression was misleading. Subsequent officials charged with proposing revisions paid a heavy price for failing to recognize that SCAP desired more radical change than Konoe envisioned. The prince himself did not live to see the game played out. On December 6, his name appeared on an official list with those of eight others as an accused Class A war criminal. Ten days later, on the night he was to go to jail, he killed himself by taking poison.[7]

Conundrums for the Men of Meiji

The more farcical government venture in constitutional revision began on October 25, when the cabinet established its own Constitutional Problem Investigation Committee. Matsumoto Jōji, a supremely self-confident legal scholar with extensive political and administrative experience, was appointed its chair. A specialist in commercial rather than constitutional law, he was nominated at the urging of Foreign Minister Yoshida. Although Matsumoto's righteousness remained intact in the turbulent months to come, his self-assurance was to be subjected to undreamed-of tribulations.[8]

To establishment figures such as Shidehara, Matsumoto, and Yoshida, constitutional revision was a frivolous notion, one more bee in the American bonnet, and initially they did not take MacArthur's statements about it very seriously. Privately, Shidehara told both Konoe and Kido Kōichi that revision was neither necessary nor desirable. In his view, it would be sufficient to simply develop a more democratic interpretation of the Meiji charter. Publicly, the prime minister said much the same thing. Following an October 11 meeting with the supreme commander, he blithely told the press that constitutional amendment was not necessary.[9] The name of Matsumoto's "Constitutional Problem Investigation Committee" was deliberately worded to avoid mention of "revision" or "amendment," and he took care to make sure no one missed the innuendo. "The Committee does not necessarily aim at the revision of the constitution," he announced. "The purpose of its investigation is to determine whether any amendment may be necessary, and, if so, what are the points to be amended."[10] This was not mere bravado. A few years after these events had played their course, Matsumoto ruefully confided that "we thought we could handle the matter as we pleased. We even thought it might be all right to leave [the existing constitution] as it was." After all, had not the Potsdam Declaration proclaimed that Japan would be allowed to chose its future form of government in accordance with "the freely expressed will of the Japanese people"?[11]

The naiveté of such thinking would soon became painfully apparent, but at the time it was an entirely natural response for men of this class and temperament. Like Konoe, they were privileged men born in the Meiji period. For them, the essence of the Meiji Constitution—the centering of sovereignty in an "inviolable" emperor—was sacrosanct. For a decade or so beginning around World War I, moreover, this old guard had seen parliamentary politics and "Taishō democracy" flourish under that same constitution without any amendment whatsoever. From this perspective, the existing constitution seemed an adequately flexible document. Although the militarists had abused it, civilian antimilitarists could certainly put things straight again without tampering with fundamental principles. Indeed, they were not entirely wrong. Before a new constitution actually came into effect, an extensive range of reformist policies including land reform, woman suffrage, prolabor legislation, and economic democratization had been put into practice under the existing national charter. But here was the nub of the problem: what really made democratization possible was neither the old constitution nor the "moderate" old civilian elites, but the new reformist overlords, the alien Americans; and in their view, there were no constitutional protections to prevent the system from clamping shut again once they left town. This was what the Japanese conservatives utterly failed to comprehend.

Their skepticism about revision notwithstanding, Shidehara and Matsumoto assembled a distinguished committee of seventeen members, including many famous legal scholars. Although the imperious Matsumoto tended to carry by far the greatest burden, often working in seclusion, the committee held twenty-two confidential meetings between October 27 and February 2.[12] For such an eminent group of authorities, it had astonishing collective shortcomings. Prime Minister Shidehara apparently gave his advisory committee no serious instructions concerning either basic principles or simple political considerations, and the committee members themselves seemed impervious to the plain power realities of military occupation. They completely failed to grasp the larger legal and philosophical principles that lay behind American constitutional thought—and refused to even ask. Despite the Potsdam Declaration and the terms of surrender, they also failed to take into consideration what the numerous countries in the victorious Allied camp thought of Japan and might demand from it before they would consider restoring sovereignty.

Most telling, these learned men revealed themselves to be utterly out of touch with what millions of ordinary Japanese were coming to understand "democracy" to be and what they desired or would tolerate. Virtually their sole reference for revision was the Meiji Constitution itself. Not only did they ignore other constitutional models, but they did not even condescend to examine the recommendations that nonofficial groups were making public at the time.[13] The naiveté and elitism of the Matsumoto committee proved to be, from its own perspective, a disaster. The committee left its name to history as a woeful example of insular complacency and myopic expertise.

In mid-February 1946, after he had belatedly come to realize the folly of this casual attitude and was vainly struggling to regain the initiative in constitutional revision, Matsumoto attempted to persuade occupation authorities that fundamental differences between East and West were at issue here. "A juridical system is very much like certain kinds of plants, which transplanted from their native soil, degenerate, or even die," he wrote in a memorandum to GHQ. "Some of [the] roses of the West, when cultivated in Japan, lose their fragrance totally."[14] This East-is-East-and-West-is-West improvisation was less red rose than red herring, for far more was involved here than white men's flora ill suited to Eastern soil, or a simplistic clash between "Western" and "Japanese" cultures. The basic conflict lay between two Western systems of legal thinking. Put oversimply, these experts, well grounded in German legislative and administrative law and a German-style "theory of state structure," were largely indifferent to American concerns about popular sovereignty and human rights.[15]

Matsumoto ran his committee with a firm hand. Once he and his colleagues were persuaded that some constitutional revision was inevitable, they adopted as a guideline what became known as "Matsumoto's four principles." As made public in a speech to the House of Representatives on December 8, these were (1) no change in the fundamental principle that the emperor combined in himself the rights of sovereignty; (2) a broadening of Diet responsibilities and consequent limitation on the emperor's prerogatives; (3) assumption of responsibility for affairs of state by cabinet ministers who in turn would be responsible to the Diet; and (4) strengthened guarantees of the rights and freedoms of the people, with provision for redress of violations of such rights and freedoms.

The committee recommended changing only one word in the clauses concerning the emperor. Instead of being "sacred and inviolable," the sovereign would be designated "supreme and inviolable." Ten additional amendments eventually were included in the so-called Matsumoto draft adopted by the committee, but this minimal word change concerning the emperor—large in the minds of the committee members but tokenistic to others—became a symbol of the extremely conservative nature of these proposed revisions.[16] Concerning fundamental human rights, about which the Potsdam Declaration had been so emphatic, the Matsumoto group merely proposed an amendment declaring that the rights and freedoms of Japanese subjects were inviolate except "as otherwise prescribed by law." As critics within GHQ always had been quick to point out, it was precisely "by law" that the suppression of human rights and freedom had been carried out in presurrender Japan.[17]

Unlike Konoe, Matsumoto resolutely refused to inquire about SCAP's expectations. Takagi Yasaka, a scholar versed in Anglo-American law who was not included on the committee, warned Matsumoto that his proposals would be rejected. When he urged Matsumoto to consult with GHQ, he was abruptly dismissed. "Constitutional reform is to be done spontaneously and independently," Matsumoto responded. "Therefore I see no need to find out American intentions or reach preliminary understandings."[18] Prime Minister Shidehara also never ventured to ask MacArthur, to whom he had ready access, exactly what he had in mind. On this most critical of undertakings, victor and vanquished simply did not communicate until it was, from the conservative perspective, too late.

The inability of these high officials and eminent scholars to imagine what the Americans required was a revealing commentary on the limitations of elite Japanese understanding of the United States prior to 1946. For these were, to all appearances, impressively cosmopolitan men. Prime Minister Shidehara was an anglophile whose facility with English bordered on the legendary. Shakespeare and Milton, it was said, were always within his reach. Yoshida Shigeru, whose last post as a diplomat had been ambassador to London, similarly enjoyed a reputation was an "old liberal." Matsumoto also handled English capably and previously had held some of the most prestigious positions in the land, not only in academe (Tokyo Imperial University), but also in parliamentary politics (the House of Peers), in bureaucratic administration (the South Manchurian Railway and Cabinet Legislation Bureau), and in the cabinet (Minister of Commerce and Industry). According to one of his admirers, he had even been "quite a socialist in his younger days," and remained "a whole-hearted liberal."[19]

To be known as an anglophile or "old liberal," however, did not mean that one was also strongly pro-American or deeply knowledgeable about the United States. The few legal experts who actually had studied constitutional law in the United States were not invited to join the committee, and the best-known Japanese reference books associated with "liberal" constitutional theories as well as the U.S. Constitution gave but passing and superficial attention to the very area that the Potsdam Declaration had singled out for special emphasis: human rights. The writings of the most famous "liberal" constitutional theorist in presurrender Japan, Minobe Tatsukichi, were a good illustration of this blind spot. In the 1930s, Minobe had been attacked by ultranationalists, fired from Tokyo Imperial University, and expelled from his seat in the Diet because his theory that the emperor was an "organ" of the government (rather than sacred and transcendent) was deemed a perversion of the essence of the national polity. Yet Minobe's writings betrayed scant interest in those human rights issues that American-style liberal thinking deemed critical. The fifth edition of his famous study of the Meiji Constitution, published in 1932 gave a mere 27 pages (out of 626 total pages) to the subject of both the rights and duties of subjects. In an earlier book devoted exclusively to "the origins and special characteristics of the U.S. Constitution," Minobe passed over the entire Bill of Rights in eight sketchy pages.[20]

There is no need to wonder what the persecuted Minobe would have done had he been given the opportunity to participate in the revision debates—for he had this opportunity. He was a member of the Matsumoto committee and lost no time in independently making his views public. There was no need to rush to revise the Meiji Constitution, he argued with ardor as well as bluntness; and, in any case, it was inappropriate to do so while the country was under foreign occupation. In his view, the problems of the recent past had occurred not because the Meiji charter was flawed, but rather because the charter's true spirit had been warped. He did not regard the status of the emperor under the Meiji Constitution as a problem at all, pointing out that Western constitutions also referred to "holy" and "inviolable" sovereign powers.[21]

Popular Initiatives for a New National Charter

The Matsumoto committee ended up in history's dustbin largely because the civilian elites remained autocratic and antidemocratic, whereas a great many ordinary men and women were proving receptive to the sort of democracy the Americans were promoting. Many, for instance, were happy to jettison emperor worship as enshrined in the Meiji charter. In a survey published just as the Matsumoto committee was finalizing its recommendations, only 16 percent of those polled desired to keep the emperor's status unchanged.[22] Denied secure rights and power under the Meiji

Constitution, they welcomed the opportunity to better their situation. This became clear in two ways, both carefully noted by officials at GHQ. First, a number of the constitutional revisions being proposed by private organizations and individuals included liberal and progressive proposals. Second, when the Matsumoto committee's recommendations were made public—by a spectacular journalistic scoop, as it happened—the media, with strong public support, denounced them as reactionary.

Besides the Konoe and Matsumoto projects, at least a dozen other proposals for constitutional revision were presented between the fall of 1945 and March 1946. Four came from political parties: in order of appearance, the Communists, the Liberals, the Progressives, and the Socialists. The Japan Bar Association contributed to the debate by advocating limiting imperial prerogatives, expanding the powers of the Diet, abolishing the peerage, and adopting a referendum system. Several proposals came from private groups and individuals, the most influential of these being the Kempō Kenkyūkai (Constitutional Research Association), composed of liberal and left-wing intellectuals—including two distinguished scholars, Ōuchi Hyōe and Morito Tatsuo, who had been expelled from Tokyo Imperial University for their heretical views during the war. Another private group, the Kempō Kondankai (Constitutional Discussion Group), was primarily a vehicle for the ideas of a single individual, Inada Masatsugu, although it included other members such as the venerable parliamentarian Ozaki Yukio.[23]

Certain individuals also contributed to these deliberations, none more influentially than Takano Iwasaburō. A progressive intellectual who had a hand in the Socialist and Kempō Kenkyūkai drafts, Takano also published an important draft constitution of his own. A hastier and more idiosyncratic contribution came from Matsumoto Jiichirō, a veteran Socialist and leader of the severely discriminated against community of outcastes (known as *eta* before the surrender and *burakumin* afterwards). Matsumoto proposed a "Union of Japanese Republics," in which each "republic" (such as Kyushu, Kansai, Kanto, and Tohoku) would have its own president and cabinet.[24]

Only two of these proposals—the Communist Party's and Takano's—advocated abolishing the emperor system entirely. Even while supporting retention of the throne, however, several of the others drastically reduced the emperor's powers. The Kempō Kenkyūkai draft explicitly transferred the locus of sovereignty from the emperor to the people, while limiting the emperor's functions to "state ceremonies solely as an agent of the people."[25] The Socialists, divided over whether or not to abolish the emperor system, ended up advocating retention of a throne virtually all of whose powers would be ceremonial. Although the party did not publish its proposed constitutional draft until mid-February, the basic notion of a "symbolic" emperor was present in its deliberations well before the American officials in GHQ adopted the concept.[26] The Kempō Kondankai essentially followed the British notion of "the king in Parliament" by stipulating that "the sovereignty of Japan proceeds from the whole body of the people, who have the Emperor as their head."[27] Conservative groups such as the Bar Association and the Liberal Party, which emphasized preservation of the throne, nonetheless expressed support for limiting imperial prerogatives. Even the inappropriately named Progressives, the most right-wing of the major political parties, spoke of the need to "broaden and strengthen the powers of the Diet and cause the Diet to participate in the exercise of the imperial prerogative."[28]

Several of these unofficial proposals contained liberal provisions concerning human rights. The Communist Party's seven-point "Outline for a New Constitution," made public in November, declared as its fifth point that "The people shall have freedom politically, economically, and socially. Furthermore, their right to supervise and criticize the government shall be ensured." The sixth point of the Communist outline stipulated that "The people's right to live, right to work, and right to be educated shall be assured by concrete facilities." These cryptic provisions were clearly adapted from the 1936 "Stalin" constitution of the U.S.S.R.[29] Like Takano's personal proposal and the Kempō Kenkyūkai draft he helped fashion, the Socialists' proposal covered not merely the basic "freedoms of speech, assembly, association, press, religion, and communication," but also economic rights such as the protection of "livelihood in old age" and gender rights such as the guarantee of "equal rights of men and women" in marriage.[30]

Because of both its early appearance and liberal content, the Kempō Kenkyūkai's proposal attracted particular interest at GHQ's Government Section. It represented, after all, an indigenous viewpoint distinctly more democratic than that of the "moderates" or "old liberals." It was also useful in the way it called attention to the relatively recent and ideologically charged genesis of the Meiji Constitution. There was, the Kempō Kenkyūkai's proposal pointed out, no single Japanese history or tradition or culture to draw upon in charting the country's future course. It was possible to read Japan's modern experience in many ways and draw a variety of lessons from it in relation to the creation of an indigenous democracy. What this—and other—popular initiatives for a new constitution revealed was the possibility of imagining a past, as well as a future, quite different from that which the old guard was so desperately attempting to enshrine.

Those who venerated the Meiji charter naturally tended to present that document as if it were an expression of emperor-centered values that had been cherished for ages eternal. In actuality, it was less than sixty years old and represented a decision by a tiny elite to turn to Germany for a constitutional model for their emerging nation-state. The emperor became the vehicle through which German-style authoritarianism was to be Japanized. In choosing this path, the Meiji oligarchs had themselves rejected more liberal constitutional proposals from outside the government, most notably from the "liberty and people's rights movement."

The Kempō Kenkyūkai drew inspiration from that earlier opposition movement and from the more liberal and radical Western traditions it had introduced to Japan. Takano himself was a splendid example of this. Born in 1871, he was eighteen before the Meiji Constitution and the modern emperor system came into existence, and he never ceased to regard this new "national polity" as a tragic development. He made this clear in "Imprisoned People," an essay that accompanied the publication of his private draft constitution. In this, Takano dwelled on how the people had become prisoners of the emperor system under the Meiji charter. He identified the liberty and people's rights movement as a major influence on his thinking and was not alone in calling attention to this earlier radical tradition. Suzuki Yasuzō, the only participant in the Kempō Kenkyūkai who actually could be called a constitutional specialist, found similar inspiration for a more participatory democracy in this early period. After being purged from the economics faculty at Kyoto Imperial University in 1927 because of his radical views, Suzuki had devoted himself to studying the thought of the liberty and people's rights movement. In essence, these individuals were doing what the civilian old guard also did in its pointedly different way: calling attention to an indigenous tradition of "democracy" in late-nineteenth-century Japan.[31]

For the occupation authorities, such critical use of history was far more convincing than any roses-in-alien-soil arguments, especially since at least some of these reformers were familiar with such a perspective through the scholarship of the Canadian diplomat E. H. Norman, the pioneer Western historian of Japan's emergence as a modern state. As it happened, Norman, Canada's representative during this critical period, actually met

Suzuki in early September 1945 and encouraged him to develop his critique of the "national polity."[32]

Government Section's favorable response to the Kempō Kenkyūkai draft was spelled out in a confidential memorandum prepared for General Courtney Whitney, the head of the section, by Lieutenant Colonel Milo E. Rowell, later a major participant in the preparation of the new constitution. Rowell observed that certain rights were still neglected in the proposal (including restraints on law-enforcement agencies and protection of persons accused of crimes). In general, however, the draft was praised for its "outstanding liberal provisions"—including popular sovereignty, prohibition of "discriminations by birth, status, sex, race and nationality," abolition of the peerage, and a guarantee of extensive workers' benefits. Additional provisions would be required, but what was proposed was "democratic and acceptable."[33]

It was against this background that, several weeks later, the Matsumoto committee's proposals made an unexpectedly sensational debut. On the last day of January, Nishiyama Ryūzō, a reporter for the daily *Mainichi*, came on a binder containing a draft revised constitution in the room where the Matsumoto committee held its private meetings. He "borrowed" it and rushed to the newspaper office, where he and his colleagues broke it into sections and hastily hand-copied it as a team. The document was then reassembled and quietly returned—a nice exercise in formal propriety, since Matsumoto's team no longer needed it. Committee members could now obtain as many copies of the secret draft as they wished by purchasing the February 1 *Mainichi*.

There were some misconceptions at the time about the nature of the *Mainichi* scoop. Officers in Government Section believed it was a deliberate government leak—what General Whitney described to MacArthur as Foreign Minister Yoshida's "trial balloon."[34] It was also generally and mistakenly assumed that the version pilfered and published by the *Mainichi* (with some minor copying errors by the journalists) was the committee's final recommendation. This draft, as it turned out, was not so conservative as the one the committee was actually planning to submit to GHQ for its confidential response.

Even this version was widely ridiculed as cosmetic, tokenistic, reactionary, and completely out of touch with the temper and needs of the time. The *Mainichi*'s own commentary provided a fair sample of opinion on this issue. Most people, the paper editorialized, surely shared their deep disappointment at the government's draft, which "simply seeks to preserve the status quo." The draft resembled "a document drawn up by law clerks . . . devoid of the vision, statesmanship, and idealism needed for a new state structure." Revision of the constitution was "not just a legal problem," but rather "a supremely political act." Matsumoto and his colleagues simply showed "no understanding that Japan is in a revolutionary period."[35]

SCAP Takes Over

The government paid the price for its inflexibility with awesome swiftness. In a quick succession of decisions taken between February 1 and February 3, MacArthur and his top aides in Government Section concluded that the government was incapable of proposing revisions that would meet the Potsdam requirements. SCAP would have to take the lead.[36] This bold decision once again revealed the extraordinary authority MacArthur wielded, not merely vis-à-vis the Japanese but vis-à-vis his own government. On February 1, the general's staff finalized a memorandum that it had been working on for a week or so that examined the basic surrender documents and concluded that the supreme commander possessed "unrestricted authority to take any action you deem proper in effecting change in the Japanese constitutional structure."[37] The following day, MacArthur directed Government Section to prepare a gist or outline of required revisions to guide the government. On February 3, he concluded that the stubborn functionaries on the other side would be more appropriately guided by a detailed model constitution.

These steps were but prelude to Government Section's most extraordinary week. On February 4, Whitney convened his staff and informed them, according to the secret minutes of the meeting, that "in the next week the Government Section will sit as a Constitutional Convention. General MacArthur has entrusted the Government Section with the historically significant task of drafting a new Constitution for the Japanese people." It would be based on three principles that MacArthur had declared essential. As jotted down in a memo Whitney brought to the meeting, they were as follows:

I

The Emperor is at the head of the State.

His succession is dynastic.

His duties and powers will be exercised in accordance with the Constitution and responsible to the basic will of the people as provided therein.

II

War as a sovereign right of the nation is abolished. Japan renounces it as an instrumentality for settling its disputes and even for preserving its own security. It relies upon the higher ideals which are now stirring the world for its defense and its protection.

No Japanese Army, Navy, or Air Force will ever be authorized and no rights of belligerency will ever be conferred upon any Japanese forces.

III

The feudal system of Japan will cease.

No rights of peerage except those of the Imperial family will extend beyond the lives of those now existent.

No patent of nobility will from this time forth embody within itself any National or Civic power of Government.

Pattern budget after British system.[38]

And the timetable for turning these sparse guidelines into a model constitution? The draft, Whitney informed his staff, should be completed and ready for approval by General MacArthur by February 12.

No single event in the occupation better exemplified MacArthur's grand style. His aides skillfully parsed the basic Allied and American documents to confirm his sweeping authority. He seized a decisive moment to interpret his instructions in a manner no one else had even dreamed of— for no other person in or close to a position of authority had ever suggested or even imagined that the Americans might write a constitution for Japan. The grandiloquent enunciation of principles—constitutional monarchy, absolute pacifism, abolition of feudalism—also was typical, as was the delegation of the mere details to subordinates. The line between Supreme Commander and Supreme Being was always a fine one in MacArthur's mind. In these momentous days of early February he came close to obliterating the distinction entirely.[39]

But why, after months of scrupulously refraining from placing pressure on the government, did MacArthur abruptly decide to move so swiftly and decisively? Why did he not leave the Japanese to hammer out their own democratic form of government, particularly in light of the promising emergence of indigenous democratic voices? On the very same day that MacArthur directed Government Section to prepare a model constitution, polls indicated that the great majority of Japanese supported revision and wished to elect their own commission to study the problem.[40] If, as the Potsdam Declaration proclaimed, the goal of the occupation was to create a more democratic society in accord with the "freely expressed will of the Japanese people," it could be argued that these polls demonstrated promising grass-roots developments. Why, at this juncture, did SCAP take over?

The answer, as so often in these months, was to be found in considerations pertaining to the throne. MacArthur was galvanized into action because he believed such an initiative had become essential to protect the emperor. That is, he was motivated in great part by the same basic concern as the ultraconservatives against whom he took action. It was not mere happenstance that the status of the emperor appeared as the first of the supreme commander's principles. This was his foremost consideration; the renunciation of war and the abolition of feudalism were secondary, being conditions that MacArthur deemed essential for gaining global support to save the imperial system and the emperor himself. This is not to deny MacArthur's commitment to "demilitarization and democratization," for he could be messianic in these areas, too. The haste and high drama of constitutional revision, however, were motivated by the perception that the government's ultraconservatism was imperiling the goal the old guard cherished most.[41]

General Whitney made this clear in his February 4 briefing. The reason for the February 12 deadline, he explained, was that Japanese officials were scheduled to meet with him on that day for an off-the-record discussion of their draft of proposed revisions, which had not yet been formally submitted to GHQ. "General Whitney expects this draft to be strongly rightist in tone," the minutes of the briefing state. "He intends to convince the Foreign Minister and his group, however, that the only possibility of retaining the Emperor and the remnants of their own power is by their acceptance and approval of a Constitution that will force a decisive swing to the left."[42]

This argument became the leitmotif of many subsequent meetings with the government's representatives. By accepting the basic model of the "MacArthur draft," they were repeatedly told, they would be protecting themselves against an even more radical revision that might eliminate the emperor system entirely. At this moment in early 1946, the general believed that the dynasty was seriously threatened from two directions: first, from the Japanese people, whose "republican" ideas as embodied in the Takano and Communist party constitutional proposals would only grow stronger with the passage of time; and second, from outside Japan, where those in the victorious Allied camp who still harbored strong anti-emperor feelings might soon be in a position to dictate the terms of any constitutional revisions.

Where this external threat was concerned, a timetable had suddenly presented itself with the impending formation of the multination Far Eastern Commission (FEC). Indeed, on January 30, members of the preliminary "Far Eastern Advisory Commission" had interviewed MacArthur in Tokyo and inquired about the progress of constitutional revision. The FEC was scheduled to commence operations sometime in late February, and in an ominous February 1 advisory from his staff, the supreme commander was informed that "your authority to make policy decisions on constitutional reform continues substantially unimpaired until the Far Eastern Commission promulgates its own policy decisions on this subject." Thereafter, the memorandum continued, MacArthur's directives on constitutional reform also could be vetoed by any member of the four-nation Allied Council for Japan, which was scheduled to commence operations in Tokyo shortly after the FEC came into being. Suddenly, it appeared that countries hostile to the emperor and the imperial institution might be in a position to override MacArthur.[43]

In these circumstances, the challenge that suddenly confronted MacArthur was to have a draft constitution under public scrutiny before the FEC actually began operating, one that would meet the Potsdam requirements and yet preserve the throne. After Government Section had completed its model draft, when Whitney and his aides were attempting to explain the rationale behind this to Matsumoto and his shocked colleagues, preservation of the monarchy remained their major argument. Thus, when the American draft was first presented, Whitney dwelled on this at length. "As you may or may not know," he told Matsumoto and a few others,

> the Supreme Commander has been unyielding in his defense of your Emperor against increasing pressure from the outside to render him subject to war criminal investigation. He has thus defended the Emperor because he considered that that was the cause of right and justice, and will continue along that course to the extent of his ability. But, gentlemen, the Supreme Commander is not omnipotent. He feels, however, that acceptance of the provisions of this new Constitution would render the Emperor practically unassailable. He feels that it would bring much closer the day of your freedom from control by the Allied Powers, and that it would provide your people with

the essential freedoms which the Allied Powers demand in their behalf.[44]

The import of such exchanges eventually came through even to those
like Foreign Minister Yoshida, whom Whitney and others regarded as
"the most reactionary element of the Cabinet." Yoshida, who became
prime minister in May, later took care to explain to his conservative compatriots that in the circumstances of defeat and occupation, constitutional
revision was not an ideal issue of law, but a practical political matter of
saving the country, preserving the throne, and hastening the day when the
occupation would end.[45]

GHQ's "Constitutional Convention"

Government Section's "constitutional convention" lost no time in meeting. A ballroom on the sixth floor of the Daiichi Building was converted
into a collective work area with scattered clusters of desks. Twenty-four
individuals—sixteen officers and eight civilians—were assigned the task of
expanding MacArthur's three principles into a full-fledged national charter within a week.

The working group, which included four women, quickly was divided
into a steering committee and seven subcommittees. They worked intensely over the ensuing days, usually beginning around 7:00 or 7:30 A.M.
and continuing until around midnight. In the words of one participant, the
converted ballroom was like "a great big bullpen." There was constant
movement between the subcommittees and the steering committee; Whitney and through him MacArthur were kept informed of the group's
progress into the night. Time was so pressing that no one had the leisure
really to contemplate what an audacious undertaking they were involved
in.[46]

Although many members of the drafting committee were uniformed
personnel, none were professional military men or women. They included
four lawyers in addition to General Whitney (Colonel Charles L. Kades,
Commander Alfred R. Hussey, Jr., Lieutenant Colonel Milo E. Rowell,
and Lieutenant Colonel Frank E. Hays), a former Congressman and governor of Puerto Rico (Commander Guy J. Swope); a recent Princeton
Ph.D. in public administration (First Lieutenant Milton J. Esman), a
newspaper editor and publisher from North Dakota (Navy Lieutenant
Osborne Hauge), a Wall Street investor (Major Frank Rizzo), a civilian intelligence specialist (Lieutenant Commander Roy L. Malcolm), a profes-

sor of social science and a professor of business (Lieutenant Colonel Pieter Roest and Lieutenant Colonel Cecil Tilton), a foreign service officer (Navy Lieutenant Richard Poole), a historian specializing in China (Dr. Cyrus H. Peake), and a journalist with prewar experience in Japan (Harry Emerson Wildes).[47] Political sympathies ran from conservative Republican to New Deal Democrat. Whitney placed himself staunchly among the former; Colonel Charles Kades, the head of the steering committee and true leader of the team, was a proud New Dealer with extensive experience in the Roosevelt administration.

A few members of the drafting committee had been trained for military government and had a smattering of Japanese. Apart from Peake and Wildes, however, the only person on the committee with genuine knowledge of or experience in Japan was Beate Sirota, a twenty-two-year-old Jewish woman who had been born in Vienna and come to Japan with her parents as a child, when her pianist father took a teaching position at the Imperial Academy of Music. Sirota had attended the German School in Tokyo for six years, until the age of twelve, before her parents deemed it "too Nazi" and transferred her to the American School. When she graduated from high school at the age of fifteen, she was fluent in Japanese and knew four other foreign languages. By the time she entered the "bullpen" on the sixth floor of the Daiichi Building, she had graduated from Mills College in the United States, held wartime positions in the U.S. Foreign Broadcasting Intelligence Service and the Office of War Information (where she wrote and even delivered Japanese scripts for propaganda broadcasts), and been a Japan specialist for *Time* magazine. Her parents had spent the war years in straitened circumstances under detention in Karuizawa. Sirota's years of contact with Japanese children and servants, as well as with the women, artists, and intellectuals who regularly visited her parents at their home, had left her keenly aware of the intrusions on personal freedom that had been perpetuated under the existing constitution. Upon returning to Japan after the surrender, she found a position in Government Section doing research on minor political parties and women in politics.[48]

Sirota sat on the subcommittee for civil rights, and her almost serendipitous presence there provided GHQ's "constitutional convention" with the rare perspective of a young, spirited, idealistic, and remarkably cosmopolitan European Jewish woman who was attuned to both Japanese and American culture and especially sensitive to issues of repression and persecution. Serendipity of a different and more whimsical sort also played a role in the appointment of a young ensign, Richard A. Poole, as one of two persons charged with drafting the new provisions concerning the emperor. Although Poole had no particular qualifications for doing this, he had been born in Yokohama—and his birthday fell on the same day as the emperor's.[49] Matsumoto and his colleagues did not have the slightest inkling of these assignments and activities. Had they been able to peer through a window into that frenetic ballroom, they would have sobbed their hearts out.

The civilian backgrounds of the American team contributed to a generally nonhierarchical working atmosphere in which rank was overlooked and opinions were freely expressed. Kades received high praise from virtually everyone who worked under him. By all accounts, he possessed a talent for listening, a gift for drawing the best out of people, and a clear sense of where he was going. He also possessed a New Deal skepticism toward the elitism of the "old Japan hands." This emerged in a little joke he shared with Poole. Since the latter was only six and a half years old when he left Japan, Kades told him, "I suppose you're all right." Such oblique sarcasm revealed a great deal about the outlook that enabled the Americans to be so iconoclastic in promoting radical constitutional revision. As Poole later put it, "on the whole, it was healthy to have the occupation run mainly by people who were not steeped in the old Japan and who had a totally fresh approach and who perhaps for that reason were unafraid to try very new concepts on Japan."[50]

Beate Sirota was even more adamant in repudiating the argument that GHQ's actions were "arrogant." At no point, she recalled, did she ever feel that she was trying to teach the Japanese something by helping to write the constitution. Rather, she and everyone around her strongly believed they were helping to create the less oppressive society that most Japanese desired but could not obtain from their own leaders. In Sirota's case, this feeling was based on an unusual sense of identity with Japanese women, coupled with personal knowledge of their legal and marital oppression. She also had seen the "thought police" in action, for they had routinely visited her parents' house to extract information about guests from the servants and kitchen help (even collecting from them the dinner place cards that identified their Japanese as well as non-Japanese guests). Although Sirota's personal experience was unusual, her attitude was typical. An idealistic *esprit* overrode political differences in the sixth-floor bullpen—a "humanistic" spirit, participants later called it, a common sense of being in an extraordinary position to lift oppression and institutionalize democracy.[51]

This spirit was infectious. It made a difference, albeit one we never can measure precisely, that the group's interpretation of its assignment almost always was shaded toward the most generous and liberal construction of what an ideal form of constitutional monarchy might be. At the same time, Government Section's constitutional convention was guided, however loosely, by a number of statements and models in addition to the supreme commander's three grand points. The Potsdam Declaration was one. "SWNCC 228," the official U.S. guideline on "Reform of the Japanese Governmental System" (which SCAP received on January 11) was another.[52] Attention was also given to principles enunciated in conjunction with the creation of the United Nations, as well as the various draft constitutions issued by private groups and individuals. Years later, Kades took care to repudiate the notion that the GHQ draft was "a Pantagruel emerging full blown from a Gargantuan Government Section." On the contrary, he insisted, "Japanese sources were most useful."[53] In addition, the committee hastily and almost haphazardly assembled all the English-language versions of foreign constitutions it could obtain on short notice. Beate Sirota requisitioned a jeep and driver to visit university libraries, obtaining a few volumes here and a few there, some ten or twelve in all, taking care not to call attention to herself by borrowing too many from a single place.[54]

During this momentous week, MacArthur's imperial style was made manifest in the most subtle way imaginable: he remained completely detached from the day-to-day work of his subordinates, yet always aware of what they were doing; and he allowed them free rein to interpret and render concrete the basic guidelines he had declared binding. In the process, his three grand principles were reconsidered and refined. Such moments as this—when relatively obscure subordinates undertook to make MacArthur's abstractions concrete—offer a vivid sense of how little-known individuals as well as famous ones may etch their mark on history.

It was Kades' team, for example, that turned MacArthur's rather stiff prescription concerning the emperor into the radically altered first section of the new constitution following the preamble. The two-person subcommittee (Ensign Poole and another junior officer, First Lieutenant George A. Nelson, Jr.) charged with rewriting this section simply ignored MacArthur's cryptic first sentence, "Emperor is at the head of state." These young men, together with the steering committee, also redefined the emperor in a way never mentioned by the supreme commander. They described him as the "symbol" of the state and of the unity of the people. Kades and his team then went on to make explicit the idea that sovereignty resided entirely with the people. In the Japanese context, this was a rev-

As part of their campaign to educate the public about the new constitution,
occupation authorities issued a series of "before and after" posters that
included these depictions of democratic principles such as (1, *top left*) the role
of government functionaries as public servants rather than officials to be
venerated; (2, *top right*) the elimination of hierarchy and the equality of all
under the law; (3, *bottom left*) governance by the cabinet instead of the
military; and (4, *bottom right*) the end of patriarchy and the establishment of
gender equality.

olutionary concept.[55] In such ways, the Government Section team not only sharpened the supreme commander's instructions, but also pushed them toward the most liberal interpretation possible. At the same time, they also ended up framing the pivotal issue of the emperor in terms similar to those recommended by the Kempō Kenkyūkai.

In a similar manner, MacArthur's third principle, vaguely enjoining that "the feudal system of Japan will cease," became the basis for detailed provisions guaranteeing representative government and a broad range of civil liberties and human rights. The section enumerating "rights and duties of the people" was, and remains, one of the most liberal guarantees of human rights in the world. Thanks largely to Beate Sirota, it even affirmed "the essential equality of the sexes"—a guarantee not explicitly found in the U.S. Constitution.[56] The drafting committee also took the liberty of toning down the language—and intent—of MacArthur's injunction concerning demilitarization. Kades, who personally assumed responsibility for this provision, regarded the general's categorical renunciation of "war as a sovereign right of the nation . . . even for preserving its own security" as too sweeping. Any nation, he reasoned, had the right to preserve its own security against internal disruption as well from as threats from outside through the maintenance of some kind of gendarmery, coast guard, or the like. So Kades took it upon himself to revise the first paragraph of the renunciation-of-war clause to read simply: "War as a sovereign right of the nation is abolished. The threat or use of force is forever renounced as a means for settling disputes with any other nation." The second paragraph of the clause, denying rights of belligerency or the maintenance of an army, navy, or air force, remained essentially as MacArthur had dictated. Kades deliberately left vague the possibility of modest rearmament "for preserving its own security"—and, in so doing, planted the seed of decades of controversy.[57]

The constitutional renunciation of war was a brilliant example of SCAP's wedge tactic, for the sovereign linked only yesterday with war was now formally associated with a radical antimilitarism. More than just adroit political manipulation was involved here, however, for the no-war ideal had great appeal on its own merits—as well as a precise precedent in recent history. It reflected an international vision that had captured attention less than two decades earlier, before the world plunged into catastrophic war, in the form of the Kellogg-Briand Pact, or Pact of Paris, of 1928. Formally known as the General Treaty for the Renunciation of War, the Kellogg-Briand Pact provided the most obvious model for the renunciation-of-war language in GHQ's draft.

Colonel Kades had long been an admirer of the Kellogg-Briand ideals, and Prime Minister Shidehara and cabinet members such as Ashida Hitoshi and Yoshida Shigeru, all of them former career diplomats, could not fail but to recognize the familiar language.[58] Indeed, this vision was being resurrected all around them. Japan had signed the Kellogg-Briand Pact in 1928, and *violation* of its principles was emerging at that very time as a major charge to be leveled against defendants in the Tokyo war-crimes trials. In these circumstances, the Kellogg-Briand language of peace became, rhetorically and legally, a double-edged sword: used, in the new draft constitution, to protect the emperor even as it was being unsheathed to cut down his erstwhile officers and officials.

Thinking about Idealism and Cultural Imperialism

SCAP's sudden decision to prepare a "model" constitution amounted to a categorical repudiation and abandonment of the very concept of constitutional *revision*. Now, abruptly and without internal debate or public announcement, it was declared that the existing constitution was so flawed that its entire contents had to be discarded. Only the rhetoric of revision remained. The new reality was constitutional replacement, an approach almost exactly antithetical to that of the Matsumoto committee. Whereas the latter worked entirely within the Meiji Constitution, nipping here and tucking there, the Government Section team was interested in this existing charter only as a negative model, a reminder of what had gone wrong. No time at all was spent studying the existing constitution article by article.

The Japan that the Americans reinvented in the Daiichi Building ballroom was not perceived as being a little replica of the United States, however, and Kades later insisted that the U.S. Constitution was not given much attention as the drafting committee cobbled together its new charter.[59] This was, after all, to be a parliamentary government with a British-style cabinet system wrapped in an imperial dynasty. Nonetheless, the political idealism of American democracy, coupled with Allied pronouncements, left a distinctive imprint on the final product. This was especially true for the preamble, which resonated with echoes of the Declaration of Independence, the Gettysburg Address, the U.S. Constitution, and two wartime proclamations: the Atlantic Charter and the Teheran Conference Declaration.[60]

It is difficult to imagine a more exhilarating assignment for bright (and mostly young) people with political ideals. Essentially, the Americans were given a clean slate, albeit already embossed with the imperial chrysanthemum, and the secret record of their day-to-day deliberations reveals not only a keen sense of common purpose, but also a high level of technical competence and professional give-and-take. None of the lawyers was a specialist in constitutional law, but this did not deter them any more than it had the commercial-law specialist Matsumoto. That they were in no position to tolerate fundamental dissent within their own ranks, however, quickly became apparent. When Lieutenant Esman, their public-administration specialist, began to interrupt the constitution-making process to criticize both the haste and secrecy in which the project was being carried out, he suddenly found himself the recipient of a five-day "rest and recreation" pass, effective immediately. While his colleagues pushed on at breakneck speed, secretly dismantling feudal vestiges, Esman spent his time exploring the spectacular mausoleum of the founder of the Tokugawa shogunate at Nikko. When he returned, the project was all but finished, although he still had time to make a small personal contribution to the final draft. It was at Esman's suggestion that the new constitution included legislative controls over the civil service.[61]

Esman's reservations about the constitution-making process were rejected not because they were too conservative, but because they were impractical. No one could disagree that a week was an outrageously short time for the task at hand, but the timetable had come as an order from the supreme commander. In criticizing the secrecy of the project, Esman had in mind the desirability of making this undertaking more genuinely collaborative by actively enlisting the support and expertise of "Japanese scholars who were deeply committed to democracy." In this way, he believed, the resulting draft would genuinely reflect democratic sentiments within the populace and be more firmly rooted in Japanese culture and society. Like speed, however, secrecy was what MacArthur had ordered. In the supreme commander's grander perspective, the developing constitution was being kept secret not just from the Japanese government, but from just about everybody in the world: the Washington policy-making structure, possible opponents of revision within the occupation command structure, and the many nations in the Allied camp now gathering in the Far Eastern Commission.

Although Esman's departure for Nikko expedited concentration on the practical issues of revision, the remaining Americans did raise and answer to their own satisfaction questions that later critics would ask. Were they being ethnocentric? Were they cultural imperialists? Their answer, after some debate, was: in the modern world it had become both appropriate and necessary to affirm that "laws of political morality are universal"—a phrase that eventually was incorporated into the preamble to the constitution. To the more specific question of whether it was wise and feasible to try to impose such liberal ideas upon Japan, the answer was that the government, not the people, was resisting such change. If the people did not like what the Americans were proposing, they could always change it later.[62]

These arguments emerged at scattered intervals as the steering committee pondered the various proposals brought back by the subcommittees. When someone pointed out the "obvious discrepancy . . . between an ideal Constitution founded upon American political experience and thinking, and the actions and past experiences of the present Japanese government," Kades acknowledged the discrepancy but took the position that no comparable gap existed "between American political ideology and the best or most liberal Japanese constitutional thought." At another point, two of the more cautious members of the committee proposed that severe restrictions be placed on amending the constitution, and that no amendment whatever be permitted until 1955. Their reasoning was "that the Japanese people are not ready for a democracy, and that we are caught in the uncomfortable position of writing a liberal Constitution for a people who still think mystically." Kades and his steering committee quickly dismissed this. The constitution was premised on a responsible electorate, they declared, and was intended to be "not only a reasonably permanent document but a flexible one as well, with a simple rather than complicated amendment procedure."[63]

There was a certain ambiguity among the drafters concerning what exactly they were preparing. Most but not all of them appear to have taken for granted that they were drafting a real constitution for Japan—a "model" charter in the sense of being ideal, not in the sense of being just a sample or guideline. Yet it was not clear to any of them what changes their draft would undergo before the Diet approved it. At one point, they even voiced fear that the government might reject GHQ's draft "in toto."[64] From the outset, virtually every American involved assumed—incorrectly, as it turned out—that whatever charter ultimately was adopted by the Diet would be subject to Japanese review and, if deemed desirable, amended as time passed.[65]

On February 10, the sixth day after he had convened his constitutional convention, General Whitney transmitted the draft of a completely new constitution to the supreme commander. He pointed out that this draft embodied the considered and collective view of the members of Government Section, "representing nearly every form of American political thought," and that it had been written after taking the historical development of the Japanese constitution into consideration and giving studious attention to American and European constitutional principles. The draft exhibited advanced thinking in constitutional matters, he observed, but at the same time contained nothing without precedent. It established not only political democracy but economic and social democracy as well, and could be characterized as a strong and sound middle-of-the-road document. As Whitney put the matter, "It constitutes a sharp swing from the extreme right in political thinking—yet yields nothing to the radical concept of the extreme left."[66]

In a typically grand gesture, MacArthur made but a single change in the draft shown him (eliminating restrictions on amending the "bill of rights"). On February 11—serendiptously, the country's National Foundation Day—he approved GHQ's handiwork for presentation to the completely unsuspecting Japanese government.[67]

chapter thirteen

CONSTITUTIONAL DEMOCRACY: JAPANIZING THE AMERICAN DRAFT

On February 13, General Whitney and three aides visited the official residence of the foreign minister and presented the GHQ draft to Matsumoto Jōji and Yoshida Shigeru, who were accompanied by Yoshida's aide Shirasu Jirō and an official interpreter. The Japanese believed they were meeting to discuss Matsumoto's recommendations (which had finally been submitted on February 8) and were, to say the least, taken aback when Whitney peremptorily brushed those aside. Despite the presence of an interpreter, Matsumoto, Yoshida, and Shirasu understood English well. Whitney chose his words carefully and spoke with deliberate slowness. He was also ill with influenza and running a fever that day, which might have contributed to the peculiar intensity and sharpness with which he evidently expressed himself.[1]

"The draft of constitutional revision, which you submitted to us the other day," he began, "is wholly unacceptable to the Supreme Commander as a document of freedom and democracy." He then distributed copies of the Government Section draft with the explanation that MacArthur had approved this as "embodying the principles which in his opinion the situation in Japan demands." A detailed summary of this meeting jointly written immediately afterwards by Whitney's three aides notes that the

Japanese officials were "obviously stunned" and "the whole atmosphere at this point was charged with dramatic tenseness."[2]

The Americans withdrew to the garden to leave their counterparts to read the English-language text. When Shirasu joined them outside, Whitney serenely observed, "We have been enjoying your atomic sunshine"—a comment that, in its harshness, provided a shocking reminder of who was the victor and who the vanquished. In his 1956 biography of MacArthur, Whitney recounted this episode with relish, adding that by a happy coincidence a B-29 flew overhead at precisely that moment.[3]

The general regarded his remark as an effective "psychological shaft" and had several more in his quiver. After Matsumoto and Yoshida had perused the document for about half an hour, the two sides came together again and Whitney let fly his next barbs. He pointed out that acceptance of the provisions of the GHQ draft offered the best possible guarantee of rendering the emperor "unassailable." Should the government reject this position, he asserted, SCAP was prepared to bring its draft directly to the Japanese people. Although in making this assertion Whitney was exceeding his instructions, MacArthur subsequently endorsed this threat with enthusiasm. As recorded in the minutes written by the American side, Whitney added:

> General MacArthur feels that this is the last opportunity for the conservative group, considered by many to be reactionary, to remain in power; that this can only be done by a sharp swing to the left; and that if you accept this Constitution you can be sure that the Supreme Commander will support your position. I cannot emphasize too strongly that the acceptance of the draft constitution is your only hope of survival, and that the Supreme Commander is determined that the people of Japan shall be free to choose between this constitution and any form of constitution which does not embody these principles.

The Japanese, who followed this without using their interpreter, did not conceal their distress. "Mr. Shirasu straightened up as if he had sat on something," Whitney recalled. "Dr. Matsumoto sucked in his breath. Mr. Yoshida's face was a black cloud." As the bringers of bad tidings prepared to take their leave, Yoshida emerged from his dark cloud long enough to urge that these exchanges be kept completely secret.

"The Last Opportunity for the Conservative Group"

Whitney offered the Japanese one straw to grasp at in the February 13 meeting. It was not essential that the GHQ draft be accepted in its entirety, he stated, although its basic principles were not negotiable. Matsumoto did grasp at this and it was several days before the hopelessness of his predicament became entirely clear to him. Privately, he initially mocked the "amateur" quality of the draft, calling attention in particular to the impracticality of GHQ's recommendation that the Diet be made unicameral. This was, as he eventually learned, the one major matter that the Americans were willing to concede as a bargaining chip.[4]

Before it became absolutely clear that the government had lost all credibility in SCAP's eyes, both Shirasu and Matsumoto made a final effort to persuade Whitney that the conservative elites did indeed share democratic ideals with the Americans. What was at issue, they argued, was simply a matter of differing approaches. As Shirasu put it in a letter to Whitney, the American way was "straight and direct," whereas their approach was "roundabout, twisted and narrow." He even enclosed a sketch, representing the Japanese route between starting point and object as a meandering road through the mountains, while the Americans went directly to the same goal as if by airplane. Whitney, unmoved by this cultural cartography, wrote back to Shirasu that the supreme commander would permit minor changes in the draft, but none "either in principle or basic form."[5]

Matsumoto argued that tyranny and misrule result when constitutions do not accord with national circumstances (the tyranny and misrule of Japan's recent decades apparently did not give him pause on this score). Unbelievably, even when faced with GHQ's ultimatum, he continued to claim that the Japanese people needed a long, slow, careful political tutelage in the ways of democracy, and that his committee's draft had to be understood in this light. "Metaphorically speaking," he wrote Whitney, his draft was "a tablet sugar-coated for the benefit of the masses." Anything more radical would shock the moderates, provoke the extremists, and precipitate internal upheaval.[6]

This was a drearily familiar refrain to Government Section's personnel. No matter what the Americans proposed in the way of reform, the conservatives invariably responded that it would provoke "chaos, confusion, and communism." They evoked the Red peril so often, Kades later observed, that "we were vaccinated against the threat of communism."

Even the staunch Republican Whitney expressed impatience with this doomsday litany. To Matsumoto, he simply conveyed word that if the cabinet did not act on this matter within forty-eight hours, SCAP would proceed, as promised, to bring its draft directly before the people.[7] This was evidently the excruciating moment when Matsumoto finally realized that, although others might have lost the war, he had just lost the Meiji Constitution.

It had been GHQ's expectation that the meeting of February 13 would precipitate immediate cabinet deliberations. To facilitate this, Whitney and his aides had even handed over fifteen copies of the draft proposal to be distributed as Matsumoto and Yoshida deemed appropriate. The government, however, did not address critical issues in the decisive, collective manner the Americans considered natural. The cabinet was not even informed about the February 13 exchange until February 19, when Matsumoto, pale and shaken, made an initial presentation. General Whitney, he informed his colleagues, had found his draft unacceptable and presented a GHQ draft in its place. Whitney's position, as Matsumoto summarized it, was that the Americans were *not* forcing this on the government, but General MacArthur was convinced that this was the only way to protect the emperor's *person* (Matsumoto apparently used the English word) from those who opposed him.[8]

The immediate response of several ministers was that the American position was simply unacceptable. Prime Minister Shidehara agreed, but Ashida Hitoshi, who later would emerge as a key figure in Diet deliberations, offered a persuasive argument for going along. If the cabinet rejected the GHQ demands and the Americans made their draft public, as they were threatening to do, Ashida warned, then an ominous scenario could unfold. The media, being "servile," would support the Americans; the cabinet would have to resign; proponents of the American draft could be expected to come forward and do well in the impending general elections. The conservatives, in a word, had to beware of being unseated by popular prodemocracy forces.[9]

It was agreed that the matter should be given further consideration, and cabinet discussion was resumed on February 22, after Shidehara had met for three hours with MacArthur. Printed materials were distributed for the first time in the form of rough translations of the first and second chapters of the GHQ draft, dealing with the emperor and renunciation of war. (Stunned and disoriented, the government did not distribute a full translation until February 26.) Shidehara reported that the supreme commander had not been unreasonable. Declaring himself to be working heart and soul for Japan and emphasizing his deep desire "to keep the emperor safe at all costs," MacArthur had offered dire intimations on the thinking of such countries as the Soviet Union and Australia—"unpleasant," as Shidehara put it, "to a degree beyond your imagination." The prime minister also quoted the general as having expressed his belief "that Japan should take *moral leadership* [Shidehara conveyed these words in English] by declaring its renunciation of war."[10]

Shidehara still held out hope of revisions of substance in the GHQ draft, but Matsumoto discovered the same day that there was no prospect of salvaging even a few portions of the Meiji Constitution. His American tormentors bluntly informed him that using the existing constitution as a basis of revision was "impossible." When the proud scholar-bureaucrat gritted his teeth and asked, "How many of the articles in the new Constitution do you consider basic and unalterable?" Whitney responded that "the whole Constitution as written is basic. . . . Put in general, we regard this document as a unit." Lest there be any misunderstanding, Colonel Rowell added: "The new Constitution was written as an interwoven unit, one section fitting into another, so there is no one section or chapter that can be cut out." At Matsumoto's request, the Americans did agree to a bicameral Diet, with the stipulation that both houses be elected by popular vote.[11]

When Emperor Hirohito was briefed about the American draft by Shidehara and a few top officials on February 22, the final deadline Government Section had given for cabinet approval "in principle," he reportedly responded decisively. Japanese informants told GHQ that he gave the proposed revision his unreserved approval. On this matter, the emperor was perhaps understandably less hesitant than his ministers. He recognized that his "person" was being protected and his position made simpler. Unlike his loyal officials, Emperor Hirohito was free to contemplate changes in the Meiji-style emperor system without having to worry about committing lese majesty. His approval, in any case, eased the conscience of his ministers and enabled them to comply with GHQ's demands.[12]

There was a touch of patriotic astrology associated with these various dates. As General Whitney was pleased to note, GHQ's February 12 deadline for completing its draft had coincided with Abraham Lincoln's birthday; the deadline given the cabinet for accepting the draft fell on George Washington's birthday.[13] Even after the government bowed to this ultimatum, however, Government Section was informed that the cabinet remained wracked by a "furious struggle." Narahashi Wataru, a minister without portfolio who simultaneously was serving as chief cabinet secretary, was one of GHQ's major informants on these matters. He described the backstage struggles in dire terms. According to Narahashi, die-hard defenders of the old emperor system remained numerous among bureaucrats, ex-military officers, and zaibatsu leaders. The bureaucrats, whose power derived partly from their elite status as loyal servants of the throne (rather than as "civil servants," or servants of the people), feared their authority would be severely diminished. Narahashi also observed that there was genuine fear among more liberal ministers that terrorism and assassination might occur if the emperor's prerogatives were curtailed.[14]

The Translation Marathon

These developments coincided with Prince Higashikuni's shocking public suggestion that Emperor Hirohito should abdicate. The "emperor's person" and the status of the throne suddenly seemed imperiled as never before, and it was in these circumstances that, on March 4, the cabinet formally presented SCAP with what eventually became known as the "first government draft" for a revised constitution.[15] To all outward appearances, this amounted to little more than a Japanese version of the GHQ text. In fact, Matsumoto and his aides had watered down GHQ's recommendations in a variety of ways, including the use of terminology that altered the intent of the draft.

Matsumoto and his assistant Satō Tatsuo, accompanied by two translators, delivered their text to Government Section at 10:00 A.M. on March 4. In a nice reprise of the February 13 "atomic sunshine" meeting, at which they had been confronted with GHQ's English draft, they handed the Americans a Japanese text without any corresponding translation. There followed a marathon thirty-hour session during which the two sides translated the Japanese back into English together, with the Americans constantly consulting their Japanese-English dictionaries and comparing the new English version with their original draft. Throughout this long, sleepless ordeal, they fortified themselves with K rations and coffee dispensed from five-gallon containers—an unpalatable sort of sustenance for the Japanese that must have seemed, in the circumstances, depressingly symbolic.

This was not, by any stretch of the imagination, a humorous occasion. Nonetheless, it had moments of almost camp theatricality. Matsumoto and Kades soon found themselves engaged in a heated exchange concerning the relative positions of emperor and cabinet. At one point, the beleaguered royalist accused the New Dealer of trying to reinvent not merely the national polity but the Japanese language as well. Shortly after noon, Matsumoto stormed out in anger, leaving retranslation and revision to Satō and his two interpreters—who had to deal with at least sixteen American officers assisted by Nisei translators and interpreters.

Satō and Kades then had a tense moment when Kades used his fists, one above the other, to illustrate the importance of clearly placing the cabinet above the emperor. Satō was less impressed by the concept than by the pugilistic intensity of Kades' stance. Kades, in turn, concluded that the Japanese could not conceive of anyone being politically superior to the emperor, an approach he found "mystical" and contradictory. On the one hand, as Kades saw it, the Japanese were arguing that the emperor had been essentially powerless under the Meiji Constitution—a crucial argument in divorcing him from any taint of war responsibility. On the other hand, they insisted that his prerogatives as sovereign ruler must remain inviolate.[16]

Beate Sirota, whose bilingual skills gave her influence in these exchanges, found that old-fashioned favors could further the cause of feminism. At various points, the young "slip of a girl," as Kades described her, came down in support of Japanese positions. Subsequently, when Satō came to the women's rights clauses Sirota had originally drafted, Kades adroitly and successfully suggested that since she had been nice to them earlier, the Japanese should now be nice to her. Through this friendly reciprocity, one of the strongest equal-rights provisions in modern constitutional law survived. In another theatrical moment, Foreign Minister Yoshida's aide, the smooth, British-educated Shirasu Jirō, appeared on the scene and had the pleasure of letting the Americans experience a small psychological shaft. Halfway through the marathon session, well after midnight, he casually produced a rough English version of the Japanese draft which everyone was laboring to translate. He had been carrying it around in his pocket.[17]

In the course of this exhausting session, the Americans discovered that the Japanese had slipped a number of substantial changes into their "translation." The English "advice and consent," for instance, emerged in Japanese as "advice and assistance." The government's ostensible translation also dropped the preamble to the GHQ draft in which the "sovereignty of the people's will" was emphasized, deleted the provision providing for the elimination of the peerage, proposed a House of Councilors that could have restricted the authority of the House of Representatives, and altered provisions on local autonomy in a manner that facilitated greater control by the central government. In addition, they undercut many of the guarantees of human rights, sometimes by reinserting formulaic phrases of the sort associated with the Meiji Constitution. Freedom of speech, writing, press, assembly, and association were now guaranteed only "to the extent that they do not conflict with the public peace and order." Similarly, censorship was prohibited "except as specifically provided for by law." The rights of workers to organize, to bargain, and to act collectively were likewise hedged with the phrase "as provided by law." The government draft also deleted or weakened a number of unusually specific rights, including ones related to foreigners, on the grounds that these were more appropriately covered by legislation outside the constitution.[18]

In the end, the stalwart Satō, bleary eyed and exhausted, succeeded in persuading the Americans that certain rights *were* better left to enumeration through extraconstitutional legislation. He also succeeded in maintaining highly nuanced renderings of such critical words and concepts as "people" and "sovereignty." On such delicate yet fundamental points, politics, ideology, language, and culture came together in ways that rendered the Japanese draft constitution—almost inevitably—a different text from the Americans one.

This was nowhere more apparent than in the concept of "the people," which was central to the Americans' notion of popular sovereignty, with all the evocative historical and cultural connotations of "We the People" that were embedded in the American experience. The Japanese had no comparable tradition of popular sovereignty. The Meiji Constitution spoke of "subjects" *(shinmin)* rather than "people" as such, and Matsumoto and his aides were faced with the question of what word to use to use for "people" in their adaptation. One possibility was *jinmin,* the term commonly used in translations of the U.S. Constitution or Abraham Lincoln's classic formulation of "government of the people, by the people, for the people." In contemporary usage, however, *jinmin* had socialist and communist connotations and conveyed a sense of the people resisting authority.

Although an initial government translation of the GHQ draft prepared by the Foreign Ministry rendered "people" as *jinmin,* Matsumoto and Satō discarded this in favor of *kokumin,* an inherently more conservative term. Written with two ideographs denoting "country" and "people," *kokumin* is an everyday word that carries connotations of the people harmoniously merged in the nation. There is no intimation here of a potentially adversarial relationship between the people and the nation, the state, or the highest authorities—including, of course, the emperor. On the contrary, as the government subsequently took care to explain, the concept of *kokumin* embraced the emperor himself, thus signifying that the emperor and people were one. During the war years, *kokumin* had been a familiar word in propagandistic sloganeering, essentially synonymous with "the Japanese" or even "the Yamato race."

Satō Tatsuo was frank in later explaining why *kokumin*, with its consensual and nationalistic connotations, was chosen for the new constitution. He and his associates, he stated, "adopted *kokumin* because (1) we wanted to emphasize the sense of the people as members of the state, and (2) we thought that *jinmin* would convey a sense of the people in exclusion and opposition to the Emperor." Although advisors to Government Section called attention to the conservative connotations of *kokumin*, General Whitney and Colonel Kades did not deem the distinction important and allowed the rendering to stand.[19]

For "sovereignty," the logical term was *shuken*. With encouragement from Prime Minister Shidehara, however, a different term—*shikō*—was substituted in the government draft. Unlike *shuken*, *shikō* was an obscure and archaic word. The two ideographs with which it was written literally meant "supreme height," but the term carried no political weight. Indeed, it is fair to say that it meant little if anything to Japanese living in the mid-twentieth century. That was the point, of course: through such ambiguities, the conservatives desired to blunt and obfuscate the radical thrust inherent in the American notion of "popular sovereignty." They were aghast at the thought of postulating a sovereignty equal to or higher than the emperor's.[20]

In this first week of March, the survival of these deliberately warped renderings through thirty hours of American hammering was a gratifying victory for the government. In the full course of events, however, this victory proved only half as sweet; for *shikō* did not make it into the draft of the constitution that eventually was adopted by the Diet (*shuken* replaced it.) The draft that emerged from the marathon session around 4:00 P.M. on March 5 differed in roughly a dozen substantial ways from the version the Japanese had submitted the day before, and in almost every instance these changes brought it back closer to the original GHQ draft.[21]

On March 5, while Satō was staggering toward the end of his ordeal, the government moved toward a denouement, of sorts, of its own. That morning, Matsumoto, who had never returned to GHQ, addressed the cabinet at length about what had taken place since February 22. The ministers recessed for lunch and reconvened at 2:00 P.M., at which time a small, symbolic, almost ritualistic event took place. Ten English-language versions of the GHQ draft, apparently some of the copies Government Section had handed over weeks previously, were presented to the assembled ministers for the first time. There was nothing to be done with these at this eleventh hour, but they now had in their midst a concrete sign of the foreign power that governed their lives.

Around four-thirty, Shidehara and Matsumoto made their way to the palace to discuss the situation with the emperor and prepare for the release of both the government draft and an imperial rescript the following day. On returning to the cabinet meeting at 8:00 P.M., Shidehara summarized the emperor's response as being that, "under the present situation, it can't be helped." The diary of Kinoshita Michio, the imperial vice chamberlain, makes clearer what a traumatic, almost chaotic moment this was at the court. The emperor was feeling immense pressure to abdicate, he wrote, and the "atmosphere of the world" was "against the imperial system." MacArthur's headquarters had become frantic. Repeating the phrase that had made such an impression on the cabinet, Kinoshita noted that if the American draft were not accepted, it would not be possible to guarantee the emperor's person.[22]

GHQ had demanded that the cabinet decide that day whether it would accept the version agreed on with Satō. With the emperor's approval, the assembled ministers proceeded to do so. Before adjourning a little after 9:00 P.M., Shidehara made a brief closing statement, which Ashida Hitoshi recounted in his diary. "Accepting such a draft constitution is an extremely grave responsibility," the prime minister said, "that in all probability will affect our children and grandchildren and later generations. When we announce this draft, some people will applaud and some will remain silent. But deep in their hearts they surely will hold resentment toward us. Looking at things from a broad perspective, however, in the present circumstances there is no other course to take."

Hearing this, cabinet members wept while the prime minister himself brushed away tears.[23]

Unveiling the Draft Constitution

On March 6, with great fanfare, the new constitution was made known to the public in a manner that gave equal prominence to the emperor and to the ideals of democracy and peace. In the name of the emperor, Prime Minister Shidehara released a detailed "outline" for constitutional revision, accompanying this with a brief but quite eloquent endorsement of the proposed new ideals. Few observers could have guessed that hours earlier the prime minister and his cabinet had been in tears. Emperor Hirohito's imperial rescript was released simultaneously, tersely announcing the need

to revise "drastically" the existing national charter and commanding the
government to comply with his wishes. On the same day, General
MacArthur announced that this "decision of the Emperor and the Government of Japan to submit to the Japanese people a new and enlightened
constitution . . . has my full approval."[24]

These three rhetorical exercises set the tone for the ensuing debates on
creating a new monarchical democracy. Shidehara typically began with effusive homage to the sovereign, who had been "pleased to grant to the
cabinet" an imperial message. "In order that our nation may fall in line
with other nations in the march toward the attainment of the universal
ideal of mankind," Shidehara declared, "His Majesty with great decision
has commanded that the existing Constitution be fundamentally revised
so as to establish the foundation upon which a democratic and peaceful
Japan is to be built."

The prime minister then proceeded to speak movingly of the passage
of mankind from war to peace, cruelty to mercy, slavery to liberty, tyranny
and confusion to order. In a suggestive turn of phrase, he intimated that
the pacifistic nature of the proposed charter could establish a vanguard
role for Japan in the world. "If our people are to occupy a place of honor
in the family of nations, we must see to it that our constitution internally
establishes the foundation for a democratic government and externally
leads the rest of the world for the abolition of war. Namely, we must renounce for all time war as a sovereign right of the State and declare to all
the world our determination to settle by peaceful means all disputes with
other countries." The prime minister went on to express his faith that all
Japanese would honor the benevolent wish of their sovereign, and concluded by noting that the draft constitution was being made public "in
close cooperation with Allied General Headquarters."

Emperor Hirohito's rescript read in full:

Consequent upon our acceptance of the Potsdam Declaration the ultimate form of Japanese government is to be determined by the
freely expressed will of the Japanese people. I am fully aware of our
nation's strong consciousness of justice, its aspirations to live a peaceful life and promote cultural enlightenment and its firm resolve to
renounce war and to foster friendship with all the countries of the
world. It is, therefore, my desire that the constitution of our empire
be revised drastically upon the basis of the general will of the people and the principle of respect for the fundamental human rights.
I command hereby the competent authorities of my government to

put forth in conformity with my wish their best efforts toward the accomplishment of this end.

In effect, the emperor was ordering his subjects to support the proposed new constitution—a stance at variance with the idea that he never exercised real authority. From this point forward, the public process of "revising" the constitution remained tinged with old-fashioned pronouncements aimed at reinforcing a sense of imperial benevolence in granting a more democratic national charter.[25]

Like Shidehara, General MacArthur spoke with a certain grandeur about peace, democracy, and culture. He described the proposed constitution as "throughout responsive to the most advanced concept of human relations . . . an eclectic instrument, realistically blending the several divergent political philosophies which intellectually honest men advocate." He also chose to emphasize rather than minimize GHQ's close involvement in the drafting process. "This instrument has been drafted after painstaking investigation and frequent conference between members of the Japanese government and this headquarters," he stated, "following my initial direction to the Cabinet five months ago." Typically, this was not entirely truthful; but the point was made that SCAP had been closely involved in the drafting process.

On the other hand, acknowledging the draft constitution's genesis in Government Section was taboo. Japanese officials were not permitted to mention the GHQ draft and the media were not allowed to speculate openly about it. A similar make-believe aura would hang over the Diet proceedings to follow. GHQ kept a close eye on these deliberations from behind the scenes and made clear at various junctures that basic principles—the revised status of the emperor, renunciation of the right of belligerency, and popular sovereignty, as well as the highly idealistic preamble to the constitution—were, much like the emperor under the Meiji Constitution, sacred and inviolable. On occasion, GHQ secretly intervened to promote or repress certain Diet proposals. As one American privy to these activities put it, Government Section personnel "were still members of a bureaucratic agency that worked behind closed doors."[26]

This was, once again, freedom in a box. All Japanese knew the box existed, however, and where the constitution was concerned the extent of the American input was an open secret. To begin with, everyone was immediately struck by the night-and-day difference between the "Matsumoto draft" that had been more or less laughed to death on February 1 and the progressive new text the government was now claiming as its own. As the daily *Yomiuri* put it, "the reactionary Matsumoto draft" had been "blown away."[27] No one imagined that the geriatric Shidehara cabinet had undergone a collective conversion experience. It was inconceivable that these two drafts could have a common authorship.

Beyond this, the Japanese text had foreign fingerprints all over it, not only in its broad principles but also in its awkward style. Contorted syntax consorted with odd phraseology. In the upper house, whose appointed members included a number of scholars, some individuals even took to referring to an official English translation that had been provided them. The very fact that an English text was released simultaneously with the Japanese draft was revealing. The upper-house member Takayanagi Kenzō, a Harvard-trained constitutional law specialist, later observed that "the translation was easier to understand than the text of the [Japanese] original."[28]

The task of preventing media discussion of the actual paternity of the new charter fell to GHQ's Civil Censorship Detachment. "Criticism of SCAP Writing the Constitution" actually became a formal category of impermissible expression in the so-called key log that censors used as a guide, and it was explicitly stipulated that this proscribed any reference whatsoever to SCAP's role.[29] Journalists did, however, attempt to call attention to the draft's "peculiar Japanese" and "funny language." One blue-penciled line stated baldly—of the *Japanese* text—"the translation is not very good."[30] The overworked censors could not catch everything, however, and even generally supportive publications managed to smuggle sardonic observations into their editorial comments. The *Asahi,* for example, described the government draft as "somewhat ill fitted, like a borrowed suit of clothes." The *Jiji Shimpō* compared its initial response to someone who smelled the aroma of Japanese cooking coming from the kitchen and then discovered that Western dishes were being served. It was necessary to put away one's chopsticks and take up fork and knife.[31]

In these circumstances, a great deal of cynicism, as well as plain confusion, accompanied public discussion. Still, the proposed constitution held great attraction as a beacon of hope and idealism in a defeated and war-shattered land. The Japanese were told that they were to consider adopting a national charter that embodied the most advanced and enlightened "eclectic" thinking of the mid-twentieth century. In going so far as to renounce war as a sovereign right, the nation, as Shidehara put it, might even see itself as leading the rest of the world. To a proud people told they had become a fourth-rate nation, this was a comforting kind of new nationalism to grasp at.

Popular reactions to the new proposal in any case offered a sharp contrast to the overwhelmingly negative response that had greeted the Matsumoto draft. Only the Communist party opposed the draft constitution. The party's position was forthright: continuation of the emperor system was antidemocratic and, though within Japan they had suffered the most overt oppression by the militarists, it was unrealistic and discriminatory to deny any nation the right to self-defense. All the other major political parties endorsed the March draft. The Socialists even claimed that the government's new position was essentially what they themselves had been advocating.

The two conservative parties that formed the backbone of Shidehara's coalition cabinet were in no position to criticize the government's announcement, but even here support was expressed with surprising spirit. The Liberals singled out for praise the three principles they saw as characterizing the draft: preservation of the emperor system, respect for fundamental human rights and democratic principles, and establishing a peaceful country by renouncing war. Even the ultraconservative Progressive Party did a dramatic *volte face* and declared that it welcomed the new draft "heartily." Historically, the Progressives now argued, the emperor had never ruled directly and so his status under the proposed new charter actually accorded with both history and reality.[32] Stated often enough, such rationalizations easily became a new gospel. Many conservatives clearly voiced their endorsements with heavy hearts, but by mid-March most of them also had come to share General MacArthur's belief in the new charter's necessity to protect the emperor and the imperial house at a critical moment.[33]

As the weeks passed, the public gained a clearer understanding of what the proposed new constitution entailed. The detailed "outline" released by the cabinet on March 6 was still written in the ponderous formal *bungotai* style. A vernacular or colloquial text replaced the outline on April 17, a week after the general elections. A final version, known as "the fourth government draft," was formally submitted to the Diet on June 21.

Water Flows, the River Stays

For technical reasons, the new constitution was submitted to the Diet by the emperor as an "amendment" to the Meiji Constitution. To both MacArthur and the Japanese royalists, this was fortuitous: constitution making and emperor saving became part and parcel of the same undertaking. Consequently, the emperor was involved at every key stage in the process. On June 20, in accordance with established procedure, he addressed the opening of the extraordinary Diet session, declaring that he would be submitting a revised constitutional draft along with other bills and expressing hope that the Diet would deliberate on these "in a harmonious spirit."[34] Although the new constitution stipulated that sovereignty resided with the people, it was intimated that this sovereignty actually came as a gift from the emperor himself. "Revolution from above" and "imperial democracy" were fused in the most ceremonial manner conceivable.

By the time the draft constitution came before the Diet, the most ultranationalistic and reactionary politicians had already been purged. The newly elected House of Representatives was a diverse group, including women as well as men. The conservatives who still dominated the lower house were, on the whole, more flexible than their predecessors and also numbered among their colleagues a sizable contingent of liberals and socialists. In the House of Peers, seats emptied by the occupation's purge had been filled by the appointment of an unusually learned and cosmopolitan group. It could be argued that the legislature was not representative, since its most vociferously conservative voices had been silenced. But it would also be accurate to say that the Diet reflected new voices more or less in tune with the emergence of genuinely democratic aspirations.

To all appearances, the parliamentary deliberations that followed were vigorous and substantial. Discussions in plenary sessions and committee hearings in both houses consumed a total of 114 days. Kanamori Tokujirō, the minister of state who replaced Matsumoto Jōji as the cabinet's chief spokesman on constitutional issues, responded to around thirteen hundred formal questions, sometimes at great length. Transcripts of the Diet proceedings in both houses eventually totaled more than thirty-five hundred pages.[35]

By far the most compelling issue for Diet members was whether the draft constitution altered the "national polity," particularly as it involved the emperor; and if so, how? Of next greatest concern were the implications of the astonishing "renunciation of war" provisions in Article 9. In due time, however, the legislators turned their attention to every single article. Satō Tatsuo, who had represented the government at the marathon translation session, later conceded that GHQ "seemed to have great respect for the Diet as the supreme representative of the people." Deliberations in the legislature left "no portion of the draft unprobed," Satō

observed, and he estimated that "80 or 90 percent" of the changes proposed in the legislature—all of which required SCAP's approval—were allowed to stand.[36]

The government's answer to questions about whether the new constitution represented a fundamental change in the *kokutai* or "national polity"
was that it absolutely did not. Both Kanamori and Yoshida Shigeru, the
new prime minister, concentrated with an almost vaudevillian energy on
this most emotional of issues. Katō Shizue, a near-legendary feminist
who had been elected to the Diet, later summarized their act with deft
strokes. Yoshida, she said, would loudly exclaim: "The *kokutai* has been
preserved! The minister in charge will explain!" And Kanamori would take
the podium and gurgle something roundabout and impenetrable (*"gu-
ruguruguruguru"* in Katō's rendering).[37]

This was unkind, but where the emperor and the national polity were
concerned Yoshida's and Kanamori's explanations were ruled by an emotional logic rather than any legal precision or historical accuracy. Yoshida
typically declared that "there is no distinction between the imperial house
and the people. . . . Sovereign and subject are one family. . . . The national polity will not be altered in the slightest degree by the new constitution. It is simply that the old spirit and thoughts of Japan are being
expressed in different words in the new constitution." Like participants in
a *renga* or "linked-verse" performance, Kanamori, in turn, carried forward
the permanence-amid-change theme by arguing that "the water flows, but
the river stays. In this point lies our basic conception concerning the
draft constitution."[38]

Although such near-mystical affirmations were only to be expected,
they caused some consternation within Government Section. Whitney informed MacArthur in mid-July that official arguments that the new constitution involved no change in the national polity were undermining the
democratic spirit of the new charter and paving the way for a return to
authoritarianism, chauvinism, militarism, and the old mystique of Japanese "uniqueness" and racial superiority. Kades, following up on this, demanded that Kanamori clarify the constitution's defense of unadulterated
popular sovereignty. It was, indeed, at this point that *shikō* was replaced
as the term for "sovereignty" by *shuken*.[39] Still, in the eyes of many members of the parliament, the new constitution was acceptable only because
it retained the throne in its transcendent splendor. The final report of the
House of Representatives subcommittee on the constitution, headed by
Ashida Hitoshi, confirmed and sanctified these sentiments:

The first Chapter of the Revised Constitution expressly provides that the Emperor of one line unbroken through ages is assured of his position as a Monarch who on the basis of the sovereign will of the people unifies them coevally with Heaven and Earth, from eternity to eternity. Thus, it has been possible to confirm the solemn fact that the Emperor, while being in the midst of the people, stands outside the pale of actual politics and still maintains his authority as the center of the life of the people and as the source of their spiritual guidance. This accomplishment the absolute majority of the committee have received with the utmost joy and satisfaction.[40]

The emotionalism and nationalistic defiance of such reverential statements are evident. For many, however, such arguments became vehicles that enabled them, in good conscience, to travel to positions they would not have dreamed of only months earlier. Once thinking the unthinkable became inescapable, it even became possible to argue that in their new imperial democracy the emperor's position had been elevated, in that he was now above politics. Shortly after the new constitution came into effect in 1947, Yoshida wrote a personal letter to his father-in-law Makino Shinken, a former keeper of the privy seal, stating that as a consequence of the emperor's more explicit detachment from politics, his "position within"—presumably meaning his spiritual role—"will become that much more enlarged, and his position will increase in importance and delicacy."[41]

Even in the midst of these reverential discussions, however, some ministers and parliamentarians could retain a detached and humorous perspective. Among insiders, for example, the new constitution became known as the *yamabuki kempō,* or "mountain-rose constitution." The joke here was that, under the new charter, the emperor now resembled the *yamabuki* flower (*Kerria japonica,* sometimes translated as "yellow rose")—all beautiful blossom, no fruit. Similarly, two witty poems referring to Kanamori were circulated in the Diet during these ostensibly solemn debates, both punning on the homonym of *kempō* (constitution) and *ken-pō* (the way of the sword). What, one poem inquired, was this strange constitutional method (or school of swordfighting) Kanamori was using? It was, the second verse responded, the two-sword national-polity school, one sword being change and the other no change. In parrying this, Kanamori proved himself an adept fencer. His way was so skillful, he responded in a poem of his own, that one sword looked like two. Whatever their politics, these were clever and agile men.[42]

"Japanizing" Democracy

At one point during the parliamentary deliberations, Colonel Kades, visiting the House of Peers, told members that GHQ was "rather sorry that more proposals for amendment have not been made in the Diet."[43] He was sincere in this. The Americans spent a great deal of time encouraging legislators to become actively involved in the revision process, which, after all, was supposed to be an example of democracy in action, the manifestation of the Potsdam Declaration's noble ideal of creating a government that reflected the "freely expressed will" of the people. The Diet was free to make all the changes it desired—so long as they did not violate GHQ's fundamental principles.

What was not so apparent where the Diet deliberations were concerned was the long reach of SCAP's invisible hand and the extent to which revisions proposed by Japanese sometimes reflected secret instructions from GHQ—or, through GHQ, from the Far Eastern Commission, which gave considerable attention to the constitution that summer. The Americans took great care to camouflage their involvement in the day-to-day activities of the two legislative chambers. Instructions were conveyed orally rather than in writing. At SCAP's insistence, the work of the key House of Representatives subcommittee on constitutional revision was conducted in confidential session, so that American instructions could be clarified *in camera;* and no references to these interventions were permitted in the stenographic record of these secret meetings. Free discussion of the constitution per se was encouraged, both in the Diet and in the media, but until 1949 all references to SCAP's decisive shaping of the new charter were suppressed.[44]

The omnipresence of SCAP's unassailable authority was captured in a felicitous phrase after the occupation ended. In the words of the Commission on the Constitution, a prestigious Japanese committee that investigated these matters between 1957 and 1964, even when the Americans did not directly intervene in the parliamentary process, their desires were still surmised "by a sort of mental telepathy."[45] One member of the House of Peers, Sawada Ushimaro, a former Home Ministry official, resisted this duress with unusual passion. In announcing why he was voting against adoption of the draft constitution, Sawada declared that the proper time for revision was after the nation regained sovereignty. It made no sense at all, he exclaimed, borrowing the *Asahi*'s earlier metaphor, to rush to adopt this new charter, "which, in fact, is no better than a borrowed suit of clothes, patched in too many places, and, above all, insufferably misfitting."[46]

All told, the Diet made approximately thirty revisions to the government's June draft.[47] Many of the most substantial changes, however, came from SCAP or the FEC. It was pressure from the FEC via SCAP, for instance, that led the Diet to strengthen important democratic provisions such as those pertaining to universal suffrage, predominance of the legislature, and selection of the prime minister and a majority of cabinet members from among Diet members. At the insistence of the FEC, the Diet also added a clause stipulating that all cabinet members must be "civilians."[48]

Major changes initiated by the Japanese were, in the end, relatively few in number. In a surprising vote, the Diet approved a motion from the Socialist Party that eliminated the peerage (apart from the imperial family) immediately, whereas the Americans had merely called for ceasing to grant any future patents of peerage. The Socialists, partly influenced by the Weimar and 1936 Soviet constitutions, also successfully introduced provisions that "All people shall have the right to maintain the minimum standards of wholesome and cultured living" and "All people shall have the right and the obligation to work," with working conditions being regulated by law.[49]

In an interesting instance of effective grass-roots pressure, a coalition of teachers affiliated with adult-education schools and night schools succeeded in persuading the Diet to eliminate wording that would have limited compulsory education to six years of free elementary schooling. Arguing that education should not benefit only the elites, the teachers directed their lobbying activities at the Ministry of Education and GHQ as well as at politicians. The final provision guaranteed all people "the right to receive an equal education correspondent to their ability, as provided by law," and became the basis for subsequent legislation establishing the so-called six-three system, entailing nine years of compulsory schooling.[50]

One of the most truly democratic aspects of the final constitution was also prompted by a grass-roots initiative and affected the very nature of the language in which formal and official texts would be written thereafter. Prior to this time, statutes and documents, including the constitution, had been written in *bungotai*, an archaic formal style that was more or less inaccessible to ordinary people. After mid-April, the text submitted by the government was written in colloquial Japanese *(kōgotai)*. This was a change of enormous practical as well as symbolic meaning. It signified that the law, and official documents in general, were no longer to be regarded

Using an old vehicle of popular entertainment and education—the *kami-shibai* or "paper theater"—an attentive street crowd is informed about the implications of the new national charter. The banner and sign announce that this is "commemorating the new constitution coming into effect."

as the domain of a privileged elite. As a consequence, the entire corpus of civil and criminal law subsequently would be converted into *kōgotai*. The decision to introduce this far-reaching change came entirely from the Japanese side, and had its origins not within the government but among scholars and intellectuals who were lobbying for language reform.[51]

In a reactionary direction, the government and subsequently the Diet succeeded in eliminating equal protection under the law for resident aliens, thus undermining GHQ's original intent. The groundwork for this move was laid by Satō Tatsuo in the hours immediately following the marathon translation session, when he sent a seemingly trivial request to Government Section requesting permission to delete the article in question on the grounds that it was redundant, given protections guaranteed elsewhere in the draft charter. The Americans approved this, unaware that the language games the Japanese side was playing excluded foreigners from such protective coverage. The key term here was *kokumin,* the word deliberately chosen to cast constitutional references to "the people" in a more nationalistic context. Essentially, the conservatives used *kokumin* not merely to weaken the connotations of popular sovereignty, but also to limit the rights guaranteed by the state to Japanese nationals alone. Where the Americans had intended to affirm that "all persons" are equal before the law, and included language in the GHQ draft that explicitly forbade discrimination on the basis of race or national origin, Satō and his colleagues erased these guarantees through linguistic subterfuge. By interpreting *kokumin* as referring to "all nationals," which was indeed a logical construction of the term, the government succeeded in denying equal civil rights to the hundreds of thousands of resident ex-colonial subjects, including Taiwanese and especially Koreans. The blatantly racist nature of this revision was subsequently reinforced by "terminological" revisions during the Diet deliberations, and this provided the basis for discriminatory legislation governing nationality passed in 1950.[52]

Renouncing War . . . Perhaps

To the world at large, the most striking single feature of the draft constitution was its "renunciation of war," mentioned in the preamble and encoded in Article 9. Unsurprisingly, this drew a barrage of questions in the Diet. In the end, the legislators revised the wording of Article 9 in a way that left no one sure what it really meant. A miasma of ambiguity was created that would survive as one of the most perplexing of the occupation's legacies: did Article 9 permit or prohibit limited armament for the purpose of self-defense?

As submitted to the legislature, Article 9 read as follows:

> War, as a sovereign right of the nation, and the threat or use of force, is forever renounced as a means of settling disputes with other nations.
>
> The maintenance of land, sea, and air forces, as well as other war potential, will never be authorized. The right of belligerency of the state will not be recognized.

Did this mean that Japan was pledging itself to be an unarmed state in an unstable world? Many Diet members voiced concern that it did, and that it thereby placed the nation at peril. Others, attracted by the idea of eventual membership in the United Nations, asked whether that might become impossible if the country were unable to fulfill the UN requirement that all members contribute to collective security. To the direct question "does Article 9 prohibit armament even for self-defense?" the government usually answered yes, but sometimes responded no. When these convoluted proceedings were completed, it would be possible to go back over the record and exhume a quotation to bolster whatever position one wished to uphold.

On April 4, before submission to the Diet, Matsumoto Jōji addressed a confidential session of the Privy Council and was explicitly asked if renouncing the "right of belligerency" prohibited a war of self-defense. He answered that it did not. " 'The right of belligerency' implies a declared war," Matsumoto stated, "but does not purport to prohibit acts of self-defense."[53] In the opening sessions of the parliament, on the other hand, Prime Minister Yoshida said the opposite. On June 26, he indicated that Article 9 entailed renunciation of the right of self-defense as well as the right of belligerency. All aggressive wars, including Japan's recent aggression beginning in 1931, he observed, were waged in the name of self-defense.

Two days later, the prime minister had occasion to elaborate on this when Nosaka Sanzō challenged the wisdom of such a constitutional restraint. It was necessary, the Communist leader declared, to distinguish between just and unjust wars, and when this was kept in mind it became obvious that every nation had the right to self-defense. Yoshida, who prided himself on being a "realist," found himself arguing the realism of idealism. "It has been suggested that war may be justified by a nation's right of legitimate self-defense," he retorted, "but I think that the very recognition of such a thing is harmful." Japan would rely for its future security on an international peace organization. In one form or another, Yoshida reiterated this interpretation of Article 9 for several years thereafter.[54]

In the final stages of its deliberations, the House of Representatives adopted a change in the wording of Article 9 proposed by its influential subcommittee on constitutional revision, chaired by Ashida Hitoshi. Approved by the upper house, this became the final wording in the new constitution:

> Aspiring sincerely to an international peace based on justice and order, the Japanese people forever renounce war as a sovereign right of the nation and the threat or use of force as a means of settling international disputes.

In order to accomplish the aim of the preceding paragraph, land, sea, and air forces, as well as other war potential, will never be maintained. The right of belligerency of the state will not be recognized.

As was required with all such proposed changes, Ashida had first cleared the new wording with GHQ, where both Colonel Kades and General Whitney approved it right away. The three men apparently did not discuss the reasoning behind the revision.[55]

In subsequent years, the so-called Ashida amendment was used to argue that, in its final form, Article 9 did not prohibit rearmament for self-defense. The first paragraph, this argument went, established maintenance of international peace as the article's objective; this being the case, the clause that now introduced the second paragraph ("In order to accomplish the aim of the preceding paragraph") indicated that the "war potential" being renounced referred to maintaining a capacity for aggressive war that would disturb international peace. Ashida himself later claimed that it had been his purpose from the outset to open the door to future armament for self-defense through this change. This never emerged in the Diet discussions, however; and the secret records of Ashida's subcommittee, which remained classified for many decades, reveal that neither he nor his fellow committee members ever explicitly discussed their revision in terms of allowing "self-defense," nor was there any evidence of an implicit understanding that this is what was being done. As in much of the discussion that took place in the Diet generally, the air was full of phrases flying in all directions—and often impossible to follow coherently. At one point, Ashida actually explained that he was simply trying to make Article 9 a less "passive" affirmation of Japan's commitment not to maintain war potential.[56]

As the final draft headed for a vote, key spokesmen for the government confirmed that Article 9 prohibited maintenance of any war potential whatsoever. When Kanamori, who took part in some of the secret discussions in the lower house, was called on to explain the new wording of the article to the House of Peers special committee on the constitution, he stressed the categorical renunciation of all armaments. "The first paragraph of Article 9 does not renounce the right of self-defense but this right is renounced as a matter of fact under the second paragraph," he told the committee on September 14. Rephrasing this, he stated that "the practical effect of the second paragraph is that even a defensive war cannot be conducted." Former prime minister Shidehara, addressing the same committee, similarly declared without equivocation that, under the second paragraph, it was "very clear that Japan cannot possess any war potential to fight a foreign country."[57]

At this juncture, the Far Eastern Commission intervened in a way that struck many legislators as bizarre. In July, the FEC had urged General MacArthur to have an article added to the constitution stipulating that only "civilians" could hold cabinet positions. The general ignored this request, but on September 21 the Chinese representative to the FEC, sitting in Washington, took note of the new wording of Article Nine and pointed out that such ambiguous language might indeed leave an opening for some form of future rearmament. Instead of urging that the Article 9 language be tightened, however, the FEC again demanded that cabinet members be constitutionally limited to civilians. MacArthur and GHQ felt that to avoid FEC censure they must comply.

This belated change, introduced in the House of Peers on September 26, caused understandable confusion: for if Article 9 prohibited an army, navy, and air force, then it seemed logical to assume that there could be no professional military establishment from which cabinet members might be drawn. Was it possible, legislators asked, that the proposed stipulation was intended to prevent *former* military personnel from assuming cabinet positions? That would certainly discriminate against the young men who had served the country in the recent war. An upper-house committee set up specifically to look into this request concluded that such a provision was not necessary. MacArthur, in turn, sent word that it was necessary to make the FEC happy. The peers then had no choice but to turn their attention to inventing a new word which would correspond to the English "civilian." Some seven or more possibilities were considered before a newly coined compound, pronounced *bunmin*, was selected.[58]

Whatever the FEC may have intended, the strange *bunmin* provision, which became Article 66 of the new charter, had the unintended effect of weakening the argument that Article 9 prohibited the maintenance of any military potential whatsoever. After all, excluding military personnel from the cabinet assumed their existence as a functioning part of the body politic. This ambiguity was compounded when in explaining the new draft in confidence to the Privy Council on October 21, Kanamori offered an interpretation quite different from the one he had given the House of Peers a month earlier. The minutes of this elite body (slated to be abolished under the new constitution) recorded that Kanamori "interprets the keeping of arms as being allowed for the maintenance of international peace."[59] In a publication entitled *Interpreting the New Constitution* published on November 3, the day the new charter was promulgated, Ashida

Hitoshi publicly offered this same interpretation for the first time. "In reality," he stated, Article 9 "is meant to apply to wars of aggression. Therefore, its provisions do not renounce war and the threat or use of force for purposes of self-defense."[60] GHQ did not challenge this view, but neither did it become a clearly held government position.

For years afterwards, in fact, Prime Minister Yoshida spoke in a very different voice. In January 1950, he stated unequivocally, "The right of self-defense in Japan's case will be the right of self-defense without resorting to force of arms." In an extemporaneous comment to the House of Councilors (which replaced the House of Peers) that same month, Yoshida went so far as to exclaim, "If we hold somewhere in the back of our minds the idea of protecting ourselves by armaments, or the idea of protecting ourselves by force of arms in case of war, then we ourselves will impede the security of Japan." True security, the elderly prime minister suggested, lay in earning the confidence of other nations.[61]

There was certainly an element of grandstanding in such statements, for Yoshida was persuaded that the best way to hasten the end of the occupation and the country's reacceptance in the world community was to emphasize the thoroughgoing nature of its renunciation of militarism.[62] At the same time, however, Article 9 also possessed a compelling psychological attraction to a shattered people sick of war and burdened by the knowledge that much of the world reviled them as inherently militaristic and untrustworthy. The renunciation of war—the prospect of becoming a *pure* embodiment of Kellogg-Briand ideals—offered a way of retaining a positive sense of uniqueness in defeat.

Three and a half decades after these events, Charles Kades looked back on the contradictions in Japanese interpretations of Article 9 and was reminded of the observations of a fifteenth-century English judge: "The Thought of Man shall not be tried for the Devil himself knoweth not the Thought of Man."[63] Where Article 9 was concerned, confusion initially arose less from Machiavellian subterfuge than from the article's poor drafting. Under the circumstances of continued occupation, moreover, the issue of self-defense was hardly a pressing concern—until June 1950, that is, when rearmament was initiated in the wake of the outbreak of war in Korea. Then the conservatives and the Americans alike found their loophole in the murky language of the Ashida amendment, and the opponents of remilitarization rallied around the ideals of disarmed neutrality that they believed to be firmly embedded in their "peace constitution." Article 9 became the touchstone for a controversy that would wrack the body politic for decades to come.

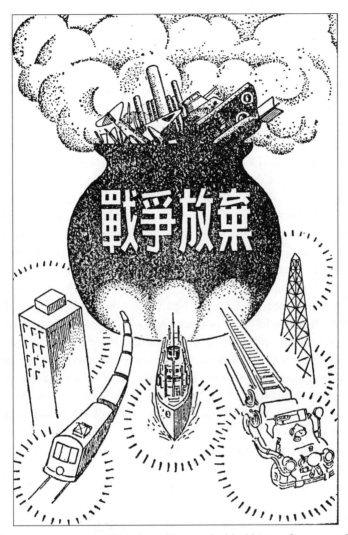

戰爭放棄

The "renunciation of war" ideal was illustrated with this soon-famous graphic in a booklet titled *The Story of the New Constitution*, which was issued by the Ministry of Education in 1947 and used as a text in middle schools for several years.

Responding to a Fait Accompli

Diet members were free to vote against the draft constitution, but in the end very few did so. In the House of Representatives, the vote for adoption was 421 to 8. In the House of Peers—where adoption meant immediate abolition of the peerage itself—the new charter was adopted over-whelmingly by a standing vote (GHQ counted 2 negative votes out of 300). Most of the Diet votes against adoption came from Communist Party representatives.

Cynics would say that this near-unanimous embrace of the conqueror's principles merely confirmed what condescending American and British analysts had been arguing all along: that the Japanese had an "ingrained feudalistic tendency" to follow authority—that, as the State Department's George Atcheson had put it at the beginning of 1946, this was the dawn of "the age of Japan's imitation of things American—not only of American machines but also American ideas."[64]

For some, this may have been the case; both Japanese skeptics and worried liberals said much the same thing at the time. The political and ideological dynamics of the situation, however, were too complex to be explained away by such simplistic notions of mass psychology. To a substantial degree, the solid vote to adopt the new constitution reflected neither conformist nor feudalistic "Japanese" values, but rather a familiar feature of democratic party politics everywhere: maintaining party discipline. With the exception of the Communists, party leaders across the political spectrum supported the revision; and party members fell into line.

Many pragmatic conservative leaders also believed that, although at the moment they had little choice but to go along with the conquerors, at a later date it would be possible to undo much of what had been done. Adopting a democratic and pacifistic national charter would hasten the day the occupation was terminated; and once independence had been regained, the constitution could be revised. Yoshida Shigeru later ruefully explained that this had been his philosophy regarding the American reformist agenda in general. "There was this idea at the back of my mind that, whatever needed to be revised after we regained our independence could be revised then," he confided. "But once a thing has been decided on, it is not so easy to have it altered."[65]

On November 3, 1946, the ninety-fourth anniversary of the Meiji emperor's birthday, Emperor Hirohito announced the promulgation of the new constitution; it was to go into effect six months later. (When it came to patriotic dating, the vanquished were as diligent as the victors.) Celebratory ceremonies were held nationwide. In Tokyo, one hundred thousand people gathered in front of the imperial palace to commemorate the occasion. As added evidence of imperial largesse, the emperor decreed an amnesty terminating the penal sentences of 330,000 individuals. This was his final grand exercise of sovereign authority.[66]

One month later, it was announced that Japan would continue to reckon time in accordance with an emperor-centered calendar. On December 5, in response to a question in the Diet, the government stated that the *"gengo* system" would be maintained, meaning that the years would continue to be numbered in accordance with the era name associated with the reigning emperor, coupled with the year of the emperor's reign. By this way of counting, the constitution was promulgated in the year Shōwa 21. This was a consoling conservative victory and a brilliant *everyday* way of reiterating that, because of their emperor system, the Japanese were unique and operated in realms not shared by others. Every time any one looked at the date on a publication, they would be reminded of the imperial presence.[67]

May 3, 1947, the day the constitution came into effect, could be remembered almost any way one chose. A Japanese brass band performing in the plaza before the imperial palace celebrated the occasion by playing *The Stars and Stripes Forever*.[68] Shimizu Tōru, the former president of the Privy Council, committed suicide by throwing himself into the ocean. The Privy Council had been the final body to vote approval of the new charter, and Shimizu left behind a note saying there was no other way he could apologize to the emperor.[69] The emperor's youngest brother Prince Mikasa, on the other hand, sent a remarkable commentary to a newspaper put out by Tokyo Imperial University, chastising the emperor and the government for the undemocratic manner in which they had conducted the day's ceremonies. He had been ill and unable to attend, but several aspects of the ceremony disturbed him. Why was his invitation addressed to him alone, and not to his wife as well; and why did it mention only the emperor and not the empress? It was no wonder, Prince Mikasa commented, that Japanese women, so recently elected to the Diet for the first time, felt they faced a difficult struggle.

He had listened to the ceremonies on the radio, the emperor's brother added, and was struck by the continued use of the distinctive, honorific language reserved only for the imperial family. If a genuine democratization were to be effected, language, too, would have to be democratized; and the proper place to begin would be to reform the special language hitherto reserved for the throne. The prince also was struck by the fact that Emperor Hirohito was not present from the outset, but rather made a grand entrance; and he was taken back by the fact that Prime Minister Yoshida greeted the sovereign's appearance by calling out "Long Live the Emperor!" *(Tennō Heika Banzai!)* three times in succession. This might be appropriate for something like an enthronement ceremony, Mikasa ob-

served, but it did not seem very suitable to a ceremony in which, presumably, sovereignty was being transferred to the people.

This was droll and iconoclastic, and it is no wonder that Emperor Hirohito, when musing on the possibility of abdicating, had dismissed his
youngest brother as a possible successor, even as regent for the crown
prince. Indeed, Prince Mikasa was not finished with his ruminations. It
might have been more appropriate, he ventured—and the reader could easily imagine him chortling here—had the planners of the ceremony instead
arranged to have the emperor lead a cheer along the lines of "Long Live
All the Japanese People!" *(Zen Nihon Kokumin Banzai!)*. Or the prime
minister might have led all the people, including the emperor, in such a
cheer. Or on behalf of the new peace-loving Japan, the emperor might
have been asked to lead a *banzai* for all the peoples of the world. In any
case, he concluded, democratizing the imperial household would be the beginning of the true task of democratizing Japan.[70]

The adoption of the new constitution propelled both GHQ and the
government into a flurry of activity. Civil laws, criminal laws, the code of
civil procedure, family law, the laws governing the imperial household—
all were subjected to substantive revision and redrafted in more colloquial
Japanese. At the same time, a massive educational campaign was launched.
On the very day the new constitution came into effect, the government
issued 20 million copies of a pocket-size booklet entitled *Atarashii Kempō,
Akarui Seikatsu* (New Constitution, Bright Life). This astonishing number was supposed to ensure a booklet for every household in Japan.

Atarashii Kempō, Akarui Seikatsu was only thirty pages long: a one-page
send-off by Ashida Hitoshi (the chairman of the lower-house subcommittee on constitutional revision), a radiant thirteen-page introduction
that included several illustrations, and the full text of the constitution itself. It was issued at the insistence of GHQ and so, like the constitution
itself, was a text written under duress. It also conveyed an idealism embraced by many Japanese. Although revision of the "MacArthur Constitution" became an ardent nationalistic cause in certain conservative circles
even before the occupation ended, the simple, optimistic rhetoric of "new
constitution, bright life" retained enough popular appeal to thwart all attempts at revision over the decades that followed.

Ashida began his brief preface with a plain but moving statement:
"The old Japan has been cast in the shadows, a new Japan has been
born." People would now respect each other on the basis of their human
qualities. They would practice democracy. Relations with other countries
would be conducted in the spirit of peace. The constitution's bold decla-

ration that "we will not do war any more" expressed a high ideal for humankind and was the only way for Japan to be reborn.

The introductory text itself began by speaking of May 3, 1947 as the birthday of a new Japan, and immediately went on to declare that the greatest "gift" of the constitution was democracy, which entailed "government by the people, for the people, and of the people." The emperor was no longer a god, but rather a symbol of the unity of the people—much in the same way that Mt. Fuji symbolized the physical beauty of Japan, cherry blossoms the gentleness of Japanese spring. The national charter was described as being a pledge never to wage war again (a point accompanied by an illustration of a trash can filled with artillery, bombs, tanks, military planes, and warships—along with a dead fish and two buzzing flies). Equality, human dignity, happiness, and the "joy of freedom" were emphasized. It was important to live in accordance with one's own conscience. Men and women were equal. (This point was illustrated by a romantic sketch of a young couple kneeling and holding hands, with overlapping valentine hearts and an exclamation point above their clasped hands. A startled old couple lurked in the background.) Officials were now public servants. The Diet was the voice of the people. The court was the guardian of the constitution. The essence of the new constitution was "people's government and international peace."[71]

This was, without question, propaganda demanded by the conquerors and expressed at an extremely simple level; and it struck a popular chord. The full measure of the compelling power of the constitutional fait accompli, however, lay in the fact that even high officials who originally had been staunch supporters of the Meiji Constitution came in time to endorse many of the fundamental principles of the new charter. The former government spokesman Kanamori Tokujirō was a fair example of this ideological sea change. Before GHQ's "constitutional convention," Kanamori had helped draft the Liberal Party's conservative proposed constitutional revision. As Prime Minister Yoshida's minister in charge of constitutional affairs, he was reluctantly compelled to present the adapted GHQ draft as the government's own handiwork. Two years after these arduous labors were done, Kanamori took it on himself to write a children's book, "The Story of the Constitution for Boys and Girls" *(Shōnen to Shōjo no tame no Kempō no Ohanashi)*. He still romanticized the emperor but also wrote with power about the great ideals of peace, popular sovereignty, and fundamental human rights. Amending the constitution, Kanamori told his young readers, should only be done with extreme care. His concluding words were these: "We must, without fail, respect and defend the constitution. And, though the road is long, let us walk steadily, step by step, toward the light of these ideals." These were not words that he had been compelled to utter.[72]

Kanamori's predecessor as minister in charge of constitutional affairs, Matsumoto Jōji, did not adjust so graciously to the fait accompli. A decade after his humiliation, by then in his eighties, he defiantly declared that he had never even condescended to read the final version of the new constitution.[73] On the other hand, former prime minister Shidehara, who had tearfully told his ministers that they could only expect contempt from subsequent generations, came in later years to claim proudly that he himself had first mentioned the ideal of renouncing war to General MacArthur. This was in all likelihood just the mistaken recollection of an elderly man—but, whether fact or fiction, his sincere embrace of the "no war" ideal gave credibility to the argument that, when all was said and done, the new constitution had indeed reflected Japanese ideals.[74]

Emperor Hirohito's intimate thoughts about the new constitution are unknown, but Colonel Kades and several members of his staff were royally thanked. Each received a small silver cup, embossed in gold with the sixteen-petal imperial chrysanthemum crest and engraved with a notation that this gift commemorated the introduction of the new constitution.[75]

chapter fourteen

CENSORED DEMOCRACY: POLICING THE NEW TABOOS

In April 1946, GHQ was informed that an entertainer in Tokyo was singing subversive songs while accompanying himself on the violin. Investigators attended a performance and were shocked. They heard lyrics like: "Seducing Japanese women is easy, with chocolate and chewing gum." More scandalous yet was this line: "Everybody is talking about democracy, but how can we have democracy with two emperors?" Democracy, Hirohito, and MacArthur lampooned, all in a single breath! The Americans banned the show.[1]

As numerous Japanese outside the music-hall circuit could attest, this was not a random act on the part of occupation authorities, who policed the country's new freedoms with a censorship bureaucracy that extended into every aspect of public expression. In the process, the Japanese quickly learned to identify the new taboos and to practice self-censorship accordingly. One simply did not challenge ultimate authority and expect to win.

The inviolability of the nation's second emperor, General MacArthur, was brought home to writers and editors in what became known as the "hero worship" incident of October 1946. Commenting on the adulation the supreme commander was receiving, the newspaper *Jiji Shimpō* offered a tempered editorial warning about "the habit of hero worship that has im-

bued Japanese minds for the past twenty centuries." The editorial was
prompted by the publication of a best-selling biography of MacArthur that
had been accompanied by a flood of adulatory letters in the press in
which the general was described in terms only recently reserved for Hirohito himself—as "a living god" and "the sun coming out of dark clouds
and shining on the world" or even as "the reincarnation of Japan's first
emperor, Jimmu." The newspaper's response, subsequently published in
the English-language *Nippon Times,* read in part as follows:

> If the conception that government is something imposed upon the
> people by an outstanding god, great man, or leader is not rectified,
> democratic government is likely to be wrecked. We fear, the day after
> MacArthur's withdrawal, that some living god might be searched out
> to bring the sort of dictatorship that made the Pacific War. . . . The
> way to express the gratitude of the Japanese people toward General
> MacArthur for the wisdom with which he is managing postwar
> Japan and for his efforts to democratize the nation is not to worship
> him as a god but to cast away the servile spirit and gain the self-
> respect that would not bow its head to anybody.

Although this eminently reasonable commentary had been approved by
GHQ authorities prior to its publication in Japanese, the English version
was immediately seized by the American military police on orders from
General Charles Willoughby, head of the Civil Intelligence Section, on the
grounds that it was "not in good taste" and tended to diminish the reputation of the occupation forces and their commander.[2] This was a rare public display of power by the ultraconservative Willoughby. At the same
time, however, his heavy-handed intervention exposed the everyday regimen of censorship, signaled a tightening of occupation controls on critical commentary that could be deemed "leftist" or even remotely critical
of American policies, and came to symbolize for many the carefully pro-
grammed and controlled nature of the democratization agenda.

The Phantom Bureaucracy

Censorship was conducted through an elaborate apparatus within GHQ
from September 1945 through September 1949, and continued to be imposed in altered forms until Japan regained its sovereignty. In the early
stages of the occupation, it was anticipated that such controls would last
only until the safety of the foreign forces could be assured and reformist
policies successfully implemented. SCAP's first formal directive on "free-

dom of speech and press," issued September 10, 1945, explicitly declared that "there shall be an absolute minimum of restrictions on freedom of speech" so long as such expression adhered "to the truth" and did not disturb "public tranquility."[3]

In practice, the censorship apparatus soon took on a life of its own. A sprawling bureaucracy was created under the Civil Censorship Detachment (CCD) within the Civil Information Section, and CCD's censors were closely abetted by the "positive" propagandists for democracy within the Civil Intelligence and Education (CI&E) Section.[4] Censorship was extended to every form of media and theatrical expression—newspapers, magazines, trade books as well as textbooks, radio, film, and plays, including the classical repertoire.[5] At its peak, CCD employed over six thousand individuals nationwide, the great majority of whom were English-speaking Japanese nationals who identified and then translated or summarized questionable material before passing it on to their superiors. Until late 1947, many publications, including close to seventy major daily newspapers and all books and magazines, were subject to *pre*publication censorship. At one point, the monthly volume of material flooding into CCD's central "PPB" (Press, Pictorial and Broadcast) section alone was estimated to average "26,000 issues of newspapers, 3,800 news-agency publications, 23,000 radio scripts, 5,700 printed bulletins, 4,000 magazine issues, and 1,800 books and pamphlets." Over the course of their four-year regime, CCD's examiners also spot-checked an astonishing 330 million pieces of mail and monitored some 800,000 private phone conversations.[6]

Censored materials included foreign as well as Japanese writings, meaning that the vanquished were not allowed to read everything the victors read. Both Associated Press and United Press wire-service dispatches were sometimes vetted before being deemed safe for consumption in translation; syndicated columnists such as Walter Lippmann encountered similar obstacles crossing the Pacific. The overall censorship operation eventually came to entail extensive checklists for taboo subjects, and in the best Orwellian manner these taboos included any public acknowledgment of the existence of censorship. Editors and publishers all received such confidential notifications as the following as soon as censorship was established:

1. The purpose of this memorandum is to make certain that all publishers in the jurisdiction of this censorship office understand fully that no publicity regarding censorship procedure is desired.

2. While it is assumed that all publishers understand that in the make-up of their publications no physical indication of censorship (such as blackened-out print, blank spaces, pasted-over areas, incomplete sentences, OO's XX's, etc.) may appear, there are some points which may not be understood clearly.

3. No write-ups concerning personnel or activities of any censorship group should be printed. This pertains not only to press censorship personnel and activities, but also to those of radio, motion-picture and theatrical censorship.

4. Notations such as "Passed by censorship," "Publication permitted by Occupation Forces" or any other mention or implication of censorship on CCD must not be made. . . .

Since censorship was never openly acknowledged to exist, its nominal termination with the dissolution of CCD in late 1949 also took place without public notice. Fittingly, as if it had been but a phantom bureaucracy, CCD passed from the scene under the confidential farewell policy that "there will be no press release on the termination of civil censorship."[7]

Contrary to early hopes that censorship would taper off fairly quickly, CCD's surveillance became both more stringent and more picayune as the months passed. In this regard, the confiscation of the press edition carrying the "hero worship" editorial signaled a moment, roughly a year after surrender, when GHQ's censorship policies hardened and simultaneously began to depart from their original focus on eliminating militaristic and ultranationalistic ideas. Robert Spaulding, who held several responsible positions in CCD, later observed that Willoughby's action had a triple legacy. It led to an expansion of the CCD staff, fostered a psychology of extreme cautiousness among the censors, and led to the proliferation of cumbersome "checking" procedures whereby officials throughout GHQ's numerous divisions and branches became more involved in controlling what the media said.[8]

Although censorship under the occupation was by no means as pervasive and stunting as that practiced in Japan in the decade and a half prior to surrender, scores of prominent literary figures ranging from Dazai Osamu (the author of *The Setting Sun*, whose suicide in 1948 caused a sensation) to the future Nobel laureate Kawabata Yasunari experienced the blue pencil. The novelist Tanizaki Junichirō, to his astonishment, had an entire short story suppressed on the grounds that it was "militaristic." He was, in this regard, in honorable company, since the translation of Tolstoy's *War and Peace* was also vetted by CCD's censors. Still, even such an acerbic literary critic as Nakamura Mitsuo concluded in the immediate wake of the occupation that, although postwar Japanese literature was largely worthless (too much sex, in his view), the literary world as a whole had enjoyed incomparably greater freedom than in the past.[9]

Journalists who had firsthand experience with presurrender and postsurrender variants of censorship were less sanguine about postwar "freedom," but usually still acknowledged that the conqueror's hand was the lighter one. Ikejima Shinpei, a former editor of the moderate monthly *Bungei Shunjū*, expressed disgust at being censored by people who didn't even speak his language, but allowed that GHQ's surveillance was a far cry from the situation under the militarists, when a transgression might even imperil one's life.[10] Matsuura Sōzō, the author of a well-known book about occupation censorship and a former editor of the left-wing magazine *Kaizō*, a favorite target of CCD, felt that even in the later period of draconian "Red purges," America's censorious "democracy" was nowhere near as oppressive as imperial Japan's "emperor-system absolutism" had been. At the same time, he looked back on the years from 1948 through 1951 as an era of darkness for progressive and left-wing writers made all the more bitter by the hopes that the occupation had encouraged.[11] Radio-show producers sometimes spoke of their long interlude under American supervision as being "still an era of unfreedom of speech" that was in some ways "more troublesome" than the wartime restrictions under which they had operated—for at least under their own thought police they were spared the burden of having to translate scripts into English for the censors' review![12]

SCAP officials were acutely aware that their give-and-take approach to democratization involved a delicate balancing act. From the outset, the censorship policy was set against a positive emphasis on freedom of speech and the dissolution of official government controls over the media. In the wake of SCAP's "civil rights" directive of October 4, editors and publishers were summoned to CI&E and encouraged to interpret this "Magna Carta" aggressively. Contrary to the past, they were told, it was now permissible to criticize the government, debate about the emperor system, and even espouse Marxism.[13] This would be a schizophrenic world, however, for the victor's censorship sometimes replicated the earlier campaigns of the imperial government against "dangerous thought" in uncanny ways, hamstringing postwar democracy from the start. This was conveyed to writers and publishers at virtually the same moment that they were being granted their "Magna Carta," for beginning on the following day the media were gradually brought under CCD's prepublication censorship and made concretely aware of the new taboos they were now required to observe.

The policy of censoring the existence of censorship itself cast a taint of hypocrisy on the Americans and compared poorly with the old system of the militarists and ultranationalists, who until the late 1930s had allowed excised portions of texts to be marked in publications with *X*s and *O*s. At least prewar readers knew that *something* had been excised; they could even count the *X*s and *O*s and try to guess what. It is not surprising, then, that some writers who experienced censorship under both systems were cynical in their appraisals of SCAP's version of free expression. One evoked an old metaphor in describing its modus operandi as like being "strangled with silk floss." Another observed, with not a little bitterness, that at least the Japanese censors had served tea.[14]

Impermissible Discourse

For publishers, broadcasters, journalists, filmmakers, and writers, SCAP's censorship operation possessed an opaque quality that made it challenging to determine how far one could go without offending the new thought police. This came, in part, from the fact that CCD's censors operated on the basis of secret "key logs" of prohibited discourse—checklists of forbidden subjects—that were never made available. In other words, the precise criteria for unacceptable expression were not conveyed to those being censored. As a consequence, those who engaged in any form of public communication had to rely on two imprecise guides in deciding what was impermissible: the very general press, radio, and film "codes" issued by SCAP in the opening months of the occupation ("News must adhere strictly to the truth. Nothing shall be printed which might, directly or by inference, disturb the public tranquility. There shall be no false or destructive criticism of the Allied Powers . . ." and so on); and imagination shaped by experience—that is, guessing what the censors would allow on the basis of what they had thus far permitted.[15] This was not only disorienting, but could prove financially disastrous if one miscalculated the censors' tolerance. Such circumstances helped foster a climate of disquieting rumors that easily spilled over into a pathology of self-censorship.

The classified key logs used as monthly checklists by CCD changed as political winds changed. Early on, they included some three score prohibited subjects. In June 1946, the "categories of deletions and suppressions" in CCD's key log were, in full, as follows:

Criticism of SCAP

Criticism of Military Tribunal [that is, of the Tokyo war-crimes trials]

Criticism of SCAP Writing the Constitution [including any reference whatsoever to SCAP's role]

References to Censorship

Criticism of the United States

Criticism of Russia

Criticism of Great Britain

Criticism of Koreans

Criticism of China

Criticism of Other Allies

General Criticism of Allies

Criticism of Japanese Treatment in Manchuria [referring to treatment of Japanese POWs or civilians by Russians and Chinese after Japan's capitulation]

Criticism of Allies' Pre-War Policies

Third World War Comments

Russia vs. Western Powers Comments

Defense of War Propaganda [described as "any propaganda which directly or indirectly defends Japan's conduct of and in the War"]

Divine Descent Nation Propaganda

Militaristic Propaganda

Nationalistic Propaganda

Glorification of Feudal Ideals

Greater East Asia Propaganda

General [Japanese] Propaganda

Justification or Defense of War Criminals

Fraternization [referring in particular to fraternization of Allied personnel with Japanese women]

Black Market Activities

Criticism of Occupation Forces

Overplaying Starvation

Incitement to Violence or Unrest [on actual censored material this often was phrased as "Disturbs public tranquility"]

Untrue Statements

Inappropriate Reference to SCAP (or Local Units)

Premature Disclosure[16]

When, say, galley proofs were censored, the offending material was returned to the publisher with blue-penciled passages to be altered or
deleted along with a standard form that simply indicated the paragraph or
paragraphs of the ten-item Press Code that these impermissible passages
violated.[17] In this manner, the concrete nature of what had been excised
became the primary means by which Japanese understood what occupation authorities really meant by their vague code commandments. Cases
that, in retrospect, may seem aberrant or even ludicrous censorial excesses
sometimes became guideposts by which the censored party decided what
the victors construed to be within the boundaries of acceptable expression.

As these internal checklists indicate, the realm of impermissible discourse was extensive. No criticism was permitted of the victorious Allied
nations (including, initially, the Soviet Union), nor of SCAP or its policies, which meant that for over six years the supreme authority in the
country remained beyond accountability. Sensitive social issues such as
fraternization, prostitution involving the occupation forces, or mixed-
blood children, to say nothing of GI crimes including rape, could not be
discussed. Public commentary about emerging Cold War tensions was, initially, forbidden. Even serious critical analysis of the black market was by
and large off limits. "Feudal" values could not be praised. Any expression
of opinion remotely resembling the propaganda of the war years was, of
course, taboo.

Controlling commentary about the recent war naturally was of utmost
importance to the victors at the outset of the occupation. They considered
it essential to suppress any rhetorical appeals that might rekindle violent
wartime passions and thereby either imperil the security of occupation
personnel or undermine their reformist agenda. In a more active rather
than reactive direction, the Americans deemed it necessary to educate the
general populace about the many aspects of Japanese aggression and atrocity that had been suppressed by their nation's own censorship machinery.

This was a reasonable mission, a formidable challenge, and a delicate
undertaking, for it posed—and ultimately failed to escape—the danger of
simply replacing the propaganda of the vanquished with that of the victors. All prior ways of speaking about the war became incorrect and unacceptable. Any criticism of the prewar policies of the victorious Allies was
categorically forbidden. All past propaganda became a portmanteau violation, as it were, of the media codes. Even controversial but entirely reasonable statements about the global milieu in which Japan's leaders
embarked on war (the shock of the Great Depression, the breakdown of
global capitalism, worldwide trends toward protectionism and autarchy, the

models as well as pressures of European and American imperialism, Western racism, and the countervailing racial and anticolonial ideals of Pan-Asianism) could be deemed not merely incitements to unrest, but also transgressions of "truth," not to speak of criticism of the occupation's policies and of the victorious powers.

What now was "true," of course, was the Allied version of the war, which the media had to endorse by acts of commission as well as omission. Publishers and broadcasters were required to present accounts of the war prepared within GHQ, especially by CI&E. Criticism of the war-crimes trials was not permitted. This meant, as noted in the key logs, that there could be no public "justification or defense" of individuals who had been indicted as war criminals. Essentially, whereas the defendants at the Tokyo trials were provided with committed defense counsel, the media were required to uncritically support the prosecution's arguments as well as the tribunal's eventual judgment.

SCAP's war-guilt campaign played an important role in the psychological demilitarization of the Japanese. The "Class A" Allied war-crimes tribunal, in particular, with its voluminous written evidence and oral testimony, revealed a secret history of intrigue and atrocity that could never have been so effectively exposed otherwise. These were critical educational undertakings, but as filtered through the censorship apparatus they taught the media and general public less positive lessons as well: that the makeup and conduct of the court were not to be questioned, for example, and that the accused were to be assumed guilty unless judged innocent. Inside the courtroom, defense attorneys were allowed to argue that Japan's leaders had believed themselves to be defending legitimate national interests, and that "victor's justice" had made these proceedings inherently biased. Outside the courtroom, the media were neither allowed to endorse such arguments nor, in a different direction, to criticize the trials for not casting a wider net by indicting many more top wartime leaders. In a familiar paradox, the Japanese learned a great deal about the war that the censorship and secrecy of their own government had withheld from them, but were not permitted to comment freely on this.

Impermissible discourse about the war extended much further, however. It went without saying that the wartime rhetoric of Pan-Asianism and fighting a holy war against "Chinese bandits" and "devilish Anglo-Americans" was intolerable, as were the paeans to "Yamato race" superiority that commonly accompanied this rhetoric. Coming to terms publicly with death, destruction, and defeat was more problematic. Here, censorship could impede reasonable and therapeutic expressions of grief. Nothing revealed this more graphically than the difficulty of coming to grips publicly with the meaning of Hiroshima and Nagasaki.

Writing about the atomic-bomb experience was not explicitly proscribed, and in the year or so following the surrender, especially in local publications in the Hiroshima area, a number of writers were able to publish prose and poetry on the subject. At the same time, however, survivors such as Nagai Takashi found their early writings suppressed, many bomb-related writings were severely cut, and the most moving English-language publication on the subject—John Hersey's *Hiroshima,* a sparse portrait of six survivors that made a profound impression when published in *The New Yorker* in August 1946—though mentioned in the media, could not be published in translation until 1949. As word spread that this was a taboo subject, a combination of outright censorship and widespread self-censorship led to the virtual disappearance of writings about the atomic-bomb experience until the end of 1948, when Nagai's books finally signaled the modest emergence of an atomic-bomb genre. In these circumstances, survivors of the bombs found it exceedingly difficult to reach out to one another for comfort, or to tell others what nuclear war meant at the human level. Beyond this, overt censorship extended to scientific writings. Many reports concerning the effects of the blasts and ensuing radiation could not be made public until the closing months of the occupation. For over six years, Japanese scientists and doctors—and even some American scientists in Hiroshima and Nagasaki who were conducting research on radiation effects—were denied access to data that might have assisted them in communicating to and helping atomic-bomb victims.[18]

The visual record of nuclear destruction was even more thoroughly suppressed. Documentary footage filmed in Hiroshima and Nagasaki between August and December 1945 by a team of some thirty Japanese cameramen was confiscated by the Americans in February 1946 and sent to Washington, with orders that not a single copy was to remain in Japan.[19] The first graphic representations of the human effects of the bombs did not appear until 1950, when the married artists Maruki Iri and Maruki Toshi published a small book of drawings of scenes they had witnessed or heard about in Hiroshima (entitled *Pika-don,* a term specific to the atomic bombs that literally means "flash-bang"). That same year the Marukis were also permitted to exhibit a stark painting entitled *Procession of Ghosts,* which became the first of a series of powerful collaborative murals depicting atomic-bomb victims. As Maruki Iri later explained, the couple was motivated to do such paintings because they feared that there might otherwise never be an indigenous visual record of the horrors of nuclear destruction.[20] It was not until after the occupation, on the seventh anniversary of the bombings in August 1952, that the public was afforded a serious presentation of photographs from the two stricken cities. The residents of the only country to experience atomic warfare thus spent the early years of the nuclear age more ignorant of the effects of the bombs, and less free to publicly discuss and debate their implications, than people in other nations.[21]

In Allied eyes, the Japanese simply had reaped what they had sown. The terror bombing of Japanese cities, culminating in Hiroshima and Nagasaki, was seen as an appropriate homecoming for the horrors Japan had visited on others throughout Asia and the Pacific. Early in 1949, when occupation authorities finally relaxed their restraints on the publication of intimate personal accounts of the effects of the atomic bombs, they conveyed this notion of righteous punishment literally. At General Willoughby's insistence, the first printing of Nagai Takashi's *Nagasaki no Kane* (The Bells of Nagasaki) had to include a lengthy American-prepared appendix about "The Sack of Manila" by Japanese forces in 1945. Such victor's logic was obtuse. It easily could be taken as suggesting that Nagasaki and Manila were comparable atrocities—hardly what the Americans intended. To the great majority of ordinary people, it was in any case emotionally impossible to accept the death of family and acquaintances or their own suffering as being deserved retribution.[22]

The need to grieve publicly, to mourn and speak well of the dead, in some instances unsurprisingly transgressed what the censors deemed proper and permissible. The most famous such case involved an elegiac prose-poem written by a former ensign in the imperial navy, Yoshida Mitsuru, who had been drafted out of Tokyo Imperial University to serve on the doomed superbattleship *Yamato*. In mid-October 1945, in an intense burst of anguished inspiration, Yoshida wrote down in intimate detail his memory of the sinking of the *Yamato* en route to Okinawa in April 1945, with a loss of almost three thousand men. Many emotions drove him. Yoshida wished to expunge the impression of meaningless death from the memory of his comrades, liberate them from shame, memorialize their sincerity and bravery, and mourn those who perished and—as would most navy men anywhere—the death of a great ship.

The twenty-three-year-old Yoshida was also wrestling with why death had not chosen him when it gathered in so many of his comrades. As one of the few survivors of the *Yamato*—and as someone, moreover, who had witnessed most of the final battle from the bridge—Yoshida essentially took it on himself to write, in a single text, an after-action report, an obituary, and a eulogy. His closing lines (as translated in the censor's report) were as follows:

> Over three thousand were the number of the crew, of which the survivors were only two hundred something. Who could surpass their ardent fighting spirit? Who could doubt their excellent training? Glorious be their end in the eyes of all the world.[23]

Yoshida's *Senkan Yamato no Saigo* (The End of the Battleship *Yamato*) now is recognized as one of the few important literary memoirs to emerge from Japan's war. Censors at the time acknowledged its impressive qualities, but also feared that this intimate evocation of the "Japanese militaristic spirit" might promote feelings of both regret and revenge among readers. As a consequence, it suppressed in 1946 and again in 1948, published only in abridged form in mid-1949, and not made available in full until after the occupation ended.

More modest efforts to grieve publicly or treat the war dead as tragic victims also encountered disapproval. In mid-1948, censors deleted the following line (the translation is the censor's) from a piece by the fiction writer Nagaiyo Yoshirō: "Under the present circumstances, she could not openly weep or express her sorrow for the loss of her only and precious son, who died an honorable death in the battle of the Solomon Seas." In this instance, the censor's rationale was "criticism of Occupation."[24] Earlier that same year, the poet Yano Matakichi failed to gain the censors' approval for a number of verses in a collection he had dedicated to his children. Yano had learned belatedly that his married daughter perished of malnutrition in Manchuria after the war and his son had died in Soviet hands as a prisoner in Siberia. A number of his poems were censored for their "anti-Soviet" sentiment. A haiku in which he spoke of having offered his son's life "for victory's sake, never never for defeat" was deemed "rightist propaganda." Another haiku, exclaiming that "the whips of defeat are too severe" and asking what crimes these young people had committed was censored as "incitement to unrest."[25]

A well-known poet, Tsuboi Hanji, provoked a more complex response among the censors, who blue-penciled a published collection of his verses. In addition to deleting lines about alienated and starving individuals groaning in the "beehive" of Japanese capitalism and warriors who had fought and perished under "the flag whose color is that of pure blood," the censors also were confronted with a poem titled "History," unpunctuated in the original, which they translated as follows:

The flag falls to the ground
and from a radio box
comes the voice of a god—
hollow, trembling, sorrowful.
This moment must be recorded in history.

Falsely created pages of myth
are closed on this day.
People's eyes are newly opened
and gaze at the reality around them.

Appallingly ruined streets,
corpses already removed without a trace,
only resentment remains.
Harboring the resentment of those who perished in the
    conflagration,
weeds spread over the ruins.

August 15 piles upon August 15.
Between those who destroyed the country
and those who would rebuild the country,
a year of vehement battle.
A history of 365 days
pours into tomorrow's time.
Let us fill tomorrow's 24 hours
as historic hours.

It is perhaps a token of the censors' own uncertainty, as well as the poet's, that they disapproved only of the third stanza of "History"—letting stand Tsuboi's opening reference to the emperor as a god *(kami)*, as well as the ambiguous implications of his concluding allusion to those who had destroyed the country.[26]

The censors had no doubts at all, on the other hand, about the complete unacceptability of "Let Us Shake Hands," by the gifted woman poet Kurihara Sadako:

"Hello, American soldiers,"
    call out little militarists,
        throwing away their toy guns.
They were busy with their game of war
    until only yesterday.

"Hello, American soldiers," they call.
In their little hearts spring out longings
    toward people of unfamiliar race.

"Hello, American soldiers!
Was it you who fought our fathers
    until only yesterday?
But you smile at us brightly:
You are not the beast
    that grown-ups had made us believe."

We want to touch your big hands,
We want to shake hands with you.[27]

Sometimes the censors' responses to allusions to the war went beyond
hypersensitivity and seemed merely dim witted. A passing reference to the
death of a suicide pilot was censored from a story by Kawabata Yasunari.
Similarly, a short article by the popular writer Sakaguchi Ango that
praised the patriotic passion of those who had volunteered to die for their
country and expressed hope that disheartened veterans could now turn
that same selfless spirit into a force for peace was suppressed as "militaristic." The censors repressed as "nationalistic propaganda" this simple,
natural statement from a text for learning English: "If the war has taught
us what peace is worth, those whom today we remember will not have died
in vain." The following haiku, evoking a familiar scene in bombed-out
urban areas where people cultivated garden plots, was suppressed as "criticism of the United States":

Small green vegetables
are growing in the rain
along the burned street.

The same rationale lay behind the deletion from a boys' magazine of a
story that used seeds sprouting in Nagasaki as a metaphor for young
people throwing their energies into constructing a new Japan out of the
ruins.

This poem too was deemed beyond the pale:

It seems to be a dream far, far away
that we wielded bamboo spears
priced at only one yen and twenty sen
against the big guns and giant ships.

An American journalist writing in the Catholic magazine *Commonweal* in 1947 singled out this particular suppression as a typical example of SCAP's censorious oversensitivity, arguing that in fact these modest lines nicely reflected "the current preference of the Japanese for sardonic comments on their political and military immaturity—an attitude that is commendable both for its common sense and its humanity." His criticism provoked a florid response from Major Daniel Imboden, chief of the CI&E press division, who referred to the Japanese as "these strange and mysterious people" and exclaimed, "I thank God that General MacArthur established censorship."[28]

One of the most consequential censorship policies pertaining to the war involved nothing more than a change of nomenclature: the Japanese were forbidden to refer to their war in Asia as the Great East Asia War *(Dai Tōa Sensō)*, the name they had given it. Instead, they were required to use the term "Pacific War" *(Taiheiyō Sensō)*. Exactly who dictated this change, and when, are unclear, although it was routinely required on manuscripts from 1946 on. Certainly, the change amounted to an act of semantic imperialism with unexpected ramifications. Whereas the Japanese phrase, for all its jingoism, had clearly centered the war in China and Southeast Asia, the new term recentered it in the Pacific and gave unmistakable primacy to the conflict between Japan and the United States. There was nothing conspiratorial in this renaming of events. It merely reflected the reflexive ethnocentrism of the conquerors, who essentially had excluded Japan's Asian antagonists from any meaningful role in the occupation and now eliminated them from the very language by which the war was to be identified. Quite the opposite of reminding the Japanese of their war guilt, such a maladroit rectification of names facilitated the process of forgetting what they had done to their Asian neighbors.

Purifying the Victors

Where criticism of the occupation and Allied powers was concerned, the censors' files contain more than a little that borders on the ridiculous. A small dog was ordered deleted from a photograph of U.S. forces on parade because it detracted from the dignity of the troops. More commonly, it was the troops themselves and all their emblems (jeeps, English-language signs, and the like) that were expunged from the visual record—as if eliminating any sign of the occupation from films and photographs would somehow help the Japanese forget that they had no sovereignty.[29]

The public was denied the opportunity to see a cartoon about the re-markable efficiency with which the GIs took over Tokyo, and as a conse-quence of this little act of suppression never was introduced to the marvelously captioned observation that "the power of chewing gum is awe-some." Nor was the public allowed to read such witty *senryū,* or satirical haiku, as this:

> Only the jeeps
> seem to receive
> the May sunshine.[30]

At a different level of suppression, for some years the media were not allowed to refer directly to the huge monetary costs that the government was required to pay for maintenance of the occupation forces—amount-ing at one point to around one-third of the regular annual national bud-get. In 1946, the press was instructed to refer to occupation costs, if at all, as "war-termination costs" *(shūsen shorihi).* The following year, at the censors' command, this was further deflated to a benign "other items" in discussions of the budget.[31] The stultifying taboo of "criticism of Occu-pation forces" also meant that the Japanese could not dwell on the con-tradiction between soaring flights of rhetoric about freedom and democracy on the one hand, and gnawing hunger on the other. The cen-sors translated and then marked "Suppress" the following poem scheduled for the February 1948 issue of *Kaizō:*

> Whenever the time comes,
> "The meal is ready, grandfather,
> The meal is ready, grandmother," we say:
> And a stale meal is carried to grandfather and
>   grandmother,
> Consisting only of "haikyu" [rations].
> When anything is said against it,
> They're told to keep their mouths shut and eat it.
> In this way,
> Their existence is just like that of the nation.
> The nation is feasting on freedom,
> And is feasting as though it is trying to see
> How long it can live no matter how it lives.
> That is "haikyu."
> One morning,
> It was still too early to eat.

The peaches were blooming in the garden
When grandfather and grandmother went down to the
    garden;
They were stretching their bent backs
And were yawning toward Heaven.[32]

This was not exactly immortal literature. But the fact that two and a half years after defeat writers could still be prohibited from expressing such views says a great deal about "the sealed linguistic space" of the occupation period, as the critic Etō Jun has called it. Those who raised cynical questions about the swiftness with which yesterday's militaristic ultranationalists became today's peace-loving internationalists sometimes (by no means always) felt the censor's hook. Those who observed that politics was gelded under the occupation were often silenced. Three years after surrender, Baba Tsunego, one of the country's best-known newspapermen, still was unable to publish an article saying that postwar cabinets were mediocre because prime ministers had no choice but to be yes-men.[33]

One small casualty of such soft dictatorship was incisive political cartooning. The turn of the century had seen the emergence of an urbane cadre of social and political cartoonists, led by a brilliant Western-influenced illustrator, Kitazawa Rakuten. Rakuten and his colleagues (who often published their graphics in humor magazines that used the English "Puck" in their titles) offered sharp lampoons of cultural foibles, social inequities, and political corruption and abuse. From the 1930s on, incisive satire of the domestic situation was suppressed and a new generation of cartoonists came to dominate the scene, led by Kondō Hidezō, a gifted chameleon who rode with the political tides but never ceased to skewer his targets of the moment in a distinctive manner. Under Kondō's leadership, cartoonists initially claimed to be politically neutral and inspired only by a "healthy nihilism." They took pride, they said, in simply producing "nonsense cartoons," but before long they became, virtually without exception, avid propagandists for Japan's war.[34]

As also happened in the film industry, cartoonists escaped the post-surrender purges virtually unscathed and declared themselves champions of democracy with scarcely a moment's pause. Symbolic of this quick conversion, the monthly magazine *Manga* (Cartoon)—a major vehicle of wartime propaganda—resumed publication in January 1946 with a cover illustration by Kondō depicting a hapless General Tōjō behind jail-house bars. Kondō and others also lent their considerable talents to new left-wing

publications such as the tabloid *Mimpō* (People's Report). Yet these cartoonists quickly learned that democracy had its limits. The same maiden
postwar issue of *Manga* was not permitted to print a Kondō graphic depicting a kimono-clad woman dancing with a big GI. Two months later,
in the March issue, the censors suppressed the graphic of another well-
known cartoonist, Sugiura Yoshio, in which a cigarette-smoking, GI-
servicing panpan prostitute stood beside a homeless man. The source of
the streetwalker's relative prosperity was not exactly disguised: she was
wearing a kimono and *haori* jacket with a Stars-and-Stripes design. "Get
a job," she told the homeless man; on the wall behind her was a left-wing
poster reading "Overthrow the Emperor System."

Sugiura's witty sally was a triple abomination to CCD. It attacked the
emperor, highlighted the economic crisis, and called attention to the fraternization of GIs with Japanese women. Nor could the victors tolerate a
clever graphic in another magazine, ridiculing the exclusion of the emperor
from the impending war-crimes trials. Depicting a large MP shepherding
Japan's wartime leaders into custody, the cartoon carried the cynical caption, "Leaving the lord behind, everyone has gone."[35]

The emperor was not formally off limits to satire, and for a while a few
publications—especially the left-wing monthly *Shinsō* (Truth)—did venture to make him a cartoon subject.[36] After 1947, however, even mild satire
about the throne largely disappeared. The more significant official restraint
on satirizing authority involved the foreigner who actually reigned over the
country. General MacArthur was as sacrosanct as the emperor had been
before his descent from heaven. (A European who worked as a censor for
CCD amused himself by privately redesignating the division SPCD as an
acronym for Society for the Prevention of Criticism of Douglas.)[37] Below
him, the occupation forces, from highest officer down to lowest-ranking
enlisted man or civilian employee, were similarly insulated from criticism—indeed, from anything but laudatory portrayal. As a matter of policy, top occupation officials also were unavailable to the media for
interviews. SCAP communicated its policies largely by press conferences
and handouts that the media were expected to report dutifully, an ex
cathedra structure of "channeled news" that foreign journalists recognized as setting a dangerous precedent.[38]

To lampoon the prospects for—or the nature of—democracy in
MacArthur's Japan was a risky undertaking. The humor magazine *Van*
learned this lesson when several cartoons were ordered deleted from its
issue of October 1947. In one, a small MacArthur faced a large but
friendly dragon labeled "Japan" with a rope around its neck and a saddle

identified as "Democracy" on its back. MacArthur was murmuring, "Well, somehow I've tamed it." For any American newspaper or magazine of the time, this would have been a commonplace depiction of the formidable challenges the occupation faced and MacArthur's partial and still uncertain success in meeting them. CCD's censors, however, interpreted the cartoon as criticizing MacArthur by representing him as being unable to get into the saddle, and so "having a difficult time in democratizing Japan."[39]

This is not to say that the period of occupation failed to stimulate clever and amusing cartoons. The greatest of postwar comic strips, Hasegawa Machiko's *Sazae-san,* made its debut in April 1946 and consistently provided an engaging, witty, and female-centered (the artist was a woman) running commentary on the ups and downs of daily family life, dominated by an exceedingly spunky wife-mother-daughter-sister named Sazae. In *Anmitsu Hime* (Princess Bean Jam), young girls were treated to an extroverted medieval cartoon princess whose silly name conveyed her passion for a popular sweet. Tezuka Osamu, the country's most inventive and venerated cartoonist, made his postwar debut in 1946 by leaving the confines of Japan for an imagined world of androids and humanoids that posed provocative questions about science, human nature, and personal identity as well as good and evil.[40]

As these examples indicate, the best cartooning was to be found outside the realm of politics. Editorial cartoonists such as the *Asahi*'s Shimzu Kon did become well known for their bemused renderings of the antics of easy-to-caricaturize politicians such as Prime Minister Yoshida. As Shimizu observed, though, even he and cartoonists like him did not really produce political cartoons, but rather "cartoons about the political world" *(seikai manga)*.[41] With but occasional exceptions, they offered no sustained political vision, no biting critique of the misuses of power and authority, no cosmopolitan world view. The occupation's modus operandi made the public development of such a critical vision next to impossible. If we were to rely on just the visual record left by cartoons, this would seem to have been an occupation virtually bereft of occupiers.

The same rationale that prohibited fundamental criticism of occupation policies extended to criticism of the Allied powers in general, for to speak badly of the victors would undermine their moral authority. This meant that the outside world, too, had to be sanitized for Japanese consumption. The left-wing monthly *Kaizō* offers a small case study in the types of statements about the victorious Allies and their world that could be deemed to be in violation of the Press Code. As Professor Furukawa Atsushi has documented, *Kaizō* was required to delete references to racial prejudices toward peoples of color among the Western Allies; mention of the surrender of Japanese troops to Kuomintang (Nationalist) rather than Communist forces in China; an allusion to the denial of voting rights to blacks in the United States; descriptions of the Soviet Union as "socialistic," the United States and Great Britain as "capitalistic," and China as "semicolonial"; mention of tension between the "democratic" U.S.S.R. and "reactionary imperialistic" United States; an expression of fear that Japan might become subordinated to international capital; a description of fascism as a manifestation of "capitalistic contradictions"; and criticism of capitalism in general (by, for example, well-known Marxist scholars such as Hani Gōrō).

Nor was this the end of the journal's transgressions. In mid-1946, *Kaizō* also was required to delete the following line from the translation of an article about Korea by the American journalist Edgar Snow: "A certain high U.S. official privately told me that 'Korea is now part of the new U.S. front line,' and this reflects the thinking of a majority of the high command." The censor marked this "untrue." In the occupation's new historiography, "general criticism of Allies" even extended back to medieval and early modern times. Thus in August 1947, *Kaizō* was required to remove a passage from an essay entitled "Dante and Columbus" which stated that in the historical development of European nations such as Spain, Portugal, Holland, and Britain, there was a predominant tendency to acquire new lands as colonies. In October 1948, the magazine, by now formally identified as "ultra-leftist" on CCD's watch list, was not permitted to state that there were plans afoot to create a committee on "un-Japanese activities" modeled on the House Un-American Activities Committee in the U.S. Congress. Although such a committee did not materialize, it was being considered at the time.[42]

Other publications were subjected to comparably close vetting. A famous turn-of-the-century Christian convert, Uchimura Kanzō, was subjected to posthumous censorship in the reprint of an autobiographical work. The offensive text referred to an early period in his life when he was in the United States and mentioned that there were more murders and alcoholics in New York than in Tokyo—to which the CCD censor responded that, although this might well be true, it was too early to let the Japanese know it.[43] Even trivia such as passing reference to the youthful poker-playing skill of former U.S. Secretary of State Cordell Hull were ordered deleted. An autobiographical account of a Japanese former POW interned at Camp McCoy in Wisconsin passed the censors' scrutiny in mid-1946 with only these sentences deleted: "The Americans give the impression of being educated, but they're surprisingly ignorant. They actually believe what they read in the papers. As gullible as the Japanese are, there's hardly one of us left who still does that." The Japanese editors of an English-language dictionary failed to smuggle in this example of the use of the verb *denounce:* "No imperialism is more denounced today than the imperialism of the United States."[44]

These remarkably close and nervous readings extended to passing comments critical of America's allies in the recent war. Censored "criticism of China" included references to the postsurrender use of Japanese troops in the Chinese civil war, abuse of Japanese repatriates, and characterization of the country as "emerging from a semi-colonial or colonial situation." Discussion of the civil war itself was not taboo, but graphic descriptions of China's chaotic upheaval could be regarded as exceeding the limits of propriety.[45]

For a while, such repression extended to negative comments about the Soviet Union. The philosopher Tanabe Hajime was censored in January 1946 for expressing apprehension about the Soviet role in the occupation, and the elderly parliamentarian Ozaki Yukio, writing in *Kaizō* in April 1946, was not permitted to speak in passing of repression in the Soviet Union. An article on Reinhold Niebuhr's book *Children of Light, Children of Darkness* in the November 1946 issue of *Shisō no Kagaku* (Science of Ideas) was heavily censored for criticizing Stalin's despotism. Even as late as September 1948, when Cold War tensions were unmistakable in occupied Japan, the following passage was deleted from the monthly *Sekai* for being "critical of Russia": "The USSR is administering her own country by an absolute, autocratic policy, so she takes the same high-handed autocratic attitude toward the smaller nations."[46]

This mystique of the immaculate Allies contributed to the fashioning of a public world that was not merely unreal, but sometimes almost surreal. Isolated from the rest of the world, the defeated Japanese were supposed to ignore the collapse of the victorious wartime alliance, the breakup of national unity in China, the renewed struggles against Western imperialism and colonialism in Asia, the decisive emergence of Cold War tensions, and the beginnings of a nuclear arms race. They were placed, as it were, in a small time warp, where the World War II propaganda of the winning side had to be reiterated even as the erstwhile victors engaged in new struggles and polemics.

In this world the Japanese could not express concern that competition among the victorious powers "in regard to atomic energy is not a welcome phenomenon from the standpoint of the establishment of world peace" (censored as "general criticism of the Allies" in May 1946); in which it was impermissible to warn that "above all, Korea today forms the contacting point of America and the Soviet Union, as well as having deep bearing with the international destinies of both countries" (censored in January 1947); in which, long after the West had adopted the rhetoric of the Iron Curtain, Japanese writers could be prohibited from reporting that "the clash of opinions between America and the Soviets is being widely circulated at present," or from expressing hopes that this would not lead to open conflict in the future (censored as "disturbing the public tranquility" in December 1947).[47]

Policing the Cinema

In the course of six and a half years of occupation, Japanese movie studios produced around one thousand feature films. Up to 1949, two copies of every screenplay had to be submitted *in English* in advance to SCAP's "advisers," and on numerous occasions a great deal of give-and-take took place before a script emerged that was satisfactory to the Americans. Some directors, such as Kurosawa Akira, flourished despite these constraints; others, such as Kamei Fumio, never found a firm postwar footing.[48]

To Kurosawa, GHQ's controls were trivial compared with those imposed by wartime censors, whom he regarded as idiots perverted by, among other things, emperor worship and repressed sexual fantasies. Kurosawa had made his directorial debut during the war, and all four of his wartime films—*Sugata Sanshirō* (the name of the film's hero) and its sequel; *Ichiban Utsukushiku* (The Most Beautiful); and the incomplete *Tora no O o Fumu Otokotachi* (Men Who Tread on the Tiger's Tail)—were included among a total of 236 "feudal and militaristic" films that SCAP ordered destroyed in November 1945.[49] This did not prevent Kurosawa from quickly emerging as the most influential cinematic innovator of the new Japan. Between 1946 and 1952 he produced eight films, beginning with the naively idealistic "democracy film" *Waga Seishun ni Kuinashi* (No Regrets for Our Youth, 1946), which was followed by a meandering tale of romance and mishap amid the ruins entitled *Subarashiki Nichiyōbi* (One Wonderful Sunday, 1947).

As the occupation unfolded, Kurosawa continued to address contemporary themes, but the hope and idealism of these films gave way to a darker vision. His prototypical protagonist became male rather than female (as had been the case in *No Regrets for Our Youth* as well as *The Most Beautiful*)—a generally humanistic individual who sometimes was cursed by the past and almost always found himself mired in a venal, duplicitous society. In film after film, this protagonist, invariably played by Mifune Toshirō, moved through an increasingly dismal milieu of gangsters (*Yoidore Tenshi*, Drunken Angel, 1948), ex-soldiers turned criminals (*Nora Inu*, Stray Dog, 1949), venal journalists (*Shūbun*, Scandal, 1950), and helpless, deranged innocents (*Hakuchi*, based on Dostoevsky's novel *The Idiot*, 1951). Even his masterful *Rashōmon*, released in 1950 and set in medieval times, held a mirror to the contemporary scene in its portrayal of sexuality, crime, and ambiguity—and the relativity of all stories people tell.[50]

Kamei Fumio's experience was the opposite of Kurosawa's. Where Kurosawa shrugged off GHQ's surveillance and moved imaginatively within the boundaries of the permissible, Kamei—more overtly idealistic and ideological—came to personify the forbidden terrain of the new censored democracy. This became clear when Kamei found it impossible to screen a short documentary titled *Nihon no Higeki* (The Tragedy of Japan) in 1946 and then was forced to make extensive cuts in *Sensō to Heiwa* (Between War and Peace), an ambitious feature film he codirected with Yamamoto Satsuo.

The Tragedy of Japan drew primarily on wartime footage to present a scathing analysis of the ruling-class forces that had led Japan into an aggressive and disastrous war. Kamei's crisp montage style, based on skillful editing of the government's own propaganda newsreels, was similar to that of Frank Capra, the premier director of propaganda films for the U.S. military during the war. There was more than a little irony in this. The *pièce de résistance* of Capra's cut-and-splice art was the anti-Japanese film entitled *Know Your Enemy—Japan*, released less than a year before Kamei's *Tragedy* appeared. Although Kamei's 1946 film hewed fairly closely to a line of Marxist analysis endorsed by the Japan Communist Party (the so-called *Kōza-ha* line), emphasizing feudal legacies and ruling-group militarism and repression under the emperor system, it was not fundamentally at variance with Capra's wartime propaganda.

By far the most memorable scene in Kamei's documentary (one that Capra surely would have applauded) was a dissolve in which Emperor Hirohito was transformed before the viewer's eyes from the nation's rigid, uniformed commander into a benign, slightly stooping civilian figure, modestly garbed in necktie, overcoat, and soft felt hat. The major studios Tōhō, Shōchiku, and Nikkatsu all refused to show the documentary in their theaters, apparently more for financial than ideological considerations, and Kamei later recalled how at early screenings some viewers hooted and one threw a wooden clog at the screen. This was a marginal film, but one just beginning to attract curious audiences—about twenty-five hundred people a day—when it was abruptly banned by GHQ in mid-August 1946.

A leftist but non-Communist film maker, Kamei had studied documentary techniques in the Soviet Union in the late 1920s. His was a unique experience of having films suppressed by both the imperial army and General MacArthur's command. His brooding 1939 documentary of the war in China, *Tatakau Heitai* (Fighting Soldiers), had been made with the official sponsorship of the military but was immediately withdrawn for being "defeatist." (The film's nickname among insiders was *Tsukareta Heitai*, or "Exhausted Soldiers.") In a roughly comparable manner, Kamei received strong support from American officials in the Civil Information and Education Section in preparing his documentary, only to have General Willoughby personally intervene and order all prints and negatives confiscated some three weeks after its release.[51]

Willoughby's intervention came at the request of Prime Minister Yoshida, who regarded Kamei's treatment of the emperor as lese majesty and succeeded in persuading two of the general's aides to view this sacrilege with him. On its own part, the Willoughby camp was more troubled by the implicit criticism of the occupation's policy of exonerating Hirohito from war responsibility. As Kamei and others later observed, the supression of the documentary essentially marked the moment when serious debate concerning imperial war responsibility disappeared. The overt rationale for withdrawing the film was that such "radical treatment of the emperor," as one of the Americans who viewed the documentary with Yoshida put it, might "well provoke riots and disturbances."[52]

Suppression of *The Tragedy of Japan* carried at least three lessons for those trying to gauge what SCAP's "democracy" meant in practice. It revealed, first of all, not merely the persistence of absolute authority, but also its arbitrariness. What GHQ had censored, after all, was a purely Japanese criticism of militarism and the abuse of authority in presurrender Japan, precisely the type of free and critical discussion the occupation claimed it hoped to promote. Kamei and his staff had been encouraged to undertake this project by CI&E officials and had then dutifully moved it through the censorship apparatus and received official approval to release it. Iwasaki Akira, the producer, was thunderstruck when told the film had been ordered withdrawn, and Willoughby himself privately acknowledged that the documentary did not actually violate censorship policy. Kamei's dry response was that he had not changed since his trouble with the Imperial Army seven years previously and apparently circumstances had not changed much either.[53]

A second lesson, carefully taken in by media people, was that serious criticism could carry an intolerably heavy price tag. Despite its reliance on already existing footage, *The Tragedy of Japan* proved expensive to produce for Nichiei, the studio that backed it. The film's suppression pushed the company close to bankruptcy and provided a compelling warning to anyone else who might be contemplating playing with controversy. Individuals working in the print media, where delays as well as outright suppression could be financially devastating, were likewise keenly attuned to the accounting costs of expressing what they truly thought.[54]

The third lesson to be gleaned from the film's abrupt suppression was ideological: the purpose of censorship was changing, moving slowly but inexorably from militaristic and ultranationalistic targets to left-wing ones. If this changing focus was still blurred in 1946, it had become much clearer by the time Kamei and Yamamoto were completing their ambitious feature film *Between War and Peace*.

CCD's lower-level censors revealed their erudition with an early notation on the screenplay to the effect that the film's title was "apparently taken from Dostoevski's famous novel." Although the title came from Tolstoy, the story line—of a soldier, long given up for dead, who returns home after the war to find that his wife has married his close friend—actually came from D. W. Griffith's innovative 1911 movie *Enoch Arden*.[55] Like *Tragedy*, the 1947 film was initially officially encouraged—in this instance by the government, at GHQ's insistence, to commemorate the ideals of the new constitution. The major studios were being urged to produce films exemplifying certain principles in the new national charter, and Kamei and Yamamoto were selected by Tōhō to direct a feature conveying the antimilitarist spirit of Article 9. After being shepherded by CI&E, the film was submitted in mid-May to the Civil Censorship Division, where it immediately came under intense criticism as a vehicle for "several Communist propaganda lines." A secret memorandum of mid-June characterized these as "glorification of demonstrations, identification of the Emperor with discreditable groups, overplaying post-surrender starvation in Japan and decadence in morals." The film, this memorandum went on to note, fell into a "sensitive" category similar to that of *The Tragedy of Japan*.

Other memos spelled out these "Communist propaganda lines" more concretely. Scenes of labor strikes and demonstrations, for example, were excised as "incitement to unrest and criticism of SCAP." As the censors put it, "Demonstrators carrying banners and posters such as 'Freedom of Speech,' 'Let us who work eat,' and watchers cheering and joining the marchers etc. are suggestive of criticizing SCAP censorship and encouraging labor strife." An episode involving thuggish strikebreakers was drastically cut on the grounds that it suggested a link (not, in fact, implausible) between right-wing strikebreakers and emperor-system ultranationalists. These scenes, it was claimed, also entailed "subtly intended criticism of U.S." by showing one of the principal characters being beaten up by the strikebreakers in a manner "suggestive of American 'gangster' methods."

The censors also discerned both criticism of the victors and a "Communist" emphasis on moral decadence in a passing shot of a man with his back to the camera negotiating with a streetwalker and in a cabaret scene in which the walls were decorated with posters of Hollywood actresses and pictures of Caucasian nudes. Although CI&E officials had assured the Japanese that kissing on the silver screen was the open and democratic thing to do, scenes that mingled promiscuous kissing with jitterbugging and other nightlife activities were here deemed "criticism of U.S. suggestive that such display of public affection is due to American influence."

Although many of the scenes that upset the censors involved unflattering portrayals of social and political conditions under the occupation, *Between War and Peace* was from start to finish a wrenching antiwar melodrama. Repatriated from China years after being declared dead, the protagonist returns to find that his wife has married his former best friend. The friend, traumatized to the point of insanity by his battlefield experience in China, has become de facto father to the protagonist's son. In miserable living conditions, the wife supports her reconstructed family by piecework. The viewer is introduced to many scenes that linger in the mind's eye: the terror of combat, the suffering and generosity of the Chinese, the air raids on Tokyo, the squalid living conditions of the postwar scene, tough street orphans and youthful prostitutes, the corruption of former military officers, the hedonistic escapism of life on the margins. Where did the responsibility for all this misery and degradation lie?

The film's answer—which unnerved the censors—was that responsibility lay with "greedy people" who had taken advantage of the emperor-centered socialization for war. When the shell-shocked ex-soldier plunged into madness after discovering his predicament and exclaimed *"Tennō Heika Banzai!"* (Long Live the Emperor!), imagining himself back on the killing fields, the censors identified this as "criticism of SCAP," on the grounds that "SCAP has recognized the Emperor system, and the scene is an attempt to belittle the system by inferring that only ex-soldiers who have gone insane ever think of their Emperor." The flashback survived, but the offending phrase was excised.

In the end, CCD backed off on a number of its reviewers' initial criticisms but required that at least seventeen sections totaling around thirty minutes be deleted from the rough cut that had been approved by CI&E in May. Even after these excisions, *Between War and Peace* still emerged as one of the grittiest postsurrender films about Japan, a rarity in the way it conveyed a visceral sense of the misery, sleaziness, tensions, hopes, and passions of those years. Despite the censors' interventions, the film's left-wing vision, driven by idealism more than ideology, remained unmistakable. Japan's Chinese victims were portrayed with a sympathy rare anywhere in Japan at that time. The film's three protagonists, their fates grotesquely twisted by the war, eventually came to exemplify an almost impossibly high order of forgiveness and love. Eloquently and with quintessential simplicity, the film's closing words—spoken against a background of children playing in a schoolyard—evoked the dream of a new generation that could be educated to cherish peace and democracy. And for all this, there was a receptive audience. Critics praised *Between War and Peace* as one of the finest films of the year, and large crowds flocked to see it. Kamei was to have no chance to repeat this accomplishment, however, for thereafter he found it increasingly difficult to get work as a director.

In ways that went beyond what had to be left on the cutting-room floor, even *Beyond War and Peace,* for all its ambition, ultimately failed to convey the political and social milieu of the time. For there were, quite simply, no Americans. There was no occupation. Alien authority was invisible. This was as it had to be. Especially in the early years of the occupation, filmmakers and other photographers and graphic artists had been instructed to turn their eyes away from the American presence. Exceptions to this injunction were tolerated, but only where the image of the conqueror was bland and benign. Soon after the occupation ended, the director Yamamoto Kajirō reminisced about how difficult it had been to film in Tokyo. Directors were supposed to avoid GIs, jeeps, English-language signs, and buildings controlled by the occupation forces, not to speak of terribly burned-out areas. Even a verbal mention of "being burned-out" was excised from one of Yamamoto's scripts, while the sound of an airplane was ordered silenced in one of his sound tracks. Since there were no Japanese planes at this time, such sound effects could only represent U.S. military aircraft—and, as such, were interpreted as signifying criticism of the occupation.[56]

The "occupied" screen did not merely offer a new imagined world. It also made things disappear.

Curbing the Political Left

Formally, SCAP censorship gradually tapered off beginning in 1947 and was terminated in October 1949, when CCD was dissolved. Traditional theater was removed from preperformance censorship in mid-1947, beginning with Bunraku puppet theater in May, followed by Kabuki in June, and Noh in September. *Chūshingura*, the classic drama of the "forty-seven loyal retainers," returned to the Kabuki stage in November with an all-star cast. (It had been feared that such tales of feudal loyalty and revenge might incite violent reprisals against the newly arrived occupation forces.) After August 1947, most radio scripts no longer required prebroadcast approval, and phonograph records were removed from prerelease strictures three months later. In October, all but fourteen book publishers were shifted from pre- to postpublication censorship, and by September 1948 the remaining companies were also freed of having to clear their manuscripts at the galley-proof stage. All but twenty-eight magazines were placed on postpublication surveillance status by December 1947, with the exceptions remaining subject to prepublication approval until October 1949. All major newspapers and news services were removed from prepublication scrutiny by the end of July 1948.

This easing of formal controls was misleading, however, for censorship assumed new forms after 1947 and did not end in 1949. CCD's sprawling bureaucracy actually peaked numerically in 1948, well after the U.S. State Department had complained that the censorship operation had "the effect of continuing the authoritarian tradition in Japan." As liberal officers increasingly left GHQ and were replaced by more conservative technocrats, censorship became more stringent, arbitrary, and unpredictable. More subtle and pernicious, in the print media in particular, the shift from prepublication to postpublication censorship had a chilling rather than a liberating effect on many publishers, editors, and writers, for it made them more vulnerable to financial disaster should occupation authorities find their published product unacceptable and demand that a newspaper, magazine, or book be recalled. Ambiguity and arbitrariness served SCAP's purposes particularly well in the context of economic instability, for few publishers could take the risk of being censored after putting their product on the market. As a consequence, caution and self-censorship became ever more apparent as the occupation progressed.[57]

The tactics of intimidation took other forms as well. While prepublication censorship was in effect, higher GHQ officials sometimes simply "held" or deliberately misplaced articles that were not technically in violation of the Press Code but nonetheless were deemed undesirable, thereby creating havoc with deadlines. This happened to many controversial articles submitted to CCD by *Akahata* (Red Flag), the official newspaper of the Japan Communist Party, and was known to be a favorite practice of Don Brown, the influential head of CI&E's Information Division, to whom CCD often referred controversial materials. GHQ officials were also able informally to reward or punish publishers by manipulating the rationing of paper, which remained in short supply for most of the occupation period. Another subtle form of leverage over what could be read was GHQ's control over the licensing of foreign books for translation, which required approval from Brown's office in CI&E.[58]

A blunter instrument lay in the ability of American officials to demand that writers or editors who displeased them be summarily fired. SCAP's early purge directives (in December 1945) had included only a small number of high-level media executives, and the formal categorical purge of influential media officials associated with militaristic and ultranationalistic propaganda prior to Pearl Harbor did not even begin until late 1947. When this astonishingly belated media purge ended in May 1948, some 2,295 individuals had been screened and 1,066 purged (of whom 857 had already resigned or retired).[59]

These public "old-war" purges had hardly ended before GHQ officials began informally demanding that management fire writers and editors whom the Americans deemed unacceptable for Cold War reasons. In October 1948, for example, Suzuki Toshisada, the publisher of the magazine *Nihon Hyōron* (Japan Review), was told by Major Daniel Imboden of CI&E to fire his assistant editor, whose offenses included trying to publish articles by the progressive Canadian historian-diplomat E. H. Norman (on free speech) and the well-known Communist Itō Ritsu (on the "new fascism"). If he failed to do this, Suzuki was told, he might well find himself being tried before a military tribunal and sent to penal service in Okinawa. The assistant editor "resigned" that month. Shortly afterward, in the so-called December Incident, four editors at *Kaizō* were forced to step down in circumstances so similar that they even involved a Nisei official from GHQ visiting *Kaizō's* offices to invoke the same threat of "hard labor" in Okinawa. Such crude threats had weight because of yet another dimension of the censorship operation: Okinawa, under the draconian control of the United States, was shrouded in secrecy as the Americans built the strategically situated island into a major Cold War military base. Throughout the occupation, and indeed until 1955, no news reports or commentaries about Okinawa were published in the press, making the image of that virtually invisible prefecture as a penal colony seem perfectly reasonable.[60]

The threat of bringing dissident editors before a military tribunal and sentencing them to hard labor was an extreme but not entirely idle one. One of the more egregious abuses of the censorship authority occurred in September 1948 in an altogether absurd incident involving a sports newspaper. The incident began with an article published in the May 27, 1948 issue of *Nikkan Supōtsu* (Daily Sports) under the headline "Mr. Thompson to Introduce American Nude Show to Big Theater." After observing a striptease in the Asakusa theater district, an official in GHQ's entertainment section was quoted as commenting to Japanese reporters that the strippers were not very impressive and he would like to introduce them to a real American burlesque show.

Although the report was accurate and had been passed by CCD's censors, it was retroactively deemed to impugn SCAP's dignity, and formal prosecution procedures were initiated. On September 1, a U.S. military tribunal sentenced the editor to one year at hard labor, suspended publication of *Nikkan Supōtsu* for six months, and levied a heavy fine of 75,000 yen on the paper—all on the formal grounds that Article 2 of the Press Code (disturbing public tranquility) had been violated. On appeal, the editor's sentence and the newspaper's suspension were overturned, but the steep fine was reaffirmed. In less frivolous proceedings a year later, three Communist editors were tried and sentenced to hard labor for publishing inflammatory propaganda.[61]

At first glance, the Thompson affair itself might appear a burlesque. To media people trying to gauge the parameters of permissible expression, however, it seemed reasonable to interpret such incidents as reflecting a deliberate, systematic arbitrariness. The outrageous striptease case, after all, went on for months, extended far beyond the foibles or momentary excesses of some GHQ underling, and dramatically revealed the heavy price that could be exacted for even petty and inadvertent transgressions of what the supreme military authorities deemed proper.

The *Nihon Hyōron* and *Kaizō* cases, on the other hand, were ideologically explicit: they made clear that the major target of censorship now was left-wing rather than right-wing thought. This was no secret in media circles. Indeed, the very process of moving away from the initial procedure of prepublication censorship had involved the explicit stigmatization of the left as the new enemy of democracy. This became a virtually open policy in December 1947, when, of the twenty-eight periodicals left subject to prepublication censorship, only two were "ultra-rightist" (with a combined readership of approximately four thousand readers). The remaining twenty-six magazines were progressive and left-wing publications with a combined circulation of over 600,000. Among them were some of the best known journals of opinion in Japan, including *Chūō Kōron* (circulation 80,000) and *Kaizō* (50,000), both of which had been suppressed by the imperial government during the war; *Sekai no Ugoki* (World Trends; 50,000), a weekly published by the *Mainichi* newspaper; *Sekai Keizai Hyōron* (World Economic Review; 50,000), which the censors characterized as being "directed toward picking out 'defects' in the capitalist system" and predicting the eventual triumph of Soviet socialism; and *Sekai* (30,000), which was regarded as moderate on domestic issues but having "adopted the usual Communist line" in its criticism of the United States, Britain, and capitalism.

The twenty-six periodicals represented only a small percentage of existing progressive and left-wing publications. The thrust of CCD policy, however, was to weaken socialist, communist, and Marxist influence by example, through the harassment and vetting of the most influential and prestigious purveyors of such views. Here, for example, is how the censors confidentially explained their decision to include the monthly *Chōryū* (The Tide; circulation 30,000) on the list. *Chōryū*, they wrote, "rates as the most important of the leftist publications. Contributors are chiefly leftist scholars who are analytical in their analyses of the world's industrial, agricultural, financial, social and political problems but whose conclusions are invariably anti-capitalistic and destructive. Their arguments are for the most part free from the bombastic outbursts peculiar to rabid Communist commentators, but are presented in such learned and exhaustive fashion as to be very effective for propaganda purposes."[62] Much the same could have been said about the often prestigious contributors to some of the other targeted journals, whose arguments went far beyond the simplistic recitation of Marxist mantras. Editors at the Iwanami publishing house, which issued *Sekai*, found that in general the censors tended to hold them to more stringent anti-Marxist standards than were applied to other publishers, on the grounds that they should be restrained from lending prestige to the political left.[63]

Robert Spaulding, who rose to be chief of the Press, Pictorial, and Broadcast Division within CCD, later acknowledged that the censors became concerned with "antidemocratic" criticism of SCAP and the United States from the left as well as the right virtually simultaneously with the proclamation of civil liberties on October 4, 1945. One of the earliest radio programs promoted by CI&E, doubly titled *The Patriot's Hour* and *Prisoners Speak Out*, was designed to give political prisoners recently released from jail an opportunity to express their views on the evils of the past and the prospects for a new Japan. In December, however, the program was dropped after it became apparent that most of these individuals were Marxists and Communists. CCD began to prepare detailed internal surveys of Soviet influence and left-wing and Communist trends in the Japanese media before the end of 1946, although it was not until around mid-1947 that "Leftist Propaganda" appeared as an explicit category on the key logs.[64]

A huge amount of leftist analysis did pass through the net—some incisive, some mind-numbingly formulaic. On the other hand, even lionized "soft" Marxist economists and industrial relations specialists such as Arisawa Hiromi, Ōuchi Hyōe, and Ōkōchi Kazuo, who were allowed to reach a large audience, all suffered minor censorship at one point or another.[65] Prominent historians such as Hirano Yoshitarō and Shinobu Seizaburō faced more sweeping suppression in mid-1947, when their long essays (on "The History of the Bourgeois Democratic Movement in Japan" and "Revolution and Counter-revolution in the Meiji Restoration" respectively) were ordered to be deleted entirely from a volume on "Tasks of the Japanese People's Revolution" in a series sponsored by Tokyo University.[66]

From the American point of view, the tapering off of formal censorship posed a dilemma, for it coincided with adoption of the conservative "reverse course" in occupation policy and a predictable heightening of left-wing criticism. On April 30, 1948, the central Press, Pictorial and Broadcast division within CCD was ordered to conduct "100 percent surveillance" of the Communist media, largely for purposes of intelligence rather than direct control. Early in 1949, the conservative government, with SCAP's concurrence, cut the rationed allotment of newsprint to official Communist publications from 86,000 to 20,000 pounds per month.[67] The "Red purge" that the Yoshida government conducted with GHQ's active cooperation beginning in late 1949 initially did not seriously affect the media, for it was carried out against radicalized employees in the public sector in the name of "retrenchment" or "rationalization" or comparable euphemisms. In the wake of the outbreak of the Korean War on June 25,

1950, however, the Red purges spilled over into the private sector and, among many other fields of activity, swept through publishing and film making, as well as public radio.

Although the beginning of the Korean War was the trigger for a media purge of "ultra-leftists," the gun had been cocked several weeks before the war began. On June 6, General MacArthur ordered that the entire Central Committee of the Communist Party be purged, and on the following day the purge was extended to seventeen top editors of *Akahata,* the official JCP newspaper. The party itself remained a legal political organization. In justifying the purge of the Central Committee, MacArthur declared that recent inflammatory statements and lawless acts by Communists "bear striking parallel to those by which the militaristic leaders of the past deceived and misled the Japanese people, and their aims, if achieved would surely lead Japan to an even worse disaster. To permit this incitation to lawlessness to continue unchecked, however embryonic it may at present appear, would be to risk ultimate suppression of Japan's democratic institutions in direct negation of the purpose and intent of Allied policy pronouncements, forfeiture of her chance for political independence, and destruction of the Japanese race."[68]

On June 26, the day after the Korean War began, *Akahata* was ordered to cease publishing (for thirty days initially, but this was later amended to indefinite suspension). Within three weeks, some seven hundred Communist and left-wing papers had been shut down, and by October 1950 such indefinite suspensions had been extended to 1,387 publications by the official SCAP account (approximately 1,700 by another calculation). Although General MacArthur and the conservative government that carried out his directives justified these purges and suppressions by equating Communist leaders with the militarists in prewar Japan, to many the more obvious historical counterpart was the prewar repression of left-wing protest against militarism and oppression. Since the media were immediately placed under immense pressure to follow the official U.S. position regarding the conflict in Korea, the parallel to imperial Japan's enforcement of a single voice for the "hundred million" seemed all the more apt.[69]

Suspension of the left-wing press was accompanied by expansion of the Red purge in the public sector and its extension into the private sector. The primary thrust of these firings was to undermine left-wing influence in organized labor, but the witch-hunts also altered what was read, heard, and seen in the mass media. Over 700 individuals were removed from journalistic circles, between 104 and 119 from broadcasting (the tally sheets vary), and 137 from the film industry. Most of these individuals had

been summarily dismissed by September. Whereas the initial GHQ suspensions had targeted "ultra-leftist" publications, many with small circu-
lations, the Red purges struck at the mainstream. The purge of public
radio, for example, was carried out in various cities on July 28, 1950 and
involved posting the names of individuals who were to be expelled immediately from the broadcasting facilities. In some cities (such as Osaka),
it reportedly was stated that this was being done in accordance with General MacArthur's orders, and American MPs participated in the expulsion
of designated individuals.[70]

The first wave of Red purges in the mainstream press took place the
same day. Where the private sector was involved, dismissals were handled
in various ways. At the *Asahi,* persons designated to be purged were summoned one by one to the office of a pale and clearly shaken company executive. At the *Yomiuri,* where bitter conflict between management and
staff had prevailed since 1946, the dismissals were announced by an official flanked by plainclothes police and company guards, and were declared to be in accordance with General MacArthur's letter of June 6. At
the Kyōdō news agency, employees who attempted to stay on after their
dismissal was announced were forced out by armed police called in by
management. In the film industry, the purges were carried out in September, after a high official in GHQ's labor section summoned studio executives and ordered them to expel all Communists from their companies,
but to take the responsibility for doing so themselves.[71]

Although GHQ never resorted to the sort of systematic suppression of
left-wing expression that the imperial government had carried out under
the Peace Preservation Law, its shutdowns, harassments, and witch-hunts
served their intended purpose. Many progressive and left-wing publications folded; others took a conservative editorial turn.[72] Beyond this, however, more than a few genuinely idealistic supporters of democracy became
disillusioned and moved from early enthusiastic support of the United
States to cynicism or outright anti-Americanism. The purges also confirmed the more doctrinaire Left in its self-righteous condemnations of
bourgeois hypocrisies.

Did SCAP's regimen of censored democracy really matter when set
against the larger developments and accomplishments of the occupation
period? The answer is: yes. Quantitatively, to be sure, the number of overt
cases of blue-pencil censorship was miniscule compared to the overall deluge of words in print. The media undeniably were vastly more lively at
the end of the occupation than they had been during the war. At the same

time, however, they became less dynamic and diversified as the occupation dragged on. Certainly to liberals and leftists who had chafed under wartime repression and had been surprised and gladdened by the vigor of the early postsurrender reforms, it was disheartening to discover the pleasure Americans took in exercising absolute authority—and dishearteningly familiar to observe the reflexive animosity they soon exhibited to those who disagreed with them.

Iwasaki Akira, who had been involved in shooting the footage of the atomic destruction of Hiroshima and Nagasaki that the Americans confiscated, and who went on to be producer of Kamei's ill-fated *Tragedy of Japan,* soon came to refer slyly to occupation authorities as the *"gunbatsu"* or military clique. "I was sickened to be made to realize how tight the undemocratic American *gunbatsu* had now drawn Japan into their clutches," he recalled feeling when he discovered that there was no way to protest the pulling of *Tragedy* from the movie houses. Satō Tadao, the incisive, self-educated dean of postwar film critics, looked back on the occupation as a two-stage epoch of "encouraged democracy" followed by "repressed democracy." To Matsuura Sōzō, who witnessed GHQ's increasingly frenzied campaign against the left at first hand as an editor of *Kaizō,* it was not until the occupation authorities actually left in early 1952 that a "renaissance of democratic journalism" was possible—an open, springlike atmosphere comparable, indeed, with the early stages of the occupation.[73] Among other things, only then was it possible to discuss the occupation itself frankly.

The deeper legacies of this censored democracy transcended ideology. Can anyone really believe that no harm was done to postwar political consciousness by a system of secret censorship and thought control that operated under the name of "free expression"—indeed, waved this banner from the rooftops—and yet drastically curbed any criticism of General MacArthur, SCAP authorities, the entire huge army of occupation, occupation policy in general, the United States and other victorious Allied powers, the prosecution's case as well as the verdicts in the war-crimes trials, and the emperor's personal war responsibility once the victors pragmatically decided that he had none? This was not a screen for weeding out threats to democracy (as official justifications claimed), but rather a new chapter in an old book of lessons about acquiescing to overweening power and conforming to a dictated consensus concerning permissible behavior.

From this perspective, one legacy of the revolution from above was continued socialization in the acceptance of authority—reinforcement of a collective fatalism vis-à-vis political and social power and of a sense that ordinary people were really unable to influence the course of events. For all their talk of democracy, the conquerors worked hard to engineer consensus; and on many critical issues, they made clear that the better part of political wisdom was silence and conformism. So well did they succeed in reinforcing this consciousness that after they left, and time passed, many non-Japanese including Americans came to regard such attitudes as peculiarly Japanese.

Part V

GUILTS

chapter fifteen

VICTOR'S JUSTICE,
LOSER'S JUSTICE

When World War II ended in Asia, the consuming sentiments of the victorious Allies were hatred and hope; and the tangle of these emotions was nowhere more apparent than in the war-crimes trials the victors conducted. The atrocities Japanese forces had committed in all theaters provoked a fierce desire for vengeance, and it was taken for granted that harsh punishment would be meted out to those found guilty of violating the established rules and conventions governing conduct in war. In formal terms, such "conventional" atrocities, or "crimes against humanity" more broadly defined, were identified as "Class B" war crimes; the planning, ordering, authorization, or failure to prevent such transgressions at higher levels in the command structure were categorized as "Class C" crimes. In practice, the two were often confused and it became common to refer to "B/C" war crimes. Thousands of Japanese were eventually accused of such crimes and brought before local military tribunals convened by the victorious powers.

With two exceptions—the hasty proceedings by U.S. military tribunals in the Philippines against generals Yamashita Tomoyuki and Homma Masaharu, both executed after being judged responsible for atrocities committed by troops under their commands—these local trials established no precedents, attracted no great attention, and left no lasting mark on popular memory outside Japan. The prosecutions that did significantly influence law and memory involved a small number of leaders accused and found guilty of *unprecedented* war crimes at the International Military Tribunal for the Far East, better known as the Tokyo war-crimes trial or the Tokyo tribunal.

Like the Allied trial of Nazi leaders at Nuremberg, the Tokyo tribunal initially captured the imagination of a war-weary world by expanding the interpretation of "crimes against humanity" and, more boldly yet, by introducing a sweeping new formulation of "crimes against peace." In the victors' idealistic rhetoric, although the Allied trials at every level would offer a model of fair and impartial justice, the showcase "Class A" tribunals at Tokyo and Nuremberg represented a momentous development indeed—in the words of B. V. A. Röling, the Dutch judge at the Tokyo trial, a moment when "international law was *en route* to banning war and rendering it a criminal offense."

To Röling and countless others, holding individual leaders personally responsible for egregious acts of state constituted a "milestone in legal development" that seemed crucial in the nuclear age. Sir William Webb, the Australian president of the Tokyo tribunal, had this in mind when he inaugurated proceedings with the observation that "there has been no more important criminal trial in all history." In an opening statement that impressed many Japanese, Joseph Keenan, the American chief prosecutor, took care to emphasize that "civilization" was the ultimate plaintiff, and civilization itself might well be destroyed if these judicial undertakings did not succeed in preventing future wars.[1] In practice, such hopes and ideals inevitably became tainted by the double standards of those who sat in judgment, as some members of the Allied camp privately acknowledged. On the Japanese side, the contradictions between judicial idealism and plain victor's justice provided fertile soil for the growth of a postwar neonationalism.

Stern Justice

It was by no means inevitable that major war-crimes trials, let alone precedent-breaking ones, would follow the war. Until 1945 many American and British officials envisioned enacting swift and summary justice against the "archcriminals" in the enemy camp. Secretary of State Cordell Hull once told his British and Soviet counterparts that, if he had his way, he "would take Hitler and Mussolini and Tojo and their arch accomplices and bring them before a drumhead court-martial. And at sunrise the following day there would occur an historic incident." Secretary of the Treasury Henry Morgenthau, thinking primarily of Germany, recommended that the Allies compile a list of top leaders who, on being captured and identified, should be executed immediately "by firing squads made up of soldiers of the United Nations." As late as April 1945, only weeks before Germany's capitulation, the British urged the Americans to approve "execution without trial" for top German leaders. Years later, some officials remained persuaded that this would have been the proper course in Japan as well.[2]

The attack on such advocacy of drumhead justice was led by Secretary of War Henry Stimson. Prompt justice based on fair legal procedures, Stimson argued, was "consistent with the advance of civilization" and would "have all the greater effect upon posterity." Stimson made clear that he had in mind trials before military commissions, which would be empowered to expedite proceedings by making their own "bare bones" rules to avoid the legal technicalities that might arise in civilian courts or even in ordinary military courts martial. The secretary of war noted that apart from meeting the "judgment of history," such trials would serve the educational and historical function of establishing a record of the enemy's transgressions. In his memoirs, published shortly after the war, Stimson declared that aggression "is an offense so deep and so heinous that we cannot endure its repetition." The Filipino jurist Delfin Jaranilla, who sat on the bench at the Tokyo tribunal, found these words so apt that he quoted them in concluding his own harsh judgment of the "Class A" Japanese defendants.[3]

When Japan surrendered, the major statement of Allied policy regarding Japanese war crimes remained what had been set forth in the Potsdam Declaration:

> There must be eliminated for all time the authority and influence of those who have deceived and misled the people of Japan into embarking on world conquest, for we insist that a new order of peace, security and justice will be impossible until irresponsible militarism is driven from the world. . . . We do not intend that the Japanese shall be enslaved as a race or destroyed as a nation, but stern justice shall be meted out to all war criminals, including those who have visited cruelties upon our prisoners.

This was highly generalized, and necessarily so, for the victors were still deliberating about how to handle Japanese war crimes right up to the end of the war. What the Potsdam Declaration conveyed most clearly was the

A Japanese nurse is sentenced to imprisonment at a trial of accused "B/C"
war criminals convened in Yokohama. She was found guilty of having
participated in eating the liver of an American airman executed at Kyushu
University, where vivisections were performed on POWs.

rage in the Allied camp over Japanese maltreatment of prisoners. Long
after the war had ended, and notwithstanding the revelation of the enormity of Nazi atrocities, great numbers of Americans, British, and Australians continued to believe that the enemy in Asia had been even more
heinous than the German one. A statistic that emerged in the course of
the trials reinforced this impression. Whereas 4 percent of American and
British servicemen taken prisoner by the Germans and Italians were calculated to have died in captivity, the incidence of death among American
and British Commonwealth prisoners of the Japanese was estimated to
have been 27 percent.[4]

Shortly after surrender, there was speculation that as many as fifty
thousand Japanese might be indicted for committing crimes against prisoners as well as atrocities against civilians in the areas their forces occupied. A year later, it was estimated that roughly ten thousand such

suspects had been identified for possible trial. Eventually, around fifty military tribunals were convened at various Asian locales—twelve by the Dutch, eleven by the British, ten by the Chinese, nine by the Australians, five by the Americans, and one each by the French and the Filipinos.[5] Other trials were conducted by the Soviet Union and, much later, by the communist regime that came to power in China.

Most of the tribunals convened outside the Soviet Union and Communist-controlled China carried out their tasks between 1945 and 1949; the last concluded in 1951. For many reasons, it is not possible to provide exact data concerning the outcomes of these proceedings. The trials took place in widely scattered locations under numerous national jurisdictions. Precise records were not always maintained or made available. Sentences, especially involving capital punishment, were sometimes reviewed and altered. Some accused prisoners died awaiting trial. Prison terms often were not served in full. Still, the overall scale of these local tribunals is clear enough. According to the most authoritative Japanese tabulation, a total of 5,700 individuals were indicted for "Class B" and "Class C" war crimes. Of this number, 984 initially were condemned to death; 475 received life sentences; 2,944 were given more limited prison terms; 1,018 were acquitted; and 279 were for one reason or another not sentenced or never brought to trial. Fifty of the death sentences were commuted on appeal, mostly by the French. Country by country (the Soviet Union excepted), the number of death sentences upheld was greatest in the trials conducted by the Dutch (236 death sentences) and British (223), followed by the Australians (153), Chinese (149), Americans (140), French (26), and Filipinos (17). The generally accepted number of those actually executed is 920.[6]

A number of the accused were officers, some of relatively high rank. With the exception of Yamashita and Homma, however, few of them were well known. Most defendants were enlisted men at the lower levels of the chain of command, including conscripted colonial subjects assigned to serve as interrogators or prison guards. The indicted suspects included 173 Taiwanese and 148 Koreans, of whom over forty were executed.[7] Some local trials involved single individuals; in others, defendants were judged collectively. The largest group trial appears to have been an Australian tribunal involving ninety-three men. The Americans collectively tried forty-six officers and men of the former imperial navy—of whom forty-one were sentenced to death. Roughly three-quarters of the defendants in these "B/C" tribunals were accused of crimes against prisoners. Whatever the charge,

The death by hanging of a convicted Japanese war criminal in Guam, 1947. Between 1945 and 1950, close to six thousand individuals accused of atrocities were brought before military tribunals convened throughout Asia by the victorious Allied Powers (not including the Soviet Union). Over nine hundred were executed.

the alleged crimes were invariably cruel and often gruesome. Although some suspects languished in their captors' hands for several years before being brought to judgment, the trials, once convened, were generally swift. Despite language problems, they averaged around two days each.[8]

At the same time, the Soviet Union conducted secret war-crimes proceedings against Japanese who had been captured in Manchuria, northern
Korea, and Karafuto (southern Sakhalin). The proceedings of one of these
trials, convened in Khabarovsk in December 1949 and involving twelve
Japanese associated with "Unit 731" in Manchuria, which had conducted
lethal medical experiments on some three thousand prisoners, was actually published in English in 1950. Secretly, the Soviets may have executed
as many as three thousand Japanese as war criminals, following summary
proceedings.[9] In the case of China, the ten formal "Allied" military tribunals that sentenced 149 defendants to death were convened by the beleaguered Kuomintang (Nationalist) regime. The Chinese Communists
subjected around one thousand Japanese prisoners to intensive "reeducation" during and after the war and brought forty-five to trial for war
crimes eleven years after Japan's defeat. Although all received prison sentences, the last of them had been returned to Japan by 1964.[10]

Showcase Justice: The Tokyo Tribunal

After a long war that saw the death of several million Japanese servicemen and civilians, the fate of these few thousand accused war criminals
in faraway places did not initially attract great attention within Japan. Although the revelation of widespread Japanese atrocities did make an impression on the general populace, many appear to have regarded these
distant exercises in Allied justice as little more than another example of
how, in war and in peace, individuals lower in the hierarchy of authority
had to pay for the misdeeds of men with real power. When all was said
and done, it was obvious that only a small number of high army and navy
officers, few high bureaucrats, no captains of the war economy, and virtually none of the civilian ideologues in politics, academe, and the media
who helped prime the pump of racial arrogance and fanatical militarism
paid for the terrible crimes that men on the front committed.

The victors channeled their concern with ultimate responsibility into
"Japan's Nuremberg," the showcase proceedings against top leaders in
Tokyo. Although the Tokyo trial proved but a murky reflection of its
German counterpart, in sheer quantitative terms it was an impressive un-
dertaking. The Nuremberg trial began on November 20, 1945, and con-
cluded some ten months later. Following months of preparation, the Tokyo
tribunal convened on May 3, 1946 and continued for thirty-one months.
One inevitable consequence of its length was increasing public ennui on

the issue of war crimes and war responsibility. "To be honest," one Japanese newspaper observed in November 1948, when the judgment was about to be handed down, "the general public's interest focused not on the proceedings but on the single point of what the verdicts would be."[11]

Eleven justices presided at Tokyo as opposed to four at Nuremberg. At its peak, the prosecution numbered around one hundred attorneys supported by a staff of over one hundred Allied nationals and almost two hundred Japanese. In 818 court sessions over 417 days, the tribunal heard testimony from 419 witnesses and accepted depositions and affidavits from an additional 779 individuals—significantly more than at Nuremberg. Thousands of hitherto secret documents were collected under its jurisdiction, providing a record of policy making that could never have been assembled under other circumstances. This was supplemented by the interrogation of scores of former civilian and military leaders. Some 4,336 exhibits were admitted in evidence, totaling around 30,000 pages. The transcript of the trial, excluding exhibits and judgments, numbered 48,288 pages. As the Canadian diplomat and historian E. H. Norman observed, the most enduring legacy of the tribunal may have been this treasure trove of documentation.[12]

Under its charter, a simple majority judgment was sufficient to convict. In fact, when these immense proceedings finally limped to their close late in 1948, the bench was divided. A lengthy majority judgment endorsed by eight justices was read aloud in court between November 4 and 12. Submitted but not read were five individual opinions, one by Justice Jaranilla, who had signed the majority judgment but took the occasion to express his view that many of the individual verdicts were too lenient. An opinion by Justice Webb, the president of the tribunal, nominally in concurrence with the majority, severely criticized aspects of the judgment and the trial. Dissenting opinions were submitted by the judges representing France, India, and the Netherlands. That of the Indian justice, Radhabinod Pal, was as long as the twelve-hundred-page majority judgment.

By majority decision, seven former Japanese leaders went to the gallows. Sixteen were sentenced to life imprisonment, one to twenty years, and one to seven years. Five of the convicted "Class A" war criminals died in prison, but none of the others served out their terms. The former foreign minister Shigemitsu Mamoru was released in 1950 and returned to politics the moment the occupation ended. The remaining twelve were paroled between 1954 and 1956. In 1958, the ten men still surviving were granted clemency following consultation with the former victor powers.[13]

A private exchange between Justice Röling and General Willoughby revealed the ambiguous nature of this "milestone in legal development." Despite their contrasting personalities, the idealistic Dutch jurist and the vigilantly conservative head of GHQ's intelligence operations had become friends as the trial unfolded and frequently played tennis together. As Röling was leaving Japan, he paid a farewell visit to Willoughby. Although he had reservations about the conduct of the tribunal and had submitted one of the dissenting opinions (voting to acquit five of the twenty-five defendants, but supporting the death penalty for three defendants who were given life sentences), Röling never questioned the overarching ideals of Nuremberg and Tokyo. A self-described peace activist to the end of his life, he maintained a "favorable opinion" about the overall purpose and fairness of the trials. Willoughby did not. "This trial," he bluntly told his friend, "was the worst hypocrisy in recorded history."[14]

Others in the victors' camp shared Willoughby's view, although it was never possible to say so publicly. Even U.S. Brigadier General Elliott Thorpe, who played a major role in deciding which high-ranking Japanese should be arrested as war criminals, privately dismissed the Tokyo tribunal as "mumbo-jumbo." As he explained it years afterward, he had

The bench at the International Military Tribunal for the Far East, where justices representing eleven countries presided over the trial of accused "Class A" war criminals.

Defendants listen with earphones to a Japanese translation of the lengthy
majority judgment being read (in English) at the Tokyo tribunal in November
1948. All twenty-five defendants were found guilty, and seven, including
former prime minister Tōjō Hideki (front row, third from left), were
sentenced to death and executed the following month.

"had the job of picking the war criminals to be tried—not the brutes and
the physical criminals and murderers, but the political war criminals,
those who came under that very disagreeable heading of those who used
war as an instrument of national policy. I still don't believe that was the
right thing to do. I still believe that it was an ex post facto law. They made
up the rules after the game was over. So we hanged them because they
used war as an instrument of national policy."

As Thorpe saw it, the "Class A" trials were fundamentally an exercise
in revenge ("we wanted blood and, by God, we had blood"). The real reason for opposing these new rules of the game, however, was that they established an alarming rather than admirable precedent, whereby in the
future anyone in a position of authority who had supported his country
in waging a lost war might well find himself accused of war crimes by the
victor. Another U.S. general who served in the occupation force later
wrote that he "went to the court many times and came away each time
with the strong feeling that it was wrong to try a man for doing his duty

for his country and government in time of war. . . . I am against it one hundred percent." He believed that these sentiments were widespread among his military colleagues.[15]

Professional soldiers were not the only ones who privately had grave reservations about the showcase trials. In March 1948, the State Department's George Kennan visited Japan and included an acid commentary, bordering on the dyspeptic, in his top-secret report to the department's Policy Planning Staff. Kennan observed that the war-crimes trials in general "have been hailed as the ultimate in international justice. There is no gain saying the fact that the trials have been *procedurally* thoroughly correct, according to our concepts of justice, and that at no time in history have conquerors conferred upon the vanquished such elaborate opportunities for the public defense and for vindication of their military acts." He then proceeded to castigate the trials in Tokyo as "profoundly misconceived from the start." Punishment of enemy leaders had been "surrounded with the hocus-pocus of a judicial procedure which belies its real nature." Interminable delays ("endless and humiliating ordeals") merely compounded the problem. He dismissed the tribunals as "political trials . . . not law." In later conversations with the British, Kennan found agreement that the trials were "ill-conceived, psychologically unsound."[16]

By the time the "Class A" trial in Tokyo ended, the world had changed. The victorious Allied alliance had been shattered by the Cold War; countries represented on the bench in Tokyo were engaged in civil wars and colonial wars in many parts of Asia; and U.S. occupation policy was in the process of turning away from the initial ideals of "demilitarization and democratization." The indicted former Japanese leaders had been denounced for attempting to argue that their incursions abroad had been partly motivated by fear of communism; yet even as this argument was being stifled, the United States was creating its own national security state dedicated to the global containment of communism. The tribunal was quickly eclipsed by what a member of the prosecution staff referred to as "the darkening shadows of current events." By 1948, hardly anyone was left who still believed that Nuremberg and Tokyo could provide the basis for a peaceful world grounded in a new order of international law and justice.[17]

This cynicism was conveyed in two symbolic acts of omission. Whereas the entire Nuremberg proceedings had been made available in a forty-two-volume bilingual (English and French) publication, no official publication ever emanated from Tokyo. Even the majority judgment, which summarized the prosecution argument in great detail, was not made readily accessible. Transcripts of the entire proceedings were distributed so haphazardly that no Allied government ever obtained a definitive set. Although the Japanese government collected materials produced by the trial, these were not readily available to the public. For all practical purposes, the record of the proceedings was buried.[18]

At the same time, led by the Americans, the victors moved swiftly to make clear that there would be no further Allied interest in the issue of ultimate responsibility for the recent war. Far more men had been arrested as "Class A" suspects and incarcerated in Sugamo Prison than were actually brought to trial, and it was initially stated that they would be indicted once the first showcase trial was concluded. Such indictments never occurred. As time passed, the number of imprisoned suspects declined, largely through dismissal of charges. As of June 1947, fifty remained in custody. By the time the Tokyo trial ended, the number had been reduced to nineteen. They included two immensely influential right-wing bosses, Kodama Yoshio and Sasagawa Ryōichi, as well as the brilliant and unscrupulous former bureaucrat (and future prime minister) Kishi Nobusuke, who had been the economic czar of the puppet state of Manchukuo and was accused, among other things, of being responsible for the enslavement of untold thousands of Chinese as forced laborers. On December 24, 1948, the day after the seven defendants were hanged at Sugamo, all nineteen remaining suspects were released on grounds of insufficient evidence. Ordinary people unversed in the subtleties of international law could be excused for failing to comprehend exactly where justice left off and political whimsy began.[19]

Tokyo and Nuremberg

Although Japanese leaders understood that they would be held accountable for war crimes, they had no way of anticipating the ambitions of the Allies in this regard. Nothing in the Potsdam Declaration indicated that the victors would put forward new norms of international law. In this regard, the Tokyo trial initially seemed to resemble the reformist occupation as a whole, being cut of new cloth and without historical precedent. Even General MacArthur was taken by surprise by the scope and innovation of this legal project—and deemed it excessive. He privately indicated that he thought justice could have been served by brief military proceedings focusing on the treacherous attack on Pearl Harbor.[20]

The Nuremberg precedent made this impossible. Although the victors in Europe hammered out the general parameters of war-crimes policy against Germany in June 1945, a month after Germany's capitulation, the "Statute of the Nuremberg International Military Tribunal" that established the basic principles for the trial of Nazi leaders was not issued until August 8—the day the Soviet Union declared war on Japan, two days after Hiroshima, one day before Nagasaki. The Japanese had no time to analyze this, and they had no indication in any case that principles explicitly designed to bring Nazi leaders to justice would be transposed with only minimal change to Japan.

In fact, it took months for the Allies to clarify their policies regarding the treatment of Japanese war criminals. While multination commissions prepared recommendations on the issue, and interdepartmental American committees refined their internal proposals—while, indeed, Japanese were being arrested for war crimes—final policy remained uncertain. Early in November, General MacArthur authorized a curt memorandum to Washington complaining that whereas the definition of war criminals had been "comparatively simple" where the Nazis were concerned, in Japan "no such line of demarcation has been fixed."[21] Only in the closing days of 1945, a month after the appointment of Joseph Keenan as chief prosecutor, did Washington inform its allies that the Tokyo tribunal would "follow the Nuremberg pattern so far as it is appropriate in the Far Eastern Theater." General MacArthur did not announce the jurisdiction and functions of the International Military Tribunal for the Far East until January 19, 1946, at which time he also issued the "Tokyo charter." These guidelines, the counterpart to the Nuremberg charter, were drafted by the American prosecution staff and SCAP's legal section. The other Allied powers were consulted only after it had been issued, and small amendments were made before the trial convened.[22]

On April 29, the prosecution formally lodged its indictment with the Tokyo tribunal. As stipulated by the rules of the court, it had previously been served on the defendants. It is a measure of both the complexity and the unwieldiness of the trial that although the indictment consisted of fifty-five counts charging the defendants with "Crimes against Peace, Conventional War Crimes and Crimes against Humanity," and although the proceedings of the trial followed this indictment for over two years, the majority judgment ultimately dismissed forty-five of these counts as superfluous, redundant, or simply obscure.[23]

In both trials, considerable time and technical argumentation was spent by the prosecution attempting to establish a prior legal basis for "crimes against peace" and "crimes against humanity" in existing international laws and treaties. Despite such arguments, no one really denied the precedent-setting nature of the two tribunals. In the Tokyo charter, the critical definition of the tribunal's jurisdiction was set forth as follows in Article 5:

> The following acts, or any of them, are crimes coming within the jurisdiction of the tribunal for which there shall be individual responsibility:
>
> a. *Crimes against Peace:* Namely, the planning, preparation, initiation or waging of a declared or undeclared war of aggression, or a war in violation of international law, treaties, agreements or assurances, or participation in a common plan or conspiracy for the accomplishment of any of the foregoing;
>
> b. *Conventional War Crimes:* Namely, violations of the laws or customs of war;
>
> c. *Crimes against Humanity:* Namely, murder, extermination, enslavement, deportation, and other inhumane acts committed before or during the war, or persecutions on political or racial grounds in execution of or in connection with any crime within the jurisdiction of the Tribunal, whether or not in violation of the domestic law of the country where perpetrated. Leaders, organizers, instigators, and accomplices participating in the formulation or execution of a common plan or conspiracy to commit any of the foregoing crimes are responsible for all acts performed by any person in execution of such a plan.

The decisive formulation of crimes against peace was framed in the first count of the indictment, which accused the defendants of having engaged in a "common plan or conspiracy" to secure "military, naval, political and economic domination of East Asia and of the Pacific and Indian Ocean," and to this end of having waged "wars of aggression" against countries opposing these purposes. This seemingly straightforward accusation rested on three bold premises. It assumed that a clear basis existed for distinguishing purely aggressive wars from wars undertaken out of genuine concern (however misguided) for the defense of legitimate national interests—and that Japan's wars all fell into the former category. It postulated a comprehensive and continuous *conspiracy* to wage such aggressive wars. And, central to the ideal of establishing an effective legal and psychological deterrent against future "crimes against peace," it affirmed that individual leaders could be held personally responsible under international law for activities previously regarded as acts of state.

Although the prosecution (following the rhetoric of the Potsdam Declaration) opened the trial by accusing the defendants of having embarked on a plan of world conquest, the majority judgment at Tokyo explicitly dismissed the notion that "the conspirators ever seriously resolved to attempt to secure the domination of North and South America." The majority, however, did endorse the prosecution's sweeping argument that top leaders had engaged in a criminal "conspiracy to wage wars of aggression" that commenced not in the period immediately prior to Pearl Harbor, as MacArthur would have had it; not in 1937, when Japan launched open war against China; not even in 1931, when the "Manchurian Incident" was used as a pretext for imposing control over Manchuria. The defendants were charged with having participated in a conspiracy that dated back to January 1, 1928, when plans to take over the Asian continent allegedly first began to be hatched.[24] Within this eighteen years of turbulence and conflict in Asia, the prosecution ultimately accused the defendants of 756 separate acts constituting crimes against peace. The bulk of the prosecution's time, and hundreds of pages in the majority judgment, were devoted to spelling out intimate details of policy making between 1928 and 1945, and arguing that virtually all of these did conform to a "common plan" to wage aggressive war.

Although "crimes against peace" thus received intense scrutiny, "crimes against humanity" remained less precisely developed as a legal concept. The latter charge had been formulated at Nuremberg primarily to enable the Allies to punish Nazi leaders for the genocidal policies that came to be known as the Holocaust. The Tokyo indictment, by contrast, contained no separate counts of "crimes against humanity." In the course of the trial these tended to be treated as essentially coterminous with "conventional war crimes" and, indeed, with plain "murder."[25] The prosecution presented testimony regarding Japanese atrocities against both prisoners of war and civilians in often horrific detail, and contended that these murderous acts were so widespread, continuous, and similar in pattern that they reflected a common policy and plan emanating from or at least tolerated by the top leadership. Here, the tribunal pursued a charge that was not part of the Nuremberg charter: the concept of negative or vicarious responsibility—that is, of criminal liability for acts of omission rather than commission. Among the counts sustained by the tribunal was not only direct participation in the perpetration of war crimes in the form of orders or authorizations (count 54), but also having "deliberately and recklessly disregarded their legal duty to take adequate steps to secure the observance and prevent breaches" of the conventional laws of war (count 55).[26]

Other differences also distinguished the Tokyo trial from its German counterpart. The four presiding judges in Nuremberg were each backed by an alternate, whereas the eleven justices in Tokyo had no backups. On more than a few occasions, this resulted in absenteeism on the bench. The prosecution was directed by four "chief prosecutors" at Nuremberg, representing the four victorious countries conducting the trial, with a clear division of labor in the charges for which each was responsible. In Tokyo, there was a single chief prosecutor, Joseph Keenan. Although Keenan was assisted by ten associate prosecutors, one from each of the other ten countries represented on the tribunal, the American control of prosecution policy and strategy bordered on the absolute.

Four languages—English, German, French, and Russian—were employed simultaneously in the Nuremberg trial. In Tokyo, while the basic languages of the tribunal were English and Japanese, at least six other languages had to be accommodated. Communication was exceedingly complicated—"beyond comparison to the German case," as a Japanese publication put it at the time—involving not only large numbers of translators and interpreters but also language monitors and arbitrators. Simultaneous interpretation proved impossible in Tokyo and, as a consequence, statements by witnesses or counsel were stopped at the end of each sentence until translations had been made. A member of the prosecution staff estimated that, "when witnesses were being examined, the speed of the trial was reduced to one-fifth of its normal pace."[27]

To many observers, the major difference between the two trials lay in the nature of the defendants and the crimes they were accused of committing. There was no Japanese cabal of leaders comparable to Hitler and his henchmen. (Emperor Hirohito was, in fact, the only person in Japan who had been at the center of power during the entire course of the alleged "conspiracy.") There were no organizational counterparts to the Nazi party and its affiliated criminal organs, such as the Gestapo and the SS (which made the charge of conspiracy easier to argue in the German case); nor, despite the horrendous litany of atrocities exposed in the Tokyo proceedings, including the massacres in Nanking and Manila, was there a real counterpart to the genocide planned and carried out by the Germans. This difference was emphasized by Justice Pal, who declared straightforwardly that "the case of the present accused before us cannot in any way be likened to the case . . . of Hitler." Justice Webb agreed that "the

crimes of the German accused were far more heinous, varied and extensive than those of the Japanese accused."[28] Despite the grievous crimes of
which they were accused, the defendants failed to exude the aura of evil
personified that choked the courtroom where their Nazi counterparts
were tried.

Of the twenty-two defendants in Nuremberg, three were acquitted and
twelve were sentenced to death (one in absentia). There were no acquit-
tals in the Tokyo tribunal, where twenty-three of the twenty-five defendants were judged guilty of participating in the "overall conspiracy"
against peace (count 1). Of the seven men sentenced to death, two were
also found guilty, among other charges, of authorizing or permitting atrocities (count 54) as well as of failing to prevent such breaches of the laws
of war (count 55), and three were judged guilty of the first but not the second of these atrocity charges. One defendant, the former general Matsui
Iwane, was given the death penalty solely on "negative responsibility"
grounds for having been derelict in preventing atrocities by troops under
his command during the Nanking massacre. To the general public, the
most surprising and shocking of the death sentences was that imposed on
the former foreign minister and prime minister Hirota Kōki, who was
found guilty of three charges, including overall conspiracy and having
failed to prevent atrocities in China. Hirota was apparently sent to the gallows on the basis of the vote of only six of the eleven judges.[29]

The public may have become bored by the trial long before it ended,
but when the verdicts were announced on November 12, 1948, there was
a great deal to talk about, including the entirely unexpected submission
of four separate opinions that were in one way or another critical of the
tribunal's conduct and conclusions. Nuremberg had not provided the
faintest precedent for this. Although the separate opinions were not read
aloud in court, their essence was noted by the media. Justice Pal had acquitted all defendants, while Justice Röling had found five (including Hirota) not guilty. Two justices, Webb and Henri Bernard of France, had
found the tribunal flawed and compromised by the decision not to bring
the emperor to trial.[30]

Given the intense campaign to present Hirohito as a champion of
peace, this high-level evocation of his war responsibility was startling. For
over two years, and with but one momentary lapse, all of the defendants
accused of "Class A" war crimes had meticulously avoided saying anything
that might seem to implicate their sovereign. Now, Justices Webb and
Bernard revealed that they had not found this vigilant loyalism persuasive.
With remarkable bluntness, Webb criticized the fact that "the leader of the

crime, though available for trial, had been granted immunity." He observed that "the Emperor's authority was required for war. If he did not want war he should have withheld his authority." Despite this, Webb supported the majority judgment, although he did suggest, albeit with no great eloquence, that the death sentences might be commuted on review.[31]

Justice Bernard found the proceedings so unfair and technically flawed that he deemed it impossible to pass any judgment whatever. He deplored the "abominable crimes" committed by the Japanese and acknowledged that at least some of the defendants bore heavy responsibility for those transgressions. The absence of the emperor, however, struck him as so glaring an inequity that condemning the defendants was impossible. Japan's crimes against peace "had a principal author who escaped all prosecution and of whom in any case the present Defendants could only be considered as accomplices." Measuring the emperor "by a different standard" not only prejudiced the case against them, but also undermined the cause of international justice.[32]

These were unsettling opinions, and the emperor and his Japanese and American entourages lost little time in defusing them. The very day the verdicts were announced, the emperor wrote General MacArthur reassuring him that he had no intention of abdicating.[33] Eight days later, Chief Prosecutor Keenan reiterated that there were no grounds for trying the emperor as a war criminal. And on November 25, the press reported three noteworthy events of the previous day. Despite pleas from representatives of several of the victorious nations that he commute the sentences, MacArthur had approved the majority verdict; Keenan had enjoyed the rare privilege of being invited to a private lunch with the emperor at the imperial palace; and Tōjō Hideki, facing death, had delivered what one paper called his "last message to the world."

Taken together, this was a memorable triptych. Had MacArthur commuted the nonunanimous death sentences, he would have given credence to Webb's argument that, as "the leader of the crime," the emperor should have been indicted; and this was inconceivable.[34] That the emperor cordially dined with the chief prosecutor on the day his loyal servants saw their sentences confirmed did not perhaps seem in the best of taste, but time was short. Keenan was leaving town. The two men spent three hours in private conversation—leaving the press to speculate that the emperor had desired to express his gratitude to Keenan for affirming his innocence.

And Tōjō? Tōjō, no more contrite than his sovereign, did not bend like him. His "last message" challenged the basic premise of the judgment: that Japan's road to war had been undertaken without provocation or legitimate national security concerns. "Peoples of all the nations of the world," Tōjō was quoted as saying, "absolutely should not abandon the right to initiate wars of self-defense."[35]

The death sentences in the Tokyo judgment were appealed to the Supreme Court of the United States, which on December 20 ruled that it had no jurisdiction in the case. Three days later, the seven condemned defendants were hanged wearing, as a SCAP press release explained, "United States army salvage work clothing completely devoid of insignia of any kind."[36] They died with the solace that they had been a shield to their emperor to the very end, and they left a legacy of lingering controversy.

Victor's Justice and Its Critics

Like Nuremberg, the Tokyo trial was law, politics, and theater all in one. Unlike Nuremberg, it "was very much an American performance," as Justice Röling put it many years later. "It was like a huge-scale theatrical production," the Dutch jurist observed. "I didn't see that at the time, and I didn't see that there were more 'Hollywoodesque' things around than there should have been."[37]

Others did see this. In its coverage of the opening sessions, *Time* magazine was impressed by how the stage was set. "Much care had gone into fitting the courtroom with dark, walnut-toned paneling, imposing daises, convenient perches for the press and motion-picture cameramen. The klieg lights suggested a Hollywood premiere." The lights dazzled everyone and often were described as almost blinding—not so much perhaps in the manner of a movie premiere as of a film being made. Indeed, much of the time the proceedings of the trial *were* being filmed. The Japanese too spoke of "lighting of the level of Hollywood," albeit with more derisive intent than *Time*.[38]

The very building in Tokyo's Ichigaya district in which the performance unfolded conveyed a certain sense of dramatic irony. Formerly the auditorium of the elite Imperial Army Officers School, Japan's counterpart to West Point, by war's end it was serving as temporary headquarters for the Army Ministry and the Combined General Staff. Following SCAP's orders, the structure was renovated by the Japanese government at a cost of almost 100 million yen, an enormous sum. Both air conditioning and central heating were introduced. Seats were provided for five hundred spectators, three hundred of them reserved for nonofficial citizens of the Allied countries and the remainder for Japanese.

The spectator's gallery provided sight lines on an enormous bullpen in which the defendants sat as a group on one side, the judges on another, and a small army of functionaries—court staff, translators, prosecutors, and the defense attorneys assigned to each defendant—filled the floor in front of them. American military police, usually wearing white helmets, checked people in and stood sentinel. Usually towering over the defendants, they provided an irresistible photo opportunity for depicting the mighty and the fallen. The defendants were quite literally dwarfed by the setting, and the relationship between the diminished elderly men in the dock and the enormity of the crimes they were accused of committing sometimes seemed to border (like so much else in the occupation) on the surreal.

The defendants not only had access to Japanese counsel, but were provided—at their own belated request—with American attorneys who assumed their duties in mid-May, shortly before the trial began. Arguing that they had not been given sufficient time to prepare their cases, six of them, including the chief American defense attorney, resigned abruptly one month later, in the trial's opening days. Those who stayed the course eventually served their clients reasonably well. When one considers wartime sentiments in favor of summary execution of the "archcriminals," the opportunity given the defendants to respond to the charges against them was impressive. Unlike the Nuremberg precedent, the Tokyo charter did not prohibit the defense from challenging the tribunal, and—led by two prominent Japanese lawyers, Takayanagi Kenzō and Kiyose Ichirō—the defendants took advantage of this to question the very legitimacy of the tribunal and to challenge the validity of the most fundamental charges in the indictment. Although these challenges were predictably dismissed, the defense lawyers laid down arguments that remained fundamental to all subsequent criticisms of "victor's justice." Later, after the prosecution spent some seven months presenting its case, the defense was given even more time (including 187 days in court) to respond.[39]

The appointment of American counsel reflected one of the controversial aspects of the tribunal: its grounding in Anglo-American trial procedure rather than the European traditions in which most Japanese legal specialists had been trained. The basic language of the trial was English, and seven of the eleven presiding judges, including the president of the tribunal, were trained primarily in Anglo-American law. Japanese attorneys operated at a severe disadvantage in this situation.[40] One strikingly Americanized dimension of the indictment was the concept of "conspiracy" that lay at the very heart of the prosecution's case. Around the end of 1944,

Secretary of War Stimson and his aides had concluded that adding conspiracy to the list of war crimes charges would expedite prosecution of Nazi leaders as well as lower-level members of Nazi organizations—something lawyers and historians have debated ever since.[41] However valid the conspiracy argument may have been in the Nazi case, it was a highly artificial basis for explaining why and how imperial Japan went to war. Justice Pal pointed out numerous instances in which it was more plausible to see Japan's leaders engaged in ad hoc responses to what they perceived as threats to their nation's security. On this particular point, subsequent scholarship generally has supported his skepticism. Declaring that documentary materials introduced revealed an eighteen-year-long "common plan" to wage aggressive war was much closer to propaganda than to serious historical analysis.[42]

The more technical criticism of the conspiracy charge was that it did not exist in international law prior to 1945. In his separate opinion, Justice Webb was unambiguous on this particular point. "International law, unlike the national laws of many countries," he observed, "does not expressly include a crime of naked conspiracy. . . . So too, the laws and customs of war do not make mere naked conspiracy a crime." Webb acknowledged that it was entirely reasonable to argue that conspiracy to commit grievous international transgressions *should* be a crime under international law. That argument did not, however, alter the fact that the tribunal in Tokyo "has no authority to create a crime of naked conspiracy based on the Anglo-American concept; nor on what it perceives to be a common feature of the crime of conspiracy under the various national laws." To do so was, as he put it, "nothing short of judicial legislation."[43] Nevertheless, Webb's court upheld the conspiracy charge as presented in count one of the indictment.

Merely by raising the issue of "judicial legislation," Webb implicitly called into question the postwar vision of establishing a new international legal order, for the ideal of outlawing "crimes against peace" posed a formidable conundrum. If the trials of Nazi and Japanese leaders were indeed precedent setting, did this not imply that these leaders were being accused of crimes that had not previously been established in international law? How was it legally possible to hold the accused responsible, as Justice Röling did in the opening words of his separate opinion, "for certain events in world history, on charges almost unknown before this war"? At issue was a sacrosanct principle familiar to all participants in these trials: that "without a law there can be no crime, without a law there can be no punishment" *(nullum crimen sine lege, nulla poena sine lege)*.[44]

Sometimes the prosecution frankly acknowledged its path-breaking agenda. In his introductory presentation, Joseph Keenan freely conceded that the trials were "without precedent" in holding individuals responsible under international law for acts of state.[45] More generally, however, as at Nuremberg, the prosecution attempted to present its indictment as but a bold reformulation of concepts and obligations already embedded in existing laws and treaties. The prohibition against "wars of aggression," it was argued, had been established in the Kellogg-Briand Pact of 1928, to which Japan had been a signatory. Furthermore, as Keenan put it in his opening statement, "the offenses of these accused resulted in the unlawful or unjustifiable taking of human lives, which constituted murder, the oldest of all crimes, and the punishment that we ask to be inflicted is punishment commensurate with such offense."[46]

In its opening challenge, the defense focused on precisely the issue of "retroactive" or "ex post facto" crimes. "Aggressive war is not per se illegal," the defense contended, "and the Pact of Paris of 1928 renouncing war as an instrument of national policy does not enlarge the meaning of war crimes nor constitute war a crime." Predictably, the defense also challenged the legality of holding individual leaders responsible for acts of state. "War is the act of a nation," it was argued, "for which there is no individual responsibility under international law." It therefore followed that the provisions of the Tokyo charter were "'ex post facto' legislation and therefore illegal." These were not frivolous arguments. In considerable part, Justice Pal's dissent rested on a strict interpretation of the limitations of existing international law vis-à-vis national sovereignty and national laws. In essence, he concluded that the defense had it right. The defendants were being tried for "crimes" that did not exist as such under international law prior to the defeat of the Axis powers.[47]

The Tokyo trial proved vulnerable to criticism on other grounds as well. A certain political capriciousness had been involved in deciding who would be indicted for "Class A" war crimes. (In the prosecution's opening statement, Joseph Keenan himself frankly and rather surprisingly acknowledged that "we have no particular interest in any individual or his punishment. They are representative in a certain sense of a class or group.") Even if one went along with the understanding that this was to be a heuristic or showcase trial in which "representative" leaders were to be held accountable for their war responsibility, the absence of certain groups and crimes was striking. No heads of the dreaded Kempeitai (the military police) were indicted; no leaders of ultranationalistic secret societies; no industrialists who had profited from aggression and had been intimately involved in paving the "road to war."⁴⁸ The forced mobilization of Korean and Formosan colonial subjects was not pursued as a crime against humanity, nor was the enslavement of several hundred thousand young non-Japanese who were forced to serve as "comfort women" providing sexual services to the imperial forces. The Americans who controlled the prosecution chose to grant blanket secret immunity to one group of Japanese whose atrocious crimes were beyond question, namely, the officers and scientific researchers in Unit 731 in Manchuria who had conducted lethal experiments on thousands of prisoners (they were exempted from prosecution in exchange for sharing the results of their research with the Americans). The prosecution also did not seriously pursue evidence concerning the Japanese use of chemical warfare in China.⁴⁹

Whimsy, or at least casualness, was also evident in appointments to the bench, where the most incisive and best-remembered justices were Röling and Pal, the authors of the two major dissenting judgments. Of the eleven judges in Tokyo, Pal was the only one with significant experience in international law. The original American appointee departed in a funk in July 1946 after learning that his qualifications had been belittled; his replacement left no mark. The Soviet judge, formerly a commissioner of justice under Lenin, had participated in the Stalinist mock trials of the mid-1930s. He spoke neither of the basic languages of the tribunal (his only two words of English, it was said, were "Bottoms up!"). The French judge had spent the interwar years in colonial service in West Africa, and according to Röling also did not speak English. The Chinese justice, educated in the United States, had published books on constitutional law but had no prior experience as a judge. The Filipino justice was a survivor of the Bataan Death March, which in a normal court would have led to his immediate disqualification. The president of the tribunal had previously been involved in prosecuting Japanese for war crimes in Australian military tribunals in New Guinea. Defense challenges to the latter two appointments were rejected.⁵⁰

Two judges, Pal and Jaranilla, were appointed at the last moment, and both clearly knew how they intended to vote before being seated. Token "Asians," they were mirror opposites.⁵¹ Justices Pal and Webb were noticeably absent from portions of the proceedings. Perhaps the most striking aspect of the conduct of the bench, however, lay in the fact that the eleven justices never collectively met in chamber to seriously discuss and deliberate the final judgment, no less how it should be argued and presented. Instead, as Röling described it, seven justices "just decided among themselves to write the judgement. . . . The seven organized the drafting, and presented the results to the other four as a *fait accompli.*"⁵²

Some disagreements concerning whether the trials were "fair" reflected differing premises concerning the proper procedures of a *military* tribunal. Even Secretary of War Stimson never imagined that such trials would be conducted with all the procedural regulations and guarantees that prevailed in civilian courts or even in military courts martial. The vehicle of the military tribunal or "military commission" was chosen precisely because it permitted the prosecution to follow procedures impermissible in other venues, particularly involving the control of admissible and inadmissible evidence.⁵³

In the context of the times, this seemed entirely reasonable. To begin with, the victors had every reason to expect the enemy to attempt to destroy or falsify evidence—as, in fact, happened.⁵⁴ The victors also feared that the defendants might attempt to use the trials as a propaganda platform to reaffirm the legitimacy of their actions. To prevent this, it was deemed necessary to place restraints on the testimony or "evidence" they could introduce in the name of self-defense. The Tokyo charter explicitly declared that "the Tribunal shall not be bound by technical rules of evidence. It shall adopt and apply to the greatest possible extent expeditious and non-technical procedure, and shall admit any evidence which it deems to have probative value." The war crimes trials were not civilian proceedings, and the "archcriminal" defendants obviously were not presumed innocent by those who drafted the charter.

The use of loose rules of evidence as defined by the victors proved, however, to be a gateway through which arbitrariness and unfairness entered the trials. The tribunal permitted the prosecution to introduce material that might have been rejected in more rigorous hearings, including hearsay, diary excerpts, unsworn statements, copies of documents where the originals were missing, and affidavits in situations where authors were not available for cross-examination. At one point, Justice Webb offered close to a lampoon of what it meant to be unbound by "technical rules of evidence." There was no way of really telling what might be admissible from day to day, he explained, because there was no way of telling who would be present on the bench. "Some times we have eleven members; some times we have had as low as seven," the president of the tribunal observed. "And you cannot say, that on the question of whether any particular piece of evidence has probative value you always get the same decision from seven judges as you would get from eleven. . . . You cannot be sure what decision the court is going to come to on any particular piece of evidence."[55]

What was sure, however, was that the prosecution commanded vastly greater resources than the defense, and could usually count on being favored by the bench on any given issue.[56] In a trial of Japanese defendants where the basic language was English, for example, access to capable translators was crucial. By one count, when the trial began the prosecution had 102 translators at its disposal and the defense three.[57] The prosecution largely controlled the submission of Japanese documents in translation, and it was only on specific request that these translations were examined. Justice Röling recalled one instance in which a text seemed odd to him and, on being rechecked, proved to have been incorrectly translated. When he asked that a corrected version be introduced into the record, his request was turned down on the grounds that it was too troublesome to reopen the issue. Testimony by the defendants reached the bench entirely through interpreters, and the English interpretations tended to be more cryptic than the original statements. No one suggested that translations and interpretations were deliberately skewed or even fundamentally inaccurate, but no one on the victor's side ever dwelled much either on what it meant to be judged (and, for seven men, condemned to death) in translationese.[58]

As Justices Webb and Bernard emphasized in their opinions, the most flagrant control of evidence involved the prosecution's single-minded campaign to insulate the emperor. The tribunal was distinguished not only by the physical absence of the emperor and the careful exclusion of any sustained references to him, but also by the absence of testimony by him.[59] The manipulation of "victor's evidence" to save him had no counterpart in Nuremberg—and received no challenge from the defense in Tokyo, even though the emperor's testimony might have benefited some of the defendants.[60] On the contrary, from the moment of their incarceration the defendants, who interacted closely in prison, resolved to do everything possible to protect the emperor—"for the future of the Japanese race," as Shigemitsu Mamoru put it. When Keenan announced on June 18, 1946, that the emperor would not be brought to trial, his loyal servants in Sugamo wept openly. Shigemitsu, the former diplomat, wrote a celebratory poem to the effect that, because his lord was a god, he was untouchable by the enemy. Kido, who had spent much time pleading the emperor's case with Keenan and the prosecution staff, rejoiced that, "with this, my mission is complete."[61]

In fact, the defendants' loyalist mission was not yet complete. Defense and prosecution alike labored to keep the emperor invisible for the next several years. On the part of the defendants, this vigilance faltered on only one occasion—December 31, 1947—when Tōjō frankly testified that it was inconceivable for him or any subject to have taken action contrary to the emperor's wishes. In response to this unintentionally candid and damaging observation, Keenan immediately arranged, through the Imperial Household Ministry, that Kido be contacted in prison and urged to tell his fellow defendant to rectify his potentially incriminating comment as soon as possible. Other intermediaries were used as well. Tōjō was happy to comply, and the opportunity to do so arose in the courtroom a week later. On January 6, in the course of an exchange with Keenan, Tōjō retracted his earlier statement.[62]

Although the defendants were happy to collude in a tacit pact to protect the emperor, the tribunal adopted other policies on impermissible testimony that ran counter to their wishes. The defense was not allowed to pursue certain lines of reasoning that most defendants believed essential to their case—for in the eyes of the victors, and in the eyes of the court, such arguments were simply "propaganda." None of the defendants accepted for a moment the accusation that they had been engaged in an eighteen-year-long conspiracy to wage "wars of aggression." On the contrary, they believed to the end with all apparent sincerity that their policies, however disastrous in outcome, had been motivated by legitimate concerns for Japan's essential rights and interests on the Asian continent. As the men in the dock saw it, their country's security had been imperiled by a succession of truly alarming developments: political chaos and economically crippling anti-Japanese boycotts in China; Soviet-led communist revolts and subversion there and elsewhere; American and European protectionist trade policies; global trends toward antarchic "bloc economies"; and coercive Western economic policies in the months prior to Pearl Harbor. Such concerns could not be excluded from mention, but the defense was not allowed to develop the case that they had validity— or that, for example, the wartime rhetoric of Pan-Asianism rested on legitimate Japanese and Asian grievances vis-à-vis the "White peril" of European and American imperialism. Nor, of course, was the defense allowed to introduce testimony or evidence purporting to show that the victors had also engaged in activities comparable to the "crimes" the defendants were accused of committing—such as breaking treaties or violating the conventional laws of warfare.[63]

Curtailing such defense arguments was fully consistent with Stimson's reasonable desire that the punishment of war crimes be stern and that trials not be allowed to degenerate into propaganda platforms for the accused. It was fully in accord with the controls over acceptable "evidence" granted the tribunal by the Tokyo charter, following the Nuremberg precedent. It was also the juridical counterpart of the general policy of occupation censorship—with all the absurdities that accompanied it. Before the Tokyo tribunal convened, Winston Churchill had already denounced the erection of an "Iron Curtain" in Europe. Before the trial was halfway over, the United States had introduced its anticommunist Marshall Plan. As the proceedings in Tokyo were drawing to a close, the Kuomintang government of China, whose representative sat on the tribunal, was fleeing to Taiwan, and American politicians were in a panic verging on hysteria at the impending "loss" of China. Yet even amid this growing sense of a global Armageddon between communist and anticommunist forces, the erstwhile "allies" of World War II were sitting in judgment in Tokyo and refusing to let the defendants pursue the argument that their policies on the Asian continent had been motivated, in great part, by fear of both chaos and communism in China.[64]

Ideologically, this was a convoluted business out of which odd bedfellows emerged. Thus, the reactionary General Willoughby found the trial hypocritical, as did Justice Pal, an Indian nationalist. What the two men shared in their scorn for the tribunal—with, indeed, its Soviet judge serenely seated on the bench—was anticommunism.[65] This was but one of the anomalies of victor's justice.

Race, Power, and Powerlessness

Even as men of good will spoke of establishing an international order in which aggression would not go unpunished, their own judicial proceedings mirrored a world still skewed by the harsh realities of race, power, and powerlessness. This was apparent in the nature of the "international" composition of the tribunal. Although the countries Japan had invaded and occupied were all Asian, and although the number of Asians who had died as a consequence of its depredations was enormous, only three of the eleven judges were Asians. Even this exceeded the original intent of the victors. Initially, only nine justices were envisioned, with only one Asian— the representative of China—among them. Justices Pal and Jaranilla were added only after agitation from their respective countries. The trial was fundamentally a white man's tribunal.[66]

The grudging inclusion of two additional Asian judges reflected specific colonial circumstances. The Philippines, an American colony since 1898, had been promised independence in 1946. India, long the crown jewel of the British empire, was to become independent in 1947; during the early part of the Tokyo trial, Justice Pal actually represented a still unliberated country. Indonesians were not so favored, although as many as a million or more of them may have died under the brutal regimen of forced labor the Japanese imposed after occupying the "Netherlands East Indies." The Dutch presumably represented the Indonesians at the Tokyo trial. Asian peoples who suffered at the hands of the Japanese in Vietnam, Malaya, and Burma also had no representatives of their own. The French nominally spoke for the "Indochinese." In theory, the British did likewise for the Burmese, the peoples of Malaya, and their colonial subjects in Hong Kong.

It was especially perverse that no Korean served as judge or prosecutor, although hundreds of thousands of colonized Korean men and women had been brutalized by the Japanese war machine—as "comfort women," as laborers forced to work in the most onerous sectors of mining and heavy industry in Japan, or as lowly conscripts in the military. Korea was not a bona fide sovereign nation at the time, nor was it clear when it would be. For the duration of the Tokyo trial, Japan's former colonial subjects remained under alien occupation in a land divided between the United States and the Soviet Union. They were not allowed to judge their former overlords and oppressors or to participate in preparing the case against them.

The plight of the Koreans was, in its way, emblematic of the larger anomaly of victor's justice as practiced in Tokyo. It called attention to the fact that the recent war in Asia had taken place not among free and independent nations, but rather on a map overwhelmingly demarcated by the colors of colonialism. Colonialism, and imperialism more generally, *defined* the twentieth-century Asian world in which Japan was accused of having conspired to wage aggressive war. Japan's colonial and neocolonial domain (Formosa, Korea, and Manchuria) existed alongside the Asian overseas possessions of four of the powers that now sat in judgment: Britain, France, the Netherlands, and the United States. China itself, nominally sovereign, had been a congeries of Japanese, European, and American "special rights and interests" and was not even formally freed from its "unequal treaties" with the United States until the war was almost over.

The tribunal essentially resolved the contradiction between the world of colonialism and imperialism and the righteous ideals of crimes against peace and humanity by ignoring it. Japan's aggression was presented as a criminal act without provocation, without parallel, and almost entirely without context. On occasion, the prosecution seemed literally blind to the Asia most Asians knew. In his opening statement, Chief Prosecutor Keenan actually claimed that the Japanese had "determined to destroy democracy and its essential basis—freedom and the respect of human personality; they were determined that the system of government of and by and for the people should be eradicated and what they termed a 'New Order' established instead."[67]

This was the sort of light-headed American effusiveness that made more sober observers among the victors cringe. It remained for Justice Pal, however, to highlight the double standards that underlay the trial. "It would be pertinent to recall to our memory that the majority of the interests claimed by the Western Prosecuting Powers in the Eastern Hemisphere including China," he observed in speaking of Japan's takeover of Manchuria, "were acquired by such aggressive methods" as the Japanese were accused of employing. He also commented, with no little sarcasm, on the ways in which the positive rhetoric of imperialism and colonialism of the Europeans and Americans became transmogrified when associated with Japan: "As a program of aggrandizement of a nation we do not like, we may deny to it the terms like 'manifest destiny', 'the protection of vital interests', 'national honour' or a term coined on the footing of 'the white man's burden', and may give it the name of 'aggressive aggrandizement' pure and simple."[68]

The Indian justice took palpable pleasure in suggesting the hypocrisy of the victors' case. He quoted England's prestigious Royal Institute of International Affairs at some length, for example, on how the Japanese had followed the precedents of European imperialism, sometimes "with almost pedantic exactitude." Similarly, in discussing the "Amau Doctrine" of 1934, in which Japan had enunciated its special rights and interests in China, Pal observed that this definition of national interest "finds obvious precedent in the conduct of the United States in pursuance of the Monroe Doctrine."[69] The prosecution's attempt to condemn the Japanese for conspiring to promote feelings of "racial superiority" through their educational system did not exactly impress him—as it had the prosecutors—as something for which the Japanese could be uniquely condemned. On this issue, he was more rueful than bitter. He quoted the historian Arnold Toynbee on how "race-feeling" had been fundamental to modern Western society, and pointed to the discrimination that Japanese and other Asians had endured in recent times at the hands of the dominant white powers. Ultimately, though, he saw the inculcation of feelings of racial superiority as "a dangerous weapon in the hands of . . . designing people from the earliest days of human history."[70]

Although Pal's dissent did not appear in translation until 1952, after the occupation ended, it resonated with the deeply held feelings of many Japanese.[71] Pal did not condone Japan's actions—nor, with hindsight, did the majority of Japanese. But apart from acknowledging the horror of "conventional" war crimes and atrocities, and apart from strong sentiment that the war had been *stupid,* many Japanese, like the Indian jurist, found it difficult to regard their country's actions as having been unique. Unsurprisingly, they were more inclined than the victors to see the war in terms of power politics in an unstable imperialist world.

That the powerless remained powerless—or, at least, the victorious "Great Powers" would have had them remain so—was apparent not only in Korea but also in the southern reaches of Asia so recently occupied by Japan, where the European victors were engaged in violent campaigns to reimpose control over their former colonies. The boggling fatuity of Keenan's opening denunciation of the Japanese for having denied the peoples of Asia "government of and by and for the people" lay not merely in the fact that nothing of the sort had existed under the old European and American imperiums, but in the fact that the French were then fighting their way back into Indochina, the Dutch into Indonesia, and the British into Malaya. No American chief prosecutor was about to argue that these bloody aggressions constituted a crime against peace and humanity— particularly since in each case his government supported these death gasps of the old imperialism.

From the Japanese perspective, the Soviet presence on the tribunal constituted a particularly egregious aspect of victor's justice. The Soviet Union, after all, had not exactly been an exemplary model of peace and justice (although many leftists believed otherwise). Closer to the bone, the Soviets were guilty of the crudest sort of hypocrisy. Japan was being accused of having violated sacred treaty obligations, but the U.S.S.R. had qualified to sit in judgment in Tokyo only by ignoring its bilateral neutrality pact with Japan in the final week of the war. And although the most harrowing revelations of the Tokyo trial involved Japanese atrocities against civilians and prisoners, it was known that the Red Army had engaged in widespread abuses of civilians in Manchuria. Throughout the duration of the trial, moreover, hundreds of thousands of Japanese prisoners remained in Soviet hands, their circumstances unknown. As it turned out, the number of Japanese prisoners who would die in Soviet hands was much larger than the number of American and British Commonwealth prisoners who perished so miserably as prisoners of the Japanese.

Against the Americans, the most predictible accusation of double standards rested on the argument that the terror bombing of Japanese cities, and the use of the atomic bombs in particular, were also crimes against humanity. Justice Pal made this argument with, even for him, unusual acidity. After bringing up a notorious statement that the German Kaiser Wilhelm II had conveyed to the Hapsburg emperor Franz Joseph in World War I ("Everything must be put to fire and sword; men, women and children and old men must be slaughtered and not a tree or house be left standing"), he introduced this statement into his dissenting opinion:

> In the Pacific war under our consideration, if there was anything approaching what is indicated in the above letter of the German emperor, it is the decision coming from the allied powers to use the atom bomb. Future generations will judge this dire decision. History will say whether any outburst of popular sentiment against usage of such a new weapon is irrational and only sentimental and whether it has become legitimate by such indiscriminate slaughter to win the victory by breaking the will of the whole nation to continue to fight. . . . It would be sufficient for my present purpose to say that if any indiscriminate destruction of civilian life and property is still illegitimate in warfare, then, in the Pacific war, this decision to use the atom bomb is the only near approach to the directives of the German Emperor during the first world war and of the Nazi leaders during the second world war. Nothing like this could be traced to the credit of the present accused.

Justice Jaranilla took strong exception to this line of argument in his separate opinion. "If a means is justified by an end, the use of the atomic bomb was justified," he wrote, "for it brought Japan to her knees and ended the horrible war. If the war had gone on longer, without the use of the atomic bomb, how many more thousands and thousands of helpless men, women and children would have needlessly died and suffered, and how much more destruction and devastation, hardly irreparable [*sic*], would have been wrought?" Taken together, Pal's and Jaranilla's comments essentially define the parameters of the controversy over the use of the bomb that persisted through the decades that followed.[72]

Pal's was an extraordinarily severe accusation, for it amounted to saying that in the war in Asia the only act comparable to Nazi atrocities was perpetrated by the leaders of the United States. No other justice went so far, but Justice Röling was also of the opinion that the air raids that culminated in the atomic bombings had violated the laws of war. Many Japanese, Röling concluded, felt similarly. In his contacts with students, he recalled, "The first thing they always asked was: 'Are you morally entitled to sit in judgment over the leaders of Japan when the Allies have burned down all of its cities with sometimes, as in Tokyo, in one night, 100,000 deaths and which culminated in the destruction of Hiroshima and Nagasaki? Those were war crimes."[73]

The hypocrisy of the victors would soon become a major thread in neonationalist thinking and Pal's dissent a well-thumbed bible for critics of the "Tokyo-war-crimes-trial view of history." That the American government itself soon embraced many erstwhile war criminals in the common cause of anticommunism—Shigemitsu Mamoru and the right-wing godfather Kodama Yoshio even before the occupation ended, and Kishi Nobusuke while prime minister from 1957 to 1960, to give but three examples—gave a perverse binational coloration to this repudiation of the Tokyo tribunal's verdict.[74]

To many Japanese, however, the crimes revealed by the trial, compounded by the perception that this was a world gone mad with violence and that such crimes against peace and humanity were not unique to Japan, reinforced the deep aversion to militarization and war that had come with defeat. The cynicism about the trial of those who took such a position cut differently from that of the neonationalists. As one left-wing intellectual wrote shortly after the occupation ended, what had begun as one of the great "revolutionary trials" of history turned into a "caricature" of justice. It became little more than a "technical trial," an exercise in retaliation against some twenty-odd men, a failure inseparable from the larger failure of the Americans to promote a fully democratic revolution. Small wonder that "too few people derived from it something that could become a true standard of behavior." However, he added, this did not mean that the ideals of peace and justice were now irrelevant. On the contrary, it was all the more important to cherish them, precisely because the trial had made their fragility so clear.[75] Where these ideals could be cherished, of course, was in the "renunciation of war" provisions of the new constitution.

Loser's Justice: Naming Names

The Japanese themselves were one of the Asian peoples excluded from participating in the prosecution of war criminals. Allied logic here was clear:

the accused should have no right to judge themselves, only to marshal a defense. The assumption, of course, was that virtually all Japanese bore some measure of responsibility for the war, and so none could be trusted to pursue the issue of war responsibility impartially where their compatriots were concerned. Such reasoning was understandable in the emotional heat of the time, particularly given the lack of serious resistance in Japan to the war regime apart from a small number of Communists. Still, excluding Japanese from any formal role in the investigation and prosecution of war criminals may have been shortsighted.

We enter here into historically perilous imaginings of what might have been. In this instance, though, we can at least turn to some participants in the events of the time who did give thought to a more active Japanese role in prosecuting war crimes. Formal involvement of this sort—possibly even extending to a presence on the bench (something Justice Röling, at least, considered, though only well after the fact)—could have removed some of the stigma of victor's justice from the trials.[76] It might also have strengthened popular acceptance of the idea that the Japanese, more than anyone else, had to take responsibility for their crimes. Failure to promote this was congruent with the larger failure of occupation authorities to recognize that their penchant for monopolizing authority could be counterproductive.

Early on, there was considerable grass-roots support for such involvement in uncovering the country's war crimes. As early as mid–September 1945, the shocking revelations of atrocities committed by Japanese troops led newspapers such as the *Asahi* to recommend that the Japanese should compile their own lists of prospective war criminals, since these would be longer than those the Allies could conceivably come up with, and possibly also conduct their own trials.[77] Many readers strongly agreed. By mid–October, the number of letters attacking "those responsible for the war"—not only the military cliques, but also bureaucrats, the police, and leaders of big business and finance—had risen sharply. The *Asahi*'s editors expressed surprise at how many people were urging that the Japanese punish their war criminals. Long before Prince Konoe and former privy seal Kido were ordered arrested, the paper was editorializing that civilians like them, and not just the so-called military cliques, should be included among the accused. Early in December, when the Allies' public list of prominent accused war criminals had reached 218 individuals, *Tensei Jingo*, the paper's most admired column, said this was far too few.[78] The confidential reports of the State Department's representative in Tokyo took note of such trends. "The general mood of the Japanese people,"

George Atcheson cabled Washington in mid-December, "is strongly in the mood of fixing war responsibility on the major suspects. Bitterness on account of Japan's defeat and an apparently growing realization that Japan should not have undertaken aggressive warfare has created a strong resentment against Japanese leaders."[79]

Such sentiments were generally endorsed on the political left. Marxists and Communists subscribed readily to a critique of Japanese "wars of aggression" dating back at least to the Manchurian Incident of 1931, and their early postsurrender campaigns called on "the people" to root out war criminals and collaborators at all levels of society. Although advocacy of people's tribunals did not become part of the Communist Party platform, prominent left-wing intellectuals such as Hosokawa Karoku gave early thought to encouraging "the trial and punishment by the Japanese people themselves of those responsible for the war." (Hosokawa actually envisioned this while in jail for thought crimes, awaiting liberation by the Allied victors.) On the eve of the Tokyo tribunal, some Japanese did succeed in warning against complacently leaving such trials to the Allies, urging that this "be done by the hands of the Japanese people as well." Others were less successful in getting this message out. At a public symposium in December 1946, a lawyer criticized the tribunal for excluding from the bench or prosecution staff Japanese who had opposed the war—and found the entire text of his speech suppressed by GHQ's censors when submitted for publication. In 1948, as the tribunal drew toward its conclusion, some progressive intellectuals renewed the call for people's courts and Japanese trials, only to find, by this date, that they could arouse no public interest whatsoever.[80]

At the other end of the political spectrum, the government also considered conducting trials. Although there was never the faintest chance that the victors would accept this idea, it nonetheless received attention in high circles before and after the surrender. It first surfaced on August 9, during an internal cabinet struggle over whether or not to surrender, when the military vainly attempted to make the right to conduct its own trials a condition for accepting the terms of the Potsdam Declaration.[81] When SCAP announced the first arrests of "Class A" suspects on September 11, the government immediately revived this idea. On September 12—shocked by the impending arrests and, related to this, Tōjō's attempt to avoid prosecution by committing suicide—the Higashikuni cabinet voted to investigate possible war crimes and conduct its own trials, regardless of what the Allies might do. Foreign Minister Shigemitsu (afterward arrested and tried for war crimes himself) conveyed the government's intent to GHQ and was informed on the following day that this would not be possible.

The cabinet proposal brought to the surface a dilemma that troubled many officials including the emperor, who observed, according to Kido's diary, that "those called war criminals by the enemy's standards, especially those in responsible positions, were all performing loyal duties, and to punish them in the name of the emperor would be unbearable." At the emperor's request, the cabinet reconsidered its decision—and reaffirmed it, finally gaining Hirohito's reluctant approval before submitting the proposal to GHQ. Kido himself found utterly implausible the notion of waging war in the emperor's name and then following with trials in the emperor's name. He also worried that this might bring out the Communists and result in people's trials, "where blood washes blood among ourselves."

Even after GHQ turned down its proposal, the cabinet did not let go of the idea. Prime Minister Higashikuni told foreign correspondents on September 18 that the government intended to investigate and punish those who had committed atrocities against POWs and other war crimes, a statement that received major coverage in the Japanese press. "Judgment of War Criminals: Begin by Our Own Hand" exclaimed one headline. Between September 1945 and March 1946, the government actually brought eight low-ranking individuals to trial for conventional war crimes in four separate trials, before SCAP intervened with a formal edict abolishing such proceedings. The presumption apparently was that once tried and sentenced, such individuals could not be subjected to double jeopardy and retried by the Allies. This hope was ill founded. The eight individuals were all retired in lower-level Allied tribunals and given more severe sentences. The relative leniency of sentences imposed in these few Japanese trials may have been a fair sample of what might have been expected if the government had been empowered to pursue war crimes at higher levels.[82]

A revealing example of official thinking on such matters can be found in the draft of an "Urgent Imperial Decree" composed sometime during these early months. This secret order never saw the light of day, but it is as vivid an example as we are likely to find of the lengths to which the ruling groups were willing to go, on their own, on the issue of responsibility—so long as such an inquiry could be coupled with reaffirmation of the emperor's virtue and innocence. Its full, baroque title was "Urgent Imperial Decree to Stabilize the People's Mind and Establish the Independent Popular Morality Necessary to Maintain National Order," and its royalist logic was elemental: the disastrous war constituted a betrayal of the emperor's trust, a tragic perversion of his abiding commitment to peace. Just as the victor nations assumed that historically and culturally *they* embodied the "civilized" ideals of respect for peace and humanity, so these authors depicted the same ideals as lying at the heart of their imperial tradition. What the Western-trained jurists laboring at Nuremberg and later Tokyo defined as "crimes against peace" and "crimes against humanity" became, in this proposed formulation, "the crime of treason."

The core of the draft decree's indictment was laid out, in cumbersome fashion, in the first three of its twelve provisions:

1. The aim of this decree is to stabilize the people's mind and establish the independent popular morality which is necessary to the maintenance of national order, and to this end to punish, remove, or dissolve those persons, institutions, or social organizations who or which, by going against the national polity, abusing their assistance to the emperor, and failing to follow his great spirit of peace, did with aggressive militarism lead or assist in leading government policies and popular trends, thus violating the instructions of the Meiji Emperor and inviting military-clique politics, with political parties knowingly aiding and abetting this, thereby instigating the Manchurian Incident, China Incident, and Great East Asia War, which destroyed the lives and assets of our people and various other peoples and endangered the national polity.

2. The following persons shall be sentenced to death or lifetime restraint for the crime of treason:

    a. Persons who without the emperor's order moved troops, needlessly initiated military activities, and commanded aggressive activities, making the Manchurian Incident, China Incident, and Great East Asia War unavoidable;

    b. Persons who violated the Imperial Rescript to Soldiers and Sailors of Meiji 15 [1882] and invited the situation of military-clique politics, going against the emperor's great spirit of peace by discarding the true essence of the national polity and engaging in despotic behavior or the like, thereby making the Great East Asia War inevitable.

3. The following persons shall receive sentences ranging from

under 10 years restraint to life for collaboration in the crime
of treason:

a. Persons directly involved in plans under provision 2a
    above;
b. Persons who agreed to the military-clique politics of
    provision 2b above, conspiring to strengthen or
    knowingly supporting this;
c. Persons who knowingly supported and cooperated
    with prowar plots and propaganda by military politi-
    cians and others, or created prowar public opinion
    contrary to the emperor's great spirit of peace, thus
    making the initiation of war inevitable.

The draft went on to indicate that in certain cases such punishments
might be commuted to what amounted to a purge from public office and
loss of the rights ordinarily accruing to subjects. Investigations, indictments, and trials would be handled under the Attorney General's office,
which would take up cases against individuals on receipt of petitions containing one hundred signatures.[83]

At first glance, it would seem difficult to imagine a greater contrast than
between this draft, still redolent with the rhetoric of wartime emperor
worship, and the ideals set forth in the Tokyo charter. For all its Japanese coloration, however, the "Urgent Imperial Decree" does suggest that
trials conducted by the Japanese would not have been altogether different
from what actually took place under the Tokyo tribunal. Like the actual
"Class A" war-crimes trials, such trials would have been showcase. A small
number of once-influential individuals would have been indicted, mostly
military officers associated with Tōjō, but also a few civilian officials such
as former foreign minister Matsuoka Yōsuke (who was indicted by the victors but died while the Tokyo trials were in progress). A documentary
record would have been established to make the case that Japanese militarism and aggression, beginning with the Manchurian Incident of 1931,
reflected "military-clique politics" rather than imperial policy. Vague
counterpart concepts to what the Allies called "crimes against peace" and
"crimes against humanity" would have been employed.

Essentially, this draft decree amounted to a rough formulation of
"loser's justice" that would have brought to the dock as scapegoats many
of the same individuals who were tried and convicted at the Tokyo tribunal. This is not mere conjecture, for in preparing its indictment, the
prosecution in the Tokyo trial relied greatly on finger pointers close to the

throne who endorsed the sentiments and tactics of the draft decree, even if they had not necessarily been directly involved in preparing it. The main purpose of the trials envisioned by the Japanese was identical to a fundamental subpurpose of the Tokyo trial: to establish the emperor as peace loving, innocent, and beyond politics. Loser's justice, like victor's justice, ultimately would have entailed arguing that Japan had been led into "aggressive militarism" by a small cabal of irresponsible militaristic leaders. Indeed, it would have involved a home-grown conspiracy theory.

However intriguing to imagine, leaving high-level war crimes trials to the Japanese themselves was inconceivable to the victors. Subsequently, the Americans rejected a more modest proposal that Japanese be included on the prosecution staff of the Tokyo tribunal.[84] It is easy to imagine the outcry this would have provoked outside Japan about letting the fox into the chicken coop; nonetheless, this was probably a genuinely promising lost opportunity. Capable and responsible lawyers were available who might have effectively staffed a contingent of assistant prosecutors, and a substantial portion of the populace—bitter about the war and hopeful for a clean start—would have supported such a role. A prosecution contingent of this sort might even have provided the nucleus for ongoing war-crimes investigations such as took place in Germany.

Lacking any formal role in prosecuting war criminals, the elites undertook informally to influence whom the victors decided to arrest and indict. Contrary (once again) to the wartime propaganda of "one hundred million hearts beating as one," the Japanese war machine had been wracked by internal conflicts. Factionalism was rife not merely between the military and civilian bureaucracies, but also within those bureaucracies— and not merely between the imperial army and navy, for example, but also within each service. By early 1945, even before the steady air raids against cities began, fingering the culprits responsible for Japan's impending defeat already had begun in earnest at the highest levels. The conquerors may have imagined themselves setting foot in a land of tight-lipped samurai bonded by blood, but what they found was closer to Byzantium, buzzing with whispers, riven with feuds.

This milieu of factional intrigue bubbled with conspiracy theories, none more immediately serviceable than the notion of "military-clique politics," which had received unusually forceful explication in February 1945 in a confidential presentation to the emperor by former prime minister Konoe Fumimaro. Subsequently known as the "Konoe Memorial," this apocalyptic presentation essentially placed all blame on Konoe's successor as prime minister, General Tōjō, and his entourage. As Konoe and *his* entourage saw it, the country had been brought to the verge of revolution by a diabolical clique of militarists and clandestine Communists. Both the militarists and leftists, his argument went, were contemptuous of capitalism and intent on bringing about a social and political revolution within Japan and throughout Asia.[85]

Konoe's conspiracy thesis amounted to a participant's rendering of the intense factional struggles that had consumed political and military circles throughout the 1930s and early 1940s. To a considerable degree, his argument followed the line taken by the *Kōdō-ha,* or Imperial Way faction, which lost power within the military after its complicity in an unsuccessful *coup d'état* in 1936. Among other things, *Kōdō-ha* supporters had been chary of taking on the United States and European powers by attacking their colonial enclaves in Southeast Asia and were more inclined to prime the country for an "advance north" against the Soviet Union. The *Kōdō-ha*'s nemesis, and Konoe's too, was the *Tōsei-ha* or Control faction headed by General Tōjō. Nothing fails like failure, and in the rubble of defeat the once-powerful Tōjō was the most vulnerable man in Japan, almost everyone's favorite target.

In the months after surrender, Konoe devoted much time and energy to conveying his perception of "military-clique politics" to the victors. At one point, he essentially gave a repeat performance of his audience with the emperor for General MacArthur. Following his suicide in December, the prince's colleagues and confederates carried on the campaign to focus Allied inquiries primarily on individuals who had been more or less aligned with the Control Faction. Konoe's private secretary Ushiba Tomohiko, later ambassador to the United States, immediately turned some seventy-five notebooks and other papers belonging to the prince over to the International Prosecution Section (IPS) and urged the victors to go after Tōjō and his supporters as well as Matsuoka Yōsuke, who as foreign minister under Konoe had been a prime mover behind Japan's alliance with Germany and Italy. Ushiba also recommended that the IPS make use of Iwabuchi Tatsuo as an informant. A prominent journalist who had been involved in the secret drafting of the Konoe Memorial, Iwabuchi worked indefatigably to promote the *Kōdō-ha* line, both in journalistic essays and briefings with the victors. He also identified the emperor's intimate adviser Kido Kōichi as bearing heavy responsibility for going along with the militarists and tendering bad advice to the sovereign. Yoshida Shigeru, another collaborator in the preparation of the memorial, also happily included Kido among the prime culprits he volunteered to the victors.[86]

Other Japanese associated with the Konoe Memorial also collaborated closely with both the IPS and GHQ's counterintelligence staff. Ueda Shunkichi, one of the most hysterical "communist conspiracy" theorists in the group, eventually submitted a list of seventy-eight names of those he deemed primarily responsible for Japan's folly and disaster.[87] Retired general Mazaki Jinzaburō, a former inspector general of military education and a leading ideologue in the Imperial Way faction, likewise cooperated enthusiastically. After being arrested as a suspected "Class A" war criminal, Mazaki essentially charmed his interrogators. He was particularly vehement in castigating Kido. Should they meet by chance, he told the Americans, he would spit in Kido's face. Although the *Kōdō-ha* firebrand had played a major role in stepping up ultranationalistic indoctrination in the army in the mid-1930s, the prosecutors who interviewed him, impressed by his "pro-American" (and virulently anticommunist) views, eliminated him from the original list of suspects designated to be tried immediately.[88]

Numerous others joined the chorus serenading IPS and GHQ investigators. Their refrain was predictable: exclude the emperor, focus on Tōjō and those close to him, and include a few obvious civilian officials such as the volatile, abrasive Matsuoka and the wily Kido. Some of these informants were insiders at the palace itself. In February 1946, Terasaki Hidenari, the emperor's indefatigable liaison with both IPS and GHQ, provided the prosecution staff with a list of forty-five names of individuals who, he claimed, bore prime responsibility for the disastrous war, buttressed with specific information concerning many of them. (Forty-two were still living.) He did not hesitate to intimate that some of his information came directly from the emperor. On one occasion, he informed his American contacts in the IPS that Hirohito had personally expressed disapproval of Matsuoka's proposal to attack the Soviet Union only a few months after the Japan–U.S.S.R. Neutrality Pact had been signed. The IPS files also contain a notation, apparently based on Terasaki's confidential conversations, to the effect that the emperor had inquired about why a certain former general, Arisue Seizō, had not been arrested.[89]

The two Japanese who had the greatest influence on the prosecution were an ex-general and the emperor's former privy seal. The IPS tuned in to former general Tanaka Ryūkichi in January 1946 and found him to be a knowledgeable, exceedingly voluble source of inside information about high-level army activity, including transgressions in China and the military's deep involvement in opium trafficking. Years after the trial, in which he appeared as a key witness for the prosecution, Tanaka explained that his rationale for incriminating so many former colleagues was "to make the emperor innocent by not having him appear in the trial, and thus maintain the national polity."[90]

More famous than Tanaka, and even more influential in naming names, was Kido, the grandson of one of the Meiji founding fathers. As privy seal from 1940 to 1945, he had not only been the coordinator of the imperial schedule and the emperor's confidant, but also a conduit of information, a processor of gossip, and a cunning intriguer. His enemies were numerous. Kido's impending arrest as a "Class A" suspect was announced on December 6, and he initially intended to shield his sovereign by taking on himself full responsibility for all imperial decisions sanctioning war. On December 10, however, following a moving farewell audience with the emperor, he was persuaded otherwise. His change in tactics was prompted by a conversation with the well-bred, young nominal Marxist Tsuru Shigeto (later a prominent economist and educator), to whom Kido was related by marriage. Tsuru, who had pursued higher education in the United States and earned a Ph.D. in economics at Harvard in 1940, explained that, given the American way of thinking, Kido's proposed tactic was grievously flawed. If he pleaded guilty, the Americans would take this as an indication that the emperor was guilty as well. To enhance the emperor's aura of innocence, it behooved him to plead innocent himself. Hearing this, Kido recorded in his diary, "I felt as if my mind has been settled."[91]

Tsuru apparently offered this advice with encouragement from his close acquaintance Paul Baran, a progressive American economist who was then in Japan with the U.S. Strategic Bombing Survey. Thus it came about that, on December 21 in his first interrogation session with the IPS (with Tsuru interpreting), Kido made known the existence of the detailed diary he had kept since 1930 and agreed to turn it over to the prosecution. He did so between December 24 and January 23 in three installments, the last being the diary entries for 1941—the period in which American investigators, fixated on Pearl Harbor, were most interested. The Kido diary quickly became known as the prosecution's "bible."[92]

It is possible that Kido vetted the diary slightly so as not to "inconvenience" his sovereign.[93] Certainly, the former privy seal was confident that his often cryptic daily entries, supplemented by what he told the prosecution by way of explanation, could be used to make the case that the emperor consistently hoped for peace and that the responsibility for resorting to war lay entirely with the government and the military. His calculated gamble paid off handsomely. Although the prosecution combed the diary meticulously in preparing its cases against the various defendants, those portions submitted as evidence were carefully screened to avoid any significant reference to Hirohito's words or actions. No part of the prosecution's unusually lengthy interrogation of Kido—thirty sessions producing approximately eight hundred pages of typed transcript—was ever introduced as direct evidence; for even Kido, notwithstanding his vigilance, occasionally made statements that could be interpreted as indicating that the emperor was a leader who bore some responsibility for Japan's course of action.[94]

In March 1946, as the final list of "Class A" suspects who would actually be brought to trial was being determined, the IPS decided to include, wherever possible, excerpts from both Tanaka Ryūichi's interrogation and Kido's diary in the file of every prospective defendant. Of the twenty-seven defendants who joined Kido in the tribunal's original indictment, he himself had singled out fifteen as bearing prime responsibility for Japan's war.[95]

chapter sixteen

WHAT DO YOU TELL THE DEAD
WHEN YOU LOSE?

The first, formal reactions of the Japanese on learning of defeat were couched in a rhetoric that could have been uttered in ancient Greece or China. Editorialists wrote of "the autumn of the hundred million weeping together," poets about a "silent wailing" throughout the land. Hearts were burned by painful fury, eaten away by tears. A general attached to Yasukuni Shrine, the final resting place of the souls of the war dead, spoke of swords broken and arrows exhausted, a traditional trope for defeat (and, indeed, emasculation), and described the tears of the deceased falling all about him, their faces pressing on his back.[1]

A week before the first occupation forces arrived, the novelist Osaragi Jirō addressed the dead more intimately in an "apology to departed heroes" in the daily *Asahi*, recounting his sleepless night in the wake of the emperor's broadcast. The faces of acquaintances killed in the war had passed before him: a friend in publishing, an occasional drinking companion, the taciturn chef at a favorite restaurant, a man he saw only at college baseball games, a doctor skilled in writing *waka* poems. He spoke of them as stars fading away with the whitening sky of dawn, imagined them alongside an endless procession of shadows on the horizon, and asked them a question that would not leave the minds of many Japanese in the years to come: "What can we do to ease your souls?" The answer seemed clear enough to Osaragi at that moment. All one could do was rely on the emperor's decision and look forward to the dawn of a day when, "shaking off old filth," a new Japan would be built. Only then, when humiliation had been overcome, would it be possible to "dedicate a requiem" to the spirits of the dead. Only then, perhaps, would it be possible for the dead to "smile and rest in peace."[2]

A Requiem for Departed Heroes

What do you tell the dead when you lose? It was this question, rather than the moral or legal perspectives of the victors, that preoccupied most Japanese as they tried to absorb the issues of war responsibility, guilt, repentance, and atonement. This was only natural—not because of cultural differences, but because the world is different when you lose. Where the victors asked who was responsible for Japanese aggression and the atrocities committed by the imperial forces, the more pressing question on the Japanese side was: who was responsible *for defeat?* And where the victors focused on Japan's guilt vis-à-vis other countries and peoples, the Japanese were overwhelmed by grief and guilt toward their own dead countrymen. The victors could comfort the souls of their dead, and console themselves, by reporting that the outcome of the war had been great and good. Just as every fighting man on the winning side became a hero, so no supreme sacrifice in the victorious struggle had been in vain. Triumph gave a measure of closure to grief. Defeat left the meaning of these war deaths—of kin, acquaintances, one's compatriots in general—raw and open.

The Japanese—certainly most Japanese men—did not arrive at war's end without some knowledge of the depredations and atrocities of the imperial forces. Millions had served abroad and witnessed or heard about such war crimes, even if they did not necessarily behave atrociously themselves. For those unaware of such brutal behavior—or at least of its scale and enormity—the victors' propaganda machinery soon provided grim, concrete evidence. If this was difficult to listen to, it proved even harder to absorb. As Osaragi observed in his tormented essay, for each ghostly figure in the endless procession of the Japanese dead, "there is a father, a sister, a brother." One might come to curse repatriated servicemen or treat them with contempt, but the Japanese dead still cried out for some kind of requiem. The millions of deaths inflicted by the emperor's soldiers and sailors, on the other hand, remained difficult to imagine as humans rather than just abstract numbers. The non-Japanese dead remained faceless. There were no familiar figures among them.[3]

In the eyes of the victors, Japan had no "departed heroes." The Tokyo tribunal made explicitly clear that this very notion was obscene for a nation whose every military action since 1928 had been an act of aggression and, ipso facto, "murder"; and whose cruelty toward both prisoners and civilians had been so widespread as to seem almost an expression of national character. One could hold memorial services for the military and civilian war dead after the defeat, but not praise them for their sacrifices. As the censorship of Yoshida Mitsuru's invocation of the last moments of the battleship *Yamato* indicated, there could be no ringing elegies to the bravery and glory of those who died fighting for their country. Yet it was impossible for Yoshida, or Osaragi, or the angry young ex-sailor Watanabe Kiyoshi, even as he cast off the last vestiges of emperor worship, to regard their dead compatriots as other than fundamentally good men. Millions of ordinary people, who similarly comprehended their country's lost war in terms of family, friends, neighbors, and passing acquaintances, shared this heartache.

As individuals such as Osaragi and Watanabe became more knowledgeable, they did not hesitate to criticize the war or Japanese society more generally. The transparent venality, corruption, and incompetence of the postsurrender elites were sufficient in themselves to undermine respect for authority—and, with this, belief in the old "holy war" myths. Much of the victors' propaganda and "reeducation," moreover, including testimony at the Tokyo tribunal, rested on previously suppressed information about systematic Japanese depredations abroad that could not be dismissed. Although many individuals came to acknowledge that the war had been wrong and involved criminal acts, however, this did not dampen a desperate need to accommodate their own dead in a positive manner in any collective acts of repentance and atonement. Osaragi's essay pointed to a common response to this dilemma: the sacrifices of the Japanese dead might be made meaningful by sloughing off "old filth" and creating a new society and culture. As it turned out, these new paths to and from the house of the dead would prove to be winding and twisted.

Nanbara Shigeru, a Christian educator who became president of Tokyo Imperial University shortly after the war ended, was typical of many respected figures in the complex way he evoked his country's war dead. Like most educators, Nanbara bore a heavy burden of personal guilt for having encouraged his students to support the wartime mission of "our glorious nation," and his transmutation into a leading war critic and apostle for peace involved more than a small leap of logic and faith. It amounted, as was often the case, to a conversion experience. The passion and sincerity of his new-found vision found compelling expression as early as September 1, 1945 in an essay in his university's newspaper. Since the recent conflict had exposed the cruelty and inhumanity of war in unprecedented ways, he began, the great task confronting education was to realize the fundamental "ideals of humanity" *(ningensei no risō,* for which he also gave the German term *Humanitätsideal),* which essentially corresponded to the universal principles of world religions. This involved a "new battle" in which the souls of students who had been killed would be present:

> In due time, our "colleagues" will return from the continent and from the southern islands. And the day is not far off when they will again fill the lecture halls and devote themselves to learning, burning with ideals and passion for the reconstruction of the ancestral land. I feel boundless sadness, however, thinking of the many great talents who will never return. All of them fought and died courageously as warriors. But even while being warriors, to the very last day they maintained their pride as students. They must have believed firmly, without any doubts, that in the end what upholds the country is truth and justice. Today, already, their souls have returned and are with us, I believe, and will bless and guide you from now on in your new battle.

To the departed souls themselves, Nanbara solemnly reported that the university had managed to preserve important scholarly materials through the war. They would, he was confident, be relieved to hear this.[4]

In November, Nanbara had occasion to address a gathering of returned students. He told them frankly that the real victors in the war were "reason and truth" and that the United States and Britain, not Japan, had been the bearers of these great ideals. This was a victory to be celebrated, and both defeat and the supreme sacrifice of those who had died should be seen from this perspective. Out of tragedy a new national life would be born, although not without struggle. Quoting Kierkegaard, he referred to a new "war of peace" in which the antagonist would be oneself and the great challenge was to develop in democratic directions and contribute to universal freedom. He concluded dramatically by welcoming back not only those present before him, but also their "comrades in battle" who had perished. From this time forward, those who had survived the war would be engaged in a new "war of truth" together with these departed comrades whose images remained in their hearts.[5]

In March 1946 it fell to Nanbara to conduct a memorial service for students and staff killed in the war. The text of the service was published by the popular monthly *Bungei Shunjū* under the title "A Report to Students Who Fell in Battle." The memorial ceremony, he pointed out, was meant to evoke the memory of dead countrymen—and the problems of guilt, repentance, and atonement—in an essentially secular "spiritual" way. He did speak, like the emperor, of enduring—and, like the Christian he was, of bearing a cross. He told the dead bluntly that Japan had been led into war by ignorant, reckless militarists and ultranationalists; that people, including those from the university, had followed along believing that they were fighting for truth and justice; that, unfortunately, truth and justice had been on the side of the United States and Britain. On all this, the judgment of history and reason was clear. This was not the same as saying, he pointed out, that the victors were necessarily just.

The dead, he continued, had been spared from witnessing the day of defeat and the hardship and spiritual pain that had followed. They should know, however, that the grievances the Japanese now felt were not against the wartime enemy, but against themselves. Political, social, and spiritual reforms unprecedented in Japanese history were now taking place and the construction of a "true and just" country was a real possibility. Lamenting the many brilliant students who had died, he spoke of them as being "a sacrifice of atonement for the crimes of the people."[6]

There were many things Nanbara did not address in these early presentations. He did not speak of the victims of Japanese aggression, did not mention other Asians at all; nor did he dwell on his own university's active complicity in promoting the militarism and ultranationalism he now condemned. There was, moreover, a danger of elitism as well as romanticization in such eulogies to "brilliant" students, as if the war's victims could and should be calibrated on some kind of sliding scale of social worth. Such limitations notwithstanding, Nanbara helped show one way in which an unjust war could be condemned while the war dead might still be honored and reassured (or, at least, those who survived them reassured) that they had not died in vain. This was a great moral and psychological dilemma that the victors did not have to confront, and for which they had little patience or tolerance. In one form or another, Nanbara's formula became a secular litany for great numbers of Japanese. Repentance and atonement were possible only for those who devoted themselves to constructing a new Japan devoted to peace and justice; and to pursue such

ideals was to honor the dead, for they were what the dead believed they
had been fighting for.

Irrationality, Science, and "Responsibility for Defeat"

Nanbara's conversion rested on the belief that he, like the truth-seeking
students he conjured up and mourned, had been misled by Japan's leaders. In this, he was perfectly in tune with popular sentiment, for the most
ubiquitous passive verb after the surrender was surely *damasareta*, "to
have been deceived." Even the most flagrant wartime propagandists seized
upon such slippery language as a detergent to wash away their personal
responsibility. Kondō Hidezō, the talented political cartoonist who rode the
military horse right up to the gates of doom with gay abandon and then
just as gaily satirized Tōjō behind bars, was unexceptional in this regard.
Life had been good before the war started, Kondō wrote early in 1946,
and whenever he thought of this he felt "hate for those Class-A war
criminals. All of us people were deceived and used by them, and cooperated in the war without knowing the true facts. Looking back now, this
was because of ignorance and being deceived."[7] The well-known writer
Kikuchi Kan, who played a leading role in mobilizing the literary world
behind the war, similarly tried to cleanse himself of the taint of collaboration by arguing (in an essay aptly titled "Wastebasket Talk") that the
miserable defeat was brought about by foolhardy leaders who suppressed
free expression.[8]

From this perspective, the people as a whole, and not just their "departed heroes," were war victims. An elaboration of this thesis was already
a media sensation before the Tokyo tribunal convened, in the form of a
"secret history" rushed into print by a team of journalists under the title
The Twenty-Year Whirlwind: Exposing the Inside Story of the Shōwa Period.
The first volume of this bestseller, covering the years from 1926 to 1936,
appeared on December 15, 1945. Some one hundred thousand copies were
sold in the first week, sparking stories about small mountains of the volume being piled up in bookstores as queues of eager buyers waited outside for the store doors to open. The second volume, which took the war
to its conclusion, was published on March 1, 1946 and quickly sold
700,000 to 800,000 copies. A slightly revised, consolidated edition was issued later that year. In one form or another, *The Twenty-Year Whirlwind*
remained on the "top ten" bestseller list through 1947, providing a nice
send-off for the "Class A" war crimes tribunal with its own home-bred
conspiracy thesis.[9]

The book was the brainchild of Masunaga Zenkichi, the head of an obscure publishing house in Tokyo, who heard the emperor's August 15 broadcast while on a trip to the countryside and was struck by the commercial potential in this tragic turn of events as he rode the train back to the capital that same day. (The phenomenally best-selling "Japanese-English Conversation Manual" had been conceived in almost identical circumstances.) Masunaga quickly recruited a small group of reporters from the *Mainichi* newspaper, most of them in the paper's East Asia bureau, who churned out their "inside story," primarily on the basis of the newspaper's files plus their own as well as their colleagues' personal knowledge. Their approach was lively and unimpeded by deep reflection. They were not particularly interested in exposing the nature of Japan's aggression or its victimization of others (the Rape of Nanking was not even mentioned) or in exploring broader issues of "war responsibility." The fact that the journalists were able to produce an instant "exposé" based primarily on existing files and their personal and previously undisclosed knowledge did not prompt them to engage in serious self-reflection on the complicity of the media in the war they were now righteously condemning. The *Mainichi* team was intent only on pointing fingers at those leaders who were primarily responsible for the great "crime" of bringing about "miserable defeat."[10]

They rounded up the usual suspects: the "military clique," mostly associated with the army rather than the navy and operating in concert with certain right-wing thugs and academic ideologues, plus a few industrialists and politicians.[11] Following the fashion in these months, they singled out Tōjō as archvillain. The former army minister and prime minister was virtually irresistible as a scapegoat, for he had not exactly enhanced his reputation by his behavior in the wake of defeat. Ordered arrested on September 11, he had shot himself in the chest four times; was propped up in a chair by American newsmen, who placed the pistol back in his hand, said "Hold it, Tōjō," and took his photo; delivered his "final words" to a reporter while awaiting an ambulance; and then was saved by American medical personnel, thanks to a blood transfusion from some anonymous GI. In the military hospital to which he was rushed, Tōjō was so impressed by the solicitude and efficiency of the personnel who treated him that he delivered a small speech in praise of "the strength of American democracy" to Foreign Ministry officials who visited him. Shortly after these misadventures, he presented General Robert Eichelberger, commander of the Eighth Army, with a valuable sword; and then, having mended nicely, went on to plead his innocence at the Tokyo tribunal.

It had been widely assumed that Tōjō should and would take his own life without delay. After all, it had been under his prime-ministerial aegis that, in 1941, the army issued its famous field code in which fighting men were admonished to "not live to incur the shame of becoming a prisoner." Tōjō received letters urging him to "commit suicide quickly," and someone reportedly sent him a coffin. When he belatedly summoned the will to die, chose the foreigner's way of the bullet rather than the samurai's way of the sword, and then botched even this, it was more than aggrieved patriots could bear. The writer Takami Jun captured this disgust succinctly in his diary: "Cowardly living on, and then using a pistol like a foreigner, failing to die. Japanese cannot help but smile bitterly. Why did General Tōjō not die right away as Army Minister Anami did? Why did General Tōjō not use a Japanese sword as Army Minister Anami did?" On the other hand, the French literature scholar Watanabe Kazuo, who had greeted the end of the war with immense relief, found this vaudeville amusing and took pleasure in recording in *his* diary how the hapless general had now "become mixed blood."[12] Whatever one might make of it, Tōjō's spectacular transformation from prime minister to prime culprit and scapegoat helped ensure a receptive audience for *The Twenty-Year Whirlwind*.

The journalists' conspiracy theory rested less on a portrait of diabolically evil schemers, however, than on what amounted to a diagnosis of collective dementia among the nation's leaders. Here, in potboiler prose, was a seductive variation of Nanbara's argument that ordinary people had been deceived by ignorant militarists devoid of "reason and truth." As *The Twenty-Year Whirlwind* would have it, "an irrational and unreasonable mentality that bordered on illness" had permeated every level of the imperial forces by the mid-1930s, so divorcing them from reality that their planning capability became a joke. Such irrationality "revealed itself conspicuously in the extremely unscientific way the Great East Asia War was conducted." The entire military command, it now could be said, probably should have been committed to a mental hospital.[13] Tōjō, it turned out, had been the captain of a huge ship of fools.

The thesis of collective irrationality carried with it a *technological* corollary of compelling attraction, namely, that the ultimate proof of the leaders' incompetence lay in their failure to comprehend Japan's backwardness in science and applied technology. By the time *The Twenty-Year Whirlwind* arrived in the bookstores, this connection between science and the "responsibility for defeat" had become an *idée fixe*—commonly linked, in the broadest symbolic manner, to the dropping of the atomic bombs. Between

August 8, when the destruction of Hiroshima by a "new weapon" was first reported, and mid-September, when occupation authorities prohibited almost all mention of nuclear devastation, few days passed when the single-sheet daily newspapers did not include at least passing reference to the mounting horror in both cities. The first detailed survey, summarized for the public before the occupation forces arrived, pronounced Hiroshima and Nagasaki a "living hell." The macabre effects of radiation sickness— apparent survivors suddenly perishing, while the estimated death toll doubled in a mere two weeks—were described as an "evil spirit" possessing Hiroshima.[14] There was a widespread sense of having experienced a forbidding, surreal new dimension of existence which no other people could hope to comprehend. Such consciousness of nuclear destruction became an integral even if not always evident part of all subsequent attempts to come to terms with the war's meaning. It reinforced a pervasive sense of powerlessness and lent an eerie kind of specialness to what might otherwise have felt like a pointless defeat.

In the final hours of the war, Kiyose Ichirō, who would emerge as a major defense attorney in the Tokyo war crimes trial, speculated publicly that racist contempt for Japanese "monkeys" explained why the Americans used the atomic bombs against Japan but not Germany.[15] Despite widespread denunciation of the "cruel" and "inhuman" American bombings, however, no abiding strain of virulent anti-American hatred carried over into the postwar period. Even before censorship was imposed, the tone of most commentary about the nuclear devastation had turned philosophical. The weapon itself, rather than those who deployed it, largely absorbed the characteristics of being cruel and inhuman; and from this, what came to be indicted was the cruelty of war in general. Defeat, victimization, an overwhelming sense of powerlessness in the face of undreamed-of weapons of destruction soon coalesced to become the basis of a new kind of anti-military nationalism.[16]

The idea that Japan could partially atone for past failures (or crimes, or evils, or sins) by drawing on its atomic bomb experience to become a champion of a nonmilitarized, nonnuclearized world would eventually become a cardinal tenet of the peace movement; but such an idea, explicitly expressed in the language of *zange* or repentance, emerged even before the occupation began. On August 27, the head of the central government's Information Bureau issued instructions to the public on how to respond to foreign occupation. War was a relative matter, he observed, and it was invariably the losers rather than victors who engaged in serious self-reflection. This was necessary and desirable. "The 'repentance' of the

hundred million people" should be done thoroughly, and perhaps by taking a leading role in prohibiting the future use of nuclear weapons, the
Japanese could turn themselves from the "losers of war" into the "win-
ners of peace."[17]

The terrible power of nuclear weaponry proved as mesmerizing as it
was terrifying, however, for nothing better exemplified America's superior
scientific, technological, and organizational capabilities. And so, in its peculiar way, the bomb became simultaneously a warning about future wars
and a beacon illuminating a path to future Japanese empowerment. On
August 16, on being named prime minister, Prince Higashikuni explained
that the biggest shortcoming of the war had been "science and technology." The next day, the outgoing minister of education thanked schoolchildren for their wartime efforts and told them that henceforth their task
was to elevate the nation's "science power and spiritual power" to the
highest level. Two days later, headlines trumpeted that under the new minister of education, Maeda Tamon, there would be "emphasis on basic science" in the postwar school system. "We lost to the enemy's science," an
article in the *Asahi* declared bluntly on August 20; "This was made clear
by a single atomic bomb dropped on Hiroshima." The article, headlined
"Toward a Country Built on Science," took care to emphasize that "science" had to be understood in its broadest sense as involving "reason" and
"rationalization" in all spheres of organization and at all levels of society—
the very idea that Nanbara Shigeru and countless others would seize on
and develop. A few days later, the *Asahi* reemphasized how irrationality
and nonscientific attitudes had spread throughout the political, economic,
and social spheres and had guaranteed defeat.[18]

"Science" soon became almost everyone's favorite concept for explaining both why the war was lost and where the future lay. Baron Wakatsuki
Reijirō, a former prime minister, urged his countrymen to have courage
and then proceeded to offer a depressing catalog of why they would need
it: because the former enemy possessed superior wealth, machinery, and
industrial skills, besides being more advanced in applied science, as witness the horrifying bombs. Two days after the surrender in Tokyo Bay, the
Ministry of Education announced that it was establishing a new bureau of
scientific education. In a speech to young people, Education Minister
Maeda explained that "the cultivation of scientific thinking ability" was
key to "the construction of a Japan of culture." Revised textbooks, it was
announced, would emphasize science. The government soon made known
that 500 million yen was being diverted from former military funds to pro-

mote science in everyday life.[19] General Yamashita Tomoyuki, about to go on trial in the Philippines, reiterated the familiar refrain with no frills. In an article translated from an American publication, the general was asked what he regarded to be the fundamental cause of Japan's defeat, and responded with the only English word he used in the entire interview. "Science," he said.[20]

Beyond doubt, this pragmatic fixation on "responsibility for defeat" was inherently conservative and self-serving. It was, however, like the loose thread that can unravel a tapestry—in this case, the fabric of the imperial state. The primary victimizers of the people were no longer the demonic Allied powers, but irresponsible leaders operating out of inherently backward, irrational, and repressive institutional structures. Thus, both the consciousness of having been victimized and the question of "responsibility for defeat" led inexorably to a commitment by many people to a more pluralistic, egalitarian, democratic, accountable, *rational* society—essentially what the occupation reformers were hoping to put in place. It was in this light that President Truman also found a receptive audience in Japan when he declared that the invention of the atomic bomb reflected what could be accomplished by a free society. Science could flourish only under a "spirit of freedom."[21]

Japanese scientists, many of them trained in Europe and the United States, applauded this new commitment. One of the first contingents of American scientists to arrive in Japan encountered a wonderful expression of these sentiments in the form of this makeshift notice, handwritten in English on brown wrapping paper and affixed to the front door of a major oceanographic institute outside of Tokyo:

> This is a marine biological station with her history of over sixty years.
> If you are from the Eastern Coast, some of you might know Woods Hole or Mt. Desert or Tortugas.
> If you are from the West Coast, you may know Pacific Grove or Puget Sound Biological Station.
> This place is a place like one of these.
> Take care of this place and protect the possibility for the continuation of our peaceful research.
> You can destroy the weapons and the war instruments
> But save the civil equipments for Japanese students
> When you are through with your job here

Notify to the University and let us come back to our scientific home

The notice was signed "The last one to go."[22]

Buddhism as Repentance and Repentance as Nationalism

The concept of "repentance" was placed at the center of public debate on August 28, the day the first advance contingent of Americans arrived at the Atsugi air base. Asked by Japanese journalists about the "cause of defeat," Prime Minister Higashikuni carefully explained that many factors had contributed, including restrictive laws, errors by military and governmental authorities, and a decline in popular morals as evidenced, for example, in black market activities. Then, borrowing a phrase from the statement by the head of the Information Bureau the previous day, he declared that "the military, civilian officials, and the people as a whole must thoroughly self-reflect and repent. I believe that the collective repentance of the hundred million *(ichioku sōzange)* is the first step in the resurrection of our country, the first step in bringing unity to our country."[23]

Since military and civilian officials had spent the previous two weeks destroying incriminating documents, there was a certain perverse truth to the notion that "responsibility" was, at that very moment, being leveled and collectivized. No one wanted it, no one claimed it. A few years later, the political scientist Maruyama Masao cleverly compared the government's "collective repentance" campaign to the cloud of black ink a squid squirts out in its desperate attempt to escape a threatening situation.[24] Although some individuals and groups did take the issue of personal responsibility seriously and engage in harsh self-criticism, the official version of collective repentance—the squid's ink, as it were—essentially faded away. Few individuals really believed that ordinary people bore responsibility for the war equal to that of the military and civilian groups. "This war was begun while we farmers knew nothing about it," one irate rural man exclaimed, "and ended in defeat while we believed we were winning. There is no need to do repentance for something we weren't in on. Repentance is necessary for those who betrayed and deceived the people." Another member of the hundred million was even terser. "If collective repentance of the hundred million means those in charge of the war are now trying to distribute responsibility among the people," he wrote to a newspaper, "then it's sneaky."[25]

While the government was promoting its version of collective repentance, Tanabe Hajime, one of the country's most influential philosophers, was completing a book-length manuscript on the same subject. Tanabe's treatise amounted to an intensely personal confession of doubt, spiritual crisis, and conversion by an intellectual whose austerity and aloofness were legendary, and whose aura of certitude had long seemed unbreachable. Despite a convoluted style that reflected his training in German philosophy, his text was an often ecstatic expression of faith in the redemptive wisdom of a thirteenth-century Japanese thinker, the Buddhist evangelist Shinran, whose prophetic language—resonating with suffering and emptiness, despair and negation, conversion and rebirth—seemed uncannily in tune with the ambiance of the defeated country.

One could hardly imagine a sharper contrast than that between Tanabe's densely reasoned disquisition on *zange*, or repentance, and the government's bromides on the same issue—with the exception of the fact that Tanabe's "repentance," too, was intensely nationalistic. His passionate reworking of Shinran's vision emphasized not just self-criticism or criticism of Japan, but criticism of all contemporary nations and cultures. Tanabe accepted defeat, acknowledged wrongdoing and despair, demanded repentance, envisioned rebirth—and did all this in a way that emphasized the unique, even superior, traditional wisdom of Japan. He claimed to be illuminating a singular Japanese path to redemption, a transcendent wisdom greater than anything Western thought had produced. For many thoughtful and tormented patriots, here was a sophisticated philosophy of contrition that snatched a kind of moral victory from the jaws of defeat. In the ruins of the most destructive war the world had ever known, for which Japan admittedly bore great responsibility, the path to redemption—and to global salvation as well—lay in the words of a Japanese prophet.

Tanabe did not develop these thoughts in reaction to the surrender. His "way of repentance" grew out of his experiences in the final months of 1944, when he was preparing his valedictory lectures on retiring from the prestigious chair in philosophy at Kyoto Imperial University. Long an ardent nationalist, whose "nonpolitical" philosophical theories neatly buttressed the militarists' racial and state-centered ideology, the rigidly disciplined Tanabe unexpectedly found himself falling to pieces. The country faced ruin and dishonor, and the death of a number of his students caused him to acknowledge his personal responsibility and, indeed, his sinfulness. "Weak-willed as I was," he confessed years later, "I found myself unable to resist [wartime thought control] and could not but yield to some degree to the prevalent mood, which is a shame deeper than I can bear. The already blind militarism had led so many of our graduates precipitously to the battlefields; among the fallen were more than ten from philosophy, for which I feel the height of personal responsibility and remorse. I can only lower my head and earnestly lament my sin."[26]

Tanabe withdrew into almost complete seclusion in February 1945; wrote furiously during the cataclysmic months of collapse; and saw his opus published in April 1946, just before the Tokyo tribunal convened. Its title was *Zangedō to shite no Tetsugaku*, "Philosophy as the Way of Repentance"—or, in more philosophical terms, "Philosophy as Metanoetics."[27] In his preface (dated October 1945), Tanabe described his state of mind as the war ended in terms familiar to students of both clinical psychology and religious conversion. He spoke of a deepening anxiety, suffering, and torment; of sorrow and pain, indecision and despair, an overwhelming sense of disgrace and failure; of reaching an intellectual impasse and being "driven to the point of exhaustion." In the opening pages of the treatise itself, he indulged in a paroxysm of self-denigration—characterizing himself as "evil and untruthful by nature," insincere, impure, vain, foolish, perverse, wicked, dishonest, and shameless.[28]

The most charismatic exemplar of such self-flagellation in the native tradition was Shinran, a master of self-loathing and ecstatic proselytizing who had founded the True Pure Land Sect, Japan's most popular Buddhist denomination. Tanabe's denunciation of his evil self actually read a bit like a crib from the master, for Shinran had aimed much the same abusive lexicon at himself. What Shinran offered beyond self-hatred was a language of transcendence that seemed to address the crisis of 1944–1945 with all the force it had possessed in the prophet's own day. The brilliant medieval evangelist offered the momentarily disoriented contemporary philosopher an embracing vision of negation, transcendence through conversion *(ōsō)*, and affirmative return to the world *(gensō)* that restored his confidence and brought him surprising joy. Tanabe felt himself reborn and regained his old dogmatic self-assurance. But he now saw the world anew. There could be no repentance without pain, he wrote, but the heart of *zange* "is the experience of conversion or transformation: sorrow and lament are turned into joy, shame and disgrace into gratitude. Hence when I say that our nation has no way to walk but the way of *zange* . . . I do not mean that we should sink into despair and stop there, but that we can hope to be transformed through resurrection and regeneration."[29]

For readers in occupied Japan, many of the Buddhist allusions in Tanabe's treatise undoubtedly carried double meanings, whether intended or not. He spoke of "self-surrender," of power and powerlessness, of Other Power *(tariki)* as opposed to Self Power *(jiriki)*—all fundamental to Shinran's strain of Buddhism, but also echoing with the idea of America-as-Other-Power. He spoke of transcending the false teachings and "evil institutions of the past," vintage Shinran-isms that rang as if they had been forged in the furnace of yesterday's defeat.

What made Tanabe's "way of repentance" even more striking was the knowledge that he had previously been known as a major interpreter of Kantian and Hegelian philosophy. He had studied in Germany with Heidegger among others, and his reputation had rested primarily on his identification with European thought. Tanabe was reputed never to have smiled, never to have made casual conversation, never to have left his house for frivolous purposes, never to have gone sight-seeing in his beautiful native city of Kyoto, never to have deigned to travel even to neighboring Osaka—and, despite his nationalism and some prior engagement with Buddhist thought, never to have rebelled against his European philosophical gods. Now, at the moment of gravest crisis and humiliation in his country's history, he used his new-found theory of repentance to declare the *inferiority* of the Western philosophical tradition.

On this critical issue, Tanabe departed dramatically from intellectuals such as Nanbara who equated repentance with embracing the "reason and truth" that were to be found in Western thought. Just as Shinran had showed him the way through his personal crisis, he wrote, the great teacher could show Japan the way out of its vale of doubt and tears. For Shinran's wisdom transcended Kant's, Hegel's, or Kierkegaard's—transcended, indeed, anything Western philosophy or religion had to offer. The evangelist's writings offered "a positive principle . . . not readily seen in any of the systems of Western philosophy." They made it possible "to develop a social doctrine inaccessible by way of Western philosophy alone." Indeed, Shinran showed the way to "the final culmination of the Kantian critique of reason."[30]

While so many others were extolling "science" and "rationality" as the keys to national redemption, Tanabe argued that Western reason had become trapped and "shredded" in antinomy, implacable contradiction. It had reached a dead end. It was a flower that blooms seven times only to wilt eight. That final wilting or negation, however, could be the last death before a Shinran-esque resurrection into a world beyond the impasse of Western logic. Tanabe took pains to underscore that Shinran's teachings did not offer only the ecstatic negation and transcendence *(ōsō)* of the conversion experience. They also emphasized a "returning to this world" *(gensō)* as a transformed individual capable of showing others the path of wisdom and compassion. Just as the born-again medieval convert to Shinran's "True Pure Land" teachings continued to participate in the mundane world, albeit now with an awakened heart and mind, so the Japanese penitent of 1946 likewise could turn to pressing social and political tasks with new vigor and insight. It was Tanabe's fervent hope that "in the current face-off between democracy and Marxist socialism," his own experience and logic could "offer a middle way from a standpoint that transcends them both."[31]

With this intellectual declaration of independence, Tanabe affirmed that there was a Japanese tradition not only capable of redeeming Japan after its wartime folly, but pregnant with the potential for saving the world. Through the very experience of defeat and repentance, Japan might be in a position to show the victors, already divided into capitalist and socialist camps, a proper middle path to a saner planet. Tanabe frequently strangled words, but he did not mince them, and his criticism of the victors was remarkably frank. "There can be no doubt that democracy and liberalism are producing the inequality of today's capitalist societies," he declared. "Socialism, meanwhile, sets up equality as its goal, but there is no disputing the fact that the socialist system invariably limits freedom and in that sense negates it." Shinran's "return to this world" provided the basis for formulating a new social ideal in which "people should be bound together by a brotherhood . . . that synthesizes the freedom of capitalistic society and the equality of the socialist state." To show the world "some concrete principle that will enable us to overcome the dichotomy of conflicting principles represented by the United States and the Soviet Union" was nothing less than "the historical mission that fate has accorded our country of Japan."[32]

This was an audacious use of old religious teachings for new ideological purposes. Tanabe turned Shinran's "unity of freedom and equality" into a point of departure for defending the creation of "social democracy," a theme he developed in other writings as well. In a similar manner, he turned the Buddhist critique of egoism into a standpoint from which to attack the "individualistic hedonism" of advanced capitalism, and fused Shinran's vision of "transindividual" love with another of the transcendent goals of this moment of defeat: "absolute peace."[33] He offered his many readers a way of criticizing their country *from within*, a "way of repentance" that escaped the hegemony of "Western" thought and cast critical light on other countries and peoples. He even managed to smuggle into his treatise disdainful comments about the conqueror's faith in imposing fundamental reform from above, observing that "a liberalism imposed from the outside is both nonsensical and contradictory."[34] Despite his previously fawning veneration of the throne, moreover, his new stance led him to a position entirely antithetical to the government's "repentance of the hundred million" campaign with its promotion of a sense of collective guilt toward the emperor for defeat. In Tanabe's view, the emperor above all others had an obligation to demonstrate repentance and assume responsibility for the war vis-à-vis both other countries and his own people, a position far more critical of his sovereign than that of the occupation authorities—and vastly more critical than the victors, with their rigid notion of the national mindset, ever acknowledged possible for Japanese. Tanabe even urged that the immense wealth of the imperial household be confiscated and turned over to the poor.[35]

Tanabe was regarded by contemporaries to be the most influential Japanese philosopher of the early postwar years, and the source of his appeal is not hard to discern. His tone was confessional yet formal. He preached repentance and rebirth, and resurrected an indigenous culture hero. While the victorious Allies were denouncing his country as a failed culture and archcriminal aggressor state, he accepted Japan's wrongdoing and guilt but denied their uniqueness, rejecting also the idea that traditional culture had nothing to offer. "Surely our own misguided nationalism stands in need of metanoesis," he wrote, "but at the same time so do the nationalistic perversions that infect democratic and socialist states alike." The defiant closing lines of his 1946 opus made the same point: "Obviously we are not the only country that needs *zange*. Other nations, too, should undertake its practice in a spirit of sincerity and humility, each acknowledging its own contradictions and faults, its own evil and sin. *Zange* is a task that world history imposes on all peoples in our times."[36]

The ways of thinking about repentance and atonement that prominent intellectuals like Nanbara and Tanabe offered had enduring legacies. Between late 1947 and 1950—as the Tokyo tribunal drew to a close, censorship tapered off, and an indigenous peace movement began to coalesce in opposition to Cold War militarization—the elite student war dead whom Nanbara had eulogized and Tanabe had mourned were resurrected through their own poignant wartime letters. December 1947 saw the publication of *In Distant Mountains and Rivers*, the controversial collection of writings by students from Tokyo Imperial University who were killed in the war. Two years later, *Listen—Voices from the Deep* appeared, containing wartime letters, poems, and diary entries from seventy-five student war dead affiliated with Tokyo and other universities. The editors of this best-selling collection acknowledged that they had taken care to exclude more nationalistic writings in favor of intimate words by the doubters and dreamers.

The endpapers of their volume reproduced sketches from the notebook of a student conscript who had starved to death on a Pacific island, and its emotional preface and postscript addressed fears that these texts might be misused "by those who once again plot war."

The pessimism of the time lay heavy on this collection, in sharp contrast to the dreams of a bright, peaceful future that had accompanied such evocations of dead students shortly after the defeat. In his brief preface, Professor Watanabe Kazuo of Tokyo University asked readers to imagine a field of white wooden crosses, steeped in blood, and exclaimed that "such crosses must never be erected again. Not even one." The postscript by Odagiri Hideo of Tokyo University painted a bleak picture of a Japan in which genuine democratic revolution had already been thwarted and the acrid smell of war again floated in the air. As the poignant wartime writings in *Listen—Voices from the Deep* indicated, Odagiri explained, the demands of humanity and reason had to be upheld by defending peace at all costs. "The blood that was shed," his appeal concluded, "can never be atoned for except by ensuring that such blood is never shed again." By this date, there could be little doubt that it was primarily the Americans whom the compilers had in mind when they spoke of "those who once again plot war." Essentially, the pure and noble dead were being recruited anew to stand against America.[37]

Other writings that appeared around the time the Tokyo trial ended reinforced such reconstructions of the war's meaning. One of the most famous of these was Takeyama Michio's *Harp of Burma (Biruma no Tategoto)*, an enormously popular novel (soon made, like *Listen—Voices from the Deep*, into a movie). Takeyama attempted to do through fiction what Tanabe Hajime had ventured through philosophy: to convey the meaning of the war—the themes of suffering, guilt, and atonement in particular—by way of Buddhism. The book's protagonist, a former soldier named Mizushima Yasuhiko, became the great fictive consoler of the souls of the country's war dead. His response to the horrors he witnessed in the final, hopeless stages of the war in Burma was to refuse repatriation and become a priest, wandering the jungles to search out and bury the remains of soldiers who had starved to death or been annihilated in combat. Possessed of a beautiful singing voice with which he had entertained his comrades, the gentle Mizushima often accompanied himself on the hand-held stringed instrument of the novel's title. Here, in another guise, was the Japanese soldier as near-saint. In a letter at the end of the novel, Mizushima explained his actions this way:

I want to learn the Buddhist teachings, to think and make them my own. Truly, we, our countrymen, suffered. Many innocent people became meaningless sacrifices. People who were like young trees, pure and clean,[38] parted from home, left their places of work, went out from their schools, and ended up leaving their bones in distant foreign lands. The more I think about it, the more unbearably regrettable it is.

Tormented by the question, so central to Buddhism, of why there is so much suffering and misery in the world, Mizushima concludes that humans will never understand perfectly. Still, Japan had brought its recent suffering upon itself.

Our country waged war, was defeated, and now suffers. That is because our desires got out of hand. It is because we were conceited and forgot what is most important in being human. Because the civilization we held up was extremely shallow in some respects.

These are human problems, not just Japan's alone, Mizushima observes. For himself, he intends to devote his life to studying and thinking carefully about such matters, to serving others and trying to act as one who can bring salvation.

Although *Harp of Burma* was a serious work of literature, it almost immediately was included in a popular series of books for children (which offered phonetic readings alongside the more difficult ideographs). Takeyama appended a brief postscript to this young people's edition, in which he referred to *In Distant Mountains and Rivers* and expressed hope that his own book might, like the student letters, make some of the war dead live again.[39] *In Distant Mountains and Rivers* itself was brought back into print shortly after the appearance of *Listen—Voices from the Deep*, with Nanbara Shigeru's March 1946 "report" to students who had fallen in battle now included as a preface.[40] In this way, various texts and presentations about war and redemption reinforced each other and survived as minor classics of the popular culture. In time a distinctive genre of "victim" literature arose, including the recollections of atomic-bomb survivors and offered not only in the name of antimilitarism and peace, but of repentance and atonement as well.

In 1950, the top ten bestseller list included the translation of Norman Mailer's novel *The Naked and the Dead.* Generally regarded as the finest American literary portrayal of the Pacific War, Mailer's reconstruction of one brutal island campaign confirmed the impression of war in general as an act of senseless and unspeakable cruelty—and of the Americans as capable of their own kinds of atrocities. As the novelist Shiina Rinzō observed after the Hollywood version of *The Naked and the Dead* had been screened in Japan, Mailer's depiction made clear that even Christians could not squarely confront the problem of guilt that arose in connection with killing in war.[41] Several eminent Japanese literary figures drew similarly on their personal military experiences to produce distinguished antiwar novels. Noma Hiroshi's *Zone of Emptiness (Shinkū Chitai)*, published in 1952, shocked readers with its portrayal of degradation and brutality in the imperial army and was widely praised as an immediate classic. Ōoka Shōhei's brilliant *Fires on the Plain (Nobi)*, about a straggler in the Philippines who encounters cannibalism by fellow Japanese and ultimately descends into madness, appeared the same year.[42]

Responding to Atrocity

People in all cultures and times have mythologized their own war dead, while soon forgetting their victims—if, in fact, they ever even give much thought to them. Many Japanese were sensitive to the dangers of such a myopic fixation even as they eulogized their dead compatriots as tragic victims of forces beyond their control. When liberal and left-wing intellectuals began to organize a formal peace movement in 1948, they acknowledged this to be a problem but nonetheless concluded that victim consciousness was the only foundation on which a more universal peace consciousness could eventually be built. Psychologically and ideologically, the argument went, the surest way to mobilize antimilitary sentiment was to keep alive the recollection of intimate loss and suffering. The image was one of gradually expanding concentric circles of antiwar consciousness: from personal to national to international. Transcending national and racial introversion, it was argued, would take time.[43]

In fact, victim consciousness never was transcended and the outer ring of these imagined circles never came to be sharply defined. Still, the stance of the "innocent bystander" that so many individuals adopted came under attack from various directions. Sometimes such criticism became highly theoretical, as in the intense debates among intellectuals concerning the weakness of a "subjective" consciousness of personal responsibility in Japanese culture.[44] On occasion, the critique was plain spoken. In mid-1946, the conservative educator Tsuda Sōkichi acknowledged that the people had been deceived by a combination of legal oppression and military propaganda; but he went on to call attention to the fact that Japan had had an elected parliament all through this period. "The people" themselves bore responsibility, he concluded, for "the fact that their intellectual ability was so weak as to be deceived, and they lacked the fortitude to repel or fight against oppression."[45] The critic Abe Shinnosuke, responding to the conclusion of the Tokyo war-crimes trial, similarly observed that "the majority of Japanese," having been deceived by the military leaders, "must bear responsibility for having been stupid."[46]

Most leftists evaded the issue of the responsibility of "the people." The more doctrinaire among them were intent on portraying the masses as victims of exploitation by the state and its oppressive ruling elites; some progressives also argued that dwelling on the criminal complicity of ordinary individuals could too easily be confused with both the self-serving "collective repentance" ideology associated with the government and the evocations of racial homogeneity that presurrender leaders had so assiduously cultivated.[47] More than a few ordinary people, however, spoke with feeling about such matters. In the publication of a local youth association, a young woman in Nagano prefecture observed that "after the defeat, newspapers wrote in unison that this was the crime of the military. . . . Naturally the government that deceived us is bad, but are we people who were deceived without crime? That stupidity, I think, is also a kind of crime."[48] As the Tokyo trial drew to a close, a farmer wrote the press that this was an occasion when all Japanese should reflect on their own thoughts and behavior during the war, and not simply look as a third party on the trials. "We must be aware that we, who were too weak and blind to authority, also are being judged," he observed. When the seven defendants sentenced to capital punishment were executed, a professor at a teachers' college in Osaka similarly urged his compatriots to recognize that this by no means brought the issue of war responsibility to an end. "The leaders alone could not have fought such a large-scale war," he pointed out. "We people were manipulated, and went along into a wrongful war of aggression, and invited miserable defeat. The crime is not that of the leaders alone, but rather all of us must bear responsibility." Henceforth, he went on, the people had to sit in judgment on themselves, and self-reflection on their war responsibility should continue forever. To this end, he proposed making the day of execution a day of national self-reflection.[49]

Such commonplace observations were sometimes coupled with an acknowledgment of Japanese atrocities. While a massive and prolonged act of barbarism such as the Rape of Nanking had been witnessed by the Japanese press corps and publicized internationally, it was not disclosed in

Japan. As the *Asahi*'s daily *Tensei Jingo* column contritely observed when
the massacre came up at the start of the Tokyo trials, "it is shameful that
not one line of truth was reported in the papers."[50] Other mass murders,
extending to the Rape of Manila in early 1945, were also suppressed. The
first detailed reports of atrocities, which focused on the Philippines and
China, shocked the Japanese greatly—so greatly that other atrocities paled
by comparison (with the possible exception of accounts of cannibalism by
Japanese soldiers that emerged in the course of the Tokyo trial). Conventional war crimes against Caucasians were nowhere near as unsettling, no
doubt at least partly because the massive presence of victorious white men
in occupied Japan made it impossible to visualize them as victims. Crimes
against Koreans and Formosans, Japan's former colonial subjects, were of
comparatively slight interest to either the victors or the vanquished. The
huge number of Indonesian "laborers" who were worked to death by the
imperial forces hardly seems to have registered at all.[51]

Between September 1945 and the end of the Tokyo trial, in any case,
atrocities were well publicized and more than a few people responded with
genuine horror. When the slaughter of civilians in Manila was made
known, the mother of a soldier wrote an astonishing letter to the national
press declaring that "even if such an atrocious soldier were my son, I could
not accept him back home. Let him be shot to death there." A young
woman, infusing the government's self-serving "collective repentance"
campaign with personal meaning, responded to these same revelations
with a letter declaring that "I understood the meaning of collective repentance for the first time when I heard about this." Some soldiers repatriated from the Philippines publicly expressed regret for their crimes,
even while recalling the hellish deaths of their own comrades there.[52]
Feminist reformers such as Hani Setsuko used the revelation of the Manila
atrocities to emphasize that this was by no means an aberration. War reflected the cultural level of a nation in every respect, Hani observed, and
she had been aware of comparable atrocities from the time she ran a
school in Peking. As she saw it, these atrocities toward civilians revealed
the low position of women in Japanese male psychology, as well as the general disregard Japanese held toward other people's children.[53]

Such perceptions carried the issue of "war responsibility" to the heart
of cultural considerations. In an article titled "Is the Morality of the People Low?" the left-wing magazine *Taihei* suggested that insensitivity to
atrocious behavior toward other peoples was rooted in the absence of "a
morality of common life" grounded in subjectively free and equal indi-

viduals.[54] The political scientist Maruyama Masao attributed such behavior to a predictable "transfer of oppression" in an inequitable, highly stratified society. The *Asahi*'s editorialists and columnists saw a social pathology here that reflected not merely racial arrogance, but also fundamental weaknesses in education and morality—possibly even a lacuna at the core of Japanese religious beliefs, which lacked a strict code of moral behavior.[55] For Marxists such as Nakanishi Kō, the barbaric behavior toward oppressed Asian peoples revealed a "feudalistic capitalistic exclusionism and selfishness rooted at the bottom of our hearts."[56]

Others responded less analytically to revelations of atrocity. In a bitter pun based on same-sounding ideographs, a contributor to a petroleum-industry publication observed immediately after the Tokyo trials began that the Imperial Army *(Kōgun)* had shown itself to be an "army of locusts" *(kōgun)*. "Responsibility for this war," the writer continued, "truly lies with the people as a whole."[57] Another writer, responding to revelations about the Rape of Nanking, wrote that "in every bit of food we ate, every piece of clothing we wore, a drop of the Chinese people's blood had seeped in. This is our people's crime, and responsibility must be borne by the people as a whole."[58] Ordinary people unaccustomed to writing for the public, such as housewives and farmers, wrote letters apologizing to the Chinese people and asking how the Japanese could make amends for such terrible behavior.[59] Kamei Fumio's sensitive treatment of China's sorrow in the opening minutes of his 1947 film *Between War and Peace* was the cinematic counterpart to such expressions of guilt. Such sensitivity was exceptional, but no one found it odd or out of place.

Some men and women turned to traditional short verse forms to express their feelings upon learning of their countrymen's atrocities. A poetry magazine published after the Tokyo tribunal ended included this evocation of popular responses:

> Vividly, the traces
> of the Japanese Army's atrocities are shown.
> Suddenly, a sharp gasp.

A village poetry magazine published this *waka* in early 1947:

> The crimes of Japanese soldiers
> who committed unspeakable atrocities
> in Nanking and Manila
> must be atoned for.

Saeki Jinzaburō, a poet of some repute, wrote two poems on the subject. One dealt with his immediate response to learning of the atrocities in China:

> So full of grief is this day
> that it made me forget
> the vexation of the day
> we lost the war.

The second went:

> Seizing married women,
> raping mothers in front of their children—
> this is the Imperial Army.

As it happened, the Japanese public never saw the first of these verses. The poem was suppressed by GHQ, obviously because the censors remained hypersensitive to any overt expression whatever of Japanese regret at losing the war.[60] This was unfortunate, for Saeki was of course not lamenting defeat here, but rather conveying, honestly and effectively, how his eyes had been opened and his conscience shocked by the revelation of his countrymen's crimes. His was one of the rare voices; and in the years that followed, as the Cold War intensified and the occupiers came to identify newly communist China as the archenemy, it became an integral part of American policy itself to discourage recollection of Japan's atrocities. These sensitive responses to revelation of the hands-on horrors perpetuated by the emperor's men, fragile and fragmented to begin with, never developed into a truly widespread popular acknowledgment of Japan as victimizer rather than victim.

Remembering the Criminals, Forgetting Their Crimes

In December 1947, almost a full year before the Tokyo tribunal handed down its judgments, the magazine *Van* offered a caustic observation about the fickleness of public opinion. "When those war advocates now called 'war criminals' first appeared on the stage, we welcomed them with loud applause," the popular monthly lamented. "When they fell, we followed along and spat on them. And now we have virtually forgotten about them." The magazine condemned this "laziness towards war criminals," as did other publications. To the editors of the intellectual journal *Sekai*, indifference to the trials extended right up to the sentencing and could only be regarded as one more distressing example of "the people's decadence," a fashionable term of cultural criticism at the time. From a somewhat different perspective, the *Mainichi* newspaper lamented the popular detachment that developed as the tribunal dragged on, but suggested that much the same sort of indifference could also be seen in German responses to the Nuremberg trial.[61]

As the Tokyo tribunal came to a close, the media assessed its meaning in the by now talismanic language of peace and democracy. The *Mainichi* warned that punishing war leaders did not mean that the people as a whole had been "washed and cleansed" of responsibility for crimes against peace. *Nihon Keizai Shimbun,* which catered to the business community, called for "self-reflection" and emphasized the responsibility people now bore to make sure they held their leaders to the principles of peace and democracy. The *Asahi* expressed regret that the people had not resisted dictatorial control more actively, and personal shame that the paper itself had caved in to the militarists. The task was to learn from such past failures, and on the basis of such self-knowledge resolve "to construct a peaceful democratic nation." The *Nikkeiren Taimusu,* the organ of a leading big-business association, editorialized that "all Japanese must believe in and uphold democracy, fully understand the meaning of 'crimes against peace,' and live as active peace-loving people."[62]

There was no great sense of justice having been truly carried out, however. Although some commentators sincerely welcomed the legal concept of "crimes against peace," establishing such a precedent by singling out a "representative" group of wartime leaders and executing a few of them did not impress many people by this date. Even the Marxist critic Hani Gorō responded to the capital punishments as a "grave sacrifice" that must not be wasted.[63]

The ambivalence embedded in such reactions—a strange compound of wishfulness and fatalism—was reflected in some of the *waka* poems that appeared in small publications in response to the trial's sentences and executions. An occasional verse spoke of the judgment as bringing a sense of relief, even a renewed commitment to creating a new country. A local monthly in Shizuoka, for example, carried this poem in early 1949:

> Since hearing the news
> of the execution of the seven war criminals,
> from deep within comes a power for reconstructing
>   Japan.[64]

More representative, however, was a feeling of resignation and uncertainty, nicely captured in a woman's contribution to one of the country's innumerable poetry magazines:

> Accepting the severity
> of the judgment for now,
> still there is a small feeling of hesitation[65]

Other poems spoke of hearing the news of the hangings and returning to one's inn in silence, or chewing one's tasteless food, or observing one's wife troubled by the inclusion of former foreign minister and prime minister Hirota among those executed.[66]

A *waka* by a resident of Sapporo, published in May 1949 as GHQ censorship was lapsing, suggested the sympathy that even the archvillain of the "Class A" drama, Tōjō, was then capable of eliciting:

> I agree and disagree
> with my elder brother,
> who murmurs that Tōjō is great after all.[67]

Tōjō's relative ascension in public esteem could be taken as a small barometer to the mood of the times, registering not nostalgia for the war years but an implicit critique of Allied double standards. There appears to have been a further dimension to Tōjō's little comeback, however, subterranean and ironic in the extreme. In the captive world of being occupied, he was the most prominent Japanese who openly disagreed with the Americans. Here was another surreal touch in the marathon dance of victor and vanquished. Under the "supreme command" of the Allied powers, and the Americans particularly, no public figure could openly express disagreement with occupation policy. In this situation, the freest men in the land could be said to be the accused war criminals who pleaded not guilty in the Tokyo trial. They, at least, were allowed to disagree openly with the victors. Outside the tribunal, every other public figure had to bite his tongue. Everyone else, in essence, played the sycophant.[68]

Like the sovereign to whom he was so loyal, Tōjō was a barometer in other ways as well. By singling him out as the preeminent symbol of aggression and defeat, Americans and Japanese alike made the central dimension of the war in Asia the conflict between the United States and Japan. Although Tōjō came out of the Kwantung Army and had played a major role in prosecuting the war in Asia, his identity as the "leader of the conspiracy" lay primarily in his association with the policies that culminated in war with the United States and the European powers. During the Tokyo trial, GHQ's censors had suppressed criticism that Tōjō's role had been overemphasized and that the real heart of "the problem of war responsibility" lay in aggression against China. Even after the trial ended, this critical observation remained taboo. Thus, an article by the legal scholar Kainō Michitaka that advanced this argument and was to appear in the June 1949 issue of a scholarly journal was suppressed *in toto*.[69]

By late 1948, when Tōjō and others were executed, the Americans and their anticommunist supporters in Japanese ruling circles had new reasons for downplaying China's suffering: China was "going communist" and replacing Japan in American eyes as the major enemy in Asia. By the fall of 1949, it was reliably reported that some five hundred former Japanese pilots were being recruited with SCAP's support by the ousted Chinese Nationalist regime in Taiwan for possible assistance in retaking the mainland.[70] As such clandestine recruitment revealed, the obverse side of forgetting China's ravishment was remembering how formidable and disciplined Japanese fighting men had been, how vigorously they had been indoctrinated in anticommunism—indeed, how much they knew at first hand about fighting on the Asian continent. General Robert Eichelberger, commander of the Eighth Army, expressed this publicly while the Tokyo trial was still in session when he observed that Japanese were the sort of soldiers whom officers dream of having under their command—an appalling comment.[71] Predictably, Tōjō's final written words before he went to the gallows also emphasized anticommunism. He exited an up-to-date man.

Some of Tōjō's more fortunate, unindicted fellow inmates at Sugamo Prison had the opportunity to remount the wave of anticommunism almost immediately after the trials ended and war crimes charges against them were dropped. Both Sasagawa Ryōichi and Kodama Yoshio, the rightwing godfathers who were released from prison the day after Tōjō and his six convicted colleagues were hanged, gave the impression of having proceeded directly from the prison gate to their literary agents to capitalize on the celebrity status their prison sojourns had conferred. Sasagawa's reminiscences were published in May 1949 under the title *Faces of Sugamo: Secret Stories of Imprisoned War Criminals (Sugamo no Hyōjō: Senpan Gokuchū Hiwa)*. Kodama's memoirs, titled *Gate of Fate (Unmei no Mon)* and featuring a photograph of Sugamo on the jacket, followed in October 1950.[72]

One Japanese war criminal, former colonel Tsuji Masanobu, made the transition from notoriety to celebrity status and commercial success without even making an interim stop at Sugamo. A fanatical ideologue and

December 26, 1949: Relatives of war criminals pardoned in a Christmas
amnesty by General MacArthur await their release in the snow outside the
barbed wire surrounding Sugamo Prison.

pathologically brutal staff officer, Tsuji bore heavy responsibility for massacres in both Singapore and the Philippines (including the Bataan death
march) and was also implicated in isolated atrocities extending to an act
of cannibalism following his execution of an American prisoner. Nominally one of Japan's most notorious fugitive war criminals, he had in fact
enjoyed the protection of first the Chinese, and then the Americans, before reemerging in the public eye in 1950. Following the surrender, Tsuji
escaped arrest by the British and made his way from Southeast Asia to
China, where his knowledge of military intelligence and his virulent anticommunism made him useful to the Nationalist forces under Chiang
Kai-shek. In mid-1946, he secretly returned to Japan (disguised as a
Chinese professor) and lived in concealment with the full knowledge of
General Willoughby and the support of former army colleagues whom
Willoughby was gathering under his aegis as the anticipated core of a future anticommunist Japanese military. This clandestine existence came to
an end when the United States lifted Tsuji's designation as a wanted war
criminal on New Year's Day of 1950; and, in that same year, the fruits
of his undercover life materialized in the form of not one but two best-

sellers—one purportedly recounting his "underground escape," the other dealing with the battle of Guadalcanal. Early in 1952, a third volume, on the struggle for Singapore, emerged from the old murderer's hand—and that same year, in the immediate wake of the occupation, he was elected to the House of Representatives from Ishikawa, his home prefecture.[73]

Tsuji's dark charisma as a flamboyant militarist who had outfoxed the victors, vanished like a ghost, and never spent a day in jail surely accounted for much of the popularity of his books. After four years of knuckling under to American rule, with no end to the occupation yet in sight, defiant figures such as Tsuji, Sasagawa, Kodama, and Tōjō could exercise a certain crude appeal even to people who did not share their politics. Their politics were actually part of the joke. The former Japanese and American antagonists, war criminals and their judges, were now more or less on the same side. Yet while the lifting of censorship enabled apologists for Japan's holy war such as these to speak openly, theirs were marginal voices. As an ordinary company employee observed on the fourth anniversary of Japan's capitulation, he was aware of almost no one who still truly grieved over the defeat. This was true not merely of what was said in public, but also what he heard in private conversations among close acquaintances. Such a response to a national disaster was "truly astonishing," he thought, and reflected a general awareness that war, more than anything else, crushes the dignity of the individual.[74] Virtually no one in Japan still dreamed Tsuji's old dreams of a Greater East Asia Co-Prosperity Sphere—but, by much the same token, few cared to be reminded any more about what the imperial "army of locusts" had actually done in that short-lived sphere of conquest.

In this milieu of willful forgetting, the years that followed witnessed the almost wholesale rehabilitation of "B/C" as well as "Class A" war criminals in popular consciousness. Defendants who had been convicted and sentenced to imprisonment became openly regarded as victims rather than victimizers, their prison stays within Japan made as pleasant and entertaining as possible. Those who had been executed, often in far-away lands, were resurrected through their own parting words. One remembered the criminals, while forgetting their crimes.

The treatment of inmates in Sugamo Prison provided the most blatant early example of this. In a total prisoner population of around four thousand, the several hundred convicted war criminals were accorded many amenities. From an early date, they were allowed to publish their own newspaper, the *Sugamo Shimbun,* and as time passed they were afforded what can only be described as prime access to live entertainment. A small theater that became known as "Sugamo Hall" was rehabilitated for their convenience. Beginning with a November 1950 performance by the Ishii ballet company, a literal parade of stars crossed its stage. There was a certain aura of the command performance in these presentations, as entertainers from the outside world lined up to perform for what amounted to a celebrity audience.

These programs continued for several years after the occupation ended, and were neither clandestine nor furtive. Entertainers happily posed for photos—a favorite background setting being Sugamo's distinctive wall and watch tower—and both the number of visitors and variety of their talents was impressive. By one account, at least 114 performances were offered inmates in 1952 alone, involving close to 2,900 entertainers. The well-known comedians Entatsu and Kingorō both played Sugamo Hall. So did the violinist Suwa Nejiko and some of the country's most celebrated popular singers, including the child star Misora Hibari, Kasagi Shizuko (of boogie-woogie fame), Haida Katsuhiko, Akasaka Koume, and Fujiyama Ichirō. The famous Nichigeki dance troupe entertained the convicted war criminals, as did little-known groups of geisha, prefectural folk dancers, and the like. Old-fashioned sword-fighting dramas were presented. To judge from the photographic record, the inmates also had the pleasure of being entertained by young women who displayed more naked flesh in more bizarre postures than these once dour militarists had permitted in public when they were still the arbiters of Imperial Way morality. Some prison entertainment took place outside Sugamo Hall. The Yomiuri Giants and the Mainichi Orions, professional baseball teams, helped the inmates celebrate the imminent end of the occupation with an exhibition game on March 28, 1952. The Sugamo playing field was also graced by teams from the "Japan Women's Baseball League," and by Western-style wrestlers. Equestrian teams performed and then lined up like soldiers before the crowd for a commemorative photo. Female gymnasts in shorts smiled for the Sugamo audience and for the camera.[75]

In the summer of 1952, the image of convicted war criminals as war victims reached new heights thanks to a maudlin song written by two men who had been sentenced to death for war crimes in the Philippines. Neither Daida Gintarō, the lyricist, nor Itō Masayasu, who composed the music, was actually executed. Daida claimed he had been framed and wrote his tearful lyrics early in 1952 after many of his fellow inmates at the Monten Lupa prison in the Philippines had been executed. The song's title—"Ah, the Night Is Deep in Monten Lupa"—revealed a perfect feel for the hot buttons of Japanese sentimentality, and the tune was said to be so appealing that even Filipino prison guards found themselves singing it.

The song was introduced at the prison on April 29 (the first day after Japan had regained its independence) in a performance that also included singing *Kimigayo*, the national anthem, and bowing as a group in the direction of the imperial palace in far-away Tokyo, a homage routinely performed by the imperial forces during their rampage through Asia. Through their Japanese prison chaplain, Daida and Itō succeeded in having a famous female singer, Watanabe Hamako, introduce the song in Japan, where it became a sensation.

The lyrics began by evoking the "inconsolable thoughts" that beset each prisoner in the depths of night as he recalled his "home far away." Looking at the moon, blurred by tears, each dreamed "of a gentle mother"—saw her agonizing over when her "beloved child" would return; imagined her heart flying "straight toward the southern sky," plaintively crying like a cuckoo seeking its lost offspring. And when morning finally came to Monten Lupa, the final stanza of the song exclaimed, the sun also rose in each prisoner's heart, giving all of them the hope and courage to "live strong . . . until we step again onto the soil of Japan."

There could be no more pristine rendering of "rising sun" nationalism and nostalgia than this; and, soon afterward, the desperate hopes of the condemned war criminals in Monten Lupa became reality. In July 1953, all of these prisoners were repatriated to Japan, where some went free while others were transferred to Sugamo Prison. Around twenty-eight thousand people met their ship to welcome them home. No one in the crowd breathed a word, as far as can be told, about all the mothers and children and prisoners of war whom the emperor's soldiers and sailors had murdered in the Philippines.[76]

While surviving war criminals were being pampered, projects were also under way to honor the memories of those who had been executed and restore to them a modicum of the individuality that had been stripped away when they were given the blanket label "war criminal." In a remarkably effective conservative publishing endeavor, the last written testaments of these men, their final letters to their families, their death poems and parting words were collected and made public. Between 1950 and 1954, more than fifteen edited books of this nature were published. Their compatriots were giving these men the last word in the most effective manner possible, by letting them speak as if from the grave.[77]

The most comprehensive and famous of these publications was a massive collection (741 triple-column pages) published in December 1953 under the title *Testaments of the Century (Seiki no Isho)*. In it, some 692 executed war criminals were given voice, and the variety of their personalities and opinions was impressive. The appeal of such writings was all the more compelling because—like the writings of student conscripts, the musings of Nagai Takashi in Nagasaki, or even Dazai Osamu's sensational novel *The Setting Sun*—these words reflected the thoughts and emotions of men looking death in the eye.[78]

Famous or notorious men passed judgment on their trials here. Tōjō's last words found a permanent place among these testaments, apologizing to the people and the emperor for defeat while reaffirming his innocence of international crimes. The Tokyo tribunal had been a political trial, he stated, and the Americans and British had made three grave mistakes. They had destroyed Japan as a bulwark against communism, allowed Manchuria (his old Kwantung Army base) to become Red, and divided Korea in two, guaranteeing trouble for the future (a prophetic observation a year and a half before the Korean War broke out). To end war forever, Tōjō observed—much like Takeyama Michio's fictional priest in *Harp of Burma*—required ending human desire and greed. Unlike that hopeful mendicant, however, Tōjō believed changing human nature to be impossible, and so assumed World War III was inevitable. He asked the Americans not to let Japan turn Red, and concluded his parting testament by apologizing for "mistakes" the military may have made but also asking the United States to reflect on the atomic bombs and their bombing campaign against civilians.[79]

The last letters to his family of General Homma Masaharu, who had been found guilty of "command responsibility" for the Bataan death march, spoke similarly of victor's justice. "To say that the United States is a fair country is a bald lie," he declared. Mentioning the hundreds of thousands of Japanese killed in air raids and by the atomic bombs, he morosely observed that "there is no such thing as justice in international relations in this universe."[80] Some condemned men accepted responsibility for the acts of which they were accused, but the more common response was that their trials had been essentially an exercise in revenge and double standards, with little care taken to ensure genuinely fair hearings. Several condemned men, Homma among them, quoted a cynical saying from the time of the Meiji Restoration: "Win and you are the official army, lose and you are the rebels" *(kateba kangun, makereba zokugun)*.[81]

The final words of these convicted men almost invariably revealed deep concern for the families they were leaving behind and the need to erase from the minds of loved ones as well as society at large the impression that they were really "criminals" in any ordinary sense, rather than simply victims of a tragic losing war. It would be difficult to overestimate the weight of this consideration in these final "private" epistles. Sons *had* to assure their parents—and husbands their wives, and fathers their children—that they were not murderers, not beasts; that there was an explanation for whatever it was they had been convicted of doing; that their loved ones could still hold up their heads. That a great many of these writings were intensely private communications did not necessarily guarantee their truthfulness, as the compilers of such materials would have had readers believe. But where dissembling began or ended was often impossible to say, sometimes undoubtedly for the writers themselves.

Of all the familial ties cherished in Japanese culture, the wettest and most sentimental surely is that between son and mother. The syrupy popularity of "Ah, the Night Is Deep in Monten Lupa" was testimony to this, and a good number of the writings in *Testaments of the Century* similarly revealed the deep attachment of these condemned men to their mothers. In this regard, several of the writings quoted a celebrated death poem by Yoshida Shōin, one of the most charismatic of the young samurai who mobilized to overthrow the feudal regime in the name of the emperor in the mid-nineteenth century. Yoshida was executed in 1863 at the age of twenty-seven for having attempted to assassinate an emissary of the shogun, and his poem was written on the day of his beheading:

> A parent's feelings surpass
> even our own feelings toward our parents.
> I wonder how she will hear today's news.[82]

The "rebel" and "criminal" Yoshida was apotheosized soon afterward as one of the heroes of modern Japan, a perfect symbol of purity of purpose and tragic sacrifice. To these condemned men less than a century later, about to die as apparent failures, even as monsters, his posthumous vindication could only have been a source of hope and consolation. That Yoshida also had been an outspoken critic of the imperialistic encroachment of the Western "barbarians" did not exactly lessen his appeal. His farewell poem was cherished, however, primarily because it revealed that even as fate swept him away, his final thoughts and concerns lay with his mother. He became, by this, intensely humanized. He was made gentle.

References to being a "sacrifice" *(gisei)* appeared frequently in the writings of the men condemned to death in the lower-level trials. Such a man might see himself as "a noble sacrifice for the country," or a sacrifice for the nation "paid in blood," or a sacrifice "for defeat" or "for the reconstruction of Japan" or "for the race," or more hopefully yet for "world peace."[83] There was no single, agreed-on agent of their victimization. To some, it was clearly and plainly the victorious Allies. A condemned officer in Singapore characterized himself as simply "a victim of British revenge."[84] Many others, however, portrayed themselves as victims of their own superiors, who had forced them to perform acts now judged criminal and then, in the familiar logic of irresponsibility, denied this afterwards.[85] Others saw themselves as little more than the casual victims of war itself. A Kempeitai officer executed in Burma in 1946 devoted his last words to a philosophical rumination on duty and individual responsibility, and concluded that he and others like him were simply "vague sacrifices that accompany war."[86]

Like most of the other collections of writings by such men, the vigilant conservatism of *Testaments of the Century* was reflected in the cryptic biographies that accompanied each entry, which simply mentioned where the writers were executed but not why. In fact, many men did discuss the crimes they were accused of, sometimes in considerable detail. Essentially, however, these publications were designed to humanize men who had died in apparent disgrace and to absolve them—or at least absolve many of them—of war crimes. In a curious way, such forgiveness was a natural, almost mirrorlike counterpart to the treatment the emperor had received from the Americans. Just as Hirohito had been absolved of wrongdoing or war responsibility, so now accused war criminals were implicitly forgiven—by those, of course, who had not felt the impact of their acts—for whatever they might have done in the cauldron of war. Their gentle words were quoted, while their actual deeds went all but ignored. They were presented as having lacked any real control over the events in which they participated. The emperor's celebrated "declaration of humanness" had been a step down. He was descending from "manifest deity," whatever exactly that meant, to human status. These men, on the other hand, were in the process of being escorted upwards from demonized realms into the same world of humanity. But whether it was the living god or the executed war criminals who were being humanized, the final impression conveyed was that no one, from the top to the bottom of the old imperium, was truly responsible for the terrible war and the atrocious acts that had accompanied it everywhere.

Such refashioning of history and memory, such a restoration of a human face to the entire imperial army and navy, was part of a national process of psychological mending. If even these most miserable of military men could be shown to be complex and sensitive human beings, however flawed, then the stigma of having been little more than a rapacious army of locusts might be lessened if not altogether removed. The reactionary potential of such publications was thus considerable, for these last testaments could easily be read as but another subgenre in the literature of Japanese victimization. They could also be seen, at least in part, as anti-Caucasian texts; for although these condemned men protested their innocence in every theater where war-crimes trials were held, expressions of bitterness were especially keen concerning the harshness and double standards of Dutch, British, and American captors.[87] Only in isolated cases, however, did such testaments serve as reminders of how grievously and casually the Japanese had sacrificed other Asians.

Notwithstanding this, the overall impression of collections of posthumous writings such as *Testaments of the Century* was not so much anger or even apologia, but rather of an overwhelming feeling of waste, regret, and sorrow. The final words of the war criminals were not so different as might be imagined from those of the student conscripts killed in the war that were collected and published by liberal and left-wing academics. Indeed, one of the most moving testaments of the dead that appeared in *Listen—Voices from the Deep* was written by a student of economics from Kyoto Imperial University named Kimura Hisao, who was executed as a war criminal in Singapore in May 1946 for abuse of prisoners. A biography of Kimura was published in November 1948, and his remarkable last testament, scribbled in the margins of one of Tanabe Hajime's books of philosophy, was reproduced in the student anthology along with poems he had written in jail. Kimura's entry in *Testaments of the Century* consisted of a final note to his father, together with most of these same poems.[88] One of the two death verses Kimura composed on the day before he was hanged conveyed a sense of having come to terms with dying at the age of twenty-six:

> The wind has quieted down,
> the rain has ceased.
> Fresh in the morning sun,
> I shall depart tomorrow.

The other poem would have reminded any Japanese reader of Yoshida Shōin:

> Without fear or sorrow,
> I shall go to the gallows
> cherishing my mother's face.

With but a few exceptions, the last testaments of the executed war criminals were not written for publication. They were collected and published after exhaustive appeals to family and friends of the deceased, and their public impact was contradictory—for even as they weakened consciousness of war responsibility, they intensified recollection of the terrible human costs of militarism and war. Like the writings of dead students and the memoirs of atomic-bomb victims, these last words became part of a public portfolio of intensely personalized portraits of individual Japanese whose lives were destroyed by war. They were usually beautified self-portraits, and in a strange or at least unanticipated way they helped make up what Osaragi Jirō, years earlier, had spoken of as a "requiem" to the Japanese war dead. The language of many of these last testaments was elegiac. These men may have been executed as "conventional" war criminals, but a great many of them wrote uncommonly well. The usual style and format of publication, moreover, almost always highlighted the elegiac tone.

Testaments of the Century, for example, was prefaced with a photograph of a bronze statue of Kannon, the bodhisattva of mercy and compassion. Entries were grouped according to the places where the Allied war-crimes trials had been held, and each section was titled with an evocative phrase taken from one of the personal texts that followed. "The Bond between Japan and China" was the subtitle for entries by individuals condemned to death in China; "Fate" for those tried by the British in Burma; "Welcoming Spring" for Hong Kong. The section by condemned men held in Sugamo Prison was titled "Purple Violet"; for the writings of those in Guam, simply "Humans."

Each individual entry also was given a title derived from the text by the editors and these, too, conveyed the generally sorrowful, reflective, humanistic tone that those who promoted such literature sought to convey. From the China trials, for example, came such headings as these: "From the Dark World," "Tears of Chinese Soldiers," "Beloved Japan," "Nothingness and Forgetting," "Every Day a Good Day." From the Dutch East Indies: "Margins of Life," "Friendship Extending to the Other Shore," "A Hundred Faces." From Australia: "Good and Evil." From Malaya and North Borneo: "Notice to Britain," "Returning to Mother" (the writer's mother was deceased). From Burma: "To Haruko" (a letter to a young daughter, written entirely without ideographs in the cursive syllabary). From Indochina: "Various People." From Guam: "Thoughts of a Scientist." From Sugamo Prison: "Coming Alone, Leaving Alone," "Bearing a Cross" (the writer had learned Christian hymns), "Wailing Wall," "White

Cloud," "External Peace," "Farewell."[89] Monstrous criminals to their enemies, they now became philosophers and poets to many of their countryfolk.

A short preface to a selection of entries from *Testaments of the Century* excerpted in a monthly magazine spoke of these writings as "a great bible" that could inspire the entire Japanese race and help all humankind cleanse itself. The editors exhorted their readers to take heart in remembering that the darkest hour comes before the dawn—*Akebono*, the name of the magazine itself, meant "Dawn"—and to devote themselves to establishing everlasting peace.[90] This was the rhetoric of purity and peace so often heard in the war years. It was a nationalistic plea to forgive the dishonored dead. It was a smoke screen obscuring the horrendous reality of Japanese war crimes and atrocities. But it was also, in this extraordinarily introverted world, an antiwar statement. Many of the writings by the condemned war criminals reinforced this in ways that moved readers deeply. The last letter to his young daughter from an army medical doctor was representative in this regard. He told her to try to make her way through life without ever killing a living thing, not even a dragonfly.

He had been executed after being convicted of maltreating Allied prisoners.[91]

Part VI

RECONSTRUCTIONS

chapter seventeen

ENGINEERING GROWTH

When the occupation began, most Americans including General MacArthur assumed that it should and would last no more than three years. Three years, however, turned out to be only its halfway point; and by then a great many Japanese had become transparently weary of foreign control. The supreme commander still received his fan mail; the ideal of "peace" remained precious; "democracy" continued to be offered as a touchstone for defining the good society; but the conquerors, although still possessed of extraordinary authority, had begun to be regarded as just one more interest group in a crowded Japanese political landscape.

The change was not only in the minds of the occupied. Driven by Cold War considerations, the Americans began to jettison many of the original ideals of "demilitarization and democratization" that had seemed so un-expected and inspiring to a defeated populace in 1945. In the process, they aligned themselves more and more openly with the conservative and even right-wing elements in Japanese society, including individuals who had been closely identified with the lost war. Charges were dropped against prominent figures who had been arrested for war crimes. The economy was turned back over to big capitalists and state bureaucrats. Politicians and other wartime leaders who had been prohibited from holding public office were gradually "depurged," while on the other side of the coin the radical left was subjected to the "Red purges." The notion of a genuinely democratic revolution—from above, below, or anywhere else—seemed more and more, as the cliché had it, a dream within a dream. Before the occupation ended, the Japanese media had dubbed this dramatic turn of policy the "reverse course."[1]

Public opinion polls, those heralded American contributions to "grass-roots" democratization, told the story of popular disillusionment in striking terms. In 1948, a majority of Japanese still responded affirmatively when asked if they believed their country was heading in a "good direction." By 1949, the majority response was negative. Beginning in 1949 as well, solid majorities of respondents expressed fear that Japan might again become embroiled in war.[2]

The dreams of peace, so carefully cultivated by victor and vanquished alike, suddenly seemed fragile indeed in a world in which the former Allied powers appeared to be at each other's and everybody else's throats. Although censorship had often screened the news that reached the public, that only made the awakening to the realities of the Cold War war world more shocking when it came resoundingly home. The harsh European attempts to reimpose colonial rule in Southeast Asia, the violence of Soviet repression in Eastern Europe, the stunning communist victory in the Chinese civil war, the terrifying emergence of a nuclear arms race—all these were not dream, but nightmarish reality.

"Oh, Mistake!"

On June 25, 1950, war erupted in neighboring Korea; and the United States, only four years after imposing its "peace constitution," hastened to impose remilitarization on a reluctant nation even as its war-related purchases gave a transfusion to the country's anemic economy. Everything was suddenly better—and worse—in unanticipated and unnerving ways. The occupation would still continue for almost two more years, but "the occupation" as it had previously been understood by both victors and vanquished was over. The conflict in Korea ushered in a new world; and for the first time since the surrender Japan, willing or not, was distinctly part of this world.

In this ominously unfolding atmosphere, petty incidents sometimes came to assume outsized symbolic import. In 1948, a student from elite Tokyo University was arrested for burglary. It was not the commission of the crime that drew attention, but rather his cynical defense of his actions. "Judgment of what is a crime," he said—as the Tokyo war-crimes trials were coming to an end—"cannot be made in today's society." To the editors of one of the popular lexicons of new words and expressions, this seemed a perfect example of the "confusion and emptiness" of the times.[3] (Such cynicism would soon have many sophisticated expressions, such as the increasingly dark and ambiguous films of director Kurosawa Akira which culminated in 1950 in the brilliantly framed "relative truths" of *Rashōmon.*)

Two years later, a reckless and rootless young couple gave the mass media a terser phrase and a more sensational incident to consider when a young man employed as a chauffeur at Nihon University brazenly stole university funds from a coworker and spent them on a spree with his eighteen-year-old girlfriend, the daughter of a professor. When apprehended, he responded with what quickly became one of the most famous English phrases of the occupation: "Oh, mistake!" The thief and his paramour, it turned out, were devotees of Hollywood gangster films, conversed in a curious polyglot of Japanese and broken English, had no apparent interests beyond material consumption and sexual pleasure, and felt no remorse at all for their casual crime. Social commentators hastened to turn the couple into symbols of the amorality of postwar youth, but the unforgettable phrase resonated far more broadly. In a world where everyone seemed to be scrambling to change horses, much of the recent past, war and occupation alike, seemed increasingly easy to dismiss as just a mistake.[4]

Weariness with the overweening American presence (coupled with the easing of censorship) gave rise to what amounted to a soft counterrevolution in popular culture. In popular songs, facetious lyrics became trendy, and the blatantly American boogie-woogie style that had been associated with a new sense of joy and vitality gave way to a traditional sort of sentimentality. From 1949 on, the prevailing mood in music and lyrics was one of wandering, loneliness, resignation, and a nostalgia that spilled over into inconsolable longing. The charismatic symbol of this bittersweet emotionalism was the precocious Misora Hibari, born in 1937, who rocketed to fame singing boogie-woogie but became the exemplary voice of a "native" sentimentalism before the occupation drew to a close.[5]

Chanbara, traditional swordplay dramas, returned to theaters around this time, while romanticized samurai stories and novels with medieval themes began to reappear in bookstores, led by a succession of four huge bestsellers by Yoshikawa Eiji beginning in 1948. Even the translations into Japanese that made it to the bestseller list, including Norman Mailer's searing, critical rendering of American combat in the Pacific, *The Naked and the Dead*, reflected the new conservatism. For two years beginning in

1949, the "top ten" list included Margaret Mitchell's blockbuster 1936 novel *Gone With the Wind*. It did not take great imagination to read Japan itself into this portrayal of the defeated Confederacy, where romantic evocations of a genteel civilization "gone with the wind" were counterpoised against the vicissitudes of a war-torn landscape and a postbellum society plagued by Yankee interlopers and groping for a new identity. Even Mitchell's sharply contrasted heroines could be viewed as figures in a Japanese mirror: the pure, submissive, domestic Melanie and pragmatic, opportunistic, sensual Scarlett. Victimization, struggle for survival, Scarlett's defiant vow that "I'm never going to be hungry again"—all made Mitchell's saga of the American South seem very familiar indeed.[6]

The end of the dream of genuine liberation and grass-roots democracy was reflected more directly in the fate of a popular booklet for children. *Atarashii Kempō no Hanashi* (A Chat About Our New Constitution), written in a burst of enthusiasm and idealism by Asai Kiyoshi, a Keio University professor, had been published in 1947 and widely used as a social studies text for seventh graders. Unlike the Meiji constitution, the little text stated, the new constitution represented the will of the Japanese people. The essence of the charter was threefold: international pacifism, democracy, and popular sovereignty—all of which were interrelated. Japan's renunciation of war meant that the nation would never maintain an army, navy, or air force. An accompanying full-page illustration showed materiel being melted down in the cauldron of "renunciation of war," out of which came the wonderful buildings, trains, merchant ships, fire engines, and communications towers of a peaceful nation. The booklet went on to emphasize the basic rights of freedom and equality, including equality between men and women.

Asai's little book was downgraded to a supplementary text by the Ministry of Education in 1950 and dropped entirely in 1951, even though the education system remained under close American scrutiny. The book's fate could hardly have been otherwise. By this date Japan was not only creating a new military under the eagle's wing, but also had embarked at long last on the path of economic recovery—and was utterly dependent, in this regard, on a war boom based on providing "special procurements" for American forces fighting in Korea.[7]

Visible (and Invisible) Hands

The most zealous exponents of the "Oh, mistake!" philosophy were actually to be found in policy-making positions in Washington and Tokyo, for the reversal of priorities in economic policy entailed repudiating one of the most basic instructions issued to General MacArthur as the occupation began. This order had stipulated that while the general's supreme authority extended "to all matters in the economic sphere," SCAP would "not assume any responsibility for the economic rehabilitation of Japan or the strengthening of the Japanese economy." The secret planning documents behind this policy made no bones about the punitive thinking involved. "The plight of Japan is the direct outcome of its own behavior," observed an early State-War-Navy Coordinating Committee paper, "and the Allies will not undertake the burden of repairing the damage."[8] Until 1948, in accordance with these instructions, the general's economic bureaucrats confined themselves primarily to such punitive and reformist tasks as designating factories for potential reparations, directing the dissolution of zaibatsu holding companies, compiling purge lists of top business managers, identifying "excessive concentrations of economic power" that needed to be broken up to ensure economic democracy, and orchestrating land reform and the abolition of tenancy. Although the United States eventually provided around $2 billion in economic aid, the bulk of it took the form of critical foodstuffs and materials deemed essential just to keep the economy afloat and stave off social unrest.[9]

In occupied Germany, responsibility for labor, finance, and the economy had been dispersed among separate sections within the Allied command. In Japan, these three huge spheres of activity—along with control over the fields of science and technology—were consolidated under a single Economic and Science Section (E.S.S.) that employed some five hundred economists, engineers, and former businessmen and supervised three ministries (Finance, Labor, and Commerce and Industry) as well as the enormously influential Bank of Japan and a newly created Economic Stabilization Board. The occupation authorities retained many of the control mechanisms over the economy introduced in the course of Japan's mobilization for "total war"; on occasion, they even promoted or endorsed controls that exceeded those enforced during the war. Until the closing years of the occupation, E.S.S. also exercised "centralized and authoritarian" control over Japanese trade. The influential recommendations of top-level advisory missions dispatched from Washington only reinforced the institutionalization of such top-down policy making.[10]

One striking consequence of Japan's long years of war mobilization was a high concentration of capital in the hands of a small number of zaibatsu conglomerates. Occupation authorities singled out ten of these combines for particularly close scrutiny: four famous "old zaibatsu" (Mitsui,

Mitsubishi, Sumitomo, and Yasuda), plus six "new zaibatsu" that had risen to positions of dominance by collaborating closely with the military (Asano, Furukawa, Nissan, Okura, Nomura, and Nakajima). By war's end, the "big four" had increased the 10 percent share of investment capital they controlled in 1937 to 25 percent. In 1945, the ten combines together controlled 49 percent of capital invested in mining, machinery, ship-building, and chemicals, 50 percent in banking, 60 percent in insurance, and 61 percent in shipping.[11]

Despite such war-induced concentration and growth, the leaders of big business were generally happy to see the war end. Their overseas investments had been lost, a great part of their holdings in the home islands lay in ruins—and that was only the half of it. Most big capitalists had come to see the war as a struggle for survival against *internal* enemies— that is, against militarists and economic bureaucrats of a "national socialist" persuasion intent on imposing virtually total state control over the private sector. The prospect of being occupied by true believers in capitalism thus seemed, at first blush, a welcome turn of events, particularly to the many executives who had enjoyed prewar personal and business relationships with Americans and British.

These sentiments were openly acknowledged in corporate circles. Executives at the Mitsui combine, the largest of the zaibatsu, convened two days after the surrender broadcast in an atmosphere of confidence about the prospects for converting to peaceful production under the Americans. As one of them, Edo Hideo, recounted, there was general agreement that "the Americans and British won't treat us badly and everything will go well." After all, they congratulated themselves, had not Mitsui been criticized by militarists and ultrarightists for being "pacifistic, liberal, and pro-American"? Similar views were expressed at a secret meeting of heads of industry held shortly before the occupation forces arrived. Asano Ryōzō, a Harvard graduate who was president of a large steel company, went so far as to blurt out in English, "Our friend is coming." Japan was fortunate that the United States would lead the occupation, he exclaimed, and this could even provide an opportunity for the country to "strive to achieve the American standard of living." Most business leaders shared this naive optimism. "We dreamed neither of the zaibatsu being dissolved," recalled another executive present at this meeting, "nor of our business leaders being purged."[12]

Although capitalists were more likely than economic bureaucrats to welcome the conquerors, neither group had prepared for impending defeat with concrete plans. In this regard, the Japanese exited from the war in

much the same dazed manner in which they entered it. When Japan attacked Pearl Harbor in 1941, its military and civilian leaders had engaged
in no serious long-term projections concerning the industrial potential of
the United States or the probable course of the colossal conflict that lay
before them. "Sometimes," Prime Minister Tōjō stated at the time, referring to a famous hillside temple in Kyoto, "one simply has to leap off
the terrace of Kiyomizu-dera." As the war ended, the elites revealed
themselves to be no less casual when it came to planning ahead. Only a
few individuals had given serious thought to how to convert from a
wartime to a peacetime economy, or what such an economy might look
like. Bureaucrats, businessmen, and politicians alike still seemed to be operating under the Kiyomizu-dera delusion: somehow, like a movie run in
reverse, they would just jump back onto the terrace. One way or another,
things would work themselves out.

Most of the jumping that actually greeted the emperor's broadcast was
frenetic and destructive. Military stockpiles as well as production materials in the hands of private contractors were either hidden or moved directly into the black market. Army, Navy, and Munitions Ministry officials
immediately began withdrawing enormous sums to pay off contractors or
line their own pockets and the pockets of favored associates. The Finance
Ministry and the central Bank of Japan turned to the printing presses and
flooded the country with freshly inked currency to provide severance pay
to millions of laid-off workers and demobilized servicemen. At the same
time, to mollify popular anxiety, wartime restrictions on withdrawals from
personal savings accounts were relaxed. Serious bookkeeping was abandoned, and records were deliberately destroyed. The result was fiscal and
economic chaos and the beginning of the ravenous inflation that ultimately drained the economy.[13]

To the leaders of big business, this flailing and thrashing seemed of no
great import. The crushing blow to their morale came not with the un-
tidiness of defeat, but from the revelation of the punitive and reformist
economic policies the victors had in mind. When executives like Asano
spoke confidently of their American "friends," they were thinking of the
conservative businessmen and clubbish diplomats they had known before
the war. The New Deal–style reformism and trust-busting fervor that so
influenced initial occupation policy was simply beyond their imaginations.
Mitsui, for example, greeted the arriving occupation authorities with ambitious plans for a "Mitsui Reconstruction Company." This new undertaking, they explained, would ensure continued work for their employees
and subsidiary firms by engaging—even at a loss, if necessary—in projects

such as housing construction and land reclamation aimed at increasing farm acreage. They were shocked when SCAP officials dismissed this as a ruse meant to obfuscate the zaibatsu's war responsibility—and chagrined beyond measure when the first head of E.S.S., who ordered their holding company dissolved, turned out to be a former department-store executive who confessed that he could comprehend neither Japanese psychology nor the country's "structure of business."[14]

The same aura of wishful thinking permeated a report submitted to the Ministry of Commerce and Industry by leading representatives of the business community in the week following formal surrender. Blithely ignoring the harsh reality of unconditional surrender, the report emphasized the "totally voluntary attitude of the Japanese" in carrying out the terms of the Potsdam Declaration and urged the government to "negotiate" firmly with the victors to ensure Japanese control over economic developments. Among their great miscalculations, the authors of the report assumed that, in order to pay reparations, the country would be encouraged to rehabilitate its heavy and chemical industries and resume trade and overseas business operations throughout Asia.[15] Comparably roseate proposals for converting war-related factories to production for the civilian economy continued to be advanced until early December, when the Americans—in a chilling pronouncement by their reparations spokesman, Edwin Pauley—made clear that they were more interested in *removing* such plants as reparations than in converting them for Japan's own internal consumption. On the basis of these initial U.S. recommendations, some eleven hundred large enterprises concentrated in the chemical and heavy industry sectors were soon designated as possible reparations. Some of these plants were allowed to produce for the civilian economy, but with the understanding that they be physically ready for removal at a moment's notice; others were forced to stand idle. Most designated facilities remained in this uncertain status until the end of 1950.[16]

Where the antitrust agenda was concerned, SCAP moved swiftly to clarify its policy of dissolving zaibatsu holding companies and eliminating zaibatsu family members as dominant share holders and officeholders. On the other hand, delay in implementing its broader "economic deconcentration" policy placed major productive facilities in an uncertain status for as long as three to four years. An "economic purge" of wartime executives was delayed until January 1947 (resulting in the resignation or ouster of over fifteen hundred individuals); the giant Mitsui and Mitsubishi trading companies were broken up the following July; and it was only in December that the Diet received and passed a basic "deconcentration law." A list of 325 large firms designated for possible breakup under this law was finally made public in February 1948, two and a half years after the surrender. By this time, reverse-course economic policies were already gaining ascendance, and in the months that followed most of these companies were dropped from the list. ("Deconcentration" ended in August 1949 with a mere eleven enterprises ordered to be broken up.) As a major survey of postwar management put it, these circumstances unsurprisingly contributed to a drastic decline in "the will to produce" on the part of big businessmen.[17]

In certain unplanned ways, economic chaos did abet reform and encourage initiative. Hyperinflation significantly diminished corporate and personal debts while enabling SCAP to dispossess rural landlords and dissolve family-held zaibatsu holdings in a manner that amounted to virtual confiscation.[18] At the same time, the pessimism and passivity that settled over big business left the entrepreneurial initiative to small and medium-size enterprises. More flexible and less vulnerable to being designated for reparations or deconcentration, they were able to respond creatively to the postwar crisis.

The majority of small and medium-size companies that flourished in the ashes of defeat catered to consumer demands, and some of their innovative accomplishments soon acquired a storybook quality. A year after the surrender, the *Tokyo Shimbun* published an article headlined "Bombs Reborn as Hand Warmers," itemizing the ways in which former producers of war materials had altered their production lines to meet peacetime demands. The hand warmers in the headline referred to the traditional charcoal-burning *hibachi,* now being made from decapitated bomb casings sitting on their fins. The newspaper's long catalog of similar conversions included rice containers made from large artillery casings and tea containers from smaller-caliber shells. A former manufacturer of mirrors used in searchlights was now engaged in producing window glass and glass lampshades; a subcontractor who produced pistons for fighter planes had retooled his product to work in irrigation pumps.[19]

Similar examples could be multiplied many times over, occasionally with names that became corporate hallmarks of the postwar economy. The president of the Komatsu company, a maker of tank parts and anchor chains for warships, was inspired by the sight of American bulldozers leveling an airfield to make the bulldozer his company's literal vehicle for recovery. The successful postwar camera manufacturers Canon and Nikon had been producers of optics for the war effort. In 1946, Honda Katsuichirō, who had been a small wartime subcontractor supplying piston rings to Toyota, began motorizing bicycles with tiny engines the military had used in communications devices. Hugely popular among small-shop owners and petty black-market operatives, these motorbikes led to the marketing of a motorcycle named "Dream" in 1949 and marked the beginning of the Honda Motor Company empire. Many successful postwar electronics firms had their genesis in middle-size companies that had manufactured communications equipment for the military. Within weeks of the surrender, Ibuka Masaru, a former employee of one such a company, had collaborated with a few colleagues to produce a popular device that converted shortwave transmissions to normal broadcasting frequencies—laying the basis for the great Sony corporation.[20]

SCAP stimulated certain areas of entrepreneurship in both deliberate and unplanned ways. Favorable consideration was given to industries that produced textiles, fertilizer, electrical appliances, and the like. GI demand boosted not only the Suntory whiskey company, but also the sales and good reputation of Canon and later Nikon cameras. By happenstance, the occupation force also helped revitalize the construction and ceramic industries. Roughly 50 percent of the huge "war termination costs" that SCAP exacted from the government for its own maintenance went to construction expenses (including toilets, sinks, tile, and the like), providing employment for a host of contractors. With their talent for turning foreign words to native use, the Japanese quickly began to refer to the process of obtaining SCAP building contracts, which were negotiated at local levels nationwide, as a transaction governed by the "three Ps": petitions, parties, and presents.[21]

Entrepreneurial activity of this sort was hardly sufficient to restore economic vitality, however, and the government soon felt compelled to identify and promote strategic industrial sectors. SCAP's support of this was noteworthy. Early in 1947, General MacArthur himself went so far as to tell the prime minister that it was essential to pursue "an integrated approach across the entire economic front." As interpreted by W. Macmahon Ball, the Australian representative on the Allied Council that met in Tokyo, this amounted to "an unequivocal statement by SCAP that in the existing situation it was essential that 'free enterprise' should be replaced by a directed economy." By the time the supreme commander issued this dictum, the government already had committed itself to an interventionist program known as "priority production."[22]

The brainchild of academic economists of various ideological persuasions, priority production received broad bipartisan support. Essentially, it stood on three "legs": allocation of labor and scarce resources to key industrial sectors; direct government subsidies to those sectors; and policy-guided loans through a newly created Reconstruction Finance Bank (RFB). Such industrial targeting aimed at stimulating overall recovery by channeling resources to the most basic energy producers (coal and subsequently electric power) and the most pivotal heavy and chemical industries (iron and steel, and to a lesser degree fertilizer). Shipbuilding and textiles also received favored treatment as crucial to any future export recovery. Until 1949, around one-quarter of all outside funding in these six targeted sectors had come from the government through the RFB, with a mere ninety-seven firms receiving 87 percent of all RFB loans.[23]

This proved a system ripe for graft, and businessmen, bureaucrats, and politicians lost no time in abusing it. Bribes led to funds, and portions of those funds in turn went into payoffs and further bribes. Particularly large sums flowed from big coal operators to conservative politicians, but the sewer of illicit payments spilled over in all directions and even stained GHQ itself. This came to public attention in a sensational manner with exposure of the "Shōwa Denkō scandal" in 1948, which revealed the enormous web of corruption cast by a single fertilizer company in the course of obtaining huge RFB loans. First mentioned in a journalistic exposé in April 1948, the scandal caused the collapse of the cabinet headed by Ashida Hitoshi in October and, by the end of the year, had resulted in the arrest of sixty-four prominent individuals including former prime minister Ashida himself, a former finance minister (currently head of the Economic Stabilization Board), high officials in the Ministry of Commerce and Industry as well as the Ministry of Agriculture and Forestry, leading bankers, well-known politicians in the two dominant conservative parties, and a top figure in the Socialist Party (accused of accepting a bribe to water down the Diet investigation of the case). The scandal was so murky as to defy full exposure (it dragged on in the courts for thirteen years), but it offered all the ingredients that aficionados of dirty dealing could hope for (competing factions, black-market transactions, a geisha-turned-mistress, an elegant upper-class woman who moved between company executives and high officers in GHQ, and double bookkeeping that revealed vague expenditures for the "entertainment" of GHQ officials). In effect, RFB abuses succeeded the end-of-war looting and hoarding as a new stage in wholesale corruption.[24]

Corruption, however, was just the fallout from priority production. By 1949, output in targeted sectors had risen fairly substantially, and in this more positive climate hoarded goods began to move back into the production cycle. Yet the costs of the "weighted" policy also were obvious.

Inflation continued unabated, "RFB inflation" becoming a dreary new catchphrase as the Bank of Japan became a primary purchaser of RFB bonds and increased its issuance of yen notes accordingly. In the meantime, nonfavored industries found themselves starved for funds. Bottlenecks of all sorts cropped up, even in the transportation sector, which was critical for moving coal, iron, and steel about. Small and medium-size enterprises suffered particular hardships and lost some of the competitive advantages they had enjoyed. Ordinary citizens continued to be caught in a wage-price spiral, and labor militancy rose accordingly. By mid-1948, the very premises of priority production were beginning to be called into question. "The scheme to check inflation by means of increasing production," the argument went, "should be changed into one for increasing production by means of checking inflation."[25]

As the life and death of policy lines go, priority production passed from the scene relatively quickly, lasting a little more than two years. Nonetheless, the legacy of this first postwar macroeconomic policy was long lasting. It focused attention on the critical heavy and chemical industrial sectors, instituted the postwar cult of top-level industrial policy making, bridged or fused a variety of economic ideologies, and brought the government and big business into an ever closer embrace.[26] The ground had been prepared for the reconsolidation of big capital and a new stage in economic planning.

Planning a Cutting-Edge Economy

Well before priority production had run its course, Japanese planners were coming to embrace a vision of their future economy that contrasted sharply with that of the victors. The Americans, even when they turned their attention to promoting reconstruction, tended to think in terms of a neutered version of the old Japanese economy—of a trading nation, that is, weaned from massive military production and turning out cheap exports of the five-and-dime-store variety (ceramics, glassware, figurines, and toys), "Oriental" specialties (silk and tea), or labor-intensive products largely made from imported raw materials (textiles, paper goods, simple electric items, and the like). The new Japan, according to this back-to-the-future view, would be similar to the Japan of the 1920s and early 1930s rather than to the country that had geared up its economy for all-out war.

There would be changes, of course. The "social dumping" of cheap exports that had enabled prewar Japan to penetrate and disrupt foreign markets would be eliminated. This, in fact, had always been one goal of the occupation's reformist economic policies, including its land and labor reforms. Improving the lives of the working population by promoting higher wages, higher incomes, and a more equitable distribution of wealth, the argument went, would create a larger domestic market and inhibit the dumping of underpriced goods abroad. Still, no matter how strongly American priorities shifted toward rehabilitating Japan economically—even to the point of proclaiming it the country's destiny to become the "workshop" of noncommunist Asia—the image always remained of a fundamentally second-rate economy at best. It was taken for granted that Japan's future markets lay primarily in the less-developed countries of Asia, not in the United States or Europe. At a cocktail party in Tokyo only days before the Korean War began, President Truman's special envoy John Foster Dulles blithely but typically told a high Finance Ministry official that the country should consider exporting things like, well, cocktail napkins to the United States. Four years later—with the occupation over and the economy booming thanks to the Korean War—Dulles, then secretary of state in the Eisenhower administration, was still privately and "frankly" telling Japanese leaders that their country "should not expect to find a big U.S. market because the Japanese don't make the things we want. Japan must find markets elsewhere for the goods they export."[27]

Although Japan's planners endured years of anxiety, they never really shared this perception of their country as a future producer of technologically inferior products. No one could deny that the war had been a disaster. Unlike the Americans, however, Japanese analysts tended to base their projections not on the prewar economy but on the advances of the war years. In their eyes, the most striking legacy of the "fifteen-year war" that began with the takeover of Manchuria in 1931 was the revolution in the heavy and chemical industries that occurred under wartime pressures—and the creation of a huge cadre of engineers, middle managers, and skilled workers capable of carrying this revolution forward. The key to a prosperous future lay in the promotion of science, the mastery of advanced technology and managerial techniques, and the production of high-value-added manufactures. No one on the Japanese side focused on cocktail napkins.

Iwasaki Koyata, the powerful head of the Mitsubishi zaibatsu, captured this outlook in a letter sent to one of his executives the day before the first Americans arrived. It was important, he wrote, to have "a great hundred-year plan" (a hoary phrase from the canon of ancient Chinese writings) and not be overwhelmed by the problems of the moment. In this regard, his own recent thoughts concerned the notable progress Japan had made in technological fields during the war years. The only way "to compete with other countries" in the future would be by emphasizing "thoroughness of research, improvement of production techniques, and improvement of managerial efficiency." The leaders of the country's largest business associations struck a comparable note when offering advice to the government in early September.[28]

The most incisive early formulation of this vision of an economy based on cutting-edge technology appeared in a March 1946 mimeographed draft report produced by a special advisory committee to the Ministry of Foreign Affairs and entitled "Basic Problems for Postwar Reconstruction of the Japanese Economy." The committee, comprising about twenty members including both academic economists and business leaders, met approximately forty times before producing its draft and issued a revised, book-length version the following September. Although never elevated to the level of official policy, this lengthy study proved as close to a long-term blueprint for subsequent policy making as one can find.[29]

While strongly endorsing the "antifeudal" and antimilitaristic policies of the occupation, the report staked out a distinctly independent course where basic issues of the political economy were concerned. It acknowledged that postwar democracy would inevitably assume a certain "American coloration," but emphasized that Japan's particular circumstances made any "mechanical application" of foreign models of economic democratization inappropriate. It was necessary to "create a new type of democracy" appropriate to the country's own situation and to conditions in Asia.[30]

In the committee's view, global trends indicated that the era of laissez-faire capitalism had ended and that the world had "at last entered an era of State capitalism or an age of controlled, organized capitalism." The Americans and the British could be expected to continue to emphasize free competition, but even their idealized economic freedoms were in reality "restricted by planning." The importance of central planning, in fact, could be readily observed not only in Britain, the Soviet Union, and the United States of the New Deal, but also (a nice touch) close at hand in SCAP's demands, "one after another," for government plans concerning such diverse matters as food, trade, unemployment relief, and public finance.[31]

In the wake of defeat, Japan's entire productive structure had come to a standstill "as if a big wheel had stopped turning." The challenge was to get this wheel moving again by mobilizing big capital in optimally ratio-

nal ways. Although the committee was critical of the zaibatsu and supportive of occupation plans to break up the economic stranglehold of such
"monopoly capital," it recognized that the zaibatsu had played a critical
role in accumulating capital, expanding trade, promoting technological
innovation, and fostering the growth of heavy and chemical industry.
With their decline, it seemed obvious "that a democratized government itself may have to perform this mission."[32]

In the postwar international economy, Japan had no alternative, the
committee agreed, but to accept the dominant role of the United States.
Indeed, Japan had much to gain from this; but once the country was again
sovereign, it was essential to avoid becoming "economically colonized." In
the new world order, it was to be expected that countries such as China
and India would emerge as producers and exporters of textiles and other
light industrial products, depriving the Japanese of these traditional markets. Japan had no choice, then, but to seek its export niche elsewhere,
namely, in the production of high-value-added manufactures that simultaneously required a heavy input of labor. As time passed, Japan's relatively
cheap labor advantage (compared with the developed Western countries)
would decrease, requiring further technological advances.[33]

On this central point, the report was exceedingly clear. Although traditional exports such as tea, raw silk, and textiles would remain important,
in the future Japan would have to depend "to a fairly high degree on the
export of machinery and chemical goods" including electrical and communications equipment, mining machines and farm machinery, rolling
stock, meters and other precision instruments, scientific and optical apparatus, watches and clocks, bicycles and vehicles, and various chemical
products. With an uncharacteristic touch of irony, the report linked such
manufactures to the "many valuable lessons and souvenirs" that the war
economy had bequeathed Japan.[34]

The responsibility of central planners in making all this possible was
strongly emphasized. The new mandarinate would ensure that production
served the interests of the whole nation, assume many of the functions
hitherto performed by the zaibatsu, provide credit to worthy enterprises,
encourage export competitiveness in small and medium-size businesses,
adopt policies to prevent basic industries from being overwhelmed by foreign capital, and maintain optimum employment stability (especially where
jobs might be lost due to global competition). Foreign trade would be
planned and guided by the state, while "modern scientific management"
in the civil service would replace the "feudalistic" practices of the bu-

reaucrats of the *ancien régime*. The educational system would be mobilized to produce students competent in statistics and the gamut of technical skills required for an advanced industrial society.[35]

Several of the distinguished members of the committee that produced this report had been purged from university positions during the war for their avowedly leftist sympathies, and all of them were acutely sensitive to the great ideological as well as technocratic and technological trends of the time. Their commitment to domestic welfare, national prosperity, and the creation of a nonmilitarized economy was strongly stated; their commitment to "capitalism" per se was another matter. At one point the report candidly left open the question of whether Japan would adopt a capitalist or a socialist system in the future. Whatever the case, "gradual transition to a socialization of the economy" seemed not only inevitable but desirable.[36]

What remained to be seen was how this would transpire.

Unplanned Developments and Gifts from the Gods

In December 1948, Washington announced nine principles of economic stabilization that were to be imposed on Japan, and then two months later dispatched to Tokyo a highly publicized mission aimed at putting the country back on its feet as a viable market economy. The mission was headed by a dictatorial "economic czar," Joseph Dodge, whose conservative "Dodge Line" was vigorously imposed until the outbreak of the Korean War. Under Dodge's stern supervision, the nine principles quickly became known as the "Nine Commandments"; and in this near-theological atmosphere, the redoubtable Detroit banker essentially joined Douglas MacArthur as another supreme being in occupied Japan. At the very least, the country now found itself with a third sovereign, wryly identified by Theodore Cohen as "the Imperial Accountant." Under the Dodge Line, the spigot of RFB loans was shut off, government subsidies were curbed (at least in theory), and the cabinet and parliament were forced to adopt an "overbalanced" budget that actually showed a surplus.

Stabilization, economic recovery, self-sufficiency—these new watchwords all depended, in the imperial accountant's eyes, on curbing inflation and domestic consumption while promoting a vigorous export sector. To this end, in April 1949 Dodge virtually single-handedly established a fixed exchange rate of 360 yen to the dollar, undervaluing the yen somewhat to stimulate exports by making Japanese manufactures cheaper on the world market. A month later, the Ministry of Commerce and Industry and the Board of Trade were merged to create the unprecedentedly powerful Ministry of International Trade and Industry (MITI). Antimonopoly legislation was revised to relax restrictions on intercorporate stockholding, mergers, and multiple directorships; at the same time, over the course of 1949 and 1950 basic laws giving the government strong control over trade, currency, and investment were moved through the Diet. Concurrently, the labor movement was weakened through the "Red purges," watered-down labor laws, and enterprise "rationalizations" that resulted in the dismissal of scores of thousands of workers.

By 1950, the Dodge Line had succeeded in reining in inflation, but at costs that Japanese across the political spectrum found increasingly unpalatable. Public works, welfare, and educational budgets were cut. Unemployment rose. Domestic consumption was suppressed. Bankruptcies increased among smaller enterprises, and the media began devoting attention to suicides among small businessmen. And still the economy remained moribund. Due partly to unfavorable international conditions, exports did not expand significantly. The production of durable goods, a telltale sign of new investment, actually declined. The stock market dropped, and popular disquiet rose palpably. The government's Economic Stabilization Board, critical of the austerity program from the outset, warned of a "vicious spiral of contraction" that was eroding the country's industrial base and threatening social stability. "Stabilization panic" became the new economic catchword. In late April 1950, *U.S. News and World Report* described Japan as being on the "verge of an economic depression" and labeled the deflation policy "economic suicide."[37]

Whether Dodge's policies would have culminated in a bona fide depression is moot, for the outbreak of the Korean War on June 25 ended the stabilization panic and brought in its place a war boom stimulated by U.S. "special procurements." The conflict that now ravaged Japan's former colony was, as Prime Minister Yoshida and a great many others liked to say, "a gift of the gods"—an ironic phrase when one considers how only a few years earlier peace and democracy were being described as "gifts from heaven." In both instances, at any rate, these gifts arrived by way of the Americans and reached every corner of society.[38]

Most industrial sectors were stimulated by these procurements, starting with metal products and extending (in roughly descending order of expenditure) to fossil fuels and machine oils, cloth and finished textile goods, medicines, vehicles, primary metal products, raw materials (excluding food and energy sources), nonmetallic minerals, electric machines and installation parts, clothing and shoes, building components (including plumbing and heating), lumber and cork products, nonelectrical machinery, drink and tobacco, paper and paper products, food, and rubber products. In addition, the Americans turned to Japan for ammunition, light weapons, and napalm bombs, although in theory such manufactures were still proscribed. "Special procurements" also extended to services provided for the U.S. forces engaged in the war, of which repair work on tanks, aircraft, and military vehicles was by far the most profitable. Up to this point, of course, Japanese workers had been told in no uncertain terms that they were never again to employ their skills for such direct military purposes. The Japanese also constructed, expanded, and provisioned facilities for a new influx of American military personnel and their families—whose personal and recreational expenditures, which fell outside the formal tally sheets, also amounted to a small bonanza.

All told, "special procurements" brought an estimated $2.3 billion into Japan between June 1950 and the end of 1953, a sum that exceeded the total amount of aid received from the United States between 1945 and 1951 and was all the more valuable because most payments came in the form of dollars. Even after the Korean War ended in 1953, military-related U.S. purchases continued under the rubric "new special procurements," bringing in an additional $1.75 billion from 1954 through 1956, a major portion of the country's "export" income during these years. This prolonged windfall enabled Japan to increase its imports greatly and virtually double its scale of production in key industries.

Even this, however, fails to convey the breadth and nature of the war boom, for the Korean War triggered global economic changes that served Japan well. Trade patterns were disrupted, recessions elsewhere came to an end, and both developments stimulated foreign purchases of a variety of Japanese manufactures. At the time, Japan was the only industrialized country with spare engineering capacity, and orders poured in for its machine products. Because Western shipyards were fully extended, the country was presented with a golden opportunity to develop its shipbuilding industry as a leading export sector. Even the end of hostilities had a plus side, for Japan was allowed to participate in and so profit from the U.S.-directed reconstruction of South Korea.

Various indices convey a sense of this heady economic revival. A stagnant stock market rose 80 percent between the outbreak of war and December 1951. Steel production increased some 38 percent in the first eight months of the war, while steel exports tripled. The automobile industry was revived by large U.S. purchases of trucks and other vehicles. Toyota, for example, boosted production 40 percent. "These orders were

Toyota's salvation," the president of the company later recalled. "I felt a mingling of joy for my company and a sense of guilt that I was rejoicing over another country's war."[39]

Many companies used this windfall not merely to import more raw and semifinished products, but also to upgrade equipment and acquire advanced foreign technology. This was the beginning of Japan's systematic acquisition of rights to American commercial licenses and patents—an immensely beneficial transaction that the U.S. government strongly supported as crucial for the economic well-being of its still-fragile Cold War associate. The war boom also facilitated the adoption of the "quality control" methods espoused by W. Edwards Deming, an American statistician and former World War II advisor to the U.S. government who found himself speaking to a diminishing audience in his native land. In 1949, pessimistic about the effects of the Dodge Line, middle-echelon Japanese scientists and engineers, groping for an "edge" that would enable them to compete in global trade, invited Deming to conduct a seminar in Tokyo. Deming agreed to do so on being assured that the participants would include personnel who might seriously influence corporate policy regarding production procedures. As fate would have it, he made his inaugural presentation to such a group in July 1950, just after the war began. Had there been no war, Deming's gospel of quality control might have had far less impact, for the simple reason that there would have been no foreign demand for Japanese products and thus no substantial mass production to which to apply his techniques. This almost serendipitous conjunction of desperation and opportunity enabled Deming's Japanese admirers to integrate his ideas about quality into the inaugural stages of new productive cycles and new entrepreneurial ventures in ways that would have lasting consequences over the ensuing decades.[40]

These were heady developments after so many years of economic stagnation, but many high-level economic planners nonetheless viewed the war boom as a decidedly mixed blessing. They were appalled by the prospect of again becoming involved in an economy dependent on military demands; and they warned that the boom threatened to exacerbate economic "dualism" by benefiting primarily larger, more modern enterprises. The 1953 *Economic White Paper* published by the new Economic Planning Agency went so far as to refer to the "sin of special procurements." At the same time, the widespread positive effects of the boom were undeniable. Many small and medium-size enterprises did prosper. Real wages in manufacturing industries increased significantly. By 1952, ordinary people were beginning to experience what the *White Paper* called a "consumer

boom." Food consumption regained prewar levels, and inexpensive clothing became widely available. Basic household amenities such as refrigerators and sewing machines were more accessible, as were such luxury items
as radios and cameras. Personal savings rose, which in turn increased the
funds available for industrial investment.[41]

This was a new world indeed. "Production prostration" and the "-
bamboo-shoot existence" seemed to belong to a different era. Even the
harshness of the Dodge Line had almost fallen from memory. Yet Dodge's
legacy was considerable, in unintended as well as deliberate ways.
Theodore Cohen, who admired Dodge, candidly described the imposition
of his austerity policy as a "ruthless operation, without regard for Japanese views three and a half years and two democratic elections after the
war." As the war boom pushed the ruthless operator from center stage, his
role as economic czar essentially was collectively inherited by the Japanese bureaucracy. The Ministry of International Trade and Industry was
one such institutional beneficiary of this legacy, constituting a greater cen-
tralization of economic authority than had been achieved at the peak of
Japan's mobilization for war. The Ministry of Finance, through which
Dodge imposed most of his directives, was another. Dodge worked particularly closely with Finance Minister Ikeda Hayato, Yoshida's right-
hand man (and later a prime minister himself); and for decades to come,
the ministry continued to exercise exceptional prerogatives vis-à-vis other
ministries and the Diet in controlling budgetary and monetary policy. As
Cohen pointed out, Dodge also "constituted the first postwar channel between the conservative Japanese big business elements and their bureaucratic and political allies in Japan and the top level of officials in the U.S.
government. From then on the Japanese conservatives were plugged into
the top in the United States." It had taken more than three years, but the
friends from America whom the leaders of big business had anticipated
had finally arrived.[42]

The "special characteristics" of the postwar economy largely took shape
during these turbulent years of the Dodge Line and the war boom. Capitalism emerged triumphant, resolving the question the Foreign Ministry's advisory committee had left open in 1946—a capitalism
characterized by high levels of capital concentration (which the planners
had worried about) coupled with a high tolerance of bureaucratic intrusion (which they had relished). Central to these developments were a
handful of private "city banks" that had grown enormously during World
War II, often as intimate parts of the various zaibatsu. Although the
American trust busters had identified these large banks as posing "an un-

usually grave problem," the financial sector escaped the early years of reformism virtually untouched. When Dodge terminated the financing of strategic industries through the RFB, these commercial banks stepped in as major sources of investment capital and soon found themselves extending more loans than their deposits warranted and covering the gap largely by borrowing from the Bank of Japan. In time, these "overloans" became standard procedure, buttressed with a variety of monetary measures that strengthened central influence over the banks. At the same time, the overloans accelerated the reconsolidation of intimate ties between industry and finance, sometimes along the kinship lines established in the presurrender era and sometimes in new configurations.[43]

Shortly after the war boom tapered off, Martin Bronfenbrenner, an astute economist formerly affiliated with E.S.S., observed that key city banks had begun to replace the dissolved holding companies "as nerve-centers of the zaibatsu."[44] What this development portended was the emergence of a distinctive postwar system dominated by so-called *keiretsu*—an old word that suddenly acquired specific and potent economic connotations. The keiretsu (the word is written with two ideographs literally signifying "lineage queue") were powerful groupings of commercial and industrial enterprises that essentially replaced (without doing away with) the zaibatsu-centered agglomerations of industrial and financial capital that had long dominated the economy. By the early 1950s, six such major concentrations of economic power had emerged, all centering on city banks: Mitsui, Mitsubishi, Sumitomo, Fuji, Daiichi, and Sanwa. All but the Sanwa keiretsu represented reclusterings or reconfigurations of the old zaibatsu.[45]

This was not presurrender Japan redux. A major portion of the economy remained outside these concentrations, and the keiretsu groups themselves differed in important ways from the presurrender zaibatsu empires topped by family-dominated holding companies. Whereas the old zaibatsu were rigidly pyramidal groupings, keiretsu relationships tended to be more horizontal, open, and internally competitive. Hereditary family influence had been largely eliminated, and stockholding was more diversified. Keiretsu banks dealt with outsiders, and group affiliates might also deal with outside banks. As a rule, such postwar enterprises were more dependent than in the past on state funds (and state directives).[46]

In the decades to come, this new capitalism would prove to be more flexible and competitive than the old zaibatsu-dominated economy had been, and far more capable of responding to global economic and technological challenges than almost anyone had imagined. At the time, however, the combination of defeat, occupation, and the tainted "gift from the gods" that came from the war next door seemed to have spawned a strange and misshapen creature—what the Economic Planning Agency referred to apprehensively as "the abnormalization of Japan's economic structure."[47] This was a creature as unfamiliar as it was familiar, as unplanned as it was planned, as vulnerable as it was formidable. In its parentage, it was as binational as it was national—the offspring, as it were, of an unprecedented encounter at a unique moment in history.

In later decades, when alarm concerning "the Japanese threat" arose in the United States and elsewhere, the binational genesis of this state-led, keiretsu-dominated economy was all but forgotten. Early reformist policies such as land reform, encouragement of labor, and the dissolution of zaibatsu holding companies were given credit, and appropriately so, for contributing to the emergence of a more vigorous and vibrant domestic economy. At the same time, however, flagrant acts of *omission* such as the occupation's failure to promote deconcentration of the banking structure also had enormous long-term consequences. The political and ideological rationale behind the economic "reverse course," moreover, was to ensure Japan's emergence as a strong anticommunist bastion, and this necessarily entailed support of the most conservative and corporatist elements in Japanese society—and, as it happened, the continued American parenting of this "abnormal" market economy.

The most striking American contribution to this new mercantilist state was largely unwitting. It derived from neither the early reformist policies nor the reverse course per se, but rather from the very operational essence of the occupation regime. While policy objectives changed dramatically from reform to reconstruction, the economy remained closely controlled from above. More than a few erstwhile reformers found bitter irony in this. Leon Hollerman, an economist who served with E.S.S., ruefully concluded that although the occupation had set itself the task of promoting democracy, "in part, it actually promoted bureaucratism" and "its bureaucratic legacy was mainly economic." This occupation-era structure, jerry built on the presurrender state's own ponderous wartime bureaucracy, was shrewdly perpetuated by the Japanese to protect their new capitalism after 1952. In this manner, as Hollerman put it, "in liquidating the Occupation by 'handing back' operational control to the Japanese, SCAP naively presided not only over the transfer of its own authority, but also over the institutionalization of the most restrictive foreign trade and foreign exchange control system ever devised by a major free nation."[48]

epilogue

LEGACIES/FANTASIES/DREAMS

In the course of the war next door, Japan gained an army and lost a supreme commander. The United States moved swiftly to rearm the erstwhile enemy. Remilitarization was initiated without constitutional revision, without enthusiastic cooperation from the conservative Yoshida government, without great joy in business circles (although rearmament lobbies did arise), and without enough popular support to permit calling an army an army or even a tank a tank. The ground forces, inaugurated in July 1950, were identified only as a "National Police Reserve" (NPR), and tanks rolled through their manuals as "special vehicles." Colonel Frank Kowalski, who played a major role in training these new forces, described them organizationally and technologically as "a little American Army." Yoshida's refusal to acknowledge publicly that the country had now embarked on serious remilitarization left Japan, in Kowalski's view, "in a kind of twilight zone of rearmament. The Prime Minister had acknowledged that the constitution would have to be revised before the nation could acquire 'fighting potentiality,' but the NPR, in the meantime, continued to be equipped with artillery, tanks and aircraft." In a poll conducted in February 1952, 48 percent of respondents said the prime minister was lying when he denied rearming, 40 percent were not sure, and only 12 percent believed him.

Yoshida's posture enshrined sophistry concerning remilitarization as official policy, but his position was understandable. His *caution* actually served as a brake on the Americans, who in the heat and panic of the Korean War secretly urged Japanese leaders to hasten to create an army of between three hundred thousand and three hundred fifty thousand men. This was a reckless, almost insane, demand. Such precipitous remilitarization, Yoshida argued, would overwhelm and distort the economy, provoke violent protest throughout the country, and seriously agitate the many peoples of Asia who, unlike the Americans, had not suddenly forgotten the horrors of Japan's recent war.

Yoshida also believed, with good reason, that if Japan remilitarized quickly it would come under immense pressure to fight alongside U.S. forces in Korea. So great was his alarm at the extreme nature of these American importunities that at one point, while John Foster Dulles was visiting Tokyo to tighten the rearmament screws, Yoshida sent clandestine emissaries to two Socialist Party leaders urging them to hold protest demonstrations outside his office to impress the American emissary. This little exercise in political show and tell, he hoped, would help drive home his genuine fear that all-out rearmament would tear the social fabric of the country apart. Under Yoshida, the Japanese held the size of the NPR to seventy-five thousand men for the duration of the occupation.[1]

On April 11, 1951, came an announcement that struck the country like a thunderclap: President Truman had dismissed Douglas MacArthur as commander of the United Nations forces in Korea on grounds of insubordination. The general was removed from all his commands, including that over occupied Japan, for publicly advocating a more aggressive military policy than the president had adopted vis-à-vis the People's Republic of China (which had entered the war on the opposing side the previous December). In a terse radio address, Truman stated that he had acted in order to avoid World War III. In theory, the supreme commander's recall was a stunning object lesson in civilian control of the military. In practice, his disgrace was generally perceived to be an astonishing and tragic event. Public expressions of regret were heartfelt and immediate. On the day after the president's announcement, the liberal *Asahi* newspaper published an editorial "Lament for General MacArthur" that struck many familiar chords:

We have lived with General MacArthur from the end of the war until today. . . . When the Japanese people faced the unprecedented situation of defeat, and fell into the *kyodatsu* condition of exhaustion and despair, it was General MacArthur who taught us the merits of democracy and pacifism and guided us with kindness along this bright path. As if pleased with his own children growing up, he took pleasure in the Japanese people, yesterday's enemy, walking step by step toward democracy, and kept encouraging us.

MacArthur left Japan for the United States on April 16, and savored a hero's departure. Prime Minister Yoshida visited to thank him for his great contributions, and wrote the general privately expressing "shock and sorrow beyond words." The emperor himself paid a last, heartfelt visit to MacArthur's residence against the advice of high court officials who argued that the general, stripped of official position, should have visited him. It was the eleventh time the two had met—and, for the first time, MacArthur accompanied the emperor to his limousine when he left. Keidanren, the powerful federation that now served as the resurrected voice of big business, issued a public statement of gratitude. The speakers of both houses of the Diet did likewise, praising the general's "righteousness, sympathetic understanding and intelligent guidance" and thanking him in particular for making the legislature the highest organ of the state. The Tokyo municipal assembly expressed gratitude in the name of "6,300,000 Tokyo residents," while the press reported that legislation would be enacted making it possible to make the general an "honorary citizen." It was suggested that a "MacArthur Memorial" be erected, perhaps even a statue in Tokyo Bay.

The general's departure was broadcast live by NHK, the public radio station, with an announcer sorrowfully repeating "Good-bye, General MacArthur" while the melody of "Auld Lang Syne" played in the background. Schoolchildren were excused from classes, and by MacArthur's account 2 million people lined the streets to bid him adieu, some with tears in their eyes. As the Tokyo police calculated it, the number was closer to a still-sizable two hundred thousand—which seems plausible, the general being always inclined to inflate things by roughly an order of ten. Yoshida and other cabinet members came to Haneda Airport to see him off. The emperor was represented by his grand chamberlain, the Diet by leaders of both houses. The general's departure "against the white clouds" on his personal airplane *Bataan* moved the *Mainichi* newspaper to an extraordinary effusion. "Oh, General MacArthur—General, General, who saved Japan from confusion and starvation," the paper keened. "Did you see from your window the green wheat stirring in the wind? The harvest will be rich this year. That is the fruit of the general's five years and eight months—and the symbol of the Japanese people's gratitude."

In the United States, MacArthur also received a hero's homage, albeit a peculiarly partisan American one led by Republican politicians; and the Japanese followed his return closely. On April 19, he addressed a joint session of Congress, concluding with a widely quoted line from a military ballad popular when he was a West Point cadet: "Old soldiers never die, they just fade away." Sentimentalists in Japan found this every bit as moving as patriotic American sentimentalists did. They were less moved, however—or, rather, *differently* moved—by his observations before a joint committee in the Senate on May 5 at the very end of three exhausting days of testimony, during the course of which he had in passing made highly complimentary comments about not only the admirable qualities of the Japanese people and the "great social revolution" they had undergone, but also the superb spirit of their fighting men in World War II. It was MacArthur's intention to argue that the Japanese could be trusted more than the Germans. Here was the way he put it when asked if the Japanese could be counted on to defend the freedoms they had gained under the occupation:

Well, the German problem is a completely and entirely different one from the Japanese problem. The German people were a mature race.

If the Anglo-Saxon was say 45 years of age in his development, in the sciences, the arts, divinity, culture, the Germans were quite as mature. The Japanese, however, in spite of their antiquity measured by time, were in a very tuitionary condition. Measured by the standards of modern civilization, they would be like a boy of twelve as compared with our development of 45 years.

Like any tuitionary period, they were susceptible to following new models, new ideas. You can implant basic concepts there. They were still close enough to origin to be elastic and acceptable to new concepts.

The German was quite as mature as we were. Whatever the German did in dereliction of the standards of modern morality, the international standards, he did deliberately. He didn't do it because of a lack of knowledge of the world. He didn't do it because he stumbled into it to some extent as the Japanese did. He did it as a considered policy in which he believed in his own military might, in which he believed that its application would be a shortcut to the power and economic domination that he desired. . . .

But the Japanese were entirely different. There is no similarity. One of the great mistakes that was made was to try to apply the same policies which were so successful in Japan to Germany, where they were not quite so successful, to say the least. They were working on a different level.[2]

The full transcript of the three-day MacArthur hearings came to around 174,000 words, and these remarks attracted almost no comment in the United States. In Japan, a mere five words in this passage drew obsessive attention: *like a boy of twelve.* The phrase came like a slap in the face and marked the beginning of the end of the MacArthur mystique. As Sodei Rinjirō, MacArthur's biographer, has observed, these words in their starkness awakened people to how they had snuggled up to the conqueror. Suddenly, many felt unaccountably ashamed. From this point on, the former supreme commander began to be purged from memory, much as wartime atrocities had been purged. Plans for a memorial were abandoned. No statue would be built. The designation of "honorary citizen" never materialized. Several large companies even responded by publishing a joint advertisement headlined "We Are Not Twelve-Year-Olds!!— Japanese Manufactures Admired by the World." This was more wish than reality, of course, but what these entrepreneurs immediately grasped was that the general's disquisition on the evolutionary backwardness of Japan fit perfectly with the patronizing and dismissive appraisals others were offering of the country's economic immaturity.[3]

Although the old soldier himself might fade away in Japanese consciousness, more quickly and gracelessly than he had ever imagined possible, the issue he unwittingly brought so floridly to the fore would not and could not be dispelled. After all, the Japanese had routinely spoken of themselves as MacArthur's children—that, indeed, had been the very essence of the *Asahi*'s emotional April 12 editorial.[4] The entire occupation had been premised on acquiescing in America's overwhelming paternalistic authority; and even as sovereignty drew near, even as the nation was being rehabilitated as a Cold War partner, the Americans never had any real expectation that an equitable relationship would be the result. The new military was a "little American army," obviously destined to remain under U.S. control. The new economy was inordinately dependent on American support and indulgence. Much of the rest of the world—on both sides of the Cold War divide—was, in fact, appalled and alarmed by the haste with which the democratization agenda had been abandoned, the old guard resurrected, and remilitarization promoted. In such circumstances, it was still difficult to imagine a sovereign Japan as anything other than dependent on and subordinate to the United States for the foreseeable future—a client state in all but name.

A full year elapsed between MacArthur's dismissal and the formal termination of the occupation. In most respects, this proved to be a year devoid of the joy and exhilaration one might have expected with independence almost at hand. Although in the end the peace treaty would involve scores of nations, the Americans controlled the peacemaking process; and the exact price Japan would be called on to pay for incorporation into a Pax Americana became apparent only bit by bit. Rearmament under the American "nuclear umbrella" was but one part of that price. The continued maintenance of U.S. military bases and facilities throughout the country was another. Okinawa was excluded from the restoration of sovereignty (just as it had been exluded from the occupation reforms) and consigned as a major U.S. nuclear base to indefinite neocolonial control. Because the Soviet Union was not part of the peace settlement, its disputed but de facto control over islands north of Hokkaido remained unresolved.

The peace treaty itself, which was nonrestrictive and generous to Japan, was signed by representatives from forty-eight nations. It was clear from an early date, however, that the communist countries would refuse to participate in a settlement that locked Japan so tightly into U.S. containment policy. In the parlance of the day, Japan had been given the choice of a "separate peace" or no peace treaty at all; although Japanese progressives and leftists called with great passion for an "overall peace" coupled with Japan's disarmed neutrality, this was not a realistic option in the ferociously Cold War atmosphere of the time. It was only after embracing the separate peace and passing through the grand ceremony of a formal peace conference in San Francisco in September 1951, however, that the Yoshida government learned how high the costs of independence would actually be. As it turned out, the U.S. Senate refused to ratify the peace treaty unless Japan agreed to sign a parallel treaty with the Nationalist Chinese regime in Taiwan—and, beyond this, to adhere to the rigorous American policy of isolating and economically containing the People's Republic of China. This shocked Japanese businessmen and economic planners, who had taken the China market for granted, and became yet another reason to argue for the importance of a state-directed, top-down industrial policy. The U.S.–Japan security treaty and a related "administrative agreement" that accompanied it also turned out to be more inequitable than any other bilateral arrangement the United States entered into in the postwar period. The Americans retained exceptional extraterritorial rights, and the number of military installations they demanded was far in excess of what anyone had anticipated. Hanson Baldwin, the oracular military commentator for the *New York Times,* accurately pronounced this the inauguration of "a period when Japan is free, yet not free."[5]

To the conservatives, this was a high but unavoidable price to pay for independence and security in a dangerously riven world. To much of the populace, the difference between occupation and the limbo of "subordinate independence" was hardly discernible and certainly nothing to cheer about. Officially, sovereignty was restored at 10:30 P.M. on April 28, 1952. The streets, everyone reported, were strangely quiet. Perhaps twenty people gathered before the imperial palace and shouted *Banzai!* A department store in the Ginza sold about one hundred rising-sun flags. Signs and insignia denoting SCAP and GHQ were removed, but there was no exodus of American military personnel, since almost everyone was staying on. Early the following day, on his fifty-first birthday, Emperor Hirohito released two celebratory poems. One expressed a wish for peace. In the other, the emperor rejoiced that Japan had survived bitter defeat and emerged essentially unchanged:

> The winter wind has gone
> and long-awaited spring has arrived
> with double-petalled cherry blossoms[6]

In a poll conducted shortly afterwards, only 41 percent of the people asked if Japan had now become an independent nation answered yes.

Here was a country divided—literally so where Okinawa was concerned—and at the same time temperamentally torn and uncertain in its feelings about Japan's new place in the world. The most dramatic divide, however, was ideological. Yoshida Shigeru later appropriated an image from the partition of Korea to describe this. The occupation, he said, had left a "thirty-eighth parallel" running through the heart of the Japanese people. The reference was to the emergence of a liberal and left-wing opposition that espoused allegiance to the original occupation ideals of "demilitarization and democratization," opposed Japan's incorporation into the Pax Americana, and was severely critical of the new constellation of conservative politicians, bureaucrats, and big businessmen that the Americans now patronized. Many prominent intellectuals took this critical stance, as did much of the mass media and a still-strong left-wing contingent within organized labor. So did the increasingly militant adherents of the Communist Party, which, harassed and shorn of its leadership, still survived as a legal organization.

Three days after the peace treaty came into effect, more than a million people took part in some 330 May Day rallies nationwide. Six years earlier, such observances had been marked by hope bordering on euphoria on the part of many participants. The unprecedented popular demonstration known as "Food May Day" had taken place in the plaza before the imperial palace in the wake of that long-ago celebration. May 1, 1952, however, entered history as "Bloody May Day." Because the Yoshida government had forbidden the use of the imperial plaza (and defied a subsequent court order nullifying this ban), the major May Day rally in Tokyo took place under the auspices of the Sōhyō labor federation on the spacious grounds of the well-known Meiji Shrine. An estimated four hundred thousand individuals gathered there in the morning and vocally endorsed such resolutions as "Oppose rearmament—fight for the independence of the race." Thousands of banners and placards peppered the crowd, promoting workers' economic demands and opposing remilitarization, war, U.S. military bases, the seizure of Okinawa, and "April 28—the Day of National Disgrace." A few hand-drawn placards portrayed the faces of Stalin, Mao Tse-tung, or the purged leaders of the Japan Communist Party; a few displayed "Go home, Yankee," lettered in English.

As the rally was ending, a cry arose to march to the forbidden plaza in front of the palace—to the "people's plaza," as it had been dubbed ever since the demonstrations of 1946. Several groups formed, perhaps ten thousand people in all, led by radical associations of Communists, Koreans, and students. White-collar as well as blue-collar workers joined in, women as well as men. They jogged to the palace chanting antigovernment and anti-American slogans. When a contingent of around six thousand demonstrators forced their way through a large police cordon and paused to regroup in front of the famous "double bridge" over the palace moat, violence erupted. Without warning, the police attacked with tear gas and pistols. A municipal employee and a university student were killed in the melee that followed, and a total of twenty-two demonstrators were struck by bullets. Violence and property damage continued as people fled to the side streets, and the toll of those injured on both sides was shockingly high. More than eight hundred policemen sustained injuries (out of five thousand who eventually became involved), and almost double that number of demonstrators (many of whose injuries came from the back as they attempted to flee). A score or so American-owned automobiles, most of them parked alongside the moat, were overturned and burned; three GIs were thrown into the moat and stoned before other Japanese rescued them. A small number of American soldiers were later treated for minor injuries. Bloody May Day branded the image of a divided country on the national consciousness.[7]

On May 2, Emperor Hirohito and Empress Nagako led a ceremony in memory of the nation's war dead at Shinjuku Park. This was the first time such a public observance had taken place since the occupation began. The government attempted to turn the following day, "Constitution Day," into a dual celebration of the 1947 constitution and the return of sovereignty. Attendance was relatively sparse. Perhaps fifteen thousand people gathered at the imperial plaza, where the emperor read a brief message. He recalled accepting the terms of the Potsdam Declaration almost seven years earlier in order "to inaugurate peace for our nation for all time," and expressed his deepest sympathies and condolences for the war's "innumerable victims." He warned against repeating the mistakes of the past, called for "building a new Japan" in the democratic spirit of the new constitution, spoke of the Japanese "family," and exhorted his subjects to "combine the cultures of both East and West." In conclusion, he announced that, heavy though the burden was, he had no intention of abdicating.

One month later, Emperor Hirohito journeyed to the Grand Shrine at Ise to report the restoration of sovereignty to Amaterasu, the sun goddess and imperial progenitor.[8]

The emperor and the general had presided as dual sovereigns through the years of defeat and occupation. They shared a great deal in common, but like the poles of a magnetic field they carried the charges of different roles and missions; and the field itself, the body politic of the defeated land, had been electric with creative tensions. This seems clearer now, with the passage of time. It was not so obvious when the occupation ended.

For all his positive words about peace and constitutional democracy, Emperor Hirohito remained first and foremost the living manifestation of historical, cultural, and racial continuity—and of the ideal of a hierarchical and patriarchal society. In defeat as in war, the emperor remained the great shaman of symbolic politics, and his poem celebrating Japan's recovery of independence confirmed the deftness of his touch and the traditionalistic thrust of his new "symbol monarchy." The occupation had been bleak and bitter; only now could the true, pure Japan reappear, as timeless as the cherry blossoms that followed winter's chill. When asked by a journalist in 1975 whether Japanese values had changed, the emperor expressed the same sentiment in plainer language. "I understand that since the conclusion of the war people have expressed various opinions," he responded, "but, looking at this from a broad perspective, I do not think there has been any change between prewar and postwar." And, indeed, was not his own incredible survival—for he continued to reign until his death in 1989—proof of this?[9]

General MacArthur's genius as a wizard of representation was better known than the emperor's among non-Japanese, and his portrayal of the defeated people differed markedly from Hirohito's. True, he was given to grand pronouncements about "the Oriental mind," and his "boy of twelve" emerged from a colonial mentality that commonly dismissed the capacity of non-Western peoples to change fundamentally. That was not his rhetorical intention, however. On the contrary, where the emperor consistently dwelled on continuity, the general never ceased to extol the revolutionary transformation that the Japanese had undergone. In his celebrated "old soldiers never die" address, he told the members of Congress that "the Japanese people since the war have undergone the greatest reformation recorded in modern history," and went on to embellish this assertion in extravagant terms. These words were not meant for Americans alone. He had said the same thing many times from his pulpit in Tokyo. In emphasizing how much the despised enemy had changed during his interregnum as supreme commander, MacArthur obviously was burnishing his own reputation. As far as one can tell, however, he sincerely believed these claims.[10]

Outside Japan, few took such observations seriously. "Japan Is Little Changed," read a subhead in a commentary on the restoration of sovereignty that appeared in the *New York Times*. After all, the explanation went, "one does not alter national characteristics in six years." Unlike when the emperor expressed such views, the meaning here was patronizing. In this same spirit, the *Times* represented the end of the occupation with a cartoon depicting the gigantic, godlike hands of the victors releasing a tiny figure labeled "Japan" onto the road of "Independence." He wore a traditional laborer's short coat and wooden clogs, and the path before him meandered erratically before vanishing in darkness.[11]

This tottering little figure was, of course, the more common rendering of MacArthur's "boy of twelve"—an old image of innate backwardness and stunted development that was reassuring to many Westerners, being neither militarily nor economically threatening. This childlike maker of knickknacks and cheap appliances would wander the byways of the American and European imaginations until the late 1960s—when, all of a sudden it seemed, Japanese automobiles and quality electronic goods surged onto Western markets and the little men were transformed into economic "miracle men" and "supermen" almost overnight. The response then was much as it had been a quarter-century earlier, when imperial Japan went to war and caught the Western powers by surprise: the genie had come out of the bottle again, only this time in a business suit rather than in khaki.

For two decades, the spectacle of this unexpected economic superpower would fascinate and alarm much of the world, provoking a great deal of high language about a so-called Japanese model. The notion of "Japan as Number One," the title of a 1979 book by a Harvard professor, simply took people's breath away. Part of the shock lay in the intimation that the heyday of Western global domination was over, but equally shocking was the fact that the accolade "number one" was being attached to a country that only recently had lain in ruins and been dismissed as a "fourth-rate nation." Pundits asked how this transformation could be explained, and usually answered that one must look to the country's deep history and traditional values. Critics coined pejorative phrases such as "ethno-economics." Eurocentric cultural determinists polished up the old "clash of civilizations" rhetoric.[12]

"New born" had been one of the pet Japanese phrases of the early years of defeat. But actually to be reborn so spectacularly within a lifetime, in the eyes of one's erstwhile detractors no less, went far beyond what anyone *in* Japan had dreamed possible. This was redemption with a vengeance, and it provoked a linguistic euphoria on the Japanese side that frequently called to mind the "leading race" rhetoric of the war years, not to speak of an arrogance reminiscent of the hubris that had accompanied the early years of the Greater East Asia Co-Prosperity Sphere. Intoxicated by their country's sudden eminence, academics and cultural critics threw themselves into interminable discussions about what "being Japanese" really meant. Popular through the 1970s and 1980s, this so-called *Nihon-jinron* discourse soon became a game of antonyms, with the Ur-Japanese being defined in terms of values or orientations that were the polar opposite of those assigned to the Ur-Westerner (group harmony versus individualism, particularism versus universalism, subjectivity and intuition versus extreme ratiocination, conciliation versus litigation, vertical as opposed to horizontal social relationships, and so on). There was more than a whiff here of the wartime fixation on a unique "Yamato spirit."

Such persistent and grandiose fixations on blood and culture demand attention in part because they are already *given* such inordinate attention in so many contemporary societies; in Japan as elsewhere, race, culture, and history are the stuff out of which collective identities and ideologies are invented. To understand the Japan that stands at the cusp of the twenty-first century, however, it is more useful to look not for the *longue durée* of an inexorably unfolding national experience, but rather at a cycle of recent history that began in the late 1920s and essentially ended in 1989. When this short, violent, innovative epoch is scrutinized, much of what has been characterized as a postwar "Japanese model" proves to a hybrid Japanese-American model: forged in war, intensified through defeat and occupation, and maintained over the ensuing decades out of an abiding fear of national vulnerability and a widespread belief that Japan needed top-level planning and protection to achieve optimum economic growth. This bureaucratic capitalism is incomprehensible without understanding how victor and vanquished embraced Japan's defeat together. To borrow one of the humorous neologisms that floated around during the immediate post-war years, the so-called Japanese model could have been more aptly de-scribed as a "SCAPanese model."

The short cycle of Japan's modern experience coincides almost perfectly with Emperor Hirohito's reign. He was the ever-present ideological touch-stone of these decades—the symbol of a seamless transition from unbri-dled militarism to imperial democracy, the most obvious rallying point, in peace as in war, for those who would emphasize the racial and cultural "unity of the people." For his subjects, Hirohito's death in 1989 signaled the literal end of an era: the Shōwa period was over, the calendars had to be changed. What marks this year as the true end of an epoch, however, is the confluence of other momentous events. The Berlin Wall came down, signaling the last days of the Cold War. And Japan's economic bub-ble burst. This was the moment when it became evident to all that while Japan had attained its single-minded goal of "catching up" to the West economically and technologically, the vision and flexibility necessary for charting a new course were lacking. The system that had created the su-perpower was breaking down. With his typical good fortune, the emperor was spared this. He had departed just in time.

Over the years, a number of dates were singled out by contemporary chroniclers as marking the end of Japan's postwar era. In 1955, a govern-ment economic agency announced with relief that "the 'postwar' has ended," basing its premature obituary notice on the fact that the overall index of production had finally returned to the prewar level. Nineteen sixty, when the government crushed the last great protests by radical labor unionists and Prime Minister Ikeda Hayato inaugurated his vaunted "income doubling" program, was another year designated as marking the transition from one era to another.[13] So was 1979, when the "number one" frenzy took off. Still, when all is said and done, 1989 is the year that will stand as the true end of the "long postwar" that had started the moment the emperor's voice was first heard by his subjects. It had lasted forty-four years.

Nineteen forty-five was unquestionably a watershed year—as momentous as 1868, when the feudal regime was overthrown and the new Meiji government established. There is always a Japanese audience for books focusing just on 1945—for books, indeed, that look only at the month of August; or only at the events of August 15. Yet it is now clear that the structural legacies of wartime Japan to the postsurrender decades were enormous. Imperial Japan had begun mobilizing national resources for possible war after the onset of the Great Depression; the concept of establishing a "total war" capacity (that is, of having the ability to harness all sectors of the nation in the eventuality of war) was strongly promoted in military and bureaucratic circles from the early 1930s; and such industrial and financial consolidation finally materialized, quite belatedly, in what is sometimes called the "1940 system." This was the bedrock on which the Allied occupation of Japan rested—and it was a system that the Americans who controlled the occupation largely perpetuated.

The institutional arrangements that were carried over from the war system were not inherently militaristic. Corporate subcontracting networks were part of this system, for example, along with increasing dependence on a small number of private banks for financing. All this became the heart of the postwar keiretsu structure. Emphasizing employee security (including "lifetime employment") over stockholder dividends in large companies, often singled out as a distinctive feature of the postwar Japanese system, had its real genesis in the war years. So did the government's intimate role in providing "administrative guidance" to business and industry. In the maw of defeat, confronted by a staggering *postwar* crisis, it seemed logical to most Japanese to maintain these arrangements; and with the good grace of their American overlords, that is essentially what they did. Much of what later became identified as the "Japanese model" and was then shrouded in a vapor of rhetoric about Confucian values was simply a carry-over of arrangements that had been spawned by the recent war;

and postwar planners maintained and adapted this inheritance not because
they were secret samurai, but because they believed this was a rational way
to promote maximum economic growth in an ominous world.[14]

The guiding hand in this system was the mandarinate, and it is in this
regard that one of the most consequential acts of the occupation period
was an act of omission: the failure to curb the bureaucracy's influence,
particularly where economic affairs were concerned. The American reformers did change the political economy of Japan in significant ways,
most notably through land reform, the dissolution of family-controlled zaibatsu holding companies, and the promotion of legislation that gave unprecedented rights to organized labor. They also imposed certain specific
bureaucratic reforms of lasting importance, eliminating the military establishment and breaking up the powerful Home Ministry that had exercised control over the police and local governments. But they did preserve
the rest of the bureaucracy, and the "1940 system" more generally, as a
matter of convenience. To work through existing channels made implementing occupation policies easier; to fundamentally change the system
would have created turmoil in an already confusing situation.

This was only the half of it, however, for the victors also were responsible for strengthening the already powerful bureaucratic authoritarianism
they encountered—and it is here that the essentially hybrid nature of the
postsurrender "model" is to be seen. From the moment of their arrival,
the Americans bolstered the role and prestige of the bureaucracy by their
patronage. When Cold War considerations took over and the "reverse
course" in occupation policy was launched, it was the Americans who promoted the administrative "rationalization" that resulted in an even greater
concentration of bureaucratic authority. The creation of the powerful
Ministry of International Trade and Industry three years before the occupation ended was the most visible example of this.

Standing above and beyond all this, moreover, was the bureaucratic
model that SCAP's own modus operandi provided. The Americans did arrive as an "army of liberation," as even the Communists acknowledged for
a while. They did initiate an impressive agenda of reform. But they ruled
as mandarins themselves. General MacArthur's authority was "supreme."
The directives issued through his General Headquarters could not be
challenged. Suggestions from even low-ranking GHQ minions carried the
force of informal commands. The entire governing structure ensconced in
Tokyo's "little America" was rigidly hierarchic. There was no "trans-
parency" in this supergovernment, no accountability to *anyone* in Japan itself. The journalist who attempted to write that his country's prime

ministers were weak because they could only be yes-men found that he could not do so thanks to the blue pencils of GHQ's censors. As it turned out, one did not have to be the bearer of a Confucian cultural heritage to promote autocracy, hierarchy, harmony, consensus, and self-censorship.

The anomaly of SCAP's neocolonial revolution from above was thus that it cut both ways—toward genuinely progressive change *and* toward a reaffirmation of authoritarian structures of governance. To speak of the war system being buckled to the postwar system is to be reminded that SCAP itself was the buckle. The conquerors gave new authority to the Diet, but chose to draft and present legislation bureaucratically. They promoted the creation of a responsible civilian cabinet, and then by their own practices gelded it. While it is commonplace and accurate to speak of Japan being under the control of fundamentally authoritarian and militaristic governments from the early 1930s until 1945, the fact is that it remained under military control until 1952.

This was democracy in a box, and General MacArthur's extraordinarily solicitous treatment of Emperor Hirohito compounded the problem by retarding rather than advancing the cause of genuine pluralism, participation, and accountability. And yet, despite all this—the binational bureaucratic cult, the old-style corporatism that survived the passage from war to peace, the mystique of nonaccountability symbolized by the sovereign, the stunted aspects of the new imperial democracy—MacArthur was quite accurate when he spoke of a society that had undergone significant change. Postwar Japan was a vastly freer and more egalitarian nation than imperial Japan had been. Its people had become chary of militarism and war to a degree matched by few other societies in our world. A healthy sense of the absurd pervaded popular culture (although foreigners rarely appreciated this). While centrists and conservatives maintained firm hold on the levers of power, the spectrum of public debate continued to embrace socialists and communists in a manner unthinkable in the United States.

This too was a hybrid legacy, full of contradictions and mixed messages; and nothing better exemplified these tensions and complexities than the debates that continued to swirl around the remarkable new constitution. There would have been no such national charter without the conquerors, and there was nothing to prevent the Diet from amending it once the occupation ended. Indeed, the Americans themselves soon came to desire and lobby for such revision: Article 9, which made remilitarization so problematical, naturally made them rue the week when GHQ had conducted its secret little "constitutional convention." When the fiftieth anniversary of the new charter's coming into effect was observed in 1997, however, not a word had been changed. Conservatives could never marshal the two-thirds vote necessary for revision, or face up to the public outcry that would have ensued.

The constitution may well be revised in the near future, but the issues involved still tell a great deal about popular political consciousness in contemporary Japan. Although Article 9 has been battered and bent to permit an increasingly expansive interpretation of what is permissible in the name of maintaining a "self-defense" capacity, it has survived (together with the strong antiwar language of the preamble) as a still-compelling statement of the ideal of nonbelligerency. The "no war" vision touched the hearts of people all over the world in the wake of World War II, but it was never encoded in another nation's constitution or laws. Every contretemps about rearmament has necessarily entailed reengagement with basic issues of war and peace (and law and constitutional guarantees in general) in a way inconceivable elsewhere. In such unplanned ways, the early occupation ideals of "demilitarization and democratization" have remained a living part of popular consciousness for over a half-century.

Japan's dreams of peace have not been consoling, for they have rested primarily on indelible memories of the horrors of World War II—of how several million Japanese gave their lives in vain; how the war came home first in the form of massive air raids and then, of course, Hiroshima and Nagasaki; how for years after the defeat it was often unclear where the next meal would come from; and how impossible it has been to publicly mourn the war dead—fathers, husbands, brothers whom the world still reviles as murderers. This deep sense of suffering and victimization has been intensified by a growing and not altogether unreasonable belief that Japan is being judged by standards that other nations do not apply to themselves. The sense of double standards and victor's justice that tarnished the Tokyo war crimes trial has only become stronger with the passage of time (abetted by revelations of the atrocities, denials, and false memories of other countries). Even Japanese peace activists who endorse the ideals of the Nuremberg and Tokyo charters, and who have labored to document and publicize Japanese atrocities, cannot defend the way the war-crimes trials were carried out; nor can they defend the American decision to exonerate the emperor of war responsibility and then, in the chill of the Cold War, release and soon afterwards openly embrace accused right-wing war criminals like the later prime minister Kishi Nobusuke.

Throughout the long postwar, the elites who engineered Japan's impressive recovery came almost entirely from the several generations who experienced war and defeat first-hand. They looked back on the war as stupid, given their country's relative backwardness in science, technology, and material resources. They were obsessed with avoiding the repetition of such a disaster, and acutely sensitive to the global protest that would arise if Japan undertook to become a bona fide military power, bristling with the nuclear weapons it could so easily produce. Some of them shared the self-critical sentiments of the progressive and left-wing academics who emerged as a "community of remorse" in the wake of defeat. Some comprised a community of regret at having been defeated. More than a few held the "Great East Asia War" in memory as one waged against communists and warlords in China, and against European and American imperialists in Southeast Asia. Many, where the most horrendous Japanese atrocities are concerned, remained in denial. Virtually all recalled, with genuine grief, friends and acquaintances who had died serving the country. They also remembered the bemusement with which the white victors tended to look down on them as "little men" for years following their defeat.

This cadre of leaders has all but departed the scene now, leaving behind a miserable record when it came to offering a clear and unequivocal acknowledgment of and apology for the depredations committed during the first two decades of Hirohito's reign. To do so, in their minds, would have involved swallowing the "Tokyo war-crimes trial view of history," which seemed inconceivable to them. Their patriotism has drawn the scorn and mistrust of much of the outside world upon their country. At the same time, these elites also bequeathed to their successors the unresolved question of whether Japan can ever be taken seriously by other nations and peoples without possessing its own independent capacity to wreak horrible destruction on others. This is the "Article 9" legacy, the "separate peace" legacy, the "U.S.–Japan security treaty" legacy. It is the legacy of subordinate independence under which the occupation was terminated and Japan regained its nominal sovereignty. Professing fidelity to the spirit of Article 9 invites international ridicule (as was made painfully apparent to the Japanese during the Gulf War in 1991, when Japan was derided for offering money but not troops for the attack on Iraq). Abandoning Article 9 will, beyond any doubt, provoke intense outcries of Japanese revanchism; for no one, except the Japanese conservatives, has forgotten the rape of Nanking. Japan's peculiar dreams of peace have come to involve a gnawing sense of entrapment.

These tangled legacies of defeat and occupation played out in a circular fashion. Consigned to military and therefore diplomatic subservience to Washington's dictates, the only real avenue of postwar nationalism left to the Japanese leadership was economic. National pride—acute, wounded, wedded to a profound sense of vulnerability—lay behind the single-minded pursuit of economic growth that created a momentary superpower a mere quarter-century after humiliating defeat. That this quest was characterized by a mercantilist mentality and an almost pathological network of protectionist defenses does not seem all that surprising. Who, in the end, could one really trust but oneself?

All this is in the air now. No one is certain where Japan will land, and no one is murmuring "number one" any more. The uncertainty is disquieting, but the lowering of expectations is surely healthy—and yet, in other ways, sad. Why? Because what has become discredited along with the Japanese (or "SCAPanese") model are also certain dreams that reflected the idealism of the early occupation agenda of "demilitarization and democratization." The Japanese economists and bureaucrats who drafted the informal 1946 blueprint for a planned economy were admirably clear on these objectives. They sought rapid recovery and maximum economic growth, of course—but they were just as concerned with achieving economic demilitarization and economic democracy. And to a considerable degree the guided capitalism they promoted succeeded in realizing these objectives. Japan became wealthy. The standard of living rose impressively at every level of society. Income distribution was far more equitable than in the United States. Job security was assured. Growth was achieved without inordinate dependence on a military-industrial complex or a thriving trade in armaments.

These are hardly trivial ideals, but they are now being discarded along with all the deservedly bankrupt aspects of the postwar system. The lessons and legacies of defeat have been many and varied indeed; and their end is not yet in sight.

NOTES

Abbreviations and Title Citations Used in the Notes

With one exception, full citations are given for sources the first time they appear for each chapter in the notes that follow; for chapters 13 and 14, which both deal with the drafting and promulgation of the new constitution, citations that appear in full in chapter 13 are not repeated in full at their first appearance in chapter 14. For convenience, the following acronyms and citations by title have been used:

FRUS   *Foreign Relations of the United States.* The official series of de-
            classified historical U.S. State Department documents,
            grouped by place and calendar year.

GI   "Gibney Interviews." Transcripts of interviews with Amer-
            ican participants in the preparation of a draft Japanese con-
            stitution, conducted by Alex Gibney in conjunction with
            his 1992 Annenberg/CPB television documentary series *The
            Pacific Century.*

JCC/FR   *Japan's Commission on the Constitution: The Final Report,*
            translated and edited by John M. Maki (Seattle: University
            of Washington Press, 1980). The final report of the so-called
            Takayanagi Commission, which conducted extensive hear-

ings on the origins of the postwar constitution between 1957 and 1964.

Koe   Edited by Asahi Shimbunsha and published in several vol-
               umes by Asahi Bunko (Tokyo, 1984). *Koe* [Voice] is the
               name of the *Asahi* newspaper's Letters to the Editor section,
               and these volumes contain selected letters beginning in 1945.

NTN   *Nihon Tōkei Nenkan* [Japan Statistical Yearbook]. A basic an-
               nual series issued by the Prime Minister's Office [Sōrifu].

Osaka Hya-   Official hundred-year history of Osaka Prefecture, published
kunen Shi   by Osaka-fu [Osaka Prefecture] in 1968.

PM   *Philosophy as Metanoetics* (Berkeley: University of California
               Press, 1986). This is the full translation (by Takeuchi Yoshi-
               mori) of *Zangedō to shite no Tetsugaku,* a seminal 1946 trea-
               tise on "the way of repentance" by the philosopher Tanabe
               Hajime.

PRJ   Supreme Commander for the Allied Powers, Government
               Section, *Political Reorientation of Japan, September 1945 to
               September 1948* (Washington, D.C., 1949), 2 volumes. A
               basic official commentary (volume 1) and documentary col-
               lection (volume 2) covering the first three years of the oc-
               cupation.

SNNZ   *Shōwa: Niman Nichi no Zenkiroku* [A Complete Record of
               the Twenty Thousand Days of the Shōwa Era], compiled
               and published by Kōdansha (Tokyo, 1989). This densely il-
               lustrated multivolume series provides a day-by-day view of
               the period of Emperor Hirohito's reign (1926–1989).

SSS   *Shōwa Sesō Shi—Dokyumento, Sengo-hen* [History of Life in
               the Shōwa Period: Documents: Postwar], edited and pub-
               lished by Heibonsha (Tokyo 1976). Contains lively media
               pieces.

SZS   *Sengo Zaisei Shi* [Financial History of the Postwar Period].
               This is the multivolume official Ōkurashō [Ministry of Fi-
               nance] history of the occupation period. The *SZS* notation
               in the notes here refers to volume 19 of this series, which is
               one of the most authoritative collections of statistics for this
               period (Tokyo: Tōyō Keizai Shimbun, 1978).

Tennō *Hyakuwa*	A two-volume collection of writings pertaining to Emperor Hirohito, edited by Tsurumi Shunsuke and Nakagawa Roppei (Tokyo: Chikuma Bunko, 1989).
TJ	*The Tokyo Judgment: The International Military Tribunal for the Far East (I.M.T.F.E.), 29 April 1946–12 November 1948,* edited by B. V. A. Röling and C. F. Ruter, 2 volumes (Amsterdam: APA–University Press, 1977).
TOT/RP	Takayanagi Kenzō, Ōtomo Ichirō, and Tanaka Hideo, eds., *Nihonkoku Kempō Seitei no Katei,* 2 volumes (Tokyo: Yūhikaku, 1972). A bilingual collection of basic documents pertaining to the American drafting of a new Japanese constitution and deriving from the papers of Milo Rowell, a GHQ participant in the drafting process (thus *RP,* for "Rowell Papers").
TYKS	*Tokyo Yamiichi Kōbō Shi* [The Rise and Fall of the Tokyo Black Market], edited by Tokyo Yakeato Yamiichi o Kiroku Suru Kai (Tokyo: Sōfūsha, 1978). A basic source on the black market.
TWCT	*The Tokyo War Crimes Trial,* edited by R. John Pritchard and Sonia Magbanua Zaide (New York and London: Garland, 1981). Citation in the notes here refers to volume 1 of this twenty-two volume transcript.

INTRODUCTION

1. Quoted in George Sansom, *The Western World and Japan* (New York: Knopf, 1965), p. 407.

2. Nominally, the occupation was supervised by all the victors. Two international bodies exercised advisory powers—an eleven-nation Far Eastern Commission that met in Washington and a four-nation Allied Council convened in Tokyo. General MacArthur's formal title was Supreme Commander for the Allied Powers. In practice, the United States dictated policy.

3. I have tried here, as best as possible, to avoid repeating topics discussed in my earlier writings, which include the following related publications: *Empire and Aftermath: Yoshida Shigeru and the Japanese Experience, 1878–1954* (Cambridge, Mass.: Council on East Asian Studies, Harvard University, 1979); *War Without Mercy: Race and Power in the Pacific War* (New York: Pantheon, 1986); and *Japan in War and Peace: Selected Essays* (New York: The New Press, 1993). In the last collection, see especially the treatment of wartime legacies in "The Useful War"; of top-level U.S. strategic planning in "Occupied Japan and the Cold War in Asia"; of racial and psychological dimensions of the U.S.–Japan relationship in "Race, Language, and War in Two Cultures" as well as "Fear and Prejudice in U.S.–Japan Relations"; of car-

toons in "Graphic Selves/Graphic Others"; and of the Japanese conservative tradition in "Yoshida in the Scales of History." Occupation legacies are addressed in "Peace and Democracy in Two Systems: External Policy and Internal Conflict" in *Postwar Japan As History*, ed. Andrew Gordon (Berkeley: University of California Press, 1993), pp. 3–33.

4. A confidential Home Ministry intelligence report dated September 4, 1945, emphasized the following American characteristics (using English for the key words themselves): (1) Practical, businesslike; (2) Straightforwardness; (3) Speedy action; (4) Self-conceited mind; (5) Adventurous spirit; (6) Punctuality; and (7) Vulgarity. The report is reprinted in *Haisen Chokugo no Seiji to Shakai, 1*, ed. Awaya Kentarō, vol. 2 in the documentary series *Shiryō: Nihon Gendai Shi* (Tokyo: Ōtsuki Shoten, 1980), pp. 313–17. "Presurrender planning" was virtually nonexistent in Japan, where it was treasonous even to speak of the possibility of defeat until the very last moment. On the American side, in contrast, such planning was carried out in great detail for several years prior to the surrender. Participants such as Hugh Borton and scholars led by Marlene Mayo, Akira Iriye, and Robert Ward have published valuable studies of this fascinating baseline to the years addressed in the present study.

CHAPTER 1. *SHATTERED LIVES*

1. Letter by Aihara Yū in *Asahi Shimbun*, August 14, 1994. Technically, this was not the first time the emperor's voice had been carried over the airwaves. In December 1928, a small scandal ensued when broadcasters covering a military review inadvertently picked up and transmitted his words as he read a rescript to the assembled troops; *Asahi Shimbun*, May 16, 1995.

2. As a general rule, confidential Japanese accounts of the emperor's activities must be treated with great caution in that they rely on notations and recollections by close aides devoted to burnishing his image. The earliest official account of high-level activities leading up to the emperor's broadcast was conveyed to U.S. occupation authorities in November 1945 by Sakomizu Hisatsune, chief secretary to the cabinet at the time of surrender and personally involved in drafting the rescript. Sakomizu emphasized that the emperor made the decision to broadcast the capitulation message personally; see U.S. Department of State, *Foreign Relations of the United States, 1945*, 6:702–8. (Henceforth this basic documentary series is cited as *FRUS.*) The most convenient compilation of Japanese sources on this matter—and on Emperor Hirohito generally—is a thick, two-volume collection edited by Tsurumi Shunsuke and Nakagawa Roppei; see *Tennō Hyakuwa* (Tokyo: Chikuma Bunko, 1989), esp. vol. 1, pp. 683–99, which includes the full text of the rescript (697–99) as well as corroborative testimony regarding the emperor's initiatory role (690). The text itself passed through several hands, including review by two academic specialists in classical Chinese who not only checked for proper cadence and grammar, but also suggested apt classical phrases; ibid., pp. 684–87. For many decades, the basic accounts of the surrender in English remained two early publications: U.S. Strategic Bombing Survey, *Japan's Struggle to End the War* (Washington, D.C.: U.S. Government Printing Office, 1946), and Robert J. C. Butow's *Japan's Decision to Surrender* (Stanford: Stanford University Press, 1954). These accounts have been critically revised in Herbert Bix, "Japan's Delayed Surrender: A Reinterpretation," *Diplomatic History* 19.2 (spring 1995): 197–225.

3. For samples of this familiar argument, see the editorial in *Asahi Shimbun*, August 16, 1945; letter to *Asahi Shimbun*, October 21, 1945; and Hidaka Rokurō, *Gendai Ideorogii* (Tokyo: Keisō Shobō, 1960), pp. 230–31.

4. The fear that revolutionary upheaval would accompany defeat was conveyed to the emperor in the famous "Konoe Memorial" in February 1945. On these fears, see John W. Dower, *Empire and Aftermath: Yoshida Shigeru and the Japanese Experience, 1878–1954* (Cambridge, Mass.: Council on East Asian Studies, Harvard University, 1979), chs. 7 and 8; also "Sensational Rumors, Seditious Graffiti, and the Nightmares of the Thought Police," in *Japan in War and Peace: Selected Essays,* by John W. Dower (New York: The New Press, 1993), pp. 101–54.

5. Kido Kōichi, *Kido Kōichi kankei Bunsho* (Tokyo: Tokyo Daigaku Shuppankai, 1966), p. 137.

6. In the immediate wake of the defeat, it was estimated that more than three hundred army and fifty navy personnel committed suicide; Kusayanagi Daizō, *Naimushō tai Senryōgun* (Tokyo: Asahi Bunko, 1987), p. 16. By another calculation, between the emperor's broadcast and October 1948, a total of 527 army and navy men, plus a small number of civilians, took their lives as a gesture of responsibility for the defeat; Tsurumi and Nakagawa, 1:714–16.

7. Marlene Mayo, "American Wartime Planning for Occupied Japan: The Role of the Experts," in *Americans as Proconsuls: United States Military Government in Germany and Japan, 1944–1952,* ed. Robert Wolfe (Carbondale: Southern Illinois Press, 1984), p. 34 (on Grew). See also Roger Buckley, "Britain and the Emperor: The Foreign Office and Constitutional Reform in Japan, 1945–1946," *Modern Asian Studies* 12.4 (1978): 557–58, and Shigemitsu's account of these events in Tsurumi and Nakagawa, 2:23–25.

8. The various texts and speeches pertaining to the formal surrender are reprinted in the September 2, 1945 issue of the *New York Times.* The positive Japanese response is noted, among other sources, in Nihon Jānarizumu Kenkyūkai, ed., *Shōwa "Hatsugen" no Kiroku* (Tokyo: Tōkyū Agency, 1989), pp. 100–1.

9. General Walter Krueger, *From Down Under to Nippon: The Story of the Sixth Army in World War II* (Washington, D.C.: Combat Forces Press, 1953), p. 339.

10. Nihon Jānarizumu Kenkyūkai, pp. 100–1; *New York Times,* September 12, 1945. MacArthur went on to note that Japan might reemerge as the commercial leader of Asia, but could never become a leading world power. Several weeks later, Fleet Admiral William Halsey (after expressing regret that the war "ended too soon because there are too many Nips left") declared that if MacArthur's policies were carried out, "Japan will never rise above a fifth or sixth place power"; *New York Times,* September 25, 1995.

11. U.S. Department of the Army, *Reports of General MacArthur,* volume 1, supplement, *MacArthur in Japan: The Occupation: Military Phase* (Washington, D.C.: U.S. Department of the Army; originally prepared by MacArthur's General Staff in 1950, but not published until 1966), p. 131. On September 21, MacArthur was again widely quoted as telling the president of the United Press that Japan's "punishment for her sins, which is just beginning, will be long and bitter." He took this occasion to reemphasize that the country could "never again" become a world power; *New York Times,* September 22, 1945.

12. Edwin A. Locke, Jr., memorandum for the president, October 19, 1945, Box 182, President's Secretary File, Papers of Harry S. Truman, Truman Library, Independence, Mo. I am grateful to Miura Yōichi for providing me with a copy of this memorandum.

13. The most-often quoted single observation made by the U.S. Strategic Bombing Survey was that Japan "certainly" would have been forced to capitulate by the end of 1945, and "in all probability" prior to November 1, "even if the atomic bombs had not been dropped, even if Russia had not entered the war, and even if no invasion

had been planned or contemplated"; see the Survey's *Summary Report (Pacific War)* (Washington, D.C.: Government Printing Office, July 1946), p. 26, and also by the Survey, *Japan's Struggle to End the War* (July 1946), p. 13. Whether this was correct is a matter of dispute.

14. The basic cumulative set of data on war damages in Japan was issued by the Economic Stabilization Board (Keizai Antei Honbu) in April 1949 and has been widely reproduced. See, for example, the official Ōkurashō (Ministry of Finance) history of the occupation period, *Sengo Zaisei Shi* (Tokyo: Tōyō Keizai Shimbun, 1978), vol. 19, pp. 15–19.

15. See Dower, *Japan in War and Peace*, pp. 121–22, for fuller statistical detail and annotation.

16. *FRUS 1946*, 8:165. See also Ōkurashō, op. cit., and Takafusa Nakamura, *The Postwar Japanese Economy: Its Development and Structure* (Tokyo: University of Tokyo Press, 1981), p. 15. None of these calculations include the loss of Japan's Asian empire, in which vast private and public resources had been invested over the course of some four decades.

17. Russell Brines, *MacArthur's Japan* (Philadelphia and New York: Lippincott, 1948), p. 40. See also William C. Chase, *Front Line General: The Commands of Maj. Gen. Wm. C. Chase* (Houston: Pacesetter Press, 1975), p. 127.

18. See, for example, Brines, pp. 26, 39–40, 117.

19. Harry Emerson Wildes, *Typhoon in Tokyo: The Occupation and Its Aftermath* (New York: Macmillan, 1954), p. 2. A vivid description of such scenes in Osaka appears in *Osaka Hyakunen Shi*, edited and published by Osaka-fu [Osaka Prefecture] (Osaka, 1968), p. 907.

20. *Reports of General MacArthur*, 1: supplement: 117–30, 148–93; for area breakdowns, see the cartographic plate on p. 148. Cf. Kōdansha, ed., *Shōwa: Niman Nichi no Zenkiroku* (Tokyo: Kōdansha, 1989), vol. 7, p. 274. (Henceforth this multivolume day-by-day account of the Shōwa period is cited as *SNNZ*.)

21. *SNNZ* 7:300.

22. *SNNZ* 7:132.

23. Hundreds of these abandoned children, invariably poor and speaking only Chinese, began to come to Japan on officially sponsored trips in the 1980s to try to reestablish contact with their families. Even where reunions did occur, they were excruciatingly painful.

24. *Reports of General MacArthur*, 1, supplement: 162, 165, 173, 174, 176.

25. Ibid., pp. 158–59, 161n, 173, 178–79; see also *FRUS 1946*, 8:311–12. The British also delayed the return of surrendered Japanese from Hong Kong.

26. *Reports of General MacArthur*, op. cit., pp. 158, 170–76, 191–93.

27. In November 1948, for example, an uproar occurred when Japanese repatriated from the Soviet Union on the ship *Eiho Maru* burst into Communist songs, delivered Communist speeches, and initially refused to cooperate with occupation authorities. Similar incidents took place in June and July 1949.

28. Early estimates of the number of Japanese in Soviet-controlled areas are given in *FRUS 1946*, 8:306. A general treatment of the subject, presenting the figures accepted by U.S. authorities, is given in *Reports of General MacArthur*, op. cit., pp. 179–91. The list of Japanese names turned over by the Soviets early in 1991 is reproduced, with commentaries, in a special July 1991 issue of *Geppan Asahi*, entitled *Chinkon Shiberia: Yokuryū Shibōsha Yonmannin Meibo*.

29. The 1950 cartoon is reproduced in Hasegawa Machiko, *Sazae-san*, volume 7 (Tokyo: Shimaisha, n.d.), p. 68.

30. Sodei Rinjirō, *Haikei Makkāsā Gensuisama: Senryōka no Nihonjin no Tegami* (Tokyo: Miraisha, 1982), pp. 173–74.

31. *Mainichi Nenkan 1949*, pp. 96–97. Returnees to Japan also included several thousand Japanese Americans who had been incarcerated on racial grounds in the United States and requested repatriation when the war ended. In addition to first-generation Issei, who were ineligible for U.S. citizenship and retained strong loyalties to their homeland, this number also included a number of second-generation Nisei, whose birth in the States gave them American citizenship. Most of the latter were "Kibei Nisei" who had lived in Japan for many years before returning to the United States prior to Pearl Harbor; see Sodei Rinjirō, *Watakushitachi wa Teki Datta no ka* (Tokyo: Ushio, 1978), pp. 55, 73–78.

32. *Reports of General MacArthur*, op. cit., pp. 89–115. See p. 108 on the Kyushu vivisections, and p. 109 for passing reference to the *kind* treatment some POWs received from lower-level camp attendants. By one count, a total of 32,624 Allied POWs were released within Japan, from a total of 127 camps (pp. 102–4).

33. Ibid., pp. 169–70, 173n.

34. Ibid., pp. 169–70.

35. Kuramitsu Toshio, "Uraga," *Bungei Shunjū*, January 1946; reprinted in *Shōwa Sesō Shi: Dokyumento: Sengo-hen*, ed. Heibonsha Henshūbu (Tokyo: Heibonsha, 1976), pp. 148–53. (This collection is cited below as *SSS*.)

36. Kuramitsu Toshio, "Hikiage Koji," *Bungei Shunjū*, December 1946; reprinted in *SSS*, pp. 153–59.

37. *SNNZ* 7:280.

38. *SNNZ* 7:274; NHK Hōsō Bunka Chōsa Kenkyūjo, *GHQ Bunsho ni yoru Senryōki Hōsō Shi Nenpyō (1946)* (Tokyo: NHK, 1989), pp. 58, 69, 73, 76.

39. *Reports of General MacArthur* 1: supplement: 187n.

40. Asahi Shimbunsha, ed., *Koe*, vol. 1: 1945–1947 (Tokyo: Asahi Bunko, 1984) p. 182. *Koe* ("Voice") is the name of the *Asahi* newspaper's letters to the editor section, and this volume is the first in a series of selected letters printed in the postwar period; this source is henceforth cited as *Koe*.

41. *Koe* 1:200–2.

42. Awaya Kentarō, ed. *Shiryō: Nihon Gendai Shi*, vol. 2 (Tokyo: Ōtsuki Shoten, 1980), pp. 38, 41, 76, 82–83, 109, 175, 197. This is a valuable collection of internal reports from the period following capitulation. See also Awaya Kentarō and Kawashima Takamine, "Gyokuon Hōsō wa Teki no Bōryaku Da," *This Is Yomiuri*, November 1994, p. 52.

43. The phrase "living war dead" *(ikite iru eirei)* is noted in Noda Mitsuharu, "Horyo no Ki," *Shinchō*, January 1947; reprinted in *SSS*, p. 139. Japanese taken prisoner during the war commonly were reported to their families as having been killed, since official policy placed such a social stigma on falling into enemy hands. Thus, incorrect reports of death in battle reflected deliberate as well as unwitting misrepresentations.

44. *Koe* 1:102–4, 152, 191–92.

45. *Koe* 1:266–67.

46. *SNNZ* 7:288–89.

47. *Sunday Mainichi,* May 30, 1948, in *SNNZ* 7:309; *Sengo Taiken* (Tokyo: Kawade Shobō, 1981; this is a volume in the *Jinsei Tokuhon* series), pp. 91, 96. *Kane no Naru Oka* ("The Hill Where the Bell Tolls"), a radio program that dealt with war orphans, offers clear evidence of how sentimentality coexisted with neglect. Although the program was introduced in 1947 at the order of occupation authorities (inspired by a visit by Father Flanagan, head of the Boy's Town orphanage in the United States) and continued until 1950 at SCAP's insistence, it did enjoy considerable popularity. See *Sengo Taiken,* pp. 83–85.

48. Hayashi's article is reprinted in Bungei Shunjū, ed., *"Bungei Shunjū" ni Miru Shōwa Shi* (Tokyo: Bungei Shunjūsha, 1988), vol. 2, pp. 26–34.

49. *Asahi Hyōron,* December 1948; reproduced in *Sengo Taiken,* p. 134.

50. *SNNZ* 7:288–89. The Japanese for "institution creatures" is *shisetsu no mono.*

51. *Koe* 1:70–72.

CHAPTER 2. *GIFTS FROM HEAVEN*

1. This exchange is recounted by Kades in a lengthy interview with Takemae Eiji, "Kades Memoir on Occupation of Japan," *Journal of Tokyo Keizai University* 148 (November 1986): 306. This became an almost ritualized exchange between American reformers and their numerous critics and doubters; for another example, see B. V. A. Röling, *The Tokyo Trial and Beyond: Reflections of a Peacemonger,* ed. Antonio Cassese (Cambridge: Polity Press, in association with Blackwell Publishers, 1993), p. 83.

2. Katō's *Okurareta Kakumei* was published in a series of pocket-sized booklets called *Rakkii Bunko* (which also carried the English title "Lucky Series") (Tokyo: Kobaruto-sha, November 1946). I am grateful to Hisayo Murakami for calling my attention to a copy of this now-rare book in the Gordon Prange collection of occupation materials in McKeldin Library, University of Maryland. For a reproduction of Katō's 1942 poster, see John W. Dower, "Race, Language, and War in Two Cultures: World War II in Asia," in *The War in American Culture: Society and Consciousness during World War II,* ed. Lewis A. Erenberg and Susan E. Hirsch (Chicago: University of Chicago Press, 1996), p. 195. A sanitized selection of his wartime graphics is included in *Katō Etsurō Mangashū* (Tokyo: Katō Etsurō Kankōkai, 1960).

3. For examples of such hand-of-God American cartoons, see John W. Dower, *Japan in War and Peace: Selected Essays* (New York: The New Press, 1993), p. 289. Harry Emerson Wildes, an occupation participant, titled one chapter "Revolution from Above" in his *Typhoon in Tokyo: The Occupation and Its Aftermath* (New York: Macmillan, 1954). Justin Williams, who supervised U.S. policy toward the Diet, titled his memoirs *Japan's Political Revolution under MacArthur: A Participant's Account* (Athens: University of Georgia Press, 1979).

4. Junnosuke Masumi, *Postwar Politics in Japan, 1945–1955,* Japan Research Monograph 6 (Berkeley: Center for Japanese Studies, Institute of East Asian Studies, University of California, 1985), pp. 88–89.

5. The Japanese terms were *okurimono* (gift), *puresento* (present), *Potsdam kakumei* (Potsdam revolution), and *amakudari no kaikaku* (reform from on high). See, for example, Kuyama Yasushi, ed., *Sengo Nihon Seishin Shi* (Tokyo: Sōbunsha, 1961), p. 7; Heibonsha Henshūbu, ed., *Shōwa Sesō Shi–Dokyumento, Sengo-hen* (Tokyo: Heibonsha, 1976), p. 8 (hereafter this source is cited as *SSS*).

6. Kawakami's cynical phrase *(haikyū sareta jiyū)* provoked criticism from many liberals and leftists; see, for example, *SSS,* p. 8; Hidaka Rokurō, *Sengo Shisō no Shup-*

patsu, vol. 1 in the series *Sengo Nihon Shisō Taikei* (Tokyo: Chikuma Shobō, 1960), pp. 76–79; Maruyama Masao, *Kōei no Ichi kara—"Gendai Seiji no Shisō to Kōdō" Tsuiho* (Tokyo: Miraisha, 1982), p. 114.

7. Yamazaki Masakazu and Kuroi Senji, "Waga Sengo Taiken," *Sengo Taiken,* special issue of the journal *Jinsei Tokuhon* (Tokyo: Kawade Shobō Shinsha, 1981), pp. 247, 255. On the logic of irresponsibility, see, for example, the 1960 discussion involving Sumiya Mikio, Inoki Masamichi, Nishitani Keiji, and others in Kuyama, pp. 91–96.

8. Nanbara Shigeru, *Nanbara Shigeru Chosakushū,* vol. 7 (Tokyo: Iwanami, 1973), pp. 299–317; Nanbara's disillusion with subsequent developments is expressed in the original 1957 preface in ibid., pp. 5–10.

9. Kamei Katsuichirō, "Haisen no Tsurasa," in *"Bungei Shunjū" ni Miru Shōwa Shi* (Tokyo: Bungei Shunjūsha, 1988), vol. 2, pp. 202–6. The article originally appeared in May 1952.

10. See, for example, Robert Wolfe, ed., *Americans As Proconsuls: United States Military Government in Germany and Japan, 1944–1952* (Carbondale: Southern Illinois University Press, 1984), and James C. Thomson, Jr., Peter W. Stanley, and John Curtis Perry, eds., *Sentimental Imperialists: The American Experience in East Asia* (New York: Harper & Row, 1981). Galbraith's phrase referred specifically to the generally young economic planners (including himself) who administrated the wartime American economy; see his *Journey Through Economic Time: A Firsthand View* (Boston: Houghton Mifflin, 1994), p. 118.

11. The two basic international bodies associated with occupation affairs were the eleven-nation Far Eastern Commission, which met in Washington, D.C., and the four-nation (United States, Australia, China, and Soviet Union) Allied Council, which sat in Tokyo. See *Activities of the Far Eastern Commission: Report by the Secretary-General, February 26, 1946–July 10, 1947,* U.S. Department of State Publication 2888, Far Eastern Series 24, 1947; *The Far Eastern Commission: Second Report by the Secretary-General, July 10, 1947–December 23, 1948,* Department of State Publication 3420, Far Eastern Series 29, 1948; *The Far Eastern Commission: Third Report by the Secretary-General, December 24, 1948–June 30, 1950,* Department of State Publication 3925, Far Eastern Series 35, 1950; and the excellent summary report by George Blakeslee, *The Far Eastern Commission: A Study in International Cooperation, 1945–1952,* Department of State Publication 5138, Far Eastern Series 60, 1953. Meetings of the Allied Council usually degenerated into an exchange of Cold War polemics, although the distinguished Australian representative to the Council by no means sided predictably with the United States; see W. Macmahon Ball's first-hand account: *Japan: Enemy or Ally?* (New York: John Day, 1949).

12. These documents are reproduced in various publications, including the basic official source for the first three years of the occupation: Supreme Commander Allied Powers, Government Section, *Political Reorientation of Japan, September 1945 to September 1948,* volume 2 (Washington, D.C.: U.S. Government Printing Office, 1949), pp. 413, 423–39. On the question of exactly when MacArthur received draft copies of the basic early policy documents, see Marlene Mayo, "American Wartime Planning for Occupied Japan: The Role of the Experts," in Wolfe, op. cit., pp. 4, 47, and 468–72 (notes 93, 97, 99). On the central importance of the secret Joint Chiefs of Staff directive (known as JCS 1380/15) to GHQ staff in Tokyo, see Theodore Cohen, *Remaking Japan: The American Occupation as New Deal* (New York: Free Press, 1987), pp. 4, 10–13. The fact that this directive was not declassified until November 1948 is noted in Edwin M. Martin, *The Allied Occupation of Japan* (New York: American Institute of Pacific Relations, 1948), p. xi; this book, written by a

State Department officer and reflecting the official U.S. position, includes JCS 1380/15 as an appendix.

13. Mayo's densely documented essay in Wolfe (pp. 3–51, 447–72) is excellent on this. See also Cohen, pp. 3–48, and Akira Iriye, *Power and Culture: The Japanese-American War, 1941–1945* (Cambridge, Mass.: Harvard University Press, 1981).

14. See, for example, Mayo, pp. 41, 48.

15. Dean Acheson, *Present at the Creation: My Years in the State Department* (New York: Norton, 1969), p. 126.

16. Kades in Takemae interview, pp. 289–90.

17. The transcript of MacArthur's Senate testimony is reprinted in the *New York Times*, May 4, 1951.

18. One should keep in mind the special nature of the occupation of Japan when confronting the large body of commentary by American writers that points to it as a representative example of America's fundamental idealism and generosity—as contrasted, for example, with Japanese occupation policies during World War II and postwar Soviet policies in Eastern Europe. When security considerations dictated policy, the United States did not seriously pursue reformist occupation policies— as seen in southern Korea and Okinawa. Japan proper had the good fortune to be excluded from such overriding Cold War security considerations in the immediate aftermath of the war.

19. B. V. A. Röling, "The Tokyo Trial and the Quest for Peace," in *The Tokyo War Crimes Trial: An International Symposium*, ed. C. Hosoya, N. Andō, Y. Ōnuma, and R. Minear (Tokyo: Kodansha and Kodansha International, 1986), p. 130.

20. *Asahi Shimbun*, September 17, 1945.

21. On October 10, some three thousand individuals indicted under the Peace Preservation Law were freed. Of this number, around eight hundred, mostly Communists, were in prison, the others under house arrest or some other form of detention; Joe Moore, *Japanese Workers and the Struggle for Power, 1945–1947* (Madison: University of Wisconsin Press, 1983), p. 14. On the Japanese government's opposition to release of political prisoners, see Masumi, p. 44.

22. Yoshida Shigeru expressed this outlook succinctly before the occupation forces arrived; see his brief communication of August 27, cited in Inoki Masamichi, *Hyōden Yoshida Shigeru*, vol. 3 (Tokyo: Yomiuri Shimbun, 1978–1981), p. 61.

CHAPTER 3. KYODATSU: *EXHAUSTION AND DESPAIR*

1. Tsurumi's insightful essays on the Japanese experience in the war and early postwar years appear in her *Social Change and the Individual: Japan Before and After Defeat in World War II* (Princeton, N.J.: Princeton University Press, 1996). Ara is quoted in J. Victor Koschman, "The Japan Communist Party and Literary Strategy," in *Legacies and Ambiguities: Postwar Fiction and Culture in West Germany and Japan*, ed. Ernestine Schlant and J. Thomas Rimer (Washington, D.C. and Baltimore: Woodrow Wilson Center Press and Johns Hopkins University Press, 1991), pp. 175–77. Even intellectuals opposed to the war tended to believe that "since we have come this far, there is no alternative but to fight until death"; see, for example, Watanabe Kazuo's diary entry about a friend in his *Haisen Nikki* (Tokyo: Hakubunkan Shinsha, 1995), p. 39. Watanabe himself seriously contemplated commiting suicide before such a final battle came to pass.

2. *Sengo no Shingo Kaisetsu* (publisher unclear; page proofs dated November 1946), p. 71. The proofs of this book, complete with censorship markings, can be found in the censorship files of the Gordon Prange Collection, McKeldin Library, University of Maryland.

3. From the memoirs of Yoshihashi Kaizō, quoted in Herbert Bix, "Japan's Delayed Surrender: A Reinterpretation," *Diplomatic History* 19.2 (spring 1995): 211.

4. *Osaka Hyakunen Shi*, edited and published by Osaka-fu [Osaka Prefecture] (Osaka: 1968), pp. 638–42. On food shortages and factory absenteeism, see Jerome Cohen, *Japan's Economy in War and Reconstruction* (Minneapolis: University of Minnesota Press, 1949), pp. 197–98, 274, 342–45.

5. Tsūsan Daijin Kanbō Chōsaka [Ministry of International Trade and Industry], ed., *Sengo Keizai Jūnen Shi* (Tokyo: Shōkō Kaikan Shuppanbu, 1954), p. 37. Most of the figures are for 1939 or 1940.

6. *Osaka Hyakunen Shi* reproduces the full list of recommended dietary supplements on pp. 642–43.

7. On estimates of calorie intake, see Rekishigaku Kenkyūkai, ed., *Haisen to Senryō*, vol. 1 in *Nihon Dōjidai Shi* (Tokyo: Aoki Shoten, 1990), p. 196; Yomiuri Shimbun Osaka Shakaibu, ed., *Shūsen Zengo* (Tokyo: Kadokawa Bunko, 1984), pp. 122–23; *Yomiuri Shimbun,* May 5, 1946; also figures and citations in John W. Dower, *Japan in War and Peace: Selected Essays* (New York: The New Press, 1993), p. 122. The smaller size of children in 1946 is noted in Tokyo Yakeato Yamiichi o Kiroku Suru Kai, ed., *Tokyo Yamiichi Kōbō Shi* (Tokyo: Sōfūsha, 1978), pp. 80–81; henceforth this valuable study of the black market is cited as *TYKS*.

8. Heibonsha Henshūbu, ed., *Shōwa Sesō Shi—Dokyumento, Sengo-hen* (Tokyo: Heibonsha, 1976), pp. 55–56. This lively collection of writings on postwar popular culture is cited below as *SSS.*.

9. Letter to *Asahi Shimbun,* August 23, 1990.

10. Kōdansha, ed., *Shōwa Niman Nichi no Zenkiroku* (Tokyo: Kōdansha, 1989), vol. 7, pp. 158, 161, 212. This day-by-day account is cited below as *SNNZ*.

11. *SSS*, p. 80; *SNNZ* 7:161, 166; *TYKS*, pp. 12–14.

12. *Asahi Nenkan 1947,* p. 169; *Osaka Hyakunen Shi*, pp. 913–14. Beginning in January 1946, shipments of wheat were brought into Japan from no-longer-needed U.S. military stocks in the Pacific area; much of this was turned into hard rolls (known as *koppepan*) and used to supplement the rice ration. Formal U.S. aid was initiated in July 1946 under the GARIOA (Government and Relief in Occupied Areas) program, which in 1948 merged with the modest and more industrially oriented EROA (Economic Recovery for Occupied Areas); these were earmarked as loans rather than donations. Under another aid program known as LARA (Licensed Agency for Relief of Asia) and administered by the United Nations, powdered skim milk was distributed to elementary schools throughout Japan. GARIOA shipments were not restricted to foodstuffs, but included basic materials such as raw cotton, fertilizer, fuels, and medicines. Typically, data concerning these materials are not always consistent, but in 1961 the Ministry of International Trade and Industry accepted the the total value of U.S. aid during the occupation as having amounted to between $1.7 and $1.8 billion, of which $1.05 billion came in the form of foodstuffs and $511 million as raw materials and fuel. In January 1962, Japan agreed to repay $490 million of this total over a period of fifteen years; see Fuji Bank, *Banking in Modern Japan* (1961; this is a special issue of *Fuji Bank Bulletin* 11.4), p. 209. This was a substantial contribution (although still considerably less than the estimated $5 billion spent by the Japanese government over the same period as "war termination

costs" in support of the occupation forces). It not only met the basic GARIOA objectives—defined as being "to prevent such starvation and widespread disease and
civil unrest as would (1) clearly endanger the occupying forces, and (2) permanently
obstruct the ultimate objectives of the occupation"—but also constituted a major
portion of Japan's total imports. One account by a former economist with the occupation estimates that this aid accounted for 77 percent of imports in 1947, 67 percent in 1948, and 59 percent in 1949; Sherwood M. Fine, *Japan's Post-war Industrial
Recovery* (New Delhi: Far Eastern Pamphlets #13, 1952), pp. 41–42, 57. Another former SCAP economist calculates that these shipments made up 58 percent of total
Japanese imports through 1950; Leon Hollerman, "International Economic Controls
in Occupied Japan," *Journal of Asian Studies* 38.4 (August 1979), p. 710. See also
SNNZ 7:212, 326; *Tsūsan Daijin*, p. 58; Cohen, pp. 477–79, 492–94; U.S. Department of State, *Foreign Relations of the United States, 1946*, vol. 8, pp. 349–50;
and the Ōkurashō [Ministry of Finance] series on occupation finance, *Sengo Zaisei
Shi* (Tokyo: Tōyō Keizai Shimbun, 1978), vol. 19, pp. 136–37 (table 52). This last
source, a basic official compilation of statistical data for the occupation period, is
cited below as *SZS*. In scale, the United States never provided aid to Japan (or Asia
more generally) remotely comparable with that directed toward Europe under the
Marshall Plan; for a detailed treatment, see William S. Borden, *The Pacific Alliance:
United States Foreign Policy and Japanese Trade Recovery, 1947–1955* (Madison: University of Wisconsin Press, 1984).

13. Yamaoka Akira, *Shomin no Sengo, 1945–1951: Sengo Taishū Zasshi ni Miru* (Tokyo:
     Taihei Shuppansha, 1973), pp. 41–46.

14. Kōdansha, ed. *Kōdansha no Ayunda Gojūnen (Shōwa hen)* (Tokyo: Kōdansha, 1959),
     pp. 560–62. The August–September 1945 issue of *Shōjo Kurabu* also emphasized
     that girls should continue wearing *monpe* pantaloons as a way of discouraging sex-
     ual advances by GIs.

15. Yamaoka, pp. 34–35.

16. *SZS* 19:140, 142–43 (tables 54 and 57).

17. *SNNZ* 7:164, 166, 264, 297; Takahashi, p. 97; *TYKS*, pp. 65, 289; Asahi Shim-
     bunsha, ed., *Koe* (Tokyo: Asahi Bunko, 1984), vol. 1, pp. 305–6. This last source is
     cited below as *Koe*.

18. *SNNZ* 7:272, 301; *SSS*, p. 266; *TYKS*, pp. 62, 117; Lucy Herndon Crockett, *Pop-
     corn on the Ginza: An Informal Portrait of Postwar Japan* (New York: William Sloane,
     1949), pp. 186–87.

19. The basic minimum standard of 2,200 calories was established in the Japanese gov-
     ernment's first "economic white paper," published in 1947. See Rekishigaku
     Kenkyūkai, *Nihon Dōjidai Shi*, p. 196; *SNNZ* 7:191, 323; Yomiuri Shimbun, *Shūsen
     Zengo*, pp. 122–23.

20. From an editorial in *Ura no Ura*, March 1948; quoted in Yamaoka, p. 223.

21. *Koe* 1:57–61.

22. *Koe*, 1:268–69.

23. "Kokumin Seikatsu to Yami Hōrei," *Toppu*, April 1947; quoted in Yamaoka, pp.
     222–23.

24. Yomiuri Shimbun, *Shūsen Zengo*, pp. 151–71; *SNNZ* 7:114.

25. *Koe*, 1:335–37; Asahi Shimbunsha, ed., *"Shūkan Asahi" no Shōwa Shi* (Tokyo: Asahi
     Shimbunsha, 1989), pp. 119–20.

26. *SSS*, pp. 43–44; see also p. 159 for a later, similar account of the hardships borne
     by women in particular. *Asahi Shimbun*, February 8, 1949, cited in *TYKS*, p. 323.

27. *SSS*, pp. 242–49. See also *Koe*, 1:72; *SNNZ* 7:203.

28. *SSS*, pp. 162–63, 197, 199.

29. Takahashi, p. 105.

30. *Nihon Tōkei Nenkan 1955/56* (Tokyo: Sōrifu), p. 477 (table 269). This is the authoritative "Japan Statistical Yearbook" published by the Prime Minister's Office, hereafter cited as *NTN*. See also *SNNZ* 7:228.

31. *NTN 1955/56*, p. 269 (table 269); cf. *NTN 1950*, pp. 440–41 (table 234). Reliable data for not only tuberculosis, but also birth rates and infant mortality are lacking for the turbulent period from 1943 through 1946.

32. *NTN 1950*, p. 436 (table 233). In 1948, public health centers alone reported having consulted on 932,604 tuberculosis cases; the figure for 1949 was 907,462.

33. *Shisō no Kagaku*, July 1990, p. 51 (n. 6).

34. *SSS*, p. 80.

35. See "Sensational Rumors, Seditious Graffiti, and the Nightmares of the Thought Police," in Dower, *Japan in War and Peace*, pp. 101–54; also "Revolution" (chapter 8) in John W. Dower, *Empire and Aftermath: Yoshida Shigeru and the Japanese Experience, 1878–1954* (Cambridge, Mass.: Council on East Asian Studies, Harvard University, 1979), pp. 273–303.

36. *Koe*, 1:248–49.

37. *TYKS*, pp. 283, 304, 312; Takahashi, pp. 106–8.

38. Kon Hidemi, "Shūdan Miai wa Ika ni Okonawareta ka," *Fujin*, July 1948; reprinted in *SSS*, pp. 231–34. See also Tsurumi Shunsuke, et al., *Nihon no Hyakunen* (Tokyo: Chikuma Shobō, 1967), vol. 1, pp. 200–2; *SNNZ* 8:121; Kanaya Chizuko, "Shūdan Miai," in *Sengo Shi Daijiten* (Tokyo: Sanshōdō, 1991), p. 415. For demographic data, see *SZS* 19:9.

39. *SNNZ* 7:275, 322.

40. *SNNZ* 7:275, 301; *TYKS*, p. 329.

41. See the letter to the *Asahi* by the famous writer Shiga Naoya on this subject, as well as readers' responses to that letter; *Koe*, 1:107–11.

42. *Koe*, 1:159, 197–98, 199.

43. *Sengo Taiken*, special issue of *Jinsei Tokuhon* (Tokyo: Kawade Shobō Shinsha, 1981), p. 48.

44. *SNNZ* 7:248, 278; *TYKS*, pp. 226–27.

45. *SNNZ* 7:230.

46. *SNNZ* 7:230, 290, 294, 308.

47. *NTN 1955/56*, pp. 496–97 (tables 279, 280, 281); *TYKS* p. 325.

48. See, for example, Hara Yasuo's rendering of child's play in the wartime cartoon collection *Kessen Mangashū* (Tokyo: Kyōgakkan, 1944).

49. *SNNZ* 7:2, 13, 181, 217, 243, 308; *TYKS*, p. 319; *SSS*, p. 266; *Koe* 1:293–94.

50. For basic sums, see *SNNZ* 7:214–15. An interesting insider account by the economist and early postsurrender Diet member Kimura Kihachirō appears in *Shōwashi Tanbō*, ed. Mikuni Ichirō and Ida Rintarō (Tokyo: Kadokawa Bunko, 1985), vol. 5, pp. 223–37. The findings of Japanese investigations into the diversion of military stockpiles into the black market are translated and reproduced in Supreme Commander for the Allied Powers, *Political Reorientation of Japan, September 1945 to September 1948* (Washington, D.C.: U.S. Government Printing Office, 1949); see vol.

1, pp. 311–13, and vol. 2, pp. 727–33. See also the coverage of Diet investigation of the scandal in SCAP's monthly *Summation: Non-Military Activities in Japan* (available on microfilm from Scholarly Resources, Inc.), summations 27 (December 1947) through 35 (August 1948), especially 27, pp. 23–32. Unless otherwise noted, much of the discussion that follows here derives from these last two sources. Post-surrender economic policies in general are discussed in chapter 17 below.

51. For the fiscal year 1946, before accounting procedures were routinized, it is calculated that occupation costs consumed at least one-third of the general accounts budget; see Keizai Kikakuchō Sengo Keizaishi Henshūshitsu, ed., *Sengo Keizai Shi (Keizai Seisakuhan)* (Tokyo: Ōkurashō Insatsukyoku, 1960), p. 73. Thereafter, these "war termination costs" accounted for two-fifths (39.8 percent) of the regular budget in 1947 and one-quarter (23.9 percent) in 1948. The figures for 1949 through 1951 were 17.1, 18.4, and 14.1 percent; see Tsūsan Daijin, appendix, pp. 15–17. On this generally neglected subject, see also *SZS* 19:186–87 (table 71); *Asahi Nenkan 1951*, p. 374; Watanabe Takeshi, *Senryōka no Nihon Zaisei Oboegaki* (Tokyo: Nihon Keizai Shimbunsha, 1966), pp. 42–43; and personal recollections of former Finance Ministry officials in the ministry's unpublished oral history transcripts entitled *Sengo Zaiseishi Kōjutsu Shiryō*, esp. vol. 1, entries 2 (p. 30), 3 (p. 17), 5 (pp. 11, 15–16), and 6 (pp. 28–29). The "regular" budget is to be distinguished from the supplemental budget.

52. These matters are touched on, albeit as inconveniences to the Americans, in Russell Brines, *MacArthur's Japan* (Philadelphia: Lippincott, 1948), pp. 295–96. On Japanese without homes of their own as of 1948, see *Sengo Taiken*, p. 64.

53. *SZS* 19:42–43 (table 12) and, for indices of consumer prices, 19:52–54 (tables 17-1 and 17-2). See also Yamaoka, pp. 34–35; Miki Torirō, "Fūsetsu no Yūmoa 'Jōdan Ongaku'," in Mikuni and Ida, p. 285.

54. *SZS* 19:64–65 (table 22); *Mainichi Nenkan 1949*, p. 536.

55. *SZS* 19:58–61 (table 20).

56. These very crude figures are extrapolated from scattered estimates concerning the value and tonnage of stockpiles mentioned in the report of the Diet investigation committee. Under the best of circumstances, official financial data for these chaotic years is problematic. In the case of the hoarded-goods scandal, massive, deliberate concealment obviously compounded the problem. At the same time, of course, the inflationary spiral makes it almost impossible to assign stable or meaningful yen values to these goods. The best one can do with these vexing numbers is place them in a rough comparative perspective to convey an impression of the enormous scale of the scandal.

57. *SZS* 19:90–93 (table 34).

58. *SNNZ* 7:227.

59. Published in the January 1946 issue of the poetry magazine *Bungei Sōshi* and reprinted in *Asahi Shimbun*, August 16, 1996.

CHAPTER 4. *CULTURES OF DEFEAT*

1. For typical examples, see *Asahi Shimbun*, letters, August 14, 1994; Kōdansha, ed., *Shōwa: Niman Nichi no Zenkiroku* (Tokyo: Kōdansha, 1989), vol. 7, p. 128; this source is cited below as *SNNZ*.

2. Yasuda Tsuneo, "Kioku to yū Jiyū," *Shisō no Kagaku* 130, July 1990, p. 7.

3. The popular term "third-country people" *(daisankokujin)* in itself provides interesting insight into racial discrimination in postwar Japan. *Gaijin*, the conventional

term for "foreigner," was reserved for Caucasians and carried a less pejorative intonation than *daisankokujin*, which was reserved for non-Japanese Asians, particularly Koreans and Formosans. "Third-country people" were understood to be "third-tier" people—below the Japanese, and below the second-tier Caucasians.

4. *Mainichi Shimbun*, September 29, 1946; quoted in Takahashi Nobuo, *Shōwa Sesō Ryūkōgo Jiten* (Tokyo: Obunsha, 1986), p. 111.

5. Heibonsha Henshūbu, ed., *Shōwa Sesō Shi—Dokyumento, Sengō-hen* (Tokyo: Heibonsha, 1976), pp. 59–62; this source is cited as *SSS* below.

6. Awaya Kentarō, ed., *Haisen Chokugo no Seiji to Shakai*, vol. 2 in *Shiryō: Nihon Gendai Shi* (Tokyo: Ōtsuki Shoten, 1980), pp. 219–20. See also the statement to the same effect in Michihiko Hachiya, *Hiroshima Diary: The Journal of a Japanese Physician, August 6–September 30, 1945*, trans. Warner Wells (Chapel Hill: University of North Carolina Press, 1955, 1995), p. 194.

7. The most widely cited author dealing with prostitution in postwar Japan is Kanzaki Kiyoshi, whose various findings are summarized in his *Baishun: Ketteiban Kanzaki Repōto* (Tokyo: Gendaishi Shuppankai, 1974). See especially pp. 127–62, as well as the detailed chronology at the end of the book; some of the data in this valuable "report" must be used with care. The account given here also draws on the following sources: Yoshimi Kaneko, *Baishun no Shakai Shi* (Tokyo: Yūzankaku, 1992), pp. 185–215; Nishi Kiyoko, *Senryōka no Nihon Fujin Seisaku* (Tokyo: Domesu Shuppan, 1985), pp. 34–39; *SNNZ* 7:270–71, 313–16; Isoda Kōichi, *Sengo Shi no Kūkan* (Tokyo: Shinchō Sensho, 1983), pp. 51–55; Makabe Hiroshi, "Ikenie ni Sareta Nanamannin no Musumetachi" in Tokyo Yakeato Yamiichi o Kiroku Suru Kai, ed., *Tokyo Yamiichi Kōbō Shi* (Tokyo: Sōfūsha, 1978), pp. 192–217; Takahashi Kazuo, "Yami no Onnatachi" in ibid., pp. 218–34. This last book is cited hereafter as *TYKS*.

8. Makabe, pp. 196–99; Yoshimi, pp. 185–88, 197–98; Kanzaki, pp. 131–33. Ikeda, who served as finance minister later in the occupation and was the architect of Japan's "income-doubling" policy as prime minister from 1960–1964, was quoted in the September 1, 1949 issue of *Sunday Mainichi*.

9. Yoshimi, p. 189.

10. Makabe, pp. 200–1.

11. Yoshimi, p. 188; Nishi, p. 36.

12. Kanzaki, pp. 136–38; Yoshimi, p. 193–94.

13. Makabe, pp. 205–8; Takami Jun is quoted in Isoda, pp. 51–52.

14. Sumimoto Toshio, *Senryō Hiroku* (Tokyo: Mainichi Shimbunsha, 1952), vol. 1, pp. 67–68.

15. Makabe, pp. 207–8; *SNNZ*, 7:270–71.

16. According to one calculation, the number of rapes and assaults on Japanese women amounted to around 40 *daily* while the R.A.A. was in operation, and then rose to an average of 330 a day after it was terminated in early 1946; Yoshimi, p. 198. See also Fukushima Jūrō, *Sengo Zasshi Hakkutsu* (Tokyo: Yōsensha, 1985), pp. 125–26. For a disturbing first-hand account of rape and assault by Australian forces in occupied Hiroshima, see Allan S. Clifton, *Time of Fallen Blossoms* (London: Cassell, 1950), ch. 20.

17. *SNNZ* 7:270–71; Yoshimi, pp. 196–97, 210–12; Kanzaki, pp. 384–86; Takahashi, p. 226; Sumimoto, p. 67.

18. Makabe, pp. 212–16; Isoda, p. 52.

19. *SNNZ*, 7:270. For the duration of the occupation, estimates of the incidence of venereal disease among prostitutes ranged from 30 to 60 percent.

20. *SNNZ*, 7:270–71, 325; Yoshimi, p. 198; *TYKS*, p. 85; *SSS*, p. 223. Lower estimates of the number of prostitutes are given *Asahi Nenkan 1947*, p. 281 (16,000 in 1946) and Kanzaki, p. 386 (38,840 in 1948).

21. *SNNZ* 7:271; *TYKS*, p. 320. Male prostitutes received some notoriety in December 1948, when one of them physically assaulted the metropolitan chief of police, who was personally inspecting the incidence of prostitution in Tokyo's Ueno area; Kanzaki, p. 386. This subject, as well as the broader topic of homosexual relations among Japanese and members of the occupation forces, remains unexamined.

22. *Van*, December 1947; reproduced in *Sengo Taiken*, a volume in the *Jinsei Tokuhon* series (Tokyo: Kawada Shobō Shinsha, 1981), p. 67.

23. For a feminist analysis of the new sexuality, especially as seen in films, see Joanne Izbicki, "The Shape of Freedom: The Female Body in Post-Surrender Japanese Cinema," *U.S.–Japan Women's Journal: English Supplement* 12 (1997), pp. 109–53.

24. *SSS*, pp. 223–29; *TYKS*, p. 223; *Asahi Nenkan 1947*, p. 281; Yoshimi, p. 210. A major wave of arrests in Tokyo in May 1947 netted some 5,225 prostitutes, of whom 2,450 gave "hardship" as the reason for selling their bodies, while 1,263 blithely said "curiosity."

25. *Sengo Taiken*, pp. 60–61; see also pp. 61–63 for another personal account.

26. *SNNZ* 7:301.

27. The comment, by *Yomiuri* journalist Suetsugu Setsuko, is reprinted in Yomiuri Shimbun Osaka Shakaibu, ed., *Shūsen Zengo* (Tokyo: Kadokawa Shoten, 1984), p. 114.

28. Sumimoto, 1:70. This two-volume "secret history" of the occupation, published in 1952, was in its time a famous exposé of matters that could not be discussed frankly while the Americans ruled Japan. Sumimoto, a journalist, estimated that occupation personnel spent some $185 million on personal matters, of which "almost half" went in one form or another to the panpan.

29. The concept of westernization "from the side" is suggested in *TYKS*, p. 242.

30. Sumimoto, pp. 70–72.

31. *Manga*, May 1948.

32. The liveliest study of the black market is *TYKS*. For a concise overview, see *SNNZ* 7:282–84. The *shobadai* argot is noted in Yomiuri Shimbun, *Shūsen Zengo*, p. 138.

33. Asahi Shimbunsha, ed., *Koe* (Tokyo, Asahi Bunko, 1984), vol. 1, p. 19; see also the letter of August 15 in ibid., pp. 25–26. This collection of letters to the *Asahi* newspaper is cited below as *Koe*.

34. *TYKS*, pp. 15–17.

35. Yomiuri Shimbun, *Shūsen Zengo*, p. 134.

36. *SNNZ* 7:155, 282–84; *TYKS*, pp. 15–22.

37. Yomiuri Shimbun, *Shūsen Zengo*, pp. 132, 137–39.

38. The summary of the Matsuda-gumi activities given here follows a 1946 report reprinted in *Sengo Taiken*, pp. 75–79.

39. *SNNZ* 7:279, 283–84. In early 1946, it was estimated that around sixteen thousand "third-country people," mostly Koreans and Formosans, were actively involved in illegal black-market activity. The "Shibuya incident" also turned the question of jurisdiction over these resident Asians into an international issue (with China claim-

ing jurisdiction over the Formosans in Japan and the Formosans themselves endorsing this, while the Japanese government attempted to affirm its authority). See "Problems Regarding the Treatment of Formosans in Japan Raised by the Shibuya Incident," in *O.S.S./State Department Intelligence Reports, II: Postwar Japan, Korea, and Southeast Asia* (Washington, D.C.: Microfilm Project of University Publications of America, 1977), reel 4, document 6.

40. Yomiuri Shimbun, *Shūsen Zengo*, pp. 135–36.

41. Yomiuri Shimbun, *Shūsen Zengo*, pp. 134, 140–46.

42. *TYKS*, p. 52.

43. *SSS*, p. 63; *Koe* 1:175, 221, 292.

44. *TYKS*, pp. 20–22, 33, 93–94, 251–54. The argument that the black market represented important elements of liberation is emphasized particularly strongly here by Ino Kenji.

45. *Koe* 1:275–77.

46. Before being identified as "kasutori magazines" in 1946, the postwar pulps were variously called "pink magazines" *(momoiro zasshi; pinku zasshi)* or *"ero-guro* magazines" *(ero-guro zasshi).* The latter designation links this postsurrender phenomenon directly to an interwar interlude of bourgeois decadence which in the late 1920s and early 1930s took the form of an *"ero-guro-nansensu"* vogue—a Western-inspired phrase referring to the erotic, grotesque, and nonsensical. Postdefeat decadence had clear prewar roots. The basic study of postsurrender magazines is Fukushima Jūrō's valuable *Sengo Zasshi Hakkutsu* (Tokyo: Yōsensha, 1985 edition). The discussion of kasutori magazines here derives largely from Fukushima (esp. pp. 163ff.); Tabuki Hideki, "Kasutori Zasshi Bunka," in *Haisen to Nihon no Shakai: Minshūteki Shiza ni yoru,* a special issue of *Rekishi Kōron,* December 1967, pp. 40–47; and *SNNZ* 8:1–3, 36–37. Since "kasutori" literally refers to the sake lees from which the crude "kasutori shōchū" liquor was made, writers in English sometimes render the counterculture, and the pulps associated with it, as "the dregs."

47. Tabuki, p. 42; for a broader categorization of topics, see Fukushima, p. 190.

48. Kyoko Hirano, *Mr. Smith Goes to Tokyo: The Japanese Cinema under the American Occupation, 1945–1952* (Washington, D.C.: Smithsonian Institution Press, 1992), pp. 154–65; *TYKS*, pp. 155–56; *SNNZ* 7:257.

49. *SNNZ* 8:34.

50. *SNNZ* 8:38–39; Ozaki Kōji, "Kuni Yaburete Hadaka Ari," reprinted in Bungei Shunjū, ed., *"Bungei Shunjū" ni Miru Shōwa Shi* (Tokyo: Bungei Shunjūsha, 1988), vol. 2, pp. 46–47, *SSS,* p. 284; *TYKS,* pp. 160–61. The ideal of the "westernized" body was by no means new. In the Meiji period, early post-Restoration enthusiasts of modernization such as Mori Arinori even went so far as to recommend improving the physical stock of the Japanese by intermarriage with Caucasians. In Meiji-period woodblock prints, idealized Japanese figures were not merely clothed in Western garb, but also given Western stature, bodily proportions, and so on. This is particularly evident in prints from the Sino-Japanese and Russo-Japanese wars (in 1894–1895 and 1904–1905 respectively), where the physical contrast of Japanese to Chinese and their corresponding resemblance to Russians (or other "Westerners") is striking. Similarly, popular prints depicting the Meiji empress in Western dress tended to render this "very petite, dainty, and slender" woman "as a towering and statuesque form . . . Westernized in physique as well as dress"; see Julia Meech-Pekarik, *The World of the Meiji Print: Impressions of a New Civilization* (Tokyo: Weatherhill, 1986), pp. 133, 138, and the many prints reproduced there.

51. Sakakibara Shōji, *Shōwago: 60-nen Sesō Shi* (Tokyo: Asahi Bunko, 1986), p. 99. The phrase "love in old age" *(oiraku no koi)*, taken from Kawada's poem, became a popular catchphrase.

52. One of the photos reproduced here is featured in Hayashi Tadahiko, *Kasutori Jidai: Renzu ga Mita Shōwa 20-nendai: Tokyo* (Tokyo: Asahi Bunko, 1987), p. 146. This little book is one of the best collections of kasutori-culture photos.

53. *Nihon Bungaku no Rekishi* 12:368; quoted in Jay Rubin's valuable essay "From Wholesomeness to Decadence: The Censorship of Literature Under the Allied Occupation," *Journal of Japanese Studies* 11.1 (1985): 71–103 (see p. 77).

54. Ango Sakaguchi, "Discourse on Decadence," trans. Seiji M. Lippit, *Review of Japanese Culture and Society,* 1 (October 1986): 1–5; this is an excellent full translation of Sakaguchi's "Darakuron." The essay is reprinted in Sakaguchi Ango, *Darakuron* (Tokyo: Kadokawa Bunko, 1957), pp. 91–102.

55. J. Victor Koschmann has addressed the "subjectivity" debates in impressive detail. See his *Revolution and Subjectivity in Postwar Japan* (Chicago: University of Chicago Press, 1996); "The Debate on Subjectivity in Postwar Japan: Foundations of Modernism as a Political Critique," *Pacific Affairs* 54.4 (winter 1981–1982): 609–31; and "The Japanese Communist Party and the Debate over Literary Strategy under the Allied Occupation of Japan," in *Legacies and Ambiguities: Postwar Fiction and Culture in West Germany and Japan,* ed. Ernestine Schlant and J. Thomas Rimer (Washington, D.C. and Baltimore: Woodrow Wilson Center Press and Johns Hopkins University Press, 1991), pp. 163–86.

56. Tamura's first critically acclaimed publication was a short novel titled *Nikutai no Akuma* (Devil of the Flesh), published in September 1946. This was followed by *Nikutai no Mon* in March 1947 and an essay titled "Nikutai ga Ningen de Aru" (Flesh Makes the Human) the following May. The theatrical version of *Nikutai no Mon* premiered in August and set a record of some seven hundred sold-out performances in various Tokyo theaters over the course of the next year. The Tōhō film version that appeared in 1948 was the first of several cinematic adaptations. The "gate to modernity" *(kindai e no mon)* comment is quoted in Okuno Tatsuo's commentary in the 1968 edition of Tamura Taijirō, *Nikutai no Mon / Nikutai no Akuma* (Tokyo: Shinchō Bunko, 1968), p. 221.

57. The photo appears in Hayashi, p. 144.

58. *Shayō* was serialized in 1947 and published in book form that December. Some thirty thousand copies had been sold by the time of the author's suicide in June 1948, after which a "Dazai boom" ensued. On the "bestseller" success of the novel, see Asahi Jānaru, ed., *Besutoserā Monogatari* (Tokyo: Asahi Shimbunsha, 1967), pp. 44–52. *Shayō* is reprinted in volume 9 of Dazai's collected works, *Dazai Osamu Zenshū* (Tokyo: Chikuma Bunko, 1989) and has been translated into English by Donald Keene as *The Setting Sun* (Rutland, Vt.: Tuttle, 1981; originally published by New Directions in 1956). The translations of Dazai that follow here are mine.

59. *Dazai Osamu Zenshū,* 9:180–81 (cf. Keene trans., pp. 114, 124–25).

60. *Dazai Osamu Zenshū,* 9:414–20. See also the translation of *Ningen Shikkaku* by Donald Keene as *No Longer Human* (Rutland, Vt.: Tuttle, 1981; originally published by New Directions in 1958), pp. 65–70, 73. The key terms rendered "illegitimate" and "legitimate" here *(higohō, gohō)* are interpreted as implying "irrational" and "rational" by Professor Keene.

61. Isoda, pp. 37–38; Rubin, p. 95–96.

62. *Dazai Osamu Zenshū,* 9:236 (cf. Keene trans. pp. 129, 131, 172–75).

63. *Dazai Osamu Zenshū,* 9:208, 218, 237 (cf. Keene trans., pp. 142, 150–51, 174–75).

64. Cited by Ozaki Hideki in his essay on the public reception of *The Setting Sun* in Asahi Jānaru, *Besutoserā Monogatari*, 1:44–52 (see p. 47).

65. Masao Maruyama, "From Carnal Literature to Carnal Politics," in his *Thought and Behavior in Modern Japanese Politics* (Oxford: Oxford University Press, 1963), pp. 245–67. For other contemporary denunciations by prominent liberal and progressive critics, see Shimizu Ikutarō, "Kikai Jidai," *Shisō*, August 1950, and the special August 1951 issue of *Shisō* on popular entertainments, which includes another article by Shimizu. These developments are briefly summarized in Toshihiro Tsuganezawa, "Postwar Trends of Studies in Japanese Popular Culture," *Occasional Papers*, East-West Center, University of Hawaii (1966): 19–23.

66. Nakamura's essay, published in *Bungaku* in June 1952, is summarized in Rubin, pp. 75–76.

67. See Maki Shōhei's discussion of *The Complete Marriage* in Asahi Jyānaru, *Besutoserā Monogatari*, 1:16–24. The original German title was *Die Volkommene Ehe: Eine Studie uber ihre Physiologie und Technik*.

68. Komagome Kōhei, "*Fūfu Seikatsu* Shimatsuki" in *"Bungei Shunjū" ni Miru Shōwa Shi*, 2:322–31; an abridged version of this article appears in *SSS*, pp. 288–92. See also Fukushima, pp. 180–86.

69. Fukushima, p. 189.

70. Fukushima, pp. 105, 177–78.

71. The photo appears on the cover of Hayashi's *Kasutori Jidai*.

CHAPTER 5. *BRIDGES OF LANGUAGE*

1. Kōdansha, ed., *Shōwa: Niman Nichi no Zenkiroku* (Tokyo: Kōdansha, 1989), vol. 7, pp. 155, 167, 227, 237, 267, 281, 287, 325; Tokyo Yakeato Yamiichi o Kiroku Suru Kai, ed., *Tokyo Yamiichi Kōbō Shi* (Tokyo: Sōfūsha, 1978), pp. 16, 34–35, 112–13. These two sources are cited below as *SNNZ* and *TYKS*. I am indebted to Herbert Passin, who served with the occupation forces, for the liquor anecdote.

2. *SNNZ* 7:281.

3. *TYKS*, p. 43; *SNNZ* 7:198–99.

4. *TYKS*, pp. 34–35; *SNNZ* 7:167.

5. Asahi Shimbunsha, ed., *Koe* (Tokyo: Asahi Bunko, 1984), vol. 1, pp. 253, 264–65; this source is cited below as *Koe*. See also the "Picture of Tokyo" quoted in *TYKS*, pp. 55–57. In another parody, the lyrics of the rousing war song *Genkō* (which had been featured in Kurosawa Akira's patriotic home-front film *The Most Beautiful*) were changed from fighting off foreign invaders to fighting off beggars.

6. See, for example, the use of these various proverbs in *Kyōryoku Shimbun*, January 1946.

7. For suggestive runs of *karuta*, including those published as pure political satire after the surrender, see *Bessatsu Taiyō—Iroha Karuta* (Winter 1974), esp. pp. 85, 87, 102–4; *Kyōryoku Shimbun*, January 1946 (although the name suggests this was a newspaper, it was a short-lived progressive magazine); *Manga*, January 1947; *Nihon Yūmoa*, January 1948; and reproductions in the 1936–1945 and 1946–1950 sections in the unpaginated *Shōwa Manga Shi*, ed. Mainichi Shimbunsha (Tokyo: Mainichi Shimbunsha, 1977).

8. "The Apple Song" is discussed in virtually all cultural histories of the early post-surrender period. See, for example, Heibonsha Henshūbu, ed., *Shōwa Sesō Shi:*

Dokyumento: Sengo-hen (Tokyo: Heibonsha, 1976), pp. 265–78 [cited below as *SSS*]; *TYKS*, pp. 150–51; *SNNZ* 7:155, 203; *Sengo Taiken* (Tokyo: Kawade Shobō, 1981; from the *Jinsei Tokuhon* series), pp. 55–59; Nihon Jānarizumu Kenkyūkai, ed., *Shōwa "Hatsugen" no Kiroku* (Tokyo: Tōkyū Agency, 1989), pp. 104–5.

9. Takemae Eiji, "Sengo Demokurashii to Ei-kaiwa—'Kamu Kamu Eigo' no Yukuwari," in Shisō no Kagaku Kenkyūkai, ed., *Kyōdō Kenkyū: Nihon Senryō* (Tokyo: Tokuma Shobō, 1972), pp. 131–46. Takemae, the dean of Japanese scholarship on the occupation period, was personally deeply influenced by this radio program. See also *SNNZ* 7:207.

10. For a useful compendium of prewar and wartime slogans, see Morikawa Hōtatsu, *Teikoku Nippon Hyōgoshū* (Tokyo: Gendai Shokan, 1989).

11. Kōdansha, ed., *Kōdansha no Ayunda Gojūnen (Shōwa hen)* (Tokyo: Kōdansha, 1959), p. 562; Morikawa, p. 81. See also the quotation from the November 1945 issue of Kōdansha's *Kōdan Kurabu* in Fukushima Jūrō, *Sengo Zasshi Hakkutsu* (Tokyo: Yōsensha, 1985), pp. 102–3.

12. See, for example, the letters from repatriated soldiers in *Koe* 1:102–3, 107–8.

13. *Koe* 1:262. The wartime "Momotarō paradigm" is analyzed in John W. Dower, *War Without Mercy: Race and Power in the Pacific War* (New York: Pantheon, 1986), pp. 251–57.

14. See the extended discussion of the postwar concept of "culture" in Hirano Kenichirō, "Sengo Nihon Gaikō ni okeru 'Bunka,' " in *Sengo Nihon no Taigai Seisaku*, ed. Watanabe Akio, (Tokyo: Yūhikaku, 1985), pp. 339–66.

15. Morikawa, pp. 14, 15, 45, 93; see also ibid., 17, 41, 84. The slogan "Rising Sun Land, Superior Culture" rested on a homonymic pun on "rising sun" and "superior," both rendered in the spoken language as *hiizuru*.

16. I have drawn here on an unpublished index to periodicals in the Gordon Prange collection of occupation-period publications at the McKeldin Library, University of Maryland.

17. Morikawa, p. 18; see also ibid., 15, 24, 33, 80, 85.

18. *Kyōryoku Shimbun*, January 1946. The phrasing of the "roundtable discussion on 'changing the world' " *(yonaoshi zadankai)* tapped a late feudal millennial tradition of "world renewal" *(yonaoshi)*.

19. Censorship is discussed in chapter 14. Material obstacles to publishing are noted in Kōdansha, p. 559; see also Shiozawa Minobu, *Shōwa Besutoserā Sesō Shi* (Tokyo: Daisan Bunmeisha, 1988), p. 114.

20. *SNNZ* 7:192–93; Fukushima, p. 52; Shiozawa, p. 114.

21. Fukushima, pp. 40, 260–62.

22. Kōdansha, pp. 509–10; Fukushima, pp. 90–97.

23. Fukushima, pp. 23–24, 53–55; *SNNZ* 7:192–93; Eizaburō Okuizumi, comp. and ed., *Microfilm Edition of Censored Periodicals, 1945–1949* (Tokyo: Yushodo Booksellers, 1982), p. 24. The last of these sources is a guide to the invaluable collection of Japanese publications submitted to the occupation's censorship section and now maintained at the McKeldin Library at the University of Maryland.

24. *Nihon Tōkei Nenkan 1955/1956*, p. 459 (table 257); Okuizumi, pp. 23, 25. The number of translations is noted in an unpublished paper by Nicholas J. Bruno, "Press Reform in Occupied Japan (1945–1952)," Eighteenth Annual Meeting of the Mid-Atlantic Region Association of Asian Studies, October 21, 1989. The figures come from a report included among the papers of the Press and Publications Branch,

Civil Information and Education Section, in the SCAP archives in the National Archives (Box 5256, folder 12).

25. Fukushima, pp. 199–201. This valuable source reproduces the statements of purpose and tables of contents from the first postsurrender issues of many magazines (pp. 199–527).

26. Fukushima, pp. 202–3, 376–79; see also pp. 55–57 on the women's magazine *Josei*.

27. Fukushima, pp. 218–23.

28. Fukushima, pp. 242–47.

29. Fukushima, pp. 264–67.

30. Fukushima, pp. 279–82. On the 1944 suppression of *Kaizō* and *Chūō Kōron*, see ibid., pp. 82–85.

31. *Sekai*, January 1946, pp. 4–6. Interestingly, *Sekai*'s inaugural statement did not mention prewar oppositional movements in Japan, as progressives and leftists usually did, but rather followed the conservative line in citing the "Charter Oath" of 1868 as the prime example of the existence of an indigenous democratic tradition.

32. Shiozawa, pp. 97–100; *SNNZ* 7:155; Asahi Jānaru, ed., *Besutoserā Monogatari* (Tokyo: Asahi Shimbunsha, 1967), vol. 1, pp. 7, 145. The conversation book was surpassed as Japan's all-time bestseller in 1981 by Kuroyanagi Tetsuko's *Madogiwa no Totto-chan*. The "top ten" bestsellers from 1946 through 1987 are listed in Shiozawa, pp. 264–74.

33. Mita Munesuke, *Gendai Nihon no Seishin Kōzō* (Tokyo: Kōbundō, 1965), pp. 72–85, esp. 77–79. See also Ueda Yasuo, *Gendai no Shuppan* (Tokyo: Risō Shuppansha, 1980), pp. 156–59.

34. See the translation of *Sorekara* by Norma Moore Field: *And Then* (Putney, Vt.: Tuttle, 1988), p. 187.

35. See the translation of *Mon* by Francis Mathy: *Mon* (Putney, Vt.: Tuttle, 1972), p. 34; cf. pp. 61, 127, 134–36, 169.

36. Asahi Jānaru, 1:25–34.

37. In 1947, another volume of Miki's essays, originally published in 1941 and collectively titled *Jinseiron Nōto* (Notes on Life), replaced *Tetsugaku Nōto* on the bestseller list.

38. Chalmers Johnson, *An Instance of Treason: Ozaki Hotsumi and the Sorge Spy Ring* (Stanford: Stanford University Press, 1964), p. 36. This book is an incisive study of Ozaki's thought and activities.

39. Asahi Jānaru, 1:36–37; Johnson, pp. 205–6.

40. Johnson, p. 198; cf. 201, 214, 286.

41. For a vintage sample of Ozaki's utopianism, see Johnson, pp. 195–96.

42. Asahi Jānaru, 1:35. Ozaki was the model for the hero of Kurosawa Akira's first postwar film, the 1946 *Waga Seishun ni Kuinashi* (No Regrets for Our Youth).

43. For an insightful essay on Miyamoto's "feminist-humanist" vision, especially as expressed in *Banshū Heiya*, see Susan Phillip, "Beyond Borders: Class Struggle and Feminist Humanism in *Banshū Heiya*," *Bulletin of Concerned Asian Scholars* 19.1 (1987): 56–65; see also Noriko Mizuta Lippit, "Literature, Ideology and Women's Happiness: The Autobiographical Novels of Miyamoto Yuriko," *Bulletin of Concerned Asian Scholars* 10.2 (1978): 2–17.

44. Asahi Jānaru, 1:71–80. Nagai is accessible in English through William Johnston's translation of *Nagasaki no Kane;* see *The Bells of Nagasaki* (Tokyo: Kodansha Inter-

national, 1984). See also Paul Glynn, *A Song for Nagasaki* (Hunters Hill, N.S.W., Australia: Catholic Book Club, 1988). Nagai's apocalyptic statement is quoted in Glynn, p. 117.

45. Asahi Jānaru, 1:108–17. These writings are discussed further in chapter 16.

CHAPTER 6. *NEOCOLONIAL REVOLUTION*

1. Faubion Bowers, "How Japan Won the War," *New York Times Magazine*, August 30, 1970; Bowers, "Japan, 1940–1949: A Tumultuous Time Remembered," *Japan Society Newsletter* (New York), October 1995; Geoffrey Perret, *Old Soldiers Never Die: The Life of Douglas MacArthur* (New York: Random House, 1996), esp. p. 488. MacArthur's "adulate a winner" observation was offered during his testimony before a joint committee of the U.S. Senate in April 1951, the full text of which is given in the *New York Times*, May 6, 1951.

2. Bowers (1980); Theodore Cohen, *Remaking Japan: The American Occupation as New Deal*, ed. by Herbert Passin (New York: Free Press, 1987), pp. 100–1. In Cohen's view, critical staff amounted to around five hundred in April 1946 and nine hundred by January 1948.

3. Edwin M. Martin, *The Allied Occupation of Japan* (New York: American Institute of Pacific Relations, 1948), p. 47. Martin's important role in drafting the early reformist policy is documented in Cohen, pp. 34–36, 42–47.

4. *Osaka Hyakunen Shi*, edited and published by Osaka-fu [Osaka Prefecture] (Osaka: 1968), p. 1257.

5. NHK Hōsō Bunka Chōsa Kenkyūjo, *GHQ Bunsho ni yoru Senryōki Hōsō Shi Nenpyō (1946)* (Tokyo: NHK, 1989), p. 67; Nihon Hōsō Kyōkai, ed., *Hōsō Yawa (Zoku): Zadankai ni yoru Hōsō Shi* (Tokyo: Nihon Hōsō Kyōkai, 1970), pp. 13, 23, 27; Kōdansha, ed., *Shōwa: Niman Nichi no Zenkiroku* (Tokyo: Kōdansha, 1989), vol. 9, pp. 176–78 [this source is cited as *SNNZ* below]. On "Joe Nip," and occupation media policy generally, see Marlene Mayo, "The War of Words Continues: American Radio Guidance in Occupied Japan," in *The Occupation of Japan: Arts and Culture*, ed. Thomas Burkman (Norfolk, Va.: Douglas MacArthur Foundation, 1988), pp. 45–83.

6. For a perceptive, witty, little-known memoir, see Margery Finn Brown, *Over a Bamboo Fence: An American Looks at Japan* (New York: William Morrow, 1951; published in Tokyo in 1954 by Charles Tuttle), esp. chs. 5 and 6.

7. Faubion Bowers, "Discussion," in Burkman, op. cit., (1988), pp. 203–4. For a wicked parody of the slavish obedience of "liberated" Japanese to anything demanded "by order of the Occupation Forces," see the humor magazine *Manga*, February 1948, pp. 4–5.

8. On display of the Japanese flag, see Tsurumi Shunsuke et al., eds., *Nihon no Hyakunen* (Tokyo: Chikuma Shobō, 1967), vol. 1, pp. 279–82.

9. Cohen, p. 101; Brown, pp. 15–20.

10. Lucy Herndon Crockett, *Popcorn on the Ginza: An Informal Portrait of Postwar Japan* (New York: William Sloane, 1949), p. 186. This first-hand account amounts to an uncommonly sustained racist diatribe; see esp. ch. 19.

11. Brown, pp. 16–17; Bowers (1988), p. 203.

12. Cohen provides good thumbnail sketches of these and other GHQ personalities in *Remaking Japan*, ch. 5.

13. See, for example, Asahi Shimbunsha, ed., *"Shūkan Asahi" no Shōwa Shi* (Tokyo: Asahi Shimbunsha, 1989), vol. 2, p. 296.

14. "Babysan" was a popular cartoon creation of Bill Hume in the early 1950s, aimed at GIs in Japan. A postoccupation collection of Hume's graphics was titled *Babysan's World: the Hume'n Slant on Japan* (Tokyo and Rutland, Vt.: Tuttle, 1954). The great Japanese patron of mixed-blood children was Sawada Miki, an upper-class woman who saw a dead half-black baby on a train in February 1947 and thereafter devoted herself to providing for unwanted children born of American-Japanese liaisons. In February 1948, Sawada established an orphanage for such children named the Elizabeth Sanders Home, which she financed primarily by selling her personal possessions. Eventually, she helped many of these children relocate in Brazil. See Tsurumi, 1:293–96, and Elizabeth Anne Hemphill, *The Least of These: Miki Sawada and Her Children* (New York and Tokyo: Weatherhill, 1980).

15. The original "Blacklist" orders calling for establishment of direct military government in the eventuality of a Japanese surrender were received by MacArthur's command on August 2, 1945. These orders were not revised until August 30, the day U.S. forces physically arrived in Japan. See, for example, the inside account of military planning in General Walter Kreuger, *From Down Under to Nippon: The Story of the Sixth Army in World War II* (Washington, D.C.: Combat Forces Press, 1953), pp. 335–38. MacArthur probably got word of this change a few days earlier; see Marlene Mayo, "American Wartime Planning for Occupied Japan: The Role of the Experts," in *Americans As Proconsuls: United States Military Government in Germany and Japan, 1944–1952*, ed. Robert Wolfe (Carbondale: Southern Illinois Press, 1984), esp. 470–72 (n. 97).

16. The negligible reforms imposed on the bureaucracy are discussed in T. J. Pempel, "The Tar Baby Target: 'Reform' of the Japanese Bureaucracy," in *Democratizing Japan: The Allied Occupation*, ed. Robert E. Ward and Yoshikazu Sakamoto (Honolulu: University of Hawaii Press, 1987), pp. 157–87. The classic case study of bureaucratic continuity, including increasing empowerment in the occupation period, is Chalmers Johnson, *MITI and the Japanese Miracle: The Growth of Industrial Policy, 1925–1975* (Stanford: Stanford University Press, 1982).

17. Mutual images of the Japanese and Anglo-American antagonists in World War II are addressed in John W. Dower, *War Without Mercy: Race and Power in the Pacific War* (New York: Pantheon, 1986), and Dower, "Race, Language, and War in Two Cultures," in *Japan in War and Peace: Selected Essays* (New York: The New Press, 1993), pp. 257–85.

18. This guide is quoted at length in John La Cerda, *The Conqueror Comes to Tea: Japan Under MacArthur* (New Brunswick: Rutgers University Press, 1946), pp. 31–33.

19. SCAP's criticism of the original film is noted in La Cerda, p. 48.

20. The War Department's counterpart film to *Our Job in Japan* was entitled *Your Job in Germany*, with a script by Theodore Geisel (later to become famous as the author of the "Dr. Seuss" children's books). The treatment of the defeated enemy here departed from the usual "bad German/good German" approach and was uncompromisingly harsh. Rather than the German brain, it was German *history* that was pulled forward as the central motif—the history of a modern nation that continually waged war and then lulled non-Germans into a false sense of security with bucolic images of a culture filled with rustic pleasures. Virtually every German, it was emphasized, had supported the Nazis; and every German—especially the young— was a potential source of future revaunchism. This harsher treatment of the Germans and their potential for rehabilitation, as contrasted to the Japanese in *Our Job in Japan*, was atypical. In part, the difference can be attributed to the fact that *Your*

Job in Germany was produced very shortly after Germany's defeat, whereas the final version of the Japan film came out around a half year after Japan's surrender. In part, the difference also probably lies in the personal influence of Geisel (who also scripted a harsh but never-released War Department film about Japan entitled *Design for Death*). The *Saturday Evening Post* article appeared in the December 15, 1945 issue.

21. U.S. Department of State, *Foreign Relations of the United States, 1945,* vol. 6, p. 545 (May 28, 1945) for Grew; Mayo (1984), pp. 32–33, 50 for Dooman and Ballantine. On Grew and the "Japan crowd," see Cohen, pp. 16–20; Waldo Heinrichs, Jr., *American Ambassador: Joseph C. Grew and the Development of the United States Diplomatic Tradition* (Boston: Little, Brown, 1966); and Howard B. Schonberger, *Aftermath of War: Americans and the Remaking of Japan, 1945–1952* (Kent, Ohio: Kent State University Press, 1989), ch. 1, esp. pp. 21–28, 38. Cohen calls attention to the many American Japan specialists who in one way or another were doubtful of Japan's capacity to become a democratic nation; see esp. p. 478 (n. 13).

22. Royal Institute of International Affairs, *Japan in Defeat: A Report by a Chatham House Study Group* (Oxford: Oxford University Press, 1945). Emphasis on the "strongly developed herd instinct" of the Japanese was routine in intelligence evaluations; see the "Anglo-American Outline Plan for Psychological Warfare Against Japan" (C.C.S. 539/4) of May 1944 in box 3 of the Bonner Fellers papers at the Hoover Institution, Stanford University. The "African tribe" comment is cited, alongside other comparable observations, in Roger Buckley, "Britain and the Emperor: The Foreign Office and Constitutional Reform in Japan, 1945–1946," *Modern Asian Studies* 12.4 (1978): 567.

23. Grew's voluminous Japan diaries, among other sources, make this clear. I have addressed this issue in *Empire and Aftermath: Yoshida Shigeru and the Japanese Experience, 1878–1954* (Cambridge, Mass.: Council on East Asian Studies, Harvard University, 1979), pp. 104–12. One Western "old Japan hand" who was uncharacteristically sympathetic to the lower classes was the Canadian diplomat and historian E. H. Norman. The "monstrous beehive" phrase is picked up in a lengthy (103 double-column pages) and extremely interesting guidebook classified "Restricted" and distributed to U.S. occupation personnel: U.S. Army, *Guide to Japan* (CINCPAC-CINCPOA Bulletin No. 209-45; dated Sept. 1, 1945 on the title page but probably printed in April 1946); see p. 65.

24. H. M. Spitzer, "Considerations of Psychological Warfare Directed Against Japan," December 9, 1944, Office of War Information files, Record Group 208, Box 443, entry 378, National Archives, Washington, D.C. I am grateful to Amy Richards for this document. The "national character" studies are analyzed in Dower (1986); see esp. pp. 118–46.

25. Theodore Cohen's memoir takes the New Deal influence as a central theme. See especially pp. 32–48, as well as the subtitle of the book itself *(The American Occupation as New Deal).* Charles Kades later summarized the essence of being a "thorough New Dealer" as involving the belief that the government should intervene in times of crisis, introducing radical measures where necessary, but always within the framework of a free, competitive, capitalist society. This emerges in an unpublished interview with Kades conducted in conjunction with the Jigsaw Productions documentary film "Reinventing Japan," program 5 in the 1992 Annenberg/CPB series *The Pacific Century;* I am grateful to Alex Gibney for sharing interview transcripts from this production. See Kades-Gibney interview, transcript 2, pp. 15–16.

26. T. A. Bisson, "Japan as a Political Organism," *Pacific Affairs,* December 1944, pp. 417–20. See also "T. A. Bisson: the Limits of Reform in Occupied Japan," in Schonberger, pp. 90–110.

27. Andrew Roth, *Dilemma in Japan* (Boston: Little, Brown, 1945). Roth and Bisson, along with the journalist Mark Gayn, who would go on to write perceptively about the early years of the occupation, were all implicated in the so-called *Amerasia* case of mid-1945, involving the unauthorized acquisition of classified U.S. government documents; see Harvey Klehr and Ronald Radosh, *The Amerasia Spy Case: Prelude to McCarthyism* (Chapel Hill: University of North Carolina Press, 1996). The Institute of Pacific Relations subsequently became a major target of the anticommunist witch hunts conducted by the U.S. government in the late 1940s and early 1950s.

28. Owen Lattimore, *Solution in Asia* (Boston: Little, Brown, 1945). Lattimore went on to serve as a major adviser to the first reparations mission to Japan in 1945–1946. In the early 1950s, he became a major target of the McCarthyist inquisition of the Asia field.

29. On the complex subject of presurrender planning and policy struggle, see Cohen, chs. 2 and 3 (pp. 14–48); Akira Iriye, *Power and Culture: The Japanese-American War, 1941–1945* (Cambridge, Mass.: Harvard University Press, 1981); Mayo (1984), pp. 3–51, 447–74; and, for an important insider account, two publications by Hugh Borton: "Preparation for the Occupation of Japan," *Journal of Asian Studies* 25.2 (1966): 203–12, and "American Presurrender Planning for Postwar Japan," *Occasional Papers of the East Asian Institute,* Columbia University (1967). Many of the wartime and early postwar intelligence reports and position papers on Japan were of high analytical quality.

30. Edwin A. Locke, Jr., Memorandum for the President, October 19, 1945, box 182, President's Secretary file, Papers of Harry S. Truman, Truman Presidential Library; *New York Times,* May 6, 1951 (on "racial characteristics"); Walter Millis, ed., *The Forrestal Diaries* (New York: Viking, 1951), pp. 17–18 (quoting MacArthur on "the next ten thousand years"); Bowers (1995); Perret, p. 482 (on pictures in office).

31. Kades-Gibney interview, transcript 2, p. 61.

32. Cohen, p. 104.

33. Alfred C. Oppler, *Legal Reform in Occupied Japan: A Participant Looks Back* (Princeton, N.J.: Princeton University Press, 1976), p. 12.

CHAPTER 7. EMBRACING REVOLUTION

1. From an interview with Kobayashi conducted by Peter Grilli in conjunction with the 1994 documentary film *Music for the Movies: Toru Takemitsu;* see the translation by Linda Hoaglund in *Positions* 2.2 (Fall 1994): 382–405.

2. Sodei Rinjirō and Takemae Eiji, eds., *Sengo Nihon no Genten: Senryō Shi no Genzai* (Tokyo: Yūshisha, 1992), vol. 1, p. 184.

3. Yoshida Shigeru, *Ōiso Zuisō* (Tokyo: Sekkasha, 1962), pp. 42–43. See also Yoshida's "Jūnen no Ayumi," *Mainichi Shimbun,* August 9, 1955, and J. W. Dower, *Empire and Aftermath: Yoshida Shigeru and the Japanese Experience, 1878–1954* (Cambridge, Mass.: Council on East Asian Studies, Harvard University, 1979), ch. 9 (pp. 305–68).

4. The ramifications of postwar conservatism centered on *junpū bizoku* consciousness are examined in Hidaka Rokurō, *Gendai Ideorogii* (Tokyo: Keisō Shobō, 1960), pp. 229–59.

5. Harry Emerson Wildes, *Typhoon in Tokyo: The Occupation and Its Aftermath* (New York: Macmillan, 1954), p. 19.

6. Sodei Rinjirō, *Haikei Makkāsā Gensui-sama: Senryōka no Nihonjin no Tegami* (Tokyo: Ōtsuki Shoten, 1985), ch. 1. The discussion that follows here derives primarily from this engaging compilation and analysis, although I also have drawn on the letters in "Subject File 1945–52," Civil Intelligence Section, Security Division, Assistant Chief of Staff, G-2, RG 331 (boxes 232–236) in the National Archives, and "Personal Correspondence from Japanese, Koreans and Others, 1945–1950" in RG 10 (boxes 172–174) in the archives of the MacArthur Memorial, Norfolk, Va. For an analysis of letters to SCAP between December 1949 and June 1951, see Okamoto Kōichi and Tsukahara Tetsuya, "Senryōgun e no Tōsho ni Miru Senryō Makki no Nihon," in *Sengo Taisei no Keisei*, ed. Nihon Gendaishi Kenkyūkai (Tokyo: Ōtsuki Shoten, 1988), pp. 251–74; this includes a breakdown by topical category (p. 252). Selected early letters to MacArthur were made available to American journalists at the time; see Richard Lauterbach, "Letters to MacArthur," *Life*, January 14, 1946, pp. 4, 7.

7. Sodei, pp. 171, 191, 261.

8. See, for example, Sodei, pp. 84, 256. MacArthur received many Buddhist paintings and statues representing deities associated with wisdom and mercy.

9. Sodei, pp. 49–51, 174–75.

10. Gifts to MacArthur are treated in Sodei, chs. 7 and 8. Their volume and variety is extraordinary, and goes far beyond what is itemized here.

11. Analyses and statistical breakdowns of these communications were presented irregularly in SCAP's internal intelligence reports such as the Civil Intelligence Section's regular publication *Occupational Trends: Japan and Korea;* see, for a sample, ibid., no. 25 (June 2, 1946), pp. 13–14. Other categories of letters involved expressions of anti-communist as well as anti-Korean sentiment; see Okamoto and Tsukahara, pp. 258–60, 266–68.

12. These various examples are taken mostly from Professor Sodei's compilation. The "I want to have your baby" phrase comes from Grant Goodman, who worked as a translator with these materials (Sodei, pp. 141–42).

13. Maruyama Masao, *Kōei no Ichi kara—"Gendai Seiji no Shisō to Kōdō" Tsuihō* (Tokyo: Miraisha, 1982), pp. 120–21.

14. By one estimate, of the approximately 200,000 individuals purged, only 268 were scholars and writers; Sodei, p. 24.

15. Maruyama, pp. 113–19; the Japanese phrase for "community of remorse" is *kaikon kyōdōtai*.

16. For a good early example of the debates over creating a "modern self," see the roundtable discussion in the aptly named journal *Ningen* (meaning "Person," "People," "Human Beings"), April 1, 1946, pp. 150–66. The appeal of writers such as Natsume Sōseki, Kawakami Hajime, Miki Kiyoshi, and Ozaki Hotsumi, discussed in chapter 5, derived in considerable part from the perception that they had possessed such individual autonomy and integrity.

17. Shimizu's article appeared in the April 17, 1946 issue of the newspaper *Tokyo Shimbun* and is quoted in Hidaka, p. 249.

18. The important role of Arisawa and others emerges in Laura Hein, *Fueling Growth: The Energy Revolution and Economic Policy in Postwar Japan* (Cambridge, Mass.: Council on East Asian Studies, Harvard University, 1990). On the prewar Marxist debates, see Germaine Hoston, *Marxism and the Crisis of Development in Prewar Japan* (Princeton, N.J.: Princeton University Press, 1986).

19. Quoted in Kinbara Samon and Takemae Eiji, eds., *Shōwa Shi: Kokumin no naka no Haran to Gekidō no Hanseiki* (Tokyo: Yūhikaku Sensho, 1982), p. 290. Book titles appear in an advertisement in *Bungaku Jihyō*, March 1946.

20. *Shin Nihon Bungaku,* March 1946 (see especially the inaugural proclamation on pp. 62–65); Odagiri Hideo, "Bungaku ni okeru Sensō Sekinin no Tsuikyū," *Shin Nihon Bungaku,* May–June 1946, pp. 64–65; Nakano Shigeharu, "Hihyō no Ningensei," part 2, *Shin Nihon Bungaku,* June 1947, pp. 2–9; Fukushima Jūrō, *Sengo Zasshi Hakkutsu* (Tokyo: Yōsensha, 1985), pp. 110–12; Kōdansha, ed., *Shōwa: Niman Nichi no Zenkiroku* (Tokyo: Kōdansha, 1989), vol. 7, p. 225. This last source is cited below as *SNNZ.*

21. Maruyama dwells on the "moralistic" acquiescence to Communist Party discipline bred of the prewar experience of apostasy in *Kōei no Ichi kara,* p. 117.

22. *Asahi Shimbun,* September 12, 1945. Etō Jun, among others, quotes this in his conservative critique of the occupation; see his *Wasureta Koto to Wasuresaserareta Koto* (Tokyo: Bungei Shunjū, 1979), pp. 58–59.

23. Asahi Shimbunsha, ed., *Koe* (Tokyo: Asahi Bunko, 1984), vol. 1, p. 158; this selection of letters to the *Asahi* is cited below as *Koe.*

24. *Koe,* 1:116–17 (December 24, 1945); see also pp. 70 and 132.

25. The comment, by journalist Suetsugu Setsuko, is reprinted in Yomiuri Shimbun Osaka Shakaibu, ed., *Shūsen Zengo* (Tokyo: Kadokawa Shoten, 1984) p. 114.

26. Heibonsha Henshūbu, ed., *Shōwa Sesō Shi—Dokyumento, Sengo-hen* (Tokyo: Heibonsha, 1976), pp. 307–11. GHQ missed the satire of this proposed skit and censored the witty exchange for being "right-wing." See the similar derision of propagandists who touted the "holy war" on December 8, 1941 and "democracy" on August 15, 1945 in *Ningen,* April 1946, p. 156.

27. Stafford L. Warren, M.D., "The Role of Radiology in the Development of the Atomic Bomb," in Kenneth D. A. Allen, ed., *Radiology in World War II* (Washington, D.C.: a volume in the series *Medical Department of the U.S. Army in World War II,* issued by the Surgeon General's office in 1966), p. 890 (for a commemorative photo of the research team and doll); Joanne Izbicki, "The Shape of Freedom: The Female Body in Post-Surrender Japanese Cinema," *U.S.–Japan Women's Journal: English Supplement,* 12 (1997), p. 109 (describing a photo of the "Miss Atomic Bomb" contest); Tokyo Yakeato Yamiichi o Koroku Suru Kai, ed., *Tokyo Yamiichi Kōbō Shi* (Tokyo: Sōfūsha, 1978), p. 137; Sodei, pp. 285–86.

28. Tsurumi Shunsuke, et al., *Nihon no Hyakunen* (Tokyo: Chikuma Shobō, 1967), vol. 1, p. 197.

29. *SNNZ* 7:160, 263–64; Rekishigaku Kenkyūkai, ed., *Haisen to Senryō,* vol. 1 in *Nihon Dōjidai Shi* (Tokyo: Aoki Shoten, 1990), pp. 230–31.

30. *SNNZ* 7:154; Rekishigaku Kenkyūkai, pp. 231–32. Male officials within the Home Ministry began addressing the prospect of introducing woman suffrage almost immediately after the surrender. This is sometimes cited as one of the postwar reforms that provoked *least* resistance on the Japanese side. See Kusayanagi Daizō, *Naimushō tai Senryōgun* (Tokyo: Asahi Bunko, 1987), pp. 40–41; *Asahi Shimbun,* May 25, 1995.

31. Joe Moore, *Japanese Workers and the Struggle for Power, 1945–1947* (Madison: University of Wisconsin Press, 1983), pp. 33–41.

32. Rekishigaku Kenkyūkai, pp. 263–64.

33. Heibonsha Henshūbu, p. 266.

34. See, for example, surveys in *Mainichi Shimbun,* November 12, 1945 (governor's elections), December 23, 1945 (*tonarigumi,* or neighborhood associations), May 27, 1946 (new constitution), December 16, 1946 (Yoshida cabinet); also *Asahi Shimbun,* December 5, 1945 (land reform), December 9, 1945 (emperor system), August 5, 1946 (Yoshida cabinet and backing of political parties), December 9, 1946 (family incomes and daily livelihood).

35. NHK Hōsō Bunka Chōsa Kenkyūjo, *GHQ Bunsho ni yoru Senryōki Hōsō Shi Nen-pyō (1946)* (Tokyo: NHK, 1989), esp. pp. 25, on daily listening time; 38, 44, 47, 64, 69, 76, 78, 93, 118–19, 127, on *Truth Box;* and 35, 65, 75, 107 on *Broadcast Discussion*. See also Russell Brines, *MacArthur's Japan* (Philadelphia: Lippincott, 1948), pp. 243–46.

36. Nihon Hōsō Kyōkai, ed., *Hōsō Yawa (Zoku): Zadankai ni yoru Hōsō Shi* (Tokyo: Nihon Hōsō Kyōkai, 1970), pp. 85, 89.

37. *SNNZ* 7: 201.

38. Alfred C. Oppler, *Legal Reform in Occupied Japan: A Participant Looks Back* (Princeton, N.J.: Princeton University Press, 1976), pp. 116–17, 318; see also pp. 74, 149, 156, 172, 222, 233.

39. Theodore Cohen, *Remaking Japan: The American Occupation As New Deal* (New York: Free Press, 1987), pp. 100, 214–15, 236–39.

40. Cohen, pp. 231–33. Cohen's summary of this middle-echelon bureaucrat's motives is revealing. Teramoto, Cohen writes, "had conceived the idea of a comprehensive labor protection code only a few weeks after the war's end, when it would have seemed rather far down on Japan's list of priorities, if indeed a wrecked economy could ever afford it. But Teramoto thought that was exactly the right time, when ultra-conservative obstructionists would be demoralized, when liberal employers would see that it was necessary to promise the workers a better life in the future, and when many enterprises were so badly off that almost nothing would make things worse. Finally, he might be able to get SCAP's help, if we were serious about democratizing the country. It was remarkable foresight." That a former member of the Home Ministry's "thought police" would entertain such progressive ideas is not in fact so anomalous as might first appear to be the case. The wartime bureaucracy contained a strong contingent of so-called new bureaucrats, or "renovationist bureaucrats," with decidedly reformist ideals, many of whom would contribute to post-surrender reforms in areas such as labor, land reform, zaibatsu dissolution, local government, and education. On labor policy specifically, see Sheldon Garon, "The Imperial Bureaucracy and Labor Policy in Postwar Japan," *Journal of Asian Studies* 43.3 (May 1984): 446–48; Garon, *The State and Labor in Modern Japan* (Berkeley: University of California Press, 1987), pp. 235–37. Such convergences are discussed and annotated more fully in "The Useful War" in John W. Dower, *Japan in War and Peace: Selected Essays* (New York: The New Press, 1993), pp. 9–32.

41. Yuri Hajime, "Kyōkasho no Haisen Taiken," *Shisō no Kagaku*, April 1969; reprinted in *Sengo Taiken*, a special issue of the journal *Jinsei Tokuhon* (Tokyo: Kawada Shobō Shinsha, 1981), pp. 39–44; Wataru Kurita, "Making Peace with Hirohito and a Militaristic Past," *Japan Quarterly* 36 (1989), p. 188. Deletion of militarist phrases from textbooks was first ordered by the government on August 26, 1945; see Yoko Hirohashi Thakur, "Textbook Reform in Allied Occupied Japan, 1945–1952" (Ph.D. dissertation, University of Maryland, 1990), p. 146.

42. Mombushō, *Shin Kyōiku Shishin* (Tokyo: Mombushō, May 1946). Excerpts from this guide are included in Kaigo Tokiomi and Shimizu Ikutarō, eds., *Kyōiku/Shakai*, vol. 5 of *Shiryō: Sengo Nijūnen Shi*, (Tokyo: Nihon Hyōronsha, 1966), pp. 9–15. I am also grateful to Aketagawa Tohru, who provided me with a copy of the preface and opening chapters of this guidebook, which he found among the papers of his grandfather, who had been a public high school teacher. The Ministry of Education's initial policy, before any conspicuous direct U.S. influence, was issued on September 15, 1945 by Maeda Tamon, an "old liberal" who had just been named to head the ministry. The policy stressed three major objectives: defending the *kokutai* or national polity, creating a peaceful nation, and developing science; Kaigo and Shimizu,

p. 2. For a concise outline of early education developments, see *SNNZ* 7:298–99. Academic studies tend to emphasize the importance of Japanese initiatives in the postwar educational reforms. See Gary H. Tsuchimochi, *Educational Reform in Postwar Japan; The 1946 U.S. Educational Mission* (Tokyo: University of Tokyo Press, 1993); also Edward R. Beauchamp and James M. Vardaman, Jr., eds., *Japanese Education Since 1945: A Documentary Study* (Armonk, N.Y.: M. E. Sharpe, 1994).

43. Shinohara Shigetoshi, *Shōnen Shōjo no tame no Minshu Tokuhon* (Tokyo: Kokumin Gakugeisha, April 1947), pp. 1–32. This text is in the Prange Collection, McKeldin Library, University of Maryland.

44. Yuri, p. 43. In a diary entry on September 12, 1945, Watanabe Kazuo recorded hearing about an elementary school teacher who told his students to grow up to be soldiers and take revenge on the Americans. If GIs offered them candy, he instructed, they should say "thank you" while harboring hatred in their minds; see his *Haisen Nikki* (Tokyo: Hakubunkan Shinsha, 1995), p. 85.

45. For a generally critical evaluation of teachers' responses, see Rekishigaku Kenkyūkai, *Haisen to Senryō*, pp. 228–30.

46. Satō Fujisaburō, "Yamabiko Gakkō o Megutte—Sonogoro no Mura to Kyōiku," *Rekishi Kōron*, December 1977, pp. 50–56. For a good sample of the positive contemporary response to *Yamabiko Gakkō*, see the June 1951 article reprinted in Asahi Shimbunsha, ed., *"Shūkan Asahi" no Shōwa Shi* (Tokyo: Asahi Shimbunsha, 1989), vol. 2, pp. 223–38.

47. *Osaka Hyakunen Shi*, edited and published by Osaka-fu [Osaka Prefecture] (Osaka: 1968), p. 1257.

48. *Osaka Hyakunen Shi*, p. 1260. See, for example, the definition of "adult education" given in *Gendai Yōgo no Kiso Chishiki, 1948* (Tokyo: Jikyoku Geppōsha; issued as special volume no. 14 of the journal *Jiyū Kokumin*), p. 134; also Shin Jānarizumu Kyōkai, ed., *Jikyoku Shingo Jiten* (Tokyo: Seibunkan, 1949), p. 100.

49. *Sengo no Shingo Kaisetsu* (Publisher unclear; page proofs dated November 1946 are in the censorship files of the Prange Collection, McKeldin Library, University of Maryland); *Gendai Yōgo no Kiso Chishiki, 1948; Jikyoku Shingo Jiten*, op. cit.; Shingo Kenkyūkai, ed., *Shingo Jiten: Toki no Kotoba* (Tokyo: Tenryūdō, 1949); "Sengo Yōgo Jiten," *Rekishi Kōron*, December 1977, pp. 153–68.

50. Unpaginated editor's preface, *Gendai Yōgo no Kiso Chishiki, 1948*.

CHAPTER 8. *MAKING REVOLUTION*

1. Fujiwara Akira, ed., *Senryō to Minshū Undō*, vol. 10 in *Nihon Minshū no Rekishi* (Tokyo: Sanshodo, 1975), pp. 61–62; Nosaka Sanzō, *Nosaka Sanzō Senshū: Sengohen* (Tokyo: Shin Nihon Shuppansha, 1967), pp. 3–19; Shakai Undō Shiryō Kankōkai, ed., *Nihon Kyōsantō Shiryō Taisei* (Tokyo: Odosha, 1951), pp. 52–56; Rekishigaku Kenkyūkai, *Haisen to Senryō*, vol. 1 in the series *Nihon Dōjidai Shi* (Tokyo: Aoki Shoten, 1990), pp. 221–23.

2. These official figures are available in many sources. See, for example, Ōkōchi Kazuo, *Sengo Nihon no Rōdō Undō*, rev. ed. (Tokyo: Iwanami Shinsho, 1961), p. 75; also Nihon Kyōsantō Chōsa Iinkai, ed., *Senryōka Nihon no Bunseki* (Tokyo: Sanichi Shobō, 1954), pp. 205–7. The latter source is an official Communist critique of the occupation.

3. Ōkōchi, p. 41; Nihon Kyōsantō Chōsa Iinkai, p. 207.

4. The basic English-language study of production control is Joe Moore, *Japanese Workers and the Struggle for Power, 1945–1947* (Madison: University of Wisconsin

Press, 1983). A statistical overview appears on p. 104 of this work. See also Ōkōchi, p. 48, and the yearbook *Asahi Nenkan, 1947,* pp. 234–35.

5. Miriam Farley, *Aspects of Japan's Labor Problems* (New York: John Day, 1950), pp. 82–85, 97.

6. Shigeru Yoshida, *The Yoshida Memoirs: The Story of Japan in Crisis* (Boston: Houghton Mifflin, 1962), pp. 75, 200, 228. For the broader context of Yoshida's fear of the left, see J. W. Dower, *Empire and Aftermath: Yoshida Shigeru and the Japanese Experience, 1878–1954* (Cambridge, Mass.: Council on East Asian Studies, Harvard University, 1979), ch. 8.

7. Junnosuke Masumi, *Postwar Politics in Japan, 1945–1955,* Japan Research Monograph 6 (Berkeley: Center for Japanese Studies, University of California, 1985), pp. 96–97.

8. Kōdansha, ed., *Shōwa: Niman Nichi no Zenkiroku* (Tokyo: Kōdansha, 1989), vol. 7, pp. 238–39; this source is cited below as *SNNZ*. See also Moore, pp. 170–77, and, for a first-hand account, Mark Gayn, *Japan Diary* (New York: William Sloane, 1948), pp. 164–69.

9. Gayn, pp. 196–200; *SNNZ* 7:250–51; Rekishigaku Kenkyūkai, pp. 226–27.

10. The full document, which appears in the minutes for the Allied Council for Japan, is reproduced in Moore, pp. 178–79.

11. *SNNZ* 7:260; Gayn, pp. 226–31.

12. The full text of the memorial is reproduced in Asahi Jānaru, ed., *Shōwa Shi no Shunkan* (Tokyo: Asahi Shimbunsha, 1974), vol. 2, p. 160. See also *SNNZ* 7:258–60.

13. Asahi Jānaru, p. 166. A full translation of the emperor's message is reproduced in SCAP, General Headquarters, *Summation: Non-Military Activities in Japan* 8 (May 1946), p. 31.

14. The key section in the U.S. "Initial Post-Surrender Policy for Japan" read as follows: "The policy is to use the existing form of government in Japan, not to support it. Changes in the form of government initiated by the Japanese people or government in the direction of modifying its feudal and authoritarian tendencies are to be permitted and favored. In the event that effectuation of such changes involves the use of force by the Japanese people or government against persons opposed thereto, the Supreme Commander should intervene only when it is necessary to insure the security of his forces and the attainment of all other objectives of the Occupation."

15. Gayn, p. 231. MacArthur's full statement is reproduced in Moore, p. 184; see also Government Section, Supreme Commander for the Allied Powers, *Political Reorientation of Japan, September 1945 to September 1948* (Washington, D.C., 1949), vol. 2, p. 762. GHQ's own confidential but widely distributed intelligence summation noted that "[t]he May Day celebrations were unprecedented. They demonstrated the new freedom which the Occupation has given the Japanese people and the political vitality of the working class which, properly guided, can be a potent force in the democratic reconstruction of Japan." In a separate entry on "law and order," the summation stated that "[d]espite the large number of demonstrations the Home Ministry reported a complete absence of mob violence or disorder throughout Japan." Regarding MacArthur's statement, it was observed that "[t]he temper of the people as a whole was clearly peaceful. Few instances of violence occurred and none of a serious nature, but the situation held such possibilities that on 20 May the Supreme Commander issued a strong warning against the dangers of mass violence and physical processes of intimidation by disorderly minorities. His statement was prominently displayed in the Japanese press and reactions indicated that it had had the desired effect. There was a striking decline in the number of mass demonstra-

tions following the message"; *Summation: Non-Military Activities in Japan* 8 (May 1946), pp. 29–30, 37.

16. Moore, pp. 179–80.

17. *SNNZ* 7:260. According to some accounts, the name of Matsushima's company and "Japan Communist Party" also were written in small lettering on the placard; see, for example, Asahi Jānaru, p. 166. The last line ("Imperial sign and seal") was written out; that is, there was no mock imperial seal.

18. Matsushima's placard was not the only one that mocked the emperor. A young female demonstrator was observed waving a crudely and rudely rendered sign that read, roughly, "Hey Old Man, I'll die if I don't eat, and I don't buy dying"; *SNNZ* 7:257.

19. *Sengoshi Daijiten* (Tokyo: Sanshodo, 1991), p. 804; *SNNZ* 7:260, 266, 281, 302, 308, 312. GHQ's position on this incident is briefly referred to in Alfred C. Oppler, *Legal Reform in Occupied Japan: A Participant Looks Back* (Princeton, N.J.: Princeton University Press, 1976), pp. 74, 165–68.

20. Sanichi Shobō Henshūbu, ed., *Shiryō—Sengo Gakusei Undō* (Tokyo: Sanichi Shobō, 1968), vol. 1, pp. 51–52. See also *SNNZ* 7:263.

21. Rekishigaku Kenkyūkai, pp. 193–98, 213.

22. Labor developments through the abortive February 1 strike are covered in detail in Moore, pp. 185–243. For GHQ's hostile position, see Theodore Cohen, *Remaking Japan: The American Occupation as New Deal* (New York: Free Press, 1987), pp. 277–300. For Japanese sources, including Ii's comments quoted here, see Rōdō Undō-shi Kenkyūkai, ed., *Senryōka no Rōdō Sōgi* (Tokyo: Rōdō Junpōsha, 1972), pp. 9–69, esp. pp. 48–55; also Satō Ichirō, *Ni-ichi Suto Zengo* (Tokyo: Shakai Hyōronsha, 1972), esp. p. 241. Ii's retrospective observations appeared in the January 1951 issue of *Sekai*. One of the famous photographs is reproduced in *SNNZ* 8:45.

23. *Asahi Nenkan, 1947*, p. 103; Rekishigaku Kenkyūkai, pp. 220–28, 236–38.

24. The broad context of these developments is given in Dower, pp. 306–68. "Depurge" already was listed as a basic contemporary term in 1948; see *Gendai Yōgo no Kiso Chishiki, 1948* (Tokyo: Jikyoku Geppōsha, issued as a special vol. 14 of the journal *Jiyū Kokumin*), p. 29.

25. Nikkan Rōdō Tsūshinsha, ed., *Sengo Nihon Kyōsanshugi Undō* (Tokyo: Nikkan Rōdō Tsūshinsha, 1955), pp. 55–60; Shakai Undō Shiryō Kankōkai, pp. 391–95; Rodger Swearingen and Paul Langer, *Red Flag in Japan: International Communism in Action 1919–1951* (Cambridge, Mass.: Harvard University Press, 1952; reprinted by Greenwood Press, N.Y., 1968), pp. 199–212.

CHAPTER 9. *IMPERIAL DEMOCRACY: DRIVING THE WEDGE*

1. The *Senjinkun* was issued to all soldiers in January 1941; the quotation here is taken from an official translation distributed by the Japanese military in the Philippines. An official translation of *Shinmin no Michi* is included as an appendix in Otto B. Tolischus, *Tokyo Record* (New York: Reynal & Hitchcock, 1943), pp. 405–27.

2. On December 5, 1946, the government announced that the era-name *(gengo)* system would not be revised; see Kōdansha, ed., *Shōwa: Niman Nichi no Zenkiroku* (Tokyo: Kōdansha, 1989), vol. 7, p. 324. This source is cited as *SNNZ* below.

3. See, for example, Takahashi Hiroshi, *Heika, Otazune Mōshiagemasu: Kisha Kaiken Zenkiroku to Ningen Tennō no Kiseki* (Tokyo: Bunshun Bunko, 1988), pp. 212, 217.

4. Grew's comment, which appeared in a letter dated October 25, 1945, is quoted in fuller context in Masanori Nakamura, *The Japanese Monarchy: Ambassador Joseph Grew and the Making of the "Symbol Emperor System," 1931–1991* (Armonk, N.Y.: M. E. Sharpe, 1992), p. 85.

5. John W. Dower, *Empire and Aftermath: Yoshida Shigeru and the Japanese Experience, 1878–1954* (Cambridge, Mass.: East Asian Studies Research Center, Harvard University, 1978), p. 321.

6. Unless otherwise noted, the Bonner F. Fellers papers cited here are held in the Hoover Institution of War and Peace at Stanford University. "The Psychology of the Japanese Soldier" and "Answer to Japan" can be found in box 1 in this collection; the communication (dated November 1944) is in box 3.

7. Form letter by Fellers dated December 31, 1944; box 3 in the Fellers papers.

8. "Psychological Warfare Against Japan, SWPA, 1944–1945," p. 6. See also "Basic Military Plan for Psychological Warfare Against Japan," April 12, 1945, p. 18; box 3, Fellers papers.

9. Office of Strategic Services, Research and Analysis Branch, R & A No. 2395, "Objective H" (July 28, 1944). A photocopy of this short memo (from the U.S. National Archives, Diplomatic Branch) is in the archives of the Ministry of Finance, Japan.

10. Fellers, "Basic Military Plan for Psychological Warfare Against Japan" (April 12), p. 19.

11. Fellers, "Answer to Japan," pp. 22–23.

12. Fellers, "Basic Military Plan for Psychological Warfare Against Japan, with appendices and minutes of the Conference on Psychological Warfare Against Japan," Manila, May 7–8, 1945, pp. 2–3, 7–10, 14; box 4 of Fellers papers. For an early ten-point version of the mantra, see the O.S.S. paper on "Basic Military Plan for Psychological Warfare in the Southwest Pacific Theater" dated June 9, 1943, in ibid. See also the August 2, 1944 update of the "Basic Plan," p. 1, in ibid. (Many of these documents are also included in box 1 of "U.S. Army Forces in the Pacific, Psychological Warfare Branch," in the Hoover Institution).

13. Fellers, "Basic Military Plan for Psychological Warfare Against Japan" (May 7–8), pp. 10, 11, 13, 18, 22, 31–32.

14. Fellers, "Basic Military Plan," p. 32. Fellers regarded Mashbir as one of his three "most outstanding authorities on Japanese psychology and language"; see letter of December 19, 1944 in box 3 of the Fellers papers. Mashbir's eccentric account of his views and activities is presented in Sidney Forrester Mashbir, *I Was an American Spy* (New York: Vantage, 1953).

15. Fellers, "Basic Military Plan for Psychological Warfare Against Japan" (April 12), pp. 7, 15.

16. The English versions of these radio scripts, broadcast between July 19 and August 13, 1945, are reproduced in Mashbir, pp. 354–68.

17. The comments on loving Japan and on killing Japanese attempting to surrender appear among the Bonner Fellers Papers in the MacArthur Memorial, Norfolk, Va. See RG 44a, box 4, folder 23 for the former; box 1, folder 5, and box 6, folder 9 for the latter. Fellers's memorandum criticizing the bombing of Japan appears in box 3 of the Fellers papers in the Hoover Institution.

18. Fellers memorandum, August 7, 1945, in box 1 in "U.S. Army Forces in the Pacific, Psychological Warfare Branch," Hoover Institution.

19. Robert O. Egeberg, "How Hirohito Kept His Throne," *Washington Post*, February 19, 1989; also cited in Stephen S. Large, *Emperor Hirohito & Shōwa Japan: A Po-*

litical Biography (London and New York: Routledge, 1992), pp. 135–36. D. Clayton James, *The Years of MacArthur* (Boston: Houghton Mifflin, 1975), vol. 2, pp. 773–74. Mashbir, pp. 308, 333. In late January 1946, the British diplomat and Japan expert George Sansom confidentially reported MacArthur as having stated that the emperor "had been from the beginning to the end a puppet, a 'complete Charlie McCarthy,' who had neither begun the war nor stopped it" (the reference was to a ventriloquist's dummy immensely popular on the American *Edgar Bergen and Charlie McCarthy* radio program); see Roger Buckley, "Britain and the Emperor: The Foreign Office and Constitutional Reform in Japan, 1945–1946," *Modern Asian Studies* 12.4 (1978), pp. 562–63.

20. Quoted in Herbert P. Bix, "The Shōwa Emperor's 'Monologue' and the Problem of War Responsibility," *Journal of Japanese Studies* 18.2 (1992): 302. This valuable essay draws on a wealth of Japanese materials published in the wake of Emperor Hirohito's death in 1989.

21. Quoted in Ōkubo Genji, *The Problem of the Emperor System in Postwar Japan* (Tokyo: Nihon Taiheiyō Mondai Chōsakai, 1948), p. 9; see also Bix, p. 303.

22. Shigemitsu's comments are reprinted in Tsurumi Shunsuke and Nakagawa Roppei, eds., *Tennō Hyakuwa* (Tokyo: Chikuma Shoten, 1989), vol. 2, pp. 27–29; this excellent collection of emperor-related materials is cited below as *Tennō Hyakuwa*.

23. *Tennō Hyakuwa*, 2:33–37.

24. The emperor's far more ambiguous role up to the final moments of the war is addressed in Herbert Bix, "Japan's Delayed Surrender: A Reinterpretation," *Diplomatic History* 19.2 (Spring 1995): 197–225.

25. *Tennō Hyakuwa*, 2:39–40.

26. On the emperor's obsession with the regalia, see Terasaki Hidenari and Mariko Terasaki Miller, eds., *Shōwa Tennō Dokuhakuroku—Terasaki Hidenari Goyōgakari Nikki* (Tokyo: Bungei Shunjūsha, 1991), p. 126; also Fujiwara Akira, Awaya Kentarō, Yoshida Yutaka, and Yamada Akira, *Shōwa Tennō 'Dokuhakuroku'* (Tokyo: Ōtsuki Shoten, 1991), pp. 16–17.

27. Kinoshita Michio, *Sokkin Nisshi* (Tokyo: Bungei Shunjūsha, 1990), pp. 48–49. Kinoshita's book is an invaluable diary-journal by the emperor's vice chamberlain.

28. *New York Times*, September 22, 1945; cf. Buckley, p. 562n, citing the *London Times*.

29. *New York Times*, September 25, 1945; *Tennō Hyakuwa*, 2:47. Frank Kluckhohn, the *Times* reporter, spent ten minutes speaking through an interpreter with the emperor, observing the ground rules that he would "ask no questions" at this unprecedented personal meeting.

30. Kinoshita, p. 34. Kinoshita recorded this report in his diary on November 8. See also Fujiwara Akira, "Tōsuiken to Tennō," in *Kindai Tennōsei no Kenkyū II*, ed. Tōyama Shigeki (Tokyo: Iwanami Shoten, 1987), p. 219. The fact that Emperor Hirohito approved the final decision to launch war against the Allied powers and knew of the plan to attack Pearl Harbor actually emerged fairly clearly in the Japanese press; see, for example, *Asahi Shimbun*, October 9 and 27, 1945.

31. *Tennō Hyakuwa*, 2:42–44; Mashbir, p. 333; Matsuo Takayoshi, "Shōchō Tennōsei no Seiritsu ni tsuite no Oboegaki," *Shisō*, April 1990, p. 8. See also Matsuo's incisive treatment of this first meeting between the emperor and supreme commander: "Shōwa Tennō—Makkāsā Gensui Dai-ikkai Kaiken," *Kyoto Daigaku Bungakubu Kenkyū Kiyō* 29 (March 1990): 37–94.

32. Shigemitsu in *Tennō Hyakuwa*, 2:47. For an example of how the meeting and photograph became the symbol of utter capitulation and defeat, see Watanabe Kiyoshi, *Kudakareta Kami: Aru Fukuinhei no Shuki* (Tokyo: Asahi Sensho, 1983), p. 32.

33. Faubion Bowers, "The Day the General Blinked," *New York Times,* September 30, 1988; see also the interview with Bowers in both the Japanese-language *Yomiuri Shimbun* and English-language *Daily Yomiuri,* October 27, 1988.

34. The secrecy of records of Japanese interpreters at these meetings is vigilantly maintained in the Imperial Household Agency and Foreign Ministry; see Hata Ikuhiko, "Tennō no Shinsho," *Bungei Shunjū,* October 1978, pp. 381–82. Hata calls attention to a summary of a May 6, 1947 meeting. The transcript of the September 27, 1945 meeting is discussed below.

35. Bowers, "The Day the General Blinked"; Douglas MacArthur, *Reminiscences* (New York: McGraw-Hill, 1964), p. 288.

36. *New York Times,* October 2, 1945.

37. Okumura's transcript is reproduced in Kojima Noboru, "Tennō to Amerika to Taiheiyō Sensō," *Bungei Shunjū,* November 1975, pp. 115–19. On the emperor's response, see Kido Kōichi, *Kido Kōichi Nikki* (Tokyo: Tokyo Daigaku Shuppansha), vol. 2, p. 1237; also Matsuo (April 1990), p. 10.

38. The October 1 brief, prepared by John Anderton, is included in the Bonner Fellers papers at the MacArthur Memorial; see RG 44a, box 1, folder 1.

39. Fellers memorandum to commander in chief, October 2, 1945, in box 3 of the Fellers papers in the Hoover Institution. This also is reproduced in William P. Woodard, *The Allied Occupation of Japan, 1945–1952, and Japanese Religions* (Leiden: E. J. Brill, 1972), pp. 360–61.

40. International opinion concerning the emperor is summarized in Kiyoko Takeda, *The Dual Image of the Japanese Emperor* (New York: New York University Press, 1988). Deliberations on the U.S. side are addressed in Nakamura, op. cit. A major portion of the voluminous U.S. archival record on these matters appears in the U.S. Department of State series *Foreign Relations of the United States [FRUS].* See especially *FRUS 1945,* vol. 6, pp. 497–1015, and *FRUS 1946,* vol. 8, pp. 85–604. For polls, see also Buckley, p. 554; Hadley Cantril, ed., *Public Opinion, 1935–1946* (Princeton, N.J.: Princeton University Press, 1951), p. 392.

41. Ota Kenichi, ed., *Tsugita Daizaburō Nikki* (Okayama-shi: Sanyō Shimbunsha, 1991), p. 118; quoted in Bix (1992), pp. 329–30. The Imperial Army officer was Lieutenant General Haraguchi Hatsutarō, and this episode remained unknown until the diary of the then chief cabinet secretary Tsugita Daizaburō was published after the Shōwa emperor's death. See also Herbert P. Bix, "Emperor Hirohito's War," *History Today* 41 (December 1991): 18.

42. Takahashi Hiroshi and Suzuki Kunihiko, *Tennōke no Misshitachi: Senryō to Tenshitsu* (Tokyo: Bunshun Bunko, 1989), pp. 48–53.

43. Wm. C. Chase, *Front Line General: The Commands of Maj. Gen. Wm. C. Chase: An Autobiography* (Houston: Pacesetter Press, 1975), p. 146–47. For a nice photo treatment of these affairs, see "Imperial Duck Hunt," *Life,* January 7, 1946, pp. 96–98.

CHAPTER 10. *IMPERIAL DEMOCRACY: DESCENDING PARTWAY FROM HEAVEN*

1. The lines of the children's song ran: "The first bridge has fallen / The second bridge has fallen / The double bridge below the imperial palace has fallen / And finally the imperial palace burned down"; Tsurumi Shunsuke and Nakagawa Roppei, eds., *Tennō Hyakuwa* (Tokyo: Chikuma Bunko, 1989), vol. 1, p. 571. For other examples of lese majesty, see ibid. 1:566–79; also John W. Dower, "Sensational Rumors, Seditious Graffiti, and the Nightmares of the Thought Police" in Dower,

Japan in War and Peace: Selected Essays (New York: The New Press, 1993), pp. 101–54. The two-volume Tsurumi and Nakagawa collection of emperor-related materials is cited below as *Tennō Hyakuwa.*

2. Awaya Kentarō, ed., *Shiryō: Nihon Gendai Shi* (Tokyo: Ōtsuki Shoten, 1980), vol. 2 *(Haisen Chokugo no Seiji to Shakai)* pp. 87, 246, 336–37; see also pp. 40, 194.

3. Awaya, 2:248; Awaya Kentarō and Kawashima Takamine, "Gyokuon Hōsō wa Teki no Bōryaku Da," *This Is Yomiuri,* November 1994, pp. 64–65. For the gallows rumor, see the discussion between Awaya Kentarō and Watanabe Kiyoshi dated October 1980 and published as an insert in Awaya, *Shiryō.* For other examples of the treasonous anti-imperial thoughts scattered throughout the police reports, see Awaya, *Shiryō,* 2:198, 205, 218, 229, 246–48, 251–52; ibid., 3:169. The government's alarm at these developments was so great that an enlarged four-thousand-member personal guard for the emperor was established; *Asahi Shimbun,* October 27, 1945.

4. Awaya 2:38, 197; 3:89–94.

5. Masanori Nakamura, *The Japanese Monarchy: Ambassador Joseph Grew and the Making of the "Symbol Emperor System," 1931–1991* (Armonk, N.Y.: M. E. Sharpe, 1992), p. 176.

6. Civil Intelligence Section, SCAP, *Occupational Trends: Japan and Korea,* January 9, 1946 (pp. 4–5); January 23, 1946 (p. 18); January 30, 1946 (p. 18). U.S. Strategic Bombing Survey, *The Effects of Strategic Bombing on Japanese Morale,* (Washington, D.C.: July 1947), p. 149; Awaya, 2:121–35.

7. Sodei Rinjirō and Fukushima Jūrō, eds., *Makkāsā: Kiroku—Sengo Nihon no Genten* (Tokyo: Nihon Hōsō Shuppan Kyōkai, 1982), p. 158; Takahashi Nobuo, *Shōwa Sesō Ryūkōgo Jiten* (Tokyo: Obunsha, 1986), p. 89; Akira Iwasaki, "The Occupied Screen," *Japan Quarterly* 25.3 (July–September 1978): 320. Even in the war years there were instances of servicemen speaking casually and scatologically about the emperor. Navy veterans on the battleship *Musashi,* for example, groused openly about Hirohito's "tight-ass" stinginess after he visited the ship and gave only a small portion of *sake* to each seaman; Awaya and Watanabe, op. cit. Before as well as after the surrender, it was not uncommon to refer to the emperor as *Ten-chan* or "Little Emp," an affectionate but decidedly unawestruck appellation.

8. Civil Intelligence Section, SCAP, *Occupational Trends: Japan and Korea,* February 27, 1946 (p. 15).

9. Kōdansha, ed., *Shōwa: Niman Nichi no Zenkiroku* (Tokyo: Kōdansha, 1989), vol. 7, p. 200; this source is cited below as *SNNZ.* The "Emperor Kumazawa" story received publicity in the U.S. army newspaper *Stars and Stripes* on January 18, 1946, and in *Life* magazine's issue of January 21, pp. 32–33. Kumazawa claimed to be the eighteenth generation descended from Emperor Go-Kameyama of the southern court. In January 1951, he unsuccessfully attempted to bring suit against Emperor Hirohito, but the suit was rejected on the grounds that the emperor could not become the object of judicial proceedings. The dispute over the legitimacy of the northern or southern lines actually became a topic of controversy in 1911, and was settled by an ambiguous government decision that seemed to acknowledge the claims of the *southern* line while nonetheless upholding the legitimacy of the northern line with which Hirohito's grandfather the Meiji emperor was associated.

10. *SNNZ* 7:190–91.

11. The international Far Eastern Commission exempted the emperor as a war criminal on April 3, 1946; the prosecution at the International Military Tribunal for the Far East did so publicly on June 18. Formal U.S. policy consideration of "treatment of Hirohito" was removed from the agenda of the State-War-Navy Coordinating Committee on June 12.

12. The official translation of the rescript appears in U.S. Department of State, *Foreign Relations of the United States 1946*, 8:134–35.

13. William P. Woodard, *The Allied Occupation of Japan, 1945–1952, and Japanese Religions* (Leiden: E. J. Brill, 1972), p. 251; this useful source, which includes documentary appendices, is by a former SCAP official responsible for occupation policy toward religion. Otis Cary, *War-Wasted Asia: Letters, 1945–46* (New York: Kodansha International, 1975; subsequently reprinted under the title *From a Ruined Empire: Letters—Japan, China, Korea, 1945–46*, pp. 272–88); Nakamura, pp. 109–10 (for Reischauer's memo, dated December 18). On wartime American theories regarding the emperor and Japanese psychology in general, see Willard Price, *Japan and the Son of Heaven* (New York: Duell, Sloan & Pearce, 1945); Alexander H. Leighton, *Human Relations in a Changing World: Observations on the Use of the Social Sciences* (New York: Dutton, 1949); Alexander Leighton and Morris Opler, "Psychiatry and Applied Anthropology in Psychological Warfare against Japan," *American Journal of Psychoanalysis* 6 (1946): 20–34, reprinted in Robert Hunt, ed., *Personalities and Cultures: Readings in Psychological Anthropology* (Garden City, N.Y.: Natural History Press, 1967), pp. 251–60; Clyde Kluckhohn, *Mirror for Man: The Relation of Anthropology to Modern Life* (New York, McGraw-Hill, 1949); Iokibe Makoto, excerpted in *Tennō Hyakuwa*, 1:581–603.

14. The disestablishment of Shinto in general is addressed in Wilhelmus H. M. Creemers, *Shrine Shinto After World War II* (Leiden: E. J. Brill, 1968). The December 15 directive is reproduced in Creemers, pp. 219–22. See also Helen Hardacre, *Shintō and the State, 1868–1988* (Princeton, N.J.: Princeton University Press, 1991), pp. 167–70.

15. Hardacre, p. 137; Kinoshita Michio, *Sokkin Nisshi* (Tokyo: Bungei Shunjūsha, 1990), pp. 83–84.

16. On Henderson and Blyth, see the afterword by Takahashi Hiroshi in Kinoshita, pp. 333–41.

17. Blyth's role emerges clearly in the Kinoshita diary. Some of the court's "liaison" with the victors was carried out by individuals who had been deeply involved in militaristic and ultranationalistic activities and now devoted themselves to courting GHQ officials with food, drink, women, and presents such as swords, formal Japanese apparel, pearls, and cameras. Two such backstage manipulators, Andō Akira and Suchi Yōsai, emerge in the diary of the emperor's vice chamberlain as part of a self-styled "American Puritan club" with close and effective ties to the top levels in CI&E; see Kinoshita, pp. 91–97, 352–55, and Yoshida Yutaka, *Shōwa Tennō no Shūsen Shi* (Tokyo: Iwanami Shinsho, 1992), pp. 65–72.

18. See Creemers, pp. 121–32, especially the "Henderson memo" on pp. 223–25; Woodard, pp. 250–68, 315–21 (this account relies on the "Henderson memo" plus interviews).

19. Although Japanese sources, both primary and secondary, delight in delineating the drafting process, these accounts are sometimes contradictory (and sometimes, in the case of reminiscences, deliberately obfuscatory) and it is impossible to reconstruct the process with certainty. In addition to sources cited above, see Matsuo Takayoshi's careful treatment in "Shōchō Tennōsei no Seiritsu ni tsuite no Oboegaki," *Shisō*, April 1990, pp. 11–18; Takahashi Hiroshi and Suzuki Kunihiko, *Tennōke no Misshitachi: Senryō to Tenshitsu* (Tokyo: Bunshun Bunko, 1989), pp. 81–84; Togashi Junji's 1962 article reproduced in *Tennō Hyakuwa*, 2:199–210; Maeda Tamon's 1962 account reproduced in ibid., 2:211–26, and also in Bungei Shunjū, ed., *"Bungei Shunjū" ni Miru Shōwa Shi* (Tokyo: Bungei Shunjūsha, 1988), vol. 2, pp. 18–25; Kinoshita, pp. 88–96. The official English version of the final text is reproduced in U.S. Department of State, *Foreign Relations of the United States, 1946*, 8:134–35.

20. The English text of Blyth's memo, reproduced in Matsuo, pp. 13–14, contains some small grammatical errors and thus may not be a precise copy.

21. The Charter Oath, as quoted in full in the official translation of the rescript, reads: "(1) Deliberative assemblies on a wide scope shall be convened, and all matters of government decided by public opinion. (2) Both the high and the low shall with a unity of purpose vigorously engage in the conduct of public affairs. (3) All the common people, no less than the servants of state, civil and military, shall be enabled to fulfill each his just aspirations, lest discontent should infect their minds. (4) All the evil practices of the past shall be eliminated, and the nation shall abide by the universal rules of justice and equity. (5) Wisdom and knowledge shall be sought throughout the world to promote the prosperity of the Empire." Emphasizing the Charter Oath was well established by this date. In his widely publicized press conference on August 29, 1945, the new prime minister Prince Higashikuni had concluded by reciting the five-article oath; the press conference is reproduced in Hidaka Rokurō, *Sengo Shisō no Shuppatsu* (Tokyo: Chikuma Shobō, 1968), pp. 53–58.

22. *Tennō Hyakuwa*, 2:208, 218–20; Kinoshita, p. 89.

23. The emperor's reminiscence, in a press interview on August 23, 1977, is reproduced in Takahashi Hiroshi, *Heika, Otazune Mōshiagemasu: Kisha Kaiken Zenkiroku to Ningen Tennō no Kiseki* (Tokyo: Bunshun Bunko, 1988), pp. 252–54. See also Takahashi in Kinoshita, pp. 345–46.

24. Kinoshita, p. 84; Maeda in *Tennō Hyakuwa*, 2:218; Woodard, pp. 253–54, 266.

25. None of the men intimately involved in drafting the declaration thought that it compromised the emperor's position, and all were prepared to argue that foreigners simply had misunderstood how the Japanese regarded their sovereign. He never had been considered, they argued, a "god" in the Western sense. This was true but also disingenuous. Historically, the emperor (and empresses in earlier times) had fulfilled numerous and changing roles: as shamans and agrarian ritualists in earliest times; as priest-leaders at their peak of power in the eighth century; as arbiters of high culture thereafter, although during the long centuries of feudalism the emperors frequently were powerless, poor, and maltreated. Myths first put into writing in the eighth-century chronicles *Kojiki* and *Nihon Shoki* recorded the direct descent of the imperial line from the sun goddess Amaterasu, and court rituals perpetuated the emperor's priestly role. Ascension ceremonies made clear the divine relationship between the sun goddess and the hereditary ruler, and imperial visits to the shrine of the sun goddess in Ise or the tomb of the mythic "divine" first emperor Jimmu (grandson of the grandson of the sun goddess) in Nara were identified as visits of homage to the imperial family's divine ancestors. Until the mid-nineteenth century ordinary Japanese were indifferent to the throne, however, if indeed they even knew or thought about it. With the exception of a small number of intellectuals, the more literate elites were scarcely more concerned.

All this changed with the Meiji period (1868–1912) and the long reign of Emperor Hirohito's grandfather, for it was at this time that the emperor system was creatively "restored" as the central ideological axis of modern nationalism. Under the direct guidance of the great Meiji statesman Itō Hirobumi, the modern emperor system was explicitly created as a Japanese counterpart to the Judeo-Christian tradition; the eighth-century mytho-histories were resurrected as political gospel; Shinto, hitherto largely a decentralized folk religion, was turned into a state religion, and some 120,000 shrines were brought directly under the control of the imperial household. (In English, see, for example, Emiko Ohnuki-Tierney, "The Emperor of Japan as Deity (Kami)," *Ethnology* 30.3 (1991): 199–215.) Most significantly, the Meiji emperor was declared to be a "manifest deity" *(arahitogami* or *akitsumikami)*, and to the Meiji statesmen who were fashioning this new figure of veneration—and keenly scrutinizing the West for models—this formulation clearly was meant to create an analog, however ambiguous, to the "Almighty God" of the Judeo-Christian tradition. (Cf. Ohnuki-Tierney, 204; Woodard, p. 370.) These pseudoreligious formulations were encoded in the Meiji Constitution of 1890, which declared the emperor to be "sacred and inviolable." Exactly what this meant was explained as follows in Itō Hirobumi's definitive "Commentaries," which were issued simultaneously with the promulgation of the constitution:

> The Sacred Throne was established at the time when the heavens and earth became separated *(Kojiki).* The Emperor is Heaven-descended, divine and sacred. He is pre-eminent above all His subjects. He must be reverenced and is inviolable. He has indeed to pay due respect to the law, but the law has no power to hold Him accountable to it. Not only shall there be no irreverence for the Emperor's person, but also shall He neither be made a topic of derogatory comment nor one of discussion.

It was during Emperor Hirohito's reign that the theocratic authoritarianism resident in these Meiji constructs was fully realized. Hirohito had been educated to believe that "sovereignty" resided in the state *(kokka shuken)*, and privately subscribed to the biological analogy that he was the highest "organ" of the state, best likened to the brain (a metaphor Itō also used in his commentaries). Between his ascension to the throne in 1926 and the end of the war, whatever his private sentiments may have been, the Shōwa emperor lent himself readily to the rituals and rhetoric of deification. His loyal philosophers solemnly explained that unlike the divine right of kings in Europe or the "mandate of heaven" in China, the emperor was *himself* a "heavenly sovereign," his edicts were "heavenly mandates" (cf. Creemers, p. 118, quoting the influential philosopher Watsuji Tetsurō). His loyal bureaucrats clarified this in official texts that became mandatory reading, such as the famous *Kokutai no Hongi* (Cardinal Principles of the National Polity) issued by the Ministry of Education in 1937. Here it was carefully and precisely explained that the emperor was not divine in the Western sense of an omnipotent and omniscient God, but rather in a uniquely Japanese way:

> [T]he Emperor is a deity incarnate who rules our country in unison with the august will of the Imperial Ancestors. We do not mean, when respectfully referring to him as deity incarnate—marvelous deity—or humanly manifested deity, the so-called absolute God or omniscient and omnipotent God, but signify that the Imperial Ancestors have manifested themselves in the person of the Emperor, who is their divine offspring, that the Emperor in turn is one in essence with the Imperial Ancestors, that he is forever the fountainhead for the growth and development of his subjects and the country, and that he is endlessly a superbly august person. (Creemers, p. 123)

What all this meant to individual Japanese varied from person to person, but no one was unaware that the "Son of Heaven" *(Tenshi* or *Tenshi-sama)* did not merely reign but was transcendent. Under the Peace Preservation Law passed in 1925, when Hirohito was serving as regent for his mentally incapacitated father, it was lese majesty to deny that the emperor was suprahuman. Those who did so were imprisoned, and the emperor, who voiced opinion on a great many issues, is not known to have said a word against this. During World War II, many Japanese Seventh-Day Adventists and Holiness Christians were arrested for refusing to acknowledge that the emperor was unlike ordinary humans. In secret cabinet meetings in 1942, Prime Minister Tōjō Hideki solemnly observed that "The Emperor is the Godhead. . . . and we, no matter how hard we strive as Ministers, are nothing more than human" (quoted in Large, p. 140). In keeping with imperial rhetoric, the emperor's August 15 surrender broadcast formally was referred to as the *seidan*—literally, "holy decision"—to end the war.

The high-ranking officials who led the campaign to protect Emperor Hirohito and "maintain the national polity" represented, in considerable part, the pro-Western "moderates" whom American and British dignitaries such as Joseph Grew and George Sansom admired. Without exception, they regarded the emperor as a transcendent being. Shigemitsu Mamoru, on learning (while in prison) that the emperor would not be indicted for war crimes, joyously exclaimed, "There is nothing wrong in the Japanese people worshiping the emperor as a living *kami*" [*Tennō Hyakuwa*, 2:130]. Prime Minister Shidehara Kijurō spoke reverently of his sovereign's "sacred character" *(shinkaku)* in the very midst of drafting the denial of divinity (Woodard, p. 254; this term actually had appeared in early translations of the Blyth text as what the emperor was supposedly *denying*).

26. Kinoshita, pp. 89–91; *Tennō Hyakuwa*, 2:202.

27. Matsuo, p. 17.

28. *New York Times*, January 2, 1946. For MacArthur, see Government Section, Supreme Commander Allied Powers, *Political Reorientation of Japan: September 1945 to September 1948* (Washington, D.C.: 1948), vol. 2, p. 471; Woodard, p. 268. MacArthur was given to such hyperbole in private as well where the emperor was concerned. He told Brigadier General Courtney Whitney, head of Government Section and his most trusted aide, that "the Emperor has a more thorough grasp of the democratic concept than almost any Japanese with whom I have talked"; Courtney Whitney, *MacArthur—His Rendezvous with History* (New York: Knopf, 1956), p. 286. It helped that MacArthur did not talk with many Japanese.

29. *Tennō Hyakuwa*, 2:224.

30. Kase Hideaki, *Tennōke no Tatakai* (Tokyo: Shinchosha, 1975), p. 207.

31. The emperor's New Year's verse for 1947 nicely captured the image of reconstruction. It ran as follows: "The day dawns hopefully / Upon the town of Mito; / The sound of the hammer / Is heard clearly." Then, in welcoming in 1948, Emperor Hirohito returned to virtually the identical image and message of his first postsurrender verse. On this occasion, two poems by the emperor were made public. One offered the image of pine trees on the seashore withstanding the fierce sea breezes of the four seasons. The other spoke of learning from the evergreen pine in a lonely garden that does not change its color even in winter's decay. (Translations printed in the *New York Times* on January 24, 1947 and January 2, 1948 are reprinted in Arthur Tiedemann, ed., *Modern Japan*, rev. ed., (New York: Anvil/Van Nostrand, 1962), pp. 184–86.)

The emperor's "declaration of humanity" did not put an immediate end to certain aspects of socialization that were closely identified with the inculcation of emperor worship in the presurrender educational system. It was not until April 6, 1946, for example, that the Ministry of Education issued a directive stating that obeisance to the emperor's portrait, housed in school shrines, was no longer required; the shrines themselves were not actually abolished until July. And it was not until September 29, 1946, that the ministry reached a decision to prohibit the reading of the Imperial Rescript on Education of 1890 on ceremonial school occasions. Even then, it was stipulated that this document—the very core of emperor-centered morality—could still be studied in classrooms because it contained "words of truth and not because it comes from the Emperor." See the secret Department of State report titled "Progress in the Field of Education in Japan since the Surrender," December 9, 1946, pp. 27–28; this is available on microfilm in *O.S.S./State Department Intelligence and Research Reports, II—Postwar Japan, Korea, and Southeast Asia* (Washington, D.C.: University Publications of America, 1977), reel 3, number 28.

CHAPTER 11. *IMPERIAL DEMOCRACY: EVADING RESPONSIBILITY*

1. Kido Kōichi, *Kido Kōichi Nikki* (Tokyo: Tokyo Daigaku Shuppankai, 1966), vol. 2, pp. 1230–31; Herbert Bix, "The Shōwa Emperor's 'Monologue' and the Problem of War Responsibility," *Journal of Japanese Studies* 18.2 (summer 1992): 304.

2. Kinoshita Michio, *Sokkin Nisshi* (Tokyo: Bungei Shunjūsha, 1990), pp. 12, 160.

3. Takahashi Hiroshi and Suzuki Kunihiko, *Tennōke no Misshitachi: Senryō to Kōshitsu* (Tokyo: Bunshun Bunko, 1989), pp. 37–38. Vice Chamberlain Kinoshita's opposition to these developments emerges in his diary. See Kinoshita, p. 225; Bix (1992), p. 333.

4. *Asahi Shimbun*, October 25, 1945; Hata Ikuhiko, "Tennō no Shinsho," *Bungei Shunjū*, October 1978, p. 376; *New York Times*, March 4, 1946.

5. Ashida Hitoshi, *Ashida Hitoshi Nikki* (Tokyo: Iwanami Shoten, 1986), vol. 1, p. 82; the passage is quoted at greater length in Herbert Bix, "Inventing the 'Symbol Monarchy' in Japan, 1945–52," *Journal of Japanese Studies* 21.2 (summer 1995): 338.

6. Kinoshita, pp. 160, 163–65.

7. Masanori Nakamura, *The Japanese Monarchy: Ambassador Joseph Grew and the Making of the "Symbol Emperor System," 1931–1991* (Armonk, N.Y.: M. E. Sharpe, 1992), pp. 118, 175; the issue of abdication is a major theme in this study. Tanabe's argument is summarized in Kuyama Yasushi, "Postwar Japanese Thought: 1945–1960," *Japan Christian Quarterly* 47.3 (summer 1981): 132–44; this is excerpted from Kuyama's edited volume *Sengo Nihon Seishin Shi* (Tokyo: Sōbunsha, 1961). See also chapter 16 below on Tanabe.

8. Miyoshi's well-known essay is reproduced in Tsurumi Shunsuke and Nakagawa Roppei, eds., *Tennō Hyakuwa* (Tokyo: Chikuma Shoten, 1989), vol. 2, pp. 323–31; see esp. pp. 325–28. A lengthy excerpt is translated in Bix (1992), p. 314. The Tsurumi and Nakagawa anthology is cited below as *Tennō Hyakuwa*.

9. Takahashi and Suzuki, p. 35.

10. Kinoshita, pp. 94, 97–99. Among other things, Dyke also proposed that the crown prince be sent to study in the United States, and that a popular referendum on the emperor system be held once the food crisis had been alleviated.

11. Kinoshita, p. 167.

12. The Fellers-Yonai conversation, on March 6, is recorded in a memorandum probably written by Mizota Shūichi, Yonai's interpreter. This is quoted and annotated in Bix (1995), pp. 343–44. On March 22, Mizota recorded another conversation in which Fellers identified the chief "un-American" voice as Benjamin Cohen, "a Jew and a Communist," who had been one of Franklin Roosevelt's New Deal advisers and currently was close to Secretary of State James Byrnes.

13. Kinoshita, pp. 222–24; Takahashi and Suzuki, pp. 38–39.

14. U.S. Department of State, *Foreign Relations of the United States, 1946*, vol. 8, pp. 395–97.

15. See, for example, Shigemitsu's discussion of the "Sugamo gang" in *Tennō Hyakuwa*, 2:123–28.

16. Tanaka Ryūkichi, "Kakute Tennō wa Muzai ni Natta," originally published in *Bungei Shunjū*, August 1965, and reprinted in Bungei Shunjū, ed., *"Bungei Shunjū" ni Miru Shōwa Shi* (Tokyo: Bungei Shunjūsha, 1988), pp. 84–91. Tanaka, a former general who testified at the trial and had close personal connections with the chief

prosecutor, Joseph Keenan, was used as an intermediary to persuade Tōjō to revise his testimony. See also the pertinent excerpts concerning the emperor from Tōjō's trial testimony in *Tennō Hyakuwa*, 2:115–22. See also chapter 15 below.

17. Fujiwara Akira, "Tōsuiken to Tennō," in *Kindai Tennōsei no Kenkyū, II*, ed. Tōyama Shigeki (Tokyo: Iwanami Shoten, 1987), pp. 195–226; Ienaga Saburō, *Sensō Sekinin* (Tokyo: Iwanami Shoten, 1985), pp. 37–47. For a sense of the controversy on this point, see the exchange between Hata Ikuhiko and Kojima Noboru in "'Dokuhakuroku' o Tettei Kenkyū Suru," *Bungei Shunjū*, January 1991, pp. 142–44.

18. Quoted in Roger Buckley, "Britain and the Emperor: The Foreign Office and Constitutional Reform in Japan, 1945–1946," *Modern Asian Studies* 12.4 (1978): 565–66. The zeal of both SCAP and the IPS in divorcing the emperor from the war extended to vetting or deliberately ignoring available materials that might incriminate him. One of the main prosecution sources for the trials, for example, was the detailed diary of former privy seal Kido, a gold mine of inside information. When the diary was translated for trial use, several entries that were deemed potentially harmful to the emperor were excised before the translation was made available. More flagrantly, extensive private interrogation of Kido, amounting in the end to some eight hundred pages of English transcript, was ultimately not introduced by the prosecution because it was feared that even this scrupulously careful confidant of the emperor unwittingly might have implicated his sovereign in some of his recollections of past policy making. See Awaya Kentarō, "Tokyo Saiban to Tennō," in *Shōchō Tennōsei to wa Nani ka*, ed. Nihon Gendaishi Kenkyūkai (Tokyo: Ōtsuki Shoten, 1988), pp. 35–36.

19. The Bonner Fellers papers at the MacArthur Memorial in Norfolk, Va., contain an undated twelve-page memorandum from Terasaki that summarizes Emperor Hirohito's version of events since 1927 and almost certainly derives from the emperor's extended recitation to his aides; RG 44a, box 4, folder 23 ("Terasaki, Terry & Gwen"). See also Arnold C. Brackman, *The Other Nuremberg: The Untold Story of the Tokyo War Crimes Trials* (New York: William Morrow, 1987), p. 78; Bix (1992), pp. 358–60. The long-suppressed "monologue" *(dokuhakuroku)* itself, along with the small deluge of primary and secondary materials pertaining to the emperor that followed Hirohito's death in 1989, is closely analyzed by Bix (1992), who provides extensive citations to pertinent other Japanese sources. For the published Japanese text, with commentary, see Terasaki Hidenari and Mariko Terasaki Miller, eds., *Shōwa Tennō Dokuhakuroku—Terasaki Hidenari Goyōgakari Nikki* (Tokyo: Bungei Shunjūsha, 1991). An interesting collection of short responses to this transcript by one hundred individuals was published in *Rekishisho Tsūshin* 75, February 1991 (Tokyo: Rekishisho Konwakai), pp. 3–21. For numerous other short responses, see *Bungei Shunjū*, January 1991, pp. 94–147. Although the monologue tends to confirm the impression of Hirohito as an individual who engaged in little if any serious self-reflection about his personal responsibility for the disastrous policies carried out under his aegis, it also reveals him to be loyal to a few individuals, such as Tōjō, who emerged as archvillains in the conspiracy theories that the prosecution sought to develop at the war-crimes trials.

A substantial body of critical historical scholarship in Japanese offers a corrective to the gilded view of the emperor's role conveyed in his monologue as well as in SCAP's sanitized version of Hirohito's responsibility. Documented treatments include Fujiwara Akira, *Jūgonen Sensō to Tennō* (Tokyo: Azumino Shoten, 1988); Fujiwara, "Tennō to Sensō Shidō," *Kagaku to Shisō* 71 (January 1989): 676–93; Hata Ikuhiko, *Hirohito Tennō no Itsutsu no Ketsudan* (Tokyo: Kōdansha, 1984): Chimoto Hideki, *Tennōsei no Shinryaku Sekinin to Sengo Sekinin* (Tokyo: Aoki Shoten, 1990); Yamada Akira, *Shōwa Tennō no Sensō Shidō* (Tokyo: Shōwa Shuppan, 1990). See also

Kentarō Awaya, "Emperor Shōwa's Accountability for War," *Japan Quarterly* 38.4 (October–December 1991): 386–98.

20. "Oral Reminiscences of Brigadier General Elliott R. Thorpe," May 29, 1977, RG 49, box 6, MacArthur Memorial, Norfolk, Va., p. 8; U. S. Department of State, *Foreign Relations of the United States, 1946,* vol. 8, pp. 87–92, esp. 90–91.

21. "Buzen naru Sesō no Ben," *Shūkan Asahi,* May 16, 1948, reprinted in Asahi Shimbunsha, ed., *"Shūkan Asahi" no Shōwa Shi* (Tokyo: Asahi Shimbunsha, 1989), vol. 2, pp. 110–121, esp. p. 112; Yoshimi Yoshiaki, "Senryōki Nihon no Minshū Ishiki—Sensō Sekininron o Megutte," *Shisō,* January 1992, pp. 91–93; Hata (1978), pp. 386–87. See also the materials from June 1948 in the papers of Laurence E. Bunker, MacArthur's aide-de-camp, in RG 5, box 77, folder "OMS Correspondence," MacArthur Memorial.

22. Fellers's letter to Terasaki, dated July 8, 1948, appears in RG 44a, box 4, folder 23, MacArthur Memorial. For Sebald, see letters of October 26 and 28, 1948, in RG 5, box 107, folder 2, MacArthur Memorial; also William J. Sebald and Russell Brines, *With MacArthur in Japan: A Personal History of the Occupation* (New York: Norton, 1965), pp. 161–65. See also Hata (1978), pp. 386–92; Nakamura, pp. 114–15; *Tennō Hyakuwa,* 2:141–50 (from Sebald's memoirs), 384, 405–9, 414.

23. Kido's message was discovered by Awaya Kentarō and first published in 1987; the translation appears in Bix (1992), pp. 315–16.

24. Nakamura, pp. 114–17; Awaya Kentarō, "Tokyo Saiban to Tennō," pp. 37–38; idem., *Tokyo Saiban Ron* (Tokyo: Ōtsuki Shoten, 1989), pp. 160, 195–97. Lese majesty laws were not reintroduced after the occupation, but taboos took their place. As Hirohito grew older and Japan became more prosperous, it became if anything increasingly "improper" to question his personal war responsibility. Certainly many individuals who had been close to him withheld publishing their diaries or memoirs until he passed away. Thus, it was not until after Hirohito's death in the opening days of 1989 that the issue of his war role and responsibility was reopened at a serious new level in both scholarly circles and the media.

Hirohito's own exceedingly unreflective thoughts on these matters were conveyed in a famous press conference on October 31, 1975, following his return from an unprecedented state visit to the United States. Asked about his thoughts on the issue of "war responsibility" by a Japanese journalist, the emperor responded: "Concerning such a figure of speech, I have not done much study of these literary matters and so do not understand well and am unable to answer." The emperor also expressed regrets that he still had never visited Okinawa (which was devastated under his war strategy and then, with his active support, turned into a neocolonial American military base after the occupation). Okinawa, he said blandly, had "various problems in the past," but he hoped its residents would do well in the future. Perhaps the most notorious moment in the press conference came when Hirohito was asked what he thought about the atomic bombing of Hiroshima, which by this date he had visited three times. It was regrettable that the bomb was dropped and he felt sorry for the citizens of Hiroshima, but since this happened during war, it "could not be helped." The Shōwa emperor went to his death with a frozen moral compass. The press conference is reproduced in Takahashi Hiroshi, *Heika, Otazune Mōshiagemasu: Kisha Kaiken Zenkiroku to Ningen Tennō no Kiseki* (Tokyo: Bunshun Bunko, 1988), pp. 226–27; also *Tennō Hyakuwa,* 2:636–37.

25. The tours are covered in considerable detail in Takahashi and Suzuki, pp. 210–61 (see esp. pp. 210, 213, 216, 241); see also Bix (1995), pp. 346–59. Kinoshita Michio's diary entry for November 29 made passing reference to the emperor speaking of a recent imperial trip to Kansai (where he paid homage at the purported tomb of his mythic progenitor "Emperor Jimmu," the grandson of the sun goddess's grandson),

and exclaiming how effective this had been in improving his relations with the people; Kinoshita, p. 64. See also Kōdansha, ed., *Shōwa Niman Nichi no Zenkiroku* (Tokyo: Kōdansha, 1989), vol. 7, pp. 218–19.; this source is cited as *SNNZ* below.

26. Takahashi and Suzuki, pp. 211–12.

27. Blyth's memo is reproduced in English in Kinoshita, pp. 111–13.

28. Kishida Hideo, "Sengo Junkō no Puromōttā," *Shūkan Asahi*, June 26, 1956; reprinted in Asahi Shimbunsha, ed., *"Shūkan Asahi" no Shōwa Shi* (Tokyo: Asahi Shimbunsha, 1989), pp. 14–15. According to Ōgane (sometimes read Ōkane) Masujirō, who planned the tours on the Japanese side, General MacArthur was the only person of influence who gave total support to the idea.

29. In the Meiji period, the imperial tours had been inaugurated to offset the "liberty and people's rights movement," which peaked in a series of radical uprisings in the early 1880s. People close to the Shōwa emperor predictibly stressed his sense of duty *(ninmu)* and genuine concern for the people in undertaking the tours; see Ōgane Masujirō in *Tennō Hyakuwa*, 2:294; *SNNZ* 7:218; Takahashi and Suzuki, p. 218.

30. Cf. Ōgane in *Tennō Hyakuwa*, 2:295–97, 309. Countless contemporary sources corroborate this impression.

31. Russell Brines, *MacArthur's Japan* (Philadelphia: Lippincott, 1948), pp. 82–83.

32. Takahashi and Suzuki, pp. 219–21.

33. Ōgane, pp. 296–99. For sample responses, see Yoshimi, pp. 94–99; Asahi Shimbunsha, ed., *Koe* (Tokyo: Asahi Bunko, 1984), vol. 1, pp. 85, 102–4, 239, 254–55.

34. Brines, p. 91.

35. Kishida, pp. 10, 14.

36. The Kumazawa anecdote is noted in Bix (1995), p. 348.

37. An emperor-as-broom cartoon from the magazine *Shinsō* (September 1947) is reproduced by Sodei Rinjirō in his illustrated essay "Satire under the Occupation: The Case of Political Cartoons," in *The Occupation of Japan: Arts and Culture*, ed. Thomas W. Burkman (Norfolk, Va.: General Douglas MacArthur Foundation, 1988), pp. 93–106. The GHQ report is cited in Bix (1995), p. 352. Carmen Johnson, a devoted occupationaire working on women's affairs at the local level, recorded her astonishment on encountering preparations for a visit by the emperor in her diary ("People busy cleaning up a stream. Stones being removed and muck cleared out. I presume the stones will be washed and replaced"); see her *Wave-Rings in the Water: My Years with the Women of Postwar Japan* (Alexandria, Va.: Charles River Press, 1996), p. 113. Justin Williams, among others, calls attention to the devastating effect of the tours on local finances; see his *Japan's Political Revolution under MacArthur: A Participant's Account* (Athens: University of Georgia Press, 1979), pp. 55–56.

38. Takahashi and Suzuki, pp. 234–36.

39. Quoted in Lucy Herndon Crockett, *Popcorn on the Ginza: An Informal Portrait of Postwar Japan* (New York: William Sloane, 1949), p. 239.

40. *Tennō Hyakuwa*, 2: 419–22.

41. *Tennō Hyakuwa*, 2:429.

42. Watanabe Kiyoshi, *Kudakareta Kami—Aru Fukuinhei no Shuki* (Tokyo: Asahi Sensho, 1983). It is not clear how much, if any, editing Watanabe's journal underwent before being published. I am indebted to Professor Takao Toshikaze for introducing me to this remarkable text.

CHAPTER 12. *CONSTITUTIONAL DEMOCRACY: GHQ WRITES A NEW NATIONAL CHARTER*

1. Douglas MacArthur, *Reminiscences* (New York: McGraw-Hill, 1964), p. 302.

2. *Guide to Japan* (CINPAC-CINPOA Bulletin No. 209–45, September 1, 1945), p. 35.

3. The volume of primary and secondary materials on the drafting of the postwar Japanese constitution is extensive. An invaluable bilingual source on these matters is Takayanagi Kenzō, Ōtomo Ichirō, and Tanaka Hideo, eds., *Nihonkoku Kempō Seitei no Katei*, 2 vols. (Tokyo: Yūhikaku, 1972). This reproduces, in the original English, the papers of Milo Rowell, a SCAP official who participated in the drafting process and assembled most of the internal documents pertaining to the actual proceedings when GHQ undertook to write a new constitution. Much of the account that follows is based on these primary documents, which hereafter are cited as *TOT/RP* (for Takayanagi, Ōtomo, and Tanaka/Rowell Papers).

Between 1957 and 1964, Takayanagi, one of Japan's most distinguished legal scholars, headed a Commission on the Constitution that held extensive hearings on the origins, problems, and prospects of the postwar charter. All told, the commission published some forty thousand pages of transcripts and documents. Major portions of the lengthy summary report of this committee are available in English; see John M. Maki, trans. and ed., *Japan's Commission on the Constitution: The Final Report* (Seattle: University of Washington Press, 1980). For a succinct summary of the various positions taken on the general issue of the enactment process, see Maki, pp. 220–31. This source is cited below as *JCC/FR*. Takayanagi's brief recollection of these investigative findings is given in his "Some Reminiscences of Japan's Commission on the Constitution," reprinted in Dan Fenno Henderson, ed., *The Constitution of Japan: Its First Twenty Years, 1947–67* (Seattle: University of Washington Press, 1968), pp. 71–88. For a concise summary of the conservative movement to revise the constitution in the 1950s and 1960s, see H. Fukui, "Twenty Years of Revisionism," in Henderson, pp. 41–70.

The pioneer Western study of the drafting of the 1946 constitution is Theodore H. McNelly's 1952 Columbia University Ph.D. dissertation, "Domestic and International Influences on Constitutional Revision in Japan, 1945–1946"; this includes many useful translations of basic Japanese materials. Professor McNelly's analysis of the constitution-making process after many subsequent years of research is summarized in his "'Induced Revolution': The Policy and Process of Constitutional Reform in Occupied Japan," in *Democratizing Japan: The Allied Occupation*, ed. Robert E. Ward and Yoshikazu Sakamoto (Honolulu: University of Hawaii Press, 1987), pp. 76–106. This same Ward and Sakamoto text includes three other pertinent essays: Robert E. Ward, "Presurrender Planning: Treatment of the Emperor and Constitutional Change" (pp. 1–41); Tanaka Hideo, "The Conflict between Two Legal Traditions in Making the Constitution of Japan" (pp. 107–32); and Susan J. Pharr, "The Politics of Women's Rights" (pp. 221–52). In a much earlier essay, Robert Ward offered an extremely harsh critique of the authoritarian manner in which the constitution was imposed on the Japanese, concluding that the charter was "hopelessly unsuited to the political ideals or experience of a vast majority of the population"; see "The Origins of the Present Japanese Constitution," *American Political Science Review* 50.4 (1956): 980–1010. See also Hideo Tanaka, "A History of the Constitution of Japan of 1946," in *The Japanese Legal System: Introductory Cases and Materials*, ed. Hideo Tanaka and Malcolm D. H. Smith (Tokyo: University of Tokyo Press, 1976), pp. 653–68; and Tatsuo Satō, "The Origin and Development of the Draft Constitution of Japan," published in two parts in *Contemporary Japan* 24.4–6

(1956): 175–87, and 24.7–9 (1956): 371–87. Satō played a key inside role on the Japanese side during the revision process, and his writings in Japanese are utilized by McNelly (1952) and Ward (1956).

A thoughtful and revealing account, prepared by Alfred Hussey, who participated in the GHQ drafting process, is included in Government Section, General Headquarters, Supreme Commander for the Allied Powers, *Political Reorientation of Japan: September 1945 to September 1948* (Washington, D.C.: U.S. Government Printing Office, 1949), vol. 1, pp. 82–118; a few key documents are reprinted in ibid., vol. 2, pp. 586–683. This source is cited as *PRJ* below. In this and the following chapter, I also have drawn on the transcripts of interviews with American participants in the drafting process that were conducted by Alex Gibney's Jigsaw Productions in conjunction with the production of his 1992 documentary film *Reinventing Japan* (program 5 in the Annenberg/CPB series *The Pacific Century*); these interesting interviews, generously made available by Mr. Gibney, are cited below as *GI* (for Gibney Interviews). Charles Kades offers his version of events in "The American Role in Revising Japan's Imperial Constitution," *Political Science Quarterly* 104.2 (1989): 215–47. Kades' recollections also appear in the transcript of a lengthy interview with Takemae Eiji: "Kades Memoir on Occupation of Japan," *Journal of Tokyo Keizai University* 148 (November 1986): 243–327; see especially pp. 272–85 on constitutional revision. The Gibney interviews also include a long and particularly interesting interview with Kades. Justin Williams, who did not participate in the drafting sessions but handled GHQ liaison with the Diet, devotes several chapters to the new constitution in his memoir *Japan's Political Revolution under MacArthur: A Participant's Account* (Athens: University of Georgia Press, 1979), pp. 98–143.

The most highly regarded recent Japanese scholarly analysis of the "birth" of the new constitution is Koseki Shōichi, *Shin Kempō no Tanjō* (Tokyo: Chūō Kōronsha, 1989). For an English edition of this incisive study, edited and translated by Ray A. Moore, see *The Birth of Japan's Postwar Constitution* (Boulder: Westview Press, 1997). This appeared as the present book was being finalized, and citations here are to the original Japanese edition. I also have drawn on two English-language writings by Professor Koseki: "Japanese Constitutional Thought: The Process of Formulating the 1947 Constitution," unpublished paper presented at the annual conference of the American Historical Association, December 1987; and "Japanizing the Constitution," *Japan Quarterly* 35.3 (July–September 1988): 234–40. The most influential critiques of the constitution as an alien charter imposed on the Japanese by the victors have been published by Etō Jun; see his *1946-nen Kempō no Kōsoku* (Tokyo: Bungei Shunjūsha, 1980). For an analysis of linguistic differences between the Japanese and English-language versions of the constitution, see Kyoko Inoue, *MacArthur's Japanese Constitution: A Linguistic and Cultural Study of Its Making* (Chicago: University of Chicago Press, 1991). This also includes a helpful although not comprehensive bibliography of materials in both Japanese and English.

4. Ward (1956), pp. 982–83; *PRJ* 1:89–90.

5. The basic subsequent U.S. directives supporting constitutional revision were (1) the U.S. Initial Post-Surrender Policy for Japan of September 6, 1945; (2) JCS 1380/15 of November 3, 1945; and (3) SWNCC 228 of January 7, 1946. The latter, which was submitted to SCAP on January 11, appears in U.S. Department of State, *Foreign Relations of the United States, 1946*, vol. 8, pp. 99–102; this series is cited below as *FRUS*. See also the February 1, 1946 memo to MacArthur in *TOT/RP* 1:94. For GHQ's own independent internal critique of the existing constitution, see the "Rowell report" of December 6, 1945, in *TOT/RP* 1:2–25; also *PRJ* 1:82–88, 92, 112.

6. *FRUS 1946* 8:99–102 (SWNCC 228).

7. Konoe's twenty-two-point outline is translated in McNelly (1952), pp. 382–86. For detailed discussions of the Konoe initiative, see McNelly (1952), pp. 22–61; Koseki (1989), pp. 8–29; and Dale Hellegers, "The Konoe Affair," in *The Occupation of Japan: Impact of Legal Reform*, ed. L. H. Redford (Norfolk, Va.: General Douglas MacArthur Foundation, 1977), pp. 164–75. Apart from developments within Japan, on October 26, 1945, the *New York Times* printed a letter from Nathaniel Peffer, a well-known Asia scholar, that described SCAP's relationship with Konoe as "grotesque." At roughly the same time, E. H. Norman was preparing a devastating internal report on Konoe's war responsibility.

8. For general discussions of the Matsumoto committee, see Koseki (1989), pp. 59–80; McNelly (1952), pp. 62–117. On Matsumoto's background and personality, see Tanaka (1987), p. 112; Koseki (1987), p. 25 (n. 23).

9. Hellegers, p. 170; McNelly (1987), p. 77.

10. Tanaka (1976), p. 656.

11. *JCC/FR*, p. 69; Tanaka (1987), p. 107; *TOT/RP* 1:xxviii.

12. The overwhelmingly dominant role played by Matsumoto is noted in Koseki (1987), p. 6. The committee held seven general meetings and fifteen work sessions; Koseki (1989), p. 64. For committee members, see *PRJ* 2:603–4.

13. Koseki (1989), pp. 75–76.

14. *TOT/RP* 1:358; see also *PRJ* 1:106.

15. This theme is treated incisively in Tanaka (1987); see also Satō, p. 371.

16. Satō, pp. 180–81; Tanaka (1987), p. 110.

17. *TOT/RP* 1:84; see also *PRJ* 1:100.

18. Tanaka (1987), p. 130 (n. 48); *JCC/FR*, p. 69; Koseki (1989), p. 75.

19. *TOT/RP* 1:338. I have dealt with Yoshida and the anglophiles and "old liberals" in two sources: *Empire and Aftermath: Yoshida Shigeru and the Japanese Experience, 1878–1952* (Cambridge, Mass.: Council on East Asian Studies, Harvard University, 1979); and "Yoshida in the Scales of History," in *Japan in War and Peace: Selected Essays* (New York: The New Press, 1993), pp. 208–41.

20. Tanaka (1976), pp. 656–57; Tanaka (1987), pp. 112–15. As Professor Tanaka has shown, this was typical. Another basic prewar source on the U.S. constitution, Fujii Shin'ichi's mammoth 1926 analysis, devoted only six of its 808 pages to human rights.

21. See, for example, Minobe's views in *Asahi Shimbun*, October 15, 1945 (also October 20, 21, and 22); also Williams, pp. 119, 131; McNelly (1952), pp. 144–45, 275–76.

22. Koseki (1989), p. 153.

23. Inada originally proposed—but to his later regret deleted—a constitutional clause making Japan a "disarmed nation of culture"; Koseki (1989), p. 57.

24. McNelly (1952), pp. 149–50. For the various drafts, see McNelly (1952), pp. 118–53, 387–403; Koseki (1989), pp. 30–58; *PRJ* 1:94–98.

25. McNelly (1952), p. 145.

26. Koseki (1989), p. 51; McNelly (1952), pp. 139–40.

27. McNelly (1952), p. 152.

28. McNelly (1952), pp. 132–34.

29. McNelly (1952), p. 120; Koseki (1987), p. 3.

30. McNelly (1952), p. 141, 401–2.

31. Koseki (1989), pp. 35, 46, 58; Koseki (1987), pp. 3–5.

32. Takano and his colleagues also studied the U.S., Soviet, Weimar, and Swiss constitutions. For general treatments of the Kempō Kenkyūkai, see Koseki (1989), pp. 32–45; McNelly (1952), pp. 144–46. For Norman's work and influence, see John W. Dower, ed., *Origins of the Modern Japanese State: Selected Writings of E. H. Norman* (New York: Pantheon, 1975).

33. *TOT/RP* 1:26–41; the text does not specify this is the Kempō Kenkyūkai, but it is. Cf. Koseki (1987), p. 8 (n. 18); Tanaka (1976), p. 655.

34. *TOT/RP* 1:42; Tanaka (1987), p. 128 (n. 16).

35. Koseki (1989), pp. 68–74; Tanaka (1976), p. 658; Tanaka (1987), p. 120; *TOT/RP* 1:xxiv. The *Mainichi* article and published draft are translated in *TOT/RP* 1:44–75.

36. For GHQ's top-secret internal critique of the Matsumoto committee's draft, see *TOT/RP* 1:40–44, 78–90; *PRJ* 1:98–101 and 2:605–16.

37. *TOT/RP* 1:90–98; *PRJ* 2:622–23; Kades (1989), pp. 220–22. The only restriction on MacArthur's authority involved removal of the emperor, in which case he was required to consult with the Joint Chiefs of Staff.

38. MacArthur's guidelines appear in many sources; see *PRJ* 1:102; *TOT/RP* 1:98–102; *JCC/FR*, pp. 72–73; Kades (1989), pp. 223–24; Kades (1986), pp. 277–78. Whitney came out of his meeting with MacArthur with these famous "three principles" written in pencil on a yellow pad. Kades, who then typed them, assumed the writing was MacArthur's but acknowledged it could have been Whitney's, for their handwriting was similar.

39. Kades later commented, surely correctly, that "except for MacArthur's leadership, probably no such document would ever have been drafted"; Kades interview *(GI)* 2:19. For a sample of MacArthur's righteous (and none too forthright) defense of his actions, claiming he had "meticulously" acted in accord with instructions from the U.S. government, see his lengthy cable of May 4, 1946, to the Joint Chiefs of Staff in *FRUS 1946*, 8:220–26. The utter surprise of the State Department's representative in Tokyo when the GHQ draft subsequently emerged in the guise of a Japanese government proposal can be seen in *FRUS 1946*, 8:172–74. Naturally, GHQ's liberal draft shocked the old-guard Japan hands who believed the Japanese incapable of democracy. In Washington, policy makers voiced fear that the Japanese people were not politically mature enough to meet the responsibilities granted them in the new constitution and this might lead to instability, which would facilitate "a reversion to bureaucratic government"; see the secret State Department report reproduced in the microfilm collection *O.S.S./State Department Intelligence and Research Reports* (Washington, D.C.: University Publications of America, 1977), reel 2, entry 23. The British diplomat George Sansom, a distinguished cultural historian of Japan, dismissed the draft constitution as "idiotic"; see Roger Buckley, *Occupation Diplomacy: Britain, the United States, and Japan, 1945–1952* (Cambridge: Cambridge University Press, 1982), p. 68.

40. *JCC/FR*, p. 68.

41. *TOT/RP* 1:xxv, xxix–xxx. After the occupation ended, MacArthur himself was emphatic in emphasizing this point. For example, in response to a query from Takayanagi Kenzō, chairman of the Commission on the Constitution, he stated flatly that "The preservation of the Emperor system was my fixed purpose. It was inherent and integral to Japanese political and cultural survival. The vicious efforts to destroy the person of the Emperor and thereby abolish the system became one of the most dangerous menaces that threatened the successful rehabilitation of the

nation." See *JCC/FR*, pp. 73–74; Takayanagi, p. 79. Japanese as well as American scholars tend to agree that a major motivation behind Article 9 was to alleviate criticism of the retention of the imperial system. See, for example, Hata Ikuhiko and Sodei Rinjirō, *Nihon Senryō Mitsushi* (Tokyo: Asahi Shimbunsha, 1977), vol. 2, pp. 8–11; Hata, *Shiroku: Nihon Saigunbi* (Tokyo: Bungei Shunjūsha, 1976), pp. 47–78; McNelly (1982), p. 30.

42. *TOT/RP* 1:102–4.

43. *TOT/RP* 1:xxv, xxix–xxx, 90–98 (esp. 94–98); *PRJ* 2:622–23.

44. *TOT/RP* 1:326–28. This message was repeated to the Japanese side in unequivocal terms in the days that followed; see ibid., 1:334–46, 372.

45. *TOT/RP* 1:374; Koseki (1989), pp. 204 (Shidehara) and 205 (Yoshida); Yoshida Shigeru, *Sekai to Nihon* (Tokyo: Banchō Shobo, 1963), pp. 94–99.

46. For personnel and committees, see *TOT/RP* 1:110. Kades notes the hours maintained in *GI* 2:22. The "bullpen" term appears in Milton Esman interview *(GI)*, p. 20. *TOT/RP* is the major primary source for GHQ's "constitutional convention." For a detailed day-to-day summary based on the confidential official record of the session, prepared long afterward (December 16, 1947) by Ruth Ellerman on the basis of minutes taken at the time, see Williams, pp. 108–13.

47. Kades (1989), p. 225.

48. Beate Sirota Gordon, "Present at the Creation: Women's Rights Under the Japanese Constitution," public lecture at Harvard University, October 7, 1997; Beate Sirota interview *(GI)*, pp. 20–23, 27–28. Sirota's role in the Government Section "constitutional convention" is discussed in detail in Pharr, in Ward and Sakamoto. In Japanese, see Doi Takako and B. Sirota Gordon, *Kempō ni Danjo Byōdō Kisō Mitsuwa* (Tokyo: Iwanami Booklet No. 400, 1996).

49. Kades interview *(GI)*, 2:69; Sirota interview *(GI)*, p. 34; Richard Poole interview *(GI)*, p. 5.

50. Poole interview *(GI)*, pp. 5–7.

51. Sirota interview *(GI)*, pp. 7–8, 20–23, 29–30, 40–42. This attitude is implicit in the summary of Government Section's outlook in *PRJ*, where "popular pressure for greater participation" in self-governance is taken far more seriously than ever emerged in the prognostications of most mainstream Asia specialists.

52. The whole modus operandi of the Government Section drafting session suggests how impressionistically so-called guiding texts may be used. Although SWNCC 228 was the product of intensive bureaucratic labor in Washington, for example, it appears to have been given only cursory attention by GHQ; see, for example, Theodore McNelly, "General Douglas MacArthur and the Constitutional Disarmament of Japan," *Transactions of the Asiatic Society of Japan*, third series, vol. 17 (1982), pp. 16–17.

53. Kades (1989), pp. 227–28. See also Kades (1986), pp. 274–75; Kades interview *(GI)*, 1:9–10, 2:23–25.

54. Sirota interview *(GI)*, pp. 24–25. See also Esman interview *(GI)*, pp. 11–12.

55. Poole interview *(GI)*, p. 17. The eventual Government Section draft of Article 1 read, "The emperor shall be the symbol of the State and of the Unity of the People, deriving his position from the sovereign will of the People, and from no other source"; *TOT/RP* 1:268. In the constitution as finally adopted by the Diet, the wording is, "The Emperor shall be the symbol of the State and of the unity of the people, deriving his position from the will of the people with whom reside sovereign power." Nakamura Masanori examines English and American thinking about

the "symbol" monarchy in detail in *The Japanese Monarchy: Ambassador Joseph Grew and the Making of the "Symbol Emperor System," 1931–1991* (Armonk, N.Y.: M. E. Sharpe, 1992).

56. See Pharr, in Ward and Sakamoto, on women's rights.

57. In his interesting interview with Takemae Eiji in 1986, Kades observed apropos of his alteration of MacArthur's instructions that, if he had given more thought to it at the time, "I probably would have written it in: 'except to repel invasions or suppress insurrection.' But we worked under great pressure, you know"; Kades (1986), pp. 277–82, esp. 279. See also Kades (1989), pp. 236–37; *TOT/RP* 1:272. A great deal of ink has been expended in speculating on who first broached the idea of incorporating the renunciation-of-war ideal into the new constitution. This issue is carefully analyzed by McNelly (1982), who persuasively rejects the argument that the idea originated with Prime Minister Shidehara. Kades or Whitney may have suggested something of the sort to MacArthur, but when all is said and done the basic decision clearly was MacArthur's. It must be kept in mind, however, that a number of wartime American and British pronouncements called, in one form or another, for the "complete and permanent" demilitarization of Germany and Japan once the two Axis enemies had been defeated. Such language was reiterated in the policy documents governing Japan, including the Potsdam Declaration and the basic Joint Chiefs of Staff directive to MacArthur (JCS 1380/15).

58. Ashida Hitoshi, *Ashida Hitoshi Nikki* (Tokyo: Iwanami Shoten, 1986), 1:78–79; see also Ashida's testimony in *Kempō Chōsakai Daishichi Sōkai Gijiroku*, April 5, 1957.

59. Kades interview *(GI)*, 2:76.

60. McNelly (1952), pp. 203–6.

61. Esman interview *(GI)*, pp. 10–11, 14–15, 21, 47.

62. See the internal debates in *TOT/RP* 1:248–52.

63. *TOT/RP* 1:128, 134–36.

64. *TOT/RP* 1:206.

65. Poole interview *(GI)*, p. 20. Subsequent developments pertaining to constitutional review are addressed in *JCC/FR*, pp. 15–16, 84; *FRUS 1946*, 8:267–73, 342–47, 350–53.

66. *TOT/RP* 1:258–60.

67. *TOT/RP* 1:262; McNelly (1952), p. 165. MacArthur's change was fully supported by the steering committee.

CHAPTER 13. *CONSTITUTIONAL DEMOCRACY: JAPANIZING THE AMERICAN DRAFT*

1. Kades (1986), pp. 282–83. [Citations in this chapter follow the full citations given in the preceeding chapter.]

2. The aides were Colonel Kades, Lieutenant Colonel Hussey, and Commander Rowell. The full official account appears in *TOT/RP* 1:320–36. See also Kades (1989), pp. 228–30; Kades interview *(GI)*, pp. 34–40.

3. Courtney Whitney, *MacArthur: His Rendezvous with History* (New York: Knopf, 1956), p. 251; *TOT/RP* 1:324.

4. Koseki (1989), p. 127.

5. *TOP/RP* 1:336–40, 346; *PRJ* 2:624.

6. *TOP/RP* 1:352–64. In certain ways, the confrontation between the Matsumoto group and the Government Section group replicated the confrontation between the "Japan crowd" and "China crowd" in Washington as World War II came to an end.

7. Kades (1986), p. 288; *TOT/RP* 1:366–370; *PRJ* 1:106. GHQ's deadline was subsequently extended to February 22.

8. The key Japanese source on these cabinet meetings is the diary of Ashida Hitoshi, which was not published until 1986; see *Ashida Hitoshi Nikki* (Tokyo: Iwanami Shoten), 1:77 (February 19, 1946). In 1954, Matsumoto publicly presented a harsher version of Whitney's position, claiming that the general had said that if the government did not accept the GHQ draft, it would not be possible to guarantee the emperor's "body" *(shintai)*. In phrasing it this way, Whitney appeared to be blackmailing the Japanese by suggesting that if they did not accept the GHQ draft, SCAP itself might take action harmful to Emperor Hirohito. This highly dubious account has made for bad history but lively polemics. See Iriye Toshirō, *Kempō Seiritsu no Keii to Kempōjō no Shomondai* (Tokyo: Daiichi Hōki, 1976), p. 199; *JCC/FR*, pp. 75–77; Takayanagi, pp. 77–78; Koseki (1989), pp. 129–31; Kades (1989), pp. 229–30; Etō (1980), pp. 33–38.

9. Ashida, 1:77 (February 19, 1946).

10. Ashida, 1:78–79 (February 22, 1946). See also Ashida's testimony in *Kempō Chōsakai Daishichi Sōkai Gijiroku*, April 5, 1957; *TOT/RP* 2:392 (Whitney's statement to Matsumoto on February 22); McNelly (1982), p. 23.

11. *TOT/RP* 1:380–98.

12. Koseki (1989), pp. 134–35; *TOT/RP* 1:406. There is some debate on what the emperor actually said; see Bix (1995), p. 339.

13. Whitney, pp. 250, 253.

14. *TOT/RP* 1:402–410.

15. The Japanese government eventually produced four drafts. These are reproduced in *PRJ* 2:625–48.

16. Kades interview *(GI)*, 1:11–12, 2:45–47. Satō places this incident at a later date; see Inoue, *MacArthur's Japanese Constitution*, pp. 172–73.

17. Kades interview *(GI)* 2:34–35, 40–45; Koseki (1989), pp. 144–46.

18. Williams, pp. 115–16; Koseki (1989), pp. 138–51, esp. 140–44; McNelly (1952), pp. 171–94; *PRJ* 2:625–36 (the drafts can be compared here). On the rights of aliens, see Koseki (1987), pp. 11–13; Koseki (1988), pp. 235–36; Koseki (1989), pp. 148, 160. On local government, see Akira Amakawa, "The Making of the Postwar Local Government System," in Ward and Sakamoto, op. cit., pp. 259–60.

19. Inoue discusses these linguistic issues in some detail, and includes the citation from Satō in her treatment; pp. 184–205, esp. 188–90. The problematic nature of the term *kokumin* was emphasized to Whitney and Kades by a team of advisers consisting of T. A. Bisson, Cyrus Peake, and Kenneth Colegrove; this is discussed on pp. 188–93 of a manuscript by T. A. Bisson entitled "Reform Years in Japan, 1945–47: An Occupation Memoir," which has been published in Japanese translation but not in English; see Nakamura Masanori and Miura Yōichi, trans., *Nihon Senryō Kaisō-ki* (Tokyo, Sanseidō, 1983).

20. Inoue introduces many excerpts from the subsequent Diet debates on "popular sovereignty" in *MacArthur's Japanese Constitution*, pp. 205–20. See also Koseki (1989), p. 151.

21. The two drafts are reproduced in *PRJ* 2:625–36. The twelve points are summarized in McNelly (1952), pp. 192–93.

22. Kinoshita Michio, *Sokkin Nisshi* (Tokyo: Bungei Shunjūsha, 1990), pp. 163–64 (March 5, 1946).

23. Ashida, 1:90 (March 5, 1946). See also Satō Tatsuo's account in *Jurisuto*, August 15, 1955, p. 34.

24. *PRJ* 2:657; English versions of the Japanese documents can be found in McNelly (1952), pp. 195–99.

25. For a commentary on the imperial aura of the constitutional revision process in general, see Isoda Susumu, "Shinkempōteki Kankaku o Minitsukeyo," *Sekai*, August 1947, pp. 22–27, esp. 24.

26. The "behind closed doors" comment appears in Bisson's unpublished manuscript, p. 196.

27. *Yomiuri Shimbun*, March 8, 1946; cited in Williams, p. 134.

28. Takayanagi, p. 77; cf. Satō, p. 385.

29. See, for example, the key log for November 25, 1946, reproduced by Etō Jun in "One Aspect of the Allied Occupation of Japan: The Censorship Operation and Postwar Japanese Literature," occasional paper of the Wilson Center, Smithsonian Institution (Washington, D.C., 1980), pp. 17–20.

30. Recalled by Robert Spaulding, a former official in GHQ's censorship section, in L. H. Redford, ed., *The Occupation of Japan: Impact of Legal Reform* (Norfolk: Douglas MacArthur Foundation, 1977), p. 58.

31. For these and other press responses, see Williams, pp. 133–40; McNelly (1952), p. 271. A confidential study by the Foreign Ministry found the immediate public response to be more or less one of perplexity. See Koseki (1989), p. 162; Etō (1980), pp. 60–61.

32. McNelly (1952), pp. 271–76. For the mixed responses of the Japanese media, see Williams, pp. 133–42.

33. See, for example, *JCC/FR*, p. 78.

34. Text in McNelly (1952), p. 317.

35. Inoue, pp. 32, 35; Williams, p. 142.

36. Satō, p. 384. See also Satō as quoted by Tanaka (1987), p. 124; Takayanagi, pp. 80–81; Yoshida Shigeru, *The Yoshida Memoirs* (Boston: Houghton Mifflin, 1962), p. 143.

37. Katō delivered these observations at the age of ninety-nine in an interview in *Asahi Shimbun*, January 25, 1996. It is a telling sign of the passage of time that after mention of the term *kokutai* in this article, the *Asahi* felt compelled to insert a parenthetical definition ("national structure with the emperor at center") for readers who had no idea what it meant. A half-century later, the most ideologically resonant word of the war years, the concept under which an entire nation had been mobilized and for which the conservatives later struggled and wept, had simply disappeared from contemporary discourse. The Diet debates of 1946 really mark the last gasp of *"kokutai"* as a central concept in the public espousal of national identity, and an interesting study could be made of the marginalization of the concept thereafter, until eventually it became primarily associated with extreme right-wing ideologues.

38. The *kokutai* interpellations are discussed in Dower (1979), pp. 318–29; see also *PRJ* 1:93.

39. Dower (1979), p. 327; Inoue, p. 206; Koseki (1989), pp. 213–21; McNelly (1987), pp. 90–91.

40. Dower (1979), p. 326.

41. Dower (1979), p. 329.

42. Koseki (1989), pp. 210, 212.

43. Takayanagi, p. 80; cf. Kades interview *(GI)*, 1:15; Kades (1986), p. 277.

44. McNelly (1987), pp. 84, 89–90, 96–97; Etō Jun, "The Constraints of the 1946 Constitution," *Japan Echo* 8.1 (1981), pp. 44–50; Satō, p. 384. The publication of *PRJ* in 1949 astonished many observers with its frank revelation of SCAP's role in preparing the original draft constitution. The confidential hearings of the House of Representatives subcommittee on the constitution (the so-called Ashida Committee) were not made public until 1995, at which time six gaps were discerned in the stenographic record. The media did not specifically relate these lacunae to GHQ interventions, however; see *Asahi Shimbun*, October 1, 1995. For the published subcommittee deliberations themselves, see Shūgiin, Daikyūjukkai Teikoku Gikai, *Teikoku Kempō Kaiseianiin Shōiinkai Sokkiroku* (Shūgiin Jimukyoku, Ōkurashō Insatsukyoku, 1995).

45. *JCC/FR*, p. 81. Takayanagi Kenzō, who chaired this committee, nonetheless became a strong supporter of what he called the "collaborative theory" of the constitution's origins, by which he had in mind two grand points. Japanese input into the creation of the constitution, both direct and indirect, he concluded, was more substantial than was usually acknowledged; and, beyond this, the constitution accurately reflected the aspirations of the Japanese people. See *JCC/FR*, pp. 224–25; Takayanagi, pp. 71–88.

46. Quoted in Satō, p. 387. See also Sawada's impassioned defense of the Meiji Constitution translated in Inoue, pp. 199–200. Sasaki Sōichi also opposed the new constitution on the floor of the House of Peers; McNelly (1952), p. 364.

47. These are enumerated, without commentary, in U.S. Department of State, *Foreign Relations of the United States* [hereafter cited as *FRUS*], *1946*, vol. 8, pp. 359–64.

48. *Asahi Shimbun*, January 22, 1996 (p. 12); this covers newly declassified materials on the "civilian" issue, as well as a declassified statement by Kanamori outlining changes demanded of the Diet by GHQ. See also McNelly (1952), ch. 7 (esp. pp. 267–69). Contrary to intense fears expressed in February and March concerning the "international" threat to the imperial system, the FEC did not take a critical stand on this. On the contrary, on April 4, 1946, the FEC exempted Emperor Hirohito from possible indictment for war crimes.

49. Cf. McNelly (1987), p. 92; Koseki (1987), p. 15; Koseki (1989), pp. 225, 233; Kades (1986), pp. 284–85. Katayama Tetsu, a Christian Socialist who participated in the deliberations in the lower house and later presided over a short-lived coalition cabinet in 1947–1948, offered a succinct rebuttal to those who would argue that the constitution was an alien imposition. It was, he said, imposed on the reactionaries, but not on the people; cited in McNelly, "The New Constitution and Induced Revolution," p. 159.

50. Koseki (1989), pp. 228–33; *Asahi Shimbun*, October 1, 1995, p. 17. When the secret records of the House of Representatives subcommittee on the constitution were finally opened in 1995, it was observed that no other article in the constitution was so directly affected by the "people's voices."

51. Koseki Shōichi, "Japanizing the Constitution," *Japan Quarterly* 35.3 (July–September 1988), pp. 239–40. The impetus for rendering the constitution in colloquial Japanese came from a lobby calling itself the National Language Alliance (Kokumin no Kokugo Renmei), which included the novelist Yamamoto Yūzō as well as a former judge and bureaucrat, Miyake Shōtarō, who had been purged by SCAP.

52. Koseki (1988), pp. 235–36; Koseki (1989), pp. 160–61; *Asahi Shimbun*, January 22, 1996 (p. 12). Furukawa Atsushi suggests that Satō was "abnormally" concerned

about the possibility of treating foreigners equally under the constitution; see Sodei Rinjirō and Takemae Eiji, eds., *Sengo Nihon no Genten* (Tokyo: Yūhisha, 1992), vol. 1, p. 168.

53. Minutes of Second Meeting of the Examination Committee of the Privy Council on the Subject of Referring the Draft Revision of the Imperial Constitution to the Imperial Diet, April 24, 1946; cited by Charles Kades in his interesting "Discussion of Professor Theodore McNelly's Paper, 'General Douglas MacArthur and the Constitutional Disarmament of Japan,' " *Transactions of the Asiatic Society of Japan*, third series, vol. 17 (1982), pp. 35–52; see esp. p. 39.

54. Yoshida's position on Article 9 is discussed in Dower (1979), pp. 378–83.

55. Kades (1982), pp. 39–41; Kades (1989), pp. 236–37; Kades interview *(GI)*, 2:66–68.

56. The secret subcommittee records, declassified in September 1995, were given extensive coverage in *Asahi Shimbun*, September 30 and October 1, 1995. The general contents of the subcommittee discussions have been known to Japanese scholars since 1983, when an English translation of most of the secret hearings was discovered in the U.S. archives. The impression that Ashida himself did not at the time have a keen sense of introducing language that would allow later rearmament for self-defense is confirmed by the generally frank and detailed Ashida diaries (published in 1986), which also contain no such commentary. See also Koseki (1988), pp. 237–38.

57. Minutes of the Special Committee of the House of Peers on the Revision of the Imperial Constitution, September 14, 1946, no. 12, pp. 36, 78–82; cited in Kades (1982), pp. 41–42.

58. The House of Peers special committee hearings that culminated in Article 66, the "civilian" or *bunmin* provision, were not declassified until January 21, 1996. This is covered in detail in *Asahi Shimbun*, January 22, 1996.

59. Minutes of the Second Meeting of the Examination Committee of the Privy Council, October 21, 1946; cited in Kades (1982), p. 45.

60. Cited in Koseki (1988), p. 237.

61. Cited in Dower (1979), pp. 382–83.

62. Koseki indicates that as early as April 1947, even before the new constitution came into effect, Asakai Koichirō, one of Yoshida's henchmen, was privately talking to Canadian and Australian diplomats about reconstituting a Japanese army in the neighborhood of one hundred thousand men; Koseki (1987), pp. 19–20.

63. Kades (1982), p. 46.

64. *FRUS 1946*, 8:92.

65. Yoshida Shigeru, *Ōiso Zuisō* (Tokyo: Sekkasha, 1962), pp. 42–43; see also Yoshida's "Jūnen no Ayumi," *Mainichi Shimbun*, August 9, 1955.

66. *SNNZ* 7:312.

67. *SNNZ* 7:324.

68. Mark Gayn, *Japan Diary* (New York: William Sloane, 1948), p. 488.

69. Koseki (1987), pp. 20–21.

70. Mikasa's reflections were published in *Teikoku Daigaku Shimbun*, May 8, 1947; they are reprinted in *Fukusatsuban: Teikoku Daigaku Shimbun* (Tokyo: Fuji Shuppan, 1985), vol. 17, p. 354.

71. Kempō Fukyūkai, ed., *Atarashii Kempō Akarui Seikatsu* (May 3, 1947). The distribution of the booklet to every household is noted in *Osaka Hyakunen Shi*, edited and published by Osaka-fu [Osaka Perfecture] (Osaka: 1968), p. 912.

72. Kanamori Tokujirō, *Shōnen to Shōjo no tame no Kempō no Ohanashi* (Tokyo: Sekaisha, 1949).

73. Cited in Koseki (1987), p. 20.

74. McNelly (1982), pp. 1–7. For Takayanagi Kenzō's acceptance of Shidehara's claim, see *JCC/FR*, pp. 74–75; Takayanagi, pp. 79, 86–88.

75. Kades interview *(GI)*, 2:72.

CHAPTER 14. *CENSORED DEMOCRACY: POLICING THE NEW TABOOS*

1. From an interview by Kyoko Hirano with Seymour Palestin, a former SCAP official, cited in Hirano's *Mr. Smith Goes to Tokyo: Japanese Cinema under the American Occupation, 1945–1952* (Washington, D.C.: Smithsonian Institution Press, 1992), pp. 72–73.

2. On the "hero worship" incident, see Robert M. Spaulding, "CCD Censorship of Japan's Daily Press," in *The Occupation of Japan: Arts and Culture*, ed. Thomas W. Burkman (Norfolk, Va.: Douglas MacArthur Foundation, 1988), pp. 6–7; William J. Coughlin, *Conquered Press: The MacArthur Era in Japanese Journalism* (Palo Alto: Pacific Books, 1952) pp. 51–52.

3. Coughlin, p. 147–49; the key document (SCAPIN 16) is reproduced here.

4. For a good case study of CI&E's "positive" regulation of the media, see Marlene Mayo, "The War of Words Continues: American Radio Guidance in Occupied Japan," in Burkman (1988), pp. 45–83.

5. By December 1945, SCAP's censors had reviewed 518 "classic or neoclassic" plays and banned the performance of 322 of them, the great majority in the Kabuki repertoire; see General Headquarters, Supreme Commander for the Allied Powers, *Theater and Motion Pictures (1945 through December 1951)*, monograph 16 in *History of the Nonmilitary Activities of the Occupation of Japan* (1952: National Archives microfilm), pp. 4–5. In the same series, see also monograph 15 *(Freedom of the Press)* and monograph 33 *(Radio Broadcasting)*.

6. For a detailed basic chronology in English of CCD censorship activity, see Furukawa Atsushi, "Nempyō—Senryōka no Shuppan, Engei, Hōsō Ken'etsu," *Tokyo Keidai Gakkaishi (The Journal of Tokyo Keizai University)* 118 (December 1980): 231–51. The most comprehensive overview of censored materials is Eizaburō Okuizumi, comp. and ed., *Microfilm Edition of Censored Periodicals, 1945–1949*, Part 1 of *User's Guide to the Gordon W. Prange Collection, East Asia Collection, McKeldin Library, University of Maryland at College Park* (Tokyo: Yushodo Booksellers, 1982). This is a massive bilingual guide to the huge CCD archives, which were transferred to the East Asia collection at the University of Maryland after the occupation; the Japanese title is *Senryōgun Ken'etsu Zasshi Mokuroku: Kaidai*. Unfortunately, due to the deteriorating condition of materials, the Prange Collection has been essentially closed to researchers since the early 1990s. Burkman (1988), which reproduces papers and discussion from a 1984 conference on arts and culture under the occupation, offers a range of perspectives on the significance of censorship in different fields. The major archives-based research in English has been published by Marlene Mayo. In addition to Mayo (1988), see her "Civil Censorship and Media Control in Early Occupied Japan," in *Americans As Proconsuls: United States Military Government in Germany and Japan, 1944–1952*, ed. Robert Wolfe (Carbondale: Southern Illinois University Press, 1984), pp. 263–320, 498–515; also Mayo, "Literary Reorientation in Occupied Japan: Incidents of Civil Censorship," in *Legacies*

and Ambiguities: Postwar Fiction and Culture in West Germany and Japan, ed. Ernestine Schlant and J. Thomas Rimer (Washington, D.C. and Baltimore: Woodrow Wilson Center Press and Johns Hopkins University Press, 1991), pp. 135–61.

Etō Jun has developed a sharp critique of occupation censorship, based on archival materials, in several publications. See "One Aspect of the Allied Occupation of Japan: The Censorship Operation and Postwar Japanese Literature," occasional paper of the Wilson Center, Smithsonian Institution (Washington, D.C., 1980); "The Civil Censorship in Occupied Japan," *Hikaku Bunka Zasshi* 1 (Program in Comparative Culture, Tokyo Institute of Technology, 1982), vol. 1, pp. 1–21; and "The Sealed Linguistic Space: The Occupation Censorship and Post-War Japan," *Hikaku Bunka Zasshi* 2 (1984), vol. 2, pp. 1–42. Many of Etō's influential essays on censorship, including Japanese versions of the preceding articles, have been collected in *Ochiba no Hakiyose: Haisen, Senryō, Ken'etsu to Bungaku* (Tokyo: Bungei Shunjūsha, 1981). Etō's emphasis on the harm caused to postsurrender literature by the censorship policy is challenged in Jay Rubin, "From Wholesomeness to Decadence: The Censorship of Literature under the Allied Occupation," *Journal of Japanese Studies* 11.1 (1985), pp. 71–103. See also Rubin in Burkman (1988), pp. 167–74, and a less sanguine commentary on the benign legacy of censorship by Yoshiko Yokochi Samuel in Burkman (1988), pp. 175–80. Many citations of censored literary passages are also given in Samuel's "Momotarō Condemned: Literary Censorship in Occupied Japan," an unpublished paper presented at the 1982 New England regional conference of the Association of Asian Studies.

The pioneer Japanese study of censorship of the print media, first published in 1969 and subsequently expanded, is Matsuura Sōzō, *Senryōka no Genron Danatsu,* rev. ed. (Tokyo: Gendai Jānarizumu Shuppankai, 1977). See also Haruhara Akihiko, "Senryō Ken'etsu no Ito to Jittai," published in two parts in *Shimbun Kenkyū,* issues 395 and 397 (June 1984 and August 1984), pp. 80–101 and 88–96 respectively; Haruhara, "The Impact of the Occupation on the Japanese Press," in Burkman (1988), pp. 21–31; Jim Hopewell, "Press Censorship: A Case Study," *Argus* 6.6 (University of Maryland, May 1971): 19–20, 58–64; Fukushima Jūrō, *Sengo Zasshi Hakkutsu,* (Tokyo: Yōsensha, 1985), pp. 122–53. The monthly case load quoted for PPB is given in Spaulding, p. 5. Mail and phone surveillance, which occupied a good portion of CCD's Japanese staff, is noted in U.S. Army, *Reports of General MacArthur: MacArthur in Japan: The Occupation, Military Phase,* vol. 1, Supplement (Washington, D.C.: U.S. Government Printing Office, 1966), pp. 238–39. By one estimate, a total of around eleven thousand magazine articles were subjected to censorship in one form or another; Mayo (1984), p. 512.

7. Coughlin, pp. 47–49 (on censorship of non-Japanese materials); Okuizumi (1982), pp. 33–39 (the basic memo); Rubin, p. 85 (the silent-departure quote).

8. Spaulding, pp. 7–8.

9. On the censorship of well-known writers, see Mayo (1991); Rubin (1985); Samuel (1982); Kimoto Itaru, *Zasshi de Yomu Sengo Shi* (Tokyo: Shinchō Sensho, 1985), pp. 19, 56, 116–18; Matsuura, pp. 21–25, 185. The Tanizaki story was "A Fujin no Tegami" (Mrs. A's Letter). On Tolstoy, see Hopewell, p. 63 (citing an article by David Conde, a former CI&E official, in *St. Louis Post Dispatch,* July 13, 1947). Hopewell's little-known article, one of the first to draw extensively on the CCD archives, contains many interesting quotations from the actual reports of the censors. Nakamura is quoted in Rubin (1985), pp. 75–76.

10. Matsuura, pp. 130–31. Since much of the translating on which GHQ relied was conducted by Nisei to whom Japanese was a second language, more than a little Japanese resentment concerning inaccurate or incomplete communication with the conquerors became directed against these second-generation Japanese-Americans.

These ethnic tensions comprise a sensitive and generally unexplored subtheme in the occupation. See, for example, Nihon Hōsō Kyōkai, ed., *Zoku: Hōsō Yawa* (Tokyo: Nihon Hōsō Kyōkai, 1970), p. 17; Akira Iwasaki, "The Occupied Screen," *Japan Quarterly* 25.3 (July–September 1978): 308, 315; Kyoko Hirano, "The Occupation and Japanese Cinema," in Burkman (1988), pp. 146, 148, and the response of Frank S. Baba to such criticisms in Burkman (1988), p. 164.

11. This is a basic thesis in Matsuura; see pp. 5–6, 17–18, 57–58, 323–24, 349, 354–55, 403.

12. Nihon Hōsō Kyōkai, pp. 13–18. The same critics also acknowledged positive aspects in the Americans' broadcasting agendas.

13. Haruhara (1988), p. 28.

14. Cf. Matsuura, pp. 5–7, 64–73; Asahi Jānaru, ed., *Besutoserā Monogatari* (Tokyo: Asahi Shimbunsha, 1967), vol. 1, p. 146. The use of *fuseji* (Xs, Os, and so on usually replacing deleted ideographs in a one-for-one manner) began around 1925 and was abandoned around 1937–1938—partly, it appears, because the thought police concluded it was inadvisable to suggest to Japan's external enemies that there might be criticism or disagreement with the war policy within the country.

15. The Press Code is reproduced in Coughlin, pp. 149–50, among many other places.

16. Reproduced in Furukawa Atsushi, "Zasshi '*Kaizō*' ni Miru Senryōka Ken'etsu no Jittai," *Tokyo Keidai Gakkaishi* 116–17 (Tokyo Keizai Daigaku, September 1980): 136–37. For an almost identical key log for November 25, 1946, with fuller original commentary, see Etō (1980), pp. 17–20; Etō (1982), pp. 5–6. The bracketed clarifications here are mine, reflecting both commentary in the November key log and actual censors' notations. For prohibited subjects in films (as stipulated in November 1945), see Hirano (1992), pp. 44–45; also 49, 52–58, 75, 78.

17. See Okuizumi, pp. 41–42, for a sample form.

18. On the censorship of atomic-bomb literature and scientific data, see Matsuura, pp. 167–212; Horiba Kiyoko, *Genbaku: Hyōgen to Ken'etsu—Nihonjin wa Dō Taiōshita ka* (Tokyo: Asahi Sensho, 1995); Committee for the Compilation of Materials on Damage Caused by the Atomic Bombs in Hiroshima and Nagasaki, comp., *Hiroshima and Nagasaki: The Physical, Medical, and Social Effects of the Atomic Bombings*, trans. Eisei Ishikawa and David Swain (New York: Basic Books, 1981), pp. 5, 503–13, 564, 585; Glenn D. Hook, "Roots of Nuclearism: Censorship and Reportage of Atomic Damage and Casualties in Hiroshima and Nagasaki," *Bulletin of Concerned Asian Scholars* 23 (January–March 1991): 13–25; Monica Braw, *The Atomic Bomb Suppressed: American Censorship in Occupied Japan* (Armonk, N.Y.: M. E. Sharpe, 1991), esp. ch. 8; Mayo (1991), pp. 150–52. Dr. James Yamazaki, an American researcher assigned to Nagasaki from 1949 to 1951 to study radiation effects, especially on children *in utero* when the bombs were dropped, discovered virtually on the eve of leaving Japan that pertinent earlier U.S. reports and studies had been withheld from him; this emerges at numerous places in his *Children of the Atomic Bombs: An American Physician's Memoir of Nagasaki, Hiroshima, and the Marshall Islands* (Durham, N.C.: Duke University Press, 1995). Regarding censored treatment of the atomic bombs in movies, see Hirano (1992), pp. 59–66. The publication of a considerable number of bomb-related writings in 1945–1946 is noted in Rekishigaku Kenkyūkai, ed., *Haisen to Senryō*, vol. 1 in *Nihon: Dōjidai Shi* (Tokyo: Aoki Shoten, 1990), pp. 237–38. For a detailed overview, see the thirty-article series on atomic-bomb literature during the occupation published in *Chūgoku Shimbun* between June 30 and August 12, 1986. Horiba, who witnessed the effects of the Hiroshima bomb, emphasizes the extent to which self-censorship compounded the restrictions imposed by outright censorship; see, for example, pp. 32–35, 54, 164–72.

See also *Asahi Shimbun*, May 16, 1994 (reporting the benign reminiscences of some former CCD censors).

19. A copy of the banned footage was hidden by Nichiei, the producing studio, which released a small portion of it at the time the occupation ended, but refused to make the entire footage available. See Iwasaki Akira, *Nihon Gendaishi Taikei: Eiga Shi* (Tokyo: Tōyō Keizai Shimpōsha, 1961), pp. 226–27; Iwasaki was coproducer of the Hiroshima-Nagasaki filming project. After being declassified by the U.S. government in 1966, excerpts from this confiscated footage became the source of a short documentary film in English entitled *Hiroshima-Nagasaki, August 1945*, released in 1970 under the supervision of Eric Barnouw. See Barnouw's "Iwasaki and the Occupied Screen," *Film History* 2 (1988): 337–57; Matsuura, pp. 192–95.

20. The collaborative paintings of the Marukis are reproduced in John W. Dower and John Junkerman, eds., *The Hiroshima Murals: The Art of Iri Maruki and Toshi Maruki* (New York: Kodansha International, 1985).

21. The first major publication of photographs was in August 6, 1952 issue of the magazine *Asahi Gurafu*. The most extensive series of photos of the immediate effects of the nuclear bombs was taken in Nagasaki by Yamahata Yosuke, a government propaganda photographer, who secretly retained over one hundred negatives. Published in Japan shortly after the occupation ended, these were not made available in an English-language publication until 1995; see Rupert Jenkins, ed., *Nagasaki Journey: The Photographs of Yosuke Yamahata, August 10, 1945* (San Francisco: Pomegranate Artbooks, 1995). See also John W. Dower, "The Bombed: Hiroshimas and Nagasakis in Japanese Memory," in *Hiroshima in History and Memory*, ed. Michael J. Hogan (Cambridge: Cambridge University Press, 1996), pp. 116–42.

22. Braw, pp. 94–100; Matsuura, p. 189. Upon encountering the fait accompli of the Nagasaki-Manila juxtaposition, Robert Spaulding was one of the few who noted how easy it would be for Japanese to conclude from this that "our action cancels out their guilt"; Mayo (1991), pp. 151–52.

23. Yoshida eventually revised his text several times. The censor's translation of the original version, quoted here, is reproduced in Etō (1982), pp. 9–10. For an excellent complete translation of the final, postoccupation version, see Yoshida Mitsuru, *Requiem for Battleship Yamato*, translated and introduced by Richard Minear (Seattle: University of Washington Press, 1985). Etō Jun has used the censorship of Yoshida's text as a major illustration of what he calls "the sealed linguistic space" of the occupation period; see Etō (1984). Another writer about the *Yamato* who attempted to express "the heavy shameful feeling that we survived while many of our brothers sacrificed their lives" also found such sentiments suppressed; Mayo (1991), p. 149.

24. Deleted from the August 1948 issue of *Kaizō;* see Furukawa (1980), pp. 176–77.

25. File on Yano Matakichi, *Haisen no Shimoto* (Whips of Defeat), Prange Collection censorship files, McKeldin Library, University of Maryland.

26. *Tsuboi Hanji Shishū* (Tokyo: Shinrisha, 1948); from a marked copy in the Prange Collection. The poem was published, with required changes, in July 1948.

27. Reproduced in Samuel (1988), p. 177. The censors also suppressed a powerful poem by Kurihara denouncing the bestiality of "any war"; see Samuel (1982), pp. 11–12.

28. Kimoto, pp. 52, 116, 118, 140; Hopewell, p. 20; Mayo (1984), p. 301. For the 1947 exchange, see Paul Vincent Miller, "Censorship in Japan," *Commonweal*, vol. 46 (April 25, 1947), pp 35–38, and Imboden's response in the June 13 issue (pp. 213–15). Miller also gave examples of the censorship of private correspondence, as

well as quotations from Japanese pointing out the hypocrisy of such practices by people who were preaching "freedom and equality."

29. Spaulding, p. 9; Matsuura, p. 196. As with other aspects of the porous censorship operation, there were exceptions to this practice. Jeeps, English signs, and occupation personnel can indeed be found in visual representations, but the relative paucity of such images is striking.

30. The cartoon is noted in Kimoto, p. 52; the poem is from the Prange Collection.

31. Coughlin, pp. 52–53.

32. Reproduced in Furukawa (1980), pp. 168–69. The author of the poem was Yamanoguchi Baku.

33. See Kimoto, p. 51 (on the magazine *Hope*); Matsuura, p. 21 (on Baba, whose article was ordered deleted from the August 1948 issue of the monthly *Chūō Kōron*).

34. See Rinjirō Sodei, "Satire under the Occupation: The Case of Political Cartoons," in Burkman (1988), pp. 93–106, and my accompanying commentary to this essay, pp. 107–23.

35. These three censored cartoons are described in Kimoto, pp. 137–39.

36. Four cartoons on the emperor are reproduced in Sodei, pp. 104–5.

37. Klaus H. Pringsheim, "Wartime Experience in Japan," unpublished paper presented at the "Violent Endings, New Beginnings" conference, National Archives and University of Maryland, October 1995.

38. Russel Brines, *MacArthur's Japan* (Philadelphia: Lippincott, 1948), pp. 246–49.

39. Sodei, pp. 96–97; the three censored cartoons from *Van* are reproduced on p. 103.

40. *Sazae-san* debuted in the newspaper *Yūkan Fukunichi* on April 22, 1946 and moved to the evening edition of the *Asahi Shimbun* in December 1949. *Anmitsu Hime* appeared in the girls' magazine *Shōjo;* see also the brief commentary in *Asahi Gurafu*, November 23, 1990. Tezuka Osamu's extraordinarily diversified oeuvre is reproduced in considerable detail, along with bilingual Japanese and English critical analysis, in the lavish exhibition catalog *Tezuka Osamu Shiten* (Tokyo: National Museum of Modern Art and Asahi Shimbun, 1990). The single most popular comic strip in early occupied Japan probably was the translated version of *Blondie,* by the American artist Chip Young, which made its first appearance in the June 2, 1946 issue of the weekly magazine *Shūkan Asahi* and later was featured in the morning edition of the daily *Asahi.* Along with Hollywood movies, *Blondie* had immense influence in shaping the popular image of "America"—in this instance, as a bountiful land of full refrigerators and marvelous household appliances, where wives splurged on fancy hats, salary-man husbands were more or less hapless but still could afford an automobile and private home, and even children and the family pets lived free of oppressive patriarchal authority. In the course of the occupation, six volumes of collected *Blondie* comic strips were published. This seductive window on American-style conspicuous consumption also served as an appealing primer in conversational English. While Japanese replaced English in the dialogue baloons, the original English was reproduced underneath. Students of the arcana of political symbolism might find significance in the fact that the *Asahi* dropped *Blondie* from its morning edition almost immediately after MacArthur was recalled in 1951, and replaced it with *Sazae-san,* which until then had appeared in its less authoritative evening edition.

41. Quoted in Sodei, p. 99. Shimizu's cartoons depicting Yoshida have been collected in Shimizu Kon, *Shimizu Kon Ga: Yoshida Shigeru—Fūshi Mangashū* (Tokyo: Hara Shobō, 1989).

42. Furukawa's valuable article "Zasshi *'Kaizō'* ni Miru Senryōka Ken'etsu no Jitai" reproduces censored portions of *Kaizō* between January 1946 and the end of formal censorship in late 1949.

43. Kimoto, p. 14; Matsuura, p. 103.

44. Hopewell, pp. 61, 63; Rubin, pp. 87–88 (quoting the Camp McCoy reminiscence, in a story by Ohinata Aoi which appeared in *Shinchō*, August 1946).

45. Hopewell, p. 59; see also Furukawa (1980), pp. 143, 151, 153, 177.

46. Kimoto, pp. 16–17; Furukawa (1980), p. 143; Hopewell, p. 58.

47. All quoted in Hopewell, pp. 60–63.

48. Hirano's excellent *Mr. Smith Goes to Tokyo* is the standard reference for film under the occupation; her balanced but generally positive appraisal of the liberation of cinema under the occupation is concisely presented in Hirano (1988), pp. 141–53. See also Iwasaki (1961), ch. 7; Iwasaki (1978), pp. 302–22; Imamura Shōhei et al., *Sengo Eiga no Tenkai*, vol. 5 in *Kōza: Nihon Eiga* (Tokyo: Iwanami, 1987); Satō Tadao, *Nihon no Eiga: Hadaka no Nihonjin* (Tokyo: Hyōronsha, 1978); Satō, *Kurosawa Akira no Sekai* (Tokyo: Asahi Bunko, 1986); Joseph L. Anderson and Donald Ritchie, *The Japanese Film: Art and Industry*, expanded ed. (Princeton, N.J.: Princeton University Press, 1984), ch. 9.

49. For a list of the Japanese films destroyed, see "Annex No. 1" in General Headquarters, *Theater and Motion Pictures*, op. cit.

50. Kurosawa's exceedingly brief recollections of the war years and early postsurrender period are found in his *Something Like an Autobiography*, trans. Audie Bock (New York: Knopf, 1982). For close analysis of all of his films, see Donald Richie's fine standard reference, *The Films of Akira Kurosawa*, rev. ed. (Berkeley: University of California Press, 1984).

51. This episode is well documented in Hirano (1992), ch. 3; Hirano's "The Japanese Tragedy: Film Censorship and the American Occupation," *Radical History Review* 41 (May 1988): 67–92; and Furukawa Atsushi, "Senryōka no Masu Media Tōsei: *Nihon no Higeki* no Jōei Kinshi o Megutte," *Tokyo Keidai Gakkaishi* 122 (Tokyo Keizai Daigaku, October 1981): 200–38. For a participant's perspective, see Iwasaki (1978), pp. 314–22. A disappointingly thin, posthumous "autobiography" by Kamei, consisting primarily of edited excerpts of materials by him, appears under the title *Tatakau Eiga: Dokyumentarisuto no Shōwa Shi* (Tokyo: Iwanami Shoten, 1989).

52. Hirano (1992), p. 135.

53. Furukawa (1981), pp. 236–37; Hirano (1992), p. 136; Iwasaki (1978), pp. 314–18; Kamei, *Tatakau Eiga*, p. 117.

54. Nichiei estimated its costs for producing *Tragedy* at 557,000 yen, a large amount for the time. See Etō (1982), p. 15; Hirano (1992), pp. 140, 143.

55. Imamura (1987), p. 101. *Between War and Peace* is the standard English rendering of the film title; the literal translation is simply, like the title of Tolstoy's opus, "War and Peace." For extended discussions of the censorship of *Between War and Peace*, see Hirano (1992), pp. 54–55, 172–75; Iwasaki (1961), pp. 228–31; and Etō (1982), pp. 12–16. Etō's essay reproduces several of the key CCD memos quoted here, but sometimes fails to note that certain deletions recommended in these memos were not actually imposed. Griffith's *Enoch Arden* was a pioneer undertaking, being two reels long whereas previous American films had been held to a single reel.

56. Yamamoto's reminiscence, in June 1952, is cited in Matsuura, p. 196. See also Hirano (1992), p. 54; Hirano (1988), p. 145. In *Late Spring (Banshun)* by Ozu Yasujirō, a line of dialogue complaining that Tokyo "is full of burned sites" was changed

to "It's so dusty all over." Despite the censorship the film sustained, one of the striking aspects of *Between War and Peace* is the extent to which graphic scenes of the U.S. air raids on Tokyo were allowed.

57. See, for example, Mayo (1984), pp. 308–10, 313–14; Coughlin, pp. 81–84; Matsuura, p. 13, 125–28.

58. See Spaulding, p. 8, on *Akahata;* Coughlin, p. 106; Mayo (1984), p. 315; Matsuura, p. 274. For an archival sample of Brown's cavalier treatment, see exchanges concerning censorship of the April 1947 issue of *Shisō no Kagaku* in the Prange Collection.

59. Mayo (1984), pp. 307, 318–19.

60. Matsuura, pp. 253–57; Hidetoshi Katō, *Japanese Research on Mass Communication: Selected Abstracts* (Honolulu: University Press of Hawaii, 1974), pp. 95–96, summarizing an article by Shinzaki Seiki in *Shimbun Kenkyū* 215 (June 1969). On censorship in occupied Okinawa, see Monna Naoki, *Okinawa Genron Tōsei Shi* (Tokyo: Gendai Jānarizumu Shuppankai, 1970). Because of the entirely separate U.S. administration of Okinawa, none of the examples or cumulative data in this present chapter (or in Japanese studies of censorship in "occupied Japan" in general) include the much harsher repressions that took place there; cf. Okuizumi, p. 529.

61. Haruhara (August 1984), pp. 94–95; General Headquarters, *Freedom of the Press,* pp. 27–28. In August 1949, a Korean editor in Osaka, Kim Won Kyun, was sentenced to five years at hard labor followed by deportation for accusing the U.S. military in Korea of killing members of the political opposition before holding a bogus general election. In September 1949, another Korean editor, Euan Muam, was sentenced to two years' imprisonment for a similar violation. The third and most famous case, also in September, involved a Japanese editor of a Tokyo-based news service, Morioka Shichirō, who was sentenced to two years at hard labor for reproducing Tass reports about British atrocities in Malaya, persecution of Communists in the United States, and the United States' turning Japan into a base for military aggression in the Far East.

62. "Magazines To Be Retained on Precensorship," November 26, 1947; this basic CCD document, describing all twenty-eight periodicals retained on prepublication censorship status, is reproduced in Okuizumi, pp. 512–25.

63. Matsuura, pp. 101–2, 104.

64. Spaulding, pp. 3–4; Mayo (1988), p. 61; Furukawa (1980), pp. 242–46; Furukawa (1988), pp. 154–55. See also Coughlin, chs. 7 and 8; Hirano, ch. 6. During the first two years of occupation, the twenty-six periodicals that were designated "ultra-leftist" in December 1947 had been subjected to a total of at least 1,280 deletions and 70 suppressed articles; compiled from CCD's "Magazines To Be Retained on Precensorship" in Okuizumi, pp. 512–25.

65. Matsuura, p. 18.

66. The essays by Hirano and Shinobu were deleted from Hirano Yoshitarō, Shinobu Seizaburō, Kimura Kenko, and Iizuka Kōji, *Nihon Minshū Kakumei no Kadai,* projected as volume 1 of *Tōyō Bunka Kōza,* sponsored by Tokyo Teikoku Daigaku Tōyō Bunka Kenkyūjo. For an example of unacceptable left-wing criticism of land reform, see the deletions demanded in June 1947 from a book by Sugō Toyoji titled *Nōson wa Dō Naru Ka: Nōson Kakumeihō no Kaiketsu* (Chūō Daigaku Shuppansha). Marked proofs of both these texts are in the Prange Collection.

67. Furukawa (1980), p. 250; Coughlin, p. 106.

68. Rodger Swearingen and Paul Langer, *Red Flag in Japan: International Communism in Action 1919–1951* (New York: Greenwood, 1968), pp. 209–12.

69. For a typical recollection of the pressure GHQ put on the Japanese media to support uncritically the American position on the Korean conflict, see Hasebe Tadashi, "Senryōka no Shimbun," in *"Shūkan Asahi" no Shōwa Shi* (Tokyo: Asahi Shimbunsha, 1989), vol. 2, pp. 43–44.

70. General Headquarters, *Freedom of the Press*, pp. 151–57; GHQ, *Theater and Motion Pictures*, p. 51; GHQ, *Radio Broadcasting*, p. 49; Matsuura, pp. 301, 315, 335; Mayo (1984), p. 317.

71. Matsuura, pp. 302, 309–11; Imamura (1987), pp. 21, 83–84.

72. See, for example, Matsuura, pp. 323–24.

73. Iwasaki (1978), pp. 304, 317–18; Satō (1978), p. 116; Matsuura, pp. 349, 354–55.

CHAPTER 15. *VICTOR'S JUSTICE, LOSER'S JUSTICE*

1. For Röling, see B. V. A. Röling, "The Tokyo Trial and the Quest for Peace," in *The Tokyo War Crimes Trial: An International Symposium*, ed. C. Hosoya, N. Andō, Y. Ōnuma, and R. Minear (New York: Kodansha International, 1986), p. 130; Röling, *The Tokyo Trial and Beyond: Reflections of a Peacemonger*, ed. Antonio Cassese (Cambridge: Polity Press, in association with Blackwell Publishers, 1993), esp. pp. 65–68, 86–91. Webb's statement appears in B. V. A. Röling and C. F. Ruter, eds., *The Tokyo Judgment: The International Military Tribunal for the Far East (I.M.T.F.E.), 29 April 1946–12 November 1948* (Amsterdam: APA–University Press, 1977), vol. 1, p. xi, and vol. 2, p. 1045; this source, hereafter cited as *TJ*, reproduces in two volumes all of the judgments in the Tokyo trial, including the majority judgment, two concurring but critical opinions, and three dissenting judgments. Keenan's opening presentation to the Tokyo tribunal on June 4, 1946, is reproduced in the multivolume basic transcript of the trial proceedings, *The Tokyo War Crimes Trial*, ed. R. John Pritchard and Sonia Magbanua Zaide (New York and London: Garland, 1981), vol. 1, pp. 383–475; see esp. 384, 392, 459. This source is cited below as *TWCT*. For samples of the positive Japanese response to identifying the trials with the cause of "civilization" itself, see the editorials in *Yomiuri Shimbun*, May 15 and June 5, 1946, and *Mainichi Shimbun*, June 6, 1946; also the statement by Hani Gorō, a Diet member and Marxist scholar, when the verdict of the tribunal was announced, in *Mainichi Shimbun*, November 13, 1948.

2. The wartime background to the trials is concisely summarized and annotated in Richard L. Lael, *The Yamashita Precedent: War Crimes and Command Responsibility* (Wilmington, Del.: Scholarly Resources, 1982); see esp. chapters 2 and 3. On early Allied thinking, including expressions of support for summary execution of top Nazi leaders, see also Telford Taylor, *The Anatomy of the Nuremberg Trials* (New York: Knopf, 1992), esp. pp. 28–40; Michael R. Marrus, ed., *The Nuremberg War Crimes Trial, 1945–1946: A Documentary History* (Boston: Bedford Books, 1997), pp. 18–38.

3. Stimson's wartime thinking, formulated primarily in the context of policy toward Nazi war criminals, is succinctly summarized in Lael, op. cit. Justice Jaranilla's citation of Stimson appears in *TJ* 1:514–15.

4. The Tokyo tribunal accepted the prosecution's calculation that 9,348 of a total 235,473 U.S. and U.K. prisoners died while in the hands of the Germans and Italians, whereas the corresponding figures for the Pacific theater were 35,756 deaths out of a total of 132,134 prisoners of the Japanese; *TJ* 1:385. There appear to be no estimates in kind for the fate of Asian prisoners of the Japanese, who suffered comparably and in greater numbers. The huge numbers of Soviet prisoners who died in German hands are rarely mentioned when the comparison between the Axis part-

ners is made, and the Holocaust was usually dealt with as an aberrantly separate issue.

5. See the valuable Winter 1989 special issue *(Bessatsu)* of the magazine *Rekishi Tokuhon,* which is entitled *Mikōkai Shashin ni Miru Tokyo Saiban* and devoted entirely to the issue of Japanese war crimes trials. The local trials, including a map of tribunal locations, are addressed on pp. 114–21.

6. The official Japanese figures, compiled by the Ministry of Justice, are reproduced in convenient table form (without attribution) in Kōdansha, ed., *Shōwa: Niman Nichi no Zenkiroku* (Tokyo: Kōdansha, 1989), vol. 7, pp. 220–21; this source is cited below as *SNNZ.* See also Awaya Kentarō, *Tokyo Saiban Ron* (Tokyo: Ōtsuki Shoten, 1989), p. 288; Awaya offers a concise summary of Japanese literature on this subject in ibid., pp. 282–97. Other tabulations giving comparable but not identical figures appear in *Bessatsu Rekishi Tokuhon* (1989). The major English-language overview of the local trials is Philip R. Piccigallo, *The Japanese on Trial: Allied War Crimes Operations in the East, 1945–1951* (Austin: University of Texas Press, 1979). A concise summary treatment can be found in Stephen Large's entry on "Far East War Crimes Trials" in I. C. B. Dear, ed., *The Oxford Companion to World War II* (New York: Oxford University Press, 1995), pp. 347–51. On the Yamashita trial, the classic critical account (by one of the general's defense attorneys) is A. Frank Reel, *The Case of General Yamashita* (Chicago: University of Chicago Press, 1949); Lael (1982) takes issue with Reel's argument. For grim case-study accounts of Japanese war crimes, see Yuki Tanaka, *Hidden Horrors: Japanese War Crimes in World War II* (Boulder: Westview, 1996); Gavan McCormack and Hank Nelson, eds., *The Burma-Thailand Railway: Memory and History* (St. Leonards, Australia: Allen & Unwin, 1993); Gavan Dawes, *Prisoners of the Japanese: POWs of World War II in the Pacific* (New York: William Morrow, 1994); and Robert La Forte, Ronald Marcello, and Richard Himmel, eds., *With Only the Will to Live: Accounts of Americans in Japanese Prison Camps, 1941–1945* (Wilmington, Del.: SR Books, 1994).

7. *SNNK* 7:221. Awaya places the combined number of Koreans and Formosans tried at 326, of whom 42 were executed; Awaya (1989), p. 291. Yuki Tanaka calls attention to a September 17, 1945 imperial army order instructing officers to blame Korean and Formosan prison guards for crimes against POWs; see his *Hidden Horrors,* p. 71. The issues raised by Koreans and Formosan Chinese being tried for war crimes commited in the service of the Japanese is addressed in Utsumi Aiko, *Chōsenjin BC-kyū Senpan no Kiroku* (Tokyo: Keiso Shobō, 1982).

8. The 5,700 accused "B/C" war criminals were brought to trial in a total of 2,244 tribunals. The Australian trial is noted in Large, p. 350; the U.S. trial in U.S. Department of State, *Foreign Relations of the United States, 1948,* vol. 6, p. 873; this series is cited below as *FRUS.* The estimate of trials lasting an average of two days appears in *SNNZ* 7:221. Many of the "B/C" war criminals, including those sentenced to life terms, were released from prison in the 1950s.

9. The 535-page English transcript of the Khabarovsk trial was published under the title *Materials on the Trial of Former Servicemen of the Japanese Army Charged with Manufacturing and Employing Bacteriological Weapons* (Moscow: Foreign Language Publishing House, 1950). Awaya Kentarō, drawing on Japanese Ministry of Justice materials, gives the estimate of three thousand Japanese executed for war crimes in the Soviet Union in his postscript to the Japanese translation of *Sud v Tokio,* a 1978 Soviet study of the Tokyo war crimes trial; see L. N. Smirnov and E. B. Zaitsev, *Tokyo Saiban,* trans. T. Kawakami and A. Naono (Tokyo: Ōtsuki Shoten, 1980), p. 517.

10. Awaya (1989), p. 293.

11. *Mainichi Shimbun,* November 5, 1948.

12. For cumulative data, see *TJ* 1:xii, 22; also Solis Horowitz, "The Tokyo Trial," *International Conciliation*, no. 465, November 1950, p. 542. Horowitz was a member of the prosecution staff, and his long article (pp. 473–584) remains one of the few detailed overviews of the Tokyo tribunal in English. The size of the prosecution staff is noted in Arnold C. Brackman, *The Other Nuremberg: The Untold Story of the Tokyo War Crimes Trials* (New York: Morrow, 1987), p. 56; Brackman covered the prosecution's (but not defense's) presentations at the trial as a journalist. Norman's observation, made in 1948, appears in the Japanese edition of his collected writings; see E. H. Norman, *Herbert Norman Zenshū*, trans. Ōkubo Genji (Tokyo: Iwanami Shoten, 1977), vol. 2, p. 391.

13. Twenty-eight Japanese originally were indicted for "Class A" war crimes, of whom two died during the course of the trial and one was excused on grounds of mental incompetence. See the chart of verdicts and sentences in Horowitz, p. 584; this is reproduced, with useful added data on deaths and parole dates, in Richard Minear's entry on "War Crimes Trials," *Kodansha Encyclopedia of Japan* (Tokyo: Kōdansha, 1983), 8:223–25. The granting of clemency in 1958 is noted in Minear, *Victors' Justice: The Tokyo War Crimes Trial* (Princeton, N.J.: Princeton University Press, 1971), p. 175.

14. Röling (1993), pp. 54, 85–86, 90. See also Röling's introduction to *TJ* 1:xiii–xvii.

15. "Oral Reminiscences of Brigadier General Elliott R. Thorpe," May 29, 1977, RG 49, box 6, MacArthur Memorial, Norfolk, Va., pp. 10–12. Wm. C. Chase, *Front Line General: The Commands of Maj. Gen. Wm. C. Chase* (Houston: Pacesetter Press, 1975), p. 144. Chase went on to observe that "We used to say in Tokyo that the U.S. had better not lose the next war, or our generals and admirals would all be shot at sunrise without a hearing of any sort."

16. *FRUS 1948*, 6:717–19, 794. Kennan's broadside did not derive from any sympathy with the Japanese side, as was the case with professional soldiers such as Willoughby, Thorpe, and Chase. Rather, he was contemptuous of the ability of the Japanese to comprehend the concepts of justice and fairness underlying the trials. Kennan belonged to the camp that believed summary punishment would have been more appropriate. "It would have been much better received and understood," he stated in his top-secret report, "if we had shot these people out of hand at the time of surrender."

17. See, for example, Horowitz, pp. 574–75.

18. Judge Pal published his dissenting opinion privately in India in 1953. The full corpus of majority, concurring, and dissenting judgments was first published privately in 1977; see *TJ*. The full proceedings of the trial were made available in a twenty-two volume commercial library edition in 1981; see *TWCT*.

19. Declassified documents concerning the release of unindicted "Class A" suspects received media attention in Japan in 1987; see, for example, *Asahi Shimbun*, December 27; *Japan Times*, December 28. Released "Class A" suspects were not free to return immediately to public life, but rather fell under various purge designations. However, Kodama, whose wartime activities had placed him in possession of vast stores of precious commodities, quickly emerged as a fixer in deals involving the C.I.A.; see Howard Schonberger, *Jyapanizu Konekushyon: Kaiun-ō K. Sugahara Den* (Tokyo: Bungei Shunjūsha, 1995), pp. 214–28, on Kodama's role in supplying hoarded tungsten to the United States at the time of the Korean War. See also Awaya's comments in Hosoya, pp. 82–84.

20. MacArthur told this to Justice Röling; see Röling (1993), p. 80, and Röling in Hosoya, p. 128.

21. *FRUS 1945*, 6:591–92, 962–63. The protracted deliberations on this issue are conveyed in ibid., 6:898–989.

22. *FRUS 1945*, 6:988–89. Both MacArthur's January 19 proclamation and the Tokyo charter (in its final form, officially dated April 26, 1946) are reproduced in Minear (1971), pp. 183–92.

23. *TJ* 1:19–22, 439–42. For a concise technical comparison of similarities and dissimilarities between the two trials, see *The Charter and Judgment of the Nurnberg Tribunal: History and Analysis* (Lake Success, N.Y.: International Law Commission, General Assembly, United Nations, 1949), pp. 81–86.

24. *TJ* 1:31–32; 439–42; ibid. 2:527–30. Kennan's opening address to the tribunal made frequent mention of Japan's conspiracy "to dominate the world"; see *TWCT* 1:386, 392, 435, 449.

25. This point is often overlooked, perhaps because the Tokyo charter, like the Nuremberg charter, dwelled equally on crimes against humanity and crimes against peace. See, however, *The Charter and Judgment of the Nurnberg Trial*, p. 82; Röling (1993), pp. 55–58; Horowitz, pp. 498–501, 551–52. In the original fifty-five-count indictment, counts 37 to 52 were categorized as "Murder," and counts 53 to 55 as "Conventional War Crimes and Crimes Against Humanity."

26. The fundamental issue of "command responsibility" actually was first introduced in the trial of General Yamashita; see Lael (1982).

27. Horowitz, p. 538. The Japanese observation appears in the yearbook *Mainichi Nenkan 1949*, p. 101.

28. *TJ* 1:477 (for Webb) and 2:1036 (for Pal). See also Röling (1993), pp. 46–47.

29. Hirota's death sentence appears to have been prompted primarily by the conclusion that, as foreign minister in 1937, he had been "derelict in his duty in not insisting before the Cabinet that immediate action be taken to put an end to the atrocities" in Nanking; *TJ* 1:446–48. Justice Röling is the source of the conclusion that Hirota was condemned to death by a 6 to 5 vote, and denounced this as "a scandalous way of arriving at the penalty of hanging"; Röling (1993), p. 64. Röling himself acquited Hirota.

30. See, for example, the November 13, 1948 press accounts in the *Asahi, Nihon Keizai,* and *Mainichi* newspapers; also the *Mainichi* of November 14. In one of the best-known Japanese accounts of the trial, Kojima Noboru notes that the four critical opinions caused confusion among the Japanese public; see his two-volume *Tokyo Saiban* (Tokyo: Chūkō Bunko, Chūō Kōronsha, 1982), vol. 2, p. 202. Justice Jaranilla's supplementary statement, supporting the tribunal against its critics and recommending harsher sentences for some defendants, did not receive as much attention.

31. *TJ* 1:477–79.

32. *TJ* 1:494–96.

33. *FRUS 1948*, 6:896; Tsurumi Shunsuke and Nakagawa Roppei, eds., *Tennō Hyakuwa* (Tokyo: Chikuma Shoten, 1989), vol. 2, pp. 671–72. This latter source is cited below as *Tennō Hyakuwa*.

34. MacArthur's acceptance without change of the majority judgment, couched in almost scriptural rhetoric, is reproduced in *FRUS 1948*, 6:908. On November 23, the day before he released this text, he met with representations of the eleven-nation Far Eastern Commission, where spokesmen for five nations (Australia, Canada, France, India, and the Netherlands) indicated in one way or another that they would welcome some commutation of sentences. On November 29, an appeal from Pope

Pius XII for commutation of the death sentences was submitted to the U.S. Secretary of State; *FRUS 1948*, 6:897–98. Justice Röling personally gave a copy of his dissent to one of MacArthur's aides but found no reason to believe that MacArthur "paid any attention to it"; Röling (1993), p. 82.

35. See, for example, the coverage of the three events of November 24 in *Nihon Keizai Shimbun*, November 25, 1948.

36. Quoted in Minear (1971), p. 172.

37. Röling (1993), pp. 20, 31.

38. *Time*, May 20, 1946, p. 24; *Bessatsu Rekishi Tokuhon*, pp. 10, 46.

39. *TJ* 1:22; Horowitz, pp. 502, 534.

40. *FRUS 1946*, 8:429; Röling (1993), pp. 36–38, 51–52, 58; *TJ* 1:xi–xii; Horowitz, p. 565. This was the same situation that arose in the revision of the constitution demanded by GHQ, where Japanese trained in European law were confronted with a text based on Anglo-American principles.

41. Lael, pp. 48–50.

42. See Pal's useful summary of both the prosecution and the defense positions on the conspiracy charge in *TJ* 2:657–66. A major portion of his dissenting opinion (2:657–950) was devoted to critical analysis of all aspects of the "over-all conspiracy" charge as presented by the prosecution. Pal did not deny the occurance of "sinister" incidents and "ill-gotten gains" on the part of the Japanese (for example, 2:717, 728), nor did he deny that for much of the period in question the country was engaged in mobilizing for war. Rather, he argued that the question before the tribunal was not whether such actions were "justifiable," but rather whether they were explicable, as charged in the indictment, as part of an overall conspiracy to engage in aggressive war (for example, 2:734, 750, 824–26, 873–80, 893, 938–40). Where the particular events leading to Pearl Harbor were concerned, Pal observed that although the Japanese position "might have been unreasonable, aggressive, and audacious," the breakdown of negotiations with the United States and the attack itself constituted neither treachery nor conspiracy. On the contrary, Japan "was driven by the circumstances that gradually developed to the fatal steps taken by her" (2:893–935, esp. pp. 903, 935).

For concise summaries of the victor's justice thesis, including repudiation of the simplistic conspiracy charge, see Minear (1983) and Large (1995). The best-known extended development of this argument is Minear's *Victors' Justice*, which recapitulates many of the arguments in Justice Pal's dissent. The most detailed and nuanced scholarly treatments of the trials are Ōnuma Yasuaki, *Sensō Sekinin-ron Josetsu* (Tokyo: Tokyo Daigaku, 1975) and numerous writings by Awaya Kentarō, especially his *Tokyo Saiban Ron* and his serialized "Tokyo Saiban e no Michi," which appeared in many installments in the magazine *Asahi Jānaru* in 1984 and 1985. See also the contributions of Ōnuma and Awaya in Hosoya, op. cit. Brackman's *The Other Nuremberg* offers a generally uncritical recapitulation of the prosecution argument that conveys some of the color and sentiments of the time. The relative paucity of writings about the Tokyo tribunal in English, in contrast to Nuremberg, is but one more indication of the trial's failure to live up to early expectations.

43. *TJ* 1:475. Many of the basic issues associated with the charge of victor's justice in the Tokyo trial, including the legal validity of the conspiracy charge, have been raised in connection with the Nuremberg trial as well. See, for example, Michael Biddiss's entry on "Nuremberg Trials" in Dear, pp. 824–28.

44. *TJ* 2:1,045. See also Hosoya, pp. 41, 43, 47.

45. *TWCT* 1:459.

46. The legal arguments concerning precedents for the charge of crimes against peace, and the stipulations of international law regarding "aggressive war," are recapitulated at considerable length in the majority judgment (*TJ* 1:35–52), as well as in the separate opinions of both Justice Pal (*TJ* 2:551–627) and Justice Röling (*TJ* 2:1048–61). For Keenan on "murder," see *TWCT* 1:473–74.

47. The defense challenge and tribunal rejection of this appears in *TJ* 1:27–28. In addition to the points quoted here, the defense also argued that the Allied Powers had "no authority to include in the Charter of the Tribunal and to designate as justiciable 'Crimes against Peace' "; that the terms of surrender, following the Potsdam Declaration, had stipulated that "Conventional War Crimes as recognized by international law at the date of the Declaration (26 July, 1945) would be the only crimes prosecuted"; that killings in belligerent operations, except as they violated the rules and customs of war, could not be construed as "murder" as charged in the indictment; and that some of the accused, as prisoners of war, should have been tried in courts martial as provided by the Geneva Convention of 1929 and not by the tribunal.

The prosecution argument that the Kellogg-Briand Pact outlawed "wars of aggression" was a tenuous one and has been challenged in many sources. It often is pointed out that as of 1944 the Allied Powers themselves had concluded, in internal deliberations, that there existed no agreed-on definition of "aggressive war," that this was in any case not a crime under existing international law, and that there also was no precedent for trying individuals for acts of state. The legal scholar Knut Ipsen argues that "crimes against peace" and the related charge of individual responsibility were indeed "*ex post facto* legislation" and thus "incompatible with the maxim *nullum crimen sine lege,* which the Tokyo tribunal itself recognized expressly as a 'general principle of justice.' " A better case can be made for the constitutionality of "crimes against humanity," he argues. See Ipsen's contribution in Hosoya, pp. 37–45.

48. For Keenan's statement, see *TWCT* 1:463. The initial U.S. lists of primary war crimes suspects did include secret society heads as well as several leading industrialists—notably Ayukawa Yoshisuke, Nakajima Chikuhei, and Fujiwara Ginjirō—who were arrested but not indicted; see, for example, *FRUS 1945,* 6:968, 978. Among the many interesting aspects of the "Class A" trials is the failure of the Soviet Union to insist strongly on indicting both the emperor and at least one "representative" zaibatsu leader. Ever since the 1920s, Soviet policy regarding Japan—clearly reflected in the pronunciamentos of the Japan Communist Party—had identified the key to Japanese repression at home and aggression abroad as residing in the twin evils of the emperor system and zaibatsu-led monopoly capitalism. When it came to exercising influence at the Tokyo war crimes trial, however, the U.S.S.R. quickly and flexibly disregarded these presumably iron-clad ideological contentions and demanded instead the indictment of two as yet unindicted individuals, former foreign minister Shigemitsu Mamoru (an astonishing selection) and former Kwantung Army general Umezu Yoshijirō. It is difficult to see in this exercise anything more than a little pointless muscle flexing. According to Russian scholars, the U.S.S.R. originally did propose indicting the three zaibatsu leaders who had been arrested (Ayukawa, Nakajima, and Fujiwara), but was told by Keenan that this was out of the question. By this date, the Soviet interpretation holds, the United States and its capitalist allies already were openly regretting the inclusion of industrialists in the Nuremberg trial; see Smirnov and Zaitsev, pp. 31–32, 122. The Soviet Union's concession on this matter was in fact consistent with its initial conciliatory policy regarding U.S. domination of the occupation in general. Essentially, Stalin appears to have hoped he could use acquiescence to U.S. control of Japan (and a low posture in China as well) as a quid pro quo for gaining American acquiescence to the Soviet "security

sphere" in Eastern Europe. See also Horowitz, pp. 495–97, on the criteria for determining whom to indict.

49. The pioneer work exposing the cover-up of Unit 731 activities was done by John W. Powell. See his "Japan's Germ Warfare: The U.S. Cover-up of a War Crime," *Bulletin of Concerned Asian Scholars* 12.2 (1980): 2–17, and "Japan's Biological Weapons, 1930–1945: A Hidden Chapter in History," *Bulletin of the Atomic Scientists* 37.8 (October 1981): 43–53. Awaya notes that the prosecution also had information about the chemical warfare activities of Unit 1644 in China; see his contribution in Hosoya, pp. 85–86, 116, and his essay in *Asahi Jānaru*, March 1, 1985 (installment 20), pp. 39–40.

50. Brackman, pp. 63–71 (where the "Bottoms up!" anecdote appears); Röling (1993), pp. 28–31; Minear (1971), pp. 75–86.

51. It was at Pal's insistence that the Tokyo tribunal agreed to accept dissenting opinions, rather than simply a single judgment as originally agreed on; see Röling (1993), pp. 28–29.

52. Röling (1993), pp. 62–63. See also *TJ* 1:494–96 (Bernard).

53. Lael, p. 48.

54. The tribunal was aware of the widespread destruction of documents by the Japanese in the weeks following capitulation; see *TJ* 1:437.

55. *TJ* 2:654–55.

56. See, for example, Röling (1993), pp. 51–52.

57. Brackman, p. 112.

58. Röling (1993), p. 53; *FRUS 1946*, 8:445; Kojima, pp. 270–77. Kojima, who notes the generally shorter versions of defendants' testimony that emerged through the court's interpreters, offers a remarkable quotation by Justice Webb to the effect that "If Japanese defense lawyers' English had been better, or the interpreters had been more capable, the judgment of the trial might have been different"; Kojima, 1:272. Kojima's book is not annotated, but one of his sources was interviews with Webb.

59. Kojima devotes a chapter to the topic of exonerating the emperor (2:91–134).

60. In the recollections he secretly dictated in March and April 1946, the emperor was in fact harsh and uncharitable concerning the great majority of those who had served him in military and political office—quite contrary to the carefully promoted image of a generous sovereign deeply concerned about the fate of his loyal servants. The two defendants who most noticeably escaped his wrath were Kido and—most interestingly—Tōjō, the number one war criminal in Allied eyes. See, for example, Herbert Bix, "The Shōwa Emperor's 'Monologue' and the Problem of War Responsibility," *Journal of Japanese Studies* 18.2 (summer 1992), pp. 299, 303, 349, 351–52.

61. See Shigemitsu's account of these matters in *Tennō Hyakuwa*, 2:123–30.

62. Takahashi and Suzuki, *Tennōke no Misshitachi—Senryō to Kōshitsu*, pp. 45–50; this is also excerpted in *Tennō Hyakuwa* 2:122. See also Kojima, 2:122–34. In the Japanese literature on the trial, this incident is known as the "Keenan-Kido move" *(Keenan-Kido kōsaku)*. The second major intermediary used by Keenan to reach Tōjō was former general Tanaka Ryūkichi, who recounts this episode in "Kakute Tennō wa Muzai ni Natta," *Bungei Shunjū*, August 1965; reprinted in Bungei Shunjūsha, ed., *"Bungei Shunjū" ni Miru Shōwa Shi* (Tokyo: Bungei Shunjūsha, 1988), vol. 2, pp. 84–91. In a letter to the *Far Eastern Economic Review* (July 6, 1989), Aristedes George Lazarus, who served as defense attorney for former general Hata Shunroku, claimed that midway through the trial he was asked by an un-

named, high-ranking representative of President Truman to arrange, through Hata, that all the defendants be coached to "go out of their way during their testimony to include the fact that Hirohito was only a benign presence when military actions or programmes were discussed at meetings that, by protocol, he had to attend." Lazarus claims he complied with this request, and "with a little subterfuge," contacted Tōjō. The letter as a whole contains numerous errors, perhaps because of Lazarus's advanced age when he wrote it, but this particular claim is at least plausible given the intense overall campaign to use the Tokyo trial to establish, by default, the emperor's innocence.

63. This was true in the Nuremberg trial also; cf. Röling (1993), pp. 54–55, 59–60; Biddiss in Dear, pp. 826–27.

64. The tribunal explicitly rejected such defense "evidence" as irrelevent on April 29, 1947; *TJ* 2:752.

65. Justice Pal's sweeping and detailed repudiation of the majority judgment at the Tokyo trial is most easily and usually attributed to his anticolonial consciousness as an Asian nationalist. This is not an unfair characterization. At the same time, the intensity and enduring interest of Pal's dissent rest on two other factors. He was the tribunal's most passionate defender of a strict interpretation of international law, its most eloquent critic of "judicial legislation." In this regard, the capsule summary of the tribunal's judgments prepared by the State Department representative in Tokyo was interesting. Justice Pal's opinion, he observed, "appears to adhere to the positivist theory of international law, which holds that national sovereignty is the basis of the international community and that consent to qualification of national sovereignty must not be presumed"; *FRUS 1948*, 6:907. The link between the Indian justice's nationalism and legal "positivism" in this regard has, to my knowledge, never been closely explored.

    Simultaneously, despite his intense anticolonialism, Justice Pal was also strongly anticommunist. In this regard, he differed from many of his anticolonial Asian compatriots, who found Marxism or communism the sharpest and most attractive vehicle through which to fight for independence. Pal's dissenting opinion returned time and again to criticism of the Tokyo tribunal's refusal to take seriously the defendants' concern with the rise of communist influence in China and Manchuria. He usually took care to suggest, however, that the issue was not so much the "correctness" of anticommunist views, but rather their worldwide pervasiveness. "When the whole world is reverberating with expressions of terror of communistic development," as he put it, "and when from every quarter we are having reports of extensive and immediate preparations, economic and military, against the apprehended menace of communistic spread, it is, I believe needless to remind that, justifiable or not, Japan's fear of this supposed menace and its consequent preparations and actions are at least explicable without the aid of the theory of any enormous conspiracy as alleged in Counts 1 to 5"; *TJ* 2:685. See also *TJ* 2:617–18, 642, 645–48, 685–86, 746, 752–55, 836, 864–65. Ienaga Saburō calls attention to Pal's virulent anticommunism in Hosoya, pp. 169–70.

66. On pressure to expand the tribunal to include India and the Philippines, see *FRUS 1946*, 8:383, 390, 393–94, 399–400, 418–20. The issue of "white men's justice" also applies to the localized trials of "B/C" war criminals, which with the exception of China and the Philippines were conducted by the European and American powers and focused primarily on crimes involving Caucasian prisoners. This point is often emphasized in Japanese writings; see, for example, Awaya (1989), p. 288.

67. *TWCT* 1:385.

68. *TJ* 2:680, 727.

69. *TJ* 2:728–29, 741–42.

70. *TJ* 2:759–64.

71. Japanese sources indicate that SCAP did not permit Pal's dissent to be translated; see *Bessatsu Rekishi Tokuhon*, op. cit., p. 48.

72. *TJ* 2:982 (Pal); *TJ* 1:510–11 (Jaranilla). Justice Pal felt so strongly about the criminality of the use of the atomic bombs that when he published his dissenting opinion privately in India in 1953, he included as an appendix reproductions of twenty-five photographs of victims and physical destruction in Hiroshima and Nagasaki that had appeared for the first time in Japan in the August 6, 1952, issue of the magazine *Asahi Gurafu* (identified in Pal's book as "The Asahi Picture News"). See *International Military Tribunal for the Far East: Dissentient Judgment of Justice R. B. Pal* (Calcutta: Sanyal, 1953).

73. Röling (1993), p. 84.

74. Justice Pal's dissenting judgment was translated and edited by Tanaka Masaaki under the title *Zenyaku: Nihon Muzai-ron* (Tokyo: Nihon Shobō, 1952); the title translates as "Complete Translation: On Japan Being Not Guilty." Tanaka also published an edited volume that same year entitled *Nihon Muzai Ron—Shinri no Sabaki* [On Japan Being Not Guilty—The Verdict of Truth] (Tokyo: Taiheiyō Shuppan, 1952). In the mid-1980s, he was still bringing to public forums the argument that "the entire trial was nothing but a farce"; Hosoya, pp. 153–54.

The inability of all conservative postwar governments to offer a clear and unequivocal apology for Japanese war crimes committed in World War II is rooted in this deep sense of double standards dating back to the Tokyo trial—more specifically, to the imputation that Japanese atrocities, as well as the policies adopted by the leaders of imperial Japan, were unique and peculiarly criminal. The failure of the victors to apply their path-breaking formulations to themselves in subsequent decades naturally reinforced such sentiments—not only where Soviet imperialism and European colonialism were concerned, but also during the American war in Indochina. The famous "Ienaga case" challenging Ministry of Education censorship of Japanese textbooks that dragged through the Japanese courts from the 1960s to the early 1990s had deep roots in this debate over the "Tokyo tribunal view of history." So, too, did the controversy that erupted in Japan in 1995, in conjunction with the fiftieth anniversary of the end of World War II, concerning whether the government would take this opportunity to "apologize" for its war responsibility. For annotated key documents on the latter, see John W. Dower, "Japan Addresses Its War Responsibility," *ii: The Journal of the International Institute* (newsletter of the International Institute, University of Michigan), 3.1 (Fall 1995): 8–11.

75. Kainō Michitaka, "Kyokutō Saiban—sono go," *Shisō* 348 (June 1953), pp. 23–31.

76. Inclusion of a Japanese justice, Röling observed in later years, "could have prevented many errors" by clarifying points and correcting biases in discussions in chamber; Röling (1993), p. 87. Röling also believed that justice would have been better served had judges from neutral countries been appointed, without suggesting which countries might have provided such judges.

77. See, for example, *Asahi Shimbun*, September 17, 18, 22, 1945.

78. *Asahi Shimbun*, October 19 and 27, 1945; *Tensei Jingo*, 1:40–41 (December 6, 1945). By early 1946, there was speculation among Japanese that between five hundred and two thousand top leaders would be arrested. See, for example, Yamakawa Masao, *Sensō Hanzai Ron* (Tokyo: Tokyo Shimpōsha, February 1946), pp. 11–12; this booklet is typical of the many publications wrestling, not unsympathetically, with the "brand new" *(ma-atarashii)* interpretation of war crimes the victors were introducing.

79. *FRUS 1945*, 6:952–53, 984–85. At the same time, Atcheson warned that this mood could change quickly.

80. See the quotations and citations in Yoshida Yutaka, "Senryōki ni okeru Sensō Sekinin Ron," *Hitotsubashi Ronsō* 105.2 (February 1991), pp. 127, 132–33. Hosokawa's view is cited by Ienaga Saburō in Hosoya, pp. 166–67.

81. This is well known; see, for example, Kido's diary entry for August 9 in *Kido Kōichi Nikki* (Tokyo: Tokyo Daigaku Shuppankai, 1966), 2:1223.

82. *Kido Kōichi Nikki*, 2:1234 (entry for September 12); Kojima, 1:46–47; Awaya (1989), pp. 67, 152–54, 189. The headline is from *Asahi Shimbun*, September 21, 1945.

83. This fascinating document was discovered by Professor Awaya Kentarō among the Makino Shinken Papers in the National Diet Library, and is reproduced in his *Tokyo Saiban Ron*, pp. 160–62; the translation here is from that work. A full English translation is appended to Awaya's contribution in Hosoya, pp. 87–88. The authorship and date of origin of the draft decree are unclear, but Awaya concludes from internal evidence that it probably was prepared under the Shidehara government, which was in office from October 1945 to April 1946.

84. See Awaya, "Tokyo Saiban e no Michi," *Asahi Jānaru*, November 23, 1984 (installment 7), p. 40.

85. The Konoe Memorial is translated and analyzed in John W. Dower, *Empire and Aftermath: Yoshida Shigeru and the Japanese Experience, 1878–1954* (Cambridge, Mass.: Council on East Asian Studies, Harvard University, 1979), ch. 8. After appearing in magazines, Konoe's postsurrender reports were published as two slight books in 1946: *Ushinawareshi Seiji—Konoe Fuminaro-kō Shuki* (Asahi Shimbunsha) and *Heiwa e no Doryoku—Konoe Fumimaro Shuki* (Nihon Denpō Tsūshinsha). Konoe's papers were immediately turned over the the International Prosecution Staff on his suicide; see Bix (1992), pp. 296, 313, and Awaya, *Asahi Jānaru*, December 7, 1984 (installment 9), pp. 37–40.

86. On Iwabuchi, see Awaya, *Asahi Jānaru*, December 14, 1984 (installment 10), pp. 32–33; also Awaya (1989), pp. 312–13. Yoshida's role is noted in Bix (1992), p. 322.

87. Awaya, *Asahi Jānaru*, December 14, 1984 (installment 10), p. 34.

88. Awaya, *Asahi Jānaru*, March 22, 1985 (installment 23), pp. 44, 46; Awaya (1989), p. 100. Mazaki and one other person (former general and prime minister Abe Nobuyuki) were dropped from the original list of those to be indicted to accommodate the individuals (Shigemitsu and Umezu) whom the Soviets insisted be brought to trial; see also Smirnov and Zaitsev, p. 122.

89. Awaya (1989), pp. 93–95; Awaya, *Asahi Jānaru*, February 15, 1985 (installment 8), pp. 41–42; Bix (1992), pp. 357–58.

90. Awaya, *Asahi Jānaru*, February 22 and March 1, 1985 (installments 19 and 20); Awaya (1989), pp. 87–88; Tanaka, "Kakute Tennō wa Muzai ni Natta," p. 85. In Japanese commentaries, Tanaka often emerges as cunning, Machiavellian, and possibly even demented.

91. Kido, 2:1252–57 (entries for November 24, December 10 and 15).

92. Awaya (1989), pp. 202–8, esp. 202–3. See also Kojima, 1:100–2. Horowitz observed, from his insider position, that Kido's diary "became the working bible of the prosecution and the main key to all further investigation"; Horowitz, p. 494.

93. Awaya, who is very careful on these matters, records hearing this from an unnamed qualified Japanese; "Tokyo Saiban to Tennō," in Nihon Gendaishi Kenkyūkai, ed., *Shōchō Tennōsei to wa Nanika* (Tokyo: Ōtsuki Shoten, 1988), p. 35; he is more circumspect in *Tokyo Saiban Ron*, p. 205.

94. See Awaya's treatments of this in "Tokyo Saiban to Tennō," p. 36; *Tokyo Saiban Ron*, pp. 207–8; *Ashai Jānaru*, January 18, 1985 (installment 14), p. 30, and January 25, 1985 (installment 15), p. 45. It was general IPS policy to refrain from interrogating sources about the emperor. H. D. Sackett, the major interrogator of Kido, apparently asked such questions occasionally for his "personal" edification. The lengthy interrogations of Kido have been translated into Japanese by Awaya and others under the title *Tokyo Saiban Shiryō—Kido Kōichi Jimmon Chōsho* (Tokyo: Ōtsuki Shoten, 1987). For a lively and often irreverent Japanese roundtable response to the Kido diary, see "Kido Nikki o Megutte," *Hyōron*, February 1948, pp. 48–64.

95. Awaya (1989), pp. 91, 207; Awaya, *Asahi Jānaru*, February 1, 1985 (installment 16), p. 41; cf. also installments 14 and 15 in ibid., January 18 and 25, 1985.

CHAPTER 16. *WHAT DO YOU TELL THE DEAD WHEN YOU LOSE?*

1. *Asahi Shimbun*, August 16, 1945. See also ibid., August 15 and 17 (for Takamura Kōtarō's poem titled "The Wailing of the Hundred Million").

2. *Asahi Shimbun*, August 21, 1945. The title "Apology to Departed Heroes" *(Eirei ni Wabiru)* was used for this and three later articles: a typical recollection of the suicide pilots by an *Asahi* reporter (August 22), an interview with the popular historical novelist Yoshikawa Eiji (August 23), and a distraught outpouring by a teacher at the Third Higher School in Kyoto (August 24).

3. Unlike the Jews of Germany, those victimized by the Japanese—even where intimate relations may have been involved, as with Korean and Chinese laborers or "comfort women" forced to service the troops—were never perceived as members of a shared community. With but rare exceptions, "Pan-Asian" rhetoric was sheer propaganda.

4. Nanbara Shigeru, *Nanbara Shigeru Chosakushū*, (Tokyo: Iwanami Shoten, 1973), 6:46–57, especially p. 55. The essay originally appeared in *Teikoku Daigaku Shimbun*, September 1, 1945, and opens with a standard expression of gratitude to the emperor for ending the war. For Nanbara's patriotic wartime exhortations, see his April 1, 1945 speech to incoming students in ibid., 6:38–45.

5. Nanbara, 6:57–66.

6. Reprinted in Bungei Shunjūsha, ed., *"Bungei Shunjū" ni Miru Shōwa Shi* (Tokyo: Bungei Shunjūsha, 1988), vol. 2, pp. 15–18. Many of these early expressions of guilt toward the dead focused on young men killed fighting, but the sentiment extended to civilians, male and female alike, killed in the air raids. On September 23, 1945, at a formal ceremony for victims of the numerous air raids on Tokyo, the souls of these departed were told that "Your lives were sacrificed for the country, and we will remember you for times to come." These sacrifices, it was pledged, would become "a foundation for the construction of a peaceful Japan"; *Asahi Shimbun*, September 24, 1945.

7. From the June 1946 issue of *Ie no Hikari;* quoted in Yoshida Yutaka, "Senryōki ni okeru Sensō Sekininron," *Hitotsubashi Ronsō* 105.2 (February 1991): 123. Yoshida's essay (pp. 121–38) makes splendid use of the voluminous Japanese-language newspapers and periodicals submitted to the GHQ censors and now deposited (but no longer readily accessible) in the McKeldin Library at the University of Maryland. As the notes that follow reveal, I have drawn heavily on quotations unearthed here by Professor Yoshida, and also by Yoshimi Yoshiaki in an equally valuable study based on these archives: "Senryōki Nihon no Minshū Ishiki—Sensō Sekinin o Megutte," *Shisō* 811 (January 1992): 73–99.

8. From Kikuchi's article "Hanashi no Kuzukago," *Kingu* 22.1 (January 1946); quoted in Yoshida, p. 123.

9. Mori Shozō, *Senpū Nijūnen: Kaikin Shōwa Rimen Shi,* 2 vols. (Tokyo: Masu Shobō, 1945, 1946); Mori was the coordinating editor of the *Mainichi* team that actually wrote the book. The best critical analysis of this famous bestseller is Ozaki Hideki, "Senpū Nijūnen," in Asahi Jānaru, ed. *Besutoserā Monogatari* (Tokyo: Asahi Shimbunsha, 1967), 1:7–15. See also Shiozawa Minobu, *Shōwa Besutoserā Sesō Shi* (Tokyo: Daisan Bunmeisha, 1988) pp. 100–2. The 1946 edition contained a number of revisions, which may have reflected GHQ censorship; Ozaki, p. 14.

10. Mori, 1:42; see also Mori, 2:88, 121, 151–152, 189 for other examples of the typical preoccupation with responsibility for defeat.

11. Mori, 1:142; see also 1:18, 120, 136–137, 167; 2:32–33, 58, 62. At one point industrialists were vaguely coupled with the military cliques as villains; ibid., 2:129.

12. *Asahi Shimbun,* September 12, 13, and 15, 1945; Asahi Shimbunsha, ed., *Koe* [hereafter referred to as *Koe*] (Tokyo: Asahi Bunko, 1984), vol. 1, pp. 35–36 (for a typical reference to the field code); Hosaka Masayasu, *Haisen Zengo no Nihonjin* (Tokyo: Asahi Bunko, 1989), pp. 246–50 (this includes Takami Jun's comment and the hospital conversation); Watanabe Kazuo, *Haisen Nikki* (Tokyo: Hakubunkan Shinsha, 1995), p. 85. The "Hold it, Tōjō!" anecdote is recounted in B. V. A. Röling, *The Tokyo Trial and Beyond: Reflections of a Peacemonger,* ed. by Antonio Cassese (Cambridge: Polity Press, in association with Blackwell Publishers, 1993), p. 34. For examples of Tōjō as archvillain in *The Twenty-Year Whirlwind,* see Mori, 1:102; 2:88, 114, 121. In a poll conducted in a Toshiba factory at the end of 1945, 80 percent of white-collar and blue-collar employees expressed hostility to Tōjō; see Yoshimi, p. 90 (plus other critical opinions on pp. 78–79, 81, 82). Years later, Tōjō's widow recalled the abuse her family received at this time. She and the children fled to her native village but still received many letters, some offering comfort but many full of hate. One letter writer, she recalled, offered to send coffins for herself and each of their children. The husband of one daughter, himself an army officer, committed suicide. The eldest son resigned from his company. The youngest two daughters changed their last names to avoid attention and derision at school. See Tōjō Katsuko, "Sengo no Michi wa Tokatta," *Bungei Shunjū,* June 1964; reprinted in *"Bungei Shunjū" ni Miru Shōwa Shi,* 2:99–111.

13. Mori, 1:149, 161.

14. *Asahi Shimbun,* August 23 and 25, 1945. Between August 8 and September 2, the effects of the bombs were discussed or at least mentioned in passing on all but five days in the *Asahi* (August 10, 24, 26, and 28, September 2). In the fourteen days between September 3 and September 16, after which censorship was in effect, the atomic bombs were discussed or at least referred to in nine daily issues (except September 4, 9, 10, 13, and 15).

15. *Asahi Shimbun,* August 14, 1945. For another example of Kiyose's sensitivity to racial issues, see Yoshida, p. 132.

16. "Cruel" *(zangyaku na)* and "inhuman" or "inhumane" *(hijindō-teki)* were the standard adjectives used to describe the dropping of the atomic bombs. I have discussed Japanese responses to the bombs elsewhere: see the foreword to the 1995 edition of Michihiko Hachiya, *Hiroshima Diary: The Journal of a Japanese Physician, August 6–September 30, 1945* (Chapel Hill: University of North Carolina Press, 1995), pp. v–xvii; "The Bombed: Hiroshimas and Nagasakis in Japanese Memory," in *Hiroshima in History and Memory,* ed. Michael J. Hogan (Cambridge: Cambridge University Press, 1996), pp. 116–42; and "Three Narratives of Our Humanity," in *History Wars: The 'Enola Gay' and Other Battles for the American Past,* ed. Edward

T. Linenthal and Tom Engelhardt (New York: Metropolitan Books, 1996), pp. 63–96.

17. *Asahi Shimbun,* August 27, 1945. See also the issues of August 18, September 12 and 16.

18. *Asahi Shimbun,* August 17, 18, 19, 20, and 22, 1945; see also issues of August 26 and 28.

19. *Asahi Shimbun,* September 5, 10, 21; October 23, 1945.

20. *Asahi Shimbun,* October 11, 1945. For other press commentaries on science and "rationality" in these early weeks, see the *Asahi* issues of September 12, 14, and 15, and October 1, 2, 18, 26, and 29, 1945.

21. *Asahi Shimbun,* September 14, 1945.

22. The original notice, which appeared on the Tokyo Imperial University Oceanographic Institute in Sagami, is now displayed in the library of the Woods Hole (Massachusetts) Marine Biological Laboratory. The notice was written by Dan Katsuma, an eminent Japanese biologist. I am grateful to Tom Benjamin for introducing me to it.

23. The press conference is reproduced in Hidaka Rokurō, *Sengo Shisō no Shuppatsu* (Tokyo: Chikuma Shobō, 1968), pp. 53–58, from *Mainichi Shimbun,* August 30, 1945. The famous *ichioku sōzange* phrase does not actually appear in the *Asahi Shimbun* transcript of the press conference (where it is *zenkokumin sōzange,* "the collective repentance of all countrymen"), but it does appear in the *Asahi's* editorial in the same August 30 issue. See also the prime minister's policy speech of September 5 in the issue of September 6.

24. Maruyama Masao, "Shisō no Kotoba," *Shisō* 381 (March 1956), p. 322.

25. *Asahi Shimbun,* October 19, 1945; these letters appear in an interesting summary of letters received by the *Asahi* in the two months after capitulation. See also the letter to the editor published in the *Asahi* on September 27 and reprinted in *Koe,* 1:39–40.

26. Quoted in James W. Heisig, "'The Self that Is Not a Self': Tanabe's Dialectics of Self-Awareness," in *The Religious Philosophy of Tanabe Hajime,* ed. Taitetsu Unno and James W. Heisig (Berkeley: Asian Humanities Press, 1990), p. 284. This book as a whole is the major collection of essays in English on Tanabe's philosophical thought. An interesting discussion of Tanabe appears in Kuyama Yasushi, *Sengo Nihon Seishin Shi* (Tokyo: Sōbunsha, 1961), pp. 170–201; this discussion is usefully excerpted in "Postwar Japanese Thought: 1945–1960," *Japan Christian Quarterly* 47.3 (summer 1981): 132–44. In the late 1930s, Tanabe had gone so far as to characterize the Japanese state as a manifestation of the true nature of the Buddha—a prototype of the ideal of the benevolent *bodhisattva*—and the subordination of the individual to the state as being, in essence, an expression of belief in the Buddha. This was bastardized Buddhism and wretched philosophy, good reason for Tanabe's subsequent feelings of shame and sin; see Kiyoshi Himi, "Tanabe's Theory of the State," in Unno and Heisig, pp. 309–10. In 1943, the year before his ecstatic conversion, Tanabe was still writing that, "In time of crisis country and individual are one; the people dedicate themselves out of necessity to the country. To distance oneself from one's country means at the same time to destroy the self itself"; quoted in Heisig, p. 283; cf. ibid., pp. 281–84. Even in his Rousseau-esque confession in his 1946 treatise, Tanabe was not really forthcoming about his significant conceptual contribution to the war effort. In 1934, for example, he had introduced a highly influential concept of "logic of species" that perfectly served the racist purposes of the militarists and ultranationalists in promoting their ideology of a racially homo-

geneous state presided over by a sacred emperor; see Himi, pp. 303–15. Nishida Kitarō, Tanabe's illustrious predecessor at Kyoto Imperial University, bluntly (and privately) observed in 1940 that "This Tanabe's stuff is completely fascist!"—a
reasonable observation that Tanabe himself, even in his most masochistic moments
of shame and sin, was never able to confess; Nishida's comment is quoted in Heisig,
p. 283. In his 1945–1946 repentance/conversion writings, Tanabe continued to reaffirm the insights of his "logic of species" theories. The extent to which his "new"
insights were rooted in his earlier thinking, and capable of being used to authoritarian ends, is a subject of continuing debate.

27. *Zangedō to shite no Tetsugaku* was published by Iwanami in April 1946. It has been
translated into English by Yoshimori Takeuchi, with a foreword by James Heisig,
as *Philosophy as Metanoetics* (Berkeley: University of California Press, 1986). Hereafter this translated source is cited as *PM*.

28. *PM*, pp. xlix–lx, 3, 26.

29. *PM*, p. lx; see also p. xxxvii.

30. *PM*, p. lvii–lviii, 20, 265, 270; see also 281, 295. Throughout his treatise, Tanabe
respectfully elucidated the superiority of his Shinran-derived thesis vis-à-vis such
Western philosophers as Kant, Hegel, Schelling, Heidegger, and Kierkegaard. This
attempt by postsurrender Japanese intellectuals to resist Western cultural hegemony is a rich subject for future research. On August 20, 1945, Tanabe's conservative "Kyoto school" philosophy colleague Kōsaka Masaaki published an adroit
essay in the *Mainichi Shimbun* praising Western "objectivity" *(kyakansei)* and "realism" *(genjitsushugi)* and criticizing Japanese "subjectivity" *(shūkansei)*, but still
maintaining that Japan had the spiritual potential to make a major contribution to
world culture. Kōsaka criticized the cultural gap between the literate elites and the
general populace; praised the excellence of Japanese morality at the state and family levels, but found Japan inferior in the "social morality" essential as a mediating
force between nation and family; spoke of a special "sacred power" running through
Japanese history; and concluded, in rather typical style, that a new Japan would reflect the rebirth and transformation of the best of old traditions. Kōsaka's essay is
reprinted in Hidaka, pp. 60–63.

31. *PM*, p. lvii, lxi–lxii, 281. The flower metaphor is noted in *Japan Christian Quarterly*,
op. cit., pp. 137, 142.

32. *PM*, pp. 261, 278–79.

33. See, for example, *PM*, pp. lxii, 263–65, 291. Tanabe developed the argument for "social democracy" in an important article entitled "The Urgent Task of Political Philosophy," published in March 1946, the month before *Zangedō to shite no Tetsugaku*
appeared.

34. *PM*, p. 296. In the introduction to the book, Tanabe offered as concise a critique
of the occupation's "revolution from above" modus operandi as one is likely to find
anywhere: "But can a nation compelled to surrender, with liberalism being forced
upon it from without and the development of culture urged from within, be expected to come up with the spiritual resources needed to create a new culture simply because the oppressive controls of the past have been removed? True freedom
is not something one receives from another; one has to acquire it for oneself. Even
should there be a flowering of new culture in such circumstances as ours, it would
be like blossoms on a hothouse plant: beautiful to the eye but too weak and shallow of root to survive in open air"; *PM*, p. lxi. It is surprising that passages such
as this (and others quoted here) passed the scrutiny of GHQ's censors. Possibly such
comments, buried in so long and ponderous a tome, simply escaped notice.

35. Tanabe called for distributing the wealth of the imperial household in his "Urgent Task of Political Philosophy" article of March 1946—the very moment when SCAP was consolidating its pro-imperial campaign.

36. *PM*, pp. 287, 296; see also lxi–lxii, 260–62. Tanabe was extremely prolific in the years following publication of *Zangedō to shite no Tetsugaku*. In addition to a number of influential articles, he published four books between 1947 and 1950: a text on the dialectics of class theory; a study of "Existenz, Love, and Praxis" that pursued the themes of repentance and love through an analysis of Western existentialism, focusing on Kierkegaard; a sympathetic study of Christian love as seen particularly in the gospels; and a general "Introduction to Philosophy" that was quite widely read.

37. Nihon Senbotsu Gakusei Shuki Henshūkai, ed., *Kike—Wadatsumi no Koe: Nihon Senbotsu Gakusei no Shuki* (Tokyo: Tōdai Kyōdō Kumiai Shuppanbu, 1949); see esp. the postscript on pp. 307–23. For examples of positive responses to the collections of student letters, see Asahi Shimbunsha, ed., *Tensei Jingo* (Tokyo: Asahi Bunko, 1981), vol. 1, pp. 261–62 (October 24, 1949); also *Koe*, 2:216 (November 4, 1949). *Kike—Wadatsumi no Koe* quickly sold around two hundred thousand copies, making it a 1950 bestseller, and remained popular in the decades that followed. By 1992, it had sold an estimated 1.8 million copies; *Asahi Shimbun*, August 15, 1992.

38. Literally, people "who did not know dirt."

39. Takeyama Michio, *Biruma no Tategoto* (Tokyo: Chūō Kōronsha "Tomodachi Bunko" edition, 1948), pp. 270–75. This children's edition went through six printings in the next two years. The novel has been translated by Howard Hibbett under the title *Harp of Burma* (Rutland, Vt.: Tuttle, 1966).

40. *In Distant Mountains and Rivers* was reissued in December 1951 with a new postscript that vividly conveyed the lingering guilt of the survivors, referring repeatedly to the editors as those who "remained living." In the original preface to this collection, Tatsuno Takashi, a scholar of French literature, offered yet another emotional expression of personal shame and torment at having survived while so many fine young students had died. He treated the defeat as a kind of divine punishment for the hubris that had gripped Japan during the half-year of sensational victories that followed Pearl Harbor, and identified the instrument of Japan's punishment as being "the material power and science of the other side." See *Haruka naru Sanga ni: Tōdai Senbotsu Gakusei no Shuki* (Tokyo: Tokyo Daigaku Shuppankai, 1951 ed.).

41. Shiina's comment is noted in Kuyama, p. 96.

42. Both *Fires on the Plain* and *Harp of Burma* were reimagined in sensitive films in the late 1950s. One of the most celebrated film treatments of the war's destruction of innocent Japanese, *Twenty-four Eyes (Nijūshi no Hitomi)*, appeared two years after the occupation ended. This film depicted an idealistic young female elementary school teacher and the fates of twelve students (thus the "twenty-four eyes") she had taught in a remote rural community before war came. As the film critic Satō Tadao astutely observed, the immense appeal of the film derived largely from its bifurcated structure. One encounters the young teacher with her attractive class, then sees her as an older woman returning after the war to the village, where she had spent only that one year, and visiting the graves of several former pupils. The impression conveyed is that those who were killed forever possessed the innocence they had as children. Viewers do not see these boys becoming young men or engaged in invasion and killing abroad. In this instance, the innocence of the child is the vehicle through which the purity of the war dead is expressed. See Satō's contribution in Tsurumi Shunsuke, et al., eds., *Sengo Eiga no Tenkai*, vol. 5 in the series *Kōza: Nihon Eiga* (Tokyo: Iwanami Shoten, 1987), pp. 46–47.

43. See, for example, the influential early statements of the Peace Problems Research Symposium (Heiwa Mondai Danwakai), reproduced in the special issue of *Sekai*, July 1985, devoted to postwar peace issues.

44. The argument that the bystander attitude reflects a general weakness of "subjective" consciousness of personal responsibility is a basic theme in postwar critical scholarship emphasizing Japanese war responsibility. This emerges strongly in the seminal articles of both Yoshida Yutaka (see pp. 122–23, 135, 137) and Yoshimi Yoshiaki (see especially pp. 76–78 on the notion of "being deceived").

45. From the combined June–July 1946 issue of *Gyōshō;* quoted in Yoshida, pp. 129–30.

46. From the January 1949 issue of *Ie no Hikari;* quoted in Yoshida, p. 135.

47. See Yoshida, pp. 129–31, 137–38.

48. Quoted in Yoshimi, p. 77.

49. Reprinted in *Koe,* 2:100 (November 13, 1948) and 2:113–14 (December 24, 1948).

50. *Tensei Jingo,* 1:97 (July 27, 1946).

51. See Yoshida, p. 134, for one of the relatively rare mentions of Korean and Formosan suffering when the issue of war responsibility came up. For a shocked response to the "thoroughgoing sin" of war, in which Japanese suffering is coupled with both the Nanking Massacre and cannibalism by Japanese troops, see *Koe* 2:107–8 (December 6, 1948). In general, apart from the strong initial response to the revelation of the 1945 atrocities in Manila, the Japanese do not appear to have been particularly sensitive to the victimization of peoples of Southeast Asia. This hierarchy of Asian victims has tended to persist even in the postwar literature of progressive scholars and activists deeply committed to exposing the extent of Japan's World War II atrocities, where primary focus has tended to be on, first, Japan's Chinese victims, and second, its Korean victims. Although it can be argued that these two peoples suffered most at Japanese hands, such emphasis cannot be explained in quantitative terms alone. Considerations of geographical, historical, cultural, racial, and psychological distancing also are involved.

52. See the press coverage of September 16, 17 and 18, 1945, in *Asahi Shimbun;* also letters in the issue of October 19, 1945, and in *Koe,* 1:103–4 (December 13, 1945) and 1:152 (February 15, 1946).

53. *Asahi Shimbun,* September 18, 1945. One of the puzzles concerning postsurrender consciousness of war crimes is why it took so long for one of the most blatant "hidden war crimes"—the sexual enslavement of non-Japanese "comfort women"—to be exposed; or, more particularly, why it took so long for Japanese women to call attention to this. The explanation certainly involves, at least in part, considerations of both race and class. Japanese women well aware of these activities, such as military nurses, generally looked down on these women as foreign whores—as did, of course, the men who used them.

54. From *Taihei,* November 1946; quoted in Yoshida, p. 126.

55. See, for example, *Asahi Shimbun,* September 17, 1945; *Tensei Jingo,* 1:95 (July 8, 1946) and 1:97 (July 27, 1946).

56. From "Ajia no Shinsei," *Genron* 1.1 (1946); quoted in Yoshida, p. 126.

57. Quoted in Yoshimi, p. 76. This play on ideographs actually was used in wartime anti-Japanese propaganda by the Chinese (and by U.S. psychological-warfare specialists who helped the Chinese prepare propaganda leaflets).

58. "Tennō no Guntai," *Jimmin Hyōron* 2.3 (1946); quoted in Yoshida, p. 126.

59. See, for example, *Koe,* 1:144–46 (February 2, 1946) and 1:211–12 (August 8, 1946).

60. All four poems are reproduced in Yoshimi, pp. 82, 86.

61. *Mainichi Shimbun*, November 5, 1948. *Van* (December 1947) and *Sekai* (February 1949) are quoted in Yoshida, p. 135.

62. *Mainichi Shimbun*, November 13, 1948; *Nihon Keizai Shimbun*, November 13, 1948; *Asahi Shimbun*, November 5 and 13, 1948; *Nikkeiren Taimusu* 25, December 1948, quoted in Yoshida, p. 124 (Yoshida criticizes this response as typically avoiding serious engagement with the issue of popular war cooperation). Yoshimi, pp. 83–84, includes several examples of censored press comment on the trials.

63. *Mainichi Shimbun*, November 13, 1948.

64. *Shizuoka Tenbō*, February 1949; reproduced in Yoshimi, p. 82.

65. By Murata Haruko in *Mizugame*, March 1949; reproduced in Yoshimi, pp. 83–84.

66. Reproduced in Yoshimi, p. 84.

67. From *Aogaki*, May 1949; reproduced in Yoshimi, p. 84. For a sample of conflicting responses to the sentence imposed on Tōjō, see Tsurumi Shunsuke, et al., eds., *Nihon no Hyakunen* (Tokyo: Chikuma Shobō, 1967), vol. 1, pp. 54–55, 61–62.

68. Justice Röling was among those who concluded that Tōjō's testimony at the tribunal, which took several days and involved a strong defense of Japan's defense of its vital interests, "restored his dignity in the eyes of the Japanese people"; Röling (1993), p. 34.

69. Yoshida, p. 134. In a panel discussion in 1948, Kainō had similarly raised the question, "Isn't there something wrong in thinking of the war trials as Tōjō's trial?" This too was censored.

70. *Tensei Jingo*, 1:256–57 (September 16, 1949). To the shock of many Japanese, General Willoughby publicly stated there might be some truth to these reports.

71. Eichelberger's notorious comment is cited by Kazuo Kawai in *Pacific Affairs*, June 1950, p. 119.

72. See, for example, *Mikōkai Shashin ni Miru Tokyo Saiban*, the interesting Winter 1989 special issue *(Bessatsu)* of the journal *Rekishi Tokuhon* devoted to the war crimes trials, pp. 158 and 159. Kodama's memoirs were later translated into English.

73. For a detailed treatment of Tsuji's notorious career, see Ian Ward, *The Killer They Called a God* (Singapore: Media Masters, 1992), esp. chs. 18–20 on his postsurrender activities. For passing reference to the unpublicized knowledge among journalists that Willoughby was protecting Tsuji between 1946 and 1950, see the comment by Keyes Beech in *The Occupation of Japan: Arts and Culture*, ed. Thomas W. Burkman (Norfolk, Va.: Douglas MacArthur Foundation, 1984), p. 43. I am grateful to James Zobel for calling my attention to these sources. Tsuji's two 1950 bestsellers were *Senkō Sanzenri* (Tokyo: Mainichi Shimbunsha) and *Jūgo tai Ichi* (Tokyo: Kantōsha).

74. *Koe*, 2:200–1 (August 15, 1949).

75. These activities are nicely captured in a photo section in *Bessatsu Rekishi Tokuhon*, pp. 24–38.

76. *Bessatsu Rekishi Tokuhon*, pp. 68–73, 87–101. The three ideographs with which cuckoo (*yobukodori*) is written literally mean "child-calling bird." Such nuances, peculiar to the writing system, seeped through to all Japanese who heard the song.

77. See the interesting bibliography of popular as well as scholarly materials about war crimes and war responsibility in *Shisō*, May 1984. Under "writings and last testaments of war criminals," this lists sixteen titles between 1950 and 1954 and a total of thirty-one through 1982. By 1954, there also had been published at least nine "in-

sider" accounts of war-criminal defendants and suspects in Sugamo Prison, one book on the U.S.–conducted Yokohama trials of "B" and "C" Class defendants, and six books about various "B/C" trials throughout Asia; twenty-nine more titles on the latter subject are listed between 1956 and 1983. The Japanese translation of A. Frank Reel's *The Case of General Yamashita*, a powerful statement of the injustice of that trial, was published in 1952, the same year the translation of Justice Pal's dissenting judgment appeared.

78. Sugamo Kisho Henshūkai, ed., *Seiki no Isho* (Tokyo: Sugamo Kisho Henshukai, 1953). In a new edition of *Seiki no Isho* published in 1984 by Kōdansha, thirty-nine of the entries in the original volume were deleted at the request of the families and heirs of the writers; the pagination of this revised edition remains unchanged.

79. *Seiki no Isho,* pp. 683–85.

80. Ibid., pp. 579–83.

81. Ibid., pp. 77–78, 101–2, 447–51, 579–83.

82. See, for example, ibid., pp. 66, 322, 483, 568, 630–33. The absence of singular or plural in the Japanese makes the poem applicable to either parent, or both. In Yoshida's case, the poem clearly referred to his mother.

83. See, for example, *Seiki no Isho,* pp. 38–39, 63–64, 88, 90–91, 407, 468, 520, 637.

84. *Seiki no Ishi,* p. 311.

85. A later conservative text on the "B/C Class" war crimes trials suggests in passing that the Japanese policy of forcing subordinates to take responsibility for atrocious acts that actually reflected official policy (such as the imperial navy's policy of killing all enemy crewmen, including civilian seamen) initially was rationalized as essential to protect the emperor by camouflaging official policy; Saka Kuniyasu, ed., *Yokohama Hōtei: B/C-kyū* (1967: Tōchōsha), pp. 102–4.

86. *Seiki no Isho,* pp. 285–90, esp. 286.

87. See, for example, *Seiki no Isho,* pp. 113–18, 168–71, 183–86, 311–15, 332–33, 453–61, 483–87 for typically harsh comments on Dutch and British cruelty and revenge. Many condemned men spoke well of the treatment they received in Nationalist Chinese jails, even when they may have felt the judgments against them were unfair. Chiang Kai-shek's politically calculated policy of treating the Japanese moderately after the war (and thus enlisting their support in his struggle against the Chinese Communists) paid handsome dividends in encouraging postwar friendly feelings toward "the Chinese" in general. See, for example, *Seiki no Isho,* pp. 8–9, 108–9; *Tensei Jingo,* pp. 33–34 (November 10, 1945). As noted elsewhere here, the Chinese Communists themselves belatedly brought a number of Japanese to trial for war crimes in the early 1950s but did not impose any death sentences.

88. The biography of Kimura is Shiojiri Kōmei, *Aru Isho ni Tsuite* (Tokyo: Shinchōsha, 1948; reprinted in 1951 by Shakai Shisō Kenkyūkai). See also *Kike—Wadatsumi no Koe,* pp. 281–304; *Seiki no Isho,* p. 433. For an abridged English translation of Kimura's testament, see Michiko Aoki and Margaret Dardess, eds., *As the Japanese See It: Past and Present* (Honolulu: University of Hawaii Press, 1981), pp. 297–303.

89. These sample entries were all reproduced in the special January 1954 issue of *Akebono* devoted to selections from *Testaments of the Century*.

90. *Akebono,* January 1954, p. 8.

91. *Seiki no Isho,* pp. 407–8. This particular entry was typical of testaments whose writers argued their innocence of the charges brought against them. In this instance, the doctor, assigned to a prison camp, claimed that in determining who was fit for work details he followed regulations precisely and treated POWs and Japanese soldiers,

many of whom were also physically debilitated, exactly the same. (This was one of the entries deleted at the request of surviving family members in the 1984 edition.)

It is impossible to exaggerate the influence of sentiments such as those conveyed in *Testaments of the Century* on postwar thinking about the war, and "war victims," in general. They embody a romanticized conservative reconstruction of the war, and their appeal to right-wing neonationalists is obvious. At the same time, they also offer reassurance to great numbers of ordinary Japanese whose kin and acquaintances fought in the war and simply can not be remembered by them as "war criminals" or men who gave their lives for an "aggressive war" and nothing more. Thus, in 1995, on the fiftieth anniversary of the end of the war, one of the largest citizens' groups calling for homage to the Japanese dead of World War II and opposing "categorical" and "unequivocal" apologies for Japan's aggression and atrocities was the Association of Bereaved Families (Izokukai). Some of these individuals would categorize themselves as pacifists; a great many certainly see themselves as antimilitarists. Their memorial services to the Japanese dead almost invariably involve appeals for peace—the appeal that there be no such Japanese "sacrifices" in the future. Unscrupulous right-wing politicians routinely exploit these sentiments, and non-Japanese routinely condemn them.

CHAPTER 17. *ENGINEERING GROWTH*

1. I have addressed U.S. reverse-course policy in detail in "Occupied Japan and the Cold War in Asia," reprinted in Dower, *Japan in War and Peace: Selected Essays* (New York: The New Press, 1993), pp. 155–207. See also Howard B. Schonberger, *Aftermath of War: Americans and the Remaking of Japan, 1945–1952* (Kent, Ohio: Kent State University Press, 1989); William S. Borden, *The Pacific Alliance: United States Foreign Economic Policy and Japanese Trade Recovery, 1947–1955* (Madison: University of Wisconsin Press, 1984); and Michael Schaller, *The American Occupation of Japan: The Origins of the Cold War in Asia* (New York: Oxford University Press, 1985).

2. Rekishigaku Kenkyūkai, ed., *Senryō Seisaku no Tenkan to Kōwa*, vol. 2 of *Nihon Dōjidai Shi* (Tokyo: Rekishigaku Kenkyūkai, 1990), pp. 194–95.

3. *Gendai Yōgo no Kiso Chishiki, 1948* (Tokyo: special issue of the magazine *Jiyū Kokumin*, published by Jigyoku Geppōsha), p. 131.

4. Zakō Jun, Tonedachi Masahisa, and Nagasawa Michio, *Shōwa no Kotoba* (Tokyo: Asahi Sonorama, 1989), pp. 318–20; Takahashi Nobuo, *Shōwa Sesō Ryūkōgo Jiten* (Tokyo: Ōbunsha, 1986), pp. 122–23.

5. Takahashi, pp. 195–97. See also the interesting October 1951 essay on Misora Hibari reprinted in *"Shūkan Asahi" no Shōwa Shi* (Tokyo: Asahi Shimbunsha, 1989), vol. 2 *(Shōwa 20-nendai)*, pp. 239–56. Hibari (her stage name) was the preeminent female vocalist of postwar Japan until her death in 1989—her charisma, if not her style, comparable to that of Judy Garland or Edith Piaf.

6. Shiozawa Minobu, *Shōwa Besutoserā Sesō Shi* (Tokyo: Daisan Bunmeisha, 1988), pp. 265–66. Yoshikawa had two "top ten" bestsellers in 1948: *Shinran*, a biography of the thirteenth-century Buddhist evangelist of that name (the same prophetic thinker who had inspired the philosopher Tanabe Hajime in his search for an indigenous concept of "repentance"), and *Shinsho Taiheiki*, a "new" rendering of a famous fourteenth-century war chronicle. In 1949, *Shinran* was joined on the bestseller list by Yoshikawa's *Miyamoto Musashi*, a romanticized biography of a near-legendary seventeenth-century swordsman that remained a bestseller in 1950. In 1951, the prolific Yoshikawa had yet another bestseller, *Shin Heike Monogatari*, a "new" render-

ing of the most cherished of all Japanese war chronicles, dealing with the late-twelfth-century civil war that ushered in long epoch of feudal rule. Also on the "top ten" lists of 1951 was Tanizaki Junichirō's brilliant rendering in contemporary Japanese of the romantic eleventh-century classic *Genji Monogatari* (The Tale of Genji).

7. Mombushō [Ministry of Education], *Atarashii Kempō no Hanashi* (Tokyo: Mombushō, 1947). This was reprinted by a Japanese peace group (Nihon Heiwa Iinkai) in 1972 and has received subsequent publicity as an example of the lost idealism of the early postsurrender period. See also the article about Asai and the origins of the booklet in *Asahi Shimbun*, May 2, 1994.

8. "Basic Initial Post-Surrender Directive to Supreme Commander for the Allied Powers for the Occupation and Control of Japan," November 3, 1945 (forwarded to MacArthur on November 8); Edwin M. Martin, *The Allied Occupation of Japan* (New York: Stanford University Press for the Institute of Pacific Relations, 1948), pp. 113, 115.

9. See chapter 3 (note 12) on U.S. aid to occupied Japan.

10. The "centralized and authoritarian" phrase is from Martin Bronfenbrenner, an economist who served with E.S.S.; see his concise summary of occupation-period economic policy in *Kodansha Encyclopedia of Japan* (Tokyo: Kōdansha, 1983), vol. 2, pp. 154–58. As noted earlier, SCAP's inordinate informal as well as formal authority is nicely conveyed by another insider, Theodore Cohen, in *Remaking Japan: The American Occupation as New Deal* (New York: Free Press, 1987). For Japanese views of the occupation's managed trade, see Noda Kazuo, ed., *Sengo Keiei Shi* (Tokyo: Seisansei Honbu, 1965), pp. 294–302; this mammoth source offers many intimate insights into postwar management.

11. Mitsubishi Economic Research Institute, ed., *Mitsui-Mitsubishi-Sumitomo: Present Status of the Former Zaibatsu Enterprises* (Tokyo: Mitsubishi Economic Research Institute, 1955), p. 6; see also the table reproduced in Dower, *Japan in War and Peace*, p. 120. The Nissan combine is sometimes identified by the name Ayukawa.

12. Interview with Andō Yoshio in Andō, ed., *Shōwa Seiji Keizai Shi e no Shōgen* (Tokyo: Mainichi Shimbunsha, 1966), vol. 3, p. 144; Kazuo Shibagaki, "Dissolution of Zaibatsu and Deconcentration of Economic Power," *Social Science Abstracts* 20 (Tokyo: Shakai Kagaku Kenkyūjo, Tokyo University, 1979), p. 21; Masahiro Hosoya, "Selected Aspects of the Zaibatsu Dissolution in Occupied Japan, 1945–1952: The Thought and Behavior of Zaibatsu Leaders, Japanese Government Officials and SCAP Officials," Ph.D. dissertation, Yale University (December 1982), pp. 17–18. The first two chapters of this dissertation provide interesting insight into the response of high executives to the surrender and early SCAP demands for zaibatsu dissolution and economic deconcentration.

13. For inside accounts of these developments, see Ōkurashō Kanbō Chōsakai Kinyū Zaisei Jitsujō Kenkyūkai, *Sengo Zaisei Shi Kōju Shiryō*, vol. 1, entries 3 and 9; this is an unpublished Ministry of Finance collection of interviews with occupation-period officials. On the printing-press inflation, see Fuji Bank, ed., *Banking in Modern Japan*, special issue of *Fuji Bank Bulletin*, vol. 11, no. 4 (1961; commemorating the eightieth anniversary of the founding of the Fuji Bank), p. 187, and the Economic Planning Agency publication Keizai Kikakuchō Sengo Keizai Shi Henshushitsu, ed., *Sengo Keizai Shi (Keizai Seisakuhen)*, (Tokyo: Ōkurashō Insatsukyoku, 1960), p. 33.

14. Hosoya, pp. 19–23, 50–54. Colonel Raymond C. Kramer, the first head of E.S.S., astonished Mitsui's executives by castigating the "blind obedience" of the Japanese people in general, giving as a prime example the way they had deferentially followed

the emperor's instructions to surrender instead of attacking the arriving U.S. occupation forces.

15. Horikoshi Teizō, ed., *Keizai Dantai Rengōtai Jūnen-shi* (Tokyo: Keidanren, 1962), vol. 1, pp. 4–11; also summarized in Hosoya, pp. 27–32. This advisory group evolved into Keidanren, the powerful "Japan Federation of Economic Organizations" that became the leading voice of big business.

16. Noda (pp. 59–66) gives an itemized total of 844 facilities still designated for reparations as of May 1, 1950 (524 operating plants and 320 idle ones), unaccountably increased to 930 as of the end of 1950. For an overview of reparations in general, see Borden, pp. 71–83. The first—and last—actual shipment of reparations goods during the occupation involved some fourteen thousand machine tools shipped to Asian claimants beginning in May 1947. In accordance with the multinational peace treaty that ended the occupation in 1952, Japan negotiated reparations settlements with claimants after regaining sovereignty, with agreed-on payments coming out of current production.

17. Noda, p. 116; see also Tsūsan Daijin, p. 14. The basic English-language study of policy toward the zaibatsu is by a former E.S.S. contributor to these policies: Eleanor Hadley, *Antitrust in Japan* (Princeton: Princeton University Press, 1970). See also Hadley's concise entries on "Zaibatsu" and "Zaibatsu Dissolution" in *Kodansha Encyclopedia of Japan* (Tokyo: Kodansha, 1983), vol. 8, pp. 361–66; Hadley, "From Deconcentration to Reverse Course" in *Americans as Proconsuls: United States Military Government in Germany and Japan, 1944–1952*, ed. Robert Wolfe (Carbondale: Southern Illinois University Press, 1984), pp. 138–54; Shibagaki (1979), pp. 1–60; Kozo Yamamura, *Economic Policy in Postwar Japan: Growth Versus Economic Democracy* (Berkeley: University of California Press, 1967); Holding Company Liquidation Commission, *Final Report on Zaibatsu Dissolution* (Tokyo: July 10, 1951); and Office of the Chief of Military History, GHQ, SCAP, "Deconcentration of Economic Power," Part B of *Reform of Business Enterprise*, vol. 10 in SCAP's unpublished *History of the Nonmilitary Activities of the Occupation of Japan* (1952; available on microfilm from the National Archives). Hosoya is insightful on the piecemeal manner in which Japanese businessmen learned about the victors' intentions.

18. For comments on "confiscation" by two former SCAP insiders, see Cohen, pp. 176–78; Hadley (1983), p. 364.

19. The article is summarized in Noda, p. 162.

20. Noda, pp. 42–44, 173–74, 192–95, 199–201.

21. Noda, pp. 113, 120–22, 175–81, 185, 193–95.

22. W. Macmahon Ball, *Japan: Enemy or Ally?* (New York: John Day, 1949), pp. 60–63 (Ball quotes a long letter from MacArthur to Yoshida dated March 22, 1947); see also Leon Hollerman, "International Economic Controls in Occupied Japan," *Journal of Asian Studies* 38.4 (August 1979): 708.

23. These developments in economic planning are nicely analyzed in Laura Hein, *Fueling Growth: The Energy Revolution and Economic Policy in Postwar Japan* (Cambridge, Mass.: Council on East Asian Studies, Harvard University, 1990); see esp. pp. 107–28. The calculation regarding the small number of firms that received RFB support is noted in Dick K. Nanto, "The United States' Role in the Postwar Economic Recovery of Japan," Ph.D. dissertation, Harvard University (December 1976), p. 236. For data on RFB loans, see Arisawa Hiromi and Inaba Hidezō, eds., *Shiryō: Sengo Nijūnen Shi* (Tokyo: Nihon Hyōronsha, 1966), vol. 2 *(Keizai)*, pp. 60–61; also Fuji Bank, pp. 193–94.

24. *SNNZ* 8:208–9; Noda, pp. 350–51; *Sengo Shi Daijiten* (Tokyo: Sanseidō, 1991), p. 435. Speculation was widespread in Japan that exposure of the Shōwa Denkō scandal was initiated by General Willoughby in SCAP's G-2 Section with the explicit intent of discrediting "radical" elements in Government Section.

25. Fuji Bank, p. 194; *Tokyo Times*, July 9, 1948, cited in Jerome B. Cohen, *Japan's Economy in War and Reconstruction* (Minneapolis: University of Minnesota Press, 1949), p. 447. For a semiofficial critique of the priority production policy by the Economic Planning Agency, see Keizai Kikakuchō, pp. 44–47.

26. This is strongly emphasized in Hein, pp. 124–28.

27. Department of State, *Foreign Relations of the United States, 1952–1954* (Washington, 1985), vol. 14, part 2, pp. 1724–25; see also p. 1693. The "workshop" phrase was introduced by Secretary of State Dean Acheson in a famous May 1947 speech advocating the reconstruction of Germany as well as Japan. The "cocktail napkin" statement was made to Watanabe Takeshi and reported in his diary-memoir *Senryōka no Nihon Zaisei Oboegaki* (Tokyo: Nihon Keizai Shimbunsha, 1966).

28. Iwasaki Koyata-den Henshū Iinkai, ed. *Iwasaki Koyata-den* (Tokyo, 1957), pp. 382–83; quoted in Noda, p. 23. See also Noda, p. 49.

29. The report was translated and published by the Japan Economic Research Center in 1977 under the title *Basic Problems for Postwar Reconstruction of Japanese Economy: Translation of a Report of Ministry of Foreign Affairs' Special Survey Committee, September 1946*. The genesis of the study was a personal report by Okita Saburō, a young engineer who became a well-known economist and later foreign minister. Actual writing of the final draft was done by Okita, Gotō Yōnosuke, Oda Hiroshi, and Hamiki Shokichi, who were too junior in status to be listed as committee members. In the summary that follows, I have followed this translation, occasionally with minor editorial alterations after comparison with the Japanese original. Laura Hein has dealt at length with postwar planning, including this report; in addition to her *Fueling Growth* (esp. chs. 5 and 6), see her "In Search of Peace and Democracy: Japanese Economic Debate in Political Context," *Journal of Asian Studies* 53.3 (August 1994): 752–78, and "Growth Versus Success: Japan's Economic Policy in Historical Perspective," in *Postwar Japan As History*, ed. Andrew Gordon (Berkeley: University of California Press, 1993), pp. 99–122.

30. *Basic Problems*, pp. 53–59, esp. 54, 56.

31. *Basic Problems*, pp. 2–6, 64–65.

32. *Basic Problems*, pp. 43–44, 56–57.

33. *Basic Problems*, pp. 7, 52–53, 60–61.

34. *Basic Problems*, pp. 48, 60, 96–100. In mobilizing for war, it was noted, Japan "had the experience of manufacturing for itself one way or another high-grade machine tools, ball bearings, optical appliances, ultrashortwave communications apparatus and . . . modern machinery of all other kinds. Further, under the pressure of actual necessity the nation trained a great number of technicians, draftees and other heavy industry workers. Now even in the remotest farm villages of the country there will be found youngsters who have returned from urban cities where they have acquired the techniques of operating lathes. These conditions will constitute valuable contributions toward the construction of a peaceful Japanese economy, dependent on the efforts that might be exerted hereafter."

35. *Basic Problems*, pp. 56–59, 65–66, 89, 91–93, 133–34.

36. *Basic Problems*, pp. 58, 65. Prominent academic economists on the committee included Arisawa Hiromi, Inaba Hidezo, Ōuchi Hyōe, Tōhata Seiichi, and Nakayama Ichirō.

37. The "Nine Commandments" dealt with taxes, credit, wage stability, price controls, foreign trade and exchange, industrial allocations and export promotion, increased production of indigenous raw materials as well as manufactures, food collection, and—first and foremost—creation of a balanced, consolidated budget. Creation of a single, fixed dollar-yen exchange rate came as a supplementary directive (the rate set in 1949 was not revised until 1972). For the Dodge Line and its effects, see Borden, pp. 92–102; Hein (1990), pp. 153–72; Theodore Cohen, ch. 23; Fuji Bank, pp. 199–206; Nanto (1976); and Tsuru Shigeto, *Japan's Capitalism: Creative Defeat and Beyond* (Cambridge: Cambridge University Press, 1993), pp. 48–56. Tensions between Dodge and the Japanese government are discussed in Dower, *Empire and Aftermath*, pp. 274–75, 416–28.

38. The popular Japanese phrase was *tenyū shinjo,* literally "heavenly aid, divine help." Another catchphrase for the war was "revival medicine."

39. Special procurements are itemized from June 1950 through 1953 on pp. 78–79 of the appendix in Tsūsan Daijin; although useful for comparative benefits reaped by various sectors, the monetary values given in this MITI publication are greatly underestimated. See also Kobayashi Yoshio, *Sengo Nihon Keizai Shi* (Tokyo: Nihon Hyōronsha, 1963), pp. 72–80; G. C. Allen, *Japan's Economic Recovery* (London: Oxford University Press, 1958), pp. 19–22, 95, 98, 203; Takafusa Nakamura, *The Postwar Japanese Economy: Its Development and Structure* (Tokyo: University of Tokyo Press, 1981), pp. 41–48; Tatsurō Uchino, *Japan's Postwar Economy: An Insider's View of Its History and Its Future* (Tokyo: Kodansha International, 1983), pp. 55–62. Toyota's president is quoted in Asahi Shimbun, ed. *The Pacific Rivals* (Tokyo: Weatherhill, 1972), p. 193.

40. See W. Edwards Deming, "What Happened in Japan?", *Industrial Quality Control* 24.2 (August 1967): 89–93; Deming, "My View of Quality Control in Japan," *Reports of Statistical Application Research* 22.2 (June 1975): 73–80. The latter journal is published by the Union of Japanese Scientists and Engineers (Nihon Kagaku Gijutsu Renmei), which sponsored Deming's decisive eight-day seminar in July 1950 and established the soon-famous "Deming Prize" the following December; see also Kenichi Koyanagi, *The Deming Prize* (1960), a pamphlet published by the Union. Deming had previously served as a consultant on sampling techniques to SCAP; he followed up his 1950 quality-control seminar with similar presentations in 1951, 1952, 1955, 1960, and 1965. See also Hein (1993), pp. 109–10.

41. Uchino, pp. 73–75; Tsūsan Daijin, pp. 74, 422–34, esp. 428, 433–34; Nakamura, p. 42.

42. Cohen, pp. 432, 441–42. The economist and policy participant Tsuru Shigeto similarly described Dodge's austerity budget as being "in the end thrust down the throat" of the government and Diet; Tsuru, p. 48. The civilian "Japan lobby" that was instrumental behind the scenes in promoting the reverse course in government and media circles in the United States is incisively analyzed in Schonberger, pp. 134–60. As prime minister in the early 1960s, Ikeda was the architect of the famously successful "income-doubling plan."

43. MITI's 1954 economic survey of the postwar years provides a succinct summary of the numerous fiscal measures the government and the Bank of Japan adopted to ameliorate the Dodge Line and stimulate the private sector, also emphasizing the key role of the Bank of Japan in promoting the overloan policy; see Tsūsan Daijin, pp. 22–23, 59–60, 315–22. The practice of commercial banks' borrowing from the Bank of Japan actually began only in 1942, when the authority of the central bank itself was greatly strengthened in the wake of the attack on the Allied Powers; Fuji Bank, pp. 157–61, 167. This is another example of wartime practices being perpet-

uated under SCAP. See Tsūsan Daijin, pp. 203–5, 208, 213–14, 220–24 on the over-loan policy in general; also Nakamura, p. 39.

44. Martin Bronfenbrenner, "Monopoly and Inflation in Contemporary Japan," *Osaka Economic Papers* 3.2 (March 1955): 42–43.

45. Shibagaki, pp. 42–50; Teiichi Wada, "Zaibatsu Dissolution and Business Group-ings," *Waseda Journal of Asian Studies* 2 (1980), pp. 13–17. The Mitsui, Mitsubishi, and Sumitomo *keiretsu* obviously came out of the old "big four" zaibatsu. The Fuji Bank group included companies associated not only with the old Yasuda zaibatsu (the smallest of the "big four"), but also with the former Asano, Nissan, and Hi-tachi combines. The Daiichi group embraced companies from the former Furukawa, Kawasaki, and Fujiyama combines, as well as independent concerns. Many interim name changes took place before the keiretsu banks settled on (or returned to) these names.

46. Shibagaki, pp. 45–55, is interesting and incisive on these matters.

47. Kobayashi, p. 75.

48. Hollerman, "International Economic Controls," pp. 707–19. Chalmers Johnson's pathbreaking *MITI and the Japanese Miracle: The Growth of Industrial Policy, 1925–1975* (Palo Alto: Stanford University Press, 1982) develops these themes in im-pressive detail.

EPILOGUE. *LEGACIES/FANTASIES/DREAMS*

1. I have dealt with these matters of remilitarization and Japan's reemergence as Amer-ica's Cold War confederate in *Empire and Aftermath: Yoshida Shigeru and the Japan-ese Experience, 1878–1954* (Cambridge: Council on East Asian Studies, Harvard University, 1979), pp. 373–400, and in "Occupied Japan and the Cold War in Asia" in my *Japan in War and Peace: Selected Essays* (New York: The New Press, 1993), pp. 155–207. On Japan's rearmament, see also Hata Ikuhiko, *Shiroku—Nihon Sai-gunbi* (Tokyo: Bungei Shunjūsha, 1976). Colonel Kowalski's interesting memoirs were published in Japanese translation (but never in English) as *Nihon Saigunbi* (Tokyo: Simul, 1969). Yoshida's solicitation of leftwing demonstrations is noted in Takeshi Igarashi, "Peace-making and Party Politics: The Formation of the Domes-tic Foreign-Policy System in Postwar Japan," *Journal of Japanese Studies* 11.2 (1985), p. 350. The United States did secretly deploy Japanese mine sweepers in the Ko-rean War, and in October 1952 Yoshida went along with expansion of the NPR to 110,000 men.

2. Although these hearings took place in closed session, transcripts were made avail-able immediately, with only negligible deletions for security purposes, and published in their entirety in newspapers such as the *New York Times*. For the formal record, see U.S. Senate, Hearings before the Committee on Armed Services and the Com-mittee on Foreign Relations, *Military Situation in the Far East*, May 1951, part 1, esp. p. 312.

3. Kōdansha, ed., *Shōwa: Niman Nichi no Zenkiroku* (Tokyo: Kōdansha, 1989), vol. 9, pp. 142–46; cited below as *SNNZ*. See also Sodei Rinjirō, *Makkāsā no Nisen Nichi* (Tokyo: Chūō Kōron, 1974). This imagery of the Japanese (and Oriental) "child" was almost reflexive among Westerners. In reporting about the anxiety many Japan-ese felt when MacArthur was dismissed (and President Truman raised alarms about "World War Three"), for example, the Sunday *New York Times* of April 15 observed that this "point of view may be silly, even childish, but there is no question that it exists."

4. The best-known Japanese film about the occupation, directed by Shinoda Masahiro and released in 1984, is titled *MacArthur's Children*.

5. *New York Times*, April 19, 1952.

6. *Tennō Heika no Shōwa Shi: 87-nenpan* (Tokyo: Futabasha, 1987), p. 131. Other translations of the emperor's poems are given in the *New York Times*, April 29, 1952, and *Facts on File 1952*, p. 132.

7. *SNNS* 9:249–51; Ōkōchi Kazuo, ed., *Shiryō: Sengo 20-nen* (Tokyo: Nihon Hyōronsha, 1966), vol. 4 *(Rōdō)*, pp. 198–200; *New York Times*, May 2, 1952. Over twelve hundred demonstrators were arrested, of whom 261 were actually indicted for causing a public disturbance and—in a court case that dragged on for an astonishing *twenty* years—around one hundred found guilty.

8. The text is reprinted in Nihon Jānarizumu Kenkyūkai, ed., *Shōwa "Hatsugen" no Kiroku* (Tokyo: Tokyū Agency, 1989), p. 134. The emperor's visit to Ise is recorded in *SNNZ* 9:262.

9. Takahashi Hiroshi, *Heika, Otazune Mōshiagemasu: Kisha Kaiken Zenkiroku no Ningen Tennō no Kiseki* (Tokyo: Bunshun Bunko, 1988), pp. 212, 217.

10. The full passage, framed in terms of the anticommunist struggle in Korea, is as follows:

> The Japanese people since the war have undergone the greatest reformation recorded in modern history. With a commendable will, eagerness to learn, and marked capacity to understand, they have from the ashes left in war's wake erected in Japan an edifice dedicated to the primacy of individual liberty and personal dignity, and in the ensuing process there has been created a truly representative government committed to the advance of political morality, freedom of economic enterprise, and social justice.
>
> Politically, economically, and socially, Japan is now abreast of many free nations of the earth and will not again fail the universal trust. That it may be counted upon to wield a profoundly beneficial influence over the course of events in Asia is attested by the magnificent manner in which the Japanese people have met the recent challenge of war, unrest and confusion surrounding them from the outside, and checked communism within their own frontiers without the slightest slackening in their forward progress.
>
> I sent all four of our Occupation divisions to the Korean battlefront without the slightest qualms as to the effect of the resulting power vacuum upon Japan. The results fully justified my faith.
>
> I know of no nation more serene, orderly, and industrious, nor in which higher hopes can be entertained for future constructive service in the advance of the human race.

11. *New York Times*, April 29 and May 4, 1952.

12. Ezra Vogel, *Japan as Number One: Lessons for America* (Cambridge, Mass.: Harvard University Press, 1979); Samuel P. Huntington, *The Clash of Civilizations and the Remaking of World Order* (New York: Simon and Schuster, 1996). The "ethno-economics" phrase is elaborated on in Murray Sayle, "How Rich Japan Misled Poor Asia," *JPRI Working Paper No. 43* (Japan Policy Research Institute, March 1998). The most incisive recent critique of Japan's deep-seated "insular mentality" is Ivan P. Hall, *Cartels of the Mind: Japan's Intellectual Closed Shop* (New York: Norton, 1998).

13. In 1960, the grossly inequitable bilateral security treaty between the United States and Japan was revised after violent street protests in Japan, constituting a third event that seemed to warrant taking that year as marking the end of the postwar era.

14. On the legacies of wartime developments, see the essay on "The Useful War" in Dower, *Japan in War and Peace: Selected Essays* (New York: The New Press, 1993), pp. 9–32; also *World War II and the Transformation of Business Systems,* ed. Sakudo Jun and Shiba Takao (Tokyo: Tokyo University Press, 1994), esp. the essays by Kikkawa Takeo ("The Relationship between the Government and Companies in Japan during and after World War II"), Sasaki Satoshi ("The Rationalization of Production Management Systems in Japan during World War II"), and Shiba Takao ("Business Activities of Japanese Manufacturing Industries during World War II"). The economist and former Finance Ministry official Noguchi Yukio emphasized "the persistence of the 1940 setup" in a dialogue with Ushio Jirō titled "Reforming Japan's 'War-Footing' Economic System," *Japan Echo* 21.2 (summer 1994), pp. 13–18.

PHOTO AND ILLUSTRATION
CREDITS

INDEX

ABOUT THE AUTHOR

John W. Dower is currently the Elting E. Morrison Professor of History at the Massachusetts Institute of Technology. Many of the themes explored in *Embracing Defeat* build on his long, scholarly engagement with issues of war, peace, power, and justice in modern Japanese history and U.S.-Japan relations. His *Empire and Aftermath: Yoshida Shigeru and the Japanese Experience: 1878–1954* was a pioneer inquiry into the linkages and discontinuities between prewar and postwar Japan. First published in 1979, this study of Japan's most influential postwar politician was a bestseller in its Japanese translation. Professor Dower's *War Without Mercy* has been widely praised as a pathbreaking comparative analysis of the racial and psychological aspects of World War II in Asia. War Without Mercy was honored with several prizes in the United States, including the National Book Critics Circle Award for nonfiction. In Japan, it won the Ōhira Masayoshi Memorial Prize for distinguished scholarship on Asia in the Pacific. In 1993 a dozen of his major essays were published under the title *Japan in War and Peace.*

Professor Dower has also broken new ground in using visual materials and other expressions of popular culture such as songs and slogans in his reexamination of modern Japan and its interactions with the Western world. In addition, he has published books on traditional design (*The Elements of Japanese Design*, 1971), on the first hundred years of photography in Japan (*A Century of Japanese Photography*, 1980); and on the collaborative political art of the painters Maruki Iri and Maruki Toshi (*The Hiroshima Murals*, with John Junkerman, 1985). In 1986, he was executive producer of a documentary film on the work of the Marukis titled *Hellfire—A Journey from Hiroshima*, which was nominated for an Academy Award. He is an elected member of the American Academy of Arts and Sciences of American Historians.